Sirenian Conservation

UNIVERSITY PRESS OF FLORIDA

Florida A&M University, Tallahassee
Florida Atlantic University, Boca Raton
Florida Gulf Coast University, Ft. Myers
Florida International University, Miami
Florida State University, Tallahassee
New College of Florida, Sarasota
University of Central Florida, Orlando
University of Florida, Gainesville
University of North Florida, Jacksonville
University of South Florida, Tampa
University of West Florida, Pensacola

University Press of Florida

Gainesville Tallahassee Tampa Boca Raton Pensacola Orlando Miami Jacksonville Ft. Myers Sarasota

Sirenian Conservation

Issues and Strategies in Developing Countries

Edited by Ellen M. Hines,
John E. Reynolds III,
Lemnuel V. Aragones,
Antonio A. Mignucci-Giannoni,
Miriam Marmontel

Foreword by Helene Marsh

This publication was made possible with grants from the United Nations Environment Programme/Convention on Migratory Species, Save the Manatee Club, and Mote Marine Laboratory Library

Copyright 2012 by Ellen M. Hines, John E. Reynolds III, Lemnuel V. Aragones, Antonio A. Mignucci-Giannoni, and Miriam Marmontel
All rights reserved
Printed in the United States of America. This book is printed on Glatfelter Natures Book, a paper certified under the standards of the Forestry Stewardship Council (FSC). It is a recycled stock that contains 30 percent post-consumer waste and is acid-free.

17 16 15 14 13 12   6 5 4 3 2 1

A record of cataloging-in-publication data is available from the Library of Congress.
ISBN 978-0-8130-3761-5

Frontispiece: West Indian manatee in rehabilitation at Centro Mamíferos Aquáticos in Itamaracá, Brazil. (Courtesy of Luciano Candisani.)

The University Press of Florida is the scholarly publishing agency for the State University System of Florida, comprising Florida A&M University, Florida Atlantic University, Florida Gulf Coast University, Florida International University, Florida State University, New College of Florida, University of Central Florida, University of Florida, University of North Florida, University of South Florida, and University of West Florida.

University Press of Florida
15 Northwest 15th Street
Gainesville, FL 32611-2079
http://www.upf.com

There are scientists who are inspirations to us all, who have shown dedication beyond what was expected of them, who have become mentors, examples, teachers; people who have shown by their example how to work with communities and politicians; people who have dedicated their lives to the conservation of endangered species. My co-editors are such scientists, and so are the contributors to this book. I thank you all and hope this book encourages others to engage in this crucial work. I more specifically include in this dedication Dr. Akoi Kouadio, who worked with West African manatees for almost 30 years and died in Côte d'Ivoire in August of 2009. I am proud to include his chapter in this book. He is an example of the scientist we aspire to be.

—Ellen Hines, July 2011, San Francisco, California

Contents

List of Illustrations ix
List of Tables xi
Foreword xiii

Introduction 1
1. The Role of Sirenians in Aquatic Ecosystems 4
   Lemnuel V. Aragones, Ivan Lawler, Helene Marsh, Daryl Domning, and Amanda Hodgson
2. Vulnerability of Sirenians 12
   John E. Reynolds III and Christopher D. Marshall

SECTION I: REGIONAL ISSUES IN SIRENIAN CONSERVATION

3. Florida Manatee Status and Conservation Issues: A Primer 23
   Charles J. Deutsch and John E. Reynolds III
4. West Indian Manatees (*Trichechus manatus*) in the Wider Caribbean Region 36
   Caryn Self-Sullivan and Antonio A. Mignucci-Giannoni
5. The Amazonian Manatee 47
   Miriam Marmontel, Fernando C. Weber Rosas, and Sarita Kendall
6. The West African Manatee 54
   Akoi Kouadio
7. Dugongs in Asia 58
   Ellen M. Hines, Kanjana Adulyanukosol, Sombat Poochaviranon, Phay Somany, Leng Sam Ath, Nick Cox, Keith Symington, Tint Tun, Anouk Ilangakoon, Hans H. de Iongh, Lemnuel V. Aragones, Shaoyong Lu, Xia Jiang, Xin Jing, Elrika D'souza, Vardhan Patankar, Dipani Sutaria, Bharat Jethva, Parimal Solanki
8. Dugongs in Japan 77
   Kazuko Ikeda and Hiroshi Mukai
9. Eastern African Dugongs 84
   Catharine E. Muir and Jeremy J. Kiszka
10. Dugongs in Arabia 91
    Anthony Preen, Himansu Das, Mohammed Al-Rumaidh, and Amanda Hodgson
11. Dugongs in Australia and the Pacific 99
    Kirstin Dobbs, Ivan Lawler, and Donna Kwan

SECTION II: RESEARCH STRATEGIES FOR SIRENIANS

12. Using Interviews in Sirenian Research 109
    Alejandro Ortega-Argueta, Ellen M. Hines, and Jorge Calvimontes
13. Tagging and Movement of Sirenians 116
    Miriam Marmontel, James Reid, James K. Sheppard, and Benjamín Morales-Vela

14. Techniques for Determining the Food Habits of Sirenians 126
    Cathy A. Beck and Mark T. Clementz

15. Individual Identification of Sirenians 133
    Cathy A. Beck and Ann Marie Clark

16. Health Assessment of Captive and Wild-Caught West Indian Manatees (*Trichechus manatus*) 139
    M. Andrew Stamper and Robert K. Bonde

17. Sirenian Pathology and Mortality Assessment 148
    Robert K. Bonde, Antonio A. Mignucci-Giannoni, and Gregory D. Bossart

18. Delineating and Assessing Habitats for Sirenians 157
    Eduardo Moraes-Arraut, Alejandro Ortega-Argueta, Leon D. Olivera-Gómez, and James K. Sheppard

19. Sirenian Genetics and Demography 168
    Leslee Parr, Fabrício R. Santos, Michelle Waycott, Juliana A. Vianna, Brenda McDonald, Susana Caballero, and Maria José de Souza Lopes

20. Boat- and Land-Based Surveys for Sirenians 179
    Lemnuel V. Aragones, Katherine S. LaCommare, Sarita Kendall, Nataly Castelblanco-Martínez, and Daniel Gonzalez-Socoloske

21. Utility and Design of Aerial Surveys for Sirenians 186
    John E. Reynolds III, Benjamín Morales-Vela, Ivan Lawler, and Holly Edwards

22. Organic Contaminants and Sirenians 196
    Dana L. Wetzel, Erin Pulster, and John E. Reynolds III

23. Manatee Rescue, Rehabilitation, and Release Efforts as a Tool for Species Conservation 204
    Nicole Adimey, Antonio A. Mignucci-Giannoni, Nicole E. Auil-Gomez, Vera M. F. da Silva, Carolina Mattosinho de Carvalho Alvite, Benjamín Morales-Vela, Regis Pinto de Lima, and Fernando C. Weber Rosas

SECTION III: STRATEGIES FOR CONSERVATION-ORIENTED SCIENCE

24. Working with Communities for Sirenian Conservation 221
    Lemnuel V. Aragones, Miriam Marmontel, and Sarita Kendall

25. Guidelines for Developing Protected Areas for Sirenians 228
    Helene Marsh and Benjamín Morales-Vela

26. The Role of Law in Protecting Sirenians and Their Habitat in Developing Nations 235
    Wyndylyn M. von Zharen

27. The Role of Scientists in Sirenian Conservation in Developing Countries 243
    Ellen M. Hines, Daryl Domning, Lemnuel V. Aragones, Miriam Marmontel, Antonio A. Mignucci-Giannoni, and John E. Reynolds III

28. A Framework for Sirenian Conservation in Developing Countries 246
    Ellen M. Hines

Notes 255
References 273
List of Contributors 313
Index 319

Illustrations

Maps

1.1. Global sirenian distribution 5
3.1. Florida manatee distribution 24
4.1. Antillean manatee distribution 37
5.1. Amazonian manatee distribution 47
6.1. West African manatee distribution 55
7.1. Southeast Asian dugong distribution 59
7.2. Dugong distribution in India, Sri Lanka, and the Andaman and Nicobar islands 73
8.1. Okinawan dugong sightings, feeding trails, and strandings since 1965 78
9.1. East African dugong distribution 85
10.1. Dugong habitat along the Arabian coasts 91
11.1. Australian dugong habitat range 99

Figures

1.1. Dugong feeding trail 8
2.1. Counter-current heat exchangers 13
6.1. Traditional manatee trap in the N'gni lagoon, Côte d'Ivoire 56
9.1. Dugong accidentally caught in a net, Kani-Be, south of Mayotte 88
10.1. Dugongs observed southeast of Bahrain, 1985–86 aerial survey 94
13.1. Manatee with peduncle tagging equipment 117
13.2. Amazonian manatee with peduncle tagging belt 118
13.3. Dugong secured alongside a catch boat for tagging 119
13.4. Comparison of locations determined via PTT and GPS tags, Florida 122
15.1. R. K. Bonde marking a Florida manatee 134
15.2. Freeze brand visible 13 years post-application 134
15.3. Florida manatee with scars from propeller blades 136
16.1. Health assessment of West Indian manatee, Puerto Rico 139
16.2. Health assessment sheet used in Florida 140
16.3. Physical examination form for captive manatees 140
16.4. Electrocardiogram monitor on West Indian manatee, Belize 141
16.5. Blood draw sampling site on West Indian manatee 145
16.6. Manatee blood draw using an extension set 145
17.1. Fatally injured manatee with propeller lesions, Florida 149
17.2. Injured manatee with propeller lesions on tail stock, Florida 150
17.3. Manatee rescued in severe state of cachexia, British Virgin Islands 152
17.4. A tanaid (*Hexapleomera robusta*) embedded in manatee's skin, Belize 154
17.5. Necropsy showing dorsal recumbency position used for examination 155
19.1 Median neighbor joining network showing three-haplotype cluster pattern 172
19.2 Median neighbor joining network showing a single-cluster pattern 173
19.3. Karyotype of hybrid manatee, northern Brazilian coast 174

19.4. Hybrids between West Indian and Amazonian manatees, mouth of the Amazon 174
19.5. PCR products from known male and female dugongs 175
19.6. Minimum spanning tree showing relationships between haplotypes, Australian lineages 176
20.1. Side-scan sonar image of manatees in Mexico 181
20.2. Sighting map for boat-based surveys 183
21.1. Cessna 172 used for aerial surveys 187
21.2. Counting manatee groups 188
21.3. "Race track pattern" distributional surveys 190
21.4. Strip transect survey in Thailand 191
21.5. GIS allows overlays of information useful to managers 194
22.1. Veterinarians take samples from a manatee in the water, Yucatán 202
23.1. Manatee in rehabilitation, Itamaracá, Brazil 205
23.2. Rescue of West Indian manatee, Crystal River, Florida 209
23.3. Routine medical examination of manatee calf, Puerto Rico 210
23.4. Bottle-feeding orphans in Puerto Rico, Brazil, Mexico, and Peru 211
23.5. Recently released manatee with satellite transmitter, Puerto Rico 212
23.6. West Indian manatee rehabilitation facility, Itamaracá, Brazil 215
23.7. Amazonian manatee rehabilitation facility, Manaus, Brazil 216
28.1. Diagram showing idealized endangered species conservation process 246
28.2. Example of integrated framework for sirenian conservation planning 247

Tables

1.1. General summary of the distribution, habitats, and diet of sirenians 7
1.2. Relative growth rates of some Australian tropical seagrasses 9
3.1. Population statistics for four subpopulations of the Florida manatee 26
3.2. Research needed to meet management needs for the Florida manatee 34
4.1. Distribution, status trend, and population estimates, Wider Caribbean Region 40
4.2. Legal protections for manatees and their habitats in the Wider Caribbean Region 41
8.1. Seagrass species in Okinawa and Sakishima islands eaten by dugongs 79
9.1. Summary of current threats to dugongs in the WIO region 87
10.1. Summary of strip-transect aerial dugong surveys conducted in the Arabian Gulf 95
11.1. Causes of live stranding or mortality of dugongs in Australia 105
12.1. Studies where interviews were used as a research method 110
13.1. Contact detail for manufacturers of sirenian tagging equipment 124
14.1. A short list of suitable biogenic materials for stable isotope analysis 129
14.2. Research laboratory contacts for stable isotope analysis of tissues and plant materials 131
15.1. Freeze branding protocol in use for Florida manatees 135
16.1. Tubes used for collecting blood during sirenian health assessments 144
17.1. Determined cause of death for 68 fresh manatee carcasses, Florida 148
17.2. Predominant cause of stranding for 121 West Indian manatees, Puerto Rico 149
18.1. Variables and instruments for sirenian habitat research 158
18.2. Satellite sensors that can be used in habitat assessments 160
18.3. Web sites with satellite imagery and computer program tutorials 161
19.1. Number of alleles in dugongs compared with the manatee 177
20.1. Beaufort Scale and accompanying wind and sea state 182
20.2. Magnification devices for sirenian surveys 183
20.3. Applications and limitations of boat-based and land-based survey methods 185
21.1. Strengths and weaknesses of different survey designs for sirenians 189
23.1. Facilities holding West Indian or Amazonian manatees for rehabilitation or display 207
25.1. Major motivations of key stakeholders in development of a protected area 231

Foreword

When I started studying dugongs in the early 1970s, much sirenian research was limited to the study of the natural history of animals that were dead or in captivity and in the United States or Australia. There are obvious limitations to each of the dimensions of this approach, and this book is testament to the modern, global, cross-disciplinary approaches used to study and inform the conservation management of wild sirenians.

The sirenians, the dugong (family Dugongidae) and the three species of manatee (family Trichechidae), are of very high biodiversity value as the world's only herbivorous mammals that are exclusively aquatic. They have all been included on the IUCN Red List of Threatened Species for decades. The other recent sirenian, the Steller's sea cow, is extinct, exterminated by humans less than 30 years after its rediscovery in the eighteenth century. The extinction of Steller's sea cow is a stark reminder of both the capacity of a species with a once vast range to become extinct and the vulnerability of relatively small isolated populations of sirenians to human impacts, particularly direct mortality.

The range of sirenians spans about 90 subtropical and tropical countries on five continents. Almost all these countries are classified as less developed. The book's editors are based in four countries from the range of three of the four extant sirenians. Eighty sirenian researchers, who are citizens of or have been based in 22 countries, have contributed to this book; more than 50 of these researchers have been or are based outside the United States and Australia. Of the 28 chapters, more than half have been co-authored by researchers from more than one country; this number is higher if the authorship of the text boxes is considered. The editors of this book, particularly Ellen Hines, are to be commended for coordinating such a large global cast of authors.

Although the study of dead and captive animals has provided important insights into sirenian biology, modern benign methods are much more powerful. Section II of this book describes a range of techniques for studying wild sirenians and their habitats to enable researchers to provide managers with robust scientific advice. Most of the methods chapters have been co-authored by researchers from more than one country. Although most methods will need to be customized for local application, the wide geographic base of the authorship increases their applicability.

Sirenian conservation is not just an issue of biology. All four species are of considerable cultural value to Indigenous and non-Indigenous peoples throughout their ranges, and sirenian conservation is an issue of conserving cultural as well as biological diversity. The extinction of sirenians will result in the local loss of cultural knowledge. Importantly, some of this knowledge is documented in this book.

The pressures on dugongs and manatees are almost certain to increase in all of their approximately 90 range states, especially those where food security is likely to be an issue. The world's human population is projected to grow from 6.8 billion in 2010 to 8.9 billion in 2050, to peak at 9.22 billion in 2075, 35% higher than in 2010. Much of the demographic change up to 2050 will take place in the less developed regions, which will account for 99% of the expected increment to world population in this period. Thus human population increase is projected to be extremely rapid in most of the countries in the range of dugongs and manatees, with increasing food insecurity. In addition, climate change is projected to increase pressure on the world's fisheries. Many of the countries where the impacts of climate change on fisheries are projected to have the greatest national economic impacts are in the ranges of dugongs and manatees. These projected changes in human population and climate are significant to the future of manatees and dugongs because the population growth rate of all sirenians is highly sensitive to changes in adult survival rate. Most local populations of sirenians cannot withstand the human-induced mortality of even a few animals per year. The future of manatees and dugongs looks bleak throughout most of their ranges in developing countries, unless the issues of food security and alternative livelihoods are addressed.

In contrast to the situation that exists for many species, however, enough is known about threats to sirenian populations to take effective steps toward their conservation, if the will exists to do so. This book will assist scientists and managers with responsibilities for dugongs and manatees, especially in these developing countries, to work with stakeholders to design and implement strategies that will reverse the declines in sirenian populations. Sirenian researchers and managers are committed to making a difference. We want our science to inform real world outcomes. This book will help us achieve that end.

Helene Marsh
James Cook University, Queensland, Australia

Introduction

ELLEN M. HINES

In October of 2003 I sent an e-mail to the sirenian scientific community to gauge interest in an edited volume on manatees and dugongs specifically in developing countries. This book as I envisioned it would emphasize conservation and management issues, research strategies, and the role of scientists in integrating their research into conservation.

Within a week I received more than 60 responses from sirenian researchers all over the world wishing to contribute. I was both excited and overwhelmed. Luckily, I also found four co-editors, with amazingly similar visions, to partner with me on organizing prospective chapters and drafting proposals to publishers.

My own research has mostly been with dugongs in Southeast Asia. My Ph.D. from the University of Victoria in Canada is based on research on dugongs along the Andaman coast of Thailand. Subsequently, I have also studied dugongs along the eastern Gulf coast of Thailand, Vietnam, Cambodia, and Myanmar; manatees in Belize; and coastal cetaceans in the Gulf of Thailand. I am an associate professor of geography at San Francisco State University with further expertise in geographic information science (geographic information systems, remote sensing, and global positioning systems).

John Reynolds has been involved in research and conservation of sirenians and other marine mammals since 1974. He received M.S. (1977) and Ph.D. (1980) degrees from University of Miami's Rosenstiel School of Marine and Atmospheric Sciences for his research involving ecology, behavior, functional morphology, and pathology of manatees. In 1989 Reynolds became a member of the Committee of Scientific Advisors on Marine Mammals for the U.S. Marine Mammal Commission, the federal agency with oversight for all research and management of U.S. marine mammals. In 1990 he became chair of the Committee of Scientific Advisors, and in 1991 he was appointed by President G.H.W. Bush to serve as chair of the Marine Mammal Commission, a position he has retained through four presidents. In 2001 Reynolds began working for Mote Marine Laboratory in Sarasota, Florida, where he serves as senior scientist and director of the Center for Marine Mammal and Sea Turtle Research. That same year he became co-chair of the Sirenian Specialist Group of the International Union for Conservation of Nature (IUCN), a post he held through 2008. For the period 2006–2008 Reynolds was elected to serve as president of the International Society for Marine Mammalogy, and he has served on the board of the International Federation of Mammalogists. Recently he has worked closely with the United Nations Environment Programme to develop and implement a Caribbean-wide Marine Mammal Action Plan.

Lemnuel V. Aragones has been involved in marine mammal research and conservation since 1988. His research has ranged from field studies on dugongs (Philippines and Australia) to manatees (Florida) to dolphins and whales (Philippines). He received his Ph.D. from James Cook University in Townsville, Australia, in 1998. A member of the IUCN Sirenian Specialist Group since 1993, Aragones is currently involved in establishing the Philippine Marine Mammal Stranding Network and Database and has worked extensively with governmental and nongovernment organizations on various aspects of marine mammal research and conservation. He is an associate professor in the Institute of Environmental Science and Meteorology at the University of the Philippines.

Antonio Mignucci-Giannoni is a biological oceanographer specializing in the biology, ecology, management, and conservation of marine mammals, particularly manatees, in the Caribbean. He is the founder and director of the international conservation organization Red Caribeña de Varamientos (Caribbean Stranding Network), dedicated to the care, treatment, and rehabilitation of injured or stranded marine mammals, sea turtles, and sea birds. Mignucci has been an executive member of the IUCN Sirenian Specialist Group since 1994. In addition to his post at the Caribbean Stranding Network, he is a research professor at Inter American University in Puerto Rico.

Miriam Marmontel is a Brazilian oceanographer who has been involved in marine mammal work since 1977. She received the M.Sc. from the University of Miami's Rosenstiel School of Marine and Atmospheric Science and a Ph.D. from the University of Florida in Gainesville. Marmontel shifted from saltwater work to the Amazon in the early 1990s to study freshwater mammals. She now leads a research group with the Mamirauá Institute for Sustainable Development in western Brazil that focuses on manatee conservation but works with pink dolphins and giant otters as well. The group pioneered an Amazonian manatee return into the wild and implemented the first community-based Amazonian manatee rescue-and-rehabilitation center. Marmontel is a member of IUCN´s Sirenian Specialist Group and Sirenian International.

Thanks to a grant from Save the Manatee Club and Dr. Paresh Desai, we were able to hire outside editor Keith Howell, with over 25 years of editorial expertise including 15 years as the publishing manager at the California Academy of Sciences. His contributions have been invaluable. This grant also enabled me to enroll Ellen McElhinny as our cartographer. I believe her excellent maps will become a standard in sirenian science. We have had several requests to use her maps in reports and presentations already. Our very patient and practical editor John Byram, as well as Meredith Morris-Babb and Nevil Parker, at the University Press of Florida, completed the editorial team. Authors from all over the world contributed to this volume; I thank you all for sharing your expertise and for your time, thoughts, and patience. Further acknowledgments are due to Sally Antrobus, Jim Valade, Ed Keith, Elliott Norse, Mariah Bellello, Bridget Watts, Winona Azure, and Lou Sian.

The response to and interest in this volume represents the growing number of sirenian researchers whose awareness of the conservation-oriented issues threatening manatees and dugongs reflects the increasing endangerment to these species as human coastal settlements rapidly grow. Anthropogenic threats to sirenians are well defined in the upcoming chapters, so I will not attempt to list them here. However, if we are to progress from awareness to realistic solutions, we must propose integrated solutions and discuss agendas and tools for conservation at all scales (global, regional, national, local).

Much has been said about the need to train a new generation of conservation-oriented scientists, but few new texts addressing these needs have been written—and none specific to sirenians. This book is meant as a resource for scientists, technicians, and managers as well as for use in the classroom. When used in environmental science, wildlife studies, conservation biology, geography, and other related programs, the book will offer students an opportunity to explore more fully the theme of sirenian conservation. The book also provides a tool for more general training of conservation-oriented scientists in government agencies and universities while using examples of applied research in diverse countries where sirenians occur. Of primary relevance in such situations are discussions of the roles that the contributing scientist-authors have played beyond the traditional tasks of biologists or ecologists. In most cases authors have created variations on the customary techniques that allow such techniques to be practical, repeatable, and cost effective in countries that are not well resourced for such studies. This adaptive process has been the case in health assessment, rescue and rehabilitation, genetics, and population and habitat assessment, to name just a few areas.

We set the stage with two opening chapters that discuss sirenians in general: their role in a coastal ecosystem, an overview of their history of endangerment, and the physiological basis of their vulnerability. The main body of the book is organized into three sections, addressing in turn the geographic issues of sirenian conservation, research strategies, and conservation-oriented science. Many of the contributions contain boxes that highlight a procedure or issue, sometimes using a specific example.

Section I consists of nine chapters focusing on different geographic regions, including three in developed countries—the U.S. (Florida), Australia, and Japan (Okinawa)—as examples of lessons learned. While this section is not as comprehensive as the excellent regional status reports published on sirenians in the past several years, research scientists experienced in each region have reported on such common themes as the history of local research and current research needs, sirenian distribution, legal status, threats, and the cultural significance of sirenians in countries and communities.

Chapters in the second section outline research strategies, addressing practical, repeatable protocols for gathering data in developing countries. The following common themes are addressed:

- What can a given technique realistically tell us?
- What should this technique not be used for? What assumptions are not realistic? When is it not practical or feasible to use this technique?
- What are its biases? How can they be addressed?
- What are the costs and benefits of adapting these strategies in developing countries?

The chapters in section III outline strategies for conservation. They offer a more general toolbox of ideas that extend past scientific research into issues of working with local communities, the roles of legislation and protected areas in supporting protection and enforcement, and, based on the issues presented earlier in the volume, the role scientists can play in applying these strategies.

Lastly, we present a framework that summarizes the commonalities among issues and tools described, upon which to organize scientific data effectively into integrated planning for conservation and management.

While this volume, especially the section on research strategies, can be considered a "how-to" or methods-oriented text, the editors and authors seek to do more than instruct. The principal term that occurs to me is that of context. We describe ongoing, active methods, within the generalized circumstances of research in developing countries. Our authors are trained in the traditional sciences and publish in the usual scientific literature. We have realized through circumstance, in developing and developed countries alike, that to save an endangered species, especially a marine mammal with specialized foraging needs that keep it perilously close to populated coastal areas, requires a sizeable step beyond traditional science. Moreover, we have learned how research in both its applied and theoretical senses has to respond to the specific contexts of the various regions and cultures where sirenians are found.

We seek to exemplify here what that "step beyond" entails. Can we derive a common framework from among the diverse methodologies to address the social, cultural, and economic as well as the ecological? What can dugong research and conservation in a coastal fishing community in southern Thailand have in common with studying manatees near Indigenous hunters in the Amazon River? Readers will naturally find commonalities in our approaches. Communities everywhere are calling for a voice in self-governance. Endangered species globally are threatened by habitat loss. The research methods and conservation issues described here are not necessarily original as they are based on those traditionally used; however, the details of how these methods are creatively practiced in diverse circumstances should be profoundly useful. The breadth of knowledge and experience that is shared by our authors is an exciting example of the dedication of these scientists to international sirenian conservation and a challenge for all sirenian scientists to use their expertise and research to address the issues that threaten sirenians.

It is our hope that the issues and strategies described in this volume create and uphold the impression that our surroundings not only affect the techniques we choose to gather and interpret data but will also influence the approaches scientists develop or need to develop to respond to the social phenomena that impact the endangerment of a coastal marine mammal.

1

The Role of Sirenians in Aquatic Ecosystems

LEMNUEL V. ARAGONES, IVAN LAWLER, HELENE MARSH,
DARYL DOMNING, AND AMANDA HODGSON

The role of sirenians in aquatic ecosystems is largely a function of their feeding ecology. Sirenians are large herbivorous aquatic mammals that often congregate and, being mammals, have high energetic requirements relative to other marine herbivores. An adult dugong can weigh from 250 to 600 kg[1], while the West Indian and West African manatees both range between 350 and 1,400kg[2], and the Amazonian manatee from 200 to 480kg[3]. Consequently, sirenians consume significant amounts of aquatic vegetation. They also display dietary preferences in regard to plant species, individual plants, and parts of plants[4,5]. Thus dugongs and manatees have the capacity to alter the nutritional quality and species composition of the plant communities upon which they feed[6].

In this chapter we provide an overview of the geographic ranges of sirenians, their food types, and their adaptations to utilizing these foods. We then consider the effects of sirenians feeding on plant communities based on small-scale studies and experiments. Finally, we discuss the likely significance of these effects when scaled up to the level of populations, and the consequential impacts on plant communities.

Distribution and Abundance

Extant sirenians range from the tropics to the subtropics, their distribution largely determined by a species' thermal tolerance and the distribution of their food (map 1.1).

The present population sizes of all sirenian species are believed to be significantly smaller than they were in even the recent past[7]. While it is reasonable to assume a consequential reduction in the role of sirenians, we believe they still significantly affect the ecology. An individual sirenian must consume about 4–25% of its body weight per day[8]. It is estimated that a dugong consumes 28–40 kg of seagrass per day[9]. In the Moreton Bay region of Australia the calculated median biomass of seagrasses on which dugongs feed is 12.3 g dry matter/m^2; each dugong overturns on the order of 401.5 m^2 of seagrass each day[10]. In the Great Barrier Reef region the biomass of the seagrasses on which dugongs feed ranges from 5.8 to 10.4 g dry matter/m^2 [11] and a dugong is estimated to overturn 263–904 m^2 of seagrass each day[12]. An adult manatee can consume about 5.9 kg/day dry weight of the seagrass *Syringodium filiforme* each day, an amount equivalent to about 50 m^2 per day[13]. Thus even an individual sirenian has some capacity to influence the dynamics of the plant community on which it feeds.

While sirenians have been reduced over most of their ranges, they may still occur at locally high densities. Herds in excess of 200 dugongs are seen in Moreton Bay (Queensland), where they were estimated to dig up more than a square kilometer of seagrass every week[14]. The winter aggregations of Florida manatees, in warm-water areas, may also cause significant grazing impacts in nearby vegetation[15].

Prehistoric sirenians were not only more abundant than modern sirenians, but they were also much more diverse in the numbers of species and morphological variation among those species. For example, five or more sympatric (occurring in overlapping geographical areas) lineages of dugongids inhabited the West Atlantic–Caribbean region during the later Tertiary (approximately 25 million years ago)[16]. Such diversity implies greater and more complex impacts on plant communities than occur today, including faster recycling of nutrients, with less primary productivity passing through the detrital (where decomposition takes place) pathway; consequent increases in plant species diversity and biological productivity; and selection pressures favoring evolutionary adaptations of plants to herbivory (including changes to growth forms, chemical defenses, life strategies, and modes of reproduction, germination, and dispersal)[17].

Diet

Dugongs are seagrass specialists, feeding almost exclusively on marine angiosperms rooted to the sea bottom[18]. In contrast, manatees tend to vary their habitat and diet.

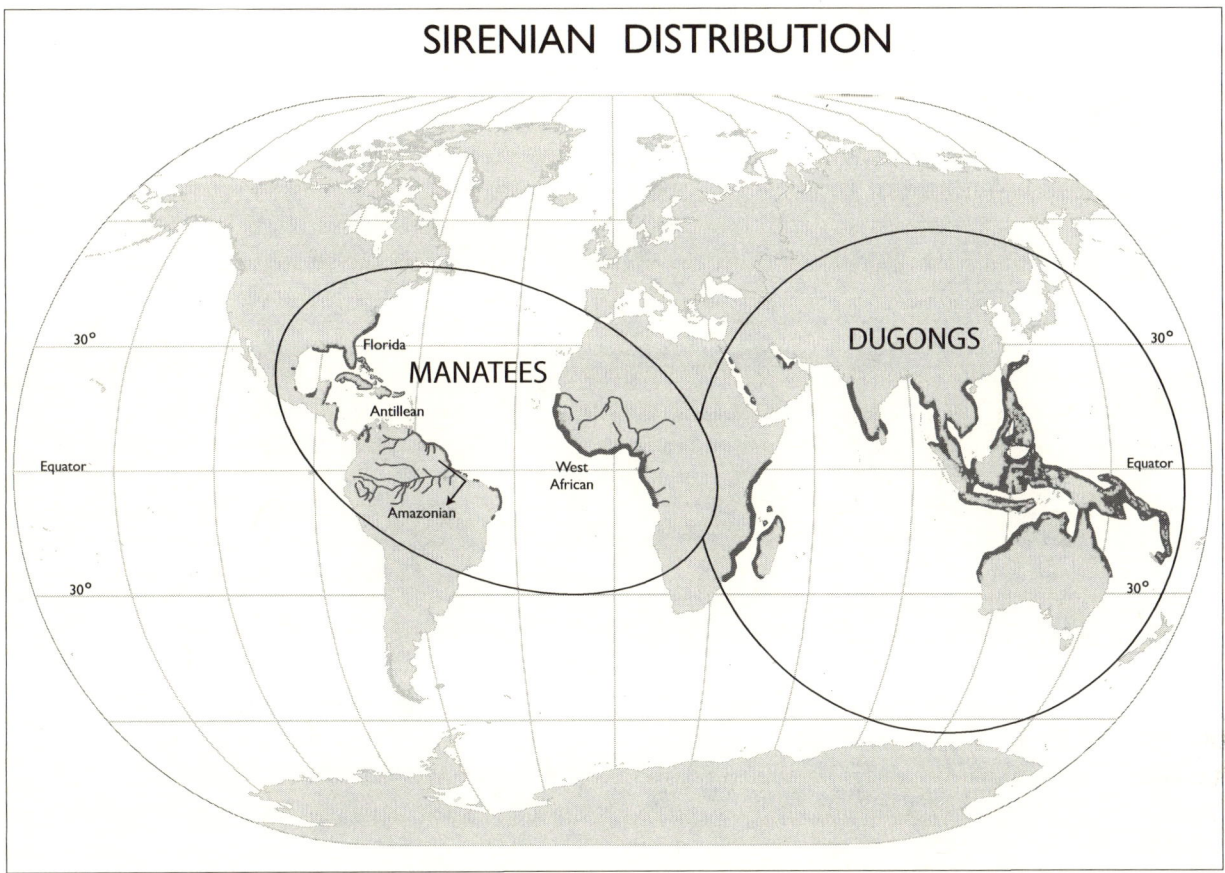

Map 1.1. Global sirenian distribution. (Map by Ellen McElhinny.)

The West Indian manatee (and presumably the West African manatee) feeds on a wide array of freshwater and marine plants[19] (see table 1.1); indeed the Florida manatee has been documented to feed on more than 60 species of freshwater, marine, and even terrestrial plants[20]. The Amazonian manatee feeds mainly on emergent freshwater plants, as the rapid reduction of light penetration inherent in the Amazonian system limits the growth of submerged vegetation[21]. The marine/freshwater dichotomy has a strong influence on the foods used by sirenians.

The facial morphology of sirenians reflects their feeding strategies and diets[22]. Dugongs have the strongest rostral deflection and are specialized for bottom feeding. The Amazonian manatee has the least deflection and prefers to forage at the surface[23], while the Antillean and the West African manatees have intermediate rostral deflections, which enable them to feed throughout the water column, from bottom feeding on seagrasses[24] to cropping emergent terrestrial grasses and herbs growing on banks[25].

The dentition of sirenians is also adapted to their diets. Steller's sea cows had no teeth[26]. The dugong's dentition is suggested to be of little use, with the horny pad playing the major role in breaking down food[27]. In contrast, the six to eight cheek teeth in each manatee (*Trichechus* spp.) jaw quadrant are constantly being replaced horizontally in an apparently limitless monophyodont (having only one set of teeth) series of supernumerary molars[28]. Despite its simple dentition, the dugong is as effective at masticating seagrasses of the genera *Thalassia* and *Halodule* as the Florida manatee[29], an achievement that presumably reflects the efficiency of its entire masticatory apparatus[30]. Domning suggested that the elaborate system of molar replacement of the three manatee species evolved in response to the tooth wear caused by siliceous phytoliths in the true grasses (Gramineae)[31]. Together with their more horizontal mouths, the more elaborate dentition of the manatees may be one of the factors enabling them to exploit a wider variety of food plants than the dugong.

Diet in Marine Environments

Seagrasses, the predominant food of dugongs and manatees, are marine vascular flowering plants (angiosperms) rather than true grasses. There are 50–60 known species

> **BOX 1.1**
>
> ### Rostral Deflection in Sirenians
>
> Daryl P. Domning
>
> A prominent feature of the sirenian skull is the enlarged snout, or rostrum, formed mainly by the premaxillary bones. This structure supports the nostrils and nasal passages; the large, fleshy upper lips and their tactile and prehensile vibrissae; and, on its underside, the horny pad that (with its counterpart on the lower jaw) serves as a cropping mechanism in feeding.
>
> This rostrum is bent downward to varying degrees, relative to the plane of the palate and cheek teeth, in different species. The degree of deflection reflects the typical diet: 15°–40° in African manatees and 25°–41° in Amazonian manatees (both of which feed largely on floating or emergent freshwater vegetation), and 29°–52° in West Indian manatees (which feed on seagrasses). The bottom-feeding dugong, a seagrass specialist, has the most downturned snout at around 70°. For swimmers with a low metabolic rate such as sirenians, constantly tipping the head up to breathe and down to feed wastes energy, while keeping the body axis horizontal as much as possible is economical. Hence, the position of the mouth is permanently adjusted to minimize movements of the body. A mouth that opens almost straight downward like the dugong's is suited to bottom-feeding, while a diet located higher up in the water column selects for a more moderate rostral deflection. This principle also provides clues to the diets of extinct sirenians.

worldwide[32]; dugongs and manatees eat about 15 species of them[33] (table 1.1).

Most information on sirenian diets comes from the dugong and the West Indian manatee, particularly the Florida manatee, and that bias is reflected in the information presented here. Dugongs show strong and consistent preferences among species of seagrasses[34]; manatees are more generalist browsers and appear to forage opportunistically but selectively where their preferred seagrass is available[35].

Generally, dugongs show preferences for species characteristic of lower seral (intermediate phase found in ecological succession) stages of seagrass communities, especially species of the genera *Halophila* and *Halodule* (see table 1.1). These genera respond well to disturbance, grow quickly[36], and invest little in structural material. The seagrass species favored by dugongs are typically lower in fiber and higher in protein than climax species such as *Zostera* or *Enhalus*[37]. When dugongs feed on *Halophila* and *Halodule*, they typically consume the whole plant, uprooting it from the substrate and leaving characteristic feeding trails[38] (figure 1.1).

In some regions dugongs feed on higher-biomass species of seagrass such as *Syringodium, Cymodocea* and *Thalassia*, and consume mostly the aboveground leaf material, especially if the substrate is too compact or the seagrass too robust to allow them to uproot whole plants. For example, in winter in Shark Bay, Western Australia, dugongs move into deeper, warmer water where their usual food species are unavailable. In these areas they switch to feeding on *Amphibolis* and strip the leaves from the stems[39]. Similarly, in Torres Strait dugongs may feed primarily on *Thalassia hemprichii*[40]. Although adult male dugongs possess tusks that could potentially be used to break up the substrate and access seagrass rhizomes, there is no evidence that they do so[41].

Manatees may choose seagrass on the basis of its accessibility and availability. *Halophila* spp. and *Halodule wrightii* are often found in shallower waters and are often easily accessible[42]. In Jupiter Sound (Florida), manatees have been observed to graze on mixed seagrasses, including *Halodule, Syringodium,* and *Thalassia*[43]. In areas devoid of seagrass because of high turbidity, and during the winter season, manatees feed opportunistically on any available vegetation including algae, mangrove leaves, and other terrestrial vegetation[44], especially when they aggregate in warm-water refuges. The seagrasses in winter refuges are at their lowest seasonal biomass[45] and are vulnerable to depletion by feeding manatees. Freshwater plants such as *Ruppia maritima* and cord grass are other possible alternatives[46].

There are important exceptions to the sirenians' focus on seagrasses. At the high latitude limits of their range, dugongs have been recorded feeding on ascidians and polychaetes during winter and spring, perhaps a response to their increased energy requirements due to lower temperatures and the seasonal reduction in seagrass biomass[47]. While animal material may be found in the stomach contents of tropical dugongs, analysis of stomach contents suggests that it is consumed incidentally while seagrass foraging[48]. West Indian manatees have also been reported to consume

Table 1.1. General summary of the distribution, habitats, and diet of sirenians.

Species	IUCN Status	Distribution	Habitats	Diet	Source of Information
Dugong (*Dugong dugon*)	Vulnerable	Tropical and subtropical Indian and Pacific Oceans	Seagrass meadows; coastal waters	Seagrasses: *Halophila ovalis, H. minor, H. spinulosa, H. decipiens, Halodule uninervis, H. pinifolia, Syringodium isoetifolium, Thalassia hemprichii, Zostera capricorni, Cymodocea serrulata, C. rotundata, Enhalus acoroides* Algae (intermittently)	Wake 1975; Marsh et al. 1978, 1982; Lanyon 1991; Preen 1993; Aragones 1994, 1996; de Iongh 1995; Suwanpanid 1999; Spain and Heinsohn 1973; Heinsohn 1981; Whiting 2002
Steller's sea cow (*Hydrodamalis gigas*)	Extinct	Subtropical to cold temperate Pacific Ocean	Kelp beds	Algae likely included in diet: *Agarum cribrosum, A. pertusum, Thalassiophyllum clathrus, Nereocystis luetkeana, Halosaccion glandiforme, Constantinea rosa-marina, Alaria praelonga, Laminaria saccharhina*	Domning 1978
West Indian manatee (*Trichechus manatus*)	Vulnerable	Tropical to subtropical western Atlantic Ocean (southeastern USA to southern Brazil), including Orinoco basin	Riverine and coastal waters	Seagrasses: *Halophila ovalis, H. decipiens, H. johnsoni, Halodule wrightii, Syringodium filiforme, Thalassia testudinum, Zostera marina* Algae (genera only): *Acetabularia, Chaetomorpha, Chara, Cladophora, Ectocarpus, Enteromorpha, Gracillaria, Halimeda, Hypnea, Oscillatoria, Penicillus, Polysiphonia, Sargassum, Spirogyra, Udotea, Ulva* Other vegetation: *Alternanthera, Eichhornia, Hydrilla, Lemna, Pistia, Ruppia, Salvinia, Spartina*	Hartman 1971, 1979; Thayer et al. 1984; Lefebvre et al. 1989; Provancha and Hall 1991; Lefebvre and Powell 1990; Hartman 1971; Campbell and Irvine 1977; Bengtson 1981; Ledder 1986; Hurst and Beck 1988
West African manatee (*T. senegalensis*)	Vulnerable	Tropical to subtropical eastern Atlantic Ocean (Senegal to Angola and Niger-Benué basin)	Riverine & coastal waters	Seagrasses: *Cymodocea nodosa, Halodule wrightii* Grasses (genera only): *Alternanthera, Echinochloa, Paspalum, Pennisetum, Phragmites, Pistia, Polygonum, Rhizophora, Ruppia, Typha, Vossia*	Reeves et al. 2002
Amazonian manatee (*T. inunguis*)	Vulnerable	Amazon River and its tributaries	Riverine	Aquatic and semi-aquatic vascular plants	

ascidians[49], bryozoans and hydroids[50], and to scavenge fish from nets[51].

Marine sirenians feed incidentally on algae[52] when seagrass resources are reduced. Following cyclones, which cause seagrass losses from wave action and sedimentation or turbidity blocking light, dugongs in Australia have been recorded eating significant amounts of algae[53]. However, large undigested fragments in stomach contents and in feces indicate that these are poorly digested[54]. Whiting provides the only account of tropical dugongs consistently feeding on algae in Australia, but the number of dugongs involved was very low and seagrass was locally scarce[55].

The only other modern dugongid is the giant (9–10 m in length) Steller's sea cow (*Hydrodamalis gigas*), which was exterminated by 1768, 27 years after its discovery. Steller's sea cow was also exclusively marine but mainly browsed on kelp, the large brown and red algae that dominates the cold-water, high-energy habitats of its former North Pacific range[56]. Steller's sea cows followed

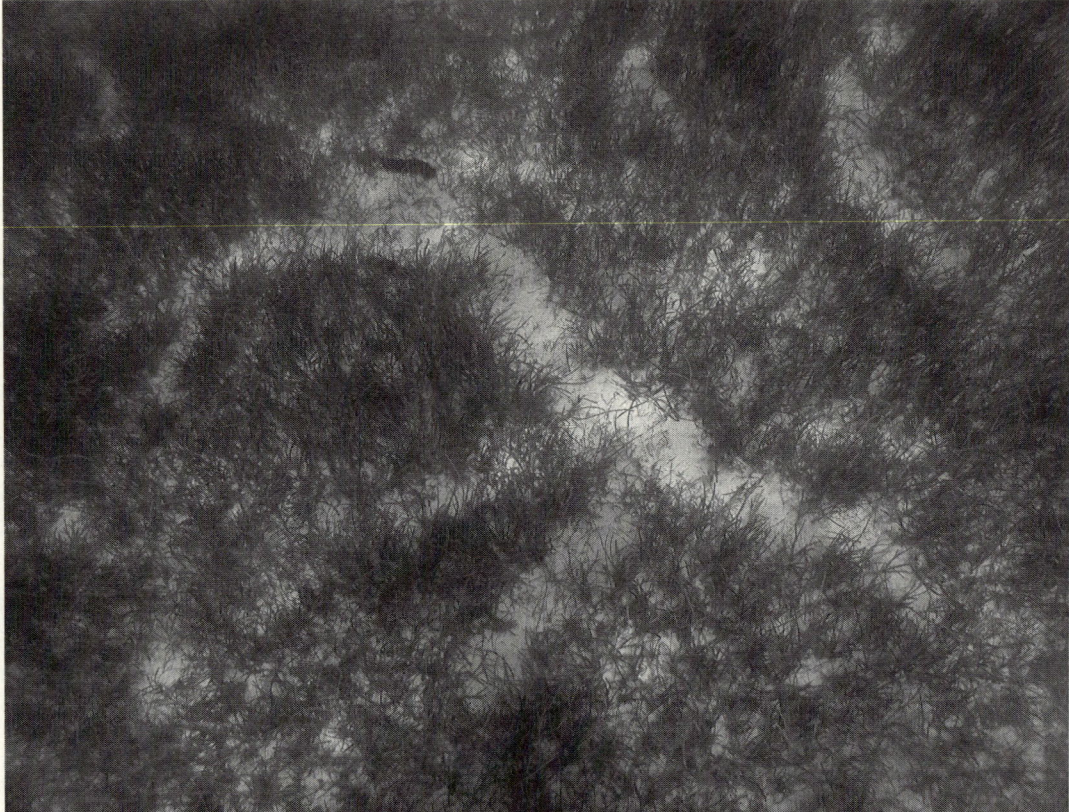

Figure 1.1. Dugong feeding trail. (Courtesy of Taro Hosokawa.)

the general sirenian pattern of resorting to an algal diet only when angiosperms were unavailable: the ancestors of *Hydrodamalis* ate seagrass before this resource was eliminated by habitat change in the North Pacific[57].

Diet in Freshwater Environments

In freshwater systems, manatees have access to a variety of aquatic plants ranging from floating and emergent to submerged forms[58]. Species of terrestrial true grasses and shoreline plants are also potential food items, especially when they are plentiful. These grasses are rooted macrophytes found underwater and along river banks. Other available plant parts, such as tree leaves, are also eaten[59].

The only exclusively freshwater sirenian, the Amazonian manatee, eats a wide variety of aquatic and semi-aquatic vascular plants[60]. Food availability in the Amazon basin is affected by seasonal changes in water levels. In the rainy season (December to June), water levels are high and food is abundant. In the dry season (July to November), water levels drop drastically, making food scarce[61]. In response, Amazonian manatees may feed on dead vegetation or fast[62].

Both West Indian and West African manatees are capable of thriving in freshwater systems for extended periods and are even thought to be dependent on access to freshwater[63]. The West African manatee feeds primarily on emergent grasses from the genera *Vossia*, *Echinochloa*, and *Paspalum*[64]. In freshwater systems, Florida manatees apparently feed on any dense vegetation they can access[65], including *Hydrilla*, a not-so-nutritious submerged aquatic plant (~92% water)[66], eelgrasses (*Vallisneria*), and cord grass (*Spartina*) (see table 1.1, and see Hurst and Beck[67] for a comprehensive list). Manatees in the Blue Spring area, a natural spring with sparse floating and submerged vegetation, will even feed on acorns (mast) from the oak (*Quercus virginiana*)[68]. Mast (fruit) is a good source of fats, sugar, starch, and protein and apparently augments the low nutritional quality of freshwater vegetation.

Effects of Grazing

The main role of sirenians in the aquatic ecosystem is herbivory; that is, grazing and/or browsing. Grazing is the act of ingesting a large proportion (≥90%) of the plant structure in grasses and other monocotyledons. Browsing is the act of ingesting leaves and branches of trees, shrubs, and forbs. Most if not all sirenians are capable of destructive grazing and browsing. Grazing is the more damaging, and bottom feeders such as the dugong and the West Indian and African manatees can uproot whole plants. Amazonian manatees are accomplished grazers and browsers on submerged and emergent aquatic vegetation.

Herbivory influences plant morphology, productivity, distribution, and community structure in terrestrial[69] and aquatic[70] systems. The effect of sirenian herbivory on seagrass depends on grazing intensity.

Effects of Grazing on Plants

Our main approach in explaining the role of sirenians in the ecosystem is to draw generalizations and parallels from information on dugong-seagrass interactions. Most of this information comes from field experiments conducted by Preen[71] and Aragones[72]. Full details of the experimental design and effects on seagrass communities are more widely available in Aragones and Marsh[73], and effects on nutrient composition are in Aragones et al.[74]. In these experiments two levels of dugong grazing and turtle cropping were simulated in seagrass beds in tropical Queensland, Australia. One level was "intensive dugong grazing," which represented a favored dugong feeding site, wherein almost all aboveground biomass was removed, leaving a small amount of belowground biomass. Another level, "light intensity dugong grazing," was simulated by removing three evenly-spaced 15 cm wide feeding strips (each resembling a typical dugong muzzle width) within each experimental unit (1.0 m^2).

Effects of Grazing on Biomass

The herbivory experiments showed that dugong grazing can change the biomass of seagrass beds, sometimes in counterintuitive ways. A favorite seagrass species, *Halophila ovalis*, increased its aboveground biomass, almost equaling its belowground biomass 10 months after intensive grazing[75]. The leaves of *H. ovalis* are some of the most important food items for dugongs, based on stomach content analysis[76] and observational data[77]. Also, it has one of the highest concentrations of nitrogen among tropical seagrasses[78].

Effects of Grazing on Community Structure and Composition

The experiments showed that dugong grazing can also have significant effects on seagrass community structure and dynamics. The structure of a tropical seagrass meadow in Australia was altered by both intensive and less intensive dugong grazing. A meadow at Ellie Point, Queensland, changed its species composition from predominantly *Zostera* and *Cymodocea* to *Halophila ovalis*[79]. Likewise, a monospecific seagrass meadow in Moreton Bay shifted from *Zostera* to *Halophila* and *Halodule* after it was intensively grazed by several hundred dugongs[80]. *Halophila* and *Halodule* species are adapted to disturbance because of their relatively short, opportunistic life histories (see table 1.2) which enable them to colonize spaces opened up by grazing. Areas where manatees feed regularly and intensively would be expected to show similar response. Thus grazing by sirenians on seagrass beds can short-circuit the detrital cycle, resulting in mosaics of young plants.

Effects of Grazing on Detrital Matter

Grazing by dugongs in tropical Australia altered the relative abundance of detrital matter in a seagrass meadow[81]. Intensive dugong grazing resulted in less detritus, presumably because most of the plant material was eaten instead of dying and decaying. We hypothesize that, in contrast, seagrass beds with few or no large grazers are likely detrital-based meadows. The detritus in seagrass meadows is an important source of organic matter and other nutrients, particularly in coastal areas. However, herbivory results in more rapid recycling of nutrients than does decomposition, so it should be even more beneficial to a community's productivity. Feeding by sirenians aerates the soil and mixes some of the detritus with soil, providing a substrate for bacterial nitrogen fixation[82], increasing seagrass productivity.

Effects of Grazing on Nutritional Quality

The response of seagrasses to grazing disturbance also initiates physiological processes that alter the chemical

Table 1.2. Relative growth rates, from published literature, of some Australian tropical seagrasses (from Aragones and Marsh 2000).

Species	Specific growth rate (% per day)	Turnover time (days)	Source
Halophila ovalis	4.0–9.0	11–24	Hillman and McComb 1988
Zostera capricorni	0.8–3.5	33–67	Kirkman et al. 1982
Cymodocea rotundata	2.5–4.0	25–40	Brouns 1987

composition of the plants. These changes are likely to complement the detrital cycling enhancement. However, the lack of a definitive set of determinants of food quality is a barrier to understanding the impacts of their grazing on seagrass nutritional quality. As for most herbivores, all chemical measures of food are only proxies for animal performance. For sirenians, obstacles to determining the effects of feeding strategies more precisely are ethically and logistically prohibitive as this would require experiments using captive animals. We measured a range of chemical constituents widely held to be important for a range of herbivores. We considered carbohydrates (energy), nitrogen (protein), and *in vitro* dry matter digestibility (IVDMD—a functional measure inversely related to levels of indigestible fiber). We also observed behavioral indicators from the dugongs themselves, assuming that preference for a feeding area indicates the presence of higher quality food.

In our experiments, *Halophila* and *Halodule* were the main genera that showed interesting changes in nutritional qualities as a result of grazing. The whole-plant nitrogen concentrations of *Halophila ovalis* and *Halodule uninervis* increased by 35 and 25%, respectively, even after almost a year of recovery from intensive grazing. However, these gains were tempered by diminishing returns in starch concentrations, making it difficult to conclude decisively whether the nutritional quality of these seagrasses increased or decreased.

Despite our imperfect knowledge of the determinants of nutritional quality for dugongs, we can interpret the above changes as improvements. The key nutrients for herbivores are usually energy (as starch, carbohydrates, etc.) and/or protein (measured as nitrogen, N). However, the relative importance of each will vary. Simulated and actual grazing consistently lead, broadly speaking, to reduced starch concentrations but higher N concentrations. Dugongs show a common tendency to re-graze areas[83], suggesting that they take advantage of the increased nitrogen concentration despite the concomitant decrease in starch.

Why does dugong grazing alter nitrogen and starch concentrations? The causes are twofold. First is the plant growth response. After grazing there is a simple increase in the proportion of new foliage with less structural material, which leads to increased N concentrations, while mobilization of energy reserves in rebuilding the aboveground biomass leads to reduced starch concentrations. Second, detrital cycling leads to higher bacterial N fixation rates in grazed areas[84] and, presumably, to enhanced tissue N concentrations in seagrasses.

Cultivation Grazing

The effects on seagrasses described in the preceding section explain the phenomenon of cultivation grazing[85], which occurs when herbivory, such as by dugongs, enhances the chemical attributes and digestibility of plants. Grazing dugongs produce serpentine feeding trails approximately 20 cm wide and 3–5 cm deep[86] (see figure 1.1), a strategy that presumably enables them to sample the spatially heterogeneous seagrass beds typical of the tropics yet prevents overgrazing because some belowground biomass is left as a vegetative source of regrowth. Aragones et al.[87] consider the effect of bacterial nitrogen fixation in the seagrass beds created by grazing disturbance to be the key to cultivation grazing. This behavior introduces detritus into the sediment, aerating it and providing substrate for N fixation. Sediments from grazed areas show higher N fixation rates than those from matching ungrazed areas, and these differences are explained largely in terms of aerobic N fixation rates[88]. This process has no known terrestrial analogue.

Meadows with high-quality seagrass are easier to find if they are large—and the more animals that graze, the larger the grazed area they create, which enhances further grazing. This is the most likely reason dugongs go back to the same feeding grounds and/or regularly or intermittently rotate their feeding grounds. For dugongs grazing in Moreton Bay in Queensland, Preen[89] documents variable return times ranging from 17 days to 5 months.

Dugongs and the Optimal Grazing Hypothesis

In terrestrial systems, there is a growing agreement that under some conditions, aboveground net primary productivity is maximized at some optimal grazing level[90]. The "grazing optimization hypothesis" can also apply in the marine environment, though the feedback loops may vary[91]. On land, herbivores may provide positive feedback to plants via local-scale inputs of feces and urine. In the marine environment these materials tend to be moved by currents, so positive feedbacks depend on the enhancement of the detrital cycle. Although total detritus may decrease in areas where grazing occurs, the physical action of dugong feeding introduces detritus and aeration into the sediment. Together, these two promote the activity of N-fixing bacteria. Nitrogen fixation rates in grazed seagrass are the highest recorded for any seagrass community[92].

In the study by Aragones and Marsh[93], *Halophila*

ovalis showed an increase in aboveground biomass productivity, while *Zostera capricorni* showed a decrease. As *Halophila* is favored by dugongs, while *Zostera* is not, this shows that both *Halophila* and dugongs are benefited by this effect. Plants growing at a rate close to their maximum growth capability have less opportunity to respond positively to grazing than plants with growth rates below maximum. This result suggests that *H. ovalis* has a greater capacity to compensate for dugong grazing than the other species studied and may be a species tolerant of herbivory[94].

The effect of dugong grazing on seagrass community composition is determined by how soon the dugongs come back and the relative recovery rates of individual species. Recovery of seagrasses from grazing disturbance depends on the timing and intensity, species composition and location within the bed, and occurrence of any additional disturbance[95]. In a mixed seagrass bed, *Halophila ovalis* recovered fastest, followed by *Halodule uninervis*, and then *Z. capricorni*. As shown in table 1.2, *H. ovalis* has faster growth and turnover than *H. uninervis* or *Z. capricorni*. Tropical seagrasses appear to recover quickly from grazing even when they are grazed during the winter, when growth is supposedly slowest[96]. In subtropical Moreton Bay the effect of timing of grazing on recovery was more pronounced than in tropical areas, presumably because of the more pronounced seasonality.

Conclusion: The Role of Sirenians

As we have shown for dugongs, sirenian grazing can have demonstrable effects on the community structure, productivity, and chemical composition of food plants. It seems likely that most sirenians are capable of producing similar grazing disturbances. Their importance is a function of the scale, both temporal and spatial, over their range and the numbers of animals occurring in local areas. Sirenians in the past presumably played a significant role in originally structuring the plant communities on which they feed, and they continue to do so in areas where their population densities remain high.

The widespread reduction in the sizes of most dugong and manatee populations has presumably altered plant communities, especially in areas not affected by other forms of physical disturbance. Presently, it is impossible to assess the ecosystem significance of the decline in populations as there are few data on the state of those systems prior to the reduction in sirenian populations. Perhaps the salient question is rather: do changes in plant communities after the removal of sirenians reach a threshold state beyond which sirenians are incapable of reinhabiting the area? We hope that conservation initiatives are sufficient to prevent that question from ever being answered.

2

Vulnerability of Sirenians

JOHN E. REYNOLDS III AND CHRISTOPHER D. MARSHALL

Sirenians represent one of the three living orders of mammals that include marine representatives. The other marine mammals are included in the Order Carnivora (walruses, seals, sea lions, sea and marine otters, and polar bears) and the Order Cetacea (whales, dolphins, and porpoises). Members of the general public, government officials, and scientists sometimes lump all the marine mammals together symbolically, ecologically, legislatively, and systematically. There is some merit in all of these perspectives except the systematic one.

In reality, the fact that some species of seals, sirenians, and whales exhibit common anatomical and other features reflects evolutionary convergence that occurred simply because the adaptations that led to success of these groups were "selected" by what worked best for mammals living in the water[1]. Thus the various marine mammal groups tend to be large and well-insulated (for heat retention), streamlined (to facilitate moving through the water), good divers (relative to humans and other terrestrial mammals), endowed with specialized sensory capabilities, and to possess a fluke or paddle-like appendages for locomotion. However, despite the number and variety of their similarities, the three orders of marine mammals arose from dramatically different ancestral lineages.

Factors such as food availability, climate, predators, and competition all shape which species succeed or perish in particular ecosystems. There are several traits that unite the members of Sirenia that reflect both their heritage and their environment[2]. As with other marine mammals, sirenians are very large; West Indian manatees are the largest living sirenians, with individuals approaching 1,600 kilograms in weight, but extinct sirenians such as Steller's sea cow exceeded 8 meters in length, and may have weighed as much as 9,100 kilograms. Large size provides several advantages, and some disadvantages, depending on the conditions under which a species lives. Large mammals inhabiting an aquatic environment are better able to conserve body heat than smaller, similarly shaped mammals, and heat conservation in cool or cold water is of obvious benefit to warm-blooded animals.

Like all mammals, sirenians are warm-blooded and must maintain a constant body temperature. Even though sirenians today only occupy tropical waters, even this warm water temperature is generally cooler than sirenian body temperature, so there is a tendency for the animal to lose heat to the environment rather than the other way around. Since water conveys heat from a body about 25 times faster than air does, it becomes clear why marine mammals, with their core body temperature similar to our own, have evolved attributes such as large size to help stay warm. An increase in body size is a relatively simple evolutionary solution to reduce heat loss. This is due to the physical relationships among body size, surface area, and volume. As an animal gets larger and body length increases, surface area increases proportionally to the second power, while volume increases proportionally to the third power[3]. Small animals have large surface-area-to-volume ratios whereas large animals have a low surface-area-to-volume ratio. Since body heat is lost at the interface with the environment, a lower surface-area-to-volume ratio means less heat loss for an animal.

Marine mammals are virtually free from the constraints of gravity, allowing large body sizes to be attained. For example, rorquals (baleen whales of the family Balaenopteridae) such as the blue whale *(Balaenoptera musculus)* include the largest living animals. In addition to increasing body size, marine mammals can influence heat gain or loss through various adaptations of the skin and cardiovascular systems called countercurrent heat exchangers[4] (figure 2.1). Manatees, and likely dugongs, have made use of such adaptations[5].

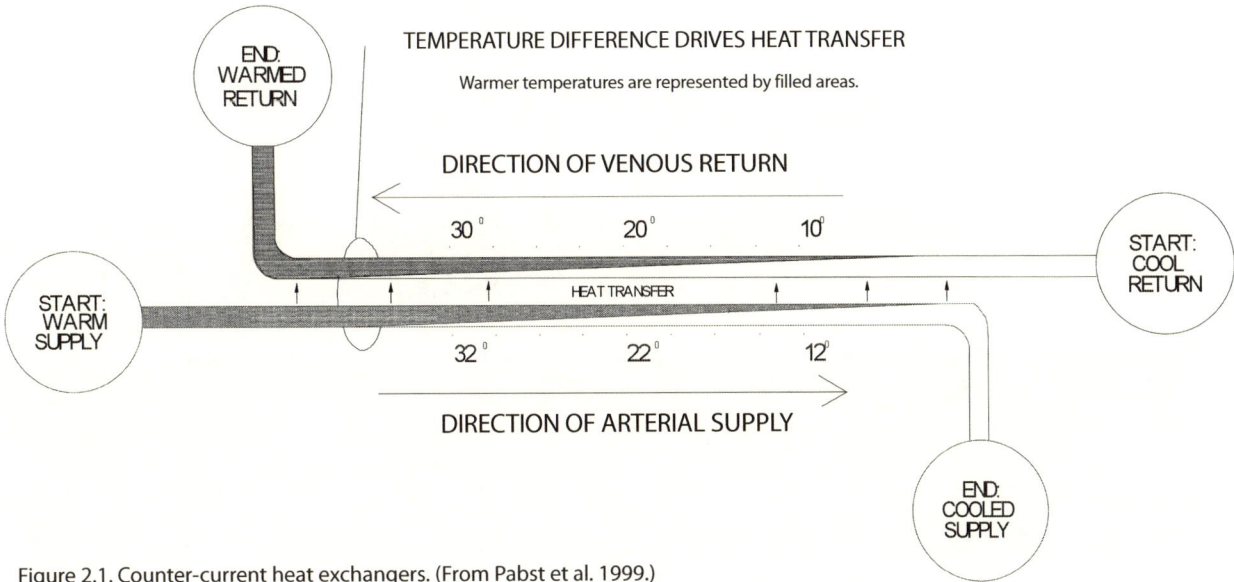

Figure 2.1. Counter-current heat exchangers. (From Pabst et al. 1999.)

Vulnerability Associated with Large Size and Other Life History Attributes

Life history can be defined as "the set of adaptations of an organism that more or less directly influence life table values of age-specific survival and fecundity; hence, reproductive rate, age at first reproduction, reproductive risk, etc[6]." Large animals of any kind have certain advantages over smaller animals (e.g., they may not have as many predators), but they are vulnerable in other ways. Most species of marine mammals, and all species of sirenians, have been exploited by commercial or subsistence hunters. As a result, some species have been dramatically reduced in numbers. It is a mistake to overlook the fact that larger species are generally not able to breed or recover easily from population declines[7]. These species are sometimes referred to in ecological terms as "K-strategists," a term describing species that have developed suites of anatomical, physiological, and behavioral adaptations or attributes that permit them to maintain relatively stable populations that hover at or near the carrying capacity (the number of individuals that can be sustainably supported) of their environment.

As well as being large, sirenians as K-strategists have long lifespans, physically develop and reach sexual maturity slowly, produce small litters (often one offspring at a time), breed numerous times in their lives (called iteroparity), provide long parental care for their few offspring, and are generally poor colonizers of new habitats. For further information on marine mammals as K-strategists and r-strategists (on the other end of the life history gradient), see Ricklefs[8].

The reproductive biology and life history attributes of dugongs in Australian waters, and of Florida manatees, have been reasonably well studied[9] and may apply to the other sirenians as well. Female Florida manatees can conceive as young as three years of age, and produce a single calf (rarely twins) every 2.5 years, although a much longer inter-birth interval can occur. Males can start to produce sperm as young as two years of age, but they may not be able to compete successfully for access to females until they mature physically and behaviorally[10]. Florida manatees can approach 60 years of age, although such a long lifespan is rarely reached due to high mortality (often caused by humans). Marsh has suggested[11] that manatee populations could, under ideal conditions, increase at a rate exceeding 6% per year. A much slower rate of increase is more likely under actual conditions[12].

Dugongs are slightly smaller than West Indian manatees, but dugong populations around Australia are likely to breed much more slowly, with sexual maturity being delayed in some cases until animals are between 10 and 15 years old. They experience significantly slower population growth, perhaps only half that of manatees. Marsh[13] and Kwan[14] have demonstrated tremendous plasticity in life history attributes of dugongs, apparently relating in part at least to availability of forage. Dugongs have been documented to live longer (up to 73 years) than manatees[15]. These life history strategies are important in conservation planning because, although complete data on all sirenian populations and species are lacking, it is clear that sirenians do not breed quickly and have trouble recovering their numbers if populations become reduced.

Humans have an unenviable history of managing resources poorly[16]. Part of the problem is that people often fail to recognize how the different adaptations of different species lead to different capabilities to reproduce and to recover from declining populations. As a result, people, including managers and representatives of government agencies, have often made nonconservative assumptions and consequently decisions that have jeopardized both species and livelihoods. As a K-strategist, an adult female West African manatee may produce only one calf every two to four years (a logical figure based on what we know of reproduction in Florida manatees). If West African manatees (especially sexually mature females) were inadvertently or deliberately overharvested, it would be biologically impossible, even under optimal conditions, to regenerate the population in a short period of time. If high harvest levels persisted for some time after the initial overharvest, West African manatees might become reduced to so few animals that recovery time could take decades, even under the best of conditions, or the population might not recover at all. For example, consider that North Atlantic right whales have not been harvested for decades, yet their numbers continue to hover at around 400 individuals[17].

Thus population simulation models that assume high species fecundity, are not conservative, and allow for occasional overharvest may condemn the K-strategists to perpetually low population numbers, as has occurred with the North Atlantic right whales. Other assumptions also affect the recovery, or nonrecovery, of similar populations or species.

One of the more common assumptions affecting recovery involves the misperception that K (environmental carrying capacity) is a constant. Nothing could be further from the truth. Natural environmental variation affects carrying capacity; so do pollution and incidental harvest of nontarget species. When people remove large numbers of certain species, remaining populations of other species are often affected. Take wolves and mountain lions out of an area, and deer and rabbit populations increase dramatically; harvest lots of deer and rabbits, and the wolves migrate or starve.

Such interdependence is also observed at the ecosystem level. For example, Dayton et al.[18] have demonstrated that due to changes brought about by human overfishing and other activities, even marine and estuarine ecosystems thought to be relatively pristine and full of wildlife are actually far removed from what is "normal." As scientists today assess such ecosystems, what should they use as appropriate natural benchmarks of ecosystem health? And without such benchmarks, what should be the goals of conservation and of restoration? Scientists and conservationists must act cautiously and conservatively when either harvesting or trying to affect the recovery of the K-strategists of the world. Conservation efforts need to consider both the direct impacts to the species in question and the indirect impacts, such as habitat destruction or any modification to the ecosystem as a whole. In the absence of such attention, it is unlikely that reduced populations will recover, even with admirable intentions, dedicated scientists and conservationists, unprecedented amounts of funds for both science and management, and ample protective legislation. The need for improved marine mammal conservation at the global scale is urgent[19].

Non Life History Attributes

Large size is not the only feature shaped evolutionarily by an aquatic lifestyle. Sirenians have evolved streamlined, spindle-shaped (fusiform) bodies lacking external protuberances that could increase drag. For example, the pelvic or hind limbs are absent, although vestiges of the pelvic bones exist deep in the muscles of sirenians. Pectoral or front limbs (called flippers) have become reduced in size and shaped like paddles. For locomotion, sirenians have powerful flukes that exist in two forms: a single, rounded fluke in the manatees, and split flukes (superficially similar to those in a dolphin) in the dugongs. In terms of energetics, the use of a fluke for swimming, as opposed to the sorts of motions humans use, is extremely efficient and permits forward propulsion on both the upstroke and the downstroke[20]. Sirenians can probably exceed 15 to 20 miles per hour in very short bursts—quite impressive, when one considers that the fastest swimming speed by a human is only slightly above five miles per hour. Although these flukes are evolutionarily efficient and make sirenians much faster swimmers than humans, sirenians are still comparatively slow relative to other marine mammals, which can make them vulnerable to boat strikes. The various adaptations mentioned and other features that induce vulnerability of sirenians are considered in greater detail in the rest of this chapter.

Proximity to People

The distribution of sirenians is linked to availability of the aquatic vegetation they require to survive. Hence sirenians of all species are found in coastal and riverine habitats close to humans. This simple fact causes sirenians to become exposed to a variety of activities that, alone or in combination, can threaten their existence[21].

Discussions fostered by the United Nations Environment Programme to create a Caribbean-wide Marine Mammal Action Plan illustrated some of the dangers experienced by inshore marine mammals[22]. The same threats can be applied, with relatively few modifications, to other habitats occupied by sirenian species. For example, people occupying rivers or coastlines where sirenians live have captured manatees and dugongs deliberately for food and other products (oil, bones for carving, leather) as well as incidentally during fishing or other activities. Subsistence hunting probably occurs at some level in many of the countries occupied by sirenians today; in some areas where sirenians are abundant (e.g., the Torres Strait, off northern Australia) takes by subsistence hunters have been estimated to number hundreds of animals per year, even in recent times[23]. In Brazil a commercial hunt for manatees existed from the seventeenth century through the middle years of the twentieth century, primarily for meat and leather. This hunt accounted for the demise of many tens of thousands of animals[24].

Incidental or accidental taking of marine mammals[25] accounts for the deaths of several thousand animals each year, and although good data do not exist for most sirenian species, Marsh et al.[26] noted that more than 800 dugongs were killed when they became entangled in nets set to protect bathers from sharks in Queensland, Australia, between 1962 and 1999. The best-documented type of "incidental taking" of sirenians occurs in Florida, where accidental collisions between watercraft and manatees kill some 100 animals each year and seriously injure many more[27]. Boat-related damage to and displacement of sirenians have become more and more widely reported.

Proximity to people also can affect the habitat of sirenians. They are the only living mammals that are marine herbivores, which means that sirenians depend on submerged, floating, or even emergent vegetation. Disruption of habitat due to dredge and fill, coastal run-off, or even scarring of vegetation by boat propellers can affect the quality and quantity of their food and can affect nutrition, growth, and reproduction. This has led the state of Florida (USA) to increase its protection of seagrass beds[28]. Increased boat traffic in shallow water over seagrasses has led to increased scarring of this habitat by propellers. Such scars lead to erosion and fragmentation of seagrass beds, ultimately resulting in loss of the complete habitat[29]. Since seagrass beds are nursery grounds for numerous marine species, loss of seagrass is detrimental not only for sirenians but to the entire ecosystem[30].

Although body burdens of contaminants of various types are poorly studied in sirenians (see chapter 22, this volume), their habit of rooting in sediment does place them in contact with persistent organic pollutants and heavy metals. In fact, a study of persistent organic pollutants in dugongs[31] found levels of octachlorodibenzo-p-dioxins and dibenzofurans as high as in carnivorous marine mammals—surprising since the herbivorous diet of dugongs means that they feed lower on the food chain than carnivores. An analysis of persistent organic pollutants in the sediment of seagrass beds near the Great Barrier Reef (Australia), common dugong foraging habitat, also found high levels, indicating that persistent organic pollutants found in dugongs were incidentally ingested during foraging[32]. Ames and Van Vleet[33] and O'Shea et al.[34] found that the level of most contaminants (organochlorines and some metals) in Florida manatees was low, although Wetzel (pers. comm.) has found PCBs in tissues of manatees sampled in relatively pristine parts of the Mexican coast[35].

Therefore chemical pollution also degrades sirenian habitat, even in rather undeveloped locations, and can affect their general health and survival. One factor in the favor of sirenians as opposed to other marine mammals is that the former occupy a low trophic level as herbivores and may be less predisposed to exposures of high contaminant loads of some (but not all) classes of toxicants than are top predators[36].

Aside from chemical pollution, sirenians in some parts of their ranges are exposed to high levels of noise pollution due to intensive boating. There is some evidence in Florida that watercraft-induced noise affects manatees' behavior and choice of habitat[37]. It appears that manatees sometimes intentionally forage and travel at night to avoid encounters with watercraft[38]. There are other, surprising ways by which contact with humans can create problems for sirenians in the shallow waters they occupy. Manatees in Sierra Leone (West Africa) are actively hunted by the Mende people, who view them as pests that ruin nets and plunder rice paddies; the Mende also enjoy eating manatee meat[39].

Simply being near people can cause sirenians to be hunted deliberately, accidentally killed or injured, exposed to noise pollution and chemical pollution, displaced from preferred habitat, and otherwise affected. The synergistic or cumulative effects of people on sirenians are unmeasured but likely to be significant.

Anatomy, Function, and Vulnerability

Additional adaptations that sirenians share include a lack of fur, having instead only sparse hairs on their bodies; lack of an externally distinct neck (another feature associated with streamlining); and extremely heavy bones, which are both pachyostotic (thickened) and osteosclerotic (hard, dense, and solid), a feature that facilitates bottom foraging[40].

Adaptations associated with their herbivorous ancestry have also played a role in the features that unite all sirenians. All living sirenian species have specialized dentition (teeth) and horny plates in the mouth to help crush and grind ingested plants. In addition, the brains of sirenians are not large, which is not surprising since herbivores tend to have relatively smaller brains than carnivores of the same body size.

Although much more is known regarding Florida manatees than dugongs and other sirenians, many sensory attributes known for trichechids may be transferred to dugongs, though with caution. Our current understanding of sirenian sensory biology demonstrates that sirenians are tactile mammals, viewing their world through the sense of touch (somatosensation). The regions of the brain (thalamus) and brainstem related to somatosensation are disproportionately large relative to other brain structures dedicated to other senses[41]. Although it appears that manatees can see in color and discriminate between grayscales and color[42], sirenian eyes are small relative to head and body size. Early work by Walls[43] suggested that manatee vision has adapted to dim lighting conditions. Much anatomical work on manatees' eyes[44] suggests that their vision is limited, particularly at close distances. In addition, the visual center of the brain is limited and the visual cranial nerve that relays the information is relatively small[45]. However, field observations and behavioral performance tests seem to indicate that manatee vision can be quite good and is used primarily for intermediate and longer distance inspection of large objects[46]. Bauer, a specialist in manatee sensory biology, feels[47] that manatees may be good at detecting motion or particular visual stimuli, but that their image forming abilities are poor compared to humans. He suggests that manatee vision is similar to that of another, better known grazer: the cow. However, manatees, and to some extent dugongs, inhabit turbid waters where vision is not of much use and other senses are likely to be extremely important.

Both manatees and dugongs are sparsely covered with hair over their entire body. The sparse density of hair makes it clear that the function of these hairs is not thermoregulation, or protection. Recently, Reep et al.[48] demonstrated that postcranial hairs, and in fact all manatees hairs, likely serve a sensory function. Sirenians are unique among mammals in that all the hairs over the head and body are follicle-sinus complexes, a type of tactile organ commonly associated with vibrissae or whiskers. Such complexes convey tactile cues from the environment to the central nervous system and are usually limited to the face and muzzle region of most mammals. The arrangement in sirenians likely represents an underwater tactile system capable of conveying detailed information regarding water currents, approaching animals, and possibly nearby large stationary features[49]. Although behavioral studies are needed to verify the sensitivity of this system, it appears to be functionally analogous to the lateral line in fish, and would be particularly useful for navigating turbid waters commonly frequented by manatees or for detecting tidal changes. The downfall of possessing such a system, and being a tactile animal, is that sensation usually occurs in close proximity to an individual. For example, it is unlikely that a water displacement detection system analogous to a lateral line system would be able to detect fast-moving boats in time to avoid a strike.

In contrast to the visual system, the brain region associated with hearing in manatees is relatively well developed. Water transmits sound much faster than air (~4.5 times faster). Although low frequency sounds in the aquatic environment travel farther than high frequency sounds, high frequency sounds are useful to aquatic animals for localizing direction of sound. An underwater audiogram of West Indian manatees indicates that a conservative estimate of their maximum hearing range is from 0.4 to 46 kHz, with the best hearing between 6 and 20 kHz[50]. The results of this study suggest that manatees may be unable to hear low frequency sounds of motorboats due to their limited sensitivity at low frequencies (most boat noise is below 1 kHz; although this greatly depends on the type of boat, boat engine, and boat speed). The audiogram data suggest that the manatee hearing range is somewhat broader than expected, based on anatomical studies of the inner ear (cochlea[51]) and electrophysiological studies of the brain activity (using evoked potential methods[52]), but still poor in the lower frequencies. Such deficits likely make manatees vulnerable to boat strikes. In contrast, evidence from field studies[53] suggests that manatee hearing may be better than these studies indicate. Wright et al.[54] and Nowacek et al.[55] suggest that manatees can respond to boat noise as far away as 65 meters but may not always be able to respond appropriately. For example, manatees may not respond in time before the strike, may not be able to distinguish between multiple sound sources, and may even move toward an approaching boat[56]. Biochemical evidence[57] and behavioral evidence using trained captive manatees[58] suggest that manatees have at least some ability to localize sound underwater. Further complicating our ability to understand manatee hearing capability, manatees inhabit shallow waters with varying topography, and in areas of high density of boat traffic, where the acoustic environment is extremely complex and variable. It is clear that manatees are vulnerable to boat strikes, likely due to their failure to detect and/or respond appropriately to these threats in a timely manner.

Sirenians exhibit a suite of adaptations for benthic foraging that influence hydrostasis, or the maintenance of equilibrium in the water[59]. They must come to the surface to breathe. Food, however, is often on the bottom, or brought to the bottom preferentially to eat[60]. Therefore sirenians are constantly moving between the two locations. Adaptations for buoyancy can be found in modifications of the whole body plan, changes in the skeletal system, lungs, and, surprisingly, the skin[61]. It is advantageous for sirenians to be slightly negatively buoyant to facilitate benthic foraging. Manatees, and to a lesser extent dugongs, have evolved thickened, solid ribs, which are near the center of the mass of the body. This ballast is compensated for by an unusual arrangement of the lungs and diaphragm. The usual condition is for the diaphragm to divide to the body into front and back (cranial and caudal) portions, but unlike in most mammals, the diaphragm of sirenians generally divides the body into upper and lower (dorsal and ventral) portions. This arrangement results in a thoracic cavity, the cavity where the lungs are located, that spans most of the length of the animal[62] and greatly changes the hydrostasis of the species[63]. Likewise the abdominal cavity, the space where the digestive tract resides, also is horizontal and spans most of the length of the animal. This is useful since manatees have a greatly elaborated digestive tract, and the horizontal position spreads its weight along the axis of the body, making changes in buoyancy easier. Surprisingly, the mass and density of manatee skin produces negative buoyancy[64]. The lungs, ribcage, and skin comprise a functional complex that has been modified to adjust buoyancy and hydrostasis, presumably to reduce the energetics for traveling between the surface and the bottom.

Although manatee bones have been termed pachyostotic (thickened bone), their bones also exhibit osteosclerosis, a condition in which less dense bone (called cancellous or spongy bone) is replaced with dense compact bone[65]. Each of these phenomena increases the mass of each bone through increased bone diameter, density, mineralization, and compactness. Therefore the long bones of manatees are best described as pachyosteosclerotic, a term that describes well those characteristics of long bones that increase ballast for the individual. Manatee long bone microstructure results in material properties that leave manatees highly susceptible to fatal injuries when struck by boats[66]. Static material tests of manatee ribs demonstrate that the bones behave as a quasi-brittle solid, similar to ceramic material. The strength and toughness of manatee bone has been tested and found to be lower than expected for other mammalian bone. Impact energy calculations show that after taking the overlying soft tissue into account, manatee bones fracture at a kinetic energy of 17kJ[67]. In real world terms this means that when a typical 17-foot boat traveling at a speed of 13–15 mph (i.e., a relatively small boat moving at modest speed) strikes a manatee, the impact could fatally fracture its ribs. Although further testing needs to be conducted, it is clear that in manatees and likely all sirenians, the skeletal adaptations beneficial for benthic foraging also make them vulnerable to boat strikes.

As noted, sirenians are unique among marine mammals in that they are aquatic herbivores. They are also hindgut (large intestine) fermenters, as are horses, elephants, and rabbits, and must spend most of the day foraging. Since aquatic vegetation is nutritionally poor, it is advantageous to be efficient in handling vegetation[68]. The sirenian snout is extremely muscular and mobile and represents a short "elephantine" trunk[69] with substantial innervation[70]. The lip region of the snout is enlarged (especially the upper lip) and is equipped with six fields of short, stout vibrissae or whiskers (called bristles in sirenians[71]). The distribution of these bristles differs slightly between manatees and dugongs likely due to their general vs. specialized foraging strategies[72]. Sirenian whiskers are unusual among mammals in that these vibrissae are used for both prehensile manipulation and sensory roles. The importance of both of these functions is indicated by the large regions in the brain and the brainstem dedicated to motor and sensory functions[73]. Both manatees and dugongs use this muscular-vibrissal complex to explore new objects or food in their environment[74]. This complex is a highly effective adaptation for ingesting the large quantities of aquatic vegetation needed to sustain sirenians. Psychophysical testing of manatee tactile discrimination power conducted by Bachteler and Dehnhardt[75] demonstrated that West Indian manatees are quite capable of using the snout, muzzle, and associated sensory hair to discriminate between objects of various different textures. The tactile resolution of manatees' muzzle and whiskers is lower than that of pinnipeds but similar to that of elephants, the closest relative of manatees. The muscular, mobile snout of sirenians is just one part of the food-gathering apparatus. Both manatees and dugongs have a horny upper and lower palate. They do not possess incisors and canines—only cheek-teeth. However, in dugongs, tusks erupt in males and occasional old females[76]. Both groups can use these structures to grind plants and transport food further into the mouth[77]. In dugongs, it is suspected that the upper and lower horny palate may do most of the mastication. The now extinct Steller's sea cow, a member of the dugong family, fed primarily on kelp and did not possess any teeth[78]. It is likely that macroalgae were processed with these enlarged upper and lower horny palates. Unlike dugongs, manatees evolved in riverine systems that contained a lot of terrestrial grasses[79]. These grasses are highly abrasive and quickly wear down teeth. All herbivores must contend with the issue of tooth wear because of the abrasive properties of plants.

The teeth of manatees are unusual among mammals in that their teeth migrate from the back of the mouth toward the front, as if on a slow-moving conveyer belt[80]. By the time a tooth has migrated from the back of the tooth row to the front, it is worn down and simply falls out of the mouth. A new tooth erupts in the back of the tooth row to replace it. The timing of tooth wear and migration depends upon how abrasive and fibrous the diet is and the amount of chewing needed to process the food. Apparently manatees have an unlimited number of replacement teeth (called supernumerary teeth). Although the sirenian feeding apparatus is efficient for foraging on aquatic vegetation, the animals must still forage for six to eight hours a day[81]. Since much of their forage is in shallow water, this makes sirenians particularly vulnerable to boat strikes and hunting.

Herbivores have expanded areas of their digestive systems which function as fermentation vats for the breakdown of cellulose (cellulolysis). They rely on a flourishing population of microbes in the gut to break down the cellulose that constitutes such a prominent component of plant biomass. Mammals lack the digestive enzymes to break down cellulose, so a symbiotic relationship with organisms that possess those enzymes is vital for mammalian herbivores. The rewards to the host are the products of cellulose breakdown by the microbes; these products, called volatile fatty acids, are absorbed from the digestive system and nourish the host.

Animals such as horses and sirenians are considered hindgut digesters; hindgut digesters cannot regurgitate fermenting materials. Plant materials are not held long in their digestive tracts[82] and tend to be incompletely broken down by the time they are excreted as wastes from the body. Hindgut digesters are not as efficient as ruminants at extracting nutrients from food. However, they can take advantage of low quality plants (such as seagrasses), whereas ruminants cannot. This has two clear behavioral and physiological consequences: hindgut digesters must constantly take in food, but hindgut digesters can survive on low quality forage.

Sirenians may spend eight hours or more feeding each day. Seagrasses and other aquatic plants are not exceptionally nutritious, but that is not really a concern for hindgut digesters. The large intestines of sirenians are enlarged fermentation vats that achieve astounding dimensions; they measure over 20 meters long, weighing with contents up to 70 kilograms, and represent an impressive 14% of the body weight[83].

Manatees and presumably dugongs have extremely low metabolic rates, about 15–20% of what scientists would expect, based on body size. Especially in Florida and in parts of dugong range, where water temperatures may be 40–50 degrees Fahrenheit lower than manatee core body temperature, staying warm is a notable challenge. A by-product of cellulolysis is heat. Rommel et al.[84] have noted that manatees in Florida have much greater girth abdominally than do manatees of the same species in Central America. This is the case even for manatees for which body length and blubber thicknesses are equal—Florida manatees tend to be bigger around than their more tropical cousins. Rommel, Reynolds, and their colleagues intend to investigate heat production and loss in manatees and speculate that through natural selection, the Florida manatees have acquired larger cellulose fermentation vats (namely the large intestines) than their warm-water relatives possess, simply as an adaptation to staying warm.

The need to process food constantly to secure additional heat from cellulolysis constitutes another point of vulnerability for sirenian populations that occupy cooler waters at the edges of their ranges, such as in Florida and in Australia for dugongs. When cold fronts occur, such animals may seek warm water to survive the lower temperatures[85]. When this happens, the animals may find little to eat near the sources of warm water, and as they fast, their internal generation of heat may decline dramatically. After the front passes, these animals may venture out to feed but, in so doing, enter cold water where they may be vulnerable without their internal "furnaces" at work.

Sirenians embody an unusual suite of adaptations. As the only living mammals that are both marine and herbivorous, they have been shaped for several tens of millions of years in ways that no other mammals have. Given the constraints imposed by both their herbivorous ancestry and an environment dramatically different from that of their ancestors, they have become an especially unusual group. Their adaptations unfortunately convey inherent vulnerability that must be recognized and accounted for if these animals are to be conserved effectively. To conserve sirenians properly, one must not only use an anticipatory and proactive approach[86] but also take into account those fundamental natural history attributes about which we already know a great deal.

SECTION I

Regional Issues in Sirenian Conservation

3

Florida Manatee Status and Conservation Issues

A Primer

CHARLES J. DEUTSCH AND JOHN E. REYNOLDS III

Manatees make headlines and television news stories on a regular basis in Florida, whether it involves the rescue of an orphan or injured animal from a backyard canal or impassioned protests at public hearings regarding proposed speed zones. The public's fascination with this charismatic aquatic mammal generates strong support for its conservation and protection. Each winter the media wait with bated breath to report the manatee count from statewide surveys, and to learn how many manatees were killed by vessel collisions in the previous year. These statistics and other biological data often end up in the courtroom, where they may form the basis and context for arguments for and against manatee protection measures. Few other species garner this attention or generate such strong emotions. Consequently, the work of researchers and the decisions of managers frequently come under the spotlight of public scrutiny.

This chapter is a primer on the status and conservation issues generated by the coexistence of an endangered sirenian with a large human population. The chapter

(1) provides an up-to-date and concise overview of manatee population status in the United States;
(2) identifies the principal threats facing the species now and in the coming decades;
(3) summarizes the findings of models that forecast manatee population dynamics decades into the future;
(4) outlines the legal protections afforded manatees by state and federal government legislation;
(5) broadly evaluates management efforts undertaken to protect manatees and their habitat in Florida; and
(6) outlines the major types of research efforts needed to address key management questions.

We conclude with a look at the challenges that lie ahead for researchers and decision makers.

Readers interested in additional information on Florida manatee biology, ecology, and conservation can refer to a number of excellent books[1].

Population Status

The Florida manatee (*Trichechus manatus latirostris*) is the northern subspecies of the West Indian manatee[2] that inhabits shallow coastal and inland waters of the southeastern United States. It is morphologically and genetically distinct from the Antillean manatee (*T. manatus manatus*)[3], although it is genetically closer to *T. m. manatus* populations in the Greater Antilles than to those in other geographic regions[4].

"How are manatees doing?" is probably the most common question manatee scientists in Florida hear. Yet it is difficult to answer concisely. How manatees are faring varies considerably across their geographic range, and there are several components to assessing population status. Two of the most commonly used measures are abundance and range because the smaller and more geographically restricted a population is, the more vulnerable it is to catastrophes and to the detrimental effects of inbreeding and demographic stochasticity[5]. The spatial structure of the population—whether it is fragmented into small, isolated subpopulations—is also crucial. Population growth rate is a key indicator of current and future status. A holistic understanding of population status must also consider the health of individuals. Finally, determining causes of mortality is essential for identifying major threats and their trends. In-depth assessments of Florida manatee population status have been completed recently[6].

Range and Distribution

Florida manatees are found only in the United States, which is the northernmost extreme of the species' range, though a few wanderers have been known to reach the Bahamas[7] and even Cuba[8] (map 3.1). Year-round range in the United States is generally restricted to peninsu-

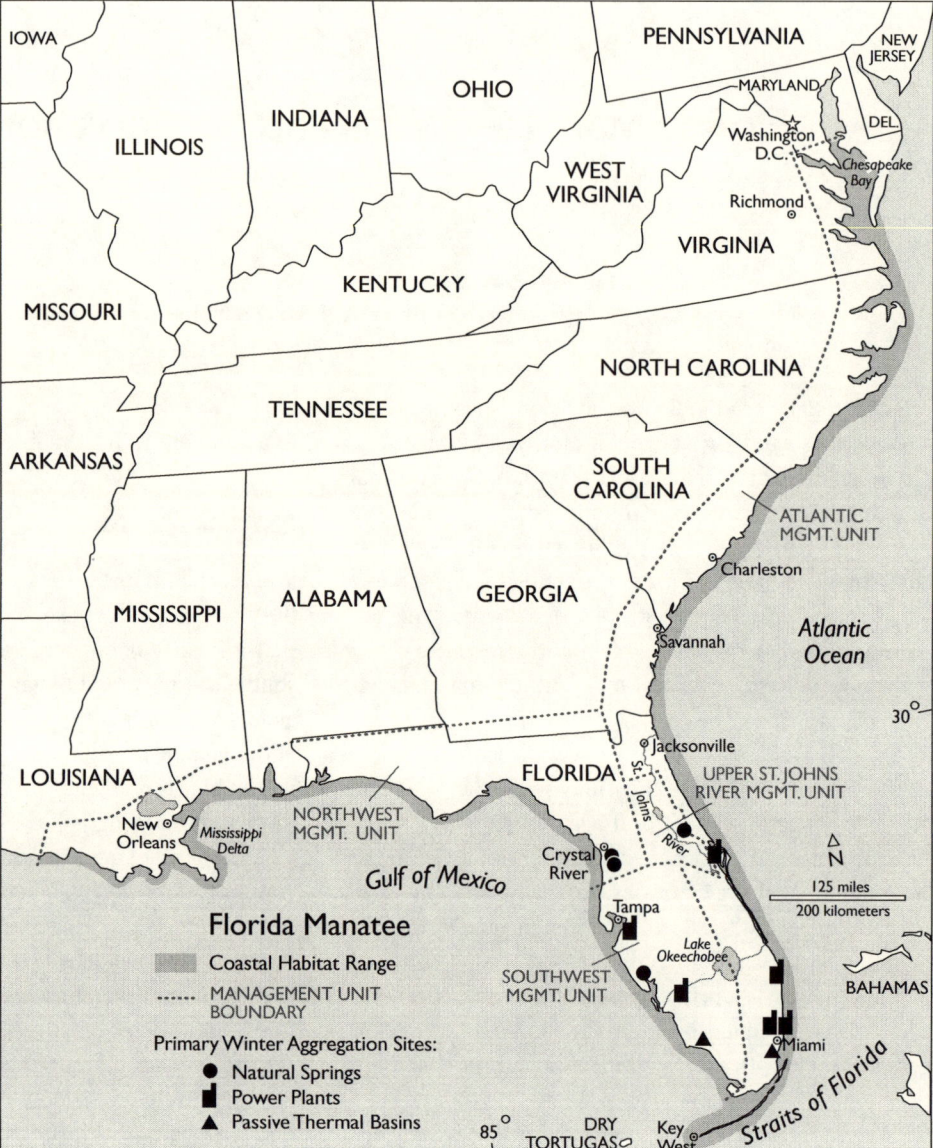

Map 3.1. Florida manatee distribution. (Map by Ellen McElhinny.)

lar Florida because manatees need warm water to survive the winter. During the warm season (March/April through October/November) when water temperatures exceed 20°C, manatees disperse throughout the shallow coastal waters, estuaries, and major rivers of Florida, and some migrate north to neighboring states including Georgia, South Carolina, North Carolina, and Virginia[9]. One satellite-tagged manatee was documented to travel from Port Everglades, Florida to Rhode Island, a distance of 2,360 km[10]. Other extralimital sightings of lone manatees have been made recently as far away as Massachusetts[11]. Along the Gulf coast west of Florida, manatees are occasionally sighted in Alabama, Mississippi, Louisiana, and Texas[12]. The source (Florida or Mexico) of the Texas manatees is not always clear, but the weight of evidence suggests most recent sightings involve the Florida subspecies[13]. The record for a manatee that swam the farthest up an inland waterway was set by one found in Memphis, Tennessee, in October 2006, about 1,400 km up the Mississippi River.

Florida manatees are highly mobile, migrating seasonally over long distances in response to seasonal fluctuation in water temperature[14]. They also are strongly philopatric to seasonal home ranges, a characteristic likely to be a general behavioral feature of manatee populations elsewhere[15]. Manatees are generalist herbivores[16] that occupy a wide range of habitats and salinity regimes. Manatee distribution constricts dramatically in the winter season when they seek shelter from the cold at a limited number of warm-water sites or areas in the southern two-thirds of Florida[17] (map 3.1). This habitat requirement is dictated by their peculiar physiology—an exceedingly low metabolic rate and relatively high thermal conductance[18]—adaptations to a lifestyle of aquatic herbivory in a tropical or subtropical climate. The primary warm-water aggregation sites currently frequented by a large proportion of the manatee population during winter include seven power plant thermal outfalls, four major artesian springs, and two passive thermal basins (areas that retain heat longer than ambient waters). Some of these sites provide thermal shelter for hundreds of manatees[19]. Other industrial outfalls, smaller springs, and thermal basins provide additional but apparently less suitable warm-water habitat.

Population Structure and Abundance

We know from the fossil record that manatees (*T. manatus*) have inhabited the waterways of present-day Florida since the early Pleistocene 1.1 to 1.5 million years ago[20]. Evidence of manatee hunting in Florida by Paleo-Indians has been found as far back as 10,000 years ago[21]. The manatee's tendency to aggregate around warm-water sources during winter probably made them vulnerable to hunters, especially in north-central Florida. Hunting by Native Americans and later by European settlers and American pioneers is speculated to have suppressed population numbers[22] and to have shifted manatee winter distribution to the southern portion of the Florida peninsula[23]. There are no estimates of historical abundance, but anecdotal evidence suggests that there are more manatees in Florida today than there have been for at least the past half-century[24].

Long-term studies of individual manatees using photo-identification techniques and radio-telemetry indicate that there are four relatively distinct regional subpopulations[25] (map 3.1). Subpopulations are defined as "geographically or otherwise distinct groups in the population between which there is little demographic or genetic exchange."[26] Each manatee subpopulation is composed of individuals that use the same network of warm-water refugia each winter and have similar distribution patterns during the warm season. Movement of individuals among these four regions, especially between the east and west coasts, appears to be limited[27]. Recently, there has been a shift to refer to these subpopulations as management units[28] because of apparently minimal genetic differentiation and documentation of some movement among regions. Ongoing genetic and photo-identification studies may shed further light on the degree of demographic and genetic exchange among regions.

The Florida manatee has a low level of genetic diversity: only one mtDNA haplotype has been found in Florida, as compared to three each in Puerto Rico, Mexico, and Belize[29], where the population sizes are far smaller. Furthermore, levels of polymorphism and allelic diversity in microsatellite nuclear DNA are also extremely low[30], evidently the result of either a founder effect when the current population was established or a major bottleneck in the past[31].

Although we have considerable data on relative abundance and distribution of manatees in Florida, there is no statistically based estimate of population size. Such an estimate needs to take into account the proportion of manatees outside the surveyed areas, the proportion present but unavailable (e.g., too deep) to be counted, and the proportion of those that were available but not observed[32]. Range-wide synoptic surveys covering warm-water aggregation sites have been conducted nearly every winter since 1991[33]. The highest synoptic count to date was 5,076 manatees in January 2010[34]. This is considered a minimum count because it does not account for the proportion of animals unobserved. Marked temporal and spatial variation in detection probability explains why the synoptic counts can vary dramatically from survey to survey, and so it is inappropriate to use these raw counts in population trend analyses. The highest synoptic counts for each of the subpopulations provide a general idea of their relative abundances, with the Atlantic and Southwest being the largest two (see table 3.1). Craig and Reynolds (2004) estimated the winter population of manatees (excluding small calves) using Atlantic coast power plants to be 1,607 (95% Bayesian credible interval = 1,353–1,972) in 2001. The highest synoptic counts in the Atlantic region around that time were 1,444 and 1,683 in 2001 and 2003, respectively.

Population Trends

A better indicator of the vigor of a population than abundance is trends in its size. This can be evaluated through an analysis of time series of absolute or relative indices of population size[35], or through statistical models that estimate population growth rate based on age-specific vital rates. Runge et al.[36] estimated growth rates for each manatee subpopulation based on a biologically realistic matrix model that incorporated stage-specific survival and reproductive rates[37]. These vital rates were estimated using mark-recapture analyses of long-term photo-identification databases that store the sighting histories of individually recognizable manatees[38].

Winter surveys and population models indicate that the Northwest (NW) and Upper St. Johns River (USJ) subpopulations have grown substantially since the 1970s (table 3.1)[39]. These findings demonstrate the level

Table 3.1. Population statistics for the four subpopulations or management units of the Florida manatee.

	NW	SW	USJ	ATL	References
Count (%) from synoptic survey with highest total range-wide count (n = 5,076, Jan 2010)	673 (13.3%)	1,623 (32.0%)	230 (4.5%)	2,550 (50.2%)	FWC unpublished data
Past average annual population growth rate (%/year), 95% CI, (years)	4.0% 2.0–6.0 (1986–2000)	-1.1% -5.4–+2.4 (1995–2000)	6.2% 3.7–8.1 (1990–1999)	3.7% 1.1–5.9 (1986–2000)	Runge et al. 2004, 2007b
Future average annual population growth rate over next 10 years (%/year), (SD)	2.2% (2.5)	-3.7% (3.5)	5.0% (1.8)	-0.1% (1.5)	Runge et al. 2007a
% of adult carcasses (known causes only) with human-related causes of death, 1990–2009 (% including unknown causes)*	52.2 (35.6)	53.5 (38.4)	80.6 (51.8)	78.0 (52.5)	FWC unpublished data

* The first value assumes animals in the unknown group died from causes in the same proportion as the known group. The value in parentheses assumes that none of the deaths in the undetermined category were due to human-related causes and so provides a minimum figure.

of population recovery that is possible when human-related mortality is kept low and adult survival is correspondingly high (~96%/year). This positive news is tempered by the knowledge that these are the two smallest subpopulations, comprising only 17.8% of the highest synoptic count in 2010. Furthermore, these regions have experienced much less impact from coastal development and waterborne human activities than more urbanized sections of the Florida coastline.

Recently updated adult survival rates for the Atlantic subpopulation provide a more positive outlook on growth rate (table 3.1)[40] than had been estimated previously[41]. The 95% confidence bounds of annual growth rate generated by this updated model generally encompass the estimated annual growth in aerial counts of manatees at Atlantic coast power plants based on a Bayesian model[42]. The population growth rate in the Southwest (SW) region is less certain than in the other regions (table 3.1). However, estimates indicate population decline at –1.1%/year, and 71% of the simulated values of growth rate were negative[43]. This reflects lower apparent adult survival in the SW[44], which is probably due to a combination of chronic mortality from vessel collisions and episodic natural mortality events caused by red tide.

Principal Threats to Manatees and Their Habitat

As discussed in preceding chapters, manatees are confronted with a variety of threats from human activities and natural events. Certain aspects of their biology, including life history features and coastal habitat requirements, contribute to increased vulnerability from human pressures[45].

Anthropogenic Mortality

Nearly half (45.2%) of documented *adult* mortality in Florida is directly attributable to human activities (table 3.1), substantially depressing manatee population growth; about three-quarters of these cases are due to vessel strikes[46]. The actual figure is probably greater because cause of death is undetermined in about one-third of carcasses; human-related activities were responsible for 65.1% of adult deaths of known cause over the past two decades (table 3.1). This is a significant finding because population growth of manatees, as in other large mammals, is most sensitive to changes in adult survivorship[47].

Watercraft collisions with manatees cause numerous injuries and deaths each year. They account for about 25% of all reported deaths and about 35% of reported deaths of known cause[48]. A recent quantitative analysis of threats concluded that vessel collision represents the greatest single threat that could lead to quasi-extinction, defined as the number of adults falling below a critical threshold number[49]. This is because it reduces the population's intrinsic rate of increase and hence its ability to recover from catastrophic population declines. In essence, the population becomes less resilient. If anthropogenic mortality is high enough to offset recruitment, then population size will be ratcheted down in a staircase fashion with each catastrophic event. Over 1 million vessels were registered in the State of Florida in 2005[50] and many more out-of-state boaters visit Florida annually. The number of registered vessels in Florida has increased by 2.9% per year over the past 25 years, doubling since 1980[51]. The risk posed by watercraft is likely to increase in the future as long as the human population continues to expand. Redesign of vessel hulls and engines has made it possible for boats to travel at higher speeds in shallower waters[52], thus potentially increasing the threat to manatees and seagrass beds.

A smaller number of manatees (6% of documented deaths) are injured and killed by other human activities or waterway structures, including crushing and drowning in navigation locks and water-control structures; entrapment in stormwater pipes, culverts, and other structures; entanglement in fishing gear; and ingestion of fishing and other debris[53]. Expensive technological modifications to most locks and water-control structures responsible for past manatee mortality have successfully reduced the incidence of such crushing deaths; retrofitting the remaining key structures with manatee protection devices is planned to be completed by 2012[54]. Entanglement in crab trap lines and monofilament fishing lines rarely results in death[55] but can cause disfiguring injuries that include amputation of a flipper[56]. Manatees often have to run a gauntlet of "active" and discarded monofilament line as they pass by spots favored by recreational fishers. Once a flipper suffers a constriction-type injury from wrapped fishing line, the individual appears to become more susceptible to re-entanglement[57].

Habitat Loss and Degradation

The most serious habitat threat to Florida manatee recovery over the long term is the predicted loss and degradation of warm-water sources currently provided by power plant effluents and natural springs[58]. Among other things, loss of warm-water habitat will lower the carrying capacity of the region and therefore reduce the buffering capacity afforded by a larger population[59]. The inexpensive once-through cooling technology that power plants have employed to dissipate waste heat has been exploited by manatees over the past 50 plus years for thermal shelter in winter. Anticipated changes in the electric utility industry—including retirement or intermittent operation of aging power plants, deregulation, and use of alternate cooling technologies required under the federal Clean Water Act—threaten the reliability of this warm-water network now used by a large proportion of the manatee population. Given the strong site fidelity exhibited by manatees[60], and the observed behavioral responses to and mortality associated with loss or interruption of warm-water effluents[61], it is generally recognized that the elimination of a few key industrial thermal refuges could have catastrophic consequences for the manatees, causing immediate mortality and a long-term reduction in carrying capacity.

As industrial warm-water sites disappear over the next few decades, manatees will need to rely more on natural springs and passive thermal basins. Unfortunately, humans have substantially altered many spring systems so that they are no longer freely accessible to manatees[62]. Furthermore, spring flows have declined from historical levels due to groundwater withdrawals and loss of recharge areas from development[63]. The human population in Florida grew by 45.3% to 18.8 million from 1990 to 2010; projections indicate that the number of residents may nearly double to 36 million by 2060[64]. Increasing water demands will likely cause further declines in spring flow and water quality. The state Water Management Districts are establishing targets for minimum flows and levels of rivers and springs to prevent significant ecological harm from permitted withdrawals. Maintenance of flows above these set minimum levels and enforcement of regulations in the face of human needs during droughts will likely be a challenge.

Rampant human development in the coastal zone of Florida over the past century has resulted in substantial loss of seagrass and other manatee foraging habitat. These losses have resulted from direct physical impacts, such as dredge and fill activities, and from indirect impacts of increased nutrient loading and reduced water clarity[65]. Within Tampa Bay, for example, only about 20% of the seagrass estimated to be present in the early 1900s was still there in 1980[66]. The manatee population does not appear to be near carrying capacity set by forage resources because there is no evidence of widespread malnourishment, declining body condition, or suppressed reproduction. Nevertheless, long-term protection of submerged aquatic vegetation near warm-water aggregation sites will be vital to manatee overwinter survival. Catastrophic large-scale die-offs of seagrass associated with extreme weather events or disease[67] also pose a serious potential threat.

Harmful Algal Blooms and Other Emerging Threats

Manatees in Florida face a number of threats from natural phenomena, including hurricanes[68], extreme cold[69], pathogens[70], and harmful algal blooms[71]. Chemical and acoustic pollution have largely unknown effects on manatee health[72], and burgeoning ecotourism is increasing

Transforming Manatee Tourism into Ecotourism

Michael G. Sorice

Each winter thousands of tourists flock to Crystal River, Florida, for the opportunity to swim with manatees. With its warm, clear, spring-fed waters the Kings Bay in Crystal River is an ideal site to encounter manatees. The animals are locally abundant during winter months, the waters provide good visibility, and most manatees are tolerant of humans. Some even approach swimmers for interaction.

Swim-with-manatee trips begin just after dawn with tourists renting boats or taking guided tours with local dive shops. Federally designated manatee sanctuaries, most created around key manatee aggregation areas (i.e., warm-water springs), prohibit human entry and allow manatees to avoid direct encounters with people and boats. Tourists in wetsuits and snorkel gear swim outside these sanctuary boundaries to observe manatees up close, and to touch, pet, and even "play" with the animals that venture out.

A number of concerns have been raised suggesting that these activities are not in line with ecotourism principles. First, there are concerns regarding the "do no harm" ethic central to ecotourism (Wearing and Neil 1999). Even with federal sanctuaries in place, some groups argue that more action must be taken to minimize the potential negative impacts of the human-manatee encounters (Sorice et al. 2006). Other than the sanctuaries there are no mechanisms to limit access or to control use spatially or temporally. Consequently, a high density of tourists is concentrated in the early morning hours at the two primary manatee aggregation areas.

Some groups, including nongovernmental organizations and some federal and state wildlife agencies, object to the interaction itself. They believe it constitutes harassment and is a violation of federal law. A quick search on YouTube.com shows videos with tourists disturbing resting manatees, separating a mother-calf pair, and crowding, poking, and riding individuals. General disturbance may result in short-term behavioral changes that can ultimately lead to an individual's reduced fitness level (Buckingham et al. 1999; King and Heinen 2004). It is, however, difficult to define and enforce specific human behaviors that are, or should be, considered harassment (Sorice et al. 2003).

Second, tourists access manatees through dive shop operators. Because these operators tend to focus their education efforts on the rules of the interaction itself, it is possible for a tourist to enter and leave the setting having learned very little about natural history or conservation issues related to manatees and the ecosystem. This education issue indicates a concern regarding the ecotourism principle of raising awareness about conservation and changing human behavior toward the environment (Kimmell 1999).

Finally, whereas local dive shops and businesses benefit from manatee tourism, they have historically made no formal effort to reinvest in manatee conservation. This lack of reinvestment does not support the principle that ecotourism should benefit the conservation of the target species and its ecosystem (Giannecchini 1993).

Manatee tourism in Crystal River could become manatee *eco*tourism by focusing on these principles of "do no harm," conservation education, and contribution to conservation. For example, as is done in some parts of the whale watching industry (Parsons and Woods-Ballard 2003), tour operators could voluntarily create a formal association and establish a set of *best practices* that contain self-imposed limits (e.g., limiting use during the day and across days of the week). The association could reduce concern about the negative impacts of human-manatee interactions by using experts to help identify specific behaviors considered to be inappropriate (see Reynolds and Wells 2003 for specific recommendations) as well as by identifying specific consequences for tourists that engage in such behaviors (e.g., removing an offending person from the water). An association may also reinvest in manatee conservation by collecting user fees from tourists that could then be used to help pay for better enforcement or to create an interpretive program in which all tourists participate. Finally, operators could voluntarily assist with efforts to monitor the effects of tourist activities on the quality of the visitor experience and on the manatees.

The primary lesson that manatee tourism in Crystal River provides for ecotourism development is that simply creating a human-wildlife interaction in nature is not, by definition, ecotourism. Beyond the attention given to minimizing impacts to a target species, ecotourism includes an ethic of enhancing conservation through education and reinvestment in the resource.

harassment of manatees at some springs used for thermoregulation[73]. For reasons of space, we here address only the "red tide" threat, which has emerged as a major cause of manatee death over the past decade, especially in southwest Florida, but we need to recognize that there may be synergistic effects at the individual and population levels from the co-occurrence of multiple stressors[74], such as increased susceptibility to pathogens due to cold-induced immuno-suppression[75].

The dinoflagellate *Karenia brevis* produces a potent neurotoxin called brevetoxin which, at sufficiently high concentrations during red tide blooms, results in massive fish kills and the deaths of other marine organisms including manatees[76]. The recent discovery that the toxin can persist on seagrass blades long after the bloom has dissipated extends the time window of the threat[77]. About 149 manatees succumbed to red tide in the spring of 1996[78]; and over a recent five-year period (2002–2006) brevetoxin was confirmed as the primary cause of death for 226 manatees and suspected in an additional 66 cases[79]. Red tide has been a part of the Gulf coast environment for at least the past 150 years[80]. Whether and how humans have contributed to the apparent increase in its frequency and duration through increased nutrient loading of coastal waters is an area of active research[81].

Future Population Status

Biologists and modelers are faced with the daunting task of taking historical and current data on population demography and threats and projecting this forward to estimate the risk of future decline and extinction[82]. Incorporating parameter and structural uncertainty into these models is critical to providing a fair representation of the range of possible outcomes[83].

Population viability analyses have recently been conducted for the Florida manatee[84]. These models were based on vital rate estimates for each of the four subpopulations and they incorporated demographic and environmental stochasticity (i.e., chance events). The models simulated scenarios based on plausible future threats, including expected declines in carrying capacity through loss of warm-water refugia, potential increases in mortality associated with projected human population growth, and natural catastrophic mortality events (harmful algal blooms, severe cold, infectious disease). Not surprisingly, the results were very sensitive to assumptions about changes in carrying capacity, adult survival, and the frequency and impact of catastrophic events.

The probability of range-wide extinction was negligible over the next 100 years in all scenarios modeled. However, without migration from adjacent regions, the SW subpopulation would have a 12% risk of extirpation over 100 years and a 61% chance of an 80% or more decline over three generations[85]. For the entire subspecies, there was a 12% chance of a 50% decline over the next three generations and a 55% chance of a 20% reduction over the next two generations. Viewed from a different perspective, the probability that the number of adults would drop below 100, 250, or 500 (possible thresholds for quasi-extinction) on *either* the east or west coast over the next 100 years was 1.0%, 8.6%, or 49.3%, respectively[86]. These models assumed that current average mortality rates would remain the same, so risk could be higher if the threat from watercraft collisions or other factors increases. Expected population growth rates over the next ten years are lower than past estimates (table 3.1), in part because they include the possibility of catastrophic events[87]. The heuristic value of these analyses does not lie in the absolute estimates of risk—which will change with updated information such as current population size—but rather as an aid in identifying the demographic parameters and threats that most influence future status. Thus this analytical approach provides a tool to focus and prioritize research efforts and to provide justification for specific management actions.

Legal Status

The Florida manatee is protected under a variety of federal and state statutes as well as international conventions[88]. Federal laws include the Marine Mammal Protection Act (MMPA) of 1972 and the Endangered Species Act (ESA) of 1973[89]. The Florida Manatee Sanctuary Act (FMSA) of 1978 and the Local Government Comprehensive Planning and Land Regulation Act of 1985 both have important provisions to protect manatees at the state level[90], and the latter explicitly addresses balancing development and resource conservation. In Florida, unlike many developing countries with scarce resources, the laws and protective regulations are actively enforced. Enforcement of manatee speed zone restrictions is a major activity of wildlife law enforcement officers.

The classification of the Florida manatee on state, federal, and international lists of imperiled species has recently undergone a period of flux and uncertainty. The species has been listed as endangered under the ESA, but in 2007 the U.S. Fish and Wildlife Service recommended reclassifying it as threatened, awaiting the outcome of the next status review[91]. In the same year the World Conservation Union (IUCN), the international body that main-

> **BOX 3.2**
>
> ### Role of Law Enforcement in Conservation of the Florida Manatee
> Jim Brown
>
> It is imperative that wildlife managers, researchers, and law enforcement officials develop a team approach to create, implement, and evaluate wildlife conservation strategies. Planning for adequate enforcement of wildlife regulations is a critical but often overlooked or underfunded management component within an imperiled species recovery process.
>
> All too often, wildlife managers become so focused on what laws and regulations are needed for adequate protection that they give insufficient consideration to how they will implement the necessary level of compliance. Inviting enforcement officials to participate in recovery planning teams at the onset will facilitate the development of enforceable laws, and law enforcement officers will develop ownership in the protections. Considerations for adequate law enforcement include the number and costs of officers needed, suitable equipment and the financial means to operate that equipment; and above all, the knowledge and willingness of officers to implement those regulations. This takes close coordination with wildlife managers and scientists to ensure that limited resources are put to the best use possible.
>
> Among various representatives serving on wildlife recovery planning teams, law enforcers often have the closest contact with the community. While conducting their routine duties, officers encounter and speak with many people every day. Florida boaters express their thoughts and ideas on everything from their myths about manatees to why they believe the laws passed to protect the species are unjust. Officers armed with facts about wildlife, conservation strategies, and motivation to counter these arguments can help change stakeholder attitudes and facilitate community buy-in. Public support and knowledge of regulations is integral to reducing injuries and deaths of manatees resulting from collisions with watercraft.
>
> Toward that goal, Florida Fish and Wildlife Conservation Commission (FWC) managers, researchers, and law enforcement officials realized that they needed to work together more closely to reduce threats to manatees and to improve communication among stakeholders. They formed stakeholder groups to increase awareness, share information and concerns, and gain consensus on issues. Also, an annual manatee law enforcement forum was created where marine law enforcement personnel from as many as 32 agencies meet with wildlife managers and scientists to learn from one another on how best to protect manatees. Law enforcement officials committed to conducting a minimum of 50,000 hours of patrols in manatee zones per year at a cost of over $4 million dollars. Law enforcement officials now stand alongside wildlife managers at public hearings to tell the stakeholders that the proposed speed zones are enforceable and they are ready to take on the task. Law enforcement is now responsible for posting the manatee speed zone signs. This has resulted in greater buy-in from the officers and has helped ensure successful prosecutions. A manatee management plan produced by managers and stakeholders was approved by the FWC in 2007, and for the first time a comprehensive state plan for future manatee conservation is in place.
>
> The jury is still out as to how much these actions have helped protect manatees, but evidence of positive gains is growing. Watercraft-related deaths continue to account for a sizeable proportion of annual manatee mortality, while the number of registered vessels in the state continues to grow each year. But the number of manatees in most areas of Florida seems to be increasing as well. With this newly formed partnership of managers and stakeholders, protection efforts have been put in place to help ensure the manatee's survival in Florida for many years to come.
>
> In summary, early inclusion of law enforcement officials during the development process of any species protection measures will likely result in greater overall effectiveness. This approach will ensure that protection efforts can and will be enforced; will enhance law enforcement officers' understanding of the needs of the species; will provide justification for the protections; and will help identify training needs to those carrying out the protections. As a side benefit, it builds camaraderie across the disciplines and builds long-term relationships that will prove valuable as we jointly strive to recover the species.

tains the Red List of globally threatened species, uplisted the status of the Florida manatee from vulnerable to endangered[92]. Several years of scientific review and contentious public debate regarding the appropriate listing category for manatees under Florida state rules—during which the Florida Fish and Wildlife Conservation Commission considered but decided against downlisting the manatee from endangered to threatened[93]—ultimately motivated a thorough review and overhaul of the state's imperiled species listing process and categories in 2010.

For species federally listed under the ESA, the state will now simply adopt the same category, avoiding confusion and unproductive controversy; therefore, for the time being, the manatee will remain endangered on the state list. Given the large increase in the synoptic survey count in January 2010—which reflects the minimum population size for manatees—followed immediately by a cold-related mortality event that was unprecedented in its magnitude and extent, we expect continued scientific and public discussion of the appropriate category under the various threatened species systems. Regardless of listing status, the manatee will remain protected under the federal MMPA and ESA, and state rules could be promulgated to protect them further under FMSA[94]. Furthermore, federal downlisting to threatened would not necessarily entail reduction in protection.

Management Efforts

The history of management and conservation efforts for Florida manatees has been well-chronicled[95]. Here we provide a brief discussion of impediments to successful management and some suggestions regarding ways by which emerging programs can benefit using the Florida experience.

The recovery program for the Florida manatee has been recognized as a model for other endangered species recovery efforts[96]. A key ingredient to its success has been the fostering of good communication and close cooperation between state and federal agencies, at both individual and organizational levels of management and research. Partnerships among state, federal, and private entities require time, dedication, and patience, but the outcome has been improved research, management, and law enforcement initiatives that take advantage of the strengths of each organization[97]. Inviting key stakeholders from boating, industry, and environmental groups to participate in revising the Florida Manatee Recovery Plan[98] has also been important in sharing perspectives and promoting acceptance from diverse groups. Starting in the late 1990s, however, there was a shift in the atmosphere from one of cooperation to conflict between stakeholders and management agencies. Even most managers and agency leaders acknowledged that the "manatee problem" in Florida had become a conservation quagmire generating unprecedented levels of controversy[99].

One of the primary impediments to successful management has been litigation associated with agencies' implementation (or perceived lack thereof) of pertinent statutes (see preceding section on Legal Status). Although it is not our intent to argue whether litigation was warranted in any particular instance, we simply note that when a conservation issue enters the courtroom, several things tend to happen: (a) issues and opposing sides become even more polarized; (b) the results of scientific studies and other information may be distorted; (c) communication among stakeholders ceases; and (d) funds and staff time that could be applied to recovery activities are used to support litigation costs. Clearly, it makes sense to attempt to promote responsible action without resorting to litigation.

Management and conservation of natural resources, however, are often carried out reactively in response to crises or public outcry[100]. Crisis management might be avoided through foresight that identifies emerging issues and results in exploration of possible alternatives well in advance of the crisis stage. Soliciting the ideas and concerns of stakeholders early in the management decision-making process can also help avoid major clashes down the road. Some progress in breaking down barriers among diverse interest groups recently occurred through the Manatee Forum, a group of 22 stakeholder organizations that includes equal representation from boating and environmental groups. Its goal is to provide a process to improve communication and understanding, cultivate trust, and search for common ground among key stakeholder groups and participating agencies.

Fortunately, a window of opportunity seems to be opening to develop a more proactive institutional culture for manatee conservation. The Marine Mammal Commission (MMC) has promoted proactive approaches to management at the federal level[101], playing a small but pivotal role as outside evaluator and advisor in the 30-year history of the Florida manatee recovery program[102]. Wallace (1994) argued that MMC has acted as an effective external agent of change and organizational learning that led to major improvements at key junctures in the program. Leaders of agencies responsible for sirenian conservation should foster a process that articulates farsighted needs and translates them into budgetary decisions and priorities in documents such as recovery and management plans. Furthermore, leaders can promote continual improvement in conservation programs by incorporating self- and external evaluations that provide objective and critical review of research and management activities and organizational structure.

Research Efforts and Needs

A history of research efforts on the Florida manatee over the past three decades has been covered in a number of recent overviews[103]. The principal tools for monitoring

BOX 3.3

Partnering for Success: Florida Manatee Photo-identification

Kari A. Rood, Sheri L. Barton, and Cathy A. Beck

Manatee photo-identification uses the unique pattern of scars and mutilations on a manatee's trunk and tail fluke to identify an individual animal over time. In Florida the scars are primarily a result of encounters with boats; however, entanglements in fishing gear, cold stress lesions, and fungal infections also can cause scarring. Photo-identification data provide insights into manatee movements, site fidelity, habitat use, behavior, intra- and interspecific associations, and reproductive parameters such as calving intervals and length of calf dependency. In addition, the capture histories produced through photo-identification efforts are used to estimate annual adult survival rates and to model population dynamics for state and federal assessments of Florida manatee status and recovery (see Beck and Clark, chapter 15, this volume, for more information). This research is realized through a partnership among the U.S. Geological Survey (USGS), the Florida Fish and Wildlife Conservation Commission (FWC), and Mote Marine Laboratory (MML). These federal, state, and private entities work collaboratively to photograph Florida manatees throughout their range, process images, identify manatees, and manage an integrated sightings database, known as the Manatee Individual Photo-identification System (MIPS).

Advantages of the photo-identification partnership have included the pooling of financial resources and equipment when working within limited budgets, the sharing of staff resources and technical knowledge on a wide range of areas from computer equipment to data analysis, and the mentoring of staff members among organizations. Additionally, the broad geographic distribution of partner offices has facilitated coverage of the Florida manatee's range and has reduced travel for fieldwork. A significant challenge associated with working in any partnership is that each organization will likely have different priorities and obligations as well as varying levels of resources to accomplish tasks. Furthermore, successful partnerships require standardization of protocols; thus the photo-identification partners have spent a significant amount of effort discussing the protocols followed within each organization, developing common procedures, and communicating when modifications are made.

The success of a partnership relies on having shared, focused objectives, frequent and open communication both within and among all levels of each organization, and specifically assigned, well-defined tasks and expectations. Without clearly articulated roles in partnerships, redundancies in effort, inefficiencies in process, and misunderstanding between organizations can result. In 2005 the photo-ID partners developed and signed a memorandum of understanding detailing their roles and responsibilities. This document facilitated the communication and understanding of partnership objectives and roles as well as expectations regarding data sharing for analysis and publication. When establishing a partnership it is important to consider the format and methods by which data and images will be shared among partners. In 2004 the three partners began using digital photography and initiated the scanning of program slides in order to facilitate the efficient exchange of image data among partners. Currently, an integrated Web-based database is being developed to allow all partners access to program data in real time. Thoughtful consideration of data flow early in the development of a partnership will go a long way in terms of facilitating an effective and efficient relationship.

The success of a partnership derives from the complementary strengths of its member organizations, as long as there are shared goals, clear expectations, and open communication. Along with the benefits of a partnership often come challenges and compromises. The manatee photo-identification partnership has overcome differing priorities, obligations, and resources to become a model of fruitful interagency research on the Florida manatee.

---

manatee populations in Florida include: photo-identification to provide capture-recapture data for estimation of survival and reproductive rates[104]; aerial surveys for relative abundance and distribution[105], useful for establishing protection zones; carcass salvage and necropsy to determine causes of death and to assess threats[106]; and population models to integrate demographic and other data[107]. Targeted research studies that have addressed specific ecological and biological questions have utilized a variety of approaches, including: behavioral observation techniques to assess manatee harassment by swimmers[108] and manatee response to vessels[109]; experiments using exclosures to determine manatee impacts on submerged aquatic vegetation[110]; satellite-linked telemetry to characterize seasonal movements, migratory behavior, and site fidelity[111]; metabolic and water turnover experiments to assess thermoregulatory and osmoregulatory capabilities[112]; functional morphological investigations on fresh carcasses to investigate cardiovascular and digestive systems[113]; psycho-behavioral experiments and anatomical studies to assess sensory abilities[114]; and a variety of molecular genetic techniques to examine population structure[115].

Although one could argue that the Florida manatee is one of the best studied marine mammals in the world, many fundamental questions regarding its biology, ecology, demography, and health status persist. Outstanding research areas (summarized in table 3.2) most relevant to current management and conservation needs include: How many manatees are there? How many can the environment support? Have slow speed zones been effective at reducing watercraft strikes? What is the best risk assessment approach to objectively identify the areas in need of protection? How will manatees respond when traditional warm-water sources disappear? What is the current health status of manatees and how could that be affected by future habitat loss and climate change? These questions may seem straightforward but are exceptionally difficult to address rigorously. Simple approaches to these problems usually incorporate untenable assumptions and biases. Our understanding of the complex topic of environmental carrying capacity (K), for example, is rudimentary. The expert consensus is that it will decline in the future, but the extent and timing of decline is a matter of opinion. Progress on this subject will require identifying and forecasting the availability of limiting resources (e.g., warm-water habitat, forage), which likely vary in time and space; quantifying physiological thermal limits, maximum densities at warm-water sites, and interannual and geographic variation in winter temperature regimes; and estimating manatee energetic needs, forage biomass, and productivity in defined areas around winter thermal refugia.

There also are sublethal threats that we know little about. Many manatees in Florida live in polluted waterways, drink from sewage treatment plant effluent pipes, are exposed to toxic algae, and suffer from repeated collisions with motorized watercraft. The potential chronic effects of these contaminants and traumas on health and reproduction are poorly known[116]. This reinforces the need to remain vigilant to new and emerging threats to manatees and habitat.

Research programs on the Florida manatee have generally been well funded and successful in pushing the frontier of biological knowledge forward. As with any long-term program, however, new challenges constantly arise, as do opportunities to reach full potential. Here we identify in broad strokes some practical advice for scientists in emerging programs to consider:

· Collaborate with researchers from diverse fields, such as seagrass ecology, hydrology, pathology, and population modeling. Not only are such interactions intellectually stimulating; they bring fresh perspectives to tackling challenging research and conservation problems, formulating hypotheses, rethinking field and analytical methods, and expanding on the knowledge base of relevant literature.
· Give sufficient consideration to proper data management (including data processing, quality control and assurance, and archival) and analysis for publication needs. The time required for these tasks is typically underestimated and undervalued, often resulting in large backlogs of data. The ideal solution is to build the necessary infrastructure into the program up front; alternatively, the services of database managers, biostatisticians, or quantitative biologists can be acquired to address specific questions of interest to managers.
· Establishing a stable funding base is crucial for long-term research. Creative, innovative funding approaches are important in developing broad public support for conservation programs. In Florida, for example, the state's long-term research and management programs on manatees have flourished because of relatively stable funding from the sale of specialty "Save the Manatee" automobile license tags and from boat registration fees. Unfortunately, tag revenues have been declining steadily for a number of years, making researchers increasingly reliant on small grant funds to undertake studies beyond core monitoring programs.
· Coordinated, long-range planning is important to reach conservation goals. Given that budgets of most organizations necessitate an annual planning horizon, long-term planning may look only three to five years out. While that may represent the outer limits of what is practical for most agencies, we submit that a broad research vision for a 20- to 30-year time span—collectively developed by the community of researchers and managers, with input from stakeholders—is essential to ensure that current efforts address questions requiring long-term data.

Table 3.2. Key areas of research needed to meet management needs for the Florida manatee.

Topic	Applications	Current Knowledge and Problems	Relevant Literature
Population size (abundance)	Models estimating future population size; probability of extinction and quasi-extinction; allowable "incidental take"; minimum mortality rate from carcass salvage; population trends	Statewide synoptic surveys provide a minimum count, but spatial and temporal variation in detection probability precludes use for trend analyses or estimation of absolute size. A new survey design is being developed to provide an estimate of abundance with associated variance.	Ackerman 1995; Lefebvre et al. 1995; Miller et al. 1998; Craig and Reynolds 2004; Haubold et al. 2006; Pollock et al. 2006; Edwards et al. 2007; Fonnesbeck et al. 2009
Carrying capacity (current and future K)	Models estimating future population size and distribution; probability of extinction and quasi-extinction; "optimum sustainable population" (MMPA); identification of limiting habitat factors	Very little is known about K; should be considered dynamic rather than a static parameter. General consensus is that warm-water habitat will likely be the first factor to limit the population in the future due to anticipated loss of such sites. Need better understanding of use of secondary warm-water sites. No evidence that manatees are near K based on forage resources.	Runge et al. 2007a; plus a number of studies on seagrass biomass and productivity, manatee energetics and thermal requirements, manatee winter movements and behavior, and warm-water aggregation sites
Vital rates (survival, fecundity, migration)	Population models, including past trends and projected future growth; factors affecting survival and reproduction	Excellent long-term data on adult survival for most regions. Major gaps include: immature survival, reproductive rate in SW, no data from far SW (Everglades); migration rates among regions; nature of density-dependence.	Langtimm et al. 1998, 2004; Langtimm and Beck 2003; Koelsch 2001; Kendall et al. 2004a; Schwarz 2007
Effectiveness of management actions and risk assessment: slow speed zones and other regulations	Evaluation of primary management tools to reduce watercraft-related manatee mortality; objective identification of areas in need of protection; educational, regulatory, and enforcement approaches to improve compliance and effectiveness	Before/after comparison of carcass counts in relation to speed zone establishment is confounded by other variables. To be effective, (1) slow speed must reduce risk of collision and/or injury (general consensus but little hard data), (2) zones must be configured correctly (risk assessments are ongoing), and (3) boaters must comply (compliance rates are quite variable). Need better understanding of manatee behavioral response to vessels, spatial and temporal patterns of vessel traffic, and factors motivating boater compliance.	Buckingham et al. 1999; Shapiro 2001; Gorzelany 2004; Nowacek et al. 2004; Laist and Shaw 2006; Calleson and Frohlich 2007; Miksis-Olds et al. 2007; Sorice et al. 2007
Manatee response to changes in warm-water network	Models estimating future population size and distribution; carrying capacity; probability of extinction and quasi-extinction; contingency planning for disruption or termination of industrial thermal effluents	Manatees have shown great adaptability over the long term but their strong site fidelity may result in maladaptive behavior in response to sudden changes in the warm-water network over the short term. Intermittent or insufficient thermal plumes can act as "ecological traps." A combination of field experimentation, opportunistic studies, and simulation modeling is needed to evaluate behavioral and population response.	Packard et al. 1989; Deutsch et al. 2000, 2003; Schlaepfer et al. 2002; Laist and Reynolds 2005a, 2005b

Note: Additional areas of vital ongoing research are not listed; for comprehensive lists of research tasks see USFWS (2001) and FWC (2007).

- A successful integrated conservation program must ensure that researchers and managers work closely, regularly share information, and jointly articulate questions amenable to scientific inquiry and of high priority to management. A recent successful example of a collaborative effort was the development of the Florida Manatee Management Plan[117], which provides the framework for state research and management activities over the next five years. Furthermore, researchers need to provide managers not just with raw data but also with the decision-support tools required to apply the data properly in management contexts[118]. While close interaction with managers is important, researchers must be separated from regulatory and management decisions in order to maintain credibility and objectivity in the public eye. This applies especially in the politically charged climate of Florida, where such decisions often face challenges from special interest groups.

Conclusions: Past Successes and the Challenges Ahead

For Florida manatees, a 35-year history of conservation efforts has resulted in positive strides toward recovery. Active, long-term research programs have provided a firm knowledge base for monitoring status and trends from which to base effective management actions. Educational programs at many levels and using a variety of media have raised public awareness of manatee conservation issues. The generally improved status of manatees in Florida is a tribute to remarkable efforts by dedicated individuals, agencies, nonprofit groups, and other organizations. It also reflects the degree to which manatees have successfully adapted to human-altered landscapes. Behavioral plasticity of individuals has been important in the manatees' ability to coexist with large human populations[119]. Other aspects of their lifestyle and biology favor such coexistence[120]. The species is a habitat generalist with a broad diet; does not compete with humans for food or other resources; is not dangerous to humans or commercially important animals; does not require wilderness or isolation from human activities to thrive; readily learns to use sanctuaries; and possesses a strong immune system, often allowing it to survive propeller strikes. These biological attributes—along with a strong legal framework and management infrastructure for protection; considerable resources devoted to support research, management, and enforcement activities; and the high value placed on manatees by the public—provide us with optimism that the manatee can remain as a natural treasure of our coasts well into the future.

There are limits, of course, on the species' ability to adapt, imposed by its physiology, anatomy, sensory biology, and life history. As stewards of our wildlife and other natural resources, we will need to modify human behaviors. Seeking an optimal approach to conservation is always difficult and, in the case of the Florida manatee, has been hindered by an aura of mistrust and divisiveness among some individuals and groups. Emerging sirenian conservation programs in other countries have the opportunity to develop without historical restrictions of this sort.

In 1988 a leading manatee biologist, Tom O'Shea, penned the following insightful words: "Florida is undergoing prodigious development, yet remnants of its fauna manage to persist in a remarkable, highly visible interface between wildlife and man. Maintenance of that interface with continued development is a great experiment in how far our society can go while still upholding principles of respect for the diversity of life"[121]. Among the many challenges faced by managers charged with protecting manatees in this "great experiment," a few stand out. Defining and protecting a network of reliable warm-water sources over the coming century will be vital to maintaining a sufficiently large population to provide a buffer against short-term stochastic events. This will likely require development or enhancement of alternative thermal sites that are not dependent on industrial outfalls (e.g., solar-heated sources, enhancing access to springs through removal of human barriers)[122]. Finding a socially acceptable and biologically viable solution for reducing watercraft collisions will continue to be a major challenge[123]. Manatees need to maintain the capacity for population growth (i.e., resilience) in order to recover from unusual mortality events, such as those caused by red tide or power plant shutdowns.

Human activities have radically changed Florida over the last century. Can we predict with any degree of confidence how the manatee's aquatic environment will change over the next 100 years? Linking those projected changes to trends in manatee demography presents the real challenge for us, as we evaluate future prospects for the manatee's long-term survival through simulation modeling[124]. Regular population monitoring and adjustment of management strategies to unexpected changes will be crucial to successfully maintain the manatee as a viable component of Florida's riverine and coastal ecosystems.

Acknowledgments

We would like to express our thanks to Ellen Hines and the other editors for their encouragement and patience in seeing this through to completion. We also thank Leslie Ward and Tom Reinert for their helpful reviews of the manuscript.

4

West Indian Manatees (*Trichechus manatus*) in the Wider Caribbean Region

CARYN SELF-SULLIVAN AND ANTONIO A. MIGNUCCI-GIANNONI

The Antillean or Caribbean subspecies (*Trichechus manatus manatus*) of the West Indian manatee is classified as endangered on the IUCN Red List because the current population is thought to be fewer than 2,500 mature individuals and is predicted to undergo a decline of more than 20% over the next two generations unless effective conservation actions are taken[1]. Yet the West Indian manatee is possibly the best understood species within the family Trichechidae. Since the late 1960s, research on the most northern subspecies, the Florida manatee (*T. m. latirostris*), has grown exponentially, driven by state and federal agencies, universities, and nongovernmental organizations[2].

In this chapter we address conservation of the remaining West Indian manatees in the Wider Caribbean (WCR), including those populations within the Caribbean Sea, the western Gulf of Mexico and along the Atlantic coasts of the Bahamas, the Greater and Lesser Antilles, and the northern and northeastern coast of South America. The common names Antillean and Caribbean are somewhat misleading. Antillean refers to the Greater and Lesser Antillean Islands; Caribbean refers to the Caribbean Sea, which borders Florida, the Gulf of Mexico, the Antilles, and Central and South America west of the Antilles. But the habitat range of West Indian manatees extends beyond both of these areas and includes the Bahamas, the Gulf coast of Mexico, the Caribbean coast of Central and South America, the Greater Antilles, and the Atlantic coast of South America as far south as Brazil (map 4.1). Moreover, at least one manatee in the Bahamas and one manatee in Cuba are emigrants from the Florida population[3]. Manatees in Guyana, Suriname, French Guiana, and Brazil are classified as a genetically distinct population from both Florida and Caribbean manatees[4]. These recent findings provide considerable evidence that West Indian manatees in the WCR are genetically distinct populations and should be managed as three biogeographic groups: (1) Bahamas, Florida, and the Greater Antilles; (2) Central and South America west of the Lesser Antilles; and (3) northeastern South America east of the Lesser Antilles. In this chapter we refer to all populations from the Bahamas to Brazil, excluding Florida, as WCR manatees. In an effort to highlight advances in each region, we have included text boxes by local scientists where research and conservation efforts have been expanded in recent years.

The WCR provides great diversity of habitat owing to geographical, environmental, social, cultural, economic, and political variation. As a result conservation strategies developed specifically for the Florida manatee may not be generally applicable to WCR manatees. Based on diversity within the region and the growing evidence that some individual manatees are wanderers, traveling hundreds of kilometers[5], WCR manatee conservation strategies are most beneficial when they are both locally derived and regionally collaborative.

Background

Had manatee meat not been an important source of food for Indigenous Americans, explorers, immigrants, and slaves, we would know very little about the species' historical range and status within the WCR. Archaeologists have documented the importance of manatee meat to pre-Columbian inhabitants. Early explorers and naturalists often wrote about the distribution, abundance, and use of manatees. Thanks to these writings we have a view into the past that enables us to estimate the historical and prehistoric distribution and abundance of WCR manatees[6].

Historical Distribution

Archaeological evidence indicates that though manatees were used by pre-Columbian inhabitants of the WCR[7], manatee remains are rare in midden deposits, possibly because they were butchered at nearshore shore or offshore sites with only the meat transported inland[8]. Given the rise in sea level since the end of the

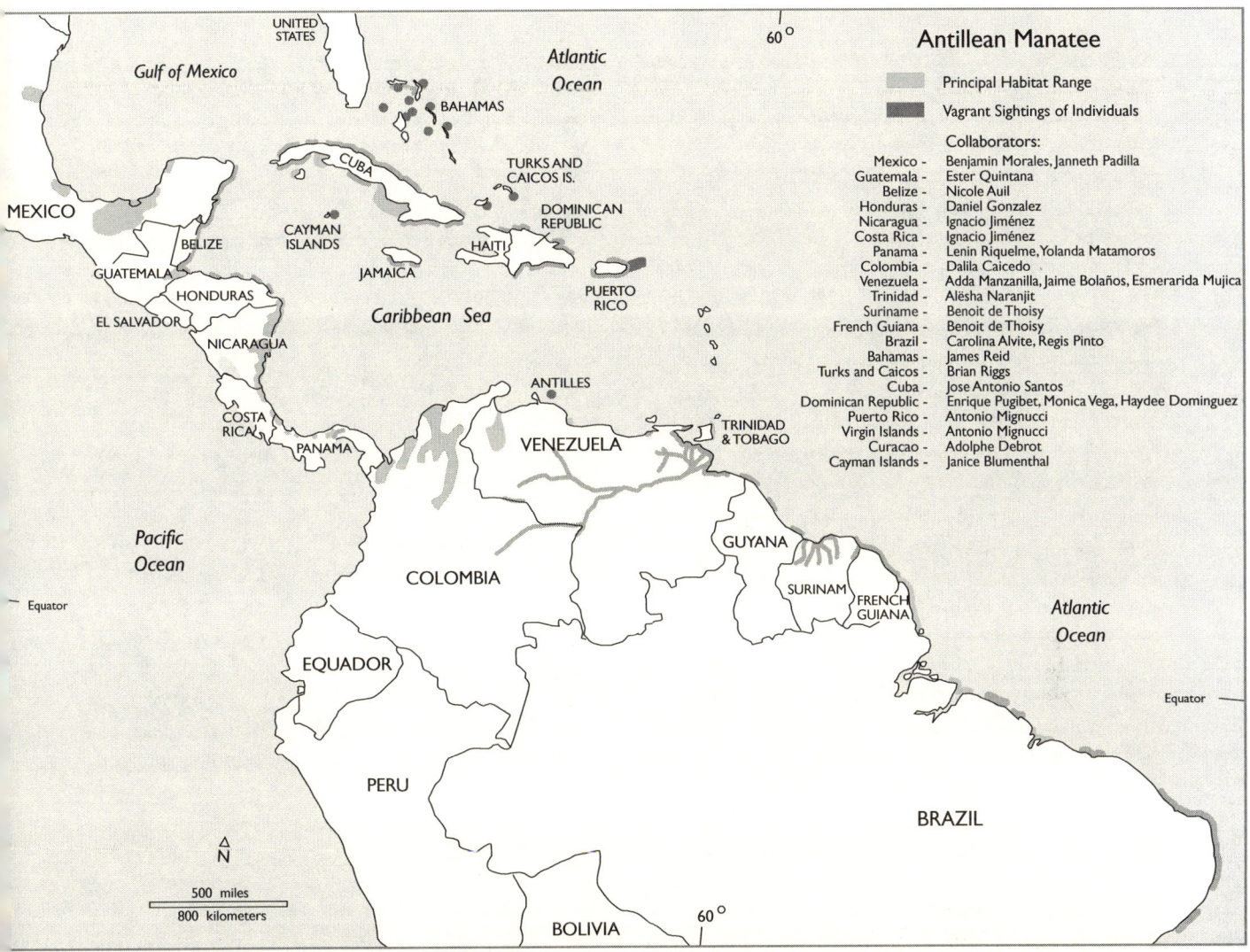

Map 4.1. Antillean manatee distribution. (Map by Ellen McElhinny.)

Pleistocene, most of these sites may be underwater or overgrown with mangrove forests[9]. Analysis of one bone midden on Moho Caye, a small island near Belize City, indicates that manatee was a primary food source for the coastal Maya[10]. The midden contained remains of manatee, mollusk, fish, turtle, and deer. Eighty-nine percent of the estimated harvest was manatee, indicating that it was the main source of meat for the Maya hunters and fishers who used Moho Caye during the Middle Classic Period (circa 400–700 AC).

Writings by early explorers and naturalists, along with historical trade documents, have led scientists to hypothesize a significant reduction in the number of WCR manatees over the past 300 years. In 1492 Columbus reported "swarms" of manatees in Cuba and also documented their presence in Hispaniola[11]. In 1520 Oviedo described hunting techniques used by both natives and Spaniards[12]. In 1699 Dampier reported manatee abundance and exploitation throughout the WCR.

Whitehead[13] provides an extensive review of the records documenting manatees as far south as 20°S latitude. As recently as 1964 a ton of manatee meat was harvested in Bahia, Brazil[14], an area where manatees are locally extinct today[15]. For a more detailed review of the archaeological and historical records see Durand and see Lefebvre et al.[16]

Historical Research

The earliest scientific investigations of Antillean manatees in the WCR were conducted in the Guianas[17]. After their first expedition there in 1962, Drs. Colin Bertram and Kate Ricardo Bertram, a husband and wife team from the University of Cambridge, U.K., dedicated four decades of their lives to sirenians, publishing more than 20 papers and bringing the dire status of these previously unstudied aquatic mammals to light[18]. Ironically, very little is currently known about the population in the Guianas.

Early scientific expeditions rarely resulted in the direct observation of living manatees. Data were more often limited to interviews with local inhabitants, counts and measurements of harvested animals, and descriptions of manatee habitat. However, interviews with local people have proven to be an essential first step in determining where manatee populations exist within the WCR[19].

During the later twentieth century a contingent of U.S. scientists followed up on interview results by working with local stakeholders to determine distribution and abundance of manatees in the WCR via aerial surveys. By the late 1970s and early 1980s, aerial surveys had become a primary tool for counting manatees in remote areas. Since that time aerial surveys have been conducted in Puerto Rico[20], Jamaica[21], the Dominican Republic[22], Haiti[23], Cuba[24], Mexico[25], Belize[26], Guatemala[27], Honduras[28], Nicaragua[29], Costa Rica[30], Panama[31], and Venezuela[32].

Broad-scale countrywide aerial surveys have become an important tool for predicting manatee presence and habitat use; however, aerial surveys have not proven useful until recently in determining actual population numbers or trends in population size[33]. In the WCR, countries are relatively small and manatees are known to cross political boundaries. Comparison of counts between countries, or even within countries over time, is also difficult owing to variations in survey techniques and the probability of detection, which depends on observer experience, habitat type, and environmental conditions. For example, in the southern Yucatán (Mexico and Belize), where aerial surveys have been conducted frequently in recent years, scientists warn that count variability may result from (a) real changes in population size and distribution, (b) short-term and random movements by manatees, (c) variation in observer reliability, (d) variation in survey methods, or (e) inconsistent detectability biases across spatial and temporal variables such as habitat type and season[34].

Most recently scientists have turned to smaller scale, site-specific studies that include live captures, boat surveys, photo-ID, remote sensing and telemetry, rescue, health assessment, and necropsy programs. For example, since Puerto Rico is a U.S. commonwealth, conservation of the manatee population falls under the jurisdiction of U.S. federal agencies; as a result the manatee population has been studied extensively using the same tools and techniques as in Florida.

In Mexico and Belize, where funding is more likely to come from nongovernmental organizations, advanced techniques have enabled scientists to perform health assessments on populations in Chetumal Bay, Northern and Southern Lagoon, the cayes near Belize City, and Placencia Lagoon[35]. Collaboration among scientists working in the region has improved our ability to estimate population numbers and identify populations at risk and has enabled the detection of seasonal variance in distribution[36].

As with all sirenians, there has been an explosion of new information on WCR manatees over the past 10–15 years, including a better understanding of the importance of habitat and breakthroughs in evolution and genetics[37]. However, if we are to ensure the survival of WCR manatees, we must move beyond traditional approaches of assessment to novel research, interdisciplinary partnerships, and an expansion of policy and conservation efforts[38].

Current Distribution

WCR manatees require habitat that provides specific resources, including fresh water for osmoregulation, warm water for thermoregulation, aquatic vegetation for foraging, quiet secluded areas for resting and reproduction, and safe travel corridors for moving between these activity centers. Many countries within the WCR provide excellent manatee habitat (map 4.1). During the past two decades, manatees have been documented in 27 countries within the WCR[39]; however, year-round populations exist in only 20 (excluding Florida; see table 4.1). Although rare manatee sightings have been reported in small islands of the Greater Antilles (Brit-

---

BOX 4.1

Manatees in Hispaniola

Haydée Domínguez Tejo

The island of Hispaniola is part of the Greater Antilles and includes two countries: the Dominican Republic (DR) and Haiti. Manatees in the DR are protected by national legislation and by international agreements. Haiti provides no legal protection at this time.

In Haiti the current status of manatees is unknown, but progress is under way. A presidential decree to establish Haiti's first Marine Protected Area is currently under evaluation. In 2007 manatees were sighted in the Port-au-Prince bay area, along the seagrass beds north of Arcahaie. The proposed protected area includes the location of the latest manatee sightings.

In the Dominican Republic manatees are commonly found in coastal marine and estuarine environments in (1) the northwest coast, from Manzanillo Bay to the Bajabonico River mouth; (2) the northeast coast, along the north coast of the Samana Peninsula, and in the south coast of Samana Bay; (3) the southwest coast, in the Neiba and Ocoa Bays, and east of the Oviedo Lagoon (see map 4.1; Husar 1977; Belitsky and Belitsky 1980; Lefebvre et al. 1989, Ottenwalder 1995; León and Ottenwalder 1997 unpubl.; Pugibet and Vega 2000 unpubl.; Domínguez 2006, 2007 unpubl.). Within these areas manatees appear to favor shallow protected waters in enclosed bays, coastal lagoons, and reef lagoons, where there are mangroves, seagrass beds, and nearby sources of fresh water at river mouths and natural springs. Manatees are occasionally reported outside these three main areas. They have been confirmed by reliable sources along the north coast close to Puerto Plata in 2007 and 2009, and on the southeast coast from Boca de Yuma to Bayahibe in 2006–2008. At the eastern tip of the island, manatee presence was confirmed in Bavaro by SCUBA divers in 2005 and 2006 and by a neonate found in 2008.

Manatee presence has been recently confirmed in at least nine of the coastal marine protected areas in the DR via (1) direct observations during land, boat, and aerial surveys; (2) carcass recoveries; and (3) reliable sighting reports from land, water, and air during commercial flights, all dating from 2004 until the present. These sightings include evidence such as still images or videos of manatees. Some individuals present small scars or markings that may be useful for photo-ID efforts. Furthermore, there are potential locations for manatee photo-ID studies on the north coast of the Samana Peninsula, at Bavaro and in Parque Nacional Jaragua, where manatees have been sighted in clear waters with excellent visibility.

Since 2006 site-specific studies have been conducted by the Marine Biology Research Center of the Autonomous University of Santo Domingo (CIBIMA-UASD) and by local and international NGOs, such as FUNDEMAR and Wildlife Trust. Current research methods include interviews, boat and land-based surveys, and most recently aerial surveys in the Samana Bay area in 2008–2009. All research includes an educational component via workshops for different audiences, and field visits, promoting manatee conservation.

Research on manatee distribution and habitat use by CIBIMA-UASD has revealed an important manatee activity center within the Marine Mammal Sanctuary of Estero Hondo. A coastal lagoon surrounded by mangroves, with calm shallow waters, abundant seagrasses, and freshwater input, has been identified as a feeding, resting, and breeding activity center, where manatees are present year-round, including mother-calf pairs (Domínguez 2007 unpubl.). At least two different sets of triads, consisting of an adult female and two calves of practically the same size, were sighted repeatedly in 2007 and 2008, suggesting the repeated occurrence of twins. Since viable twins are thought to be extremely rare in manatees, these observations invite further studies.

The Nature Conservancy (TNC) analyzed the marine protected areas of the country through a series of participative workshops in 2006–2008(Domínguez et al. 2008). Manatees and sea turtles were established as conservation objects of national priority in terms of coastal marine biodiversity. The national goal was set to protect 65% of their area of distribution within protected areas by 2010. Two proposals, under review at the time of writing, were presented to the government to fulfill this goal. CIBIMA-UASD is currently working with TNC, developing a conservation action plan for the Marine Mammal Sanctuary of Estero Hondo, with manatees as one of the conservation targets.

In spite of these efforts, there are many challenges to overcome: law enforcement is lax; there is still illegal manatee hunting; there is no national conservation and recovery plan for the species, and no ongoing manatee research and conservation efforts exist in most of the marine protected areas due to lack of funds and expertise and limited personnel capacity. To produce the needed information for manatee recovery and conservation, future plans for the Dominican Republic include boat surveys in other possible manatee activity centers along the northwest and southwest coast, nationwide aerial surveys, photo-ID, and telemetry studies.

Acknowledgments

Information regarding the current situation in Haiti was kindly provided by Jean W. Weiner, director of the marine conservation NGO Fondation pour la Protection de la Biodiversité Marine (FoProBim).

ish and U.S. Virgin Islands, Turks and Caicos, Cayman Islands), Lesser Antilles (St. Maarten), and off the coast of South America (Curaçao, Bonaire), these are thought to be wanderers from nearby populations.

All manatee populations within the WCR are locally classified as threatened or endangered, but conservation status varies widely among the 20 countries with year-round sightings[40]. In many locations population sizes and trends are unknown (table 4.1). For the first time, the 2008 IUCN Red List assessment estimated population sizes using orders of magnitude. By country, numbers range on the order of 10 (Bahamas) to 1,000 (Belize, Mexico), with most estimates on the order of 100–500[41]. Using these rough estimates, the total number of manatees in the WCR (excluding Florida) may fall somewhere between 3,000 and 6,000 individuals, including calves and independent juveniles. Extrapolating from Florida data on the proportion of mature manatees, this would put the population of reproductively viable adults at less than 2,500. However, this estimate is at best an educated guess. The revised UNEP/CEP Regional Management Plan is the most recent source of information[42]. Unfortunately, much of the data in this report is based on personal communication and gray literature.

Legal Status

Manatees and their habitats throughout the WCR are protected by both national legislation and international agreements[43]. Legal status and conservation efforts in the region were greatly enhanced when the Caribbean governments reached an agreement during the Convention

Table 4.1. Distribution, status trend, minimum population counts, and population estimates (including adults, calves, and juveniles) for the Wider Caribbean Region.

Country	Trend	Minimum Counts	Population Estimate
Bahamas	I	5	10
Belize	S/D	700	1,000
Brazil	S/D	200	500
Colombia	U/D	100	500
Costa Rica	D	30	100
Cuba	U/D	50	100
Dominican Republic	D	30	100
French Guiana	S	10	100
Guatemala	U	50	150
Guyana	D	25	100
Haiti	U	5	100
Honduras	S	50	100
Jamaica	U/D	25	50
Mexico	U	1,000	1,500
Nicaragua	D	71	500
Panama	U	10	100
Puerto Rico	S	308	618
Suriname	D	10	100
Trinidad & Tobago	D	25	100
Venezuela	D	25	100
Virgin Islands (USA)	E	vagrant	0
Virgin Islands (UK)	E	vagrant	0
Bonaire (Netherlands)	E	vagrant	0
Curaçao (Netherlands)	E	vagrant	0
Turks and Caicos (UK)	E	vagrant	0
Cayman Islands (UK)	E	vagrant	0
Sint Maarten (Netherlands)	E	vagrant	0
Totals		2,730	5,928

Sources: Quintana-Rizzo and Reynolds 2007; Deutsch et al. 2008; Self-Sullivan and Mignucci-Giannoni 2008.
Notes: The last seven locations listed have reported rare sightings of manatees in recent years.
I = possible increase
S = likely stable
D = probable decline
U = unknown (data deficient)
E = locally extinct

for the Protection and Development of the Marine Environment of the Wider Caribbean Region, held in Cartagena on 24 March 1983. The Convention established a regional policy of protection for both endangered species and their habitats. Subsequently, the Specially Protected Areas and Wildlife (SPAW) Protocol to the Convention has become a driving force for the conservation of manatees as a species of priority concern in the WCR[44].

However, legal protection alone has not ensured the survival of manatees and will not. Despite the fact that manatees have been protected by local legislation for over 50 years (table 4.2), illegal hunting and destruction of habitat continue. In additional to local laws, the Convention on International Trade of Endangered Species (CITES)[45] has been ratified by all WCR countries with year-round manatee populations except Haiti. All but three countries have one or more Ramsar sites. The Ramsar Convention on Wetlands, which was signed in Ramsar, Iran, in 1971, is an international agreement that provides a framework for the conservation of wetlands and their resources[46]. Although most countries have signed, ratified, or acceded to these and other international agreements, governmental agencies charged with managing protected species and protected areas in the WCR are generally small and understaffed[47]. Throughout the region, co-management agreements between governmental agencies and NGOs are emerging as one solution to the lack of governmental resources[48].

Threats

Historically, the most significant decline in the number and distribution of WCR manatees came as the result of hunting, which was documented with varying accuracy into the 1960s[49]. When comparing historical writings to the current population estimates, the subspecies may have been reduced by an order of magnitude over the past three centuries. Intrinsic factors, including extremely low fecundity and slow growth, and anthropogenic factors have been cited as reasons for limited recovery of manatees to their historical numbers[50].

The major threats to the survival of WCR manatees today include poaching, incidental or accidental catch, habitat degradation and loss, watercraft collisions, entanglement in fishing gear, chemical contamination and other pollution, natural disasters, and human disturbance[51]. Although threats due to hunting are diminishing in some areas, other listed threats appear to be increasing.

Because the distribution of WCR manatees is linked to

Table 4.2. Partial list of legal protections for manatees and their habitats in the Wider Caribbean Region.

Country	NL	Ramsar	CITES	SPAW
Bahamas	1968	1	1979	NK
Belize	1933	2	1981	2008(R/A)
Brazil	1967	8	1975	NK
Colombia	1969	5	1981	1990(S)/1998(R/A)
Costa Rica	1953	11	1975	NK
Cuba	1936	6	1990	1990(S); 1998(R/A)
Dominican Republic	1938	1	1987	1998(R/A)
French Guiana (FRANCE)	1986	3	1978	1990(S); 2002(R/A)
Guatemala	1959	7	1980	1990(S)
Guyana	1956	NK	1977	NK
Haiti	NK	NK	NK	NK
Honduras	1959	6	1985	NK
Jamaica	1971	3	1997	1990(S)
Mexico	1921	113	1991	1990(S)
Nicaragua	1956	8	1977	NK
Panama	1967	4	1978	1991(S); 1996(R/A)
Puerto Rico	1943	NK	1975	1990(S); 2003(R/A)
Suriname	1954	1	1981	NK
Trinidad & Tobago	1975	3	1984	1990(S); 1999(R/A)
Venezuela	1970	5	1978	1990(S); 1997(R/A)

Sources: Quintana-Rizzo and Reynolds 2010; Self-Sullivan and Mignucci-Giannoni 2008; Ramsar 2009; CITES 2011; UNEP 2009.
NK = none known
NL = earliest known date of species and/or habitat protection by local legislation
Ramsar = number of Ramsar sites
CITES = date of entry into force
SPAW = date signed (S), ratified (R) or acceded (A) to the Specially Protected Areas and Wildlife Protocol of the Cartagena Convention.

the availability of aquatic vegetation, their range, similar to growing human populations, is restricted to the coastal zone: rivers, lakes, estuaries, and seagrass beds along the coastline. The resulting shared habitat naturally results in competition for space with human populations. In areas with high boating, fishing, agricultural activity, or poverty, the competition often ends tragically, especially when humans are using motorized watercraft, gillnets, and agrochemicals.

Hunting and Incidental Catch

Historically, manatees were hunted for meat, oil, and bones. The meat provided a good source of protein, oil was used for cooking, and bones were shaped into weapons, Indigenous religious tools or ground for medicinal purposes. Today, WCR manatees appear to be poached almost exclusively for meat[52]. Depending on the market, manatee meat may sell for anywhere from US$2 to US$100 per pound. Illegal hunting, both for subsistence and profit, is a significant threat in Brazil, Colombia, Costa Rica, Cuba, Dominican Republic, French Guiana, Guatemala, Honduras, Mexico, Suriname, Trinidad, and Venezuela[53]. A favored technique uses a float tied to a harpoon. Hunters harpoon and chase a manatee by following the float until the animal becomes exhausted. Then it is dragged to shore and killed by stabbing or blunt force to the head.

Other hunters are known to place a gillnet across water between rivers and coastal seagrass beds. Incidental entanglement in nets and other fishing gear is often difficult to distinguish from such intentional hunting. Most fishers do not report cases of incidental catch or accidental entanglement[54], possibly harvesting the meat for subsistence or commercial sale.

Watercraft Collisions

With increased tourism in the Caribbean and Central and South America, competition for space between manatees, boats and jet-skis has become a significant threat. Recent studies in Belize and Puerto Rico provide a good example. Although older studies detected no scarring from boats[55], watercraft collision is currently considered one of the leading causes of manatee mortality[56]. With an exponential increase in cruise ship tourism between 2001 and 2004[57], the local perception is that more manatees are being injured or killed by boats each year, especially near Belize City[58]. Boat based studies using photo and video-ID methods indicate that more than 80% of the manatees at Basil Jones and 44% of the manatees in the Drowned Cayes bear scars from non-lethal watercraft collisions[59]. The unique scars are being used to develop a photo-ID catalogue of the manatees in the region[60].

Other Direct Human Disturbance

In addition to collisions, an increase in the number of boats and other human activities also interrupts manatees that are using the areas for feeding, resting, and nursery activities. Little is known about the long-term effects of disturbance on manatee populations; however in the short-term, boats and other watercraft are known to separate mother-calf pairs, often permanently. In Belize tour operators have been observed using small, fast, inflatable boats to bring tourists to known feeding, resting, and nursery areas in the Drowned Cayes and the Belize River, causing manatees to leave. In northeastern Brazil the stranding of live-orphaned calves is considered a primary threat to the subspecies[61]. Researchers concluded that watercraft and other human disturbance

---

BOX 4.2

Antillean Manatees in Brazil

Carolina Mattosinho de Carvalho Alvite and Regis Pinto De Lima

In Brazil sirenians were observed by the earliest European settlers in the 1500s (Whitehead 1978) ranging from Vila Velha, Espírito Santo (~20°S), to Cape Cabo Orange, Amapá (~4°N). An anonymous author traveling with the Pedro Álvares Cabral Portuguese discovery expedition described a female manatee with "ears the size of arms" in present-day Cabrália, Bahia. We can only assume the author was describing the manatee's forelimbs! Cristóvão de Lisboa, a Franciscan missionary who lived for twelve years in São Luís, Maranhão, reported groups of 300 or more in lagoons, rivers, and coves and along the northeastern coast. Goeldi (1893) reported manatees along the northernmost coastline between Cape Cabo Orange (4°25′N) and Cape Raso do Norte (1°43′N). Ferreira (1903) described manatees near Marajó Island and in rivers in the State of Grão Pará. He reported that they fed on riverside grasses and were harpooned by two or three aborigines in a small canoe. Ferreira also mentions a rare kind of manatee called a butter manatee, "peixe-boi manteiga." From these and other early explorers and writers, we know that historically, manatees were observed in abundance along the north, northeastern, and southeastern coasts of Brazil.

Today the Antillean manatee is listed as critically endangered by IBAMA, the Brazilian Institute for the Environment and Renewable Natural Resources. Population estimates lack calibration and surveys to monitor trends are not being conducted in all areas of historical occurrence. There is no rigorous information about the current population trend, but if we consider the threats and the estimated population size of ~500 individuals (Lima 1997; Luna et al. 2001), the population should be considered decreasing. The estimate of ~500 manatees represents a significant decrease over the past centuries when manatees were one of the most important sources of animal protein in the country. Indiscriminate killing finally motivated the government to prohibit hunting in 1967. However illegal hunting continued until the 1980s. Today hunting is rare, at least along the northeast coast, due to increased conservation efforts. However, manatees in Brazil continue to be threatened by entanglement in fishing nets and indiscriminate coastal development, which has degraded Brazil's aquatic environments. Additionally, increased boating activities have resulted in both lethal collisions with manatees and disruption of manatee behavior, often causing animals to leave their normal habitat.

The stranding of live-orphaned calves has been identified as the main recent threat to the species in northeastern Brazil (Lima et al. 1992; Lima 1997; Parente et al. 2004). Between 1981 and 2002, 74 stranded manatees were reported on the northeastern coast of Brazil; 58% (n = 43) were live manatees. During this period, all the live-stranded manatees were dependent calves, suggesting that that the main reason for manatee strandings along the northeastern coast is the separation of mothers from their calves. This area has become degraded due to shrimp and salt farms and uncontrolled tourism, which has reduced habitat available to manatees for calving and nursing (Lima 1997; Parente et al. 2004).

The coast of Brazil provides three distinct biogeographical habitats for manatees. The north region has a tropical climate, influenced by the South Equatorial Current and the Amazon River, which renders the waters murky and productive. Large, continuous mangrove forests dominate the coastal landscape, fringed by a *Spartina* species of seagrass, which is an important food source for the manatees. Antillean and Amazonian manatees are sympatric near the mouth of the Amazon, and hybrids have been identified using genetic analysis (Vianna et al. 2006; Garcia-Rodriguez et al. 1998). The northeastern region, where most of the research and conservation efforts in Brazil are focused, with its clear, warm waters, has many estuaries, mangrove forests, and coral reefs surrounded by marine algae and seagrass beds including *Halodule*, the preferred manatee food in the region. The southeastern region is more temperate and strongly influenced by both the cooler southern climate and the warm Brazilian Current, which flows from north to south along the coast. In recent years manatees have been reintroduced by scientists in the states of Paraíba and Alagaos. At least one has traveled as far south as the state of Sergipe (see map 4.1).

In 1972 the IUCN Red Data Book classified the species as vulnerable, with a southernmost distribution along the Atlantic coast of the Guianas, excluding Brazilian territory. In 1976 the southernmost distribution was expanded to include northern Brazil. In 1980 Projeto Peixe-Boi (the Brazilian Manatee Project, now run by IBAMA, the national environmental authority), conducted the first surveys in Brazil. They confirmed that manatees had vanished from the states of Espírito Santo and Bahia in the southeast. However, between 1990 and 1993, the Igarakue mobile unit, organized by Projeto Peixe-Boi undertook an extensive survey from Mangue Seco in Bahia to the Oiapoque River, the border between Brazil and French Guyana, conducting interviews with local people, gathering biological material, and reviewing older literature. The survey concluded that the manatee was extirpated in the states of Espírito Santo, Bahia, and Sergipe but still extant from Alagoas to Amapá.

from an increase in shrimp farms, salt farms, and tourism are causing mother-calf separation and a high number of calf strandings.

Cultural and Socioeconomic Significance

Cultural and socioeconomic significance of manatees varies within the WCR. In the Greater Antilles, manatee fat was used by Indigenous people to cook, make candles, and cure diseases. Today in the Dominican Republic, manatee meat, fat, and artisanal products are still used in localized places based on these traditions[62]. Bones have special value as medicines. The ancient Tainos of Hispaniola and Puerto Rico crafted rib bones into ceremonial instruments such as spatulas to induce vomiting[63]. In Cuba poaching does not seem to be a major threat. More than 80% of people interviewed were aware of the laws protecting manatees[64].

In Central America the ancient Maya hunted manatees for spiritual requirements as well as for the meat.

The ear bone was considered an amulet that protected its owner from evil powers. A special process was used to dry manatee meat, called *bucan*, which was thought to increase a man's strength and virility[65]. Today in Belize the living manatee is culturally and socioeconomically significant primarily as a tourist attraction. However, along the Miskito Coast of Nicaragua, Indigenous people continue to hunt manatees and may take up to 40 animals per year[66].

In South America Indigenous peoples were hunting manatees prior to European colonization, using both harpoons and nets. Specialized knowledge of manatee behavior, required to become a successful hunter, was passed down from one generation to the next[67]. In Brazil some cultures believe that manatee genitalia, skin, and ribs have magical significance. In French Guiana some cultures believe the manatee to be a water spirit; others consider the ear bones to be charms with therapeu-

BOX 4.3

Manatees in Nicaragua and Costa Rica, Central America

Ignacio Jiménez Pérez

Historical distribution of manatees in Nicaragua and Costa Rica was probably determined by water depth and accessibility of watercourses and wetlands connected to the Caribbean Sea. There is some evidence that manatees once inhabited Lake Nicaragua (O'Donnell 1981), the largest body of fresh water in Central America. It still contains other marine species, including sawfish, tarpon, and bull sharks. Despite its proximity to the Pacific, the lake drains into the San Juan River, which currently has manatees in its lower regions near the Caribbean (Jiménez Pérez 1999, 2003). However, upper regions of the river contain rapids that should prevent manatee movement to and from Lake Nicaragua, despite the fact the bull sharks, jumping like salmon, navigate the rapids. Manatees have not been observed in the Sarapiquí and San Carlos, two large rivers that drain into the San Juan from Costa Rica, since the late 1800s. Massive deforestation has been blamed for the species' absence in these two rivers, as in the Parismina, Reventazón, and Matina (O'Donnell 1981, Jiménez Pérez 2005a, 2005b). Manatees were also formerly present in the small Estrella River and Mahogany Creek in southern Costa Rica, and in the Walpasiksa River bar in Nicaragua, and may have used the lower Coco River, on the border between Nicaragua and Honduras (Jiménez Pérez 1999, 2002; see map 4.1).

However, manatees are still present in most areas of their historical range in Nicaragua and Costa Rica, though there are no good estimates of manatee abundance. They have recently been observed along the Caribbean coast, in the main rivers and lagoons near the sea, and up to 60 km upstream in the San Juan, Wawa, and Kurinwás rivers (Jiménez Pérez 1999, 2002). Aerial counts have either underestimated the population substantially, as was the case in Costa Rica (Reynolds et al. 1995), or were limited to a small fraction of the national range, as happened in surveys carried out by Carr (1994) in the Miskito lagoons of northern Nicaragua. In fact, Nicaragua may have one of the highest densities in the Caribbean, with some groups surpassing 20 individuals. Informed guesses estimate that 30–60 manatees inhabit Costa Rica, found mostly in the northeastern half of the country (Jiménez Pérez 1999), and that several hundred individuals were present in Nicaragua (Jiménez Pérez 2002). Aerial surveys and interviews indicate much larger manatee groups in northern Nicaragua than in southern Nicaragua and Costa Rica (see Carr 1994; Reynolds et al. 1995; Jiménez Pérez 1999, 2002, 2005b). Northeastern Costa Rica is the only area in both countries where there has been some systematic research on population trends of manatees. Jiménez Pérez (2005b) used standardized interviews to assess population changes in this region between 1996 and 2005, concluding that manatee abundance and group size had probably increased during the last ten years.

To understand differences in conservation status between the two countries, we should look at the history of manatee hunting. Hunting was common practice in Costa Rica during the 1960s and 1970s, becoming rare in 1980s, and was practically extinguished by the late 1990s due to scarcity of manatees and the initiation of conservation (Jiménez Pérez 1999). A similar pattern, 5–10 years later, occurred in southeastern Nicaragua (Jiménez Pérez 2003). Manatee numbers have rebounded from a minimum during the last two decades in the frontier region between Nicaragua and Costa Rica.

On the other hand, manatee hunting decreased sharply in central and northern Nicaragua during its civil war in the 1980s, only to be revived in Indigenous communities (e.g., Halouver, Krukira, Bismuna, and Rama Cay) after peace returned in the 1990s (Jiménez Pérez 2002). Between 1999 and 2001, an estimated 41 to 49 manatees were killed in Nicaragua. Present poaching rates in northern Nicaragua vary from year to year, depending on such economic and social factors as commercial fishing, logging contracts, and cocaine smuggling (Espinoza Marin 2004). Thus it is extremely difficult to provide a realistic assessment of the population status of manatees in the northern half of Nicaragua.

Both Nicaragua and Costa Rica harbor abundant, pristine manatee habitat. Northeastern Nicaragua has extensive floodplains of up to 100 km in width along its Caribbean coast, which include many slow-moving rivers, creeks, lagoons, and bays. Vegetation is abundant and ranges from tropical forest species along the river banks to large mangrove-enclosed lagoons of seagrass beds. Shallow water with extensive seagrass beds extends far offshore (Jiménez Pérez 2002).

In southeastern Nicaragua and northeastern Costa Rica the large brackish lagoons have been replaced by freshwater rivers, creeks, and small lagoons surrounded by rainforest and grass-swamps. The largest rivers in this area carry abundant sediments from the volcanic interior to the sea, creating a highly turbid coastline with few seagrass beds. As a result, manatees in this region are more abundant inland in wide, slow-moving rivers and lagoons with abundant emergent and floating vegetation, similar to habitats used by the Amazonian manatee (Jiménez Pérez 2005). Among these habitats, the Tortuguero waterways have the greatest disturbance due to an increasing ecotourism industry and pesticide runoff from neighboring banana plantations.

South of the Tortuguero floodplain there is a 45 km stretch without good manatee habitat, until seagrass beds reappear in the coastal zone close to the Panama border, and emergent vegetation becomes abundant in the Sixaola River (Jiménez Pérez 1999). This small area in southeastern Costa Rica is connected to known manatee habitat in San Changuinola, and Bocas del Toro, Panama (Mou Sue and Chen 1990).

A vast network of protected areas covers over 60% and 85% of manatee habitat in Nicaragua and Costa Rica, respectively. However, differences in enforcement of conservation policies vary widely. Protected areas in central and northern Nicaragua are little more than "paper parks" where native people tend to be unaware of the existence of reserves, and manatee poaching is common in some Miskito and Rama indigenous communities (Chacón 2000; Jiménez Pérez 2002; Espinoza Marin 2004). On the other hand, the UNESCO Rió San Juan Biosphere Reserve has significant enforcement due to governmental presence. This large reserve is adjacent to the Tortuguero Conservation Area in Costa Rica, with a longstanding tradition of protected area management. This binational network of protected areas along the Nicaragua-Costa Rica border provides one of the best conservation strategies for manatees in Central America.

---

tic properties[68]. In Venezuela manatee meat, oil, skin, and bones are thought to have medicinal value, and the manatee played a significant mythological role in some tribes[69]. In Colombia the Sikuani tribe of the Orinoco values the living manatee and believes that rivers will dry up if people eat manatee meat[70].

Research Needs

Given the paucity of data within the WCR, conservation research should focus on (1) assessment of manatee distribution and relative abundance, and (2) assessment and control of threats to manatees and their habitat. Additionally, there are reports of interesting phenomena at specific sites that warrant further behavioral research; for example, the possibility of twinning in the Dominican Republic and the seasonal use of barrier reef sites in Belize.

It is difficult to develop the standardized protocols and techniques needed for population estimates on a regional level. Optimally, assessments of status should include population estimates and trends, demographics, and identification of threats to WCR manatees. However, if data cannot be statistically analyzed or compared across spatial and temporal scales, then the time and resources invested may be wasted. Most advanced techniques are costly and labor intensive, making the probability of implementation throughout the WCR unlikely. Details of relevant research techniques are presented throughout this volume.

Regional Database

In most WCR countries, watercraft collision has been reported as a growing threat to the local manatee population. Given the high proportion of manatees bearing unique scars in Belize, the development of a photo-ID database to serve the WCR would increase our ability to evaluate the subspecies and track movements of individual manatees between political jurisdictions. A photo-ID database with fields similar to the MIPS database for Florida manatees could be modeled after the online EC-OCEAN database for whale sharks, which enables collaboration among scientists[71].

Summary

West Indian manatees are an endangered species of priority concern within the WCR. Their numbers have declined exponentially since European colonization and will continue to do so without significant changes in human behavior. Despite an explosion of new data over the past decade, we have failed to develop the interdisciplinary partnerships necessary to coordinate conservation efforts. Owing to their endangered status, time is of the essence and priority should be given to providing protection for manatees and their habitat. Improved public awareness, increased protected areas, better enforcement of laws, reduced anthropogenic mortality, and cooperation among local, national, and regional entities are essential to the success of existing conservation strategies. National recovery plans should outline and prioritize activities with a specific time-line for completion. Regional networks should be strengthened to ensure coordination of activities across political boundaries. Several organizations are dedicated to supporting such networks, including Mote Marine Laboratory, the Marine Mammal Commission, the USGS Sirenia Project, Save the Manatee Club, Sea to Shore Alliance, Sirenian International, and the Puerto Rico Manatee Conservation Center. The updated WCR management plan recommends additional conservation strategies and specific research needs[72].

From an ecological perspective, manatees are the largest primary consumer within the WCR. Their decline is an indicator of significant changes is the coastal marine ecosystem, which is essential to the health and well-being of all species, including humans. Although the legal framework for protection of manatees and manatee habitat is in place, the success of conservation efforts relies on conformance by stakeholders who share the manatee's environment. The charismatic nature of the West Indian manatee provides a unique opportunity for educational outreach with the goal of improved conformance with existing laws and conservation programs.

5

The Amazonian Manatee

MIRIAM MARMONTEL, FERNANDO C. WEBER ROSAS, AND SARITA KENDALL

Among the sirenians, the Amazonian manatee (*Trichechus inunguis*) is the only endemic species in the Amazon Basin and the only sirenian restricted to freshwater systems. Indigenous groups living in areas where the Amazonian manatee occurs have their own names for the species (*yacu-huagra* in Kichwa, *entsania-yawa* in Shuar, *siáya-wêkî* in Siona, *airuwe* in Ticuna, and *yuwara* in Cocama and Yagua). Non-Indigenous terms liken the manatee to land cattle (*vaca de água, vaca del Amazonas, manatí,* or *vaca marina* in Spanish, and *peixe-boi* in Portuguese), names that reflect the large, round nostrils both animals have in common, in addition to their shared herbivorous diet.

The Amazonian manatee is probably a branch of the trichechids that invaded the Caribbean region in the early Miocene epoch and then became isolated in the Amazon Basin after the origin of the Andes in the early Pliocene, some 5 million years ago[1]. The species inhabits lakes, rivers and channels of white, black, and clear water in the Amazon region[2] (map 5.1). However, highly productive white water is the preferred habitat of the species. Manatees have played a significant role in Amazon basin culture, having been hunted for subsistence by Indigenous people for hundreds of years[3].

Exploitation by non-Indigenous peoples apparently started in 1542 when Francisco de Orellana and crew went down the Amazon and were offered manatee meat by the Indians. Despite protective legislation currently in place, manatees are hunted to this day throughout the Amazon. While fishers with harpoons are currently the main threat, other more efficient techniques have reached the backwaters of the Amazon and may be on the increase. In particular, the use of nets is on the rise everywhere and presents a threat of both accidental and deliberate capture.

The huge dimensions and complexity of the Amazon region make estimating the size of the population a real challenge. The manatee has been under pressure from human activities for centuries (including hunting, pollution, and habitat destruction), and there is good rea-

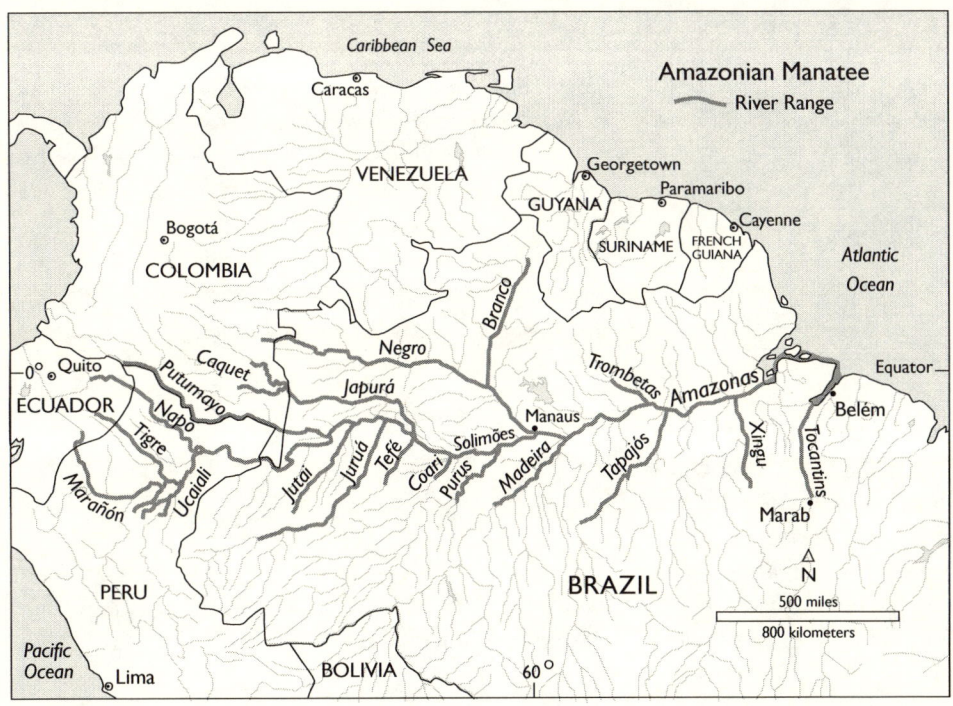

Map 5.1. Amazonian manatee distribution. (Map by Ellen McElhinny.)

son to believe the population level is below the carrying capacity of its environment[4]. In this chapter we present the general biology, habitat use, current status, and main threats and include recommendations for the manatee's conservation.

Distribution and Habitat Needs

Amazonian manatees have a wide distribution, ranging from the headwaters in Ecuador, Peru, and Colombia to the estuary in Brazil. They are typically found throughout lowland forested areas at altitudes below 300 m. Manatees are rare in some areas and have been extirpated in others[5]. The largest populations probably occur in the Brazilian Amazon, most notably in the Solimões, Negro, Japurá, Juruá, Tocantins, and Tapajós river systems. Most records in Ecuador are from the extreme northeast[6]. In Peru, Amazonian manatees occur in the Samiria, Pacaya, and Yanayacu-Pucate rivers[7] and in the Javari and Amazonas rivers near the Colombian border. In Colombia they also occur in the Amazon, Putumayo, and lower Caquetá rivers. All through their range manatees occupy a great range of black and mixed-water lakes, including large expanses of *várzea* (floodplains and seasonally flooded forest) and *igapó* (permanently waterlogged swamp forest)[8].

Amazonian manatees prefer shallow, 1–4 m deep, calm waters away from human activities with easy access to patches of aquatic vegetation. Annual variation in river levels through the Amazon Basin may reach 10–15 m. The seasonal variation of water levels profoundly influences manatee life in terms of both feeding and protection from human predation. Amazonian manatees undertake long seasonal movements, using lakes and *várzea* areas during high waters when the production of aquatic plants increases. As observed in the mid-Solimões area in Brazil and in the Colombian Amazon, when the river level drops, manatees move to deeper water bodies where they spend the dry season.

Population Dynamics

While there are no accurate population estimates available for the Amazon, there is no doubt that numbers are lower than in the past due to long-term hunting; in fact, manatee habitat is believed to be below carrying capacity[9]. Although subsistence hunting seems to be the present primary cause of decline in population, it is not the only one. From 1935 to 1954 commercial hunting was responsible for the deaths of several thousand manatees[10]. One of the most problematic and pressing questions is the lack of population estimates. The only basin-wide minimum estimate of 10,000 animals[11] must be viewed with caution. Interviews with local inhabitants suggest increased sightings in some areas and fewer sightings in others. Conditions in the region conspire against an easy answer: most waters inhabited by Amazonian manatees are very murky, and Amazonian manatees are extremely secretive, perhaps an adaptation to hunting.

The annual reproductive rate of sirenian populations is approximately 5%[12], an obstacle to recovery for an exploited population[13]. Slow reproduction rates, combined with continued subsistence hunting, suggest that the population is likely to continue to decrease. Nevertheless, genetic diversity of *T. inunguis* was found to be high[14]. Recent analyses from the mitochondrial DNA control region[15] suggest that Amazonian manatees are undergoing a population expansion, although estimates vary as to when this began. Although the Amazonian manatee is not found outside the Amazon Basin, hybridization has recently been confirmed between the *T. manatus* and *T. inunguis* species at the mouth of the Amazon River in Brazil[16].

Legal Status

In Brazil the Amazonian manatee is classified as a "vulnerable species"[17] and has been protected by law since 1967 under the Wildlife Protection Law (No. 5197 of 3 January 1967) and Edicts No. 3481 of 31 May 1973 and N-11 of 21 February 1986. In Ecuador, where it is classified as "critically endangered," the manatee is considered the most threatened Amazonian mammal and is protected by Resolución No. 105 of the Ministry of Environment (Registro Oficial No. 5 of 28 January 2000)[18]. In Colombia (*Libro Rojo de Mamíferos Amenazados de Colombia*) manatees are considered endangered (see http://www.iucnredlist.org/technical-documents/categories-and-criteria/2001-categories-criteria#categories, criteria EN A.2c, d, and A.3c, d), mainly due to loss of habitat and hunting, and are protected by Resolución 574 of 1969. In Peru Amazonian manatees are protected under the *Reglamento de Ordenamiento Pesquero de la Amazonía Peruana* (R.M. No. 147–2001-PE) of 30 April 2001.

Threats

Subsistence and Commercial Hunting

Historically, Amazonian manatees have been caught by Indigenous peoples for local consumption and trade. From precolonial times manatees were the focus of international trade, which peaked during the Industrial Revolution, when their skin was valued for building machinery parts[19]. And *mixira* (manatee meat preserved in its own fat) was commercially available and widely distributed throughout the nineteenth century.

Subsistence hunting and the illegal sale of meat still exist throughout the species' range, despite widespread awareness of the animal's protected status. Hunting and trading in manatee products are practiced by Indigenous peoples[20], colonists, and the military[21] and are the primary threat to manatees. Hunting is usually carried out by men, and the capture of a manatee may be considered an act of machismo, since it is so difficult. In the past there were specialized manatee hunters and, while a few hunters are still left, manatee hunting is now usually secondary to the capture of *paiche* (*Arapaima gigas,* a large freshwater fish)[22]. Traditional hand-held harpoon hunts account for from 55% to over 90% of hunting events. Hunting strategies include looking for manatees in feeding sites and mating areas and using captured calves as bait to attract and harpoon the mothers. Most hunters (over 75%) are between 30 and 59 years of age. Manatee products are mostly used for subsistence; the value of meat varies from US$0.40 to US$3.00/kg (for comparison, beef sells for approximately US$3.00/kg). The average annual family income is US$500.00 in the Brazilian Amazon.

It is difficult to quantify the number of manatees killed. Even expert manatee hunters may pretend not to know what a manatee is, and locals are wary of talking to outsiders, especially if it is a one-time event. Some hunters justify their acts by saying that hunting for food is allowed. Although current Brazilian legislation (Law No. 6905/98) does allow subsistence hunting, it is only for those who can prove dire need[23]. In the Colombian Amazon the Ticuna and other Indigenous communities have been granted some level of autonomy or may be so remote as to make enforcement impossible[24]. During May and June 2004 seven manatees were killed in two villages in the Samiria River Basin in Peru, suggesting high hunting pressure[25]. In Peru's Pacaya Samiria Reserve, manatees are caught by specialized fishers, usually *ribereños* (people who live near the rivers) descended from the Cocama-Cocamilla Indigenous group. In Peru and in the Colombia-Peru border area, hunters set traps remarkably similar to those used for West African manatees; traps that might be responsible for an increase in hunting.

Hunting is easier during normal low water periods and extreme droughts. During the 1995 drought records for ten towns in the Brazilian state of Amazonas showed 443 manatees killed; in 1997 a record 648 manatees were killed[26]; and in 1998 475 cases were recorded[27].

As early as the nineteenth century, the practice of setting strong nets across narrow entrances to lakes or streams to catch manatees began[28]. Nets may allow non-traditional peoples to move into areas and set specially made gillnets. A freezer boat working with a large trawl net on the Purus River in 1999 caused the death of 14 animals[29].

Fishing traps are illegal in both Colombia and Peru, but traps (*pari* or fence, with an entrance above which hangs a harpoon) are being used in Peru[30] and the Atacuari area on the Colombia-Peru border, where a dozen manatees perished between 1998 and 2002.

The use of nets and traps represents a cultural change[31]. Both allow a number of animals to be caught for sale with minimal effort, skill, or knowledge of manatees and their habits. Young people are not interested in harpoon hunting. They go to school in urban areas and spend less time in their villages, so they tend to fish with nets, which demands less time and effort; their participation in manatee hunting is usually opportunistic.

Accidental Captures in Gillnets

The second most important threat to Amazonian manatees is the accidental catch of young animals in fishing nets, which has been documented in Peru[32], Colombia, and Brazil. Young animals are particularly vulnerable to fishing nets; if the manatee survives, hunters may raise it, sell it, or give it away for consumption or as a pet. Over half of the 44 calves that have arrived at Centro de Pesquisa e Preservação de Mamíferos Aquáticos (CPPMA) in Brazil since 1992 were caught in gillnets[33]. The number of calves rescued from gillnets every year in Brazil has been increasing, but this number is certainly a small reflection of what is happening in the Amazon as a whole[34].

Habitat Alteration and Disturbance

The third most significant threat to the survival of these manatees is human activity that causes loss, alteration, and fragmentation of habitats[35], notably in Colombia[36].

Very few cases of Amazonian manatees being hit by boats have been recorded in Brazil[37]; this may be due to a tendency for the species to avoid busy, noisy places. Manatee absence from areas where they were recorded previously in Peru and Colombia may be partially attributed to increasing boat traffic[38] and temporary beach settlement during the dry season[39]. On the Tapajós River, proposed government projects to transport soybeans will greatly increase barge traffic[40]. Other activities thought to displace manatees from typical use areas include large nets set in *remansos* (calm backwaters) and channels of the Colombian Amazon, the cutting of grasses, and fishing with trot lines in floating meadows[41].

The construction of hydroelectric dams and oil exploration and production may be particularly damaging to manatee habitat. The current relatively high level of genetic diversity observed in the Amazonian manatee might change if all 80 hydroelectric power plants planned for Amazonia[42] are built. These dams will act as barriers isolating manatee populations[43]. Petrobras (the Brazilian multinational oil company) was granted permission to explore for oil in Yasuni National Park, a development that will involve considerable traffic, with the potential for oil spills and soil contamination. Another problem is fishing by Indigenous people who use dynamite and by outsiders who employ toxic substances to poison fish.

Local, National and International Uses

An adult manatee may produce more than 80 kg of meat, which is greatly appreciated in the Amazon region and is consumed for subsistence and offered for sale. The skin is also cooked and eaten with sauce[44] or added to black bean stew. The meat is usually salted and sun-dried, but it is the preparation of *mixira* that leads to greater pressure on the species, since it is highly valued and may be conserved for six months to a year. The fat is used in cooking, to fry fish and to make local dishes such as *beiju* and *tapioca*[45]. The meat is compared to bush meat, and local people claim they can distinguish seven different flavors.

Hunters are afraid of the environmental police in Brazil and, therefore, only sell manatee products to neighbors or nearby communities, although when possible they also take manatee products to town markets and sometimes even to the state capitals. An entire manatee may be ordered in the Belém (Para state) market. In Colombia people used to give away parts of the animal to other members of the community; now, due to cash needs, they sell at least part of the meat to restaurants, institutions (military, boarding schools), and others at approximately US$1.50/kg. A large manatee can provide the equivalent of a monthly urban minimum salary, "a real bonanza"[46]. Before 1998 Puerto Nariño police were among the greatest buyers. In Atacuari, on the Colombia-Peru border, manatee meat is sold to military posts or traded for favors or compensation for some tasks; in the Lagartococha river system, one of the most remote areas in Ecuador, demand for animal protein arises largely from the military posts[47].

Household and Medicinal Uses

The scapula is used to stir *farinha* (manioc flour). From the ribs, locals make *gaponga* (small pieces of rib that are thrown into the water to simulate the sound of fruit falling and thereby attract *tambaqui* fish). The skin is currently used to enclose and carry heavy materials, make braided cables or whips[48], drums[49], *rilhos* (a wooden handle with leather ring on the end, to get cocoa), and as bait to attract carnivorous fish like *tucunaré*[50]. The fat has long been used for lubricating tools[51]. Locals may use pieces of manatee bone as charms—often called *puçanga*—to give them luck when searching for a manatee to kill.

Besides food, manatee products are also used as medicine. The fat (pureed or mixed with *andiroba* oil) is used for respiratory diseases, swellings, muscle pain, bone diseases (including rheumatism), and hernias[52]. In fairs, commercial businesses, and drugstores in the state of São Paulo (Brazil) and even in Porto Alegre (southernmost capital in Brazil), creams are made of fake manatee fat[53] because of its alleged healing properties. Skin, toasted and ground, is made into a tea used to treat hernias, respiratory diseases, and impotency[54]. Tea made from the powder of the ear bone is offered as a cure for deafness; similarly, the stapes (or small middle ear bone) may be hung around the neck as treatment[55].

Captivity Issues

Calves are sold as pets or sold or given to politicians, authorities, and wealthy influential people in other Amazonian countries. Trafficking in calves in Colombia has been common for several years, and there are recent cases in the Leticia-Tabatinga-Benjamin Constant area. In the Brazil-Colombia border area, calves cost about R$300,00 (~US$143.00)[56]. There were at least three cases of calves captured in Peru and offered for sale in Colombia between 2003 and 2005[57]. Evidence for similar activities in Manaus comes from complaints about hotels using them for exhibits. When kept as pets, manatees are generally maintained in inadequate private enclosures, such as pools or small lakes. Siona and Quechua Indians keep them as pets but raise them for food[58].

Most illegal captivity sites are in the interior of the Brazilian Amazon, where animals are ordered and maintained in ponds, tanks, and small lakes by local landowners, hotels, and hunter-fishers. Animals in private captivity are a problem. IBAMA (Brazil's environmental law enforcement agency), does not have a clear policy and does not have adequate resources to move the animals to institutions—CPPMA; the National Institute for Amazonian Research (INPA, Instituto Nacional de Pesquisas da Amazônia); or the National Rubbertapper Council (CNS, Conselho Nacional de Seringueiros)—much less to incur the high costs associated with raising manatees in captivity. The release of captive-reared animals is further complicated because it is not generally known where the manatees in captivity originated and because hunting continues in all areas. A few years ago a community-based rehabilitation program involving short-term captivity followed by release in the original place of capture started in the Amanã region of Brazil[59]. The actual number of illegally kept manatees is unknown, but it is thought to be a significant problem.

Presently there are more than 100 manatees legally held in five Brazilian Amazonian institutions. Most arrived as orphans after their mothers ended up in meat markets; a few had lost their mothers and were found swimming alone, following boats, or trapped after a severe drought[60]. The Letícia Zoo held captives from approximately 1990; the last one died in 2005. Three Brazilian research centers are reviewing proposals to reintroduce captive-raised manatees back into the wild.

Cultural Beliefs

Live manatees have no central position in Ticuna mythology, but the meat is used in one of the most important rites, the *pelazón* or female puberty ceremony[61]. Ticuna stories describe how grubs transform into manatees in the giant *Ceiba* tree. The grubs grow fat on the leaves and build cocoons, which, after a heavy thunderstorm, fall into a river and float down; by the time they reach a lake they have turned into manatees[62].

Another relevant Ticuna strategy is the concept of *lagos bravos* or wild lakes: these are dangerous places protected by mythical guardians such as enormous anacondas or aquatic jaguars. People are afraid to fish there, creating unofficial aquatic reserves.

There are taboos associated with manatee meat eating. Meat is said to be noxious and cause skin diseases, diarrhea, and occasionally death[63]. This type of belief or restriction, plus low commercial value (in Peru), might provide opportunities for manatee conservation[64]. Usually the skull and bones are tossed in the river; this is done out of fear of someone using the bones to perform some kind of black magic that would cause the hunter not to catch a manatee again; that is, fear of *panema* (bad luck).

Research

At present there are relatively few manatee field projects in place, and research is being carried out in only a small portion of the species' range. Since the mid-1970s, the National Institute for Amazonian Research (INPA, Instituto Nacional de Pesquisas da Amazônia) in Manaus, Brazil, has conducted most of its work on captive manatees, addressing rescue and rehabilitation activities, health, and morphological, anatomical, reproductive, and physiological studies. In 1993 Brazil's Mamirauá Institute for Sustainable Development (IDSM, Instituto de Desenvolvimento Sustentável Mamirauá) located in Tefé, Amazonas state, started the first long-term research program on free-ranging manatees in the Amazon's two large, sustainable development reserves, Mamirauá and Amanã (over 3,500,000 ha). So far it has successfully monitored five animals for medium- to long-term periods, which helped to define migratory routes. IDSM also works very closely with the local inhabitants of the reserves, monitoring hunting levels, documenting traditional knowledge, and implementing educational programs.

The Centro de Pesquisa e Preservação de Mamíferos Aquáticos (CPPMA), established in 1992, is involved in the rehabilitation of orphaned manatees and in environmental education activities, with a view toward making locals co-responsible for the conservation and appropriate use of natural resources[65]. The Institute for Ecological Research (IPE, Instituto de Pesquisas Ecológicas) focuses on research and conservation involving wild populations in the lower Negro River region, Amazonas[66]. The Centro de Mamíferos Aquáticos (CMA, Center for Aquatic Mammals) started a project in 2001 in Pará state, that includes the rescue and rehabilitation of animals in illegal captivity and surveys on the conservation and status of Amazonian manatees in the main rivers of the Brazilian Amazon. In 1998 the Omacha Foundation started working in Colombia's Puerto Nariño area, carrying out studies on hunting, feeding ecology, distribution, and use of habitat; more recently, under the Natütama Foundation, this research has extended into abundance studies and direct observations of manatees through a co-investigation program based on local knowledge, and it includes education and awareness building as priorities. In Ecuador, studies have been occasional, as there is no institution with a project specifically dedicated to manatees. In Peru the Durrell Institute at the University of Kent maintains a long-term monitoring program in the Samiria River[67].

Conservation and Management

In 1997 Brazil's IBAMA started a campaign to protect the manatee by enforcing regulations in critical hunting areas and has covered five main rivers (middle Solimões, lower Amazonas, middle Purus, upper Juruá, and lower Uatumã). Owing to the permanent work and protection activities by the environmental program of Amazonas Energia (a private power company that manages the Balbina Hydroelectric Dam), hunting is believed to be decreasing in the lower Uatumã River (from a high of 73 in 1995 to zero in 2003 and 2004 and one in 2005)[68]. In Colombia's Puerto Nariño area the hunting trend has also been decreasing for the past five years. Between 1998 and 2003, 47 hunted manatees were recorded in the area of Puerto Nariño (Zaragoza to Atacuari)[69]. With the campaign in key communities to reduce hunting, the number of hunted animals decreased from ten in 1998–99 to four in 2003. In 2004 two animals were hunted, and in 2005 none were hunted[70]. Although legislation is important, it is not sufficient: due to educational programs about the low reproductive rate of manatees and reduced numbers in the area, most fishers agreed to stop hunting, and those who continue to do so now tend to be isolated by the community.

In Ecuador the Siona Indians are said to practice a self-imposed ban on manatee hunting because of low manatee populations[71]. However, some of the Siona do not know of this ban, and hunting probably continues[72]. There is no cultural check on manatee exploitation in Peru, where they are hunted and trapped everywhere, and it is particularly discouraging that reserve guards are avidly hunting manatees as well. Although aware of the illegality, hunters think that manatees may be taken if they have a special permit or if the take is for the purpose of a communal celebration. There is no fear of law enforcement, since detection levels, enforcement, and punishment are so weak. Protein source alternatives may reduce hunting pressures, but further research is needed to evaluate the status and sustainability of white-lipped peccary, small fish species, and agriculture for these riverine people. Educational campaigns should also be directed at hunters, focusing on pertinent biological information and the effects of hunting pressure on manatee populations[73]. Hunters have been actively involved in data collection in other regions of the Peruvian Amazon[74]. Community-based conservation might increase awareness and, therefore, increase the opportunities for changing attitudes about manatees[75].

The Mamirauá Sustainable Development Reserve, established in Brazil in 1992, had a management plan approved in 1996 that includes guidelines to reduce the number of manatees taken. Colombia has the only management plan specifically designed for manatees.

Conservation strategies in the Colombian Amazon and the Mamirauá Reserve include involving fishers and hunters in manatee research activities and conducting workshops, thus incorporating hunters into an information/conservation network with the added advantage that they also become ambassadors. Locals have additionally been incorporated as co-researchers, trained in telemetry, global positioning systems (GPS), radio communications, the use of hydrophones, photography, data analyses, etc.[76]

This approach has produced a generalized acceptance of the fact that hunting may not be sustainable and manatees need to be protected[77]. From a conservation standpoint, two important information gaps remain: locals typically do not regard manatees as a functioning part of aquatic ecosystems (e.g., their role in returning large quantities of feces and nutrients to the water) and are unfamiliar with the manatee life cycle (including information about their long gestation period, lengthy calf dependency, and extended birthing intervals)[78].

Hunters in the Puerto Nariño area have decided that it is important to exercise "self-control" and have recommended no hunting for at least ten years. In addition, calves found alive in nets should be released, and females with calves should never be hunted. While not everyone agreed, the majority thought that those who did not exercise self-control should be sanctioned (e.g., community work assigned by the local authority) but not sent to jail (except in the case of continuing offenders)[79]. The fishers/hunters also called for alternatives to compensate them for not hunting manatees, given overall economic and social pressures on their community, including increasing human populations, more boats, widespread use of fishing nets, and lack of employment of young people.[80] Although hunting has decreased and the few hunters who persist have been identified and censured, there also needs to be strong legislation upon which to base enforcement, or the commitment may weaken[81]. Captive manatees may be used to stimulate conservation, and every effort should be made to link locals to the rehabilitation and reintroduction of manatees. There is a far greater appeal in seeing a manatee taking milk from a bottle or playing than in a chunk of meat[82].

Given that manatees are distributed in such remote areas and that enforcement is so weak, educational and participative strategies are fundamental to achieving manatee conservation. In the past decade or so, working with communities has become a more widespread conservation tool throughout the Amazon countries; in Colombia's case, this includes disseminating the importance and status of the manatee, socializing information about legal protection, and creating a sense of ownership by local inhabitants[83].

Research and Conservation Needs

There is clearly a need for further research, especially in countries where few studies have been carried out, such as Peru and Ecuador. It is also important that alternative techniques, both direct and indirect, be explored to try to estimate manatee numbers accurately. The use of sonar equipment (on the high tech end) or surveys by canoe with the help of locals (on the low tech end) should be attempted. These methods have already been used in Colombia and Brazil. The collaboration of local hunters is fundamental to the success of all research projects, not only because of their traditional knowledge but also as a way to increase their awareness in favor of manatee conservation. The generalized lack of biological knowledge among local people about reproductive parameters, especially slow reproductive rates, as identified in Brazil, Colombia and Peru, makes educational campaigns vital. The effect of manatee feces fertilization on phytoplankton production could be quite important, particularly in lake systems[84], and should be investigated. The ecological impact of extirpating manatees in a given area is probably not measurable, but their serious depletion or removal undoubtedly brings costs to the environment as a whole[85].

Despite all the laws, conservation and enforcement are difficult as there are few control mechanisms, and the regions in question are very remote. Recommended conservation measures include:

- additional preserves (including areas where no adverse human activities will take place);
- evaluation of whether present protected areas contribute to manatee conservation, and appropriate adjustments, if necessary;
- research on manatee vulnerability to oil spills and human presence, and better population estimates;
- implementation of national environmental education plans, especially with people in and near areas inhabited by manatees, including discouragement of captive trade;
- full implementation of hunting and trade prohibitions (including all consumers);
- implementation of binational and regional plans, with the agreement and support of governments, and educating border garrisons to ensure that military personnel become manatee guardians;
- evaluation of the potential for the return of captive manatees to areas that could maintain healthy populations[86]; and
- future conservation strategies should take into account the likelihood of interspecific hybridization, especially when considering reintroduction of animals[87].

Outlook for the Future

Although traditional hunting still occurs throughout the area, it may be naturally slowing down with the aging of the professional hunters. However, new threats lurk on the horizon, such as the use of nets and traps. Should those practices become widespread, manatees would be facing very harsh times. Data on captivity methods should be carefully monitored and educational campaigns should be developed to address this concern.

Enforcement should be enhanced, especially in town markets and produce fairs, to reduce the illegal trade in manatees and their products. Enforcement in reserves may be conducted by trained volunteers or paid wardens, who can be on site at the time of any capture. Workshops and/or electronic meetings should be held among authorities and researchers, possibly in multinational meetings, to deal with the growing problem of illegal captivity. Community-based rehabilitation centers may help to solve the captive manatee problem and increase awareness about manatee conservation. Existing reserves that contain manatee populations must be enforced and need management/action plans to be developed and implemented in collaboration with the local inhabitants. Critical areas used by manatees, especially during dry periods, must be identified and included in such plans.

6

The West African Manatee

AKOI KOUADIO

The West African manatee (*Trichechus senegalensis*) is a slow-moving, herbivorous aquatic mammal found in shallow coastal waters, rivers, estuaries, and lagoons. Until fairly recently the West African manatee was among the "forgotten" marine mammals, the sirenian about which the least was known. Only a handful of individual scientists had attempted to carry out preliminary studies on the distribution and biology of the species.

A broad-scale survey, based mostly on information gleaned from fishermen, was first conducted by Nishiwaki et al.[1], who visited 13 African countries in July–August 1980 and January–March 1981. These authors presented a regional picture of the manatees and reported numerous animals occupying a variety of habitats. Reeves et al.[2] studied the West African manatee in Sierra Leone and Nigeria, while Roth and Waitkuwait[3] investigated manatee distribution and status in Côte d'Ivoire. More recently, Powell[4] spent nine years in West Africa studying manatee biology and management in seven countries. His report contains perhaps the best current presentation of regional information. Research on the biology and the ecology of the West African manatee was conducted by Akoi[5], who tagged and tracked 18 animals in the lagoon complex of Fresco in Côte d'Ivoire from April 2000 to September 2002.

This lack of information is in part due to the fact that the species lives exclusively in less-developed countries, where research funding is inadequate and field conditions are harsh. The conservation and management of a species for which so little information exists remains a real challenge. This chapter aims to provide some baseline information on the species' distribution, its value to people, threats to its survival, local beliefs, and conservation efforts undertaken to date.

West African manatees are very similar to West Indian manatees in their exterior morphology. However, experts familiar with the appearance of both species have noted that the West African manatee is less robust, more fusiform in shape, and its eyes protrude slightly more from their sockets. An average adult West African manatee is about 3 m in length and weighs from 450 to 500 kg, although some exceptional individuals can reach 4 m long and weigh more than 1,000 kg. Eighteen manatees (eight males and ten females) trapped and tagged in the Fresco lagoon complex in Côte d'Ivoire had a body length from 2.04 m to 2.94 m, with a mean length of 2.57±0.25 m.

West African manatees are mostly solitary animals that spend most of their time resting, traveling, feeding, and cavorting. In Gabon, Keith[6] has documented manatees sighted in groups in 22% of total sightings (n=44); groups are also reported frequently in Angola and Senegal.

Although little is known about the feeding behavior of the West African manatee, the species is believed to have a diverse diet. Recent studies suggest that their diet mostly consists of emergent grasses, plants, and even fruits that fall into the water[7].

Distribution

The West African manatee is found along Africa's Atlantic coast from the Senegal River in the north to the Longa River of Angola in the south[8]. Manatees have also been recorded far inland, some 2,000 km from the sea in the Niger River from Koulikoro to Gao, in Lakes Debo and Léré in Mali, and in Lake Tréné in Chad (map 6.1).

West African manatees are believed to inhabit practically all aquatic habitats. Optimal habitats, however, based on reported sightings in various areas, are coastal lagoons and estuaries with abundant growth of mangrove or emergent herbaceous vegetation[9].

Population Trends and Threats to Survival

A population estimate has never been produced for the West African manatee. Past and current population sizes are unknown, but it is believed that the population has drastically declined and that several local populations have been extirpated. Manatees here are subjected to a

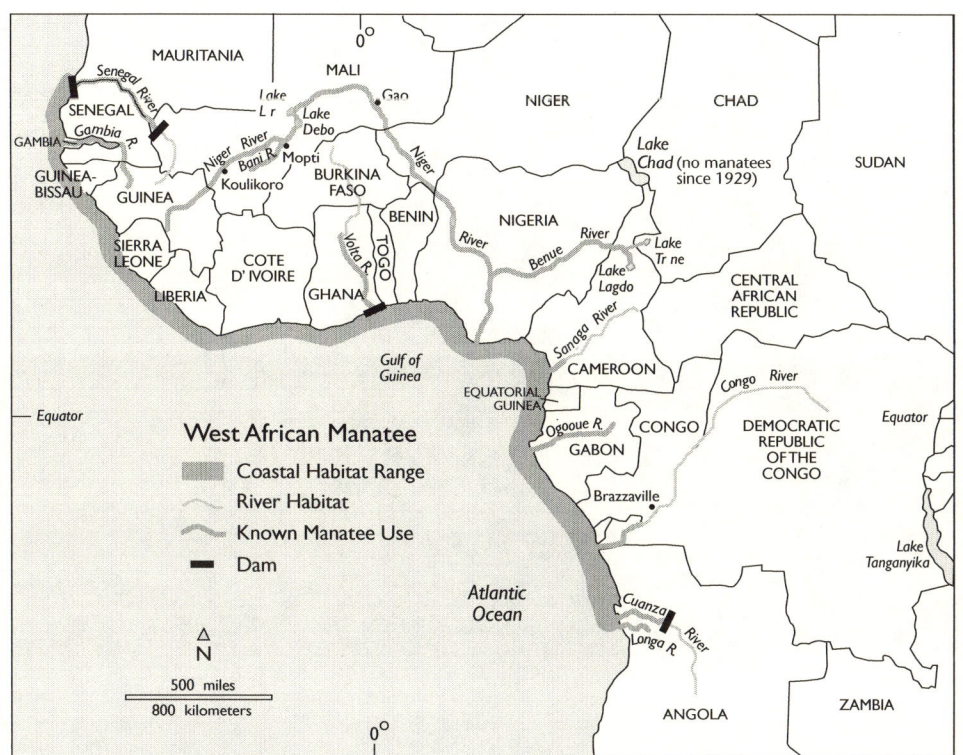

Map 6.1. West African manatee distribution. (Map by Ellen McElhinny.)

number of human impacts, and the species' long-term decline in many areas is probably caused principally by subsistence and commercial hunting. The only known significant predator is man.

The species continues to be taken for consumption throughout its range, and manatee meat is frequently sold openly in local markets and sometimes exported to other countries. In Côte d'Ivoire around six manatees are believed to be killed per village in the coastal area every year[10]. The animals are caught in traps constructed of multiple wooden sticks, secured together with vines and sunk in the lagoon bottom. They are aligned in a semi-oval 2 m long and 1.5 m wide but open at one end. At the open end a sliding door made of sticks and weighted with a large rock is constructed. The door is held open by a system of smaller stakes that are balanced together to act as a trigger mechanism. The traps are placed in a shallow area 1–1.5 m deep and about 100 m from the shoreline. The traps are then baited every day with fresh cassava peel (Manihot esculenta), which is thrown randomly inside and around the trap. When a manatee enters to eat the cassava, it accidentally pushes the trigger stick and the door falls (figure 6.1).

In Gabon, market surveys conducted by WWF from 2005 to 2008 in the Ogooue River and associated lakes have documented up to 39 manatees hunted and sold in a two-month period during the rainy season and a total of 133 manatees killed over the study period[11]. In Congo, around Lake Naga, 1–4 manatees are killed per year in the village of N'Bouyou. Manatees are primarily hunted using harpoons and specially designed nets in the southern extent of the species range.

Besides hunting, incidental entanglement in fishing nets was found to be the next most immediate threat to the population in the region[12]. Johnson[13] reported that as many as 12 manatees a day were caught in a 100-mile stretch of the Gambia River, while Powell[14] estimated that around two manatees a year were taken between 1978 and 1983 from the same area.

In all countries throughout its range, the West African manatee is protected by law. However, enforcement has not been effective, and a number of national and international protection agencies have recently become concerned by the status of manatees in their countries. A good example is the CMS action plan that was signed by 15 countries in 2008.

In recent years the numbers of people living in coastal areas and sharing habitats with manatees have spiraled. Traditional migration routes of manatees have been closed or modified by coastal development and hydroelectric and agricultural dams, and human activities have impinged on habitat quality throughout their range. For example, in the Bandama River in south Côte d'Ivoire, manatees traditionally moved from south of the river to the north of the country during the wet season. Today, due to the hydroelectric dam constructed in Tias-

Figure 6.1. Traditional manatee trap in the N'gni lagoon, Côte d'Ivoire. (Courtesy of Akoi Kouadio.)

salé (100 km north of the sea), manatee movements are restricted to the south of the dam. Mangroves are disappearing under the growing demands of urbanization, particularly around large cities. Meeting the growing resource needs of humans and West African manatees in the same habitats has become a complex challenge.

Value to People

Through the ages, people have exploited West African manatees for their meat, oil, and hides and for their ivory-like bones. According to Lela Dominique from the village of Attoutou in Côte d'Ivoire, a dead manatee can yield about US$300–350 to the hunter. Similarly, Sandrine Louis, in the Niger Delta, found that a male manatee can be exchanged for a 10 m boat plus an engine worth US$400. While in Gabon and Cameroon only the meat is used and the rest discarded, in some parts of Africa every part of a dead manatee is used. The animal's body fat and clear oil are used for lubrication and as lantern fuel. In Benin and Togo the sexual organs of a male manatee are believed to restore men's potency. The ribs are used to cure rheumatism and sprains, while the fat is employed as medicine for fever, tetanus, and suppurating otitis in children. Some parts of a manatee, such as the heart, tail, and head, are reserved for chiefs and family heads. For the Temne of Sierra Leone the tail of a dead manatee is the prerogative of the village chief. In Gabon the tail is kept by the hunter; only circumcised men can eat the head[15].

Today manatees continue to be a source of food and income for Indigenous peoples although hunting is officially banned. In the few areas where they can easily be seen, manatees are a tourist attraction. In the lagoon complex of Fresco in Côte d'Ivoire, weekend tourists from Abidjan look for manatees from banana boats. Although these tours are still very profitable, the operations need to be improved.

The West African manatee also has important traditional values in the culture, magic, and folklore of various peoples of Western and Central Africa. For the Sorko found in Niger, between the border of Mali and Nigeria, a community leader or a village chief is always chosen from among manatee hunters. For the Mande of Niger and Ebrie of Côte d'Ivoire in West Africa, the manatee is a tribal totem. The tribal name Mande is derived from the vernacular name of manatees, ma, and the word for son, nde or ndin—thus meaning "son of manatees"[16]. Members of the Ebrie tribe believe that manatees are their protectors. In the history of this tribe it is said that in the past the mortal remains of a drowned woman were brought to the beach by a manatee after two days of unsuccessful searching by experienced divers from the village. From that day, elders of the Ebrie tribe established a covenant with manatees, and the manatee is still a tribal totem for the Ebrie[17].

Throughout West Africa there are strong beliefs in Mammy-Wata, water deity of good or evil, almost always associated with manatees. The Peulh, who are found from Senegal to Chad, do not eat manatees and have strong mythical beliefs associated with the species. The Vili from Congo-Brazzaville and the Sawa from the coastal area of Cameroon believe that the manatee is the water spirit who protects riverside people. In the village of Akpasang manatees are believed to receive their power from the devil. If a person kills a manatee, the animal punishes the hunter's family[18]. For the Godie of Fresco, only a widower would attempt to kill a manatee, as the Godie believe that the spirit of a manatee killed by a married person will kill the wife of that person in compensation[19].

Research and Management Efforts

The West African manatee is listed as vulnerable in the IUCN Red Data Book (category V), in Annex II of CITES, and is legally protected by national laws in all of the countries in which it occurs[20]. For example, in Angola the West African manatee is listed in Annex 1 of the hunting law, which gives the species total protection; in Côte d'Ivoire it is considered a fully protected species under Class A, Annex I, of the Ivorian Hunting and Wildlife Protection Code (Law 65-255 of 4 August 1965).

But the laws are not working, and urgent research is required to identify the actions that will encourage recovery of the West African manatee. Short-term surveys, based mostly on questionnaires and information gleaned from fishers, have been conducted to determine the species' status and distribution. Included in these surveys are Angola, Chad, Benin, Togo, Senegal, Gambia, Guinea-Bissau, Ghana, Nigeria, Mali, Liberia, Cameroon, Gabon, and Congo[21].

The West African Manatee Conservation and Education Project in Côte d'Ivoire has been supported by the Wildlife Conservation Society in collaboration with the Ivorian Ministry of Water and Forests since 1986. This project has provided basic information on the biology and status of the West African manatee in Cote d'Ivoire, identified potential conservation problems, trained local resource managers in manatee research and conservation techniques, and initiated a public awareness and education campaign around the manatee's habitats. Currently, activities of the project are focused on the implementation of a long-term management strategy. Other long-term studies should be mentioned: Patrick Ofori-Dansen has had a research study in Ghana since 1998, there are 20-year efforts by Nigerian biologists, and research has begun in the past five years in Senegal, Togo, Benin, Cameroon, Gabon, and Angola.

It is encouraging to note that in the last two years some conservation steps have been taken. These include the Regional Conservation Project for the West African manatee supported by the IUCN, Wetlands International, World Wildlife Fund, and Fondation Internationale du Banc d'Arguin (FIBA); the Integrated Coastal and Marine Biodiversity (ICAM) project in Gambia; the West African manatee research project in Sevare-Mopti, Mali; evaluation of present distribution and condition of the African manatee in the Congo and Cuanza rivers in Angola; a countrywide study of status and distribution in Gabon; and research projects on manatees in Senegal, Togo, Benin and Cameroon.

Conclusion

In most of their major habitats, West African manatees live in aquatic systems dominated by people. Although the species is legally protected in most parts of its range, human activities continue to threaten the species, which may face extinction soon if sound and lasting protection initiatives are not undertaken. Better knowledge and monitoring of the manatee population is imperative. The manatee is a charismatic animal and an excellent flagship species for wetlands worldwide[22]. The West African manatee can play its part in Africa. High interest in manatees should be exploited to highlight the importance of wetlands and to generate more support and interest at regional, national, and international levels for its protection before it becomes too late.

7

Dugongs in Asia

COMPILED BY ELLEN HINES

Countries and Contributors

Thailand: Kanjana Adulyanukosol, Ellen M. Hines, and Sombat Poochaviranon
Cambodia: Ellen M. Hines, Kanjana Adulyanukosol, Phay Somany, and Leng Sam Ath
Vietnam: Nick Cox, Ellen M. Hines, Keith Symington, and Kanjana Adulyanukosol
Myanmar: Tint Tun and Anouk Ilangakoon
Indonesia: Hans H. de Iongh
Philippines: Lemnuel V. Aragones
China: Shaoyong Lu, Xia Jiang, and Xin Jing
Sri Lanka: Anouk Ilangakoon
India: Elrika D'souza, Vardhan Patankar, Dipani Sutaria, Bharat Jethva, and Parimal Solanki

Since World War II, increased exploitation of primary resources has been the policy of many Asian countries[1]. Especially since the 1960s, there have been high birth rates and accelerated population growth in coastal areas. The population in Asia grows by 22.5% every ten years, with 60 to 70% of people living within 50 km of the coast. This number is expected to double in the next 25–35 years[2]. Rapid development coupled with a rapidly increasing human population in coastal areas has resulted in the degradation of coastal resources that were historically sustainable. Along with this intensified population growth, there has been a dramatic increase in commercial fishing[3]. While coastal areas are vital to the needs and livelihoods of local peoples, human activities are, in many cases, degrading these areas. In South and Southeast Asia and China, as farmland becomes less available, immigration from overcrowded provinces into an open-access artisanal fishery and an often destructive and corrupt commercial fishing industry has created an atmosphere of desperation that often places the dugong and its habitat at risk[4].

Here, as in other areas, as coastal resources are overexploited, there follows a decline in the condition of these coastal ecosystems and consequent impoverishment of the people who depend on coastal resources. Besides fisheries depletion, the subsequent threats as a result of this acute pressure on coastal and marine areas include air and water pollution and the loss of wetlands and other coastal areas due to increased urbanization and agricultural and aquacultural development. Any assessment of conservation issues affecting the dugong, a species with specialized foraging needs that keep it close to these shores, must consider how these requirements create unique vulnerabilities to be considered when planning their protection[5].

In Asia, as throughout the dugongs' range, groups of dugongs along the coast are largely scattered around beds of seagrass (map 7.1). Where dugongs were historically more abundantly distributed, reduction in numbers and local extirpations have left smaller, more isolated groups[6]. The low numbers and isolation of these remnant populations expose each small group to a higher risk of extirpation, where a species becomes extinct in a specific area. The patchy distribution of seagrass meadows makes the dugong especially vulnerable to the effects of increasing habitat fragmentation[7]. Throughout most of Asia we have limited knowledge of dugong population numbers and distribution. Therefore the recolonizing ability and travel distances of dugongs in these regions are unknown. Asia is experiencing some of the highest global levels of resource use, population growth, and development[8], which could lead to a very bleak future for Asian dugongs.

There are four major threats to dugongs in this region. One is the incidental catch of dugongs in fishing nets. Both illegal fishing practices (dynamite, cyanide

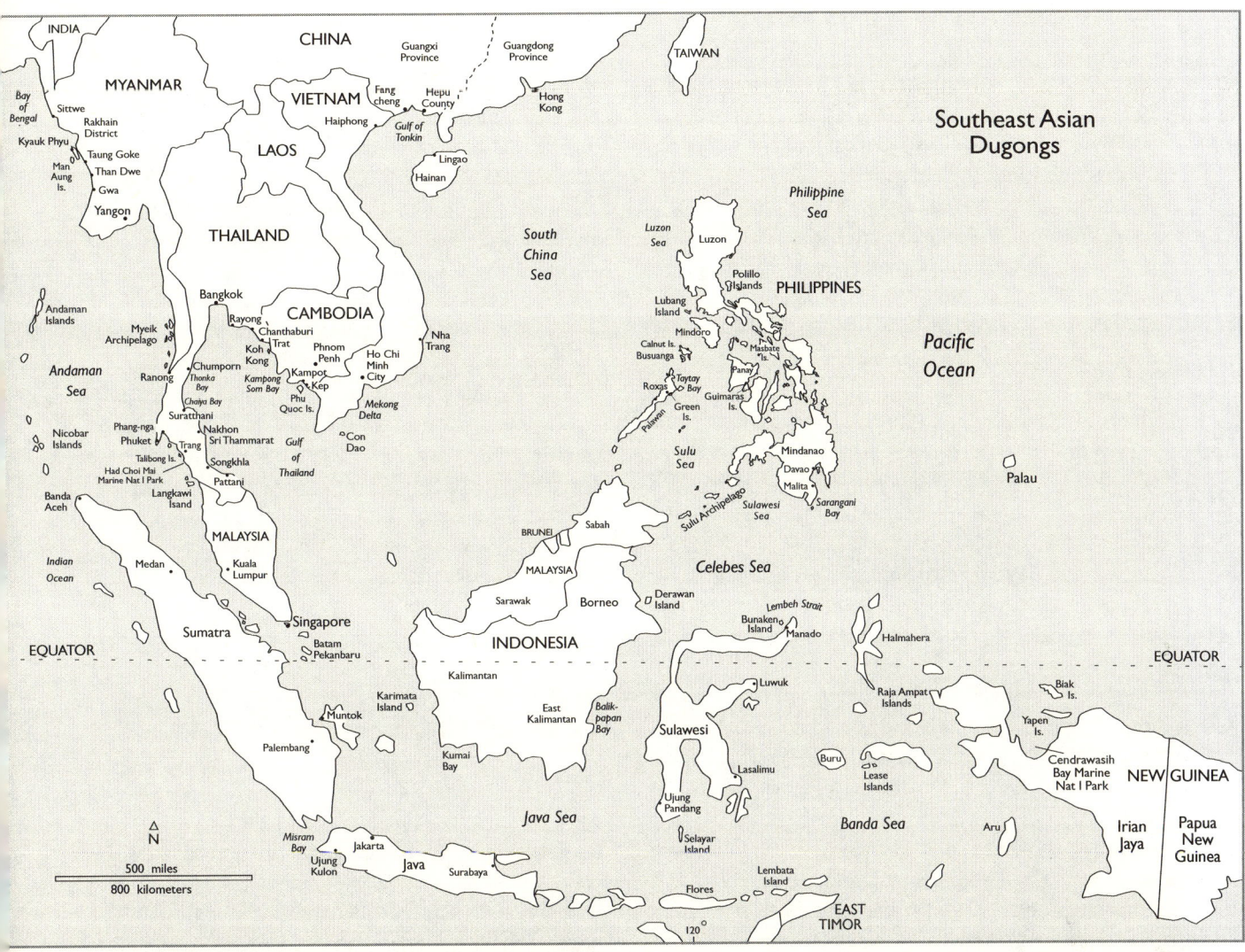

Map 7.1. Southeast Asian dugong distribution. (Map by Ellen McElhinny.)

fishing, or push nets) and legal fishing (e.g., with small mesh seines and gillnets) can directly harm dugongs and damage seagrass beds. A related key problem is the encroachment of large commercial fishing trawlers into shallow coastal waters. These boats damage seagrass beds and catch dugongs incidentally. Development and overcrowded coastal areas are the second threat. As previously discussed, destruction of seagrass beds, pollution, and increasing numbers of boats and human use of coastal areas are depleting dugong habitat areas.

The third threat, in some areas, is directed take or hunting; even in areas where hunting does not occur, dugong body parts, including meat, bones, tusks, and tears, are considered valuable and are sold as food, amulets, and medicine[9]. The fourth threat to dugong survival is the insufficient knowledge, both nationally and regionally, of the locations and numbers of dugongs and the species and distribution of seagrass. Without this knowledge, how can we determine how best to protect these animals?

In this chapter, we discuss specific issues and strategies affecting dugongs in several of the countries in this region. A separate chapter on dugongs in Okinawa follows as one of three chapters on sirenians in developed countries. For a complete status report on dugongs globally, please consult Marsh et al[10].

Thailand

History of Research

Thai scientists have been conducting dugong research since the 1980s. Most likely the largest population group of dugongs in Southeast and Eastern Asia is in Trang Province along the Andaman coast[11] (map 7.1). The first aerial population survey was conducted by Suwan Pitaksintorn of the Royal Forestry Department, who saw 61 dugongs in Trang Province in 1991 and 1992[12]. Kanjana Adulyanukosol, from the Marine Endangered Species Unit (MESU) of the Phuket Marine Biological Center (PMBC), was the first Thai scientist to interview villagers systematically[13]; she performed aerial surveys between 1997 and 1999. She and colleagues found 48 dugongs in 1997 and 38 in 1999 along the Andaman coast[14]. Information on Andaman coast seagrass beds has been available since 1994, and further surveys were conducted in 1998[15]. Since then aerial surveys, interviews with villagers, and seagrass surveys have been continued along both the Andaman coast and the eastern Gulf coast of Thailand[16]. While due to financial constraints the research has been more episodic than regularly conducted, scientists do have a general idea of dugong distribution and numbers along these coasts. A rough estimate for the Andaman coast has been given as 200 animals, with smaller populations seen along the eastern Gulf[17]. For the eastern Gulf coast, small groups of dugongs (between 7 and 36) have been seen in Rayong, Chanthaburi, and Trat provinces[18].

Along the western Gulf of Thailand, interviews were conducted in Chumporn and Suratthani provinces in 2003–2004. Respondents at that time believed there were still small numbers of dugongs in their waters. Although no dugongs were seen in aerial surveys along Suratthani Province in 2004, feeding trails have been documented in Chumporn and Suratthani provinces[19]. Adulyanukosol[20] noted isolated reports of strandings in Chumporn, Suratthani, Nakhon Sri Thammarat, and Pattani provinces, based on records kept at PMBC since 1989. In 2005 a dead dugong was found in Suratthani province, and in 2006 a stranded dugong was released in Chumporn province[21].

Present research efforts are mainly conducted along the Andaman coast by scientists from the Phuket Marine Biological Center. Aerial surveys in Trang Province in 2000 and 2001 resulted in a minimum population estimate of 123 animals[22]. Surveys were conducted in this area after the December 2004 tsunami by Adulyanukosol and Thongsukdee[23]. One hundred and twenty-six dugongs, including 17 calves, were seen in one day of aerial surveys. Based on the number of animals seen, the presence of young calves, and the good condition of seagrass beds, the authors concluded that the tsunami did not affect the Trang population adversely.

Along the Andaman coast, interviews with 145 individuals indicated that even though most respondents believed that dugongs were declining, a majority of fishers see dugongs regularly, know stories or legends about them, and have heard of and used dugong body parts for medicine and amulets. Dugongs here get trapped in commercial fishing nets, and villagers are concerned about the illegal and destructive fishing that the presence of these boats represents. Ninety-nine percent of respondents consider dugong conservation important, as dugongs represent a healthy ecosystem, and people want their children to see them. Seagrass conservation is considered very important, as habitat for larval fish, fishing grounds for local fishers, and dugong habitat[24].

Aerial surveys and interviews in fishing villages along the eastern Gulf coast of Thailand[25] show that in comparison to the results of dugong research on the Andaman coast, the eastern Gulf coast has fewer dugongs in fewer places and not as much trade in dugong body parts; the practice and knowledge of medicinal and amulet use for dugong body parts are comparatively lower. Most interview respondents here believe that dugong numbers are declining as seagrass is increasingly being destroyed by illegal trawlers, and 89% believe it is important to conserve dugongs and seagrass for their children, and because dugongs are rare. Seagrass was considered important by 65% of respondents for similar reasons as in the Andaman interviews.

Distribution

Along the Andaman and eastern Gulf coasts scientists have identified regular foraging areas for dugongs. No data on regular foraging areas are available for the coast of the western Gulf of Thailand. Although there have been no sightings of dugongs in the western Gulf during aerial surveys, based on the stranding records at PMBC and sightings of feeding trails, some dugongs are still present, most probably in Suratthani and Chumporn provinces[26].

Legal Status

The dugong has been under federal protection since passage of the Fisheries Act B.E. 2490 in 1947[27]. Three other laws apply to dugong and seagrass conservation in Thailand: Wildlife Reservation and Protection Acts B.E. 2535 (1992), Export and Import Product Acts B.E. 2522 (1979), and CITES (the Convention on the International Trade in Endangered Species), which Thailand signed in 1983[28]. All laws prohibit the killing, taking, possession, and trading of dugongs or dugong body parts in Thailand[29].

At present there are no areas designated specifically to protect dugongs. Some areas do offer protection to dugongs under various management schemes. For example, in Trang, seagrass and dugongs are protected in the

Had Chao Mai Marine National Park and the Talibong Island Non-Hunting Area, also designated in 2002 as Ramsar Wetlands of International Importance. The Thai Department of Marine and Coastal Resources (DMCR), in cooperation with the Australian government, drafted the Convention of Migratory Species (CMS) and Action Plan for Dugong in May 2006. The Dugong National Action Plan was been drafted in cooperation with WCS (Wildlife Conservation Society, Thailand) and DMCR in 2004. In June of 2011, DMCR signed a memorandum of understanding on the conservation of dugongs with the United Nations Environment Programme[30].

Threats

There have been no significant reports of deliberate dugong hunting in Thailand for the past 40 years. As is typical for the Southeast Asian region, the major threats to dugongs are habitat loss and disturbance, incidental catch, and the value of body parts as medicine and amulets. However, a serious indirect threat to dugongs is the degraded condition of mangroves, seagrass, and coral reef areas along the Andaman coast as a result of overfishing, destructive fishing methods, and removal of mangrove forests for shrimp farming (which increases water turbidity and over-enriches nutrients on seagrass beds). The rapidly increasing Thai population along the coast has caused degradation and destruction of natural resources and the marine environment. Two major threats have been identified: tin dredging near the shore and sedimentation from land-based mining. Sedimentation hampers the growth of seagrass and limits foraging opportunities for dugongs. The majority of tin mining occurs in Phuket, Phangnga, and Ranong provinces along the Andaman coast[31].

The conflict between commercial and small-scale fishers is increasing, as is the poverty of a growing number of people in coastal communities[32]. Large trawler fleets compete with increasing numbers of small-scale fishers for the diminishing fish resources, and the small-scale fishers are losing. A small percentage of trawlers catches 92% of the total catch, while a large proportion (72%) of artisanal fishers catches 8%[33]. As long as coastal fisheries are an open and unregulated resource, the conflict between commercial and small-scale fishers will grow, as will poverty in coastal communities[34]. Dugongs are caught in the middle of this conflict. They are trapped in the nets of illegal commercial gillnet and push net trawlers. If the commercial operators were to report an incidental catch, they would also have to admit to fishing within a 3-kilometer shoreline exclusion zone. Small-scale fishers who find dugongs trapped or stranded are apt to be tempted by the money they can receive for selling tusks. They can use bones for medicine, use tears as an aphrodisiac, and eat or share the meat. Thais believe that dugong tusks have medicinal properties when mixed with other materials, such as lemon juice, and use them as amulets for luck or protection[35].

Reporting the incident is often at the expense of time spent fishing. There is also the risk of being fined. Anyone found with a dead dugong could face a four-year jail term or a 40,000-baht (US$1,070) fine. Another reason these occurrences are not reported is the economic and social marginality of small-scale fishers, which creates an atmosphere that isolates fishing communities from local and regional decision makers and enforcement agencies[36]. An accurate estimate of dugong mortalities caused by fishing at this time cannot be made because many of these incidents are not reported. According to Hines et al.[37] only about 12% of dugong strandings that are found are reported to local authorities.

There are signs that this situation is changing. Three nongovernment organizations (NGOs) are actively working on community-based management on issues of small-scale fisheries and conservation of mangrove forests along the Andaman coast of Thailand: the Andaman Natural Resource Rehabilitation Project, Yadfon Association, and Wildlife Fund of Thailand.

Cultural Significance

Hines et al.[38] summarized responses from interviews conducted in local communities throughout Thailand. They found three categories of responses that imply historic and modern knowledge of and familiarity with the dugong. The first was the instance of village names derived in part or whole from words meaning dugong in Thai or local dialects. The second group of responses was the recounting of stories, legends, and musical plays about dugongs. The most common story along the Andaman or west coast of Thailand involved a pregnant woman turning into a dugong as she walked into the sea to eat seagrass. Lastly, these interviews showed that the practice of using dugong body parts for medicine and protective amulets, and the belief in the delicious taste and tonic properties of dugong meat, remain common, even though the animal has not been directly hunted for the past 50 years. Researchers believe that the actual practice of dugong body part use will decline with aging of the population of those who actually hunted dugongs.

Research Needs

Further research in Thailand needs to concentrate on regular monitoring of areas that have already been surveyed and more complete assessments of areas where knowledge is still incomplete. We recommend a three-tiered approach, including aerial surveys, seagrass surveys, and interviews in local communities. Along the Andaman coast, regular aerial surveys are needed to monitor the Trang dugongs, and further surveys are needed to get a more accurate estimate of the number of dugongs and the location of feeding sites. In order to get a more complete picture of dugong movement as input into protected area planning, scientists are looking at a tagging project with satellite PTTs and/or GPS transmitters[39]. Along the eastern Gulf of Thailand, aerial surveys have resulted in sightings of varying numbers of dugongs and should be continued in conjunction with seagrass surveys[40]. Along the western Gulf coast, aerial surveys are needed to determine dugong numbers and feeding areas.

In all areas, regular seagrass surveys should be conducted to map seagrass density and boundaries, record feeding trails, and be combined with interviews to learn more about strandings, sightings, and local conservation issues affecting dugongs. Researchers at the Phuket Marine Biological Center are using underwater videography to survey seagrass from the subtidal zone to 10 m depth and are investigating methods of restoring degraded seagrass beds.

Summary

The relatively large number of dugongs in Trang Province allows Thailand an opportunity to conserve what might be the biggest group of dugongs in Asia. While the Trang area is threatened by development and tourism, the mixture of local marine protected areas, environmental education, community involvement in nearshore conservation, and the dedication of local scientists and NGOs may be a successful combination for dugong conservation. At this time, it is critical to implement a comprehensive, integrated management campaign to conserve the remaining dugongs in Thailand.

Cambodia

History of Research

While little formal research has been conducted on dugongs in Cambodia, Nelson[41] mentioned that they were commonly seen in coastal areas until the mid-1970s, when Pol Pot and the Khmer Rouge relocated people away from the coast to inland camps. Anecdotally, dugongs have since been rumored to be both present and extirpated in various areas, but these reports have not been substantiated. Beasley et al.[42], in their boat surveys of cetaceans along the Cambodian coast, did not see any dugongs.

In 2002 an international group of researchers conducted interviews with local fishers in villages near Kampot and Kep along the eastern Cambodian coast. In 2004 aerial surveys, more interviews, and seagrass sampling were carried out along both coasts[43].

Distribution

While no dugongs were seen during the 2004 aerial surveys, abundant seagrass beds were seen around Koh Kong on the western coast, on the eastern shore of Kampong Som Bay on the central coast, and off the eastern coast of Cambodia in Kampot and Kep provinces (map 7.1). Interview respondents in western Cambodia had not seen dugongs in the wild for several years but had heard of dugong meat for sale in local markets. In eastern Cambodia, most respondents had recently seen dugongs either while fishing or stranded, and pointed out areas where dugongs could be found, especially in villages near the Vietnamese border. Most respondents believed that dugongs were declining. The most frequent reasons given were illegal and destructive fishing in the seagrass and the large amounts of local fishing activities in the seagrass. Ninety-three percent of respondents considered dugong conservation important, and as was found in the Thai interviews, people want to conserve the animals for future generations. Seagrass conservation was also considered important, as habitat for both fish and dugongs. The majority of people knew about using dugong body parts as medicine and amulets, and researchers were shown skin, bones, and tusks several times. Most of the fishers interviewed use crab nets, push nets, and traps in the seagrass; they fish very close to the shore only when the tide is at its lowest. They would not see dugongs in such shallow water. As these fishers have little knowledge of or exposure to dugongs in the wild, they might not recognize dugong feeding trails. In 2005 a dead dugong was found stranded along the coast of Kampot Province in eastern Cambodia.

Legal Status

Legislation signed by the king of Cambodia in May of 2006 declared it illegal to catch, sell, buy, or transport aquatic mammals that have been given endangered status by the Ministry of Agriculture, Forestry and Fisheries (MAFF). MAFF is also charged with protecting and conserving the habitat of these endangered species. MAFF did publicize this law, as even before the legislation was signed, several interview respondents in 2004 mentioned it as a reason why they would not hunt for dugongs[44].

Threats

Threats to dugongs along the Cambodian coast include incidental catch in both small-scale and illegal commercial fisheries; some direct catch when an animal is seen; the common knowledge of and large profit from the sale of dugong body parts as medicine or amulets; and most importantly, escalating overfishing and degradation of seagrass beds by an ever-increasing number of people living at the coast. There are serious conflicts, as in Thailand, between small-scale fishers and commercial trawlers (many from Vietnam) that fish illegally close to shore, and shrimp farming is starting right at the shoreline, destroying mangroves and seagrass beds[45].

While there are similarities to Thailand in the nature of threats to dugongs, an added threat to all marine life here is the extreme poverty of the growing number of people trying to make a living in the nearshore area.

Cultural Significance

Poverty and issues of everyday survival have understandably taken precedence here. Cambodia has yet to recover from the Khmer Rouge genocide between 1975 and 1979 that killed 2 million out of 8 million people. Though Cambodian interview respondents agreed that conservation was important, their comments when asked about protecting an area of seagrass showed contradictions: on one hand, a protected area would allow fish to grow and make sure no illegal trawlers could fish there; but on the other, there were already too many people fishing in too small an area. Answers as to how the government could help elicited requests for government regulations and enforcement to protect fishing grounds from illegal trawlers, fishers from neighboring villages, and seaweed growers. Catching a dugong would be considered an economic opportunity[46].

Research Needs

Further research on dugongs in Cambodia is definitely needed, as is further research on coastal seagrass. In western Cambodia, the healthy seagrass beds and proximity to Trat Province along the eastern Thai coast brings the possibility of the same animals using both areas for foraging. The eastern Cambodian coast is close to Phu Quoc Island in Vietnam (map 7.1), where Hines et al.[47] found dugong hunting and reports of common sightings. Respondents in Phu Quoc mentioned that dugongs and seagrass were regularly seen between their island and the Cambodian coast. Further aerial surveys here are impossible because of the expense and the lack of support infrastructure for plane maintenance. The most practical suggestion would be for annual interviews to monitor sightings and strandings, and mapping and regular monitoring of seagrass and feeding trails.

Summary

Threats to the nearshore ecosystem, the dugong, and other marine fauna and flora from the people who live along the Cambodian coast, the poverty and the needs of those people, and their reliance on a quickly degrading environment are all entwined. Any solution that attempted to address only one of these threats would be ineffective. Continuing research needs to be conducted by local agency scientists who need to be trained and supported, if not by a government with few resources, then by concerned international NGOs. International organizations are also urgently needed to help fund and train health and sanitation workers and environmental educators and to train coastal villagers in alternative, sustainable livelihoods. Legislation can be an impetus for change if improved social conditions encourage self-regulation as well[48]. The dugong could possibly be a flagship species for an educational campaign to increase environmental awareness, accompanied by efforts to improve living conditions and enforce regulations against illegal and destructive commercial fishing[49].

Vietnam

History of Research

Other than specimens found in Khanh Hoa (Nha Trang) and Con Dao provinces in the south[50], there has been little scientific research on dugongs in Vietnam. Cox[51] conducted interviews in 2000 and, in 2001–2002, land-based dugong and seagrass surveys in the Con Dao archipelago. Between November 2001 and January 2002 he had a total of 33 dugong sightings. In December of 2002 World Wildlife Fund Indochina organized interview surveys in Con Dao and Phu Quoc Island (map 7.1)[52]. The Con Dao area has been protected as a Vietnamese National Park since 1984 with regulations that protect dugongs and seagrass from direct catch and destructive fishing techniques. However, Cox heard about ten dugongs found stranded there between 1979 and 2002[53].

On Phu Quoc Island interviews revealed declining numbers of dugongs along the south and west coasts, with more frequent sightings along the northeast coast of the island. Several of the interview respondents revealed a commonly known direct hunt for dugongs, associated with a profitable market for meat and other body parts kept or sold as medicine and amulets[54].

Distribution

Anecdotal reports indicate that dugongs were historically more widely distributed along Vietnam's coast, including Quang Ninh, Haiphong, Khanh Hoa, and Binh Thuan provinces, Con Dao Island, and Kien Giang Province (Phu Quoc Island and Ha Tien near the Cambodian border; map 7.1). Unconfirmed sightings have recently been reported in Bai Tu Long National Park (Quang Ninh Province), the Can Gio Biosphere Reserve, and Bac Lieu Province[55].

Confirmed sightings have been recorded only in Con Dao and Phu Quoc Island. Cox believes there to be as few as ten dugongs remaining in the Con Dao area[56]. Dugong hunters in the northern part of Phu Quoc Island mentioned that they find as many dugongs as always, but respondents in other areas said numbers have declined greatly in recent years. As previously discussed, the region between northern Phu Quoc Island and the eastern coast of Cambodia probably houses the largest remnant dugong population in the area, though numbers cannot be estimated[57]. There have been several instances since 2002 when dugong meat has been found in the local markets in and near the Cambodian border[58].

Legal Status

Several laws and decrees are relevant to dugong protection. Legislation has been in place since 1989. Some laws include the dugong as a fisheries resource, including Group 1B updated in 2002. Species under this law are protected against hunting, trade, confiscation, and captive breeding, and against import and export unless permission is granted by the prime minister. The dugong is designated as endangered in the Red Data Book of Vietnam[59]. A Fisheries Department law mentioning marine mammal protection came into effect in July 2004[60]. In response to the official discovery of dugong hunters in Kien Gang Province (which includes Phu Quoc Island), the provincial People's Committee issued a directive prohibiting dugong, dolphin, and marine turtle hunting, transport, or consumption[61].

Threats

While in some areas seagrass beds are still abundant, degradation and loss of available habitat resulting from overfishing in seagrass beds and from coastal development are major threats. Sewage discharge into seagrass beds and destructive fishing techniques are additional problems, especially near Phu Quoc Island[62]. During the rainy season, sediment runoff into seagrass beds from nearby roads is a problem in Con Dao[63].

Directed hunting of dugongs near Phu Quoc is an extremely serious problem. In 2002 the Kien Giang Department of Fisheries began educational programs emphasizing the importance of conserving endangered marine species. Insufficient funds and personnel hamper management and enforcement of existing regulations. The department also began an attempt to keep track of dugong hunting and found 12 animals killed in 2002, 5 in 2003, and 4 in 2004[64]. All parts of the dugong are used for food, medicine, or protection, and knowledge of these uses and their potential profits is common. At this time, dugong meat is still considered the best way to offer hospitality to distinguished guests, even by government officials[65].

While there have not been reports of boat collisions with dugongs in the Phu Quoc area, and the use of trawlers in seagrass beds is prohibited, there are large numbers of fishing boats in shallow waters. This increases the threat of collisions and incidental entanglements in nets. While there is no estimate of how many dugongs are accidentally caught in fishing nets, those that are found are certainly killed and locally consumed or sold.

Cultural Significance

Interview respondents in Con Dao and Phu Quoc Island did not recall any stories or legends about dugongs. In areas where dugongs were not hunted, a majority of respondents considered dugong conservation to be important, but hunters did not see any threat or decline. Hunting and medicinal use and sales of dugong body parts in communities show more of a practical than a cultural relationship[66].

Research Needs

In all areas in Vietnam where dugongs have been seen or found stranded within the past several years, local scientists need to be educated about dugongs and seagrass. We suggest that scientists, with the support of NGOs, conduct seasonal seagrass monitoring for feeding trails and seagrass health and continue interviews with local fishers on a yearly basis. Community members can be trained to participate actively in these monitoring activities. Based on the seagrass work, a seagrass database and mapping system should be established at a centralized location, perhaps the Department of Fisheries or a university. Regional training and collaboration (aerial surveys, seagrass mapping and monitoring, stranding network, etc.) are needed among Thailand, Cambodia, and Vietnam to combine resources and account for the cross-boundary movements of dugongs. Specifically at Con Dao, long-term surveys for dugongs can be conducted by building viewing platforms near seagrass areas. This could be a project for local rangers or for a Vietnamese graduate student. A project is also needed to explore methods for stabilizing slopes near coastal roads to prevent run-off into seagrass beds.

Summary

No dugongs have been seen along the eastern coast of Phu Quoc Island by fishers or dugong hunters since 2006. The effects of the continued exploitation of animals are inherently predictable. Vietnam is an example of how legislation alone cannot protect a species that is valuable as a product. Education and community awareness about the consequences of extinction can communicate the results of unsustainable resource use in the long term. Whether this message can be conveyed in time is questionable.

Myanmar

History of Research

Dugongs are known in Myanmar as *ye-wet* (water pig), *ye-thu-ma* (mermaid) or *lin-shu*. The presence of dugongs in Myanmar waters has been known within the country since time immemorial and was documented in the 1850s by Rev. S. Benjamin[67].

A dugong was captured alive in 1966 in a fishing net on the Rakhine coast (formerly known as the Arakan coast in western Myanmar; map 7.1) and sent to the Yangon Zoological Garden, where keepers attempted to raise it in captivity. It was kept in a tank filled with fresh seawater but did not survive long[68].

Although accidental bycatch of dugongs has been reported from Rakhine and the Myeik Archipelago, no systematic research was done until 2005 and 2007, when Ilangakoon and Tun conducted interviews on dugongs along the northern coastline of Myanmar in the Ayeyawady and Rakhine divisions[69].

In early 2007 Hines et al.[70] traveled through the southern Myeik Archipelago (map 7.1). They completed 34 interviews about dugongs with Burmese and Karen settlers and Moken (sea gypsies). The Moken are nomads who live and travel on small boats during the dry season and build temporary structures for shelter in the rainy season. Nowadays, most Moken live in permanent homes in villages.

Distribution

Ilangakoon and Tun's surveys documented the continued presence of the dugong and healthy seagrass beds along the northern coast of Myanmar. In contrast, the Myeik Archipelago is not an area that could support groups (50–100) of dugongs as seen in Thailand or the Rakhine coast.

In the Myeik Archipelago interview respondents saw only the occasional dugong. Researchers found little seagrass, unlike along the Thai Andaman coast to the south. The islands are mainly limestone or granite, with steep slopes nearshore. Nearshore areas are mostly shallow-water corals or rocky, with muddy fluvial run-off at gentle easterly facing slopes and muddy mangrove swamps in sheltered areas where seagrass would be expected.

Legal Status

The State Law and Order Restoration Council of the Union of Myanmar enacted the State Law and Order Restoration Council Law No. 6/94, titled the Protection of Wildlife and Protected Areas Law, on 8 June 1994. In accordance with article 15(a) of the law, the Forest Department of the Ministry of Forestry, Union of Myanmar, issued a List of Protected Animals on 26 October 1994 in Notification No. 583/94, listing the dugong as a Completely Protected Species and calling for the ministry to designate and carry out measures for the conservation of protected species.

Threats

At present the most significant threat to dugongs in Myanmar waters is accidental bycatch in gillnets[71]. While there appears to be no cultural or religious significance attached to dugongs in Myanmar, animals that are incidentally caught are used for local consumption. While fishers from the Rakhine coast realize that dugongs are rare and protected animals, they can make a large amount of money by killing a dugong found in a net. In the Myeik Archipelago, 50% of respondents consider conservation of dugongs important because they are rare and are considered an "old animal." However, the Moken consider themselves fortunate to find and kill a dugong.

The dugong appears to be relatively safe in Myanmar waters at present, in comparison with other countries in South and Southeast Asia. However, the small number of animals remaining in both Rakhine and Myeik is a major concern.

While respondents had heard about conservation, realization of what it means was low, and most answers about the importance of conserving endangered species or systems (i.e., seagrass, coral, mangroves) mentioned that it was fine to conserve what local people did not use. Public awareness and education regarding the endangered status of the dugong in Myanmar is needed among the coastal communities. Such knowledge is lacking both among the general public and among law enforcement authorities[72].

Cultural Significance

There were no specific superstitions, myths, or religious beliefs about the dugong mentioned along the Rakhine coast. However, several stories mentioned everyday interactions between dugongs and fishers. Dugongs come and bump their heads against the wooden rudder of an artisanal fishing craft. At times they collide so violently that the rudder is damaged, so fishers carry long bamboo poles to push the dugongs away.

At Gwa, a man who used to dive for sea cucumbers reported that dugongs are curious and follow divers up and down between the surface and the substrate. This behavior makes the divers nervous, because even though the dugongs are not aggressive, they are large heavy animals.

In their surveys Tun and Ilangakoon[73] found that people of the Rakhine coast believe dugong skins and bones can be used as a remedy for diarrhea. Some keep these body parts, but they do not kill the animal for this purpose.

In the Myeik Archipelago the use of dugong body parts for medicine and artifacts was reported by only one respondent. A common story here is that when dolphins get older they walk into the seagrass and turn into dugongs. When dugongs get older they walk into the jungle and turn into pigs.

Research Needs

As systematic research on dugongs in Myanmar began only very recently, there are data gaps to be filled to protect dugongs adequately and ensure their survival in Myanmar waters. Aerial surveys along the Myanmar coast would be useful to collect quantitative data on dugong and seagrass occurrence and distribution. The lack of infrastructure to support small planes and the permitting, expenses, and safety considerations involved make aerial surveys difficult at this time in Myanmar[74]. Interviews should be continued.

An assessment of the abundance, quality, and distribution of seagrass along the Rakhine coast and in the Myeik Archipelago is another method to determine dugong distribution and foraging. Preliminary seagrass surveys were done in the southern Myeik Islands using SeagrassNet (a global seagrass monitoring network) tools and methodology[75]. Personnel from the Myanmar Department of Fisheries were trained to assess and map seagrass beds[76]. SeagrassNet methods should be continued and expanded to areas identified by satellite images and aerial photographs and in consultation with fishers. This information should lead to developing a seagrass habitat map for Myanmar, used to select and prioritize areas for dugong protection.

Summary

One of the most important needs for dugong conservation in Myanmar is systematical monitoring of the incidental catch of dugongs in gillnets. Bycatch incidents are not always reported to authorities and many may be undocumented. A system of reporting and documenting bycatch in all coastal areas of the country is needed, as is basic training in data collection for local fisheries and social sector officials. These data are vital to minimize conflicts between local fisheries and dugongs.

Public awareness and education programs should be created to inform local people about status, conservation, and bycatch reporting and the important role of coastal communities in dugong research and conservation.

Collaboration with neighboring countries Thailand and Bangladesh for dugong research would be valuable in determining regional dugong movement. Thailand has a history of dugong research and expertise, which is lacking in Myanmar. Collaboration and consultation with Thai scientists could help to build local capacity for dugong research and conservation.

Indonesia

History of Research

Indonesia is one of the largest and most varied archipelagic countries in the world. The country stretches 5,120 km from east to west and 1,760 km from north to south. It encompasses 17,508 islands, of which only 6,000 are inhabited[77]. There are five main islands (Sumatra, Java, Kalimantan, Sulawesi, and Papua); two major archipelagos (Nusa Tenggara and the Maluku Islands); and sixty smaller archipelagos (map 7.1).

The first known written record of a dugong in Indonesia was made in 1712 by Samuel Falours, a Dutchman employed by the United East Indies Company (VOC), who described how a juvenile dugong was kept for four days in a bath tub in Ambon[78].

Scientific research on dugongs in Indonesia has been very limited[79]. The main research efforts on dugong and seagrass interactions have been done in the Moluccas Province (Aru, Lease islands) and in East Kalimantan (Balikpapan Bay)[80].

Evidence gathered through aerial surveys in the study area of the Moluccas Province indicates a dispersed distribution of low numbers of dugongs in a small tropical island ecosystem with a narrow coastal shelf. The number of dugongs per survey hour in the study area was 5–11 dugongs/hour[81], which compares with the results of aerial surveys in other tropical island ecosystems; for example, 5.4 dugongs/hour in Palau[82], 9.2 dugongs/hour in the Torres Strait[83], and 1.9 dugongs/hour in the Philippines[84].

To date, the only observations on movements and home range of dugongs, using conventional and satellite telemetry, are from the Lease islands[85]. Three adult females and one immature male were tracked for between 51 and 285 days. Similar to the findings of Preen[86], the animals showed an individualistic pattern of movement, moving over large areas. Dugongs were seen in small feeding groups in certain core areas where feeding took place.

Distribution

Few data are available on dugong distribution and population numbers in Indonesia. Marsh et al.[87] estimated between 1,000 and 10,000 dugongs. A first distribution map of dugongs for Indonesia was prepared by Salm[88]. Nishiwaki and Marsh[89] published the first overview of global dugong distribution, including Indonesia. More recent sightings of dugongs have been included in the National Dugong Data Base for Indonesia[90].

Important dugong habitats are also believed to occur from Arakan Wawontulap to Lembeh Strait between Lembeh and the mainland (North Sulawesi); along the east coast of Biak Island and western Cendrawasih Bay Marine National Park (Papua Barat), the Lease and Aru islands (Maluku), and Flores–Lembata Islands[91]. Marsh et al.[92] also mention dugong presence in Kotawaringin, Karimata Island Marine Reserve, and Kumai Bay. From 2001 until 2007 students from Leiden University (Netherlands) recorded a number of dugong sightings and a large number of dugong grazing tracks in the Balikpapan Bay, East Kalimantan[93]. In 2007 one dugong was sighted in an aerial survey over Balikpapan Bay. Kreb and Budiono[94] reported observations of dugongs in the Berau Archipelago around the island of Derawan. The presence of dugongs at Derawan Island was confirmed during a survey in 2006[95].

De Iongh et al.[96] estimated between 22 and 37 individuals in the Lease islands, based on aerial surveys. This is the only known dugong population census based on aerial sightings conducted in Indonesian waters to date.

The Jaya Ancol Oceanarium also mentions anecdotal evidence for dugong presence in east, west, and south Kalimantan[97]. The Seaworld Indonesia Oceanarium reported dugongs to occur in the following locations[98]:

Bojonegara, Banten (West Java); 2000, 2002, 2003
Yapen Island, Papua; 2003
Lasalimu, Buton Island (South East Celebes); 2004, 2007
Muntok (West Bangka); 2007
Ujung Batee (Banda Aceh); 2006
Cipanon, Labuhan (West Java); 2001, 2004, 2005
Batam, Pekanbaru; 2006
Lubuk (central Celebes); 2005
Selayar Island (south Celebes); 2004

Although accurate and up-to-date data are scarce, dugongs are widely scattered and distributed in Indonesia's coastal waters. Research activities on dugongs have been restricted mainly to the Moluccas, Sulawesi, and East Kalimantan. Most sightings in other areas are from incidental records. While anecdotal evidence can give an initial indication of dugong presence, local areas have to be surveyed more thoroughly before it is possible to draw conclusions on dugong distribution.

Legal status

The Conservation of Flora and Fauna Act No. 7 of 1999 is the only legislation that directly protects Indonesian dugongs and seagrass. In appendix no. 20 of the act, dugongs are listed as protected fauna. In article 4, verse 2 measures are dictated for protection by: (a) management *in situ*, through identification and inventory of species and habitats, monitoring, management, and research; and (b) management *ex situ* through research, rehabilitation, and protection of species and habitats.

While specific laws and regulations protecting the coastal zone as an ecological entity are still nonexistent in Indonesia, a wide range of laws and regulations covering the coastal zone pertain to the dugong and seagrass ecosystems. Several regulations are relevant.

The Directorate General of Nature Conservation–Ministry of Forestry has the mandate to protect and manage dugong populations in Indonesia. However, the management of marine national parks (most of which support dugongs and their habitat) is delegated to the Ministry of Marine Affairs and Fisheries. The Directorate General for Marine, Coasts and Small Islands at the

Ministry of Marine Affairs and Fisheries has established regional marine protected areas (Kawasan Konservasi Laut Derat, KKLD). There are now 21 KKLDs established by district leaders[99]. However, the legal protection of dugongs in Indonesian waters is not very effective. Enforcement is complicated by the nation's large area and numerous islands.

Research Needs

In the Draft National Dugong Conservation Strategy and Action Plan[100] the following research needs have been defined:

- Implement aerial surveys nationwide where dugongs are known and/or suspected to occur.
- Study the impact of community-based conservation on dugong core areas for an initial term of five years.
- Continue research on the interactions between dugongs and seagrass meadows in Indonesian coastal waters, as initiated by De Iongh et al.[101]
- Use satellite telemetry to study dugong movements in Ujung Kulon and Miskam Bay, East Kalimantan, North Sulawesi and Papua.
- Initiate research to investigate dugong grazing trails in Indonesian coastal waters.

Threats

Although apart from the Aru Islands no data are available on decreasing dugong populations in Indonesia, it is safe to assume such a decrease. Several factors could have a negative effect on the present dugong population[102]:

- habitat destruction and degradation of seagrass meadows caused by local industries, boat traffic, and agricultural pollution;
- impact of oil pollution, especially near oil refineries and terminal platforms and during accidental oil spills;
- destructive fishing methods, such as sodium cyanide fishing and coral blasting;
- accidental catches in shark nets, gillnets, or tidal traps (*belat* or *sero*);
- Indigenous hunting: deliberate harpooning of dugongs is reported from the Aru Islands, but since the eighties this practiced has been abandoned; and
- boat-related impacts: mortality of dugongs by the impact of outboard engines has been reported both in Balikpapan Bay and in Ambon.[103]

Research suggests that the protection of certain core areas as dugong sanctuaries is an important conservation measure[104]. Researchers[105] have emphasized the importance of traditional management systems (called *sasi* in Indonesian) for the conservation of dugongs in Indonesia. The declaration of dugong sanctuaries should coincide with the enforcement and enhancement of traditional community-based conservation systems, like the local *sasi laut*, with protected inshore areas and restricted fishing practice. *Sasi* is a traditional practice built around the principle of prohibiting or of abstaining from catching specific resources for a specific period of time. Local elders or customary leaders may determine the timing of such temporal closures or they may be "spirited from heaven" through seasonal changes or dictated by calendar years. The institution of *sasi* has survived for 400 years in various parts of Maluku Province[106].

Cultural Significance

In Indonesia, apart from the Aru Islands, there are no reports of dugongs being actively hunted[107]. It has been suggested that in some areas local people do not hunt dugongs as they consider them sacred animals[108].

Dugongs often get caught in fishing nets and tidal traps by accident. The dugongs that get caught by accident are often killed and eaten by the local community. The meat can be consumed dried or fresh and is said to be delicious[109].

Dugong tusks are used by local people to make cigarette holders, and the bones are kept in houses or elsewhere in villages for protection or good luck[110].

Summary

Little research on dugongs or their ecology has been done in Indonesia. Further scientific research throughout Indonesia is vital for the development of a sustainable dugong conservation program. A first priority is population census by interviews, snorkeling surveys, and aerial surveys. While dugongs in Indonesia are protected by law, enforcement is still poor. A two-part National Conservation Strategy and Action Plan for the Dugong in Indonesia was published in 2009, funded by the United Nations Environmental Programme/Convention on Migratory Species, the Ocean Park Conservation Fund of Hong Kong, and the Netherlands Committee of the International Union for the Protection of Nature (IUCN), and guided by a National Steering Committee.

Philippines

History of Research

Research on Philippine dugongs started in the mid-1980s, initially conducted by the Department of Environment and Natural Resources (DENR) through the Pawikan Conservation Project (PCP) of the Protected Areas and Wildlife Bureau (PAWB). DENR's task from 1985 was first to protect the dugong and second to research its distribution. This included rescuing and rehabilitating stranded animals, now conducted in collaboration with the Philippine Marine Mammal Stranding Network (www.pmmsndatabase.upd.edu.ph).

Aragones[111] conducted the first systematic research on the feeding ecology of a local dugong population in the Philippines in Calauit Island, Busuanga (map 7.1). Further research[112] reported sighting an average of five individuals and rarely, groups of 15–24 animals. From a collaborative project between PCP and Toba Aquarium, Kataoka et al.[113] highlighted the importance of the islands of Palawan Province as critical habitat for Philippine dugongs.

Research efforts focusing on the ecology, distribution, and conservation of dugongs are currently being conducted by the DENR, WWF-Philippines, Conservation International, Silliman University and the University of the Philippines. Several local universities in Mindanao have recently started studying the dugongs in their particular areas.

Distribution

The number of dugongs in the Philippine archipelago is unknown[114]. Historically, almost all islands of the Philippines harbored dugongs[115]. Reports by Aragones and by Baltazar and Yaptinchay[116] delineate the extensive historical and modern distribution of dugongs along the coastlines of northeast Luzon, Lubang Island, Mindoro, Guimaras Strait, Panay Gulf, the Palawan islands, northern and southern Mindanao, and the Sulu archipelago (map 7.1). Recent sites with dugong sightings also include the northern Tañon Strait area[117], Semirara islands, Masbate Island, Guimaras Island, southern Panay Island[118], and Romblon islands.

Legal Status

The dugong is protected by the Philippine Wildlife Protection and Conservation Act of 2001 (Republic Act 9147). Killing, taking, and the possession of any parts of protected wildlife are prohibited. The Republic Act (RA) 9147 delineates that the dugong is under jurisdiction of the DENR, specifically the PAWB. The Department of Agriculture–Bureau of Fisheries and Aquatic Resources has jurisdiction over marine organisms, including cetaceans.

Unfortunately, RA 9147 was unable to correct deficiencies in dugong protection administration from a previous law. In 1991, the DENR had issued Administrative Order No. 55 to protect the dugong from continuous exploitation. This was the initial legal instrument used to protect dugongs from being killed, sold, collected, and traded. This administrative order initially assigned the PCP/PAWB responsibility for dugong protection, since most dugong entanglements (strandings) and similar incidents happened in seagrass communities and/or adjacent areas where their primary species of interest, the sea turtles, are also found. At that point it would have been logical for the PCP/PAWB to protect dugongs. However, people who were experienced at working with dugongs moved to other agencies. Also, sea turtle conservation and management required the focused attention of PCP/PAWB. There needs to be a single agency to deal specifically with dugong and cetacean conservation and protection effectively.

There are no protected areas specifically allocated for dugongs in the Philippines. Several places have been proposed but not established, including Calauit Island, Taytay Bay, and Roxas Bay, which includes Green Island Bay, all in Palawan Province. These areas have had intermittent strandings or entanglements of dugongs from fish corrals (*baklad*)[119]. These bays and coastal areas in Palawan Province will most likely be the last bastion for dugongs in the Philippines. Other areas identified as possible Dugong Protected Areas are located in southern Mindanao: Malita in Davao del Sur, Mati in Davao Oriental, Sarangani Bay, and the whole of the Sulu Archipelago[120].

Under the National Integrated Protected Areas System Act of 1992 (NIPAS, Republic Act 7586), it is the DENR's task to conduct suitability studies and public hearings for potential protected areas (PA). The DENR has not acted on any proposed Dugong Protected Areas.

In principle, a congressional act is required for a PA to become officially part of NIPAS so that its boundaries will be legally delineated and mapped, and funds will be allocated for its management. Another possibility is for the Philippine president, via presidential proclamation or executive order, to proclaim or designate a particular area as a protected area by virtue of its outstanding biological or physical features. The administration and management of any PA is granted to the Protected Area Management Board (PAMB), which should be composed of regional, provincial, and local officials and representatives from local tribal communities, academe, and nongovernmental organizations.

Threats

Major threats to Philippine dugongs include habitat loss and degradation, direct and indirect takes, and pollution, resulting from a steadily growing human population. The habitat loss and degradation brought about by development of resorts in pristine and remote islands in Palawan is alarming. It has become common to lease pristine islands in Palawan and develop resorts mostly catering to foreign tourists. These same islands are often the preferred feeding habitats of dugongs.

The high rate of migration to coastal areas in the Philippines has been an environmental issue since the 1980s. This trend is primarily brought about by open access to productive coastal communities, where people can find food and shelter. As the number of coastal inhabitants increases, the ecological integrity of the coastal areas deteriorates. These coastal areas suffer from sedimentation and eutrophication from improper waste disposal, negatively impacting local seagrass meadows. Though seagrass is widespread throughout the Philippines, it is not the only factor that restricts dugong distribution, as there are many healthy seagrass beds where dugongs are not found.

Hunting and incidental catch of dugongs in fishing nets and corrals will always be a problem, particularly in remote areas. The frequency of takes may be declining in less remote areas due to increasing awareness of the Philippine Wildlife Protection and Conservation Act of 2001 and/or from information campaigns by governmental agencies, scientists, and NGOs. Fishers can easily butcher a dugong whenever it gets entangled in a net or catch one by spearing or dynamite fishing. Butchering remains an easy way for fishers to get money and cheap protein. There has been a substantial leap in awareness among fishers about conserving dugongs since the early 1990s. A 2006 interview survey of local people in Guimaras Island, where there is a small population of dugongs, showed that 49% of fishers (n = 593) and 25% of the nonfishers (n = 680) were familiar with dugongs[121]. When respondents were asked if they were willing to conserve the dugongs, 56% and 88% of fishers and nonfishers, respectively, replied yes. A recent paper[122] showed that one dugong calf stranded per year from 2001 to 2009 in the Philippines. Orphaned dugong calves imply that their mothers may have been captured and butchered by local fishers. In Mati, Davao Oriental, four dugongs died from February to April 2011 from gillnet entanglements.

Pollution may be the least threatening of the factors listed, although increasing migration into coastal areas increases pollutant risks. Recent events such as the oil spill that occurred in Guimaras Island on 11 August 2006 significantly threatened an already vulnerable local dugong population. There have been no reported dugong sightings from local fishers since the oil spill.

Another threat is the increasing ecotourism activity of diving with dugongs; an example is in Club Paradise at Dimakya Island, Palawan[123]. This activity has now moved to areas far from Dimakya, as the dugongs that were usually observed feeding in a seagrass meadow adjacent to the island have not appeared. A recent program in Malita, Davao del Sur (part of Davao Gulf), is also attempting to promote dugong ecotourism.

Research Needs

Research needs for Philippine dugongs were summarized by Marsh et al.[124] as:
(1) broad-scale aerial surveys throughout the Philippines (with Palawan as a priority) to gather information on patterns of distribution and abundance to identify important habitat areas;
(2) studies on socioeconomic impediments to dugong conservation;
(3) estimates of rate of incidental catches by specific types of fishing gear;
(4) intensive interview surveys;
(5) seagrass distribution and abundance;
(6) consolidation of dugong sightings and habitat in a national data base;
(7) satellite tagging studies to provide information on movement of dugongs; and
(8) examination of the ecotoxicology of mine waste disposal on the marine food chain, including dugongs and seagrass.

Summary

Dugongs in the Philippines are extremely vulnerable to anthropogenic threats, especially due to rapidly increasing human coastal populations. The need to institutionalize the proposed Dugong Protected Area(s) and protect the remaining populations and the ecological integrity of these areas is imperative. Lack of a comprehensive national program to protect the remaining populations and address research and conservation needs aggravates the situation, and is among the reasons why dugong numbers will likely continue to decline. Given all these issues and the lack of recent sightings of large groups of dugongs, one can conclude that the dugong is one of the most critically endangered marine mammals in the Philippines.

China

History of Research

The earliest recorded sighting of a dugong in China was when Dutch explorers traveling between Nanyang and

Guangshou in the mid-seventeenth century recorded seeing an animal they called a sea cow[125]. In 1935 Shou found dugongs in the Gulf of Tonkin and, in 1955, discovered a male dugong stranded on the beach of Gaode Town, Beihai, in Guangdong Province (map 7.1)[126]. Hirasaka, in 1932, reported the earliest capture of a dugong in China, with descriptions of its morphology and basic measurements[127]. In January of 1931 a dugong was discovered stranded on Taiwan's southern coast.

Wang and Sun[128] conducted surveys of dugong distribution along China's coast in 1962, 1981, and 1984 and studied the external morphology of captured animals. Dong et al.[129] did primary anatomic and histological research on dugongs. In 2000 Zhou et al.[130] conducted ship surveys for dugongs in Beibu Gulf (Gulf of Tonkin) and found six dugongs. They also examined seagrass and determined that seagrass beds along western Hainan Island were more plentiful than in Guangxi. Five dugongs were found by fishers near Gangmen Village (Hainan Province) in September of 2000. Respondents also mentioned they had caught dugongs in November and December of 1999[131].

Workers in the Hepu National Dugong Reserve organized ship surveys within the reserve twice in 2000 but did not see any dugongs[132]. Deng and Lian[133] documented 43 sightings of dugongs in Beibu Gulf between 1978 and 1994, of which 13 were dead or stranded because of dynamite fishing.

Distribution

The dugong's distribution in China includes the coast of the Guangxi Zhuang Tribe Autonomous Region (from Hepu to Fangchenggang) in Beibu Gulf, western Leizhou Peninsula in Guangdong Province, and the western coast of Hainan Island[134] (map 7.1)

Along the Guangxi coast dugongs are found mainly offshore of Shatian town in Hepu Province, and Yingluo Bay, and are often caught in fishing nets near the town of Longtan (near the city of Beihai). Between 1976 and 2001, along the Beibu Gulf, 100 dugong strandings were reported, mostly close to Shatian town[135].

Legal Status

China's Forestry Department has established Regulations for the Protection of Wild Animal Resources, which group protected animals in China into three categories, all of which are protected from hunting. For Class I species like the dugong, capture is allowed only by permit from the Forestry Department.

The Chinese government has established several laws and regulations that are relevant to dugongs and marine reserves, such as the People's Republic of China (PRC) Natural Reserve Management Regulations, PRC Wild Animal Protection Law, Marine Environment Protection Law of the PRC, Action Plan for Marine Biodiversity Conservation in China, and Management Measures for Marine Reserves. While legislation is adequate to protect the dugong in China, enforcement is a problem[136].

Threats

As coastal populations increase, areas of dugong habitat have become degraded by development, overfishing, and destructive fishing. Dugongs were once directly harvested and incidentally caught in fishing nets[137]. Overfishing depletes fishing resources and increases incidents of bycatch and destruction of seagrass beds[138].

In one incident, during the Great Leap Forward in 1958, the community of Shatian in Hepu County organized teams to catch dugongs using nets. Between 1958 and 1962 they caught 110 dugongs to be used as medicine and food. Dugongs are valuable, as their oil is used in traditional Chinese medicine to warm lungs and dissipate coldness, invigorate the spleen, and reinforce the vital *qi*. The upper incisor can be made into medicine to treat food poisoning. Dugong meat is considered delicious, with a texture similar to pork; people used to consider it a delicacy. The skin is quite thick and was used to make leather, while fat was used as fuel. The incisor and first cervical vertebra were made into decorations[139]. Hunters used various methods to capture dugongs: luring them into cage traps using tapioca as bait; using spears, net entanglements, or harpoons to trap and kill dugongs; or setting up fences to trap dugongs during ebb tides.

In 1992 the Guangxi Zhuang Tribe Autonomous Region People's Government established the 350km² Hepu National Dugong Reserve.

This is the only dugong reserve in China; however there are urgent problems facing enforcement.

Illegal fishing, such as fishing with electricity, dynamite, and cyanide, occurs within and around the reserve. Numerous aquaculture farms are illegally located within the reserve boundaries. More than 20,000 wooden structures have been erected in the shallow sea within 10 m from the shore for the illegal aquaculture farms. These structures prevent dugongs from feeding in the seagrass beds. These fish farms also pollute nearby waters[140].

There are three towns within and around the reserve, with a total of 1,400 motor-powered fishing boats. These boats often operate within 20 m of the coastline, fishing with bottom trawlers that destroy fisheries and seagrass[141]. Since the 1980s the number of motor-powered boats in Beibu Gulf has been steadily increasing. In the past two decades the number of dugongs is believed to have decreased, and fishers rarely see the animals. Residents in this area believe dugongs either are extinct or have moved[142].

The following are suggestions to improve dugong protection in the reserve:
(1) community education about dugongs, laws, and regulations;
(2) stricter enforcement of the laws and regulations;
(3) improved management capacity and updated facilities and equipment;
(4) improved management tools such as cars, boats, protection facilities, and equipment;
(5) boundary markers or landmarks clearly establishing the nature reserve's boundary;
(6) establishment of a dugong research and nursing center; and
(7) participation in national and international exchanges for better communication of ideas.

Cultural Significance

Fishers on Hainan Island call dugongs sea cows, mermaids, human fish, or sea horses. According to legend, during the Song dynasty a man out sailing saw a mermaid he described as a married woman appearing above the sea, with red coat, thick limbs, and tangled hair.

Before the 1950s fishers regarded dugongs as "saintly fishes" and never caught them. People started hunting dugongs after the Great Leap Forward in 1958. Informal statistics show that 150 individuals were caught between 1958 and 1962, and 40–50 animals were caught from the early to mid-1970s.

Research Needs

Long-term research projects and personnel are needed to study dynamic situations such as dugong distribution, activities, and abundance. Stranding, rescue, and rehabilitation facilities are also needed for dugongs and other marine mammals.

Summary

The Chinese government has already established a series of rules and regulations and a reserve to protect dugongs. These regulations should be enforced within communities and local governments. Specifically, the following are critical: removal of illegal aquaculture in the reserve, limiting the number of fishing boats, strict enforcement of areal and temporal closures and fishing regulations, a ban on destructive fishing methods, reinforcement of seagrass bed protection measures, and minimizing anthropogenic disturbance to dugongs. More widespread educational programs are needed through media, posters, and exhibitions to increase local knowledge about protecting marine biodiversity.

The reserve could be a source of ecological, societal, and economic benefits, and the national and provincial governments should invest more in the reserve to resolve its lack of funding. Recently, a 26 million yuan (US$3.8 million) project to improve the reserve was completed. Improvements include a new research and rescue center and more patrol boats[143]. Scientists should be encouraged and funded to conduct research in the reserve. For local development to be sustainable, close cooperation between local residents and reserve management should be encouraged. To guarantee the livelihood of local communities, support is needed for traditional activities such as fisheries and sandworm digging. Areas should be designated to allow the public to carry out activities (such as aquaculture), provided that the conservation mission of the reserve is not compromised. Once the lifestyle of local residents has been improved, the conflict between conservation and the communities can be better resolved so as to protect dugongs more effectively.

Sri Lanka

History of Research

Coastal villagers have known about the dugong in Sri Lanka's waters since ancient times. The species has been the subject of scrutiny at least as far back as 1560, when dead specimens were examined and documented[144]. Since then, several sources have documented dugong catches in the Gulf of Mannar off the northwest coast of the island[145] and later expressed concern regarding the long-term survival of the species in Sri Lanka[146]. However, little systematic research has ever been carried out on this dugong population. In recent decades, research on the remaining dugongs off the northwest of Sri Lanka has not been possible due to an ongoing ethnic conflict, making the area unsafe for researchers.

The most recent surveys include brief aerial surveys of one to two days' duration in the early 1980s and an interview survey on the Gulf of Mannar coastline in 2004[147]. The aerial surveys resulted in two animals being sighted in 1981, while none were sighted in 1983[148]. Occasional records of accidental bycatch in gillnets continued to be reported throughout the 1980s and 1990s[149]. The 2004 interview survey recorded the continued presence of dugongs but reported a recent decline in numbers[150]. This survey also reports on continued illegal hunting and accidental bycatch of dugongs along the northwest coast.

Distribution

Historically dugongs were known to be abundant in the Palk Strait and Gulf of Mannar off the north and north-

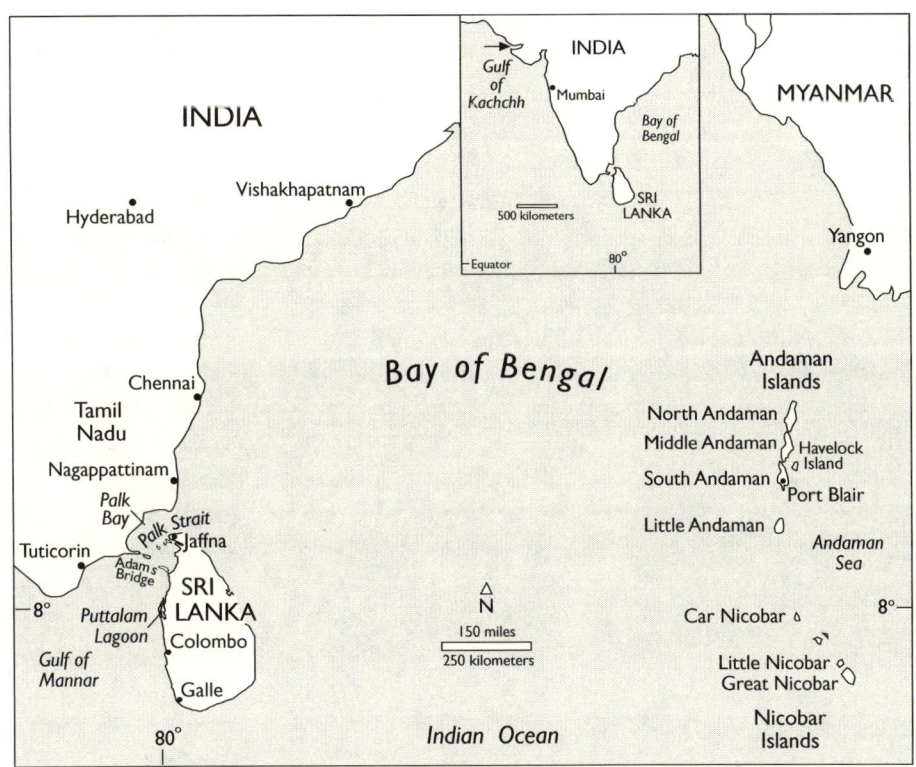

Map 7.2. Dugong distribution in India, Sri Lanka, and the Andaman and Nicobar islands. (Map by Ellen McElhinny.)

west of Sri Lanka[151] (map 7.2). Although dugongs were occasionally caught off the east coast in the distant past[152] and very rarely on the south coast[153], there are no recent records from these areas[154]. The remaining population is in the Gulf of Mannar from Adam's Bridge south toward the Puttalam lagoon and around associated islets[155]. The shallow coastal waters of the extensive continental shelf in this area still support seagrass beds that provide suitable feeding grounds for the dugong, but these beds are threatened by destructive fishing practices[156].

Legal Status

The dugong is a legally protected species in Sri Lanka, having had total protection under the Fauna and Flora Protection Ordinance since 1970. It is also afforded some protection under the Fisheries Act of 1996. Although the necessary legislation is in place on paper, law enforcement has been weak and is presently inadequate to protect the remaining dugong population[157]. Poor law enforcement is partially due to inadequate staff and resources within state agencies that have the authority to implement these laws. Besides lacking the resources for regular monitoring along the coastline, the personnel in these departments are particularly ill-equipped to deal with offenses relating to marine mammals, as they have had no training and little experience with these species. The problems of law enforcement are further exacerbated by the remaining dugong population being confined to the northwestern waters, where ongoing ethnic conflict makes it difficult for enforcement authorities to carry out their duties effectively.

Threats

The dugong has long been hunted for human consumption in Sri Lanka. Dugong meat was traditionally considered a delicacy, and the species was the target of deliberate hunting in the past. A government-sponsored dugong fishery was operated during the British colonial period, with 40–50 dugongs being caught in the Gulf of Mannar area each season[158]. This activity continued after the country became independent, and it is reported that even in 1958–59 the dugong fishery resulted in the capture of 265 dugongs in the district of Mannar alone[159]. The high demand for dugong meat among coastal communities has depleted dugong populations in areas where they were once common. It has also led to small cetacean meat being sold as dugong meat in areas where the dugong is no longer found[160].

Since the modernization of the fishery and the introduction of synthetic gillnets in the 1950s, incidental bycatch has become an additional threat to the dugong in Sri Lanka[161]. The remaining dugong habitat in the Gulf of Mannar is under intensive fishing pressure and considered a highly productive fishing ground. Even if animals that are accidentally caught are found alive, the likelihood that they would be released is extremely low, given the high popularity of dugong meat, coupled with poor law enforcement[162].

Habitat destruction has become a more recent threat, with the illegal use of explosives in certain areas that were once considered prime dugong habitat. The use of push nets and shrimp trawls in seagrass beds off the northwest coast is also destroying dugong habitats[163].

Cultural Significance

The 2004 interviews showed that the dugong has no special religious or cultural significance in Sri Lanka. Dugongs are considered a food source, with people believing that dugong meat is of superior quality and taste. No dugong parts are used in traditional medicine or for any other cultural or spiritual purpose, and there are no superstitious beliefs attached to the animal.

However, certain common stories about the dugong were independently recounted by fishers at diverse locations[164]:

> When a dugong with a calf gets encircled within a beach-seine net, the adult throws the calf into the air and over the net to safety. Older fishers had often witnessed this behavior in the past, when beach-seines were used more frequently.
>
> In the past when a dugong was sighted, a strong fisherman would jump off the boat, wrestle it to the bottom and hold its face in the sand to kill it by suffocation, before bringing it ashore.

Research Needs

Quantitative research on dugongs in Sri Lanka's waters has never been done in a consistent manner and most of the available information is qualitative or anecdotal. As a result there are many data gaps that still need to be addressed to assess the actual status of this declining population and determine its long-term survival prospects.

Both aerial and boat-based surveys are needed to make a quantitative assessment of the status of this population. Data on population size, year-round distribution, relative abundance, and habitat requirements are necessary to design management interventions and conservation actions that would minimize threats to the remaining dugongs and their habitat and ensure their long-term survival. Aerial surveys could be particularly helpful in identifying critical areas still used by dugongs. Cost-effective interview surveys should be continued periodically, to obtain qualitative information that is complementary to the quantitative data generated through sighting surveys.

Assessment of dugong habitat through initial mapping of remaining seagrass beds in the Gulf of Mannar and Palk Strait is a priority. Along with current distribution of seagrass habitats, their species composition, abundance, and quality should be assessed. A survey of dugong grazing trails should be done to determine critical areas for habitat protection.

Neither direct take nor bycatch is documented. Building on the baseline data from the 2004 questionnaire survey, an assessment of direct hunting, bycatch, and use of dugong meat is needed to quantify the annual catch rates and assess the economic value of this illegal take.

The dugong population of the entire Gulf of Mannar (Sri Lanka and India) should be considered a single unit for purposes of research, conservation, and management. Dugongs on both sides of the Gulf of Mannar face similar threats, and depletion in numbers is a problem common to both Sri Lanka and India[165]. Collaboration between Sri Lanka and India would facilitate pooling of expertise and scarce resources and enable research and management measures to help secure a dugong population that faces extirpation in both countries.

India

History of Research

The first accounts of the Indian dugong describe external features, habits, and osteology[166]. Various scientists have reported on the distribution, abundance, habits, and food of dugongs in India[167]. Mani and Silas[168] reported the occurrence of dugongs on the Saurashtra coast, and Lal Mohan[169] reported their occurrence in the Gulf of Kachchh and the Gulf of Mannar. In the 1970s James studied dugong osteology and first stressed the need for conservation[170]. However, aerial surveys in Palk Bay and the Gulf of Mannar region by Leatherwood and Reeves in 1983 did not report any dugong sightings[171]. In 2004 interviews were conducted in the Gulf of Mannar and Palk Strait region to obtain perceptions of local fishers about dugong presence and conservation[172]. Dugongs were believed to occur around the Andaman and Nicobar islands[173] but were first recorded by Das and Dey[174], who reported the presence of 40 dugongs through interviews with local fishers and dive operators. A study on the status and distribution of dugongs in the Andaman and Nicobar islands was started in 2007 and during the study, behavioral observations were made on three individuals in the wild[175]. Recently the Indian government funded a project to study dugong population status and distribution.

Distribution and Status

Dugongs have been reported from northwestern India and in southeast India in the Gulf of Kachchh through the Gulf of Mannar and Palk Bay[176]. There are no records from farther north along the east coast of India or from the Sunderbans[177], although there are records from the Chittagong coast of Bangladesh and in Burmese waters[178]. Dugongs were previously reported (as seals) along the west coast of India[179] and from saltwater inlets off the south Malabar and Konkan coasts as far north as Canara (corresponding to southern Maharashtra, Goa, Karnataka, and Kerala today). The occurrence of dugongs along the Malabar Coast was also mentioned in the Imperial Gazetteer[180]. Dugongs have been reported from the Maldives and Laccadive Islands but are now believed to be extinct there[181]. Contemporary distribution in India is patchy and restricted to three areas: the Gulf of Kachchh, the Gulf of Mannar and Palk Bay, and the Andaman and Nicobar islands[182] (map 7.2).

Though dugongs have historically been recorded along the west coast of India[183], the only records of dugong carcasses or sightings are from the southern Gulf of Kachchh[184]. However, boat-based surveys here in 2002 did not report any dugong sightings[185]. Since 2002 several strandings and one instance of a dugong caught in a trawl net have been reported in the Gulf of Kachchh[186].

As early as 1905, Annandale stated: "It is rare nowadays for more than one specimen to be taken, whereas formerly in the Gulf of Mannar flocks of hundreds were said to occur."[187] During recent interviews in the Gulf of Mannar, fishers reported that sighting a dugong today was rare, with few sightings or accidental catches of dugongs in gillnets[188].

Dugongs were common in the Andaman and Nicobar islands until the 1950s, but currently there are only sporadic sightings and poaching records[189]. Das and Dey estimated around 40 dugongs in 1994–95 based on chance encounters with fishers and dive operators[190]. D'souza and Patankar saw three dugongs in the wild at Neil, Havelock, and Kodiaghat islands in the southern Andaman Islands, and three dugongs were seen near Neil Island by Jethva and Solanki[191].

Legal Status and Management

Dugongs have the highest level of legal protection under Schedule I of the Indian Wildlife Protection Act of 1972. Under this act, hunting, capture, killing, buying, and selling of dugong meat are prohibited and punishable by imprisonment of up to seven years and a fine of Rs. 25,000 (about US$500). In April 2008 the Indian government signed a specific Memorandum of Understanding under the Convention of Migratory Species (CMS) to conserve and manage the dugong and its habitats in India. The major dugong habitats in India are protected under the Indian Wildlife Protection Act and are designated protected areas. The Gulf of Kachchh was designated as a marine protected area in 1982 and the Gulf of Mannar as a biosphere reserve in 1986. In the Andaman and Nicobar islands, two areas are specifically designated as marine national parks. In 2002 the Andaman and Nicobar administration declared the dugong the state animal of the islands.

There are no areas designated specifically as dugong conservation areas. However, the Indian government and local NGOs have initiated conservation and awareness efforts. There is a large gap in management efforts because of limited knowledge of dugong ecology and habitat needs among rangers, difficulties in accessing the habitat areas, and the absence of a monitoring protocol.

Threats

Gillnets, shark nets, and dynamite fishing are a major source of mortality. Approximately 1.28 million gillnets, each 2–3 km long, are used along the coast near the Gulf of Mannar[192]. Although dynamite fishing has been banned since the Indian Fisheries Act of 1896, it was resumed illegally in Palk Bay and was later used to kill dugongs[193]. Nair et al.[194] reported an average of 40 dugong deaths per year in the 1970s in gillnets set in Palk Bay. Jones[195] reported annual gill and shark net catches between 1957 and 1970 to be up to 175 in Palk Bay and the Gulf of Mannar.

Ilangakoon et al.[196] reported that 29% of respondents interviewed in the Gulf of Mannar–Palk Strait believed that trawling was the main cause of decline for dugongs. Accidental bycatch of dugongs in trawl nets has been recorded from the Gulf of Kachchh[197]. In the Andaman and Nicobar islands unreported numbers of dugongs are caught every year as accidental bycatch in gillnets, shore seines, and commercial shark fishing nets.

In the Gulf of Kachchh, dugong oil is valued as a preservative and conditioner for wooden boats. However, dugongs are not hunted here for personal consumption. The personal consumption of dugong meat is common near the Gulf of Mannar, although banned, and a stranded or accidentally caught dugong is sold for a high price[198]. Ilangakoon et al.[199] reported that 64% of respondents had hunted dugongs in the past 40 years, but due to declining numbers in the last 25 years, it was increasingly difficult to find the animals. These researchers reported that dugong meat was considered valuable in the region, was nutritious and delicious, and fetched a high price as it is now illegal to eat.

In the Andaman and Nicobar islands the Andamanese, Onges, and Nicobarese tribes traditionally hunt dugongs with iron harpoons tied to their boats (*dunghi*)[200]. The skull and lower jaw bones are preserved in the belief that the smell released from the dead animal attracts animals from the forest or sea, thus facilitating future hunts[201]. The Onges, the Great Andamanese, and Nicobarese hunt dugongs from dugout canoes with a special type of harpoon called a *thomae*, a thin iron rod (about 10–12 cm long) with 3–4 barbs notched at the end. The hunter pulls on an attached rope until the animal tires. The Shompens of Great Nicobar hunt by getting the animal entangled in gillnets and shore seines. The Karen community of Middle Andaman hunts dugong in a manner similar to that of the Onges; the harpoon is called a *danow*. None of the tribes, except the Great Andamanese of Strait Island, hunt regularly because of the time and effort it takes to find and kill a dugong[202].

Industrial development, toxic run-off, heavy marine vessel traffic, siltation, occasional oil spills, bottom trawling, and dredging are major causes of habitat loss in the Gulf of Kachchh and the Gulf of Mannar. The present construction of the Sethu Samudram ship canal off the coast of Tamil Nadu in India goes through dugong habitat areas. In the Andaman Islands, Das and Dey suggested habitat loss to be the main cause for decline in dugong numbers[203]. The coastal waters of the larger islands within the Andaman and Nicobar archipelagos have extremely turbid water from sediment run-off, largely due to deforestation and coastal construction[204]. Fishers stated that dugongs were found washed ashore after the cyclone of 1954, which destroyed large areas of seagrass[205]. The tsunami of 2004 had a major impact on seagrass beds in the Gulf of Mannar–Palk Strait and the Andaman and Nicobar islands[206].

Cultural Significance

Dugongs in India have varied names: in Gujarati they are *baimacchi* and *suvarmacchi*; in Tamil *owlia, kadalpasu*, and *kadalpanni*; in Hindi *pani suwar*. The Karen name is *thaw thee*, and the Telugu name is *neelu pandi*. Names used in the Nicobar Islands are *haoonelmai* (Car Nicobar), *hipot* (Nancowry), and *hippo* (Little Nicobar).

In the Gulf of Mannar interviews, most (64%) respondents had heard stories about dugongs[207]. People said that when a dugong was captured it cried like a human, and the calves swam close to their mothers and did not like being separated. Two people said dugongs look like mermaids or women in the sea. One person had heard a story about a man being rescued and brought back to shore by a dugong after he fell out of his boat. Most respondents mentioned that dugongs were like cows and fed milk to their young and took care of their young like humans do. In the Andaman and Nicobar islands, the Onges paint the pectoral girdle (*girange*) of the dugong skeleton brown and throw it away in the forest, while the mandible (*ebirange*) and the sternum (*gatta*), also painted brown, are kept in people's homes to bring luck at hunting[208]. Skeletal parts have no significance for the Nicobari tribes except for the Nicobarese of the Nancowry group, who use tusks for ornamental purposes.

Research Needs

It is important to determine the distribution and relative abundance of dugongs in the key areas: Gulf of Kachchh, Gulf of Mannar–Palk Strait, and the Andaman and Nicobar islands. But considering that populations have dwindled greatly, secondary data from interviews could guide the areas where boat-based or aerial surveys are carried out, so as to make the best use of resources. Large-scale aerial surveys can be used to survey the Gulf of Mannar–Palk Bay, including Sri Lankan waters, using techniques developed for large remote areas in Australia[209]. Mapping of seagrass beds and a survey of dugong grazing trails could help to determine critical dugong habitat for conservation and to inform subsequent management initiatives.

Summary

Sightings are rare, and the chance of saving the populations in the three regions seems low. Ecological data sources to inform conservation science are few and of low quality. More information is also needed about the changing perceptions and socioeconomic conditions of the communities who hunt dugongs or depend on fishery resources from the three regions. While awareness programs can inform communities about the need for conservation, the formation of a collaborative space between local communities and conservationists is required for the ban on dugong hunting to be successful. Conserving potential habitat in conjunction with a successful ban on hunting would be required to save the last remaining dugongs in Indian waters.

As indicated in the introduction to this account of dugongs in Asian waters, their future is jeopardized by extremely high human use of coastal resources. Although the precise details vary among countries and settings, losses derive primarily from bycatch in fishing nets and from fishing practices that harm both dugongs and seagrass beds. Moreover, growing human populations in coastal zones pose intensifying threats to dugongs and their habitats. For actions aimed at long-term dugong survival to succeed, Asian countries urgently need fuller knowledge of the remaining dugong populations and fuller inclusion of coastal communities in conservation initiatives.

8

Dugongs in Japan

KAZUKO IKEDA AND HIROSHI MUKAI

The dugongs of Japan are in dire straits. Many thought they had already been extirpated when, in the 1990s after plans for a U.S. military base threatened seagrass beds in Henoko Bay, an investigation confirmed the continuing presence of dugongs around Okinawa Island. There are critical obstructions to dugong and seagrass research in Japan. The primary problem is that U.S. military bases, closed to Japanese citizens, occupy some 20% of the Okinawa Islands, including many coastal areas. Ironically, it is also difficult to finance any research, locally, nationally, or internationally, because the number of dugongs in Okinawa is so low.

History of Research

The first aerial survey was conducted in 1998 in Okinawa, yielding ten dugong sightings[1]. Previously, sighting data were collected opportunistically by nongovernmental organizations (NGOs) such as Dugong Network Okinawa, while dugong feeding trails were recorded only incidentally by individuals. The Defense Agency of Japan also conducted preliminary surveys for dugongs and seagrass around the Henoko area of Okinawa Island in 2000 (map 8.1). They found several dugong feeding trails in seagrass beds and saw five dugongs[2].

Since 2001 research has been conducted around Okinawa by the Japanese Ministry of the Environment every five years to survey seagrass distribution, dugong distribution, and dugong feeding trails and to perform DNA and stomach contents analysis[3].

Aerial photography was used to create seagrass maps and design feeding trail surveys. Based on these maps, it was estimated that approximately 20 km² of seagrass beds in the islands were near the shore around Okinawa Island[4].

Aerial surveys of dugongs from light aircraft were conducted in 2002 and 2003, and a total of 13 individual dugongs were seen. Dugongs were mostly seen alone, occasionally in pairs[5]. In 2004 and 2005, follow-up surveys using helicopters were flown around Okinawa Island. In these surveys there were 13 sightings (17 individual dugongs). Six sightings were of the same individual, and based on photo identification, three sightings of a mother and calf pair were believed to be the same animals[6].

Surveys of dugong feeding trails were conducted from 2002 to 2006 by the Ministry of the Environment. Most trails were found in seagrass beds near Kayo and Henoko on the eastern side of Okinawa Island and the southern part of Kouri Island, off the northern coast of Okinawa Island[7] (map 8.1).

The Ministry of the Environment used DNA analysis to clarify the relationship between dugong populations in Okinawa and those in Southeast Asia. Results based on mitochondrial DNA analysis agree with Tikel (1997) that the haplotype of Japanese dugongs does not overlap that of Australian dugongs[8]. Asian populations such as in the Andaman Sea, Gulf of Thailand, Philippines, Palau, Taiwan, Sulawesi, and Okinawa are not significantly different[9].

Stomach contents analysis of stranded or net-entangled dugongs showed that dugongs feed on seven species out of ten native species of seagrass around Okinawa Island (table 8.1)[10].

Several studies using the captive dugongs of Toba Aquarium were also conducted. Hormonal levels based on urine analyses in a female dugong were measured to learn more about the ovarian cycle[11]. Cycles of approximately 50 days were reported. This research also suggested that the measurement of urinary progesterone is a useful method to detect the ovarian cycle of dugongs in captivity.

Research on seagrass digestibility was carried out by Aketa et al. (2003) and Goto et al. (2004)[12]. Both groups reported high digestibility of 80–90%. Goto et al.[13] also studied the characteristics of microbial fermentation in the hindgut of dugongs.

Ikeda used isotope analysis to research the feeding habits of wild dugongs in Okinawa. The $\delta^{13}C$ and $\delta^{15}N$ of all available species of seagrass and several dead du-

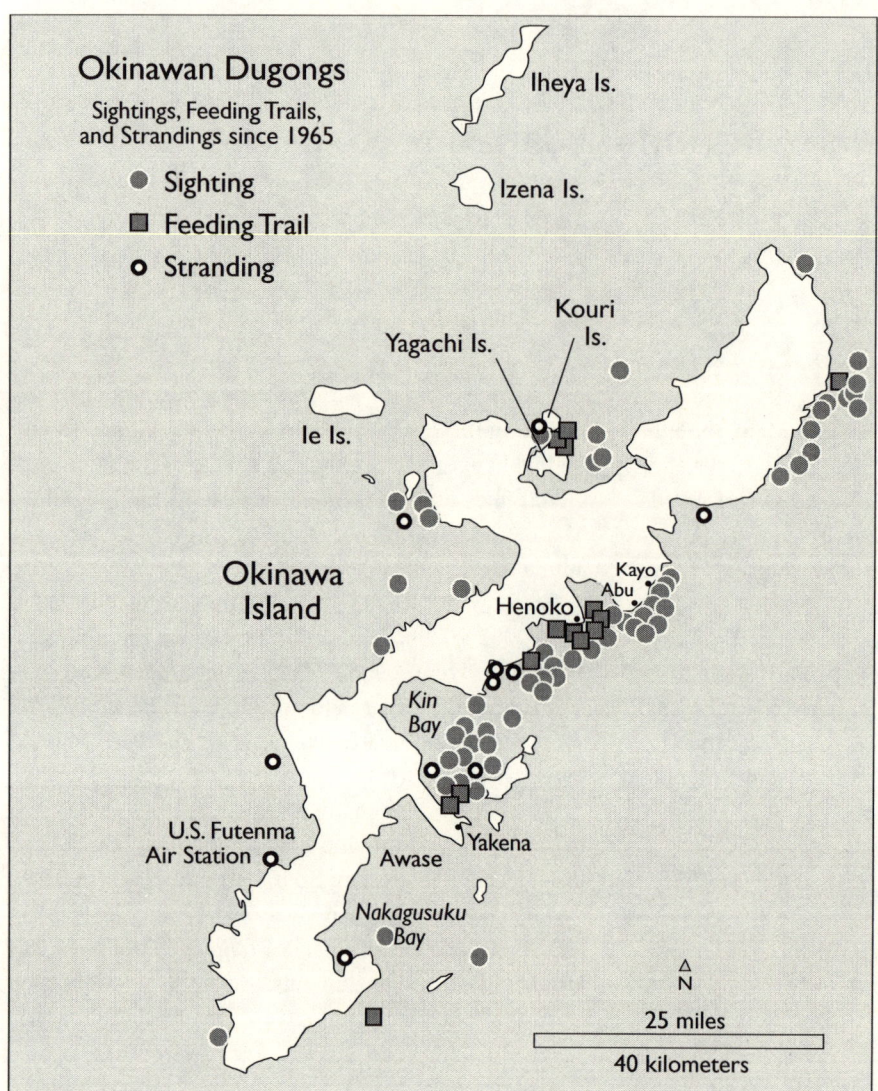

Map 8.1. Okinawan dugong sightings, feeding trails, and strandings since 1965. (Map by Ellen McElhinny.)

gongs' perioral bristles were measured to estimate the seagrass species eaten by individual dugongs. Each dugong's $\delta^{13}C$ value shows different trends, which implied that individual dugongs feed on different seagrass species[14]. Ikeda also studied seagrass recovery after dugong grazing in Okinawa Island[15].

A research group supported by the Ministry of Education, Culture, Sports, Science and Technology started studying dugongs in other islands as well: Amami-Ohshima Island of Japan, Hainan Island of China, and the Philippines[16]. The scientists also conducted a study of the cranial bones of the dugongs enshrined at Aragusuku Island in the southern Ryukyu Archipelago[17].

In 2002 the Nature Conservation Society of Japan established *Jangusa*-Watch (the word means seagrass in the Okinawan dialect) as a way for local people to learn about dugong conservation[18] and to create a rapid and easy method for mapping and monitoring seagrass habitat using volunteers. Another NGO, Dugong Network Okinawa, continues to collect dugong sighting information from small aircraft pilots, fishers and the general public.

Distribution

Dugong teeth and bones were found in a shell mound of the Jomon Period (10,000 to 3000 BC) in the Ryukyu Archipelago, which means that dugongs have inhabited this island chain for more than 10,000 years[19]. During the Ryukyu Period (1453 to 1879 CE; Okinawan Dynasty), people hunted dugongs for meat and leather, and from the end of the 1800s to the beginning of 1900s, dugongs were still hunted for their meat. According to the statistical reports of Okinawa Prefecture, 283~327 dugongs were killed by hunters between 1894 and 1916[20]. As the data are limited to meat sold in markets, and dugongs were commonly consumed within local communities, that is probably an underestimate. It is believed that dugongs once inhabited the Sakishima, Okinawa, and Amami islands, throughout the Ryukyu Archipelago. However, since 1965, dugongs are largely thought to have been limited to Okinawa Island[21].

Based on the interpretation of aerial photographs and the results of field research, the shallow waters around Okinawa Island and adjacent small islands are presently the best remaining dugong habitat[22]. Seagrass is especially abundant along the east side of Okinawa Island, such as the Awase tidal flats in Nakagusuku Bay, the south part of Kin Bay, and Henoko and Kayo. Kume and Tonaki islands, about 90 km and 60 km from Okinawa Island respectively, also have small seagrass beds. In the northern part of Okinawa Island, seagrass is found around Izena and Iheya islands.

Other than the Okinawa Islands, seagrass is seen in the Sakishima Islands, mainly in Miyako, Ishigaki, and Iriomote islands. According to the 4th National Survey of the Natural Environment, there are 56.2 km² of seagrass beds around the Sakishima Islands, including Miyako, Iriomote, and Ishigaki islands[23]. In these islands most natural areas are undamaged, and the seagrass beds are in good condition. Small but healthy seagrass beds are also found in the northern part of the archipelago in the Amami-Ohshima islands[24].

In the Ryukyu Archipelago there are ten known seagrass species[25]. Based on the stomach analysis of stranded animals, dugongs in Okinawa Island are known to feed on seven of them[26] (table 8.1). Most seagrass beds contain mixed species, though there are few monospecific seagrass beds of *Halophila ovalis*. Dugongs and feeding trails are most commonly found from the middle to northern part of the east coast where seagrass beds are abundant[27].

Today only a small relic population of dugongs remains around Okinawa Island[28]. Ten were seen in 1998[29] and six in 2000[30]. During aerial surveys by the Ministry of the Environment, three, ten, nine, and eight dugongs were seen respectively in 2002, 2003, 2004, and 2005[31]. They are mainly seen in the middle of the eastern side of Okinawa Island in Kin Bay, Henoko, Abu, and Kayo areas, and also along the northern part of the island near Yagaji Island and Kouri Island (map 8.1).

Based on interviews conducted by the Ministry of the Environment, feeding trails and several animals that were reported as dugongs have been seen by local people near Iriomote Island since 2000[32]. There is still a small possibility that dugongs inhabit the Sakishima Islands, including Iriomote Island. In 1999, when Kasuya et al.[33] conducted an aerial survey around Iriomote Island, they had no sightings.

Several dugongs were seen by divers and fishers in Kasari Bay on the northern part of Amami-Ohshima Is-

Table 8.1. Seagrass species found in Okinawa and Sakishima islands eaten by dugongs.

Family	Genus and species	Okinawa and Sakishima islands	Eaten by dugong
Potamogetonaceae	Cymodocea rotundata	✓	✓
	C. serrulata	✓	✓
	Halodule pinifolia	✓	✓
	H. uninervis	✓	✓
	Syringodium isoetifolium	✓	✓
Hydrocharitaceae	Enhalus acoroides	✓	
	Halophila decipiens	✓	
	H. ovalis	✓	✓
	Thalassia hemprichii	✓	✓
Zosteraceae	Zostera japonica	✓	✓

Sources: For seagrass species of Okinawa and Askishima islands, see Toma 1999; for seagrass species eaten by dugongs, see Aketa 2003 and Ministry of the Environment 2004b.

land in 2003. However, no evidence of a resident dugong population in Amami-Ohshima Island was found in the extended survey of 2003[34].

In 1997 the Mammalogical Society of Japan estimated the population of dugongs as fewer than 50 and listed the dugong as an endangered species[35]. The Ecological Society of Japan has commented: "The estimated number of dugongs is only about ten, and the dugong is one of the most endangered species in Japan"[36].

Legal Status

Several laws prohibit the hunting or killing of dugongs in Japan. In August 2007 the Ministry of the Environment reviewed the Red List of Japan and listed dugongs as critically endangered[37]. The dugong was designated as a Natural Monument by the Law for the Protection of Cultural Properties in 1972. Killing and hunting of a Natural Monument is prohibited. However, there are no designated areas for dugong protection under the Natural Monument legislation. The Fishery Resources Conservation Law (1951) has also prohibited the hunting of dugongs since 1993. The Wildlife Protection and Appropriate Hunting Law (1892) bans the hunting of terrestrial mammals and birds (except game species and several nuisance rodents). Dugongs and five other marine mammal species were included in a 2002 revision of this law.

These laws combined play a major role in the prohibition of hunting or killing of dugongs. However, to protect the animal, it is also necessary to regulate fishing gear, such as fixed fishing nets and gill nets, and to manage habitat modifications, such as damage caused to seagrass beds by filling and draining. There are no laws or regulations that address these actions. The Fishery Resources Conservation Law and Wildlife Protection and Appropriate Hunting Laws were written for different purposes: the former encourages the development of fisheries, and the latter promotes agriculture and the conservation of wildlife by controlling hunting.

The Law for Conservation of Endangered Species of Wild Fauna and Flora (1992) could be sufficient for the protection of the dugong, as this law institutionalizes mechanisms capable of designating endangered species formally as a National Endangered Species and instituting a variety of measures, such as the establishment of Natural Habitat Conservation Areas. However, although included in the Red List, the dugong is not currently included as a National Endangered Species under the Law for Conservation of Endangered Species of Wild Fauna and Flora. This designation is needed urgently as the basis to establish Natural Habitat Conservation Areas in dugong feeding zones along the east coast of Okinawa Island.

Protected Areas

Within the Ryukyu Archipelago, there are several terrestrial parks that include shallow coastal waters: one national park, two quasi-national parks and three prefectural national parks[38].

On Okinawa Island, Okinawa Kaigan Quasi-National Park (260.52 km^2) and Okinawa Senseki Quasi-National Park (19.32 km^2) were established on the west and southern coasts of Okinawa Island, with a Marine Parks Area (4.93 km^2) within the Okinawa Kaigan Quasi-National Park. Around the Yagaji and Kouri islands within the Okinawa Kaigan Quasi-National Park and within the Okinawa Senseki Quasi-National Park are seagrass beds in good condition. However, few dugongs or feeding trails are seen along this side of the island. Dugongs are mainly seen along the eastern side of Okinawa Island, where protected areas for seagrass and dugongs are urgently needed.

In the Sakishima Islands, Iriomote Ishigaki National Park has 206.69 km^2 of terrestrial area and 458.13 km^2 of marine area, which contains a Marine Park area (11.06 km^2; figure 3). Within this national park, although there are relatively large seagrass beds, dugong presence is uncertain.

The Natural Park Law under which these national and quasi-national parks were established does not have any restrictions on fishing gear.

Under the Wildlife Protection and Appropriate Hunting Law, National Wildlife Protection Areas (NWPA) can be designated by the Ministry of the Environment. In the Special Protection Area (SPA) within the NWPA, habitat modification and the hunting and killing of wildlife are prohibited. However, there are no regulations on fishing gear such as fixed fishing nets or gillnets, even in an SPA. There are seven NWPAs in Okinawa Prefecture, but only two of them, Yagaji NWPA (where dugongs have been seen) and Nagura-Anparu NWPA (10 km^2 and 0.60 km^2 respectively), have SPAs of marine area.

Under the Nature Conservation Law, a Special Marine Zone (SMZ) within a Nature Conservation Area was established in Sakiyama Bay (1.28 km^2) on the west side of Iriomote Island. In the SMZ, activities such as the capture and collection of designated animals and plants, dredging, land filling, mooring, etc., are basically prohibited. However, as in an NWPA, there are no regulations governing fishing activities and gear.

Threats

Unfortunately, none of the existing protected areas of Okinawa and Sakishima islands are effective in conserving dugongs and their habitat, because the most serious threats for dugongs—habitat degradation and fishing gear—are not restricted.

Although dugong hunting is prohibited by several laws in Japan, bycatch and entanglement of the dugong in fixed fishing nets and gillnets is the one of the most serious threats. There are many fixed fishing nets and gillnets around Okinawa Island and adjacent islands. Since 1965, 21 dugongs have been documented as stranded in fishing nets or on shore[39]; three of the 21 were alive and were released into the ocean. Dugong strandings due to fishing net entanglements are reported once every one or two years. It is assumed that there are more stranded dugongs that have not been reported. The last incidental entrapment of a dugong by a fishing net in Okinawa was reported in 2004; a single live juvenile dugong was found inside a fixed fishing net. Fortunately, this individual was released successfully.

Habitat degradation is another major threat. There are two developments that endanger seagrass beds. On Awase tidal flat, one of the largest seagrass beds in Okinawa Island, a landfill plan of 190 hectares is currently being undertaken in spite of the opposition of NGOs and the local people. Another far more serious project is the one that galvanized the movement to save the dugongs of Japan: the relocation of the U.S. Futenma Air Station to the extensive seagrass beds along the east coast of Okinawa Island. This plan was frozen because of strong opposition from local people and NGOs and their concern for the natural environment and dugongs. However, on 1 May 1 2006, the United States–Japan Security Consultative Committee Document was published, calling for the United States and Japan to locate the Futenma Replacement Facility (FRF) in a configuration that combines the Henoko-saki (land area) and adjacent water areas of Ohura Bay and the shallow waters of Henoko, including two runways aligned in a V shape, each runway 1,600 m long plus two 100 m overruns. The construction method will be landfill. Both the U.S. and Japanese governments said this facility ensures agreed operational capabilities while addressing issues of safety, noise, and environmental impacts. However, many scientists believe that major damage to seagrass beds and therefore to dugongs is inescapable.

Seaweed mariculture (*Cladosiphon okamuranus* or *Okinawa-mozuku* in Japanese) is believed to be a possible cause of seagrass degradation as nursing nets are spread just 20 to 30 cm above the seagrass beds. The effect of *Okinawa-mozuku* mariculture on seagrass productivity has not yet been studied, and research is badly needed as the production of *Okinawa-mozuku* is increasing as cultivation technology improves. Okinawa presently yields approximately 90% of the total production of *mozuku* in Japan. Other issues to consider include the inaccessibility of the seagrass for dugong foraging due to the nursing nets and their possible entanglements in these nets.

Additional human-caused problems include frequent boat traffic, noises caused by human activities, and use of artificial lights at night. It has not been scientifically confirmed, but local people believe that dugongs use the seagrass beds at night to avoid humans.

Local people are very aware of the need for dugong conservation, especially after the animal's designation as a Natural Monument. Presently there is no hunting or marketing of dugong meat. A crucial issue is the trapping of dugongs in fishers's gillnets or fixed fishing nets. The most reliable method to release the dugong is to cut the fishing net. However, the local government does not compensate fishers for cutting a net, nor for the harvest lost due to the release. Any delay in rescue may cause the death of a dugong. We believe that to avoid public attention, fishers report to governmental agencies inaccurate numbers of dugong deaths from fishing gear entanglements.

Besides these threats, red soil (tuff loam) run-off, port construction, agricultural chemicals, and untreated wastewater run-off are all indirect causes of seagrass degradation in the Ryukyu Archipelago.

Cultural Significance

The dugong is well known to local people and has many local names, such as *zan* or *jan* in Okinawa Island and adjacent islands[40]. Seagrass is called *zan-gusa*, or *jan-gusa*, which means the grass of dugongs. It can be said that *zan* also means tsunami, which might be based on the observation that tsunamis or inauspicious happenings occur after dugongs are captured[41]. Local people used to fear the dugong as a god of the ocean. Dugongs are also called *akangaiyu* or *yonatama*. The origin of the name *akangaiyu* is unspecified. However, in popular lore, it was named after an image of the mother dugong, which held her calf like a human, or the childlike vocalizations of the dugong. *Akanbo* means child and *iyu* means fish in the local dialect. The name *yonatama* is used in Miyako, Irabu, and Ikema islands. The origin of the word *yonatama* is also not clear. But it is said that *yona* (or *ina*, *una*) is ancient word that means ocean, and *tama* means spirit; thus *yonatama* could mean god or spirit of the ocean.

Following is one of the local legends of *yonatama* from Irabu Island. Irabu and Shimochi islands are in the Sakishima island group. The two islands are separated only by a deep narrow channel.

> Once upon a time, a fisher who lived on Shimochi Island caught a *yonatama* (dugong) that had a human face. The fisher thought it a good idea to share this unique fish meat with neighbors and started a fire for cooking. When the night came, a small child living next to the fisher's house started to cry and insisted on running away to Irabu Island. The child's mother thought something was strange and went outside with the child. They heard a voice calling from the ocean: "*Yonatama, yonatama*, why are you so late to come back? Return to the ocean." Then, a small voice from the fisher's house cried: "I was caught and almost roasted over the fire. Please bring a tsunami and save me now." The mother was very surprised and ran away with her child to Irabu Island. In a moment, a huge tsunami came and covered all of Shimochi Island, including the fisher's house and the *yonatama*.

There are also several local legends of creation about dugongs. A creation myth from Kouri Island in the Okinawa Islands (map 8.1) is known as the story of the origin of Okinawan people. This story is similar to the story of Adam and Eve.

> There were a naked man and woman on Kouri Island. One day, they saw dugongs mating in the sea, and they awakened sexually, ashamed that they were naked. After that they covered their private parts with fan-palms. From watching dugongs mating, they learned how to mate themselves, and their children became the people of Okinawa.

A creation story from Yabushi Island, on the eastern coast of Okinawa Island (map 8.1), says that the first people of Yabushi Island were the offspring of a union between a dugong and a short-finned pilot whale (*Globicephala macrorhynchus*)[42].

Dugongs were feared and admired, yet still hunted as an important food source in the Ryukyu Archipelago. Dugong bones were also used as accessories and ornaments and sometimes tools[43]. Dugong meat was very valuable in the Ryukyu Period as it was believed to be a medicine for perpetual youth and longevity[44]. The local people of Aragusuku Island, south of Iriomote Island, had to provide the meat and tanned leather of dugongs to the Ryukyu Dynasty as a tax[45].

The skulls of hunted dugongs were enshrined in *utaki*[46] of the Aragusuku Islands in the hope of a good fishing haul for the next year. Local people still regard the *utakis* of the Aragusuku Islands as holy ground. There are many *utaki* in the Sakishima and Ryukyu islands; however, the *utaki* on the Aragusuku Islands are the only places with the enshrined skulls of dugongs.

Research Needs

Procedures are needed to prevent the entanglement of dugongs in fishing gear. The Fisheries Agency of Japan has been developing a monitoring system whereby a camera would be fixed inside a fixed fishing net to check for trapped dugong. Since 2003, Dugong Rescue Training focused on freeing trapped dugongs from fixed fishing nets and gillnets has been taught to fishers by the Okinawa Prefecture and the Ministry of the Environment. Fishers listen to lectures, participate in discussion sessions, and actually rescue a dummy dugong trapped inside a fixed fishing net[47].

Detailed surveys of seagrass beds and dugong distribution in Okinawa (except Okinawa Island) are also necessary. In particular, more research should be conducted on Iriomote, Ishigaki, and Miyako islands of the Sakishima Islands, as they have seagrass beds that could possibly support dugongs.

Research on the restoration of dugong habitat as well as the recovery of dugong numbers is urgently needed. While there had been two captive dugongs in Toba Aquarium since 1979, the male died in February of 2011. If the pair had bred successfully, it would have been the first example of captive breeding in dugongs.

Summary

Dugongs in Japan are in crisis. Although no more than ten have ever been seen in any single year, there are still no effective conservation measures. The relocation of the U.S. Futenma Air Station to the extensive seagrass beds along the east coast of Okinawa Island is a major threat to the only area in the archipelago where dugongs and feeding trails have been documented by Ministry of the Environment researchers.

With two major landfill projects in Awase and Henoko poised to destroy extensive seagrass beds, protected areas or sanctuaries are urgently needed to preserve healthy seagrass beds. Island-wide planning to prevent red soil (tuff loam) run-off and to promote chemical and wastewater treatment needs to begin soon.

Spearheaded by academic researchers and NGOs, symposia and workshops have been held in various places in Japan. On Okinawa Island, NGOs have been conducting campaigns to oppose the reclamation of the Awase tidal flat and the shallow water areas of Henoko.

There is an urgent need for laws regulating fishing gear in critical dugong habitats, and to arrange financial compensation to fishers for damage to fishing nets and loss of income associated with dugong rescues. Most important for the dugong's survival will be the understanding and cooperation of local people and fishers in planning and implementing dugong conservation. We also believe that grassroots conservation activity instigated by local people including fishers is needed most and would work more quickly and effectively than depending solely on the legal system. With the support of local people for the regulation of fishing gear, legal restrictions can be more effective.

9

Eastern African Dugongs

CATHARINE E. MUIR AND JEREMY J. KISZKA

The eastern coast of Africa marks the westernmost boundary of the dugongs' global range. They are known to occur in the waters off Somalia, Kenya, Tanzania, and Mozambique (map 9.1). Their range also extends farther east off the islands of the Seychelles, Comoros, Mayotte, and Madagascar[1]. In Mauritius and Rodrigues dugongs were historically present, and in some places abundant, but declined during the eighteenth century due to hunting. Dugongs are now extinct in Mauritius[2]. The Western Indian Ocean (WIO) region is an important feeding and calving ground for dugongs as well as other endangered marine species such as sea turtles[3].

The region has a coastal population of more than 30 million people, who are among the poorest in the world and whose livelihoods are largely dependent on marine and coastal resources such as inshore fisheries and mangroves[4]. The population is increasing at a rate of 5–6% per year and is expected to exceed 40 million by 2020. This rapid human expansion is having a significant negative impact on marine and coastal environments[5].

As in many areas of their range, dugongs here are severely depleted. Their future survival is threatened by incidental catch in fishing nets, habitat loss/degradation, fishing pressure, hunting, and pollution. Vessel strikes, acoustic pollution, and ecotourism pose lesser threats. Sharp population declines in recent decades have led to escalating concern about their future survival in a region where dugongs are considered to be critically endangered[6].

This chapter explores the issues that influence dugong conservation in eastern Africa and presents a suite of possible conservation strategies in a region of rapid development.

Dugong Status and Distribution

The critical status of dugongs in eastern Africa and the lack of knowledge concerning their abundance and ecology were highlighted by Marsh et al.[7], who called for immediate and effective conservation measures to ensure their future survival. This prompted an initiative to develop a regional WIO dugong conservation strategy[8]. As part of this study, in 2003, scientists from the seven countries in the region gathered data on dugong status, distribution, and threats, working mainly from historical data (literature reviews) and qualitative surveys (questionnaire surveys and opportunistic sightings). Since then, dugong studies and conservation programs have been set up in some countries, including Tanzania, Madagascar, the Comoros archipelago (Mayotte and Moheli), and Mozambique, to collect more data on dugong abundance, biology, and ecology as well as to raise awareness among local people.

These studies indicate that populations are very small, isolated from one another, and threatened by gillnets and habitat disturbance. The mortality levels and the discrete nature of these populations underscore their critical conservation status. Mitigating the threats poses a major challenge for conservation managers, particularly as there are extensive gaps in knowledge of dugong biology, movements, population dynamics, and feeding, mating, and calving habitats. The summaries that follow for each country reflect the results from both the regional assessment and these national initiatives.

Historical records and anecdotal reports indicate that dugongs were relatively abundant off the eastern African coast in the 1950s and 1960s, with herds ranging in size from 30 to over 500 individuals[9]. However, current information suggests that dugong populations have been declining sharply since the 1960s and 1970s in Kenya and Tanzania and more recently, since the late 1980s and early 1990s, in the Comoros, Mozambique, Madagascar, and Mayotte. In the Seychelles the historical status of dugongs is not clear. In southern Somalia dugongs are reported to occur around the Bajuni archipelago, but their current status is unknown[10] (map 9.1).

Kenya's dugong population has dropped precipitously since the 1960s when large groups of animals were re-

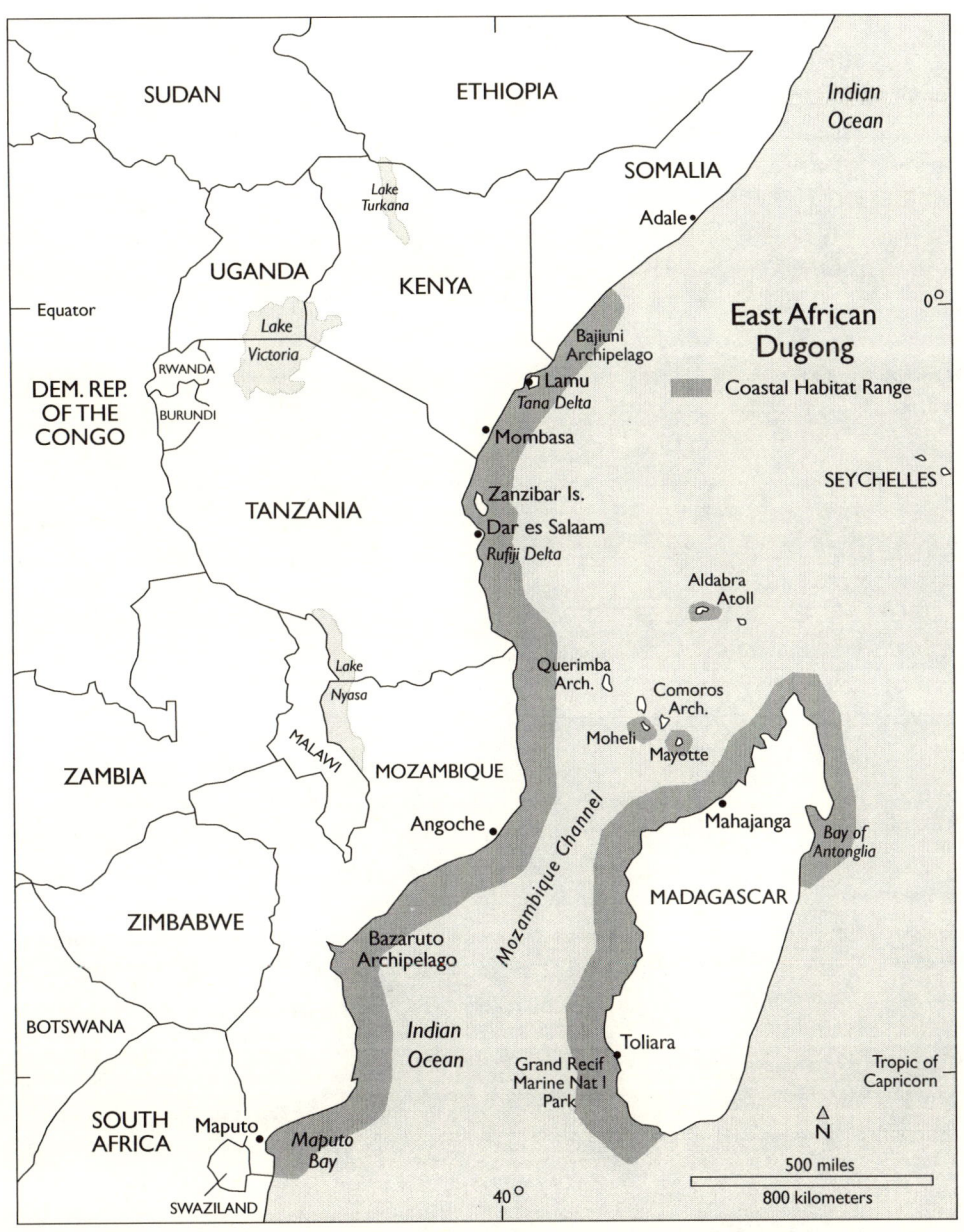

Map 9.1. East African dugong distribution. (Map by Ellen McElhinny.)

ported, the largest a group of 500 seen in 1967[11]. In 1994, ten dugongs were observed during an aerial survey[12]. During the last national aerial survey conducted in 1996, only nine dugongs were counted: six within the Lamu Archipelago in the north and three in the south near the border with Tanzania[13]. The most recent verified records are from the Tana Delta area, where two dugongs died in gillnets in September 2005[14]. Based on recent research on the possible movement patterns of dugongs[15], the extreme northerly and southerly populations may interact between southern Somalia and northern Tanzania.

In Tanzania the most important dugong habitat is off the Rufiji Delta east to Mafia Island and south to Kilwa, an area characterized by extensive shallow seagrass beds and sheltered bays and channels. Dugongs have also been reported to occur at Moa, near the border with Kenya. From January 2004 to December 2008, there have been confirmed reports of eleven animals caught in drift gillnets: ten off the Rufiji Delta[16] and one off the east coast of the Zanzibar island of Unguja[17]. The exact size and range of the population in Tanzania are unknown, but anecdotal reports and infrequent captures indicate that numbers are very small.

The largest remaining population in the WIO region is believed to be in the Bazaruto Archipelago in Mozambique, where recent aerial surveys conducted between April 2006 and December 2007 estimate 250 animals[18]. In 2005 four animals were caught in nets: three in a gillnet and one in a beach seine net[19]. Dugongs have also been sighted in the northern Quirimba Archipelago, but they may have disappeared from Maputo Bay in the south. At this writing, seagrass bed habitat surveys and bycatch monitoring are under way in Bazaruto Bay (map 9.1).

The current status of dugongs in Madagascar is unclear, but they are thought by local fishers to have declined over the past 10–15 years due to heavy exploitation for their meat. Interview surveys (116 sites visited and 195 respondents, mostly from the west coast and few from the northeast and southeast) indicate or suggest that potential dugong sites include the northeast, north, and northwest coasts[20].

Within the Seychelles Island group, dugongs have been reported as occurring only at Aldabra Atoll, where they have been observed by members of the Seychelles Island Foundation regularly since 2001. Prior to this, the last sightings were in the early twentieth century. The largest group, seen in 2005, consisted of four animals: an adult, two subadults, and a juvenile[21].

In the Comoros dugongs are no longer believed to occur off Grande Comore and Anjouan islands; however, low numbers still occur in the Moheli Marine Park, in the south of the island[22].

In Mayotte, which forms part of the Comoros Archipelago, dugongs are present in small numbers in the lagoons. The largest aggregation that has been observed consisted of three animals seen during surveys for marine turtle nesting assessment (Centre d'Etude et de Découverte des Tortues Marines, Réunion Island). Dedicated aerial surveys between July and December 2005 (21.4 hours of visual effort) resulted in four sightings: three of single animals and one of a cow-calf pair[23].

Legal Status

The dugong is protected throughout East Africa, from Mozambique to Kenya, including all islands of the western Indian Ocean. In addition, these countries have ratified a number of conventions, such as CITES. In Kenya, for example, all marine mammals are protected from hunting and harassment. The national law is galvanized by Islamic beliefs, prohibiting the consumption of certain food items[24]. In Tanzania dugongs have been protected since 1970 under the Fisheries Act no. 6. Under this law anyone found guilty of a first offence is liable to a fine of around US$300. In Mozambique the fine is as much as US$2,000, and fishing gear and licenses are confiscated.

In Mayotte, a French territory of the Comoros archipelago, the penalty is much higher for purchasing, harassing, or killing a dugong (six months imprisonment and a fine of US$13,000). As well as by direct legislation, dugongs are protected under more generic legislation, such as within marine protected areas (e.g., Bazaruto in Mozambique). However, at the regional scale, capacity to enforce national legislation is lacking due to limited resources and awareness.

Threats

Exploitation for Meat and Other Parts

In the past when dugongs were more abundant, they were often deliberately hunted for their meat (a prized source of protein), oil, and bones. Today, with populations so severely depleted, captures are mostly incidental, although the value of meat remains an incentive to kill a live dugong caught in a net[25].

Incidental Net Captures

Entanglement in legal inshore artisanal set- or drift-gillnets poses the greatest contemporary threat to dugongs in the region (table 9.1). Large mesh nets of 12–18 inches (*jarife*) are the most threatening fishing gear, although captures in smaller mesh nets (<3cm) have been observed in Mayotte, and there have been reports of captures in traditional fence traps[26] (figure 9.1). The most recent verified dugong captures in gillnets were off the Tana Delta in Kenya (two animals) and the east coast of Zanzibar, Tanzania, (one animal) in September 2005, and from Mafia Island in Tanzania in October 2005 and March 2009[27]. In all countries, the decline in dugong populations appears to be related to the introduction or increased use of nylon filament gillnets[28].

Population Pressure

The shallow, nearshore habitat requirements of dugongs and their slow rate of reproduction render them particularly vulnerable to human activities, including artisanal inshore fishing, habitat disturbance, and hunting, and to general pressures from a rapidly growing coastal population[29]. Even low rates of dugong mortality can have a devastating impact on the reproduction and future survival of the population[30].

Habitat Destruction and Disturbance

Seagrasses, the main diet of dugongs, are very sensitive to human influence, both directly (trawling, mining) and indirectly (inland and coastal clearing inducing erosion and sedimentation, and pollution by heavy met-

BOX 9.1

Dugong Uses and Myths
Catharine E. Muir and Jeremy J. Kiszka

While the primary use of dugongs is for meat, which is highly valued and has already compromised dugong survival in most countries in the region, there are other uses for dugong parts. Coastal Kenyan communities use the meat, oil, bones and tusks of dugongs as a cure for a variety of ailments including arthritis, labor pains, tonsillitis, and protection against evil spirits (N. T. Marshall 1998). In Tanzania, dugong oil is occasionally used as a cooking fat or waterproofing for boats (*sifa*) and as a cure for asthma, burns, skin ulcers, muscle pain, ear ache, and breast pain (Muir et al. 2003). The dense bones are used as a cure for skin rashes or rubbed on the legs of young children to help them walk. They are also believed by some to ward off evil spirits and are made into necklaces. According to legend, eating dugong meat perpetuates eternal life. In northern Mozambique, owing to the dugongs' similarity to humans, a prayer must be said at the mosque or church before a captured dugong can be butchered (Whittington et al. 1998).

The mermaid myth remains robust throughout the region. In southern Mozambique, for example, the local name for dugong translates as "human fish" and in Tanzania, local fishers often refer to dugongs as *binadamu* or persons. Other myths and beliefs tend to be localized. In Kenya dugongs play an important cultural role and in Lamu are referred to as the "queen of the sea." In Madagascar, sighting a dugong is interpreted as a gift or a good omen for fishing (Rafomanana and Rasolojantovo 2004).

---

als and organic pollutants)[31]. On the Zanzibar Island of Unguja in Tanzania, rapid and unplanned coastal tourist development is causing severe erosion, which in turn can have a serious impact on seagrass habitat. Nearshore licensed prawn trawling in Kenya, Tanzania, and Mozambique in areas where dugongs are most commonly seen is impacting seagrass beds and therefore their foraging areas. Seagrasses can be also destroyed by natural physical processes such as cyclones, which occur in Mozambique and Madagascar.

Political Apathy and Lack of Law Enforcement

Although dugongs are protected by national legislation in all the WIO countries, these laws are rarely enforced. The capacity of government departments responsible for enforcement of such laws is often lacking, with efforts hampered by limited personnel and lack of resources.

Regional Issues

There are a number of common regional issues that affect dugong conservation and that need to be addressed when developing conservation and management strategies. Table 9.1 summarizes these.

Political Will and Law Enforcement

There is often limited political will to invest finances and resources in species and habitat conservation or to enforce laws in developing countries. With the exception of the Seychelles and Mayotte, laws to protect dugongs are rarely enforced, despite appropriate legislation. The areas that need to be covered or regulated are vast and remote, infrastructure and training are inadequate, and there are insufficient people and equipment (boats, vehicles, radios, etc.) to implement regulations

Table 9.1. Summary of current threats to dugongs in the WIO region.

Threats	Fishing			Habitat loss/disturbance				Others	
Country	Gill/shark nets	Explosives	Other	Pollution	Coastal development	Boat traffic	Cyclones	Hunting	Lack of political will
Kenya	√		√	√	√			√	√
Tanzania	√	√	√	√	√	√		√	√
Mozambique	√		√	√	√		√	√	√
Madagascar	√		√	√	√		√		√
Seychelles	√								
Comoros	√				√			√	√
Mayotte	√			√	√	√		√	

Source: WWF EAME 2004.

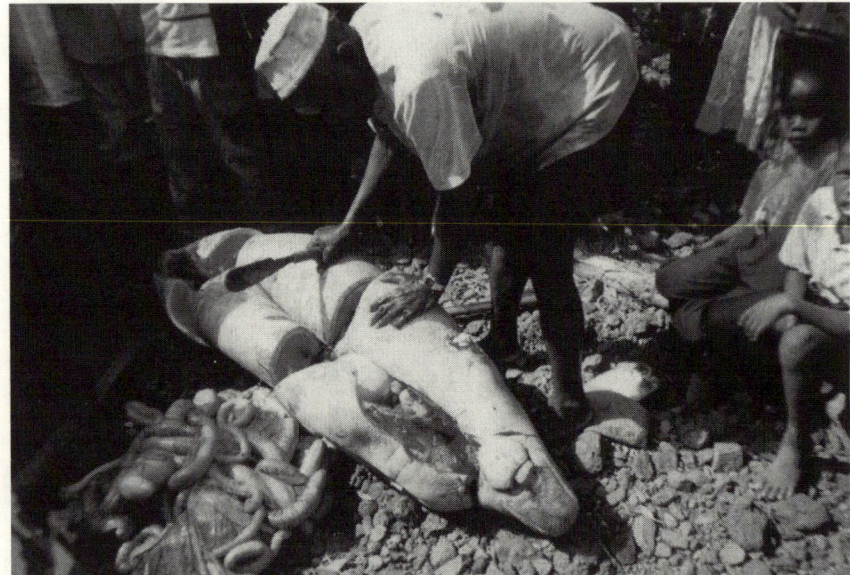

Figure 9.1. A dugong that was accidentally caught in a net being sold on the beach of Kani-Be, south of Mayotte. (Courtesy of Franck Charlier/ONCFS.)

and raise awareness. This situation is unlikely to change in the immediate future. Private sector and civil society involvement in dugong protection and monitoring is an effective way of resolving this issue. In Tanzania, for instance, a local NGO, Sea Sense, is employing local fishers to assist with community monitoring and educational activities[32]. In northern Mozambique tourist hotels and operators are employing local fishers as game scouts to support dugong conservation activities[33].

Lack of Environmental Concern

Many coastal communities in the region live a hand-to-mouth existence and are concerned primarily with daily survival. The regional dugong assessment exercise highlighted the fact that although local coastal communities are aware that hunting or killing dugongs is illegal, the animals are still killed for meat if caught in a net[34]. Local villagers are often highly suspicious of conservation intervention, especially when it may mean compromising their income (e.g., banning certain types of fishing gear) or restricting access (marine protected areas). Thus local sightings and captures often go unreported, which hinders research and conservation efforts. Without incentives, alternatives, and long-term commitment, it will be difficult to gain the confidence of local communities, and conservation is unlikely to be effective. Private sector employment of local villagers in conservation activities is one way of providing incentives. Others include leasing key seagrass habitats from local communities, which they could then patrol and manage, and establishing local dugong societies or trusts, which could become self-sustaining through membership fees and donations. The dugong could act as a flagship for marine conservation, including seagrass habitats.

Local Culture and Beliefs

Although coastal communities are aware that hunting or killing dugongs is illegal, there is a cultural demand for dugong parts. The meat is highly valued and a dugong is typically killed if caught in a net[35]. The use of other parts for medicinal purposes still occurs and cultural beliefs persist, but these are eroding as the dugong becomes less common and increasingly unfamiliar to younger generations (see text box 9.1).

Funding

Scientific research (such as aerial surveys, genetic studies, and tagging) and conservation efforts require considerable resources and long-term commitment. It may not be possible to implement effective research projects and management efforts in developing countries due to lack of funding or limited institutional capacity or continuity. Funding opportunities and successes would be greatly improved if countries in the region came together and pooled knowledge and expertise in areas like proposal writing. The development of regional projects may also considerably improve funding success. An example of such an initiative is a regional proposal currently being finalized, led by Réunion (IFREMER, via the South-Western Indian Ocean Fisheries Project or SWIOFP, funded by the World Bank), to study the movements of green turtles in the southwest Indian Ocean through satellite tagging.

Conservation Recommendations and Strategies

Existing Research and Conservation Activities

In Mozambique, aerial dugong surveys are carried out regularly in Bazaruto Bay, but additional surveys are needed in the Quirimba Archipelago and Maputo Bay. Gillnets have been banned in Bazaruto Bay. In Mayotte, regular aerial surveys were conducted between 2004 and 2007 to assess the distribution and abundance of dugongs and other marine mammals. The establishment of a marine park (covering most of the lagoon where there is seagrass) and stricter marine protected areas are planned. In Tanzania, an education campaign targeting gillnet fishers has been in effect since 2001, and aerial surveys in the Rufiji Delta area have been conducted in 2006 and 2008 by Sea Sense to assess dugong abundance and distribution[36]. In the Seychelles, regular aerial surveys in Aldabra, protected as a World Heritage Site, are being conducted to determine dugong site fidelity, movements, population size and spatio-temporal distribution[37].

Very little information is available from Madagascar. The western and northeastern coasts are probably inhabited by dugongs, but their status in the area has not been assessed despite the presence of large areas of seagrass habitat. This region may be highly significant as a potential dugong foraging area. As such, Madagascar should be prioritized for aerial and further questionnaire surveys in the near future.

Priorities for Dugong Research

In areas where no data exist, immediate questionnaire surveys are needed to help define potential dugong hotspots and assess the status of the species (especially related to bycatch and exploitation). Interviews can also help to underline key interactions between dugongs and human activities[38]. Second, if interviews reveal regular sightings, aerial surveys can then be conducted. Aerial surveys should be performed first in areas where dugong hotspots are known or suspected[39]. These surveys should be carried out often and regularly if a comprehensive picture of population trends, habitat, and distribution is to be obtained[40].

A realistic estimate of dugong mortality in gillnets and other fishing gear is needed to define population vulnerability. Experiments to investigate ways to reduce the threat from bycatch are also important; for example, reducing the soak time of the net and establishing marine protected areas where the use of certain nets is banned (such as in Bazaruto National Park, Mozambique, and in Mayotte).

Furthermore, raising awareness among coastal communities, especially fishers, should also be a priority. This will help improve the level of reporting of dugong captures and encourage better relations between local communities and research or conservation groups. In Tanzania, regular contact between NGOs and fishers has helped to quantify the impact of human activities on dugong populations[41].

Ecological studies include assessment of habitat distribution and status, feeding ecology, and habitat preference and use. Identifying seagrass distribution and species consumed by dugongs can help prioritize areas for conservation. The collection of samples from strandings or animals taken as bycatch will allow analysis of stomach content, seagrass species use, and possibly cause of death[42]. Currently only a few dugong specimens are available for biological and ecological investigation.

Research on the large, medium and fine-scale movement patterns of dugongs is needed to assess migration patterns and the degree of isolation between populations (in conjunction with genetic analyses). It is also critical to identify small-scale home range, habitat use, and preferences in sites where potential habitats, particularly seagrass beds, have already been surveyed[43].

Studies of habitat use and preferences can be done through dugong tagging. However, tagging may be risky, particularly with so few animals[44].

Using existing material in museums and biopsy surveys, genetic studies are needed to determine the genetic structure of dugong populations throughout the region and for comparison with populations elsewhere, such as Australia and the Gulf of Arabia. Such data will help determine levels of isolation and assess the mobility of individuals[45].

Priority Conservation Actions

It is clear that conservation actions—such as banning the use of threatening fishing gear in key seagrass areas, providing local fishers with alternative livelihoods, and raising public awareness about dugong conservation—should have the highest priority.

To develop effective national and regional dugong conservation and management strategies, several key steps are required. These include working with local communities and government to protect dugongs and develop conservation strategies that are appropriate, mutually beneficial, practical, and effective; raising awareness through education campaigns; improving capacity; and bringing relevant parties in the region together to develop a regional program and raise much-needed funds.

To protect the habitats where dugongs feed and breed, measures need to be put in place quickly by engaging with local communities, enforcing existing regulations, and banning threatening fishing gear. The most effective way will be to restrict or ban the use of gill and mesh nets in key dugong habitats. Other options include the establishment of marine protected areas or community-managed sanctuaries in key habitat areas where human activities such as trawling, gillnet use, and marine traffic have been identified[46]. Any management interventions should consider the needs and culture of local communities so that measures are fitting, mutually beneficial, practical, and effective.

Environmental awareness and concern are generally poor in the region. Conservation education, promotion of sustainable resource use, and provision of alternative livelihoods are critical. The use of radio as a medium for delivering messages about marine conservation and specifically dugong biology, threats, issues, and solutions is often highly effective in countries where illiteracy is high and other media are either unavailable or too expensive. Education efforts should target fishers, users of coastal areas, and school children.

Adopting the dugong as a flagship species for marine and coastal biodiversity conservation is recommended. In Mayotte children have played an important role in delivering dugong conservation messages to their families and to elders, and the dugong is regularly used as an educational symbol[47].

In countries with limited government capacity and resources, community monitors should be trained. Local villagers often have greater knowledge and cultural sensitivity and can play effective roles in raising awareness and obtaining local information. Training of relevant government authorities should also go hand in hand with capacity building at the village level. Regular communication with local communities will ensure more efficient feedback of information and understanding of conservation. In Tanzania members of the network of local fishers established by Sea Sense act as an interface between the NGO and local communities, and frequent contact is maintained to ensure strong working partnerships.

There are common issues and threats relating to dugong conservation and management, so many solutions will be similar throughout the region. A regional gathering of practitioners (scientists, conservationists, managers, etc.) is recommended to address these common themes and to find affordable, practical, and culturally sensitive ways to implement research and conservation strategies using expertise from across the region and from elsewhere in the dugongs' range.

Fund-raising success may also be more effective when international and/or regional funds are targeted through a regional initiative. Potential funding sources include the Western Indian Ocean Marine Science Association (WIOMSA) and SWIOFP. Moreover, some countries in the region that have greater financial support and resources (e.g., Mayotte is a colony of France) can help to mobilize other less affluent countries to develop regional projects and cooperation.

Summary

The dugong is a critically endangered species in eastern Africa and adjacent island states. Basic scientific knowledge remains sparse in most countries, and conservation measures are mostly inadequate due to limited funding, education, and political will.

Historical data indicate that dugongs occurred in the coastal waters throughout the region and were relatively common. Recent investigations show that dugongs have declined dramatically in recent decades, especially during the 1970s and 1980s. The reasons for this decline are still unclear, but deliberate killings, incidental catches in fishing nets, and habitat destruction are probably the most significant threats. Dugongs are still found in Mozambique, Tanzania, Kenya, the Comoros, Mayotte, the Seychelles, and Madagascar but in very low numbers, which may not be viable. However, observations of mother-calf pairs in certain areas gives reason for optimism.

Reducing mortality levels needs to be addressed immediately. The most effective short-term conservation measure will be reducing the threat from incidental net capture through restriction or banning of threatening fishing gear and the provision of alternative gear or livelihoods. In the medium to long term, education, training of local communities and relevant government bodies, and the establishment of community-managed dugong sanctuaries will also play a valuable role. Regional cooperation is imperative to coordinate efforts, target resources, and encourage the development of a more robust scientific approach. Further scientific investigations are needed to provide accurate data on the status, distribution, abundance, and ecology of the region's dugongs.

10

Dugongs in Arabia

ANTHONY PREEN, HIMANSU DAS, MOHAMMED AL-RUMAIDH,
AND AMANDA HODGSON

In the Arabian region dugongs occur in the Red Sea and the Arabian (Persian) Gulf (map 10.1). They are known locally by a variety of names: *bugarah al bahr* (cow of the sea: Bahrain, Qatar, and UAE); *arus al bahr* (bride of the sea: Gulf and central Red Sea coasts of Saudi Arabia, and Bahrain); *taweelah* (southern Red Sea coasts of Saudi Arabia and Yemen); *al jild* (skin or leather: at Wejh in Saudi Arabia and Hurgadhr in Egypt); and *naqat al bahr* (camel of the sea: northern Red Sea)[1].

Dugongs have long been utilized in this region. Documented harvesting of dugongs goes back at least 7,000 years[2]. However, the significance of dugongs in the diet and culture of the local people has lessened in recent decades, as the people became more affluent. Early literature suggested that the dugong populations in the

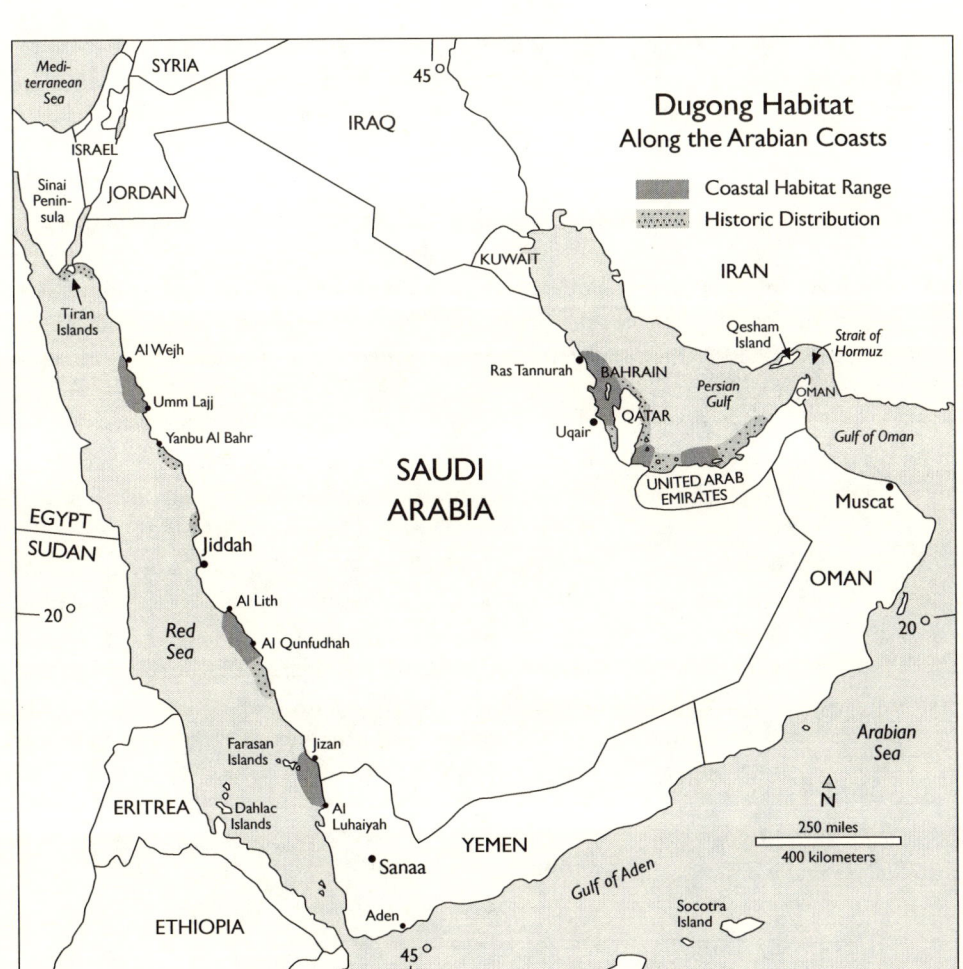

Map 10.1. Dugong habitat along the Arabian coasts. (Map by Ellen McElhinny.)

Arabian region had declined[3] and the species was seen as rare and endangered[4].

History of Research Efforts

Apart from Gohar's[5] treatise on dugong anatomy and diet, based on carcasses of dugongs caught along the northern Egyptian coast, little research focused on dugongs in the region until the 1980s, when it was stimulated by one of the world's worst oil spills—the Nowruz oil spill.

In 1983, during the Iran-Iraq war, a ship collision and military activity resulted in oil discharge from seven wells in the offshore Nowruz oilfield in the northern Arabian Gulf. Heavy crude oil discharged at an estimated rate of 15,000–20,000 barrels per day. The major spill continued from 24 January 1983 for eight months, until the first of three wells was capped[6]. By February 1984, 1.2 million barrels had been released, and although the flow had slowed, it had not stopped[7]. Among much other wildlife, 37 dugongs were found stranded along the coasts of Saudi Arabia and Bahrain.

Prior to this spill, in 1975 and 1976, a preliminary boat and helicopter survey of dugongs in the waters around Bahrain had noted dugongs on only three occasions, and the largest number seen was "about 50"[8]. After the carcasses were found following the Nowruz oil spill, the unpublished figure of "about 50" was, apparently, taken as the whole Gulf population[9]. The dugong population was believed to be at a critically low level[10]. Responding to worldwide concern, Saudi Arabia's Meteorology and Environmental Protection Administration (MEPA) initiated a Dugong Replenishment Project in 1985.

Ironically, the number of dugongs killed during the oil spill was much greater than suspected at the time—an estimated 150 following adjustment for areas not searched, the distribution of dugongs, and the dispersal pattern of the oil[11]—but the population of dugongs was also much greater than assumed.

On the assumption that dugongs in the Arabian Gulf were on the brink of extinction, the Dugong Replenishment Project initially envisaged repopulating the Gulf with dugongs caught in the Red Sea. The project was soon refined, however, to focus on assessing the dugong population through aerial survey, habitat assessment, and interview surveys. It was subsequently expanded to include the eastern coast of the Red Sea[12].

Between 1985 and 1988 the MEPA dugong study conducted three major strip-transect aerial surveys: two that covered virtually all the dugong habitat in the countries in the Arabian Gulf and a third, in 1987, that covered most of the dugong habitat of the eastern Red Sea. Many shoreline aerial surveys, beach surveys for skeletal material, and interview surveys were also undertaken.

The great strength of this project was the willingness of the Saudi Arabian government to fund survey work in other countries and the willingness of other countries to host this work. The MEPA dugong project surveyed the waters of Saudi Arabia, Bahrain, Qatar, the United Arab Emirates (UAE), and Yemen[13]. One of the great challenges was to conduct this work successfully during an active war.

Following the 1987 aerial survey there was a long hiatus in dugong research. Then in the late 1990s the United Arab Emirates' Heritage Club decided to produce an ecological atlas of the marine resources of Abu Dhabi Emirate (which contains the majority of the UAE waters and all the significant dugong habitat). This provided an opportunity, in the summer of 1999[14], to repeat the 1986 aerial survey of the southern Gulf and obtain trend information on the populations of dugongs and small cetaceans.

Around the same time, the Environmental Research and Wildlife Development Agency of the UAE (later renamed as Environment Agency–Abu Dhabi) started a dugong project consisting of four aerial surveys between 2000 and 2004 that aimed at refining the information on dugongs in Abu Dhabi Emirate to allow for more active management.

In 2005 the Bahrain Centre for Studies and Research (BCSR) started a dugong research program, modeled on the program of the Environment Agency–Abu Dhabi. Aerial surveys commenced in 2005 with the aim of documenting the year-round distribution of dugongs and their abundance. This program, which was to include interviews with fishers, identification of important feeding areas, educational activities, and the development of a management plan, was discontinued following the initial surveys. However, in 2006, GEOMATEC, a subsidiary of the BSCR, began the production of a Bahrain Marine Atlas, similar to that developed for Abu Dhabi. This prompted a formal dugong aerial survey, which repeated the MEPA survey within Bahraini international waters to update information on dugong distribution and to estimate abundance for Bahrain[15].

Abundance, Distribution, and Status

Red Sea

On the west coast the Red Sea is long, narrow, and deep. Much of the coast has a narrow fringing reef that quickly drops off. Although dugongs occur along the full length of the Red Sea, suitable habitat is patchy, often where dry creeks reach the shore, and usually covers relatively small areas. Larger areas of seagrass habitat occur around some of the archipelagos, such as the Farasan Islands, the Dhalak Islands, and the Wejh Bank[16] (map 10.1).

The strip-transect aerial survey of dugong habitat along the Saudi coastline (covering 22,371 km² of coastal waters along the eastern shore), conducted in summer 1987, provided a population estimate of 1,820 + SE 380 dugongs. Based on information from interviews with Yemeni fishers and the extent of relatively shallow waters suitable for seagrasses, the waters of Yemen—which could not be surveyed—are likely to support a further 200 dugongs[17]. The most important dugong habitats along the east coast of the Red Sea are around Sharm Munaibira south of Wejh and the Wejh Bank south to Umm Lajj; around Qishran Island and Al Lith and the surrounding area; and from Khawr al Ja'afirah north of Gizan to Luhaiyah in Yemen[18] (map 10.1).

There have been no follow-up surveys or other significant dugong research efforts in the Red Sea since 1987. The distribution of suitable dugong habitat on the African coast of the Red Sea is likely to be similar to that on the Arabian coast, due to the bilateral symmetry of the shorelines and bathymetry. A Red Sea population of some 4,000 dugongs, therefore, is possible. However, this estimate assumes similar levels of human-related mortality along each coast and separate east and west coast dugong populations. Both these assumptions are unlikely because (1) the human population of the African coast is much less affluent, and dugong hunting as well as incidental net captures are likely; and (2) the distance between east and west coasts is relatively small and well within the scale of movements documented for dugongs[19]. Therefore we are unable to draw conclusions on the present status of the dugong population(s) in the Red Sea.

Arabian Gulf

The Arabian Gulf is characterized by large areas of shallow water, which support large areas of seagrasses along the western and southern shores. The utilization of those seagrasses by dugongs appears to be limited by water temperature in winter. Hence, cold water restricts regular use of seagrass meadows in northern Saudi Arabia and Kuwait[20].

The core habitat for dugongs in the Arabian Gulf occurs in the western and southern Gulf and extends from Ras Tanura on the Saudi central coast through Bahrain and Qatar to about Ras Ghanadha, east of Abu Dhabi city in the UAE (map 10.1). Small numbers occur east of Ras Ghanadha to the Omani border, but the area of habitat is limited. Based on bathymetry and latitude, dugongs potentially occur around Qeshm Island, along the southern Iranian coast, although there is no published evidence of their presence.

The most important areas for dugongs are the Marawah Island area, between Abu al Abyad island, Jabal Dhannah, and Bu Tinah shoal in the UAE; Khawr Duwayhin, including Ghaghah Island in Saudi Arabia between Qatar and the UAE in the southern Gulf; between Bahrain and Qatar, south of Fasht Adam and north of the Hawar Islands; and between Saudi Arabia and Bahrain, south of the King Fahad Causeway and north of Uquair[21] (map 10.1).

The first strip-transect aerial survey, conducted during the winter of 1985–86 (table 10.1), covered all the waters of Bahrain and all the Gulf waters of Saudi Arabia out to a depth of about 20 m. Most of the dugongs seen were highly aggregated in the largest herd seen in modern times (figure 10.1). Such aggregation contradicts an assumption of the method used to estimate population abundance from such surveys[22], so the results of this survey were unsuitable for population estimation. Perhaps because the winter water temperature in this area is near the lower limit tolerated by dugongs[23], such winter aggregations may be due to the presence of relatively warm freshwater springs[24].

The summer survey of 1986 covered virtually all the dugong habitat in the Arabian Gulf and provided a population estimate of 5,840 (SE 903) dugongs (table 10.1). The Arabian Gulf, therefore, supports the largest known dugong population outside Australia[25].

The 1999 survey of the UAE replicated the UAE component of the larger 1986 Gulf survey. The population estimate for this area in 1986 was 3,047 (SE 704), while the estimate in 1999 was 2,691 (SE 608). There is no significant difference between these population estimates, indicating a stable population over a 13-year period[26].

The results of the surveys conducted in 2000–2004 (table 10.1) cannot be compared with the results of the 1999 survey (or the 1986 survey) as the 2000–2004 surveys covered different areas, flew different transects, and had data analyzed differently. The important finding from the latter surveys is that dugong numbers in the UAE remain fairly constant throughout the year.

A preliminary summer (June) survey conducted in Bahraini waters in 2005 observed few dugongs between the Bahrain main island and the Hawar Islands when the surface water temperature was 33°C. However, about 300

Figure 10.1. Part of an aggregation of 674 dugongs observed southeast of Bahrain during the 1985–86 aerial survey. (Courtesy of Anthony Preen.)

individuals were reported during a winter (November) survey of the same area, when the water temperature was 18°C. The systematic survey conducted in early October 2006 produced a population estimate for Bahraini international waters of 1,164 (SE 317)[27]. The highest density of dugongs occurred between Bahrain and the Hawar Islands, confirming the importance of the seagrass beds in this area. A large herd of dugongs was sighted north of Bahrain near the coast guard station, which suggests that this area may also represent important habitat. As the MEPA surveys and the recent survey covered different areas, they were not directly comparable; however, it appeared that there was no substantive change in dugong abundance between 1986 and 2006[28].

Impediments to Research

Much of the Arabian region, particularly the Gulf, is oil rich, and the resources are available for expensive work like strip-transect aerial surveys. This, however, does not mean the region is an easy place to work. Many characteristics can make it quite challenging.

War

War has been a defining feature of the Arabian Gulf for more than two decades. The history of war in the region, combined with ill-defined borders and the value of oil reserves, means the region is extremely security sensitive. Such sensitivity flows through to the difficulty of conducting field research. For example, during 1980s surveys, individual flights required simultaneous coordination and approval across several armed services in several countries; on one occasion the aerial survey aircraft was tentatively identified by a coast guard officer as an invading Iranian fighter and was at risk of being shot down by a missile; on another occasion, when the air survey helicopter lost radio contact with the air base when it landed to inspect a dead finless porpoise, it was suspected that the aircraft had been shot down, and an F16 fighter was scrambled.

Restrictions

Many areas are out-of-bounds due to military sensitivities or ownership by members of extended royal families. The 2006 survey in Bahrain, for example, missed

Table 10.1. Summary of strip-transect aerial dugong surveys conducted in the Arabian Gulf.

Year	Season	Country	Area covered (km^2)	Coverage %	Population estimate + Standard Error (SE)	Reference
1985–86	Winter	KSA, Bahrain	21,587	10.3	Aggregated[a]	Preen 1989, 2004
1986	Summer	KSA, Bahrain, Qatar, UAE	34,144	11.3	5,840 (903)	Preen 1989, 2004
1999	Summer	UAE	14,841	10.9	2,691 (608)	Preen 2004
2000	Summer	UAE	6,075	9.8	1,861 (411)	Das unpubl.
2001	Winter	UAE	6,697	10.1	2,185 (382)	Das unpubl.
2004	Winter	UAE	6,454	9.9	2,925 (410)	Das unpubl.
2004	Summer	UAE	6,454	9.9	2,291 (329)	Das unpubl.
2006	Autumn	Bahrain	3,810	10.6	1,164 (317)	Hodgson 2009

[a]The highly aggregated distribution of observed dugongs was unsuitable for the estimation of population size.
KSA = Kingdom of Saudi Arabia
UAE = United Arab Emirates

large sections of the coastline for these reasons[29]. Approval to conduct survey work over or near such areas can take considerable time to negotiate.

It is necessary to work through or in conjunction with military and/or security agencies during the planning and execution of fieldwork. As there are multiple layers of security services, it can be a slow process.

Political Boundaries

There are many countries in the area, which makes for many international boundaries. The 1980s aerial surveys in the Arabian Gulf abutted or crossed eight international borders. While the Arab states have recently resolved most of their contentious borders in the Arabian Gulf, the borders with Iran remain very sensitive and, in some areas, disputed or poorly defined.

As the ecological boundaries are unrelated to the political boundaries, the conduct of meaningful aerial surveys can be challenging. This applies particularly with a highly mobile and wide-ranging species such as the dugong.

Logistical Constraints

In the Red Sea the length and remoteness of much of the coastline imposes real logistical constraints on fieldwork. This applies especially to aerial surveys as transit times to and from fuel supplies can leave limited time to fly surveys.

The unexpected should be expected. As part of the aerial survey of the Red Sea coastline, some six months were spent negotiating a strip-transect aerial survey of Yemeni waters. While just about every contingency was covered, no one thought to check the availability of Avgas, light aviation fuel. Only after the survey team had flown their light aircraft from southern Saudi Arabia into Saana, the capital of Yemen, was it discovered there was no Avgas in Yemen. There was insufficient fuel even to return to Saudi Arabia! The transect survey had to be abandoned and replaced by an interview survey.

Habitat Status

Arabian Gulf

Only three species of seagrass can tolerate the vagaries of the Gulf's harsh marine environment: *Halodule uninervis*, *Halophila stipulacea*, and *Halophila ovalis*. These species not only survive, they thrive; hence while the Gulf seagrass meadows may not be diverse, they are productive. These seagrasses form vast meadows to a depth of about 15 m[30]. As the Gulf is very shallow, there are large areas of seagrass habitat, the most extensive of which probably occur in Bahraini and Qatari waters between the Fasht al Adhm and the Hawar Islands[31] and in the greater Marawah Island area in the UAE[32].

Much seagrass habitat, especially in the southern Gulf, coincides with areas used for human activities related to the oil industry and shipping, and some areas have been highly modified by dredging, reclamation, pipelines, oilfields, and ports.

Red Sea

Because much of the dugong habitat along the Red Sea coastline is patchily distributed (wadi mouths, or mouths of seasonally dry riverbeds, separated by extensive areas of fringing coral reef), individual patch areas are vulnerable even to relatively small local coastal developments.

The Red Sea hinterland has less oil reserves than the

Gulf coast, but oil is exported from Yemen and from pipelines terminating at Yanbu along the northern Saudi coast. The Red Sea is also a major sea route for tankers traveling from the Gulf to Europe, so oil pollution remains a threat.

Threats

Incidental and Deliberate Capture in Mesh Nets

This is the most significant chronic threat. In the UAE, net mortality was estimated to be unsustainable on the basis of the 1986 survey results and estimates of mortality levels derived from interview surveys[33]. In 1998, 12 dugong carcasses were found tied under mangroves on Marawah Island, near an area where large-meshed gillnets were set[34]. These carcasses were in the same area where the remains of 28 dugongs were reported in 1995. All had apparently died in nets[35]. Gillnets are now banned in the marine protected area that has subsequently been established around Marawah Island. However, an expansion of the shark fishery in the Gulf could result in an unsustainable bycatch of dugongs leading to a population decline. Based on the 1999 population estimate, the sustainable annual take of dugongs in the UAE is 54–107 (2–4%)[36].

In Bahrain most gillnetters use the drift technique, which is known to result in high bycatch rates[37]. This technique is prohibited, but operations are run at night, which may further increase bycatch, as dugongs have no opportunity to see the nets. The relatively small mesh size of the nets used may limit the bycatch of dugongs, but as no bycatch records are kept, there is no way of knowing the impacts of gillnetting in Bahrain. Based on the population estimate from the 2006 Bahraini survey and assuming an annual population growth rate of 3%, the maximum sustainable annual take is 14 dugongs[38].

Net mortality is also a threat in the Gizan area of the Red Sea[39], and a strip-transect aerial survey conducted in 1991 recorded fewer dugongs than seen during the 1987 survey, suggesting a local population decline[40]. However, the area surveyed may not have been large enough, relative to the scale of dugong movements, to draw reliable conclusions.

Habitat Loss

There are plans to construct a massive bridge/causeway linking Bahrain and Qatar that will pass along the edge of one of the premier dugong habitats. The extent to which this will affect current flows and salinity gradients and the extent to which these changes, plus increased turbidity, will impact the seagrasses and dugongs remain unknown.

Considerable areas of seagrass have been dredged or reclaimed along the Gulf coastline, and such activity continues apace. In Bahrain, for example, a total coastal area of 88.5 km^2 has been reclaimed, which represents 13% of the kingdom's total land area[41]. Luckily the very shallow, nearshore seagrass beds are not as important to dugongs as the more extensive beds that usually occur farther from the shoreline; however, the turbidity produced by dredging can impact seagrasses over a much greater area than that directly impacted.

Trawling is common in dugong habitat in the Gizan area, along Yemen's Red Sea coast, and in Bahrain[42], and is likely to cause disturbance to seagrass beds. Dugongs have been caught in trawl nets near Gizan[43].

Pollution

The Arabian Gulf is the most oil-polluted marine area in the world[44]. Oil extraction, treatment, and transfer are features of much dugong habitat in the Gulf. Dugongs here are particularly vulnerable to pollution events as much of their habitat is close to offshore oilfields. While dugongs and seagrasses have shown themselves to be resilient to chronic, low-level oil pollution, the likelihood of a catastrophic spill is always present.

At least three die-offs of dugongs have occurred in the western Gulf. One was related to an oil spill, but the other two may have been the result of an epidemic caused by a morbillivirus crossing from dolphins to dugongs[45]. Morbilliviruses have caused mass moralities of dolphins[46], and the possibility exists that such an event could occur with the dugongs in the Gulf.

Climate Change

The Arabian Gulf is shallow and landlocked by desert. Salinity is in the range of 40–70 $^0/_{00}$, summer water temperatures reach as high as 36°C, and the annual range of water temperatures is as much as 24°C[47]. The Gulf is a harsh environment, and many species are at or near their physiological limits. For instance, of the more than 50 species of seagrass worldwide, only three can survive in the Gulf. Because of the extreme nature of the Gulf's environments, all habitats here are vulnerable in a warming world.

Legal Status

In the UAE it became illegal in 1999 to harvest or harass dugongs, dolphins, and turtles (Federal Law no. 23), although it was widely understood that the species was protected much earlier than that (see later discussion). In the Kingdom of Bahrain dugong hunting has been banned since January 2003 (Ministerial Decree no. 4 for 2003).

Protected Area Status

A series of potential marine protected areas (MPAs), for the conservation of dugongs and associated wildlife in the Red Sea and Arabian Gulf, were identified and nominated as part of the MEPA dugong study[48]. One of the two most important locations in the Arabian Gulf is around Marawah Island in the UAE. Following the second (1999) aerial survey of the UAE, which reconfirmed the importance of the Marawah Island area for dugongs, seagrasses, and turtles, a further recommendation was made for an MPA[49]. The aerial survey conducted by the Environment Agency–Abu Dhabi in 2000 also confirmed the importance of this area for dugongs.

In 2001 the Marawah Marine Protected Area was declared, covering 4,255 km^2 of core dugong habitat in the UAE. The law authorizing this protected area (No. 18) not only prohibits the capture, harassment, or killing of wildlife but also prohibits damage to any of the habitats. This actively and professionally managed MPA will make a great contribution to the conservation of dugongs and associated species in the southern Gulf.

In the Red Sea, the Farasan Protected Area (which includes the dugong habitat along the Gizan coast) was declared in 1996, although the extent to which threatening fishing practices (large mesh nets and trawling) are restricted along the Gizan coast is unknown.

History and Attitudes

Attitudes to dugongs are changing in the region, with the United Arab Emirates leading the change. During a long shared history in this part of the Gulf, the function of humans in the relationship between people and dugongs has evolved from exploiter to proud protector. Around 4,000 years ago dugongs were a staple in the diet of the people living at Umm al-Nar, near Abu Dhabi Island[50]. On Akab Island, Umm al-Qaiwain, young dugongs were hunted seasonally 6,000 years ago[51], and there is evidence of exploitation of dugongs on Dalma Island, Abu Dhabi Emirate, around 7,000 years ago[52].

In 1986 fishers and fish sellers were interviewed at Abu Dhabi fish souk (market) to determine the extent and nature of dugong exploitation[53]. In previous decades, demand for dugong meat was high and animals were captured by herding them into shallow water, where they were clubbed to death. By 1986, however, active hunting of dugongs had ceased (at least around Mirfa, on the mainland southeast of Marawah Island, and around Abu Dhabi Island), and the only dugongs captured were those accidentally entangled in fishing nets[54]. According to the fishers interviewed at Abu Dhabi, active dugong hunting ended some time after H.H. Sheikh Zayed bin Sultan Al Nahyan had acceded as ruler of Abu Dhabi Emirate in the late 1960s. He is reputed to have said that fishers should not deliberately hunt dugongs, and only those dugongs accidentally caught in nets should be sold.

However, demand for dugong meat ensured a continued supply. In the mid-1980s between 70 and 100 dugongs were sold annually in the Abu Dhabi fish souk[55]. This was an increase over the estimated dugong sales at the same souk a decade earlier. In 1976, two members of the Emirates Natural History Group obtained separate estimates of 50–60 and 60–70 dugongs sold each year[56]. The numbers of dugongs being sold at Abu Dhabi in the mid-1980s, however, did not represent the total number being caught. Apparently because of Sheik Zayed's statement, non-national fishers, who made up a significant proportion of the fishing community if not a majority, tended not to sell dugongs they caught in their nets in order to avoid any criticism. Of the dugongs that were retained to be sold, an unknown proportion passed through the Abu Dhabi souk. In 1986, the fishers from Mirfa claimed that the one to two dugongs they caught each year were consumed locally[57]. On 14 February 1977 at least eight dugongs were landed at Butain, near Abu Dhabi city, and much of the meat was sold directly to local people, rather than going through the Abu Dhabi fish souk[58].

In the mid-1980s live dugongs were sometimes brought into the Abu Dhabi fish souk. During butchery, it was said that none of the gut contents must spill onto the meat, or it would be spoilt. The tail meat was the most favored, and the muscle, fat, and connective tissue of the facial disc was also highly desired. The flukes, flippers, viscera, and remaining head were discarded. The hide, which is very thick, was once used to make sandals[59]. The meat was eaten fresh or salted, and some parts of the dugong were used medicinally[60].

An average adult dugong carcass yields 100–150 kg of usable meat[61], which sold for much less than the cost of lamb and beef, so dugong was cheap red meat. Some restaurants in Bahrain bought dugong meat to use as an inexpensive source of "beef"[62].

Education and Levels of Environmental Awareness

Environmental awareness has been emerging among the general public of the Arabian region over the past decade. Awareness is currently greater among governments than among the people; there is thus considerable potential for promotion of environmental issues.

Today dugongs are considered to be an important part of an extensive maritime heritage in both the UAE and Bahrain. Production of education and awareness materials to foster an appreciation of dugongs is an objective of the UAE dugong program, but to date there are no community-based conservation groups or NGOs in the region.

Research Needs

In the Arabian Gulf there is a need for information on the movements of dugongs. Dugongs in the western Gulf share, and almost certainly move between, the waters of Saudi Arabia, Bahrain, and Qatar; some may even move between these countries on a daily basis. Management requires an understanding of these movements and the extent to which all countries must protect the same dugongs.

In the Red Sea there is a need for more up to date information, preferably including a repeat of the previous transect aerial surveys and interview surveys. Very little is known of the African coast.

Suggestions for Conservation

Seven candidate MPAs for the Arabian Gulf and four for the eastern Red Sea were identified in 1989[63]. Of the 11 areas, three were ranked as crucial in the Arabian Gulf and three in eastern Red Sea. Since 1989 two of these recommended areas have been established as effective MPAs: Marawah MPA in the Gulf and Farasan Protected Area in the Red Sea. The other "crucial" areas are the Ghaghah Island areas (mostly Saudi Arabian waters between Qatar and the UAE in the Gulf); the Wejh Bank area (north Saudi coast in the Red Sea); and the Al Lith area (south-central Saudi coast in the Red Sea). The remaining protected area recommendations represent the most productive conservation actions that could be undertaken.

In the absence of MPAs there is a need for alternative fishing methods for fishers who use large-meshed gillnets to catch large and pelagic species of fish. These nets, and the cumulative effects of habitat loss, are perhaps the greatest threat to dugongs in the Gulf and Red Sea and indeed throughout the species' range.

Conclusion

The Arabian Gulf is one of the few places in the world where the dugong population may be secure. This is a surprising finding, given the history of environmental disturbance in that area over the past decades. The apparent stability of the dugong population may reflect their resilience if active hunting can be eliminated. The Arabian Gulf now has a good base of data from which to monitor and manage its dugongs. Some countries have started ongoing research programs and have instituted or are planning to establish quality marine protected areas in which dugongs feature prominently.

The prognosis for the Red Sea is less optimistic. While there are some good base data for the Arabian coast, this information is now dated. On the African coast, where the impacts of humans, particularly hunting, are likely to be greatest, there is virtually no information and the need for data is urgent. Interview surveys and shoreline surveys would be the most cost-effective way of collecting such information.

11

Dugongs in Australia and the Pacific

KIRSTIN DOBBS, IVAN LAWLER, AND DONNA KWAN

In the Pacific region, dugongs occur in the coastal waters of Australia, New Caledonia, Palau, Papua New Guinea, the Solomon Islands, and Vanuatu, with occasional sightings in Guam and Yap[1] (map 11.1). This region presents a diverse array of cultures, social and government systems, conservation and threat abatement approaches, and biological habitats in relation to dugong distribution, use, and management. For the most part, dugong populations throughout the Pacific region are relict populations, and most are declining. The only locations with significant populations are northern Australia (from Shark Bay to Moreton Bay) and southern Papua New Guinea, particularly Torres Strait, where the largest remaining population of dugongs in the world is found.

The reasons dugongs have such a high profile in the region are varied: their value as a subsistence food; their importance in the maintenance of cultural protocols and activities; their iconic and intrinsic value to human populations; and their status as threatened or endangered species. Perhaps less well known, and likely very important, is their role in structuring the seagrass ecosystem[2].

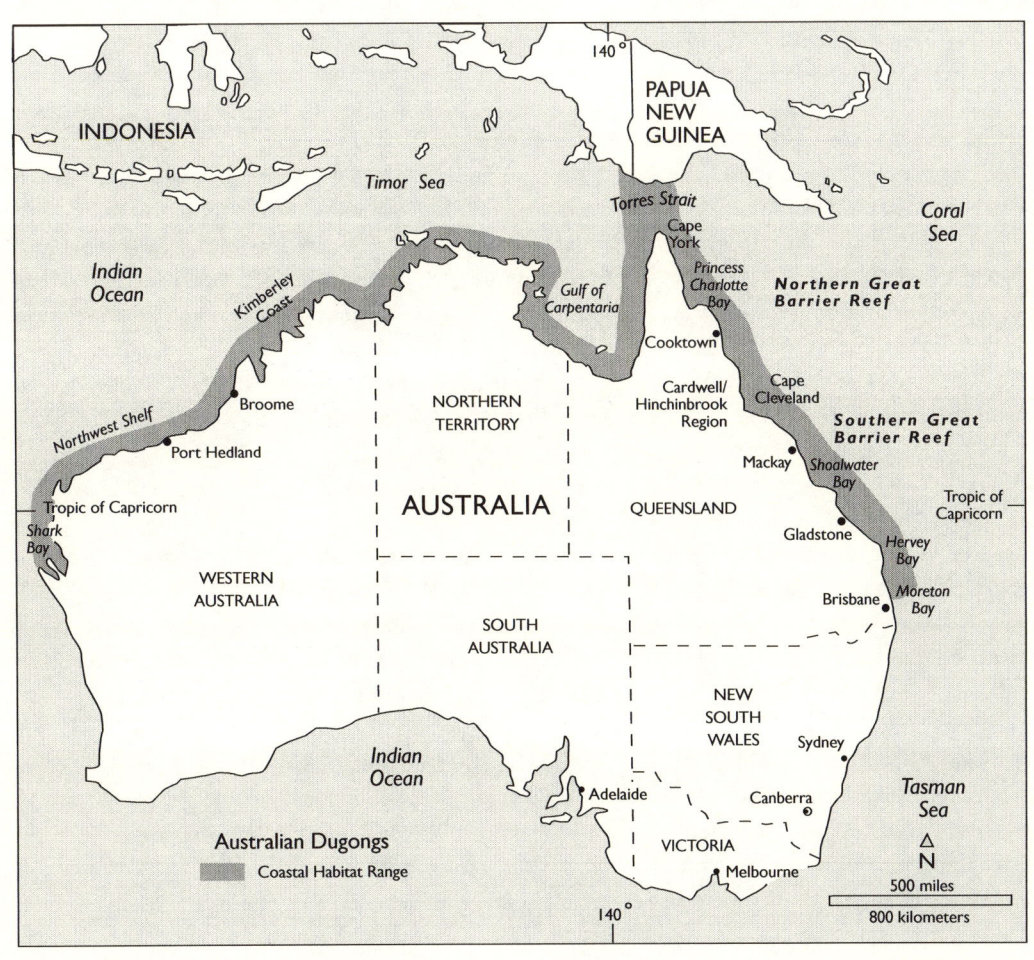

Map 11.1. Australian dugong habitat range. (Map by Ellen McElhinny.)

Cultural Significance

Dugongs are of great cultural importance to Indigenous communities and are an essential element of the people's maritime culture, featuring prominently in stories and legends. In Papua New Guinea many myths and legends tell of the origin of dugong or of the techniques and rituals used in hunting[3]. Dugongs also feature in many rituals meant to ensure hunting success, and specific parts of dugongs are believed to possess magic properties. Many Indigenous people in Papua New Guinea and northern Australia have totemic associations with dugongs. Some individual Aboriginal and Torres Strait Islander people associate their personal identity with their role as dugong hunters.

Dugongs are hunted throughout the region, both as a subsistence food source and for rituals such as weddings, funerals, and feasts. A dugong yields on average 115 kg of meat and fat and 17 liters of oil—35% of its body weight. In the islands of Torres Strait large quantities of dugong meat (estimates of up to 300 mg/person/day) are still consumed by local communities[4]. Elsewhere, where dugong populations are small, hunting is largely prohibited, and only occasional animals are taken either illegally or as incidental takes[5]. In some Pacific countries and Australia, customary law and cultural practices determine when animals can be caught and who can catch and butcher them. For example, in the Manus Province of Papua New Guinea (PNG), certain people, particularly women, are forbidden to hunt or eat dugong[6].

Material expression of the cultural and spiritual significance of the dugong is found in the paintings, prints, artifacts, and ceramics of many contemporary Indigenous artists. In Australia great importance is placed on the social sharing of the meat with members of the family. In remote coastal areas throughout the region, including Australia, dugongs have a higher social value because they provide food to communities where a nourishing diet is often expensive. In addition, marine food resources strengthen culture and demonstrate a connection with tradition and the sea.

Many Indigenous people have extensive knowledge about the biology and behavior of dugongs. Knowledge of the best tidal or weather conditions is vital for a successful hunt. In most hunting communities in Torres Strait, a good dugong hunter is highly regarded[7]; nonetheless, community elders are concerned that younger hunters seldom receive intensive training and lack hunting skills and the ability to distinguish different types of dugongs (e.g., pregnant from nonpregnant females). However, Indigenous people are keen to combine their spiritual beliefs and extensive knowledge to manage dugongs and other marine resources.

In most Pacific countries (Australia, Palau, Vanuatu, Solomon Islands, PNG), dugongs are protected by legislation and/or customary lore and practices. Such is the importance of dugongs that many Indigenous people have an inherent sense of responsibility toward ensuring that their cultural associations with dugongs are maintained. Increasingly, there is recognition that the sustainability of cultural associations is inextricably linked to the ecological sustainability of the dugong. In Torres Strait, where the large population of dugongs has enabled the persistence of one of the world's oldest maritime hunting societies[8], recent evidence of overharvesting[9] has reignited concerns for the continuity of this lifestyle.

In PNG the sale of dugong meat was banned in 1984, but the ban is not enforced. There are still reports of dugong meat being sold in the Daru market[10], and concern is widespread among the communities, researchers, and governments responsible for the Torres Strait region that the subsistence harvest in the Western Province of PNG is unsustainable. Unfortunately, a progressive, community-based management program that established the Maza Wildlife Management Area and a comprehensive catch and biological monitoring program[11] in the Western Province of PNG (especially Daru) has lapsed.

In Australia, coastal Indigenous groups have developed a variety of initiatives to continue or regain their involvement in dugong conservation, in ways that give contemporary expression to their inherited rights and obligations to their traditionally owned sea country estates[12]. Traditional Owners, as recognized under the Australian government's Native Title Act 1993, are asserting their rights over shared resources such as dugongs. Some initiatives have included voluntary agreements by groups to manage dugong hunting or even suspend it altogether.

Only relatively recently have Indigenous people in Australia had the opportunity to work with governments, wildlife managers, and scientists to develop cooperative frameworks of shared expertise and decision making, which also incorporates their cultural, social, and political needs. These initiatives, which increasingly involve partnerships with government agencies and research institutions, give local people greater authority and responsibility and hence a sense of ownership and the potential for greater commitment and compliance. A significant achievement has been the establishment of the North Australian Indigenous Land and Sea Management Alliance (NAILSMA), which provides a strategic framework for Indigenous land, sea, and natural resource management across northern Australia, from the Kimberley region to Cape York Peninsula. In 2005 NAILSMA received funding from the Australian government to develop and implement community-based dugong (and marine turtle)[13] management projects.

The Australian government has also signaled a new commitment to work in partnership with Indigenous people to ensure a sustainable harvest of dugongs. The National Partnership Approach for the sustainable harvest of dugongs and marine turtles, established in 2006, brings together key government agencies (federal, state, territory) and Indigenous people to provide advice and expertise directly to ministers about priorities and strategies. Such advice may include policy development or highlighting needs, such as building capacity, funding, or filling information gaps.

Concurrent with these initiatives, Indigenous people are calling for active involvement in all phases of management, monitoring, and research, including priority setting and the development and implementation of conservation measures[14]. They are keen to combine their traditional knowledge with scientific information in ways that address their cultural, economic, and social interests in dugong conservation. Many Indigenous groups have developed a cooperative, strategic approach. Some examples include Land and Sea Management units set up by the Kimberley Land Council and Torres Strait Regional Authority and the Saltwater Ranger Unit set up by the Girringun Aboriginal Corporation based in Cardwell, Queensland.

There is also increasing recognition among governments and research groups of the benefits of engaging Indigenous people in the collection of data. The collective experience of researchers is showing that results are more likely to be accepted if Indigenous people are themselves involved in the collection of the data[15].

Dugongs have an iconic status in the Pacific region and Australia, and the reasons for this are as varied as the reasons people take a fancy to any animal. The fact that the dugong is the only living species in the Family Dugongidae means some people believe they are a vital component of the world's biodiversity, and hence all steps should be taken to ensure their continued existence. Some communities feel privileged that the waters adjacent to their townships host this unique creature. At least three coastal townships in Queensland have erected statues of dugongs along public foreshores, raising awareness about the species and its role in the ecosystem.

Legal Protection

Dugongs are afforded legal protection by most countries in the region, and government agencies often have obligations to protect dugongs or their essential habitats or both. Within Australia, dugongs are accorded a high conservation priority because they are protected under various national and state/territory legislation. The national conservation legislation, the Environment Protection and Biodiversity Conservation Act 1999, puts into effect several international agreements and conventions to which Australia is signatory. They include the Convention for the Protection of the World Cultural and Natural Heritage (World Heritage Convention), the Convention on the Conservation of Migratory Species of Wild Animals (Bonn Convention, CMS), and the Convention on the International Trade of Endangered Species of Wild Flora and Fauna (CITES).

Dugongs are protected because they are: (1) one of the World Heritage values of the Great Barrier Reef and Shark Bay World Heritage Areas; (2) listed under Appendix II of the Bonn Convention and hence considered a "listed migratory species"; and (3) listed under Appendix I of CITES, which means the export of dugongs or dugong products requires a permit under the legislation. National and state/territory legislation also prohibits the sale of dugongs or dugong products.

The Environment Protection and Biodiversity Conservation Act 1999 also establishes an environmental impact management regime whereby actions that are likely to have a significant impact on a matter of National Environmental Significance (NES) are subject to a rigorous assessment and approval process. Matters of NES include, *inter alia*, World Heritage properties and listed migratory species. Therefore actions that may affect dugongs receive greater scrutiny and environmental assessment. Criteria developed to assist with assessments of impacts on the matters of NES (in this case for migratory species) include a determination of whether an action does, will, or is likely to:

- substantially modify (including *inter alia* by fragmenting, altering nutrient cycles or hydrological cycles), destroy, or isolate an area of important habitat;
- result in harmful invasive species becoming established in an area of important habitat; or
- seriously disrupt the life cycle (breeding, feeding, migration, or resting behavior) of an ecologically significant proportion of the population.

Where a country has various levels of government (e.g., national, provincial, local), an understanding of the legal regimes that are in effect for dugong protection can further conservation efforts. In Australia, state and Northern Territory jurisdiction extends seaward for three nautical miles until national legislation comes into effect. Dugongs feeding in intertidal waters in Queensland may be under state jurisdiction at high tide, while at low tide they may be under Commonwealth jurisdiction, highlighting the need for complementary marine protected area planning activities.

Research

The substantial research efforts in Australia have generally concentrated in Queensland and the Torres Strait (and Shark Bay, Western Australia, which is outside the Pacific focus of this chapter). This is due to a combination of factors: a nearby research university, the high public profile of dugongs as a World Heritage value of the Great Barrier Reef, the cultural importance and abundance of the species in Torres Strait, and the accessibility of dugongs along a predominantly urban/settled coast. Recent data on large-scale movements, and results of studies done in other locations, suggest that application of Australian research insights, with caution, is valid in other parts of the dugong's range. Below we identify general key issues that inform dugong conservation management.

Dugong Distribution and Abundance

Perhaps the most important information for conserving any species is simply to know where individuals are and how many are there. Given the wide distribution of dugongs, their shy nature, and low density across much of their range, aerial surveys have proven the only viable means to assess populations, particularly as we increasingly recognize large-scale movements by individuals[16,17].

After involvement in early aerial surveys with George Heinsohn[18], Helene Marsh set about developing a more rigorous method. With David Sinclair, she developed methods to estimate, and thus adjust for, perception bias (where dugongs are available to be seen but are missed by the observer) and availability bias (where dugongs are below the water surface and, because of water/weather conditions, unable to be seen when the aircraft passes over)[19]. Population estimates could be calculated in a way that took into account both spatial and temporal comparisons and important areas identified. The technique has been applied widely throughout much of Australia's coastline[20].

Despite the improvement, there has always been some concern about whether aerial surveys properly accounted for the proportion of unseen dugongs underwater. In recent years considerable effort has gone into the development of a more rigorous method. This involves modeling the diving behavior of dugongs[21] and their visibility under different conditions to determine the time for which dugongs were available to observers. These were combined to provide the first absolute estimates of dugong populations; fortuitously, these estimates were in close agreement with previous estimates using the earlier method[22].

Estimating absolute numbers is of fundamental importance to dugong conservation. Monitoring programs assume that trends, particularly declines, will be detected and that will stimulate management action(s). However, the statistical power to detect such declines for small and/or widely dispersed populations is low[23]. For such populations, even intense monitoring will fail to detect a decline until the population is imperiled, if the decline is detected at all. In recognition of this, a technique known as potential biological removal (PBR) is increasingly being adopted[24]. Marsh et al.[25] advocate the adoption of the PBR approach[26] as it allows rapid response to current conditions and is less constrained by the statistical limitations and time delays inherent in monitoring programs.

The PBR technique aims to detect the circumstances that lead to a decline before it occurs. It assumes that knowledge of the population size and its potential to increase (via fecundity) will allow for an estimate of sustainable mortality levels. As it is predicated on knowing a starting population size, an absolute (rather than relative) estimate is crucial. Already such analysis has shown that hunting levels in Torres Strait are unsustainable[27].

A word of caution should be given here. While the standardized techniques have been valuable for population estimation in Australia, they may not be applicable elsewhere. In many areas, population density may be too low to estimate size effectively. In such areas, the additional cost and effort of planning and executing such a survey may be unwarranted, and other survey methods may be more appropriate[28].

Dugong Movements

When researchers began to assess dugong distribution and abundance, there tended to be an implicit assumption that the dugongs of a particular area, such as a bay, stayed in that bay. This assumption was also reflected in management approaches that were organized at a regional office level, each office being responsible for "their" dugongs or "their" bay.

We now know that large-scale movements between widely separated habitat areas are a common feature of dugong biology. In fact, the frequency and scale of movements is such that questions of how to define a dugong "population" and at what scale to implement management actions are some of the most important questions in dugong conservation. Such questions also raise substantial logistical obstacles: the 2005 aerial surveys in Queensland, for example, employed three aircraft and surveyed areas between Torres Strait and Moreton Bay, a distance of more than 3,000 km[29].

Evidence for large-scale movements has come from three separate research approaches: (1) aerial surveys, (2) satellite tracking, and (3) genetic analysis.

Early aerial surveys of the east coast of Queensland and Torres Strait in the mid- to late 1980s established population baselines. It was agreed then that surveys would be repeated at approximately five-year intervals, as that interval reflected a trade-off between the substantial cost and logistical effort required for such surveys and the need for more frequent surveys to increase statistical power to detect population trends[30].

The dugong population of the Great Barrier Reef south of Cooktown was estimated in 1987 at 3,479 (± 459)[31]. When resurveyed in 1992, it had declined by nearly 50% to 1,875 (±292), and a similar estimate of 1,682 (±236) was obtained in 1994[32]. This substantial population decline raised serious concerns about the sustainability of the population in that region and led to a range of management actions.

When the region was resurveyed in 1999 the population estimate was 3,993 (+ 641), similar to 1987 levels[33]. Dugong populations cannot increase that quickly by breeding alone, so the only reasonable interpretation was that dugongs had moved en masse back into the region south of Cooktown, presumably from the north[34] (map 11.1). Unfortunately, the remote area north of Cooktown had not been surveyed concurrently in 1999, so the hypothesis of movement could not be demonstrated. Evidence of such large-scale shifts has now accumulated from repeat surveys of Shark Bay (Western Australia)[35], Torres Strait[36], and Hervey Bay and Moreton Bay[37].

Satellite tracking has enabled the movements of individual dugongs to be recorded. While the numbers tracked will always be limited by cost and logistics, large-scale movements have been demonstrated to be of sufficient scale and frequency to support the interpretation of aerial survey results.

BOX 11.1

Response to Dugong Declines

Management actions have been undertaken in Australian waters in response to declines in the dugong population along the urban coast of Queensland as reported in the mid-1990s from aerial surveys. Key factors that were identified as leading to the decline of dugongs in this region included incidental entanglement in nets, Indigenous hunting, habitat degradation, and vessel strikes. As a result, the following actions were implemented in the late 1990s and early 2000s.

- Establishment of 15 Dugong Protection Areas (DPAs) in the Great Barrier Reef Marine Park south of Mission Beach and one in Hervey Bay.
- Prohibition of traditional hunting permits for dugongs along the urban coast south of Cooktown.
- Review of netting practices in the Queensland Shark Control Program.
- Increase in surveillance and enforcement in conjunction with a review of penalties for offences in DPAs.
- Reapplication of a 40-knot boat speed restriction in the Hinchinbrook DPA.
- Development of a strategy for cooperative management agreements with Indigenous peoples.
- Endorsement of phasing out the use of high explosives in the Great Barrier Reef World Heritage Area.
- Use of the Dugong Research Strategy as a funding guide (Oliver and Berkelmans 1999).
- Establishment of measures to minimize the impact of land-based activities.
- Improvement of procedures for dugong carcass and live stranding reports (Eros et al. 2000).

The need for these actions was further validated when an additional study reported that the dugong population along the urban coast of Queensland was a fraction of its historical estimate in the 1960s (Marsh et al. 2001).

Dugong movements tend to be very individualistic. When several dugongs are tracked in the same area, it is not uncommon to see some stay in the area, while others cover distances up to 600 km within a few days[38]. The low numbers of individuals tracked throughout the dugong's range limit the capacity to test explicitly the factors stimulating these movements, but it does not seem that they are related to the capture itself, sex, age, or season. It is suspected that the catalyst is the individual's perception of available food resources[39] or is a function of the experience of each individual during the pre-weaning period with its mother. The nature of the large-scale movements by dugongs is strikingly similar to those of Florida manatees. In several cases, a manatee calf has shown large-scale patterns of habitat use very similar to those shown by its mother[40]. That this is a learned behavior is indicated by the tendency for both dugongs and manatees to bypass areas of suitable habitat in favor of more distant sites[41].

Genetic analyses are the third line of evidence for frequent large-scale movements. In the 1990s Tikel[42] analyzed the genetic structure of the Australian population of dugongs using the mitochondrial d-loop region. Her results showed some mixing, consistent with an isolation-by-distance model, but were generally inconsistent with the evidence for movement as described in the preceding discussion. Using the same method but aided with a greatly increased sample set from around Australia, McDonald[43] demonstrated a degree of population structuring more consistent with data from aerial surveys and satellite tracking. Owing to advances in population genetics, McDonald also used microsatellites to analyze population structure. These results indicated less structuring than the d-loop data but still showed an isolation-by-distance effect[44].

We see no inherent biological reason why the dugongs' movements would not be the same if, as we suspect, they were a response to spatial and temporal variability in seagrass resources. Individual dugongs that make long-distance movements may be more exposed to anthropogenic threats than those that move only locally, perhaps those that remain in isolated populations. There is the possibility that either the instinctive drive or the learned geographical knowledge of individuals in these populations to make long-distance movements has been reduced.

Other Key Research

Clearly for any species, ascertaining its diet and how it interacts with its food resources is vital to good management. Understanding the status and future prospects for any dugong population is clearly tied to the distribution and abundance of its key seagrass food resource. This has been the subject of considerable research[45] as well as new work by James Sheppard and colleagues[46] on dugong movements and their relationships to seagrass resources.

Accurate research on dugong abundance has necessarily been limited to the time since aerial surveys began. However, human impacts on dugong populations pre-date this data set, and an important part of management must be to determine the population level to which we should aspire. This issue has recently gained much attention, with quite surprising estimates published for what the pre-European dugong population might have been in Queensland. Anecdotal reports of dugong numbers in the late nineteenth century include one report of a herd three miles long by 300 yards wide in Moreton Bay[47]. Jackson et al.[48] took this estimate, multiplied it by the density of dugongs in modern herds photographed in Moreton Bay, and reached an estimate of dugongs in the herd. They then extrapolated the result to suggest that there may have been as many as 1–3.6 million dugongs in Queensland at that time.

Marsh and colleagues have combined two innovative approaches to arrive at a more conservative estimate of the number of dugongs that Queensland could support (31,000–165,000) but cautioned against their use as a target for recovery[49]. While we have seen dramatic fluctuations in the dugong population along the urban coast of Queensland since the 1980s, we now know that they reflect merely the tail end of a crash[50], and that even estimates of a stabilization in the decline[51] should not be taken as grounds for complacency.

Grech and Marsh[52] have recently used spatial modeling and geographic information systems (GIS) to develop a risk assessment for dugong conservation in the Great Barrier Reef World Heritage Area. They looked at the current management arrangements in the World Heritage Area, with respect to their combined capacity to protect dugongs and their habitats in the region. Zoning maps, commercial netting restrictions, information on Indigenous hunting pressure, boater registrations, habitats impacted by poor water quality, dugong distribution data (from aerial surveys), and seagrass information were integrated into a GIS. The results of this work have highlighted the adequacy of some existing management measures but also identified areas requiring improvement.

Future Research

Researchers in Australia are now increasingly concentrating on understanding disturbances and threats to

Table 11.1. Causes of live stranding or mortality of dugongs in Australia.

Natural causes of death	Human-related causes of injury or death
Disease (i.e., pneumonia, septicemia, parasites)	Bycatch in fishing gear (mostly net, some anecdotal trawl encounters)
Old age	
Shark attack	Coastal development leading to poor water quality and habitat destruction/seagrass loss
Stingray barbs pierce gut	
Weather patterns causing seagrass loss (e.g., monsoonal rains)	Harvest
	Ingestion of marine debris (fishing hooks and line)
	Trawling that can impact seagrass beds
	Vessel strike

dugongs, their responses to these factors, and how to ameliorate the effects through management. Having an ability to understand the causes of mortality, injury, and disturbance occurring in populations aids in prioritizing actions, provides justification for implementing them, and fosters public awareness of the issues associated with the species.

A range of natural and human-related mortality factors impact dugongs in Australia (table 11.1). Not all factors may be relevant for a particular population or area. The type and frequency of dugong mortality depend upon the size of the human population and uses of the area.

Summary

The Pacific region is vitally important to the long-term conservation of dugongs throughout their range. Because of the significant populations that exist in Australia, Papua New Guinea, and Vanuatu[53], we have an obligation to conserve and learn from them and to use the knowledge to conserve dugongs elsewhere. There is a high likelihood of achieving this goal, in part because of the vast amount of information in this region about dugong biology, ecology, and population status; the legal protection afforded here to dugongs and their habitats; the low human population density across the northern coastline of Australia; and the significant cultural and community values placed on the species.

Within Australia the prospect of maintaining viable populations of dugongs is good if cross-jurisdictional cooperation for management occurs, especially in collaboration with Indigenous Australians. Grassroots initiatives, such as the NAILSMA-funded project, need to be coordinated with activities that are happening at a broader scale (e.g., the Australian National Partnership Approach; regional marine protected area planning) to encompass the dugong's entire habitat.

Cooperation among jurisdictions for the protection and conservation of dugongs is also critical on an international scale. Initiatives are required to ensure that efforts in one country assist with and do not detract from those in a neighboring country. For example, many governments across the dugong's range are working together and have developed a memorandum of understanding (MOU) to promote dugong conservation. This MOU will allow for improved communication and understanding about dugong issues internationally and will establish a plan of action to conserve the species into the future. Such global cooperation can lead to improved access to information and exchange of research samples (e.g., through the CITES permitting process).

Ultimately it will take initiatives on a range of fronts to ensure the long-term survival of dugongs. However, Australia and the Pacific region are well placed to provide the information and expertise to make this happen.

SECTION II

Research Strategies for Sirenians

12

Using Interviews in Sirenian Research

ALEJANDRO ORTEGA-ARGUETA, ELLEN M. HINES, AND JORGE CALVIMONTES

A crucial step in any research on endangered species is to obtain baseline information about their geographic range, present population status, and relevant conservation issues. As sirenians are routinely found in coastal, riverine, and lagoon systems, they are often in such close proximity to human settlements that their lives and behavior are significantly affected by human activities. Sirenians are also an important food resource exploited by ancient and modern societies.

In this chapter we discuss a variety of techniques and modalities commonly used in interviews of local inhabitants, explain elements to be considered when planning and undertaking interviews, and give some practical recommendations. We include examples of case studies that emphasize working with local communities. Interviews are especially important where a strong relationship between scientists and local community members is crucial to the success of a research project[1].

As conservationists we need more information about manatees and dugongs than just biological and ecological parameters such as population, life history, or seagrass boundaries. We also need to know the cultural and economic influence of sirenians both historically and presently on the lives of people. Traditional knowledge, myths, perceptions, and opinions are important, not only for sirenian management and conservation but also for the maintenance of the surrounding environment upon which both people and wildlife depend. Here is where knowledge gained directly from local people becomes one of the most valuable methods in sirenian research. Hines et al. and Calvimontes[2] have shown the value of interviews in assessing the status of the dugong and ongoing threats to its survival, in describing the relationships of sirenians with local communities, and in developing recommendations for a workable conservation plan.

At the initial phase of a research project, interview surveys can give us a first look at the place where researchers will be working. This is especially valuable in an area not previously surveyed. Interviews can help researchers initially identify possible habitat areas, meet people in nearby communities, start identifying key informants (hunters, elders, community leaders, etc.), and start learning about local issues affecting sirenians. Examples include hunting, the incidental catch of sirenians in fishing nets, the destruction of seagrass beds by coastal development, the capture of calves to sell as pets, and the use and sale of body parts as medicine, food, amulets or tools.

Another advantage of interviews is that further research techniques can be based on the information gained[3]. While aerial surveys are usually recommended for a formal population estimate, they can be prohibitively expensive, ineffective, or dangerous in some conditions[4].

At the initial stage of a research project, especially in a large area, a first step in determining the current status of sirenians may be to determine locations of primary habitat using interviews and boat-based surveys[5]. Researchers are better able to make decisions about the need and practicality for more sophisticated and expensive methods and techniques, such as aerial surveys or tagging. Such decisions might also depend on the objectives and the type of information needed.

When conducting interviews, researchers can involve and train local villagers as participants. Interviews can be used as an opportunity to disseminate information to respondents on the importance of conserving sirenians and their habitat[6]. This can get more people involved and may raise local support for conservation.

The Interview as a Research Tool

An interview can be defined as a "conversation with a purpose"[7]. For any interview, two components are essential[8]:

1. The substantive part of the interview consists of questions and answers.
2. The participants have defined, non-overlapping roles: one person asks the questions (the interviewer) and the other answers the questions (the respondent).

Commonly used techniques include structured, semi-structured, and unstructured interviews; close-ended or open-ended questions; focus groups or group interviews; participative observation; and oral histories. Depending on the technique and quality of the data gathered, you can use qualitative and/or quantitative analyses for interpretation. For this reason, the design of a questionnaire is a critical step[9]. Table 12.1 includes examples of case studies and corresponding references relating to sirenians where interviews were conducted as a principal or complementary research method.

A structured interview is the most formal technique and can be as simple as a questionnaire with closed-ended questions, offering limited choices of answers, such as "yes," "no," or a number. For example, "Have you seen manatees in the past five years? If so, how many times? How many animals?" The advantage of the structured approach is that the resulting data can be analyzed

Table 12.1. Examples of studies where interviews were used as a research method.

	Types of information collected	References
Dugong-related case studies		
Western Indian Ocean	Dugong status, spatial distribution, abundance, uses and myths, threats, extent of traditional knowledge	WWF EAME 2004
Thailand, Cambodia, Vietnam, Sri Lanka, India, Myanmar, Malaysia	Dugong sightings, influence of dugongs in the locals' life (hunting practices, trade, traditional uses, legends, stories and beliefs), dugong mortality and threats; local opinions about conservation measures	Hines et al. 2005b, 2007 2008a; Ilangakoon et al. 2008; Ilangakoon and Tun 2007; Rajamani et al. 2006
Vanuatu	Dugong sightings, influence of dugongs in the locals' life (hunting practices, traditional uses, legends, stories and beliefs), dugong mortality and threats; local opinions about conservation measures	Chambers et al. 1989
Australia	Dugong sightings, influence of dugongs in the locals' life (hunting practices, traditional uses, legends, stories and beliefs), dugong mortality and threats; local opinions about conservation measures	Hudson 1981, 1986a, b; Kwan 2002, 2006
Manatee-related case studies		
Florida	Impact of tourism activities	Sorice et al. 2006
Belize	Distribution, abundance, threats, manatee hunting	Bengtson and Magor 1979; Auil 1998
Costa Rica	Sightings, temporal and spatial distribution, abundance, hunting, traditional uses, threats, ecology, mortality	Reynolds et al. 1995; Jiménez Pérez 2005
Honduras	Spatial distribution, hunting techniques, mortality	Rathbun et al. 1983
Nicaragua	Spatial distribution, abundance, ecology, habitats, threats, hunting techniques	Jiménez Pérez 2002
Mexico	Spatial distribution, abundance, threats, hunting, traditional uses	Colmenero and Hoz 1986; Morales-Vela et al. 2003
Puerto Rico	Spatial distribution, threats	Powell et al. 1981
Colombia	Spatial and temporal distribution, status, habitat use; conservation issues, hunting, socioeconomic importance, myths, beliefs, threats	Montoya-Ospina et al. 2001; Orozco 2001; Kendall and Orozco 2003; Castelblanco-Martínez 2004b
Venezuela	Spatial distribution, abundance, threats, hunting techniques, traditional significance (food, medicinal, folklore, beliefs, legends)	O'Shea et al. 1988
Brazil	Spatial distribution, status, natural history, ecology, behavior, hunting techniques, traditional uses, beliefs, historical use; local perception about research and conservation issues	Domning 1981; Calvimontes 2009
French Guiana	Spatial distribution, abundance, habitats, biology, threats, traditional uses, beliefs	De Thoisy et al. 2003
Cameroon	Spatial distribution, abundance, habitat, hunting, traditional uses, perceptions and attitudes	Grigione 1996

> **BOX 12.1**
>
> ### Dugongs along the Andaman Coast of Thailand
>
> Ellen M. Hines
>
> During two field seasons in 2000 and 2001, my colleagues and I conducted interviews in five provinces along the Andaman coast of Thailand that have seagrass beds known to have supported dugongs or where dugongs have been seen by villagers or scientists (Hines et al. 2005b). Interview respondents were chosen using several methods. In some areas we had contact names supplied by local nongovernmental organizations or other connections. We also sought to interview the heads of villages, who sometimes recommended others. We went to stores and restaurants and walked through villages and stopped at houses with nets outside. We purposely tried to mix ages and genders. While a more random sample would have been optimal, we were dependent on the limited availability of fishers and the guidance of contacts and translators. In Thai culture it is rare to interview a single person; respondents are more comfortable being interviewed in groups, and if people see an interview happening, they sometimes join in. Occasionally the original respondent stops answering questions or even leaves and lets the newcomer finish the interview, depending on their relative status within the community.
>
> We wrote a standardized interview form that was part semi-structured and part unstructured and exploratory. We used it both as an instrument to open up dialogue and as an empirical attitudinal survey based on a specific hypothesis and designed for quantitative analysis (Pole and Burgess 2000; Verhoeven 2000). We used a mixture of open- and closed-ended questions (Fowler and Mangione 1990; Whyte 1982). Some questions were structured and required either a fixed response or a short answer (e.g., "How many dugongs have you seen in the past year?"). Several of the fixed-answer questions were followed by a probing question (e.g., "Do you think this is important?"). Other questions encouraged respondents to speak without restraint (Backstrom and Hursh-César 1981). An unstructured question is particularly useful when the interviewer has limited information about what answers to expect, or anticipates a large range of answers.
>
> The content of the interview questions was initially based on a questionnaire survey done by Chambers et al. (1989). Questions addressed the history of interactions with dugongs and knowledge of legends or beliefs. We also asked about temporal and seasonal patterns of dugong sightings (plus sightings of whales, dolphins, and marine turtles). In other questions we inquired about past or present hunting and sources and levels of dugong mortality. We questioned the community members about their opinions regarding threats to dugongs and the importance of conserving dugongs and seagrass and of designating areas off-limits to fishing to conserve dugongs, seagrass, and mangroves (Marsh and Lefebvre 1994).
>
> The interviews were conducted in Thai. The quantitative measurement of responses for these interviews was affected by the different language skills of the interviewers and their varying reliance on the questionnaire. For most of the 2000 field season, the administration of the interviews was standardized. The translator was a Canadian woman whose knowledge of Thai was limited, especially of the southern Thai dialect, though subsequent translators in Thailand and Canada corrected most of the discrepancies. In 2001 native Thai speakers, some with prior experience, conducted the interviews. Later that year two Thai scientists from the Phuket Marine Biological Center, both of whom had prior interviewing experience and knew the local dialect, conducted a second series of interviews.

quantitatively, as the exact interview is repeated with each respondent.

Semi-structured interviews allow both the quantitative analysis of a structured survey and the opportunity to pursue interesting themes with respondents using open-ended questions[10]. As an interview is also an opportunity for researchers to learn about local issues, an open-ended question encourages respondents to comment more freely (see text box 12.1). A totally unstructured interview encourages respondents to expand without constraint on their experience and knowledge[11].

A major advantage of closed-ended questions is that they can be replicated by other researchers and comparisons can be made between different groups of people and areas. Open-ended questions are more complicated to compare and analyze. However, you can put results together into a narrative of community/traditional knowledge[12], or use computer tools, such as NUD*IST and NVIVO, for analysis.

A group or focus group interview is a discussion of interview questions led by a moderator who manages the group dynamics of eight to ten people. They might be fishing cooperatives, for example, or boat drivers, shrimp farmers, or women who might not feel comfortable being interviewed alone. First, establish a secure, confidential, and comfortable environment where participants are invited to speak openly about their opinions, experiences, perceptions, and beliefs. Employ various combinations of structured, semi- or unstructured interview questions.

Participative observation is a technique used to facilitate either the quantitative or qualitative collection of field data. It involves establishing relationships in the community or communities where the study is developed[13]. Calvimontes[14] demonstrated that when researchers live close to communities and participate in their daily lives, a more personal relationship evolves, with more useful results.

The researcher should learn to interact within the normal activities of a community as if he or she were not present. Such participation reduces reactivity, or the effect of observation upon respondent behavior. Scientists can then learn more about local cultural practices and can better understand relationships between local people and sirenians as well as local traditional uses and perceptions about the ongoing conservation status of sirenians.

Using a compilation of data from oral histories allows researchers to learn about historical relationships. The participation of people who have access to this information or extensive experience in related issues is critical. Focus on key informants[15] or people with specialized knowledge and who enjoy telling stories. Select good informants and ask them the right questions. Elders or knowledgeable people can relate events that later will be identified as indicative of the human/sirenian relationship. Compile the responses into a cohesive representation of local history. Calvimontes compiled oral histories to research historical use of the Amazonian manatee by local people in the Amanã Reserve, Brazil[16]. A major issue he examined was how hunting knowledge is transmitted from generation to generation, how skills for hunting are taught, the age when hunters learn to hunt, and reasons for hunting.

In general, types of data collected through interviews can be classified into three topic areas:

1. Biological and ecological information about sirenians and their habitat (e.g., areas or sites frequented by sirenians; types of habitat used; size of groups; observed behavior; changes in ecological and behavioral patterns across time).
2. Ethnobiological and historical information (e.g., traditional use of sirenians and their body parts; number of hunters within a local community; historical exploitation; motivation for hunting; cultural beliefs).
3. Conservation-related information (e.g., potential application of management actions; people's willingness to work with an education project; community attitudes toward a protected area designation or hunting ban; local perceptions and level of knowledge about endangered species and conservation issues; destructive fishing or activities affecting the coastal zone).

Planning the Interview

Selecting respondents requires preliminary planning. When possible, start with a pilot study of a small representative group of respondents to test your interview design and interviewing skills. A questionnaire should be designed for different groups of people, of different ages, lifestyles, and genders, and where appropriate, different communities. Choose people from different professions or roles in society who may have different perspectives.

When resources and time are limited, design an interview that is administered by teams of interviewers during short-term visits to communities[17]. With more time available, use the participative observation method with community members to gather more comprehensive data[18].

"Snowballing" is a procedure that helps to identify a sample of people with similar roles in society[19]. Ask key informants to suggest others to be interviewed. This procedure is useful when researchers are conducting a pilot survey and/or are unfamiliar with the local area. Snowballing also helps to corroborate that the right people are being interviewed if one respondent makes reference to another person already interviewed.

Possible Limitations and Biases

Interviews are limited in their ability to verify the accuracy of respondents' statements. Because of this, biological and ecological data gathered from interviews cannot be used for accurate estimates of population abundance, size, and trends. Population parameters such as sex ratio should be viewed with caution. The utility of interview-derived information will depend on the researcher's skills and experience. However, in some cases, lack of information from developing countries has obligated scientists to combine local interviews with expert opinion.

For example, in 2005 the World Conservation Union (IUCN) requested information to update sirenian conservation status worldwide. Because of the lack of systematic surveys and reliable population estimates, most of the data on manatee populations from the Caribbean and West African regions were based on combining interview data with expert opinions[20]. While not totally accurate, this method was the only means available for reviewing population numbers.

Biases from responses to a questionnaire usually arise for three main reasons[21]. First, the respondents' behavior: they may deliberately try to please the interviewer or prevent the interviewer from learning some undesirable, controversial, or possibly illegal information. The respondent may embellish a response, give a socially desirable response, or omit certain relevant information. The respondent may also err due to faulty memory. The second source of bias is found in the nature of the interview itself: the method of questionnaire administration, misunderstandings due to the wording sequence, or mistranslations. The third source of error is the interviewer, whose lack of knowledge of local culture or questioning techniques can impede communication[22].

An unstructured cross-cultural interview must be based on an atmosphere of mutual respect, where the interviewer is interested in all kinds of information. The interviewer in this case must guard both tone of voice and body language to ensure that the respondents will not "lose face" if they misinterpret or do not know the answers[23]. In some cases respondents may modify their responses based on the way the question is asked; especially by looking at the researcher's facial expression or listening to the tone of voice. It is important to minimize the cultural differences between interviewer and respondent[24]. Interviewers should appear unknowledgeable, receptive, and grateful for any information and should remain in the background. In this way an interviewer can learn unanticipated, valuable information; the disadvantage is increased difficulty in judging the reliability of responses.

Other factors that may influence interview biases:

1. Wording: Questions should be simple, clear, specific, and unambiguous. Jargon and vague words like "many" and "few" should be avoided.
2. Local language: Indigenous languages make communication difficult even for local researchers. It may be necessary to have an interpreter, which may cause misunderstandings. A good interpreter is critical.
3. Sensitivity: Questions should not force respondents to talk about controversial topics that may offend, threaten, or cause disgust (e.g., trying to interview a manatee hunter in presence of local authorities or strangers). Even calling respondents "manatee hunters" may be insensitive. The use of other words, such as "manatee experts" or similar expressions, is recommended. Such knowledge may come out only after the researcher has gained the respondent's trust.
4. Understanding of local social, economic, and cultural contexts: For example, in many developing countries sirenian poaching is still a common practice. In some rural communities of marginalized people, sirenians are considered a necessary food source. In this context, an inappropriate and potentially alienating question would be: "If you know that manatee hunting is illegal, why do you do it?"
5. The respondent's relationship with and trust of interviewers: In some places, especially in rural areas, the presence of a researcher may be intimidating. If an interviewer is from a government agency, or represents an unknown organization, responses will be guarded or the truth may be withheld. Sometimes interviews are appropriate only after the researcher has spent time—days or weeks—in the community, gaining people's trust. The use of a tape recorder or video recorder may also make people feel uncomfortable. Permission to use recorders or take pictures should always be obtained prior to the interview.
6. Gender: In many societies men and women respond differently to an interviewer. The gender of the interviewer can also be a consideration. Women in some rural areas tend to avoid talking to strangers, especially if no local men are present. Unless the researcher knows when men will come back, it may be impossible to find respondents among the women. In other circumstances where women are allowed and/or agree to participate, they may feel comfortable only with female interviewers.

Women's traditional duties may affect the extent of their exposure to sirenians. In some Mexican coastal villages women are more involved in fishing than men and may know more about the areas most visited by manatees and about their behavior; they also have more knowledge about traditional uses of manatees as food and medicine. In some areas of Thailand, women fish either with each other or with their husbands. They can be very outspoken about dugongs and conservation issues that affect their villages and families. In other areas, women tend not to want to be interviewed, either as they do not fish in boats or because they would rather have their husband give an opinion. In Brazil, women do not generally participate in manatee hunting or prepare manatee meat. The only women who can speak knowledgeably about manatees are the wives or close relatives of hunters. However, women should always be sought out for interviews. Women's opinions on nearshore conservation issues are relevant, even if they have never seen a sirenian.

An example of how to address the biases of interviewing is provided by Fontana and Frey[25]. During an unstructured interview, the researcher is often involved in an informal conversation with the respondent, maintaining a tone of friendly chat while trying to remain close to the topic. "The researcher would begin with general questions and gradually move on to more specific ones, while, as inconspicuously as possible, asking questions intended to check the veracity of the respondent's statements"[26].

The pilot survey can be used to test biases with a trial questionnaire given to a few respondents. In an early stage of the research, these preliminary interviews may help to confirm that the interview focuses the respondent on the relevant issues. Any problems with the wording of the draft questionnaire should become evident and can be corrected before the real interviews start[27].

Biases of interview surveys can be also addressed by triangulation—the use of multiple methods to cross-check and verify the reliability of a particular research tool and the validity of the data collected[28]. Usually triangulation involves combining quantitative and qualitative methods to check the accuracy of the data gathered by each interview method. Information from interviews might be verified by direct observation, a review of complementary documentation, or expert opinions. Interviewing different members of the same community or asking various respondents to talk about specific events (e.g., hunting) may also help confirm responses. Areas where respondents mention that sirenians are found may be confirmed during aerial surveys. Sites where sirenians were found stranded or slaughtered may be validated by the presence of bones.

Summary

An interview is one of the least expensive and most practical methods to conduct research on sirenians, especially compared with advanced technologies and expensive methods such as radio-telemetry or aerial surveys. They are also noninvasive, an important consideration for small, endangered populations, and applicable when you do not want local people to witness the risky procedure of an animal being captured and tagged. Interviews allow us to collect valuable primary data directly from local people.

Many researchers today are looking for a closer interaction with people in local communities, especially in projects where humans and their relationships with the conservation target are the main concern. Conservationists are becoming more conscious of the importance of social-science approaches to understanding human-sirenian conflicts (e.g., manatee and dugong hunting, boat strikes, net entanglements, and habitat destruction). The participation of local people is a fundamental component of sirenian conservation in developing countries[29]. Community participation is needed not only during interview activities but also for effective conservation planning, implementation, and monitoring.

Within this context, having good communication, trust, and close collaboration with respondents from local communities is critical for success (see text box 12.2). Addressing illegal hunting of sirenians is not only a matter of law enforcement and fines. Conservationists need to understand the socioeconomic context, beliefs, and conditions that obligate people to continue with illegal practices. In many countries, utilization of sirenian body parts still has a very important cultural and economic role in Indigenous communities, and hunters have a high social status. Planning effective conservation and management strategies can only be achieved by researchers and conservationists through close interaction and communication with local communities. Interviewing is not only an essential research technique but also a natural way to communicate and build relationships between communities and researchers.

BOX 12.2

Relationships between Amazonian Manatees and Amanã Reserve Inhabitants

Jorge Calvimontes

Between 2002 and 2004 an intensive field study was conducted to record the relationship between the inhabitants of the Amanã Sustainable Development Reserve in western Brazilian Amazonia and the Amazonian manatee. Research methods were based on Participatory Rural Appraisal techniques adapted for the study area and objectives (Chambers 1994). To obtain as complete a picture of the situation as possible, quantitative and qualitative methods were employed for data collection in an unobtrusive way.

Using Participant Observation (Bernard 1988), the research was conducted in 15 rural communities, sharing their daily life for three years in the field. The study had three phases determined by the relationship with local inhabitants and the level of exchange of information that occurred in the process.

The first phase was recognition and corresponded to the time when *I* became familiar with the area and the local inhabitants. Informal conversations with all members of the community, along with participation in community events, such as parties and local meetings, were instrumental to building trust. It is crucial to build a good relationship with locals, based on mutual trust, and an understanding of their lifestyle and culture. For approximately three months I visited the communities to make this first contact and start learning who was who within their society. I met with locals to discuss our interest in working in their territory and make contact with people knowledgeable about the manatee. In this first phase I avoided using the term *hunter*, to let people know I was passing no judgments. The process of selecting the main informants with whom to start the interviews was based on information obtained by locals previously contacted by the Amazonian Manatee Project, of the Mamirauá Institute. I first conducted exploratory interviews, which consisted of open questions about manatees, their presence, and their behavior. Our interviewees were people knowledgeable about manatees and who were or had been hunters, as well as elders who could talk about the relationship between inhabitants and the manatee, and primary school teachers, who could help us understand the perceptions children had.

I then went on to the information phase, when most of the data were collected. Interviews were conducted intensively in each community where I had a close relationship with the informants. I conducted over 150 semi- or unstructured interviews on biological and ecological characteristics of the species, its abundance and threats, the characterization and description of hunting, and beliefs, myths, and local stories about manatees. During the process new themes, not originally identified, came to light. Findings generated in the interviews were fundamental to provide feedback and contribute to improvements to the interview questions. For the hunting data I used a structured form that allowed us to analyze information quantitatively. This information was combined with the semi-structured interviews. I held conversations with a few families previously identified as traditional hunters, recording the family history in family trees. I also documented how family members have used manatees over the years and how this had changed due to socioeconomic and biological factors. Interviews were also conducted in canoes as local inhabitants showed us important areas for manatees and discussed the history of their use in the reserve. I asked questions about the perception locals had of research, researchers, and local conservation-oriented projects.

Last, I conducted a meeting with all those interested in talking about manatees, as a final data collection, exchange of information and experiences, educational opportunity on the conservation status of the Amazonian manatee, and presentation of preliminary results.

13

Tagging and Movement of Sirenians

MIRIAM MARMONTEL, JAMES REID, JAMES K. SHEPPARD,
AND BENJAMÍN MORALES-VELA

Sirenians occur in waters that range from crystal clear to chocolate-milk brown. They can live anywhere from inland small channels covered with overhanging vegetation to offshore marine waters. They may spend several months in one location or make long migrations or movements at a relatively fast pace of 20 to 50 km per day. In large portions of their range, sirenians behave very cryptically, so researchers must often rely on electronic telemetry tags for the challenging task of documenting sirenian movements, habitat use, and general behavior.

Telemetry, or the science of adapting transmitters to living beings to monitor a variety of biological parameters, has been successfully applied to sirenians since the 1970s in different parts of the world. The field of telemetry has evolved so rapidly that nowadays tracking may be conducted remotely and produce a wealth of information. When planning to use telemetry, one must first have in mind exactly which research questions to answer and tailor the telemetry tools accordingly. Each study plan should be critically analyzed beforehand as to project objectives, desired information, and level of available support, both financial and human.

Not all gear will work well in all environments, and as enticing as using sophisticated telemetry devices may be, tracking studies can be very costly. In this chapter we present the strengths and challenges of different tagging and tracking techniques that hold potential for use in developing countries, which may vary depending on species, different habitat requirements, and behaviors. Any use of trade, product or firm names does not imply endorsement by the U.S. government.

Sirenian Capture and Tagging Techniques

Several capture techniques have been used to secure sirenians. Capture by woven nylon nets of different sizes and mesh is perhaps the most common method for manatees. Study animals have been net-captured using land-based techniques at power-plant discharge canals and other sites in Florida[1], manual deployment from small craft (Brazil)[2], and open-water techniques with net deployment from specialized designed capture boats (Florida, Belize, and Puerto Rico)[3]. At some locations in Florida, manatees have been attracted to advantageous capture sites by their need to use warm-water sites or drink fresh water, even using fresh water as bait[4].

Other capture techniques have been developed that are specific to particular areas. Vegetation is used as bait for special manatee traps in Africa[5]. In clear and shallow waters of Mexico, manatees have been lassoed in the water and held for tag attachment using a rodeo method[6]. One person must jump from a moving boat to hold the lasso. Once the manatee's movement has been halted, a second person jumps from the boat to slip another rope onto the peduncle. In 2004 this technique was successfully used in clear deep water (>4m) in a coral reef area[7]. In the Amazon region of Brazil, small harpoons, similar to but dramatically smaller than the ones used by hunters, were used to restrain manatees prior to people transferring them to canoes and larger boats. Although no adverse effects were noted from this technique, its use was discontinued because of its invasive nature.

In some cases, manatees were tagged while free-swimming with an animal without the need to capture it, but this is limited to areas where the water is clear and the animals are not shy of humans. Captive sirenians have been tagged for monitoring upon release from rehabilitation facilities.

Because dugongs avoid human contact and largely inhabit turbid marine waters, they have primarily been captured using the rodeo method, which requires someone to jump from a moving boat and grasp onto a dugong that has been herded into shallow intertidal waters. Once the dugong's movement has been halted, it is secured alongside the boat within a flotation cradle that allows its well-being to be monitored while tags are attached, samples collected, and measurements taken[8].

When capturing dugongs in deep water (>3m) a 20 m padded tail rope can be attached by one of the jumpers to the animal's tail. The other end of the rope is attached to the catch boat and allows the animal to surface to breathe without escaping, until it is brought alongside the boat for tagging.

Although sirenians typically struggle to escape at some point during capture, most remain calm after being removed from the water and normally do not require excessive restraining. Nevertheless, accidents have happened, so a large crew of people is recommended to expedite handling, to avoid accidents with the capture crew and to ensure that no animal drowns from unnoticed entanglement. Respiration and pulse rate should be monitored at all times, handling time kept to a minimum (less than one hour if possible), and individuals released at or close to their capture location. Additional data recorded upon capture include morphometrics (total length and girths), sex, and photographs of scars or natural marks. Complete biometry and biological sampling (including DNA) should be performed to the extent possible, given the logistic and resource capabilities of the capture operation[9]. Additional markings or identification tags (e.g., freeze brands, PIT tags, or "cookies") may be applied at this time[10].

Sirenian Attachment Mechanisms

Although attachments and housings may vary with the type of transmitters used, all successfully tracked sirenians were tagged with a similar kind of padded belt/harness around the caudal peduncle (figures 13.1 and 13.2). With the fusiform body shape typical of all sirenians, the peduncle offers the only secure attachment point for external devices. Peduncle belts can incorporate attached transmitters capable of emitting signals in fresh water, or can accept tethered floating radio tags that enable manatees to be tracked in saltwater habitats.

Peduncle belts used on manatees consist of a length of neoprene machine belting inside one-inch internal diameter latex tubing[11]. Padding and temporary flotation are provided by applying one-component urethane foam inside the latex tubing. To allow for the different sizes and strengths of manatees, belts are built using various lengths of machine belting ranging from ¾- to 1-inch width, and 3 to 9 ply in thickness. Predetermine the peduncle girths of manatees to be tagged and build the appropriately sized belts, or build a range of possible belt sizes for various size classes. Strength of the peduncle belt is determined by the width and number of ply of belting material, which varies with belt sizes to enable

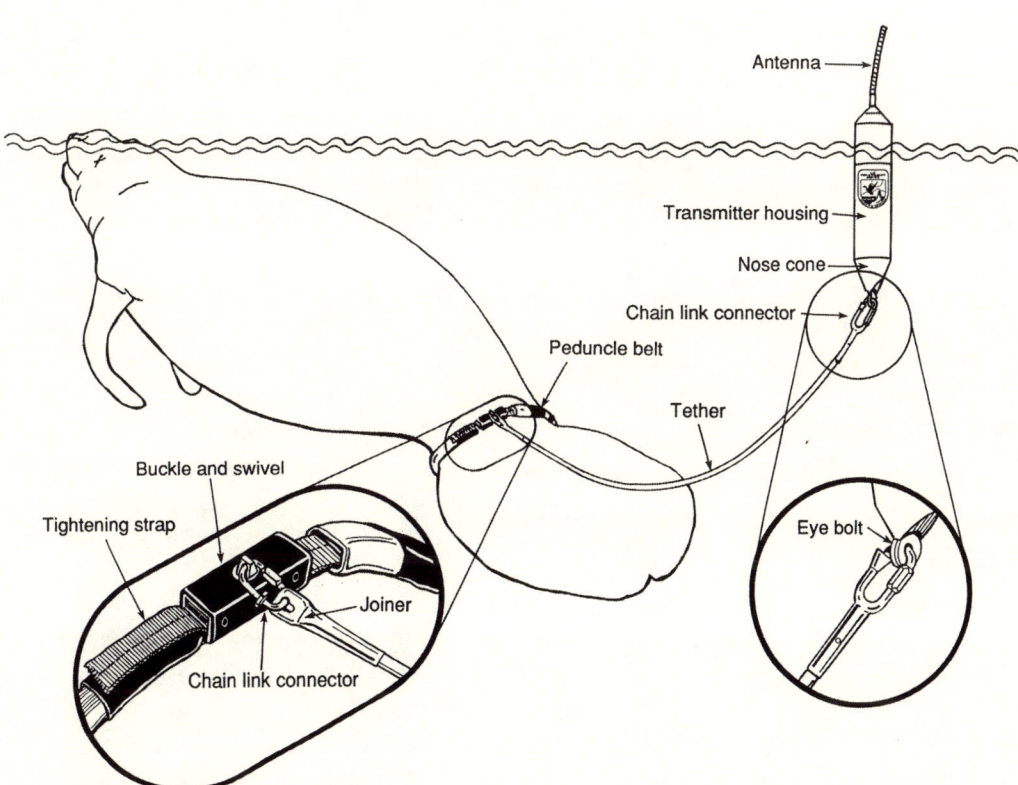

Figure 13.1. Manatee with peduncle tagging equipment. (Adapted from Reid et al. 1995.)

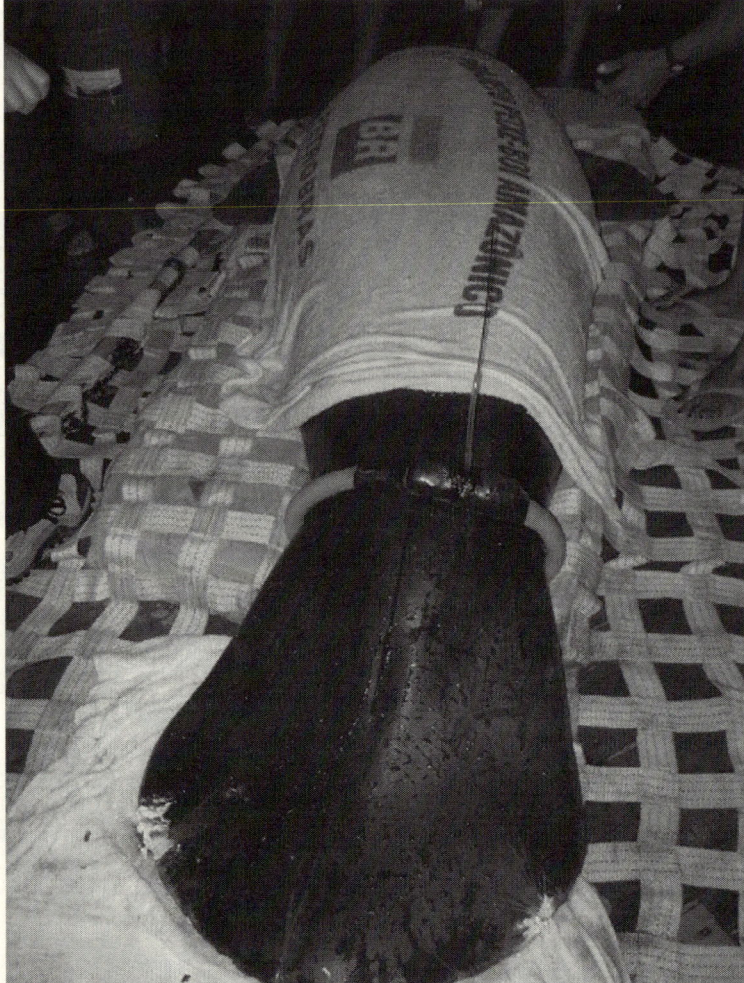

Figure 13.2. Amazonian manatee with peduncle tagging belt. (Courtesy of Miriam Marmontel.)

manatees to break free of the belts should they become entangled. Corrodible nuts and bolts of dissimilar materials allow belts to release over time.

Manatee belts used with tethered floating tags are typically secured using a spring-loaded "bear-claw" buckle, which enables a rapid attachment and provides a swivel for attaching the tether[12]. A less sophisticated but economical way to attach the belt is to use two plastic plates with corrodible nuts and bolts to secure the belt by sandwiching the ends. Likewise, this assembly can incorporate a swivel, similar to that used in the buckle but mounted within a hole in an outer stainless steel plate, for attachment of tethered tags.

Most of the floating tags for manatees, which are described in detail later, were attached using a flexible plastic rod. This "tether" between the belt and floating tag enables the tag to transmit in air, thus allowing manatees to be successfully tracked in saltwater environments. A 4- to 10-foot length of solid ⅜-inch-diameter plastic rod, made from low water absorption nylon (e.g., Nylon Type 158L), was used to construct the tether. Specially designed stainless steel connectors were attached to each end to allow for rapid attachment to the belt swivel and the floating tag. A weak link within the connector was made by drilling holes through the tether rod, which reduced the tether strength and enabled the animal to break free should the tether or tag become entangled.

Dugong tags also employed padded peduncle belts, although different construction materials were used and the belt size was significantly smaller. The harness system used to attach a satellite tag to a dugong was a modification of that previously described by Marsh and Rathbun 1990 (figure 13.3).

To ensure recovery of tethered tags, a remote release system can be built into sirenian harnesses. For a design used on dugongs, a release mechanism can be preprogrammed to send an electrical current down the attachment tether when triggered by a radio signal from a handheld transmitter at a range of 1–0.5 km (Telonics, Inc.). The current passes along an exposed wire link through which the peduncle strap has been wrapped,

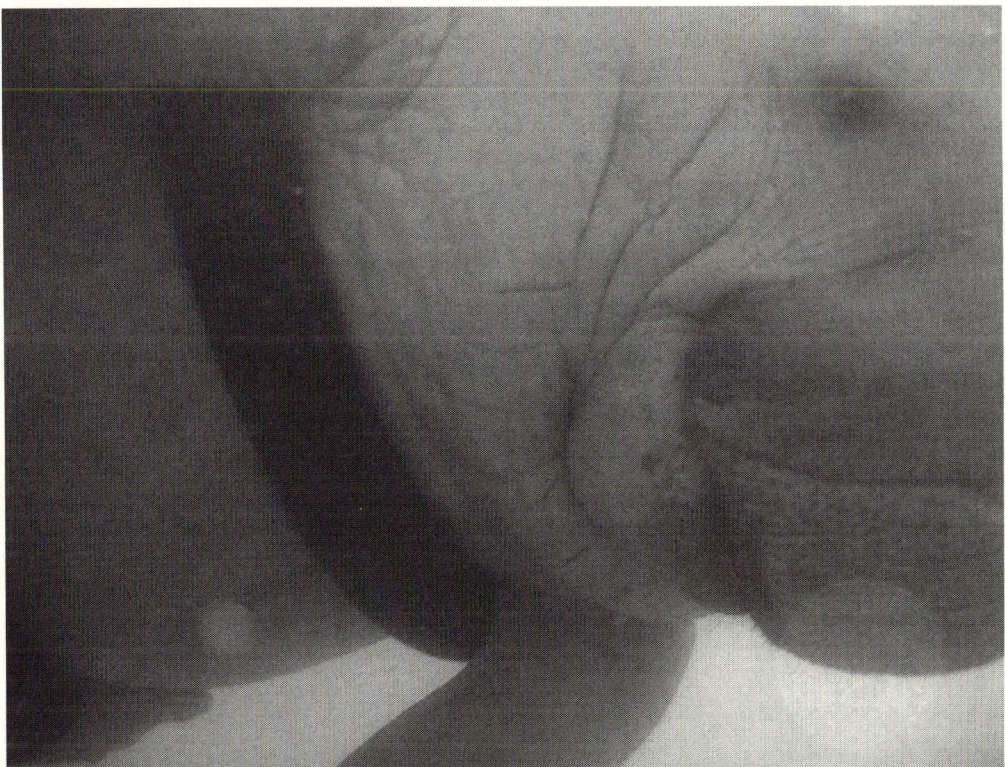

Figure 13.3. A dugong secured alongside a catch boat in a rubber cradle so that it can safely breathe while the satellite tag is attached to its tail and measurements are taken. (Courtesy of James K. Sheppard.)

corroding it rapidly (10–15 minutes) owing to an accelerated galvanic reaction with seawater. Once the link breaks, the harness with tethered tag detaches from the animal and can be retrieved. A tag release mechanism used on manatees involves a programmable device (CR-2A, Telonics, Inc.) incorporated in the peduncle belt. These programmable, self-releasing units employ a miniature pyrotechnic actuator enclosed within a machined plastic housing that will release the harness and attached tether at a predetermined date and time.

The retagging or replacement of tethered tags on sirenians by researchers while snorkeling has been accomplished frequently in the field on manatees in Florida, Puerto Rico, Brazil, and Mexico but rarely on dugongs in Australia. On these occasions the manatee was not restrained while an experienced swimmer quietly approached and removed and/or replaced a tag. Given the shy nature of most sirenians, specialized tools and tether-to-tag attachment mechanisms have been developed to expedite this process.

Telemetry

The sirenian telemetry systems most commonly used today are radio tags that transmit in the range of very high frequency (VHF), for land- and boat-based tracking, or ultra high frequency (UHF), which are satellite monitored. Recently, satellite-monitored transmitters (also called platform transmitter terminals or PTTs) have been integrated with Global Positioning System (GPS) receivers. These tags enable remote monitoring and relay of detailed GPS locations. Ultrasonic tags or "pingers," typically used for fish tracking, also can be incorporated into the belt and/or tethered tag for close range monitoring, retagging, or capture efforts and tag recovery.

VHF-Only Tags and Tracking Methods

The conventional, simplest, and least expensive tracking method has been the use of VHF radio transmitters[13]. This technology was first used to study manatees in the late 1970s in the St. Johns River of Florida[14] and in the eastern Brazilian Amazon[15]. In this attachment method, a nonbuoyant, waterproof transmitter was mounted directly onto a custom-built belt that was fitted to the animal's caudal peduncle[16]. Because the transmitter remains underwater most of the time, its use has been restricted to freshwater habitats, as salinity levels (higher electrolyte concentrations) in marine and even brackish areas prevent signal transmission through the water column. To enable sirenian radio-tracking in marine or brackish habitats, a tethered floating tag assembly was designed for manatees and dugongs[17].

Typical VHF wildlife tags are within 148–152 MHz, 163–165 MHz, or 216–220 MHz[18]. For tracking manatees, the 163–165 MHz range has been most common in Florida, Puerto Rico, Belize, and Mexico. In Brazil a range of 163–164 and 173–174 MHz has been employed within the Amazon, while 148 MHz has been used along the coast. Choices among these ranges are determined by governmental frequency allocations within the study area or country and by wildlife equipment manufacturers.

With the VHF tracking system, minimum equipment needs include radio transmitters with an appropriate attachment mechanism, a portable wildlife-tracking receiver (either manual or scanning), and a directional antenna (typically a handheld "H" or Yagi antenna). Also valuable to promote successful field tracking ventures are a good pair of headphones and a handheld GPS receiver or detailed maps and a good compass. For aerial tracking, a pair of antennae with specific brackets for attachment to an aircraft and an in-line left/right switch allow trackers to monitor either or both sides of a plane's ground track in order to localize signals.

VHF tracking is usually accomplished by "homing" (following a signal toward its greatest strength)[19], or triangulation (getting at least two signal bearings from different locations, and plotting the animal at their crossing)[20]. Homing can enable visual observations, but trackers risk disturbing the animal and causing it to change behavior[21] and position. This disturbance can be minimized by using triangulation. Triangulation requires angles of about 90° between bearings and short intervals between readings, which may not be feasible under conditions of narrow channels and surrounding dense forest. Autonomous VHF signal monitoring can be accomplished by automatic receiving stations coupled with an antenna array[22].

VHF field data sheets should include a map, with fields for recording individual manatee identification, date and time, duration of listening, platform (land, boat, tower, aircraft), level of accuracy (general area, triangulation, sighting), triangulation points (recording in UTM coordinates recommended)[23], coordinate bearings and signal strength, details of equipment, and tracker comments (e.g., weather conditions). In areas where manatees can be seen, data should also include duration of observation, physical condition, and behavior; actual or estimated group size, including notation of presence and number of calves and presence of other animal species; condition of housing and belt; and environmental information, including, if applicable, species of plants present and consumed[24]. Field data can be entered in a computer database and analyzed with the help of software such as LOAS[25] and plotted as geographic information system (GIS) maps.

There are a number of caveats associated with field-based VHF tracking: the signal may be attenuated by distance, obstacles, and dense vegetation. It demands great field effort (e.g., transportation and personnel), and bad weather can limit tracking and observation opportunities. It is not uncommon for a manatee to detect boat noise at long distances and move before it is seen. The level of results will be variable, depending on the intensity of the monitoring, but field observations often provide insights on behavior and specific resource or habitat use.

Automatic tracking—utilizing fixed receiving stations that autonomously capture the signals of animals traveling in the vicinity—is effective for continuous monitoring in relatively small study regions. Programmed frequencies are scanned at user specified intervals and received signals logged to memory by frequency with date and time. As with any VHF tracking, signal detection range improves with the height of the receiving antenna, so automatic stations/antennas are often mounted on elevated platforms. Automatic tracking involves high equipment costs and maintenance, and data typically reflect presence/absence of study animals as opposed to determining precise locations.

Tags utilizing only VHF transmitters have limited efficacy in dugong tracking. VHF tags usually allow a field observer to locate only the general vicinity of a tagged dugong (i.e., within ~80 ha). When dugongs are approached by a boat they usually remain submerged for longer periods (>5 minutes) and/or head out to deeper waters where the VHF signal cannot be located. Consequently, too few VHF signals are typically acquired to triangulate the location of the animal accurately, especially for extended periods[26].

VHF tags are best used for general information on spatial distribution patterns, frequently used areas, site-specific use by individuals, site fidelity of individuals, and general estimation of movements. Field-based tracking also provides opportunities for visual contact with the subject, allowing a scientist to gather information on general behavior, identification of forage species, and associations with other individuals. Due to the limited transmission range, these tags are not well suited for documenting timing and route of long-distance moves.

However, VHF systems may be operational for several years, providing multiple-year tracking possibilities. In Mexico, in estuarine conditions, the longest VHF transmitter batteries have lasted for 837 ± 154 days (n=3) of continued manatee tracking[27]. VHF is a desirable component to have in addition to a PTT/GPS system, as it allows ground truthing of animal behaviors once their initial location is obtained via satellite, and it facilitates easy location and retrieval of detached transmitters from the field.

Satellite-Based Tags

PTT tags

In the late 1970s the Argos system was created, using receiving stations on satellites[28]. This made it possible to monitor long-range movements in remote areas and dramatically improved the continuity of monitoring across time and animal range. The first manatee satellite tag was deployed in Florida in the mid-1980s[29].

This category of radio tag incorporates a satellite link for remote location determination and relay of sensor data. The Argos system continues to be a standard for satellite monitoring of sirenians. This system consists of animal-based Platform Transmitter Terminals (PTTs), a network of polar orbiting satellites, and ground-based data processing with user interface. The ultra high frequency (UHF) signal (centered at 401.650 MHz) emitted by the animal's PTT is picked up by individual satellites. The tag's location is calculated by Doppler shift, and recent location and sensor data may be accessed through computer interrogation on the Internet or by email or fax. In addition to location determination, remote monitoring, and near real time data availability, these tags record transmitter temperature, activity and dive periods, and other sensor data.

Tagging technology keeps improving, and different configurations are being explored, but all existing tags in this category are tethered to ensure optimal signal reception and performance. Tethered tags may be disadvantageous in areas such as rivers, where the amount of submerged branches results in increased probability of entanglement or where heavy forest cover may impede signal transmission.

To enable field tracking and allow recovery of the tag, VHF beacons have been adapted to PTTs used in manatee and dugong studies. Remote and field monitoring capabilities of combined PTT/VHF tags enhance VHF field tracking and opportunities to get visual contact with the subject. Field tracking and observations are necessary to document resources or animal behaviors associated with use areas, to implement specific complementary studies, and to monitor or replace the tag if necessary.

Argos location data may be used to obtain information on space distribution tendencies, frequently used areas, site-specific use and site fidelity of individuals, accurate estimation of displacements and movements, and strong support of other studies, such as addressing aerial survey bias and assessing habitat use.

The Argos system allows remote tracking of offshore animals, such as dugongs. Satellite-monitored tags require little field effort (except for capturing). This type of tag, which requires more energy to operate, usually has a shorter lifespan than VHF tags (6–12 months, depending on duty cycle). Because satellites have polar orbits, greater amounts of data are generated from tags deployed at higher latitudes. However, tropical sirenians can be effectively tracked with five operational satellites, which are capable of generating over 15 locations daily (satellite passes lasting five minutes or more) near the equator. Although initial investment and fees for data acquisition and processing are high, the system does not involve significant field costs in supplies and salaries (except during regular monitoring of the general condition of the housing and tether/peduncle belt attachment), and it does produce a wealth of data which might not be obtained through VHF telemetry.

GPS tags

The latest addition to wildlife telemetry involves the incorporation of GPS technology. In its basic form, a GPS receiver with an antenna mounted in a floating housing captures signals from a group of geo-stationary satellites, calculates a position, and stores it to memory at set time intervals.

Tracking may occur under any weather condition, with location fix time intervals down to a few seconds and accuracy of less than 5 m[30]. Operational time is dependent on programmed fix intervals and sensor operations, but deployments can span several months to one year, with sampling rates scaled for individual studies. Initial costs are high, but GPS tags produce highly accurate data[31]. This is a more cost-effective system than VHF in terms of the number and accuracy of data points obtained.

The data logging GPS tag, typically coupled with a VHF transmitter, must be removed from the animal or otherwise recovered to obtain the stored location data. Some researchers have incorporated preprogrammed or actively triggered release mechanisms for tag recovery as described earlier. In other GPS tag designs, data may be acquired in the field through periodic transmission of downloaded data sent by the tag via modulated radio frequencies at programmed intervals. With the Argos-

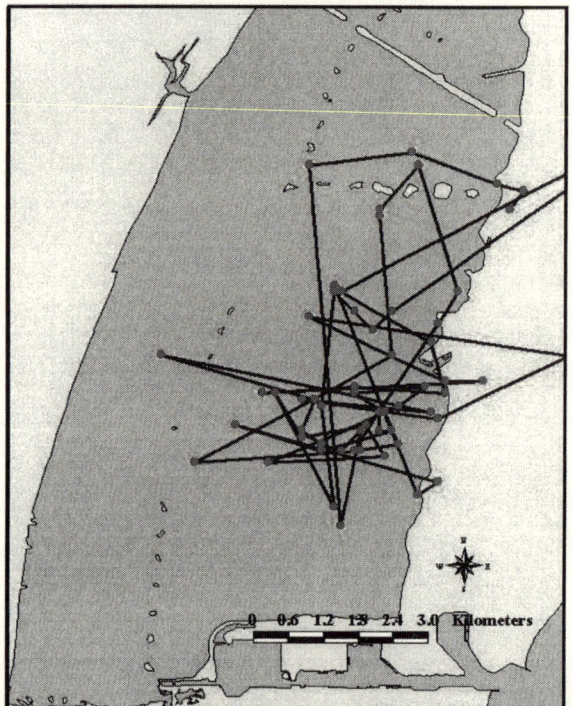 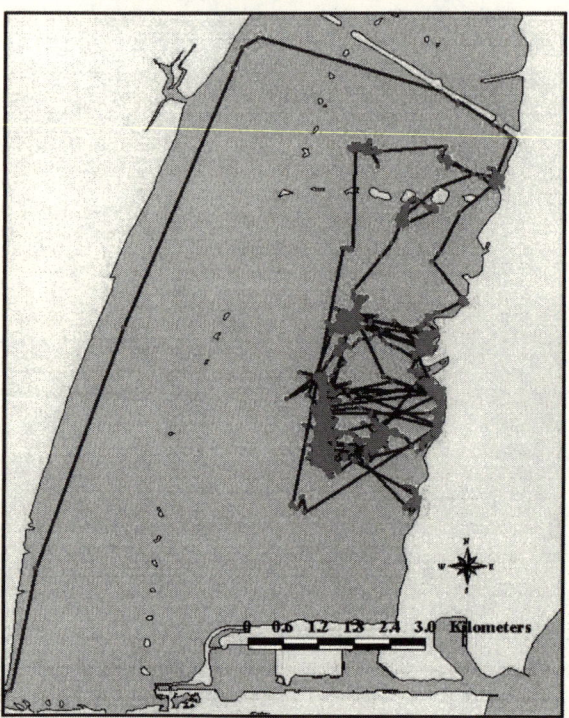

Figure 13.4. Comparison of locations determined via PTT and GPS tags deployed simultaneously on an individual in eastern Florida. (Courtesy of James Reid, U.S. Geological Survey.)

linked GPS tag, described in more detail later, GPS locations are relayed through a satellite link and acquired from the researcher's office.

Tests of GPS tags on manatees resulted in records from many locations, enabling detailed insights into the movements of the tagged animals. For 18 days, a GPS tag was deployed piggyback to an Argos PTT on a previously tagged adult manatee as it swam through the protected waters of the Banana River at the Merritt Island National Wildlife Refuge at Kennedy Space Center in Florida. Comparisons of the resulting data (figure 13.4) showed a distribution of Argos locations (mean # loc./day = 3.7) that reflected the animal's persistent use of an 18 sq km portion of the river; however, specific movement patterns are not discernable. Data from the GPS tag, operating during the same time period and programmed for ten-minute GPS fix intervals, recorded locations (mean # loc./day = 122) in shallow water along the shore at night and 1.2–1.8 km offshore within seagrass beds during the day. This diel use pattern was not evident from the Argos track[32].

GPS tags are a valuable tool in intensive investigations into how manatees utilize habitats. Compared to VHF or PTT data, these tags provide more specific information on space distribution tendencies, better definition of areas frequently used, more accurate estimation of movement and routes of displacement, and more specific data on site fidelity, all with a continuous, standardized localization method. The system works very well in most sirenian habitats, allowing researchers to follow large- and small-scale movements, and provides valuable information for ecological studies like habitat evaluation of both hotspots and general areas. Locations, when integrated in a GIS, can be correlated with seagrass habitats, bathymetry, and other detailed map coverages.

PTT/GPS tags

Perhaps the most popular tag currently employed for detailed, multi-month monitoring of sirenians is the Argos-linked GPS tag, or PTT/GPS tag. GPS locations are stored to memory, and then periodically relayed by an on-board PTT as encoded sensor data through the Argos satellite system. This combination allows both remote monitoring and fine-scale analysis of sirenian movement patterns, with user-defined sampling rates over three to nine months. Specific applications include identification of habitat hotspots, site fidelity, characterization of large-scale moves or movement highways, and characterization of foraging movements influenced by tidal cycles.

Compared to early PTT-only tags used on sirenians, Telonics PTT/GPS tags[33] are smaller, accumulate large amounts of precise location data, and can be programmed to require less energy to operate. Owing to battery/memory constraints, a trade-off must be made between obtaining temporally high-resolution fixes over a short deployment or fixes further apart over longer deployment periods. These considerations must be scaled with a duty cycle appropriate to meet study objectives. The duty cycle can be set from minutes to months depending on (1) the tag specifications, (2) battery capacity, and (3) the type of data required. For example, when early Telonics units were set to the minimum 15-minute cycle, battery power lasted around two months. A 20-minute cycle provided suitably high-resolution location data to capture the full range of dugong movement behaviors (fine and large scale) for three months at a time[34]. In manatees, a 20-minute cycle provided high-resolution locations data for five months. Recent versions of the Argos-linked GPS tags conserve significantly more power, which enables longer deployment periods or more frequent GPS fixes.

The units usually require a surface period of 4 to 40 seconds to acquire a GPS fix, depending on the version of the tag electronics. Newly incorporated Fastlock GPS tags (Wildlife Computers, Inc.) can fix within one second but provide lower position accuracy than standard GPS locations. If the animal is resident in deep water (>4m), the tag will typically spend less time at the surface and so fewer location fixes will be recorded. Similarly, when the animal is moving a long distance or otherwise continually swimming, the tag remains underwater for much of the time and there is less surface time to acquire a location fix[35]. Because the satellite tag can only acquire a location fix at the surface, to conserve battery life a saltwater switch is incorporated into the units to shut down transmission attempts when submerged (note that any antifouling compounds should be kept away from the saltwater switch terminals, as copper-based paints may conduct current and prevent the switch from operating properly). The lack of GPS location fixes acquired from dugongs tracked in deep water or while traveling rapidly can introduce a significant bias into analyses of habitat use, which must be accounted for, for example through summarization or weighting of the location data[36].

The utilization of GPS tags requires specific training and protocols to ensure proper programming and data recovery. We encourage the use of these GPS tags in collaboration with experienced research groups. Because the equipment is highly technical, tagging operations should be conducted with (reasonably) easy access to logistical support. Tag costs and maintenance, repair, and upgrading of satellite units are often prohibitively expensive. Fees for Argos monitoring may be reduced if the country has a Joint Tariff Agreement with Service Argos.

Integration of Other Equipment

Activity and mortality (lack of activity) sensors incorporated in VHF and/or satellite-monitored tags allow researchers to know when an animal is active or resting, and aid in determining tag detachment and enabling equipment recovery. Belt release mechanisms have been incorporated in dugong and manatee harnesses to allow for automated tag detachment and tag recovery; see earlier discussion. These can be self-activated at a preset time or activated by researchers within radio range.

Dugong dive profiles can be collected using a time-depth recorder (TDR: Mk9, Wildlife Computers, Ltd.) to analyze dive patterns within and between habitats. These compact units (~8 x 3 cm) can be fitted to the plastic block on the dugong harness as close to the animal's tail as possible. Current models can collect over six months of dive data with a reading taken every two seconds, and many concurrently measure light intensity, water temperature, and velocity. A sample rate of two seconds is of suitably high resolution to capture the dugong's dive profile. If the unit can also record light and temperature, these can be sampled at longer intervals (~five minutes) to conserve battery life. Dive recorders usually must be retrieved from the field to download the full-recorded dataset.

Several newly developed devices designed to record detailed observations over brief periods have been deployed on sirenians. National Geographic's Crittercam records video and audio and collects environmental data such as depth, temperature, and acceleration[37]. The Marine Mammal Behavior Laboratory at Woods Hole Oceanographic Institution developed a Digital Acoustic Recording Tag, or D-tag, to monitor continuously the behavior of marine mammals and their response to sound[38]. These tags, which can record the manatee's acoustic environment synchronized with the orientation of the animal (depth, speed, pitch, and roll) in three dimensions, have been used in studies for manatee-boat interactions.

Discussion

Insights into Sirenian Biology

The high cost of equipment and difficulties associated with tagging usually lead to small sample sizes, so caution should be taken when referring to tagged animals as representative of all animals in the region (this is common for VHF, PTT, and GPS tags). These techniques provide little information on the role of nearby animals in influencing movement patterns and resource use, and limited information on habitat characteristics or quality. Direct observations of tagged individuals can provide some insights on associations with conspecifics. Likewise, field characterization of habitat conditions can help correlate tracking data with resource needs.

GPS/PTT satellite telemetry has provided previously unobtainable fine-scale information on the movement, behavior, and habitat use of dugongs and manatees. For example, GPS/PTT tags deployed on 70 dugongs along the coast of Australia have provided detailed information on the large-scale movements of dugongs among core seagrass habitats along the coast[39]. Satellite tags have enabled the core seagrass habitats that dugongs use intensively to be identified so that they can be surveyed and mapped. Enhanced understanding of what constitutes "quality" dugong seagrass pasture will directly inform management policy for protecting important dugong habitats[40]. In Mexico, GPS tags have provided detailed information on the large-scale movements of manatees along the coast of Mexico and Belize and between distant areas of localized manatee occurrence[41]. Tagging data can also be used as baseline information to support ecological and habitat use research[42].

Tagging and Tracking in Developing Countries

Table 13.1 is a list of contact details for manufacturers commonly used by the authors. VHF is the most versatile technique. Given its low cost, long life, and reasonable accuracy, it is the natural technology to be used in developing countries and certainly a first step when starting a new tracking program. VHF is also the best option in relatively small areas like lagoons or rivers. The intensive field effort involved in conducting the monitoring and operating the equipment enables local people to be involved, which usually improves understanding and helps gain support for the project. However, in open areas too large for the reception coverage of VHF tags (with a signal range of 5 km from land or boat), the long-term intensive field monitoring effort needed may become problematic in expense, time, human participation, and administration support[43].

Though satellite tracking demands a much higher investment, it is useful and more efficient and provides higher quality data. Collaborative efforts may reduce limitations: neighboring countries sharing sirenian populations should consider collaborative research to reduce costs and improve data collection. While some PTT/GPS tags are available complete from manufacturers, most tags and the harness assembly for attaching the tag must be custom made. Technical training by scientists from countries where materials are becoming available allows for in-country belt construction. Strong coordination between regional partners is needed for training in capture techniques, the use of new software, and data analysis. Customs clearance of some materials, such as lithium batteries or transmitting devices, may be a problem at some international airports.

In Mexico, VHF-generated information on the spatial distribution of manatees supports manatee habitat use and management studies in lagoon systems[44]. It was used as the foundation for the first management plan of the Chetumal Bay Manatee Sanctuary. New and continuing baseline information about regional manatee movements between distant sites of manatee occurrence in Mexico and Belize, obtained by GPS tags, could strengthen current regional collaboration and promote new cooperation among neighboring countries with sirenian populations.

The documentation of a regular manatee movement between a preserved area of "white" (murky, sediment-laden) water environment and a large, deep blackwater

Table 13.1. Contact detail for manufacturers of sirenian tagging equipment.

GPS/PTT tags	Telonics, Inc.	http://www.telonics.com/
TDRs, GPS/PTT tags	Wildlife Computers, Ltd.	http://www.wildlifecomputers.com/
Dugong tether and harness	Ocean Industries Pty, Ltd.	http://www.oceanindustries.com.au/

lake as the water levels change in the Amazon served as further justification toward establishing a new protected area in the Brazilian Amazon.

Detailed maps of dugong movement corridors and core habitats identified from satellite tracking were directly incorporated into the Great Sandy Strait Marine Park Zoning in Queensland, Australia. The marine park was officially designated in 2006 and protects most of the dugong seagrass habitat within Hervey Bay in Habitat Protection Zones where professional fishing, development, and aquaculture can occur only with permission from the state government. Also within the new marine park are go-slow zones over the seagrass habitats identified by satellite tracking as those used most intensively by dugongs[45].

The application of radio-tracking technologies to study sirenians continues to evolve. The tagging and tracking techniques discussed here can be cost-effective and adaptable to most situations to address specific research questions or assist with captive release and other programs for sirenian management. The unique findings from radio-tracking can provide valuable information and insights about sirenian movement patterns, foraging strategies, and behavior that are unobtainable by, and yet complementary to, other research methodologies.

14

Techniques for Determining the Food Habits of Sirenians

CATHY A. BECK AND MARK T. CLEMENTZ

Sirenians, the only fully aquatic mammalian herbivores, are efficient hindgut-digesters[1], with a broadly diverse diet. Diet determination can be accomplished by various techniques, but here we offer three methods that can be employed with minimal effort and nominal expense. It is beyond the scope of this chapter to include the chemical composition of the components of all known dietary items, but constituent analyses for most food species are available in the literature.

Determination of the food habits is essential for ecological and nutritional studies of sirenians, but can be difficult because of the breakdown of vegetation due to mastication and passage through the extensive digestive tract[2]. Direct observation of feeding is seldom possible. Nonetheless, knowledge of the specific components of the diet can offer tremendous insight into availability and utilization of resources as well as preferences related to the season, reproductive condition, or simply taste and texture.

The dugong diet consists almost exclusively of seagrasses[3], although algae[4] and invertebrates[5] may be consumed. West Indian and West African manatees feed on seagrasses as well, and all three species of manatees may be particularly opportunistic feeders, with a diet that includes a wide variety of aquatic and wetland angiosperms, shore grasses, species of marine algae, and occasionally fish and invertebrates, consumed incidentally with vegetation or purposely[6]. Seasonal variation in diet choices, based on either nutritional content or availability, has been observed for the dugong[7], Amazonian manatee[8], and Florida manatee[9].

For sirenians, a straightforward method for analysis is by direct examination of the contents of the gastrointestinal (GI) tract. This method is simple, but of course can only address diet components at one point in time, and if the animal is still alive, it is very intrusive. A second technique utilizes analyses of stable isotope ratios in sirenian tissues, which can also provide insight into foraging habits over longer timescales (i.e., weeks to years). Near-infrared reflectance spectroscopy (NIRS) is a third method for estimating dietary components. Techniques for each of these methods, from sample collection to final determination, are outlined in the sections that follow. Resources for standard procedures, necessary equipment, technical assistance, and facilities that may provide analyses or assistance are also listed.

Sirenian Diet Determination by Direct Examination

Stomach and duodenum contents are easiest to identify because the fragments of ingesta have been subjected to minimal digestion. Not only are the fragments larger in the upper GI tract, but they are also the best indication of the entire range of what an animal has most recently consumed. Fecal samples, often abundant and fairly easy to obtain in known sirenian feeding areas, are more difficult to identify by direct examination. The fragments are often only a few cells in size, and the more delicate species may have been digested beyond recognition. Tougher plants, for example, those with thicker leaves or fibrous veins, will be over-represented in a fecal sample. The examiner should be aware of this potential for bias when reporting results if only fecal samples are available for diet determination. Stomach contents are

---

BOX 14.1

Equipment for Direct Examination

Essential equipment:

- containers and labels for sample storage
- microscope with 100× magnification
- glass slides and cover slips
- data sheets/field book

Recommended equipment:

- absorbent paper
- 70% ethyl alcohol
- Hertwig's clearing solution
- polarizing filter for microscope
- sieves

generally available only from salvaged carcasses but may be collected from animals at capture through the use of a stomach tube and pump. Outlined below is a step-by-step process for a food habits study based on direct examination of ingesta contents. This technique can be accomplished with a limited budget and under field conditions but will yield insight only into an animal's recent diet. Methods of analysis are the same whether the samples are from the stomach or farther down the GI tract[10].

Step 1. Establish a reference collection: Before identifying plant fragments from ingesta, a reference collection of known or potential food items within the habitat is necessary (unless there is a local herbarium with a collection of accessible plants). Although the amount of material needed is minimal, in most locales it may be necessary to obtain a permit to collect plants. Collect all parts of the plants present: leaves, stems, roots/rhizomes, and flowers, fruits, or seeds. Terrestrial plants that may be accessible should not be overlooked, as these may be consumed as well. Various species of algae and invertebrates as epiphytes or epibionts on plant material may be consumed incidentally and should also be sampled. Also consider collecting samples of algae and invertebrates (e.g., bryozoans) observed in feeding areas, as these may be directly consumed. Use local field reference guides, plant and invertebrate keys, or experts to help identify specimens. Label specimens with collector name, date, and location, minimally; salinity, depth, temperature, other plant associates, and other parameters also may be of interest later. This material will be a reference key for later comparison to the ingesta content samples.

To prevent the growth of mold, thoroughly air dry or use absorbent paper to blot and press the specimens. Absorbent papers are sold specifically for pressing and drying plants for collections. However, newsprint is an economical substitute; it is absorbent and deters fungal growth. It may be easiest to float aquatic or thin-leaved plants directly onto the paper to display the structure best. Either method may require several changes of paper before the specimen is completely dry. Place dry specimens between layers of paper or into envelopes, and store them away from insects. Consider using an insect repellent in the box or cabinet where the specimens will be stored.

Step 2. Process reference material: For each species collected, examine a small piece of each plant part—a piece of leaf, including the edge, a piece of stem, a piece of rhizome, etc. Place these on separate slides and treat with Hertwig's solution if available (see box 14.2). Thick leaf and stem material will first need to be gently scraped to remove layers of cells (this may mean peeling apart and separately examining the upper and lower leaf surfaces), and all but the thinnest, most delicate plants (e.g., fine algae, leaves of some *Halophila* species) will need to be gently pressed (smashed) using a blunt probe. This simulates mastication and exposes various structures, but do not overdo it and tear or grind the plant into tiny fragments. The goal is to have a one- to two-cell-thick fragment of material with identifiable structures apparent. The shape and arrangement of cells and veins, and the shape, presence or absence, and arrangement of spines, stomata, crystals, or specialized cells (idioblasts) that differ in appearance from surrounding cells, all help with identification.

Although there are plant keys available for specific plant types, geographic regions, and habitats[11], it is useful to create your own key of common identification characters of the plants in your reference collection by making a permanent collection of reference slides and photomicrographs. To create a permanent reference slide collection, mount known fragments using any available mounting media. It is not necessary to stain the plant tissues; doing so can make some characters harder to identify. If slides will be stored in a humid environment, choose a non-water-soluble mounting medium. Label and store slide mounts flat. For later reference, photograph specimens by capturing images through a microscope eyepiece.

Step 3. Collect ingesta samples: Stomach samples, if available from a carcass, are preferable for examination as the fragments will be larger, less digested, and easier to identify than fecal samples. However, fecal samples are useful and may be collected from captured animals or in areas where sirenians are feeding. Prior to microscopic examination, wash samples

BOX 14.2

To Make Hertwig's Solution:

19 ml 1 molar hydrochloric acid
150 ml water
60 ml glycerin
270 g chloral hydrate crystals

Add acid to water, and *then* add glycerin and crystals and mix over low heat until completely dissolved.

through a fine sieve (e.g., 0.425–0.500 mm mesh size) to remove minute pieces of debris, sand, and single cell fragments of vegetation that can easily obscure identification characters. Content samples are best stored in 70% ethyl alcohol (EtOH). If no preservative is available, treat the sample as if it were a freshly collected plant specimen and simply air dry or dry between absorbent papers, again ensuring the prevention of mold growth.

Some plant fragments, especially from the upper GI tract, can be identified without a microscope. Closely examine each sample; this is an opportunity to record the obvious presence of parasitic helminth species and any nonfood items (debris) that may have been incidentally ingested.

Step 4. Process the sample: Always wear eye protection when preparing a sample and when using Hertwig's solution. To prepare a subsample for microscopic examination, place 1–2 grams of ingesta onto a 2×3-inch (25×75 mm) glass slide. If available, add a few drops of Hertwig's solution and mix gently with a small probe. Using a clamp or clothespin, hold the slide over a low flame (alcohol burner, candle, or handheld lighter; all work equally well) and away from alcohol or any other flammables, just until the solution begins to bubble (usually less than a minute). Take great care that the plant material does not burn. If the solution does catch fire, quickly and gently blow out the flame, and the sample generally will not be affected. Heated Hertwig's solution will clear pigments from the plant cells, making the cellular structures more easily discernable.

Using the already washed and cleared ingesta sample, spread a very small amount as thinly and evenly as possible onto a clean slide. Add a few drops of 70% EtOH, and place a cover slip on top. Scan at low (40×) power to be certain that the material on the slide is evenly distributed and the cellular structure of the fragments is clearly visible. Some species may be identifiable at low power, but a higher power (100×) optimizes identification. Use the coordinates on the microscope stage as transect lines to define fields of view and ensure an even examination of the slide. If Hertwig's solution is unavailable, fragments may still be identifiable using your reference collection for comparison or using published microhistological keys (see keys referenced in Step 2).

Step 5. Identify plant fragments: Even with only a small fragment to examine, some plant fragments are easily identified by unique characteristics. Other plant species present a challenge. Here are a few suggestions to help in the microscopic identification process.

- The leaves of the red mangrove, *Rhizophora mangle*, are consumed by manatees in some parts of their range[12]. The species has idioblast cells in the leaf tissue that are a distinct H-shape. Arms of the H may be of different lengths, but once this characteristic is noted, it will not easily be missed. Idioblasts survive gut passage and may be numerous in fecal samples.
- Look closely for spines along the leaf edges and vein surfaces. Presence or absence of these may be an identifying feature or the most easily distinguishing character between two similar genera. For example, *Hydrilla verticillata* and *Egeria densa* often occur in mixed beds in aquatic habitats in Florida and are very similar in appearance; an additional aid to distinguishing microscopic fragments of these species is to look for an obvious mid-rib leaf vein with spines, often apparent on *Hydrilla* but not on *Egeria*.
- A polarizing filter over the light source on the microscope is a helpful accessory to assist in highlighting specific identifying characters of the plants in your reference collection; that is, veins, crystals, idioblasts, and spines[13]. For instance, the rectangular leaf epidermal cells of *Halodule wrightii* are stacked like a brick wall, and the leaf fragment will have edge veins that usually glow when viewed under polarized light. *Ruppia maritima* cells have a similar arrangement, but the epidermal cells are more cube-shaped and do not have brightly glowing veins evident.

Step 6. Determine the proportion of species present: For some studies it may be of interest to determine the percent occurrence of species present in a sample. We recommend this process only if using stomach content samples. Samples from lower in the GI tract have been subject to more digestion and will result in an over-representation of some less digested plants (e.g., fibrous grasses, mangrove leaves). To determine percent occurrence a modified microscope point technique may be used to record five identifications in each field of view and repeat this for five slides[14]. (Note the presence of nonfood items such as sand, parasites, debris, etc.) A sample data form for recording food items can be found in Hurst and Beck[15].

Stable Isotopes and Sirenian Diets

A second method for determination of diet involves sampling various tissues of a sirenian and submitting

Table 14.1. A short list of suitable biogenic materials for stable isotope analysis.

Material	Preparation	Stable Isotope Tracers	Turnover Rate
Blood			
Plasma	Hobson et al. 1997	$\delta^{13}C, \delta^{2}H, \delta^{15}N, \delta^{18}O$	~1 day
Red blood cells	Hobson et al. 1997	$\delta^{13}C, \delta^{2}H, \delta^{15}N, \delta^{34}S$	~1 month
Tissues			
Liver	Hobson et al. 1997	$\delta^{13}C, \delta^{2}H, \delta^{15}N, \delta^{34}S$	Weeks
Muscle	Hobson et al. 1997	$\delta^{13}C, \delta^{2}H, \delta^{15}N, \delta^{34}S$	Months
Skin	Hobson et al. 1996	$\delta^{13}C, \delta^{2}H, \delta^{15}N, \delta^{34}S$	Months
Blubber	Tieszen et al. 1983	$\delta^{13}C, \delta^{2}H, \delta^{15}N, \delta^{34}S$	Months
Keratin			
Hair	Hobson et al. 1996	$\delta^{13}C, \delta^{2}H, \delta^{15}N, \delta^{34}S$	Accreted
Vibrissae	Hobson et al. 1996	$\delta^{13}C, \delta^{2}H, \delta^{15}N, \delta^{34}S$	Accreted
Nails	Hobson et al. 1996	$\delta^{13}C, \delta^{2}H, \delta^{15}N, \delta^{34}S$	Accreted
Dentition			
Bioapatite	Koch et al. 1994	$\delta^{13}C, \delta^{18}O$	Accreted
Collagen	Koch et al. 1994	$\delta^{13}C, \delta^{2}H, \delta^{15}N, \delta^{34}S$	Accreted
Bone			
Bioapatite	Koch et al. 1994	$\delta^{13}C, \delta^{18}O$	Years
Collagen	Koch et al. 1994	$\delta^{13}C, \delta^{2}H, \delta^{15}N, \delta^{34}S$	Years

Note: Turnover rates for these tissues are based on reported rates for other mammalian species and should be considered an estimate of the possible turnover rate for sirenians.

these for stable isotope analysis (table 14.1). This method provides insight into the animal's diet over a longer period of time, although with less precision as to species consumed.

Stable isotope analysis of tissues (i.e., bone, collagen, hair, skin, etc.) has become an increasingly important proxy for ecological and dietary information from marine mammals[16]. The stable isotopes from five elements—carbon ($\delta^{13}C$), hydrogen ($\delta^{2}H$), nitrogen ($\delta^{15}N$), oxygen ($\delta^{18}O$) and sulfur ($\delta^{34}S$)—have been employed in modern and paleontological studies to address questions of marine mammal ecology. These elements are common components of marine mammal tissues, and their isotope ratio in tissues are ultimately controlled by diet and drinking water[17]. For sirenians, dietary resources are typically restricted to aquatic macrophytes, and drinking water is dependent upon the body of water in which the species lives. Since primary producer and environmental water isotope values can differ significantly between freshwater and marine ecosystems[18], the tissues of sirenians foraging in these food webs can be isotopically labeled by the vegetation and water they consume, providing a powerful tool for identifying manatee foraging habits ($\delta^{13}C, \delta^{34}S$), trophic level ($\delta^{15}N$), and migration ($\delta^{2}H, \delta^{18}O$).

Stable isotope ratios are often calculated using the delta (δ) equation:

$$\delta\ (‰) = (R_{sample} - R_{standard})/R_{standard} \times 1000$$

where R is the isotope ratio of the sample or standard.

The differences in the relative amount of one isotope to another are very small, and are expressed as parts per thousand or per mil (‰) differences relative to an international standard.

For example: Carbon isotope analysis examines the ratio of ^{13}C to ^{12}C in a sample and is reported relative to the international laboratory standard V-PDB ($^{13}C/^{12}C$ = 0.0112372). Thus a sample with a $^{13}C/^{12}C$ of 0.0112472 would have a δ-value of 0.9‰. The same equation is used to calculate the δ-value for other stable isotope systems including hydrogen ($^{2}H/^{1}H$), nitrogen ($^{15}N/^{14}N$), oxygen ($^{18}O/^{16}O$), and sulfur ($^{34}S/^{33}S$).

An important consideration is the selection of the appropriate tissue type. The temporal detail of information recorded within an animal's tissues depends upon how quickly those tissues are metabolized[19]. Preferred tissues for stable isotope analysis include materials that may turn over on the order of days (e.g., blood plasma); weeks (e.g., red blood cells, liver); months (e.g., muscle, skin, blubber); years (e.g., bone bioapatite, collagen); or not at all (e.g., hair, nails, tooth enamel, and dentine)[20].

The amount of time integrated into the dietary signal extracted from a tissue must be considered when designing the sampling protocol. For instance, collagen, the organic framework of bone, is continuously remodeled throughout an animal's life and reflects a running average of an animal's diet. As such, collagen would not likely capture the full range of dietary variation exploited by sirenians. Other materials, such as skin, cholesterol, or liver, turn over much more quickly and, if sampled repeatedly within a year, are more likely to reflect a population's true dietary range. Finally, hairs, nails, and teeth are not reworked by the body once formed and grow by the deposition of new layers of material. Since these materials grow incrementally, their isotope composition can provide a nearly continuous record of an animal's diet over several months or years.

Prior stable isotope analysis of sirenian tissues has focused primarily on analysis of tooth enamel[21], bone collagen[22], and skin and organ tissue[23]. Table 14.1 is a list of suitable materials. Results from these projects found significant shifts in stable isotope values for individuals within populations, particularly for freshwater and marine populations of Florida manatees, and testify to the usefulness of this approach for providing valuable dietary information. No published work, however, has yet looked at how the stable isotopes of other elements, most notably hydrogen and sulfur, may contribute information about sirenian diets, nor has anyone examined whether materials that grow incrementally or that turn over relatively quickly (i.e., whiskers, fats, cholesterol) can provide new insight into dietary change over shorter windows of time. Materials such as cholesterol and whiskers can be relatively easily collected from living sirenians during field surveys and would provide conservation biologists a quick and efficient means of monitoring dietary change within regional populations.

For the stable isotopes of most elements, there is a measurable difference between the stable isotope composition of an animal's tissue and that of its diet. This offset is referred to as a discrimination factor and can vary considerably between species and between tissue types[24]. For small differences (<10.0‰), the discrimination factor can be calculated as simply the difference in stable isotope value between diet and tissue (e.g., $\delta^{13}C_{tissue-diet} = \delta^{13}C_{tissue} - \delta^{13}C_{diet}$). For differences of greater magnitude (>10.0‰), it is necessary to calculate the discrimination factor (in per mil) using the following relationship:

$$\varepsilon_{tissue-diet} = (1000 + \delta^{13}C_{tissue})/(1000 + \delta^{13}C_{diet}) - 1$$

A few studies have attempted to calculate the magnitude of carbon isotope discrimination between tissues and diet for sirenians, which ranges from 3‰ for skin to 14.1‰ for enamel from manatees and dugongs[25], but discrimination factors for the isotopes of hydrogen, nitrogen, and other elements have not been determined for sirenians. Before interpretation of individual diets can be made using isotopes from these other elements, researchers need to take the time to quantify carefully the magnitude of these offsets for each tissue of interest. Until then, the stable isotope ecology of sirenians will primarily be restricted to analysis of the carbon isotope composition of tissues and diet.

Field Methods and Sample Preparation

Once particular isotopes and tissues have been selected, the next step is to collect samples from field or captive specimens. Prior to field collection, obtain permits, including specific permits for tissue collection, and determine transport, the amount of sample required, and appropriate methods of preservation and transport.

The sensitivity of isotope ratio mass spectrometers (IRMS) has increased significantly, allowing researchers to use smaller sample sizes for analysis. This amount is dependent upon the concentration of the particular element of interest within a given tissue. Most tissues have a more or less consistent concentration of carbon, nitrogen, and hydrogen, so a similar sample size of 0.5 to 1.0 mg (dried weight) is appropriate for most analyses. For other elements, such as sulfur, the concentration can be much lower and can require several milligrams per

---

BOX 14.3

Equipment for Stable Isotope Sampling

Essential equipment:

    containers and labels for sample storage (glass preferred)
    field book for recording results
    syringe, scalpel, or other instrument for tissue collection
    cooler with ice or dry ice

Recommended equipment:

    coffee grinder and/or mortar and pestle
    freeze-dryer (lyophilizer)
    desiccators

analysis[26]. In general, collection of ~100 mg of sample (wet weight) should be sufficient for most analyses and would not be too difficult to collect in the field.

Once a sample is collected, preservation of its stable isotope composition is strongly dependent upon the type of tissue selected. For instance, keratinous tissues, such as hair, vibrissae, or nails, are highly resistant to decay and can often be stored under standard room conditions. Blood and tissue samples, however, are highly susceptible to degradation and isotope alteration, so steps must be taken immediately following collection to halt this process. The best preservation methods are freezing and/or drying specimens[27]. If available, a lyophilizer or freeze-dryer is the best choice for long-term storage. In the field, these methods may not be available; alternative methods include preservation in ethanol and drying small tissue samples using prepackaged containers of silica gel desiccant. The latter method is not appropriate for samples intended for δ^2H analysis (the desiccant may alter the D/H composition of the sample).

Back in the lab, samples may be stored in the freezer or in a desiccator prior to analysis. Several labs are currently offering to perform these types of analyses (table 14.2) and can provide information on the cost and preparation.

When in the field, it is important to collect a sample of potential food items. Although considerable carbon isotope data have been published for many terrestrial plant species[28], information on the composition of other isotopes in aquatic plants is limited and can vary considerably between locations[29]. Before valid dietary interpretations can be made, the isotope composition of these food items needs to be determined. Plant samples can be collected and preserved in much the same way as tissue samples, except larger quantities (~1 g) should be selected, so that upon drying, these samples can be ground and homogenized to produce an average isotope value for each particular dietary item.

Near-Infrared Reflectance Spectroscopy

An alternative technique for determining the composition of vegetative fragments in a content sample is near-infrared reflectance spectroscopy (NIRS). This technique is a useful method for large-scale analyses of diet data from a discrete area. NIRS enables the estimation of primary vegetative components in a content sample[30] and can be used to determine chemical components as well[31].

For sirenians, this technique first entails collection of plant samples that are potential or known food items from the animals' habitat and calculation of a calibration equation for the NIRS results from each possible food item. Prior to NIRS analysis, plant samples are washed to remove epiphytes, sorted into parts (leaf, root/rhizome), dried, ground to consistently sized (1mm) fragments, and then stored in sealed containers until processing. The fragments are carefully packed into sample cups with an optical grade quartz glass cover on one side, then irradiated with NIR light, and the reflectance spectra are collected[32]. Uniform particle size is critical as a sample with varying size particles can affect the reflectance measurements. Assurance that the samples are completely dry is also critical, as water has a strong near-infrared spectral absorbance that could affect results. Analyses therefore must be conducted in a controlled environment, specifically a room maintained with known constant temperature and humidity. The NIRS result will yield a value for

Table 14.2. Research laboratory contacts for stable isotope analysis of tissues and plant materials.

Institution	Web site
University of California–Davis Stable Isotope Facility	http://stableisotopefacility.ucdavis.edu
University of Wyoming Stable Isotope Facility	http://www.uwyo.edu/sif/
University of California–Berkeley Center for Stable Isotope Biogeochemistry	http://ib.berkeley.edu/groups/biogeochemistry/
Alaska Stable Isotope Facility	http://www.uaf.edu/water/ASIF/ASIF.html
Stable Isotope Ratio Facility for Environmental Research	http://sirfer.utah.edu
Australian National University Stable Isotope Facility	http://www.rsbs.anu.edu.au/Products&Services/StableIsotopeFacility/

Note: Refer to each facility's website to address questions of sample cost and laboratory capabilities.

each known sample to which content samples, examined microhistologically and treated in the same manner, can be compared.

The advantage of this method is its potential to increase greatly the number of samples that can be analyzed quickly. André and Lawler[33] used this method to analyze a large number of dugong stomach content samples. These authors demonstrated that once the calibration equations were established for major dietary items from a sample of the total collection, the remaining samples could be estimated by NIRS alone.

Although the NIRS process requires some preprocessing of the samples, some specialized equipment, and controlled conditions, the efficiency of this technique can result in a reduced cost per sample. Researchers interested in employing this technique are advised to collaborate with facilities with the required equipment (NIR spectrophotometer) and expertise. Universities or government laboratories that analyze feed for livestock may be of assistance.

Summary

Each of the methods outlined is useful for diet determination, but the chosen method will be dependent on the objectives of a study as well as logistic and budgetary constraints. Access to samples may require permits, and the equipment needs associated with each method can vary and must be addressed before beginning a project. With these considerations in mind, however, gut content, stable isotope, and NIRS analyses are all methods available to employ for revealing the dietary preferences of sirenian populations, beyond what can be achieved by direct field observation.

Acknowledgments

Our sincere thanks to M. Marmontel, E. Hines, and two anonymous reviewers, whose insightful comments greatly improved this chapter. Any use of trade, product, or firm names is for descriptive purposes only and does not imply endorsement by the U.S. government.

15

Individual Identification of Sirenians

CATHY A. BECK AND ANN MARIE CLARK

The ability to identify an individual in a population of outwardly identical sirenians is often an important aspect of population research. Identification and monitoring of individuals can provide insights into questions of reproductive success, longevity, intraspecific social behaviors, determination of seasonal site fidelity, frequency and duration of using specific habitats, movements to new sites or regions, determination of the sex ratio of a group, survival rate of a population, and documentation of any changes in appearance over time.

There are several established techniques used to identify specific individual sirenians, although not all are practical or possible for all species and in all parts of the world. The methods, applicability, challenges, and benefits of each approach are discussed in this chapter. Techniques include (1) marks or tags applied to captured individuals (PIT tags, radio tags, freeze brands), (2) photographic documentation of unique features, and (3) genetic analysis of tissues. In the United States all these methods require federal permits. Researchers elsewhere are advised to determine whether their proposed activities require permission from local or national permitting authorities.

Applied Marks and Tags

Several methods have been tried to mark individual sirenians artificially[1]. These include marks made on the skin with oil-based crayons (e.g., Paintsticks), freeze brands, subdermal implantation of passive integrated transponder (PIT) tags, and tagging with a colored plastic strip attached to a dart (known as a spaghetti tag). Freeze branding requires capture of the individual, and PIT and radio tagging generally do as well.

All-weather crayon markings can be accomplished on wild sirenians while in the water, provided the individual is approachable. However, these marks are easily smeared or lost when animals rub against each other or other objects and are useful only for very brief monitoring, generally 1–3 days[2] (figure 15.1).

Applying spaghetti tags on sirenians is not recommended owing to the difficulty of penetrating the dense dermis and the rapid reaction of the animal to expel the tag out of the skin. Efforts to apply these tags to Florida manatees in captivity using a lance, and to wild manatees using a thrown handheld lance or crossbow, were overwhelmingly unsuccessful[3]. On Florida manatees, abscesses sometimes formed at the penetration site[4].

Freeze branding of individuals with unique characters leaves a permanent mark useful for later identification on close observation. Capture is required, and application times are critical for the brand to "take" (figure 15.2). Freeze brands are persistent if they have been applied properly, following established protocols (table 15.1). The 2-inch freeze brands are applied to two locations on the dorsum of Florida manatees, enabling long-term identification, *only* if there are no other permanent identifying features. Freeze brands have been used successfully in Florida and Puerto Rico to mark unscarred captive manatees slated for release. Discernable brands have been resighted on animals up to 22 years after application (USGS files).

Passive integrated transponder (PIT) tags have been used successfully on many species of wildlife as well as domestic animals[5]. Rice-grain-sized PIT tags generate a unique string of numbers and letters that can be read with an appropriate scanner. They have been implanted successfully under the dermis of manatees in Florida, Puerto Rico, Mexico, and Belize without any subsequent tissue reaction or long-term harm and are very useful for positively reidentifying an individual upon recapture or death. In Australia, these tags have also been successfully applied to dugongs while in the water without any detectable problems[6]. PIT tags are especially important when condition of a carcass at recovery makes photo-

Figure 15.1. R. K. Bonde applying harmless Paintstick marking to a Florida manatee. (Courtesy of James Reid, U.S. Geological Survey.)

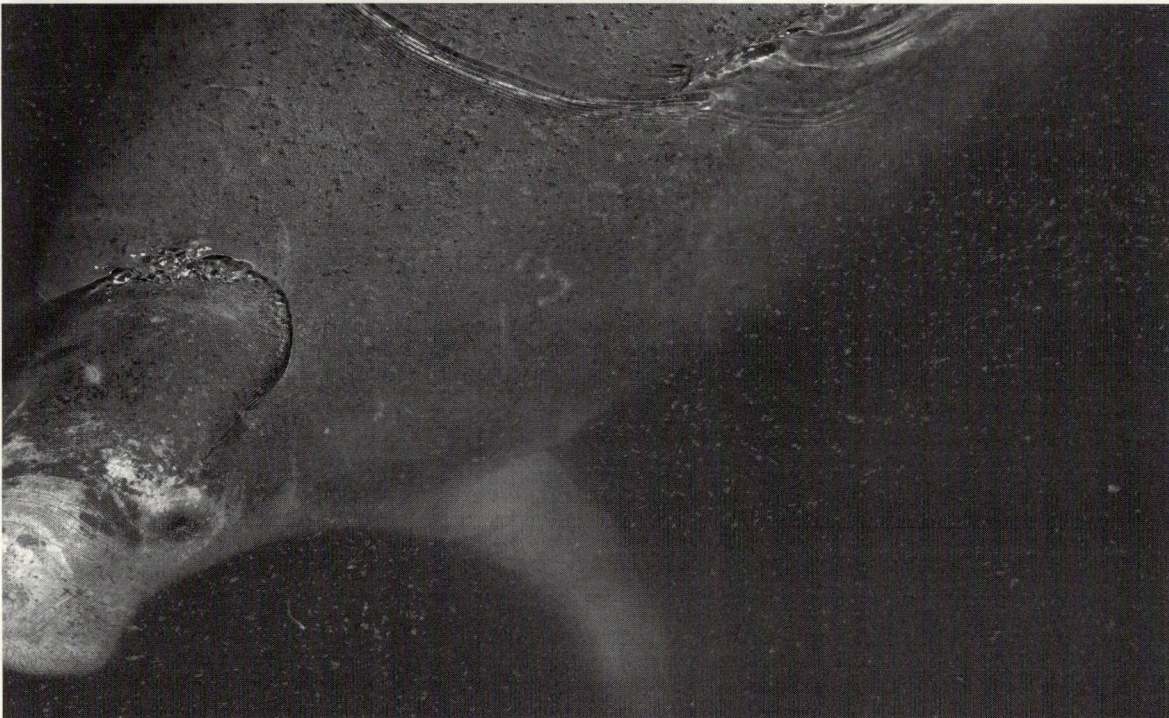

Figure 15.2. Freeze brand (38) visible 13 years post-application on Florida manatee BC393. (Courtesy of A. L. Teague, U.S. Geological Survey.)

Table 15.1. Freeze branding protocol in use for Florida manatees (USGS 2005).

Equipment	Procedure
1. Two-inch solid brass numbers/letters 2. Application handles 3. Submersion container 4. Liquid nitrogen and Dewar transfer container 5. Gloves 6. Towels 7. Antiseptic soaps 8. Freezebrand data sheet and camera	1. Determine if branding is necessary; i.e., that the individual has no other identifying marks. 2. Ensure that number, letter, or combination of these has not been assigned to another individual. 3. Begin cooling brands by submerging in liquid nitrogen; brand should be cooled for at least 5 minutes prior to application to ensure success. 4. Select branding sites on animal (usually mid-dorsum, one behind the head and another just anterior to the peduncle). 5. Orient brands in same direction with body axis. 6. Clean area with betadine or alcohol rubs and allow the skin surface to dry completely. 7. Take extreme caution to ensure there is no contact of the liquid nitrogen or brands with the skin of person applying the brands or that of bystanders. 8. Once brands are completely cooled to the core, the liquid nitrogen will stop bubbling. 9. Apply cold brands directly to the preselected area(s) and apply moderate pressure to ensure even contact with skin. 10. Hold brand on site for 25 to 45 seconds (time dependent on size and age of individual animal). 11. Remove brand and replace in liquid nitrogen if needed again. 12. Take photos to document branding prior to release. 13. Record data and submit information to appropriate authorities.

Note: Prior to initiation of use, freeze branding will likely require a permit issued from the proper authorities.

Remember that brands may not be visible when first applied; scarring may take up to two weeks, and occasionally a brand will not result in white scar tissue.

Manatees will react to branding if brand is held too long against the skin.

Take care to orient position of brands in same direction with tail being down, head up, to prevent wrong orientation of numbers; this will enable accurate reporting and recording of brands.

graphic identification impossible. The protocol for use in manatees requires implantation of two tags, one medial to each shoulder and just under the dermis. This ensures later identification in the event one should fail or break during insertion. Once successfully implanted, PIT tags are durable and longlasting. There are two commonly used brands of PIT tags, Trovan and Avid, each requiring a specific reader. Trovan tags have been used historically in dugongs in Australia and manatees in Florida, Puerto Rico, and Belize, ensuring that if these manatees moved between ranges and were recaptured and scanned for PIT tags, their earlier history would be available. If PIT tagging is undertaken, it is important to determine first which brand is in use by sirenian researchers in nearby regions, and to employ the same type to ensure compatibility.

Researchers in Australia also have applied titanium turtle tags and colorful plastic cattle ear tags to the fluke margin of dugongs, the latter to aid in individual identification without recapture[7].

Radio tagging is a successful approach for short-term identification and monitoring of individuals[8].

Individual Identification by Photographic Documentation

Precise photographic identification (photo-ID) requires the individual to have at least one permanent, unique feature. Manatees in Florida, and increasingly in other parts of their range, commonly bear scars from encounters with boats or entanglement in fishing gear (figure 15.3). Cuts from boat propellers and skegs, and entanglement in monofilament or heavier nylon lines or other debris, can result in permanent scars and mutilations. Increasingly, boat encounters with sirenians are an emerging concern outside Florida. Although gruesome

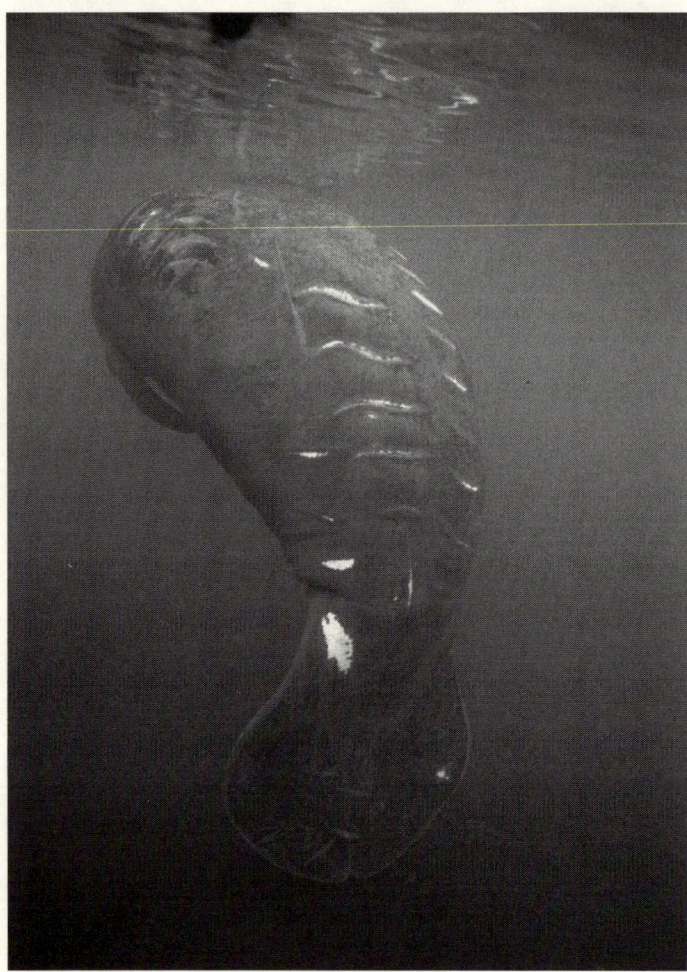

Figure 15.3. Florida manatee CR385 with several series of scars resulting from the cuts of boat propeller blades. (Courtesy of A. L. Teague, U.S. Geological Survey.)

and regrettable, such wounds, once healed, often result in unique scars that can be used for individual identification. But we hope this will not become the primary means of identifying individuals. Congenital deformities and scars resulting from fungal infections or cold lesions are less common but also may be useful for identification.

Complete photographic documentation of the entire dorsal and lateral aspects of the body and tail must be accomplished to depict an individual reliably and to avoid cataloguing one animal as two or more individuals. The advantage to photo-ID is that documentation of a scarred individual is nonintrusive, technologically simple, and fairly affordable, and it can often be accomplished opportunistically while conducting other field research. For long-term study of the population, dedicated and continued monitoring and photo-documentation are necessary, as acquisition of any new features could alter an individual's appearance, potentially making it difficult or impossible to reidentify the animal at a later date.

Challenges to photo-documentation include lack of unique markings on individuals; scars covered by algae, barnacles, or mud on the dermis; and dark or murky water not optimal for photography. The appearance of an individual may change over time as new features are added or others are obliterated. Therefore it is essential that the photo-ID effort is consistent and continued, especially in areas where acquisition of new marks is frequent. No doubt there will be individuals that have not been photographed and are therefore not in a photo-identification catalogue, and of course, some individual animals (notably young calves, but possibly older animals as well) may have no unique features. It also may take years to acquire complete photographic documentation of an individual, and a considerable time investment is needed to describe or code the features used for identification. Furthermore, a photo-identification catalogue is only as good as the photographs. Out-of-focus images will always leave some doubt and in most cases cannot be used as positive identification. Additionally, unique features used for positive identification may be difficult to discern on a carcass as decomposition progresses and the epidermis is lost. In this case, identification by other means, such as PIT tags and genetic genotyping, is of greater benefit, when possible.

A primary example of the use of photo-ID is the long-standing photographic catalogue of individual manatees in Florida since the late 1970s[9]. The Manatee Individual Photo-identification System (MIPS) is a database of sighting records and life history and feature description information for well over 2,000 Florida manatees, based solely on photographic documentation[10]. The images enable the researcher to identify specific animals at specific locations on known dates. The resulting data have enabled estimation of rates of reproduction, adult survival, and population growth[11].

Genetic Analysis

Genetic analysis can address questions that cannot be answered with conventional methods such as photo-ID, marking or tagging. If an individual is not PIT or radio tagged, has no unique markings, or has died and the carcass has decayed beyond the point of recognition, the animal cannot be identified as a particular individual without genetic analysis. Genetic analysis of tissues collected from individuals can provide a unique opportunity to examine the genetic composition of a population of sirenians and can add an additional and irrevocable method of identification and relatedness. Blood, skin, hair, bone, or other tissue samples are useful for genetically determining individual identity and providing insight into the population structure, identification of family units, and determination of the reproductive success of males as well as to answer other questions[12]. Samples for genetic analysis are collected most easily from a captive-held animal or during a capture event. Captured or captive sirenians provide a unique opportunity for a complete morphometric, photographic, and health assessment and for collection of tissues for laboratory analysis. In recent years researchers in most locales routinely draw blood when the opportunity arises, particularly to monitor various health parameters[13]. The same blood sample also can be utilized for various DNA analyses[14]. Blood collected for genetic analysis should be placed into prepared vials containing blood lysis buffer and can be stored at room temperature for extended periods of time[15]. Other tissues (e.g., skin, hairs, fecal samples, and body organs from carcasses) also can be utilized, and if collected should be stored in the appropriate reagents[16]. These samples can then be maintained at room temperature in the same manner as blood samples stored in lysis buffer.

Samples useful for genetic analysis can be taken directly from free-ranging individuals as well. A handheld cattle ear-notcher has been used successfully to collect a small tissue section (approximate thumbnail size) from the tail margin of West Indian manatees and dugongs in Australia[17]. This is easily accomplished using a local anesthetic when an individual is beached (decked) but is also possible for a skilled and stealthy swimmer to accomplish in water on a free-ranging sirenian. This technique has the added advantage of marking the individual so that the researcher is certain it has been previously "sampled," thus avoiding unnecessary duplication. Skin scrapings also yield tissue for genetic analysis but do not leave a permanent mark to prevent resampling. With either collection method, special care must be taken to not contaminate the tissue with one's own DNA (do not handle the sample without gloves). Once collected, tissue samples are stored in a tissue buffer solution; there is no need for refrigeration or other special handling prior to submission for analysis. Tissue samples also may be stored frozen or preserved in 95% ethyl alcohol.

DNA from blood in mammals is isolated from the white cells. The somatic cells in other tissue types all have nuclei and therefore yield DNA. The isolation is done using a variety of methods, such as organic reagents or kits, and there is no preferred storage method that significantly affects the quality or quantity of the DNA. The condition of the tissue at the time of collection is a much greater factor. Decomposing tissues are more difficult to work with and have a much lower yield of DNA than fresh tissues.

Interbreeding, Fitness, and Disease Issues

A database containing genetic information can readily be combined with any other identification methods, such as photo-ID and/or tagging data. The ability to track gene flow can help researchers determine whether excessive inbreeding that may be detrimental to the health of the animals is taking place. While some species (not presently documented in sirenians) seem to tolerate significant inbreeding[18], other species suffer from inbreeding depression[19] and fail to thrive when the breeding population becomes too small. One of the overt effects may be reduced fitness making the individual more susceptible to disease and less able to recover if affected. For instance, red tide has been especially problematic in Florida waters[20] with a high death toll perhaps worsened by reduced population fitness. The fecundity of females may also be affected, causing reduced reproductive capacity. Sirenians are long-lived but reproduce slowly. Further reduction in reproduction will make it more difficult for the species to recover from low population numbers.

Additionally, paternity, reproductive success, confirmation of the association between a cow and calf, identification of family units utilizing a specific habitat, gender determination of individuals, and confirmation of identity at death can all be revealed using genetics. A genetic database containing historical samples as well as contemporary samples would allow biologists to assign individuals to seasonal or feeding areas, or family units, based on allele frequencies. Removal of animals from the database through death, captivity, and emigration, and the addition of animals into the system through birth, captive release, and immigration, would give managers a better grasp of reproductive success and habitat use by free-ranging individuals.

A combination of genetics and photo-ID for individual identification has the potential to be a very powerful tool to assist in developing management strategies and accurate population modeling. A merging of these techniques will provide the background for deeper analyses of both populations and individuals and result in more effective conservation initiatives to aid each species.

Acknowledgments

The authors are grateful for helpful comments from R. K. Bonde, E. Hines, M. Marmontel, and L. Parr, which greatly benefited the clarity of this chapter. We also recognize and appreciate the accomplishments of all the researchers who have used various methods to identify individual sirenians. Any use of trade, product, or firm names is for descriptive purposes only and does not imply endorsement by the U.S. government.

16

Health Assessment of Captive and Wild-Caught West Indian Manatees (*Trichechus manatus*)

M. ANDREW STAMPER AND ROBERT K. BONDE

As human populations increase along coastlines and waterways, their various activities impact the health of sirenians in these fragile environments. Medically examining these animals in their natural habitats and gauging how both individual and overall population health alter as the environment changes serves as a tool for the conservation and management of the animals and their habitats[1]. To construct useful databases, it is critical that observations are recorded and samples taken in consistent ways. Most important is the appropriate collection and careful management of biological samples. Collection and handling of samples takes experience even when conducted in controlled situations, such as at a captive facility. Even greater skill and quality control needs to be attempted in field situations, where biologists and veterinarians often work in difficult conditions, with fluctuations in temperature, direct sunlight, rain, wind, and tides. Despite the unpredictability of fieldwork, tissues and the associated documentation must be handled carefully; otherwise biases caused by artifact interference could influence results, especially when interpreting blood analyses.

Guided by experience obtained from handling manatees in Florida, Puerto Rico, Belize, Mexico, and Brazil, and dugongs in Australia, this chapter is designed to give scientists information on the appropriate protocol to examine a sirenian for a detailed health assessment (figure 16.1).

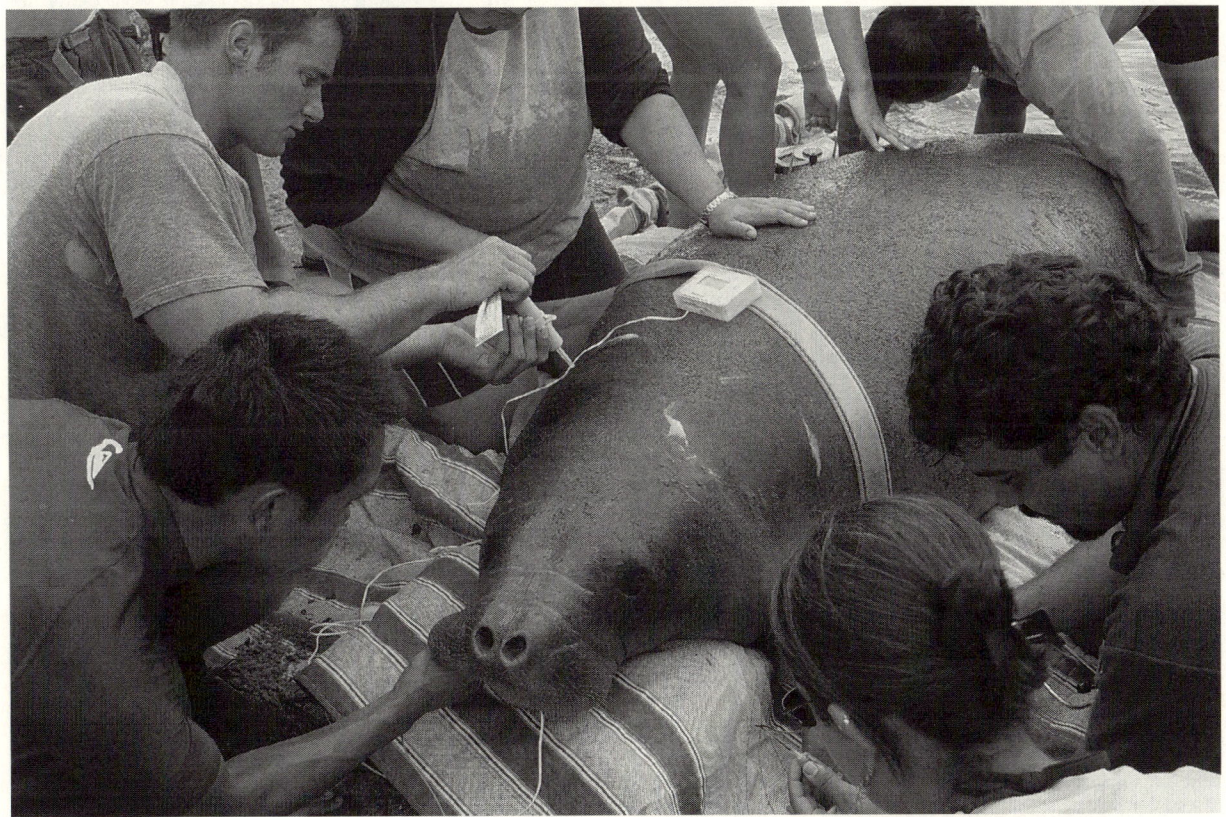

Figure 16.1. Health assessment of wild-caught West Indian manatee in Puerto Rico. (Courtesy of U.S. Geological Survey.)

Most health assessment projects develop their own data sheets. These usually include one form each for the overall examination (figures 16.2 and 16.3), specimen collection, documentation of temperature, pulse and respiration (TPR) monitoring, ultrasound recording, radio tagging, etc.

External Examination

Prior to capture, researchers and clinicians should note the general disposition of the animal. Once beached, the animal should be made as comfortable as possible and placed on foam pads. Special consideration must be made for pregnant animals (enlarged abdomen and, during late stages, distended vulva), which should not be left without appropriate support while out of water and should be processed as quickly as possible or released right away. The overall condition of the animal should be thoroughly evaluated for any evidence of lesions, nutritional status, and deformities[2]. This must be performed in a consistent and systematic method (i.e., head to tail) for every animal.

First, overall appearance should be noted, including movement characteristics (i.e., freedom of movement of the head and neck, pectoral flippers, and tail) and body condition (i.e., emaciated, thin, or overweight). Eyes and nares should be examined for abnormalities. The examiner should document any skin scarring with drawings and photographs. As part of an evaluation of body condition, determine the thickness of the adipose (fat/blubber) layer of manatees using ultrasound or a sonogram[3]. Morphometric measurements should include weight; total length (straight line and curvilinear); girths at axilla, umbilicus, anus, and peduncle; and measurements of any scars or mutilations (figure 16.1). This information, coupled with results of lab analyses, is a valuable tool for gauging health status.

In most countries where sirenian research is ongoing, all captured animals should be scanned for passive integrated transponder (PIT) tags[4]. Tag types should be standardized between projects and countries, since animals often travel across borders. The standard protocol for West Indian manatees is to place one tag in each shoulder. However, be aware that it is possible, though rare, for the implanted transponders to migrate

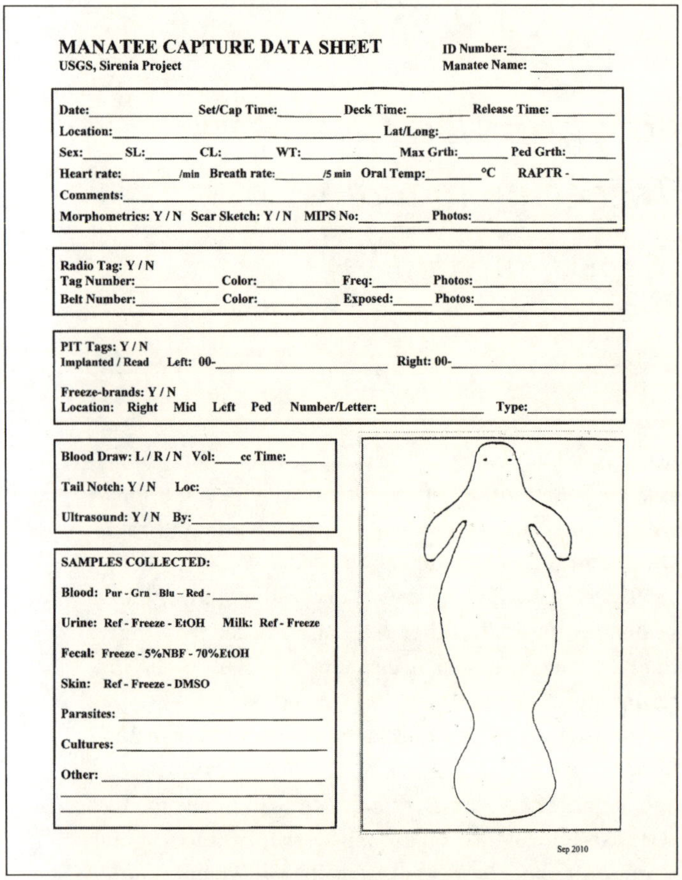
MANATEE CAPTURE DATA SHEET
USGS, Sirenia Project
ID Number: ______
Manatee Name: ______

Date: ______ Set/Cap Time: ______ Deck Time: ______ Release Time: ______
Location: ______ Lat/Long: ______
Sex: ______ SL: ______ CL: ______ WT: ______ Max Grth: ______ Ped Grth: ______
Heart rate: ______/min Breath rate: ______/5 min Oral Temp: ______°C RAPTR - ______
Comments: ______
Morphometrics: Y / N Scar Sketch: Y / N MIPS No: ______ Photos: ______

Radio Tag: Y / N
Tag Number: ______ Color: ______ Freq: ______ Photos: ______
Belt Number: ______ Color: ______ Exposed: ______ Photos: ______

PIT Tags: Y / N
Implanted / Read Left: 00-______ Right: 00-______

Freeze-brands: Y / N
Location: Right Mid Left Ped Number/Letter: ______ Type: ______

Blood Draw: L / R / N Vol: ____cc Time: ______
Tail Notch: Y / N Loc: ______
Ultrasound: Y / N By: ______

SAMPLES COLLECTED:
Blood: Pur - Grn - Blu – Red - ______
Urine: Ref - Freeze - EtOH Milk: Ref - Freeze
Fecal: Freeze - 5%NBF - 70%EtOH
Skin: Ref - Freeze - DMSO
Parasites: ______
Cultures: ______
Other: ______

Sep 2010

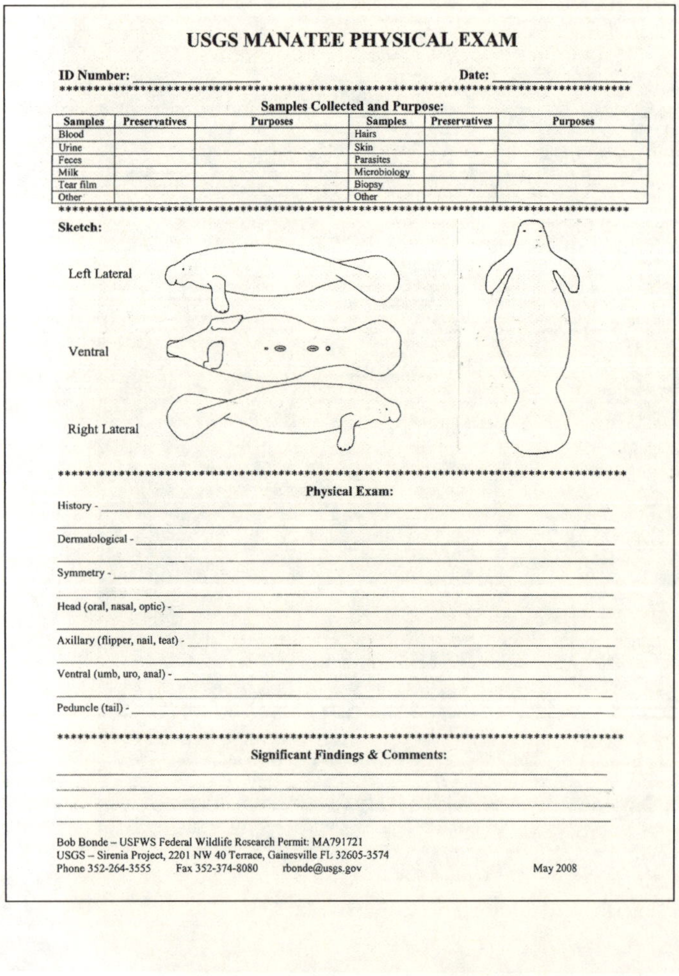
USGS MANATEE PHYSICAL EXAM

ID Number: ______ Date: ______

Samples Collected and Purpose:

Samples	Preservatives	Purposes	Samples	Preservatives	Purposes
Blood			Hairs		
Urine			Skin		
Feces			Parasites		
Milk			Microbiology		
Tear film			Biopsy		
Other			Other		

Sketch:
Left Lateral
Ventral
Right Lateral

Physical Exam:
History - ______
Dermatological - ______
Symmetry - ______
Head (oral, nasal, optic) - ______
Axillary (flipper, nail, teat) - ______
Ventral (umb, uro, anal) - ______
Peduncle (tail) - ______

Significant Findings & Comments:

Bob Bonde – USFWS Federal Wildlife Research Permit: MA791721
USGS – Sirenia Project, 2201 NW 40 Terrace, Gainesville FL 32605-3574
Phone 352-264-3555 Fax 352-374-8080 rbonde@usgs.gov
May 2008

Figure 16.2. (*top left*) Health assessment sheet used in Florida for wild-caught manatees. (Courtesy of U.S. Geological Survey.)

Figure 16.3. (*bottom left*) Example of a detailed physical examination form used for captive manatees. (Courtesy of U.S. Geological Survey.)

through tissue, and examiners should be careful to scan the whole animal. If a PIT tag is not present, then the animal should be fitted with two tags, using the protocol described in Wright et al[5].

Vital Signs

Respiration

During restraint and observation note the number of respirations per five-minute interval. Average rested animal respirations should be around one breath every minute with a range of 3–15 per five minutes[6]. Attempts can be introduced to increase breathing by pouring water over the closed nasal passages. This procedure often results in a voluntary inhalation. Describe if the inspiration and expiration are shallow or deep, and document the odor of the expiration (no odor, sweet/sour, or foul). Though this may be difficult in large animals, a stethoscope can be used to listen to each lung along the dorsum while the animal is taking a breath; note if the lung field is clear.

Heart rate and capillary refill

To obtain heart rate, either use an electrocardiography (ECG) monitor or place a stethoscope against the body at the sternum. Check the heart for palpitations, trills, or arrhythmias and evident murmur sounds. Siegal-Willott and colleagues[7] demonstrated a heart rate of 51–66 bpm for adults and 61–75 bpm for calves using an ECG monitor (figure 16.4). Capillary refill time will give an indication of blood circulation and can be determined by pressing a finger against the upper inner lip pad, then removing and noting capillary refill time when the blanched tissue returns to normal color. Notice if the gum color is pink or pale and whether the tissue appears cyanotic (bluish) or icteric (yellowish). If the animal is showing signs of distress, try supporting it in the water (if possible and safe) to see if parameters normalize. On very rare occasions, some animals may be lethargic, and these individuals should be introduced back into the water with care. If the animal does not stabilize satisfactorily, transport it to the nearest rehabilitation center if possible.

Temperature

Oral temperature in West Indian manatees is generally between 34 and 36°C. Temperature can be monitored with a flexible oral probe placed as far as possible into the posterior of the mouth between the outer cheek teeth and gum. Care must be taken since the animal's

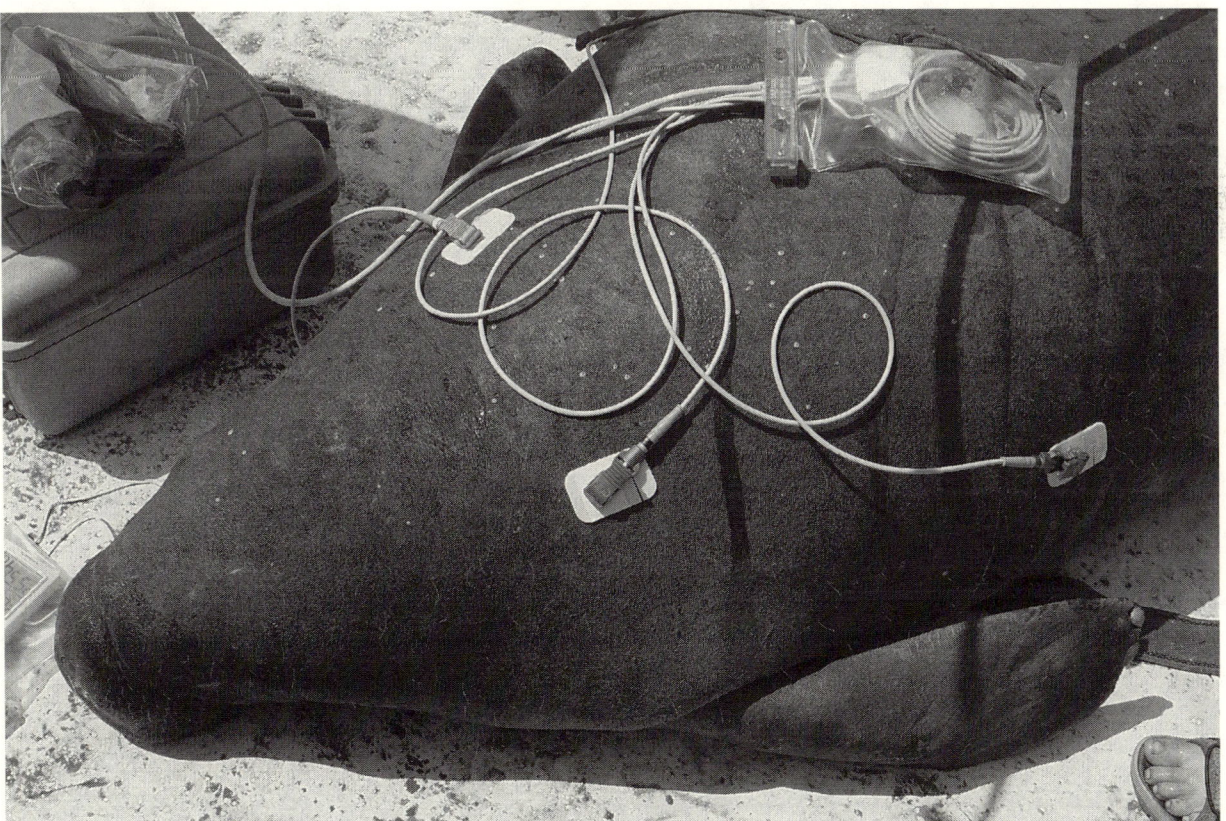

Figure 16.4. Researchers monitor a West Indian manatee in Belize using an electrocardiogram (ECG) monitor. (Courtesy of U.S. Geological Survey.)

molars can crush fingers and probes. Rectal temperature is unreliable since the fermentation characteristics of the manatee gastrointestinal system create dynamic temperature fluctuations, with rectal temperature ranging between 27 and 32°C[8]. Increases in temperature should be mitigated by shading the animal as well as applying copious amounts of water over the body, especially over the flippers and tail. In addition to cooling the animal, this also helps to keep skin from drying. Be aware that a dramatic decrease in body temperature can lead to shock. Lower oral temperature can indicate hypothermia during periods of exposure to cold ambient temperatures. In this event, attempt to raise the body core temperature by placing a layer of survival blankets over the animal.

Mentation/reflexes (reactiveness)

During handling, care should be taken to note alertness and reaction to eye reflex. Eye reflex can be examined by placing the finger adjacent to the eye, which should elicit a response.

Skin and Epibionts

Skin

The skin should be examined for abnormalities. Make descriptive notes detailing the characteristics of any abnormal tissue or lesions. Photographs of lesions are helpful to the pathologist examining tissues submitted for analysis (they can also be used for future identification). Tissues may be collected cleanly with a scalpel and forceps after a local anesthetic has been applied. Counter to intuition, skin biopsies should not be surgically prepped since this will remove portions of the tissue that need to be examined. The use of forceps must be performed carefully to prevent crushing tissue. For correct preservation, tissues should be collected in a fashion that allows efficient perfusion of formalin. Since formalin cannot penetrate more than 1 cm into tissues, this should be the maximum depth to the center of any tissue collected. Collected tissues should be representative of the surrounding normal tissue as well as any suspected pathology[9]. After removal of tissues the biopsy site should be thoroughly cleaned.

Special care needs to be taken when handling tissues for histological examination. Use a 1:10 tissue to formalin ratio to preserve tissues in 10% neutral buffered formalin. Label all samples with a field number unique to the animal; record date, organ sampled, and sampler's initials; and detail any lesion using descriptors for size, shape, density (soft, firm, hard), and color.

Parasites and Epibionts

Note the presence or absence of external parasites, which should be properly collected. Commensal associates are commonly found on the skin of sirenians. Signs of copious amounts of algae and invertebrate growth do not necessarily mean the animal is in poor condition since there are large variations between individuals and habitat types. However, there may be an underlying issue that warrants further investigation. Parasites, algae, commensal associates (e.g., barnacles), when in fresh condition, should be preserved in equal volume of 70% ethanol.

Urinary and Reproductive Systems

Urine

Urine should be clear, but it will have a strong odor if the animal is captured from a marine environment and the urine is concentrated. Semen is sometimes present in the urogenital canal of adult male breeders. A complete urinalysis includes chemistries, hormones, bacterial cultures, parasite screening and identification, and examination for blood and other cells. Generally the collection and processing methods of Pratt[10] are used, although they must be adapted to working in the field with a large mammal. Urine can be collected from the manatee by placing a sterile circular container (a Frisbee or soft-edged flying disc, for example) beneath the manatee covering the urogenital aperture. Make sure the area is thoroughly cleaned prior to placement of the collection container. Positive bacterial cultures should still be viewed with skepticism since it is very difficult to collect a sterile urine sample in this fashion. Manatees that are dehydrated and/or in marine environments do not urinate frequently. Some success has been achieved by external manual massage of the skin by applying pressure above the urinary bladder. If urine is acquired it should be placed in a sterile centrifuge tube, protected from sunlight and excessive heat, and refrigerated until analysis. To reduce the effects of chemical and cellular changes, urine should be examined as soon as possible, within two hours if fresh or six hours if refrigerated. Water contamination can also be a factor with dilution in freshwater environments, or high pH/NaCl content indicating saltwater contamination if animals are in marine systems. To examine for solid elements in the urine, one drop of 40% formalin should be added to 30 ml of urine. This test should be conducted after all chemical tests are performed, as formalin interferes with some chemical analysis, especially for urobilinogen and pH[11].

Reproductive system

An overall examination of the external genitals should be conducted. For adult females, total body length, abdominal distention in lean animals, enlarged/swollen vulva, and enlarged axillary mammary glands (teats) should be documented, as these are often indicators of near term pregnancy. Currently serum immunoassay to measure progesterone is the only reliable test for determining pregnancy in sirenians[12]. Collection of milk from lactating females is accomplished by manual massage of the mammary region on the main body, caudal to the insertion of each flipper, while gently pulling on the teat. The area should be thoroughly washed with alcohol prior to milk withdrawal. Expressed milk should placed into a sterile container and frozen as soon as possible after collection.

Digestive System

Manatees have a single stomach and some 40 m of small and large intestine. They are hindgut fermenters. Flatulence is a common function of the manatee's digestive system and should be expected.

Mouth

The mouth should be examined for vegetation, ulcers, or dental anomalies. Naturally, use caution as manatees do not tolerate oral examination well and can bite down or struggle.

Abdomen

Palpate the abdomen for tenderness and listen with a stethoscope to the lower abdomen for intestinal movement (peristalsis) and gas production.

Feces

Collect a fecal sample if the animal defecates. Describe the frequency, color, and consistency of the stool. Feces should be semi-solid, well formed, and soft and may or may not float in water. Fecal samples are used for identification of gastrointestinal tract contents, internal parasites, and bacteria and fecal hormones. Fresh fecal samples are valuable, as rapid changes occur in bacterial population and parasite eggs once they are passed from the animal's body; the death of some protozoa that may be present and identified by their movement can occur quickly[13]. Unfixed fecal samples should be refrigerated as soon as possible. For hormonal analysis, samples should be frozen. When used for vegetative content analysis or parasite identification, fecal samples should be placed in equal volume of fecal matter and 70% ethanol.

Hematology and Blood Chemistries

Value of Blood for Health Assessment

Blood provides researchers with another tool for assessing the health status of the animal. Generally, the complete blood count (CBC) is a profile of tests including the cell types, sizes, and numbers used to describe the quantity and quality of the cellular elements in blood and a few substances in serum. Common abnormalities may alert one to events such as infections, immunosuppression, homeostasis abnormalities, anemias, and/or clotting abnormalities. Serum chemistries in conjunction with other ancillary tests can indicate issues involving the liver, kidney, brain, intestines, muscle, endocrine system, and pancreas and give information on overall nutritional and electrolyte status.

Collection of Blood Samples

Blood must be handled delicately and quickly to ensure accurate results for comparisons to previous and subsequent analyses. Blood tubes, containing a variety of anticoagulants or supportive media, are used to assure accuracy and validate quality control (table 16.1). Blood should be collected as soon as possible after capture since stress-released hormones can influence body metabolism (shifting enzymes and blood cell populations). The brachial arteriovenous plexus on the medial or lateral aspect of the pectoral flipper is the preferred draw site (figure 16.5). It should be noted that an unknown mixture of arterial and venous samples will be collected at this site. This can dramatically impact some values, especially blood gases, electrolytes, tissue-derived enzymes, and pH values. Thorough cleaning of the sampling site (medial or lateral aspect of the flipper) is extremely important as manatee skin has high loads of bacteria; use alternating scrubs, three each of betadine or Nolvasan and isopropyl alcohol, employing a circular pattern, working from the center outward. Blood can be obtained using the Vacutainer method (recommended) or by syringe. Use of a Vacutainer collection method (figure 16.6) will fill multiple tubes rapidly and result in the least sampling artifact. Generally, 3.8 cm long, 18–21 gauge needles are used. An extension set (approximately 20 cm) with a Luer adapter and collar are handy and give flexibility to change tubes away from the needle insertion site. To reduce trauma to the arteriovenous plexus, use larger needles (18 gauge) for larger manatees and smaller needles (21 gauge) for calves. If a lateral approach is used, a 5 cm needle may be needed in larger manatees. Tubes with anticlotting agents should be filled first (table 16.1). To prevent damage to blood cells, the needle should be removed from the syringe (if used) prior to filling the blood tubes. The tubes should be filled slowly to the labeled line or approximately 80% full. All anticlotting tubes (i.e., green or purple/lavender tubes) should be capped and rocked gently and slowly for 15–30 seconds immediately after collection. Caps should be tightly secured.

Minimal blood collection for basic health measurements includes two 5 ml EDTA purple/lavender top tubes for complete blood count, one to three 10 ml lithium heparin green top tubes for plasma archival banking, and two to five 10 ml red top tubes for serum biochemistries and archival banking, totaling some 40–90 ml of blood (table 16.1).

To ensure proper interpretation of each processed sample, history must be carefully documented and should include times and conditions. Times to be recorded include when, how, and for how long the animal was followed, time of actual capture, and exact time blood was collected. All tubes should be labeled with the date, time, animal ID, and any other pertinent information. Use a pencil or indelible pen that will not smear.

Protecting the sample from environmental conditions once it is collected is paramount to ensuring its integrity. Blood exposed to a rise of 10°C can double the rate of chemical or enzymatic reaction. Blood should be stored as close to refrigerator temperature (4°C) as possible. Wrap the tubes in paper towels so that they do not directly touch the ice or ice packs, since this may freeze the blood cells and rupture them.

Table 16.1. Different types of tubes used in various studies for collecting blood during sirenian health assessments.

Tube top color	Anticoagulants and preservatives	Description	Diagnostic use	Minimum to collect
Purple/lavender	EDTA (Ethylenediaminetetraacetic acid)	Used for whole blood	Hematology, complete blood cell count	2 5-ml tubes
Red or red/gray	None	Used for extracting serum	Biochemistry standard panel, electrophoresis, protein evaluation, triglycerides, hormone, vitamin, mineral and contaminant analysis	2–5 10-ml tubes
Light green	Sodium heparin	Used for extracting heparinized plasma	Emergency biochemistry standard panel, electrophoresis, triglycerides, hormones, lymphocyte proliferation, cytogenetics	1 10-ml tube
Dark green	Lithium heparin	Used for extracting heparinized plasma	Emergency biochemistry standard panel, electrophoresis, triglycerides, hormones, blood gas analysis	2–4 10-ml tubes
Royal (dark) blue	None	Acid washed, zinc-free stopper. Designed for mineral and heavy metal analysis	Biochemistry standard panel, protein evaluation, electrophoresis, triglycerides, hormones, minerals, heavy metals	Optional*
Light blue white label	Sodium citrate	Used for extracting citrated plasma	Coagulation testing, fibrinogen quantization	1 5-ml tube
Light blue yellow label	Thrombin and soybean		Determining fibrin degradation products	Optional
Orange or gray/yellow	Thrombin	Used for extracting serum, faster clotting	Biochemistry standard panel, protein evaluation, electrophoresis, triglycerides, hormones	Optional
Yellow	Acid citrate, dextrose		DNA or red cell survival	Optional
Gray, no label	Diatomaceous earth		Measure activated clotting time	Optional
Gray, white label	Sodium fluoride, and/or potassium oxalate		Measure glucose and lactate	Optional

Note: Tube top color may vary according to maker/laboratory. Please contact your local lab to assure correct tube for your diagnostic use.
*Use of optional tubes should be at the discretion of the assessment team; generally only collected for special clinical purposes.

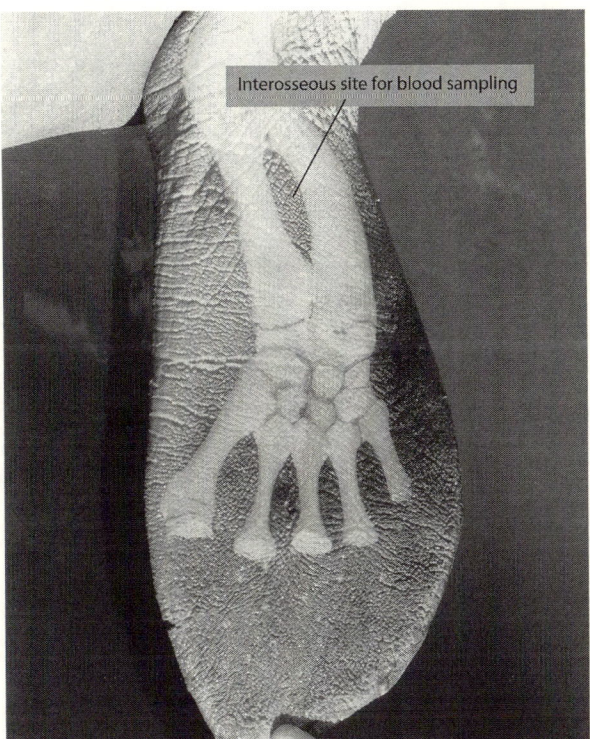

Figure 16.5. Blood draw sampling site on a West Indian manatee. (Courtesy of Mike Walsh.)

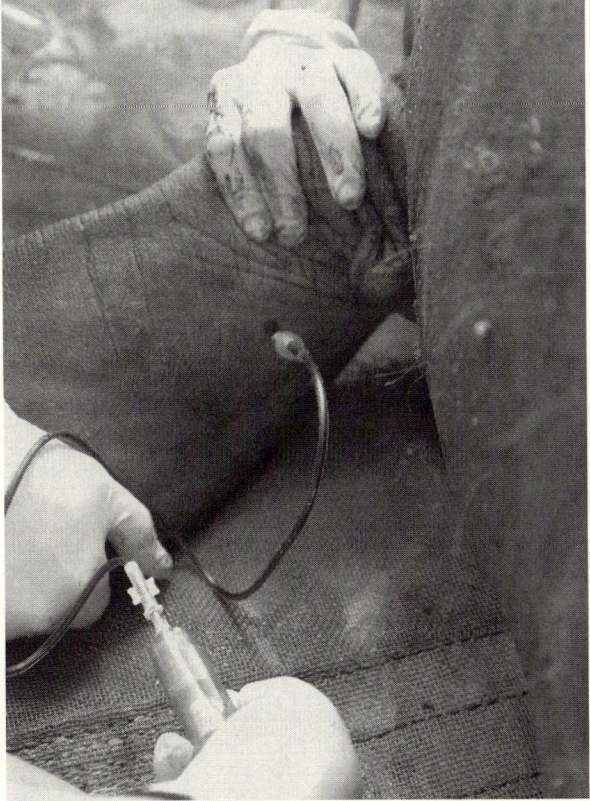

Figure 16.6. Manatee blood draw using an extension set. (Courtesy of U.S. Geological Survey.)

Processing Blood Samples

Timely preparation is vital for accurate analysis. Blood for biochemical analyses should be separated within two to three hours of collection but may still give useful information if processed within 12 hours. Separated, chilled serum and plasma are still useful for biochemical analyses four days after collection. Always check the collection protocol and test procedures with the laboratory you are utilizing.

An on-site centrifuge is necessary if blood is to be processed in the field for diagnostic analysis. An electrical outlet is essential for many units; however, some will work off a 12-volt battery. A voltage converter also can run a machine from a battery, or a small portable generator can be used. The centrifuge should be capable of operating at 2,000–3,000 RPM in a stationary position. Hematocrit centrifuges can be used to spin blood that can be used to analyze hematocrit. Total protein can be obtained using a refractometer. On the water, to avoid breaking tubes, a boat must be stationary with little movement when running these machines.

Cells should be separated from the plasma fluid phase. Cells are separated in whole blood containing an anticlotting agent (such as EDTA, citrate, or heparin) by centrifugation for approximately ten minutes at 2,000–3,000 RPM. Plasma fluid is obtained by decanting the supernatant (fluid above the blood cell pellet) from a sample tube. Excessive RPM may cause hemolysis or cell breakage. Use a sterile pipette to remove the plasma and place it into appropriately labeled containers.

Serum is plasma with fibrinogen removed during the clotting process and is obtained when a blood sample is drawn in either a thrombin or red-top tube and allowed to clot for roughly 20–30 minutes. It is then processed similarly to plasma. Serum can be used to measure hormones, vitamins, minerals, and contaminant concentrations as well as serum biochemistries and analysis of immunologic compounds. Prior to use, check with the laboratory running the desired tests to ensure that the type of blood tube used will not impact the results.

Obtaining blood smears on glass slides for hematological analysis takes experience, and personnel should be well trained before attempting this in the field. Please refer to clinical pathology textbooks to master these techniques. Make sure to label all slides with pencil as some staining techniques will remove ink. Slides made in the field should be protected at all times from moisture, flies (which will eat the blood film), and other contaminants. Blood slide holders can be obtained to assure that the slides are protected. Deterioration due to excessive humidity is common in the tropics, and samples should be kept cool and dry if possible.

Interpreting Results

Caution should be used when comparing values generated by different methods or analytical machines, as these factors can result in marked differences[14]. Manatee CBC and serum chemistries do not always follow conventional domestic or wild animal trends. Always use caution and consult experienced clinical veterinarians during all components of blood data interpretation and treatment. All interpretation should be performed in conjunction with other physical examination results. Basic clinical diagnostic manuals such as Willard et al.[15] give fundamental information on diagnostic analysis on domestic animals, and Harvey et al.[16] detail biochemistry analyses of blood from Florida manatees. Also, reported reference ranges for serum chemistry from manatees from Colombia and Puerto Rico are presented by Montoya-Ospina[17]. Walsh and Bossart[18] and Bossart[19] can be referenced to give insights into marine mammal medicine, but proper interpretation is always based on experience.

Microbiology

Bacteriology

At least 48 species of bacteria have been reported from West Indian manatees[20]. In characterizing bacteria from a wild or captive manatee, the first rule is to choose samples carefully, always mindful of potential contaminates found in the water or air or on the human collecting the sample. Samples for isolation of microbes should be collected under sterile conditions. Special culture media are available for anaerobic and aerobic pathogens, and researchers and clinicians must consult with a microbiologist for the most appropriate media given the diagnostic interest.

Bacterial samples are only worthwhile if fresh. Tissues (blocks) or fluids (several milliliters of purulent discharge, exudate, or feces) are better than culture swabs because they preserve the bacteria's environment for longer periods of time. If using tissues, pack individual tissues in separate sterile containers to avoid cross-contamination. If specific transport media are not available, use plastic bags for collection and then transfer the specimens to screw-capped, water-tight containers before sending them to a laboratory. If a swab must be used, transport medium should be used to increase the chance of isolation and identification of organisms and to prevent desiccation. If possible, refrigerate samples as soon after collection as possible. If this is not feasible, assure that the samples are not exposed to direct sunlight or extreme temperatures. Culturette brand swabs are supplied with transport media for aerobes. Because most anaerobes cannot survive exposure to air for more than 20 minutes (at most), collecting samples for anaerobic culture on swabs is not recommended. Acceptable anaerobic specimen collection techniques include: (1) blocks of tissues in a closed sterile container with the air evacuated (sealed thioglycollate broth tube is likely best), (2) material placed in Becton-Dickinson's "anaerobic specimen collector," and (3) purulent discharge and other exudate specimens drawn into a sterile syringe with the air expelled and the needle plugged with a rubber stopper or bent backward on itself. The specimens should be cultured as soon as possible after collection and refrigerated. Do not deep freeze any bacterial samples unless there will be extensive delay before the samples can be examined. Freezing often desiccates bacteria or disrupts the bacterial cell wall.

Mycology

Often fungal samples can be collected similarly to aerobic bacterial cultures. Some skin-related fungi need to be collected on special media. Care must be taken to avoid environmental contamination.

Virology

Viruses have not been extensively studied in manatees other than current work with papilloma and herpes viruses in Florida manatees[21]. If a virus is suspected, contact a veterinary specialist and individual laboratories to determine the method of collection, as each may have different requirements. A biopsy should be collected and frozen for molecular analysis. Additional samples from the lesion should be preserved in 10% formalin for supportive histological and immunohistochemical examination. Formalin fixation may not be the only preservative of choice, and researchers should contact a virologist for specific instructions.

Cytology

Health and disease diagnosis may also be accomplished through cytology or cellular diagnostics. With minimal equipment, samples can be obtained to be sent to diagnostic laboratories for analysis. The major goal is to obtain a significant number of well-stained cells reflecting the composition of the sample. Samples of deeper tissue are more likely to be diagnostic but are more difficult to obtain. Fluid or secretions should be collected in a specimen cup as well as spread on a microscope slide with a sterile applicator. Fine needle aspirates and impression smear collecting techniques are used to obtain cytology samples. Please refer to a cytology textbook to determine appropriate technique.

Cytology does have its limitations. Histopathology may be more diagnostic and definitive because more information (i.e., tissue architecture) is available from a histopathology sample than from a cytologic smear. Histopathology has limitations for assessing organisms in infected tissue or evaluating cellular detail useful in diagnosing some tumors.

Conclusion

To garner insight into human health issues as well as to identify potential impacts of anthropogenic threats such as hunting, pollution, climate change, and habitat destruction, it is important to determine proactively the health status of populations of animals in the wild. In the proactive study of wild populations, the first step is obtaining baseline information to give a reference point for future efforts. The key to this endeavor is to obtain good quality centralized data so that efforts can translate among groups in an effort to maximize our understanding of health and risk maladies in fragile sirenian populations.

Acknowledgments

We would like to thank Kendal E. Harr, DVM, MS Dipl. ACVP, of Phoenix Central Laboratory for Veterinarians, for her editorial review and clinical advice and Dr. Antonio A. Mignucci-Giannoni of the Caribbean Stranding Network for his excellent suggestions, contributions, and editing of the chapter. The results of this chapter are the combined efforts of countless hours of fieldwork provided by many excellent researchers and colleagues who gave their time and effort to help advance our understanding of sirenian health assessment.

17

Sirenian Pathology and Mortality Assessment

ROBERT K. BONDE, ANTONIO A. MIGNUCCI-GIANNONI,
AND GREGORY D. BOSSART

Previous chapters in this book have discussed how rapid technological development in recent history has accelerated human impact on sirenians. Determining the causes of the numerous threats to manatees, especially those that result in mortality or disease (tables 17.1 and 17.2) will enable implementation of appropriate protection measures. As a conservation tool, cause of death determination and interviews with the local population are vital steps for establishing successful research and conservation programs[1]. Such information can identify threats to the species and provides an opportunity to collect information on population distribution, diseases, parasites, diet, reproductive condition, genetics, and morphological anomalies.

Anthropogenic Causes of Mortality

Beyond being exploited for food[2], manatees and dugongs are faced with additional human-originated threats. In Florida many manatees are killed each year as a result of collisions with water vessels (figure 17.1). Twenty-five percent of Florida manatee mortalities are due to such collisions[3]. From 1990 to 2006, 19.8% of all known manatee deaths (n = 121) in Puerto Rico were identified to be due to boat strikes[4]. Most boat strikes are single events, affecting one individual. However, both in Puerto Rico and Florida, scientists have documented boat strikes of up to five manatees at one time, all assumed to be part of a mating herd when struck. Manatees in mating herds are preoccupied with breeding and may be especially vulnerable to collisions.

Most adult manatees in Florida, and some in Puerto Rico, bear scars as evidence of nonfatal encounters with boats, and sirenians with propeller scars are observed in other countries as well[5]. Many manatees do not appear to be permanently affected by moderate to light vessel strikes, but others suffer very serious injuries that may affect reproduction and migration or lead to death. In fatal cases the trauma can be acute or chronic in nature[6]. In acute cases, the injury is often massive, deep, or severe

Table 17.1. Determined cause of death for 68 fresh manatee carcasses from Florida by age/size and sex in decreasing order of frequency, January 1996 to January 2004.

		Adult		Subadult		Perinatal	
Cause of Death	Total	M	F	M	F	M	F
Trauma	32	7	6	12	7	.	.
Cold stress syndrome	12	1	.	4	7	.	.
Inflammatory/infectious disease	8	2	0	3	2	.	1
Suspected brevetoxicosis	6	2	1	2	1	.	.
Cachexia	4	.	.	.	.	2	2
Unknown	4	2	.	1	1	.	.
Intestinal foreign body	1	.	.	.	1	.	.
Cardiomyopathy	1	1	.	.	.	.	.
Total	68						

Source: Bossart et al. 2004, reprinted with permission.

Table 17.2. Predominant cause of stranding for 121 West Indian manatees recovered from Puerto Rico between 1990 and 2006 with comparison to previously tabulated data.

		Prior to 1990		Total		Total	
	Causes	Cases	%	Cases	%	Cases	%
Natural		6	10.9	53	43.8	59	33.5
	Dependent calf	6	10.9	28	23.1	34	19.3
	Illness	0	0	21	17.4	21	11.9
	Stillborn	0	0	3	2.5	3	0.6
	Predation	0	0	1	0.8	1	0.6
Human related		31	56.4	35	28.9	66	37.6
	Drowning	0	0	1	0.8	1	0.6
	Entanglement	1	1.8	1	0.8	2	1.2
	Gunshot	2	3.6	2	1.7	4	2.3
	Pollution	0	0	2	1.7	2	1.2
	Capture	22	40	5	4.1	27	15.3
	Watercraft	6	10.9	24	19.8	30	17
Undetermined		18	32.7	33	27.3	51	28.9
Total		55		121		176	

Source: Adapted and updated from Mignucci-Giannoni et al. 2000, with permission.

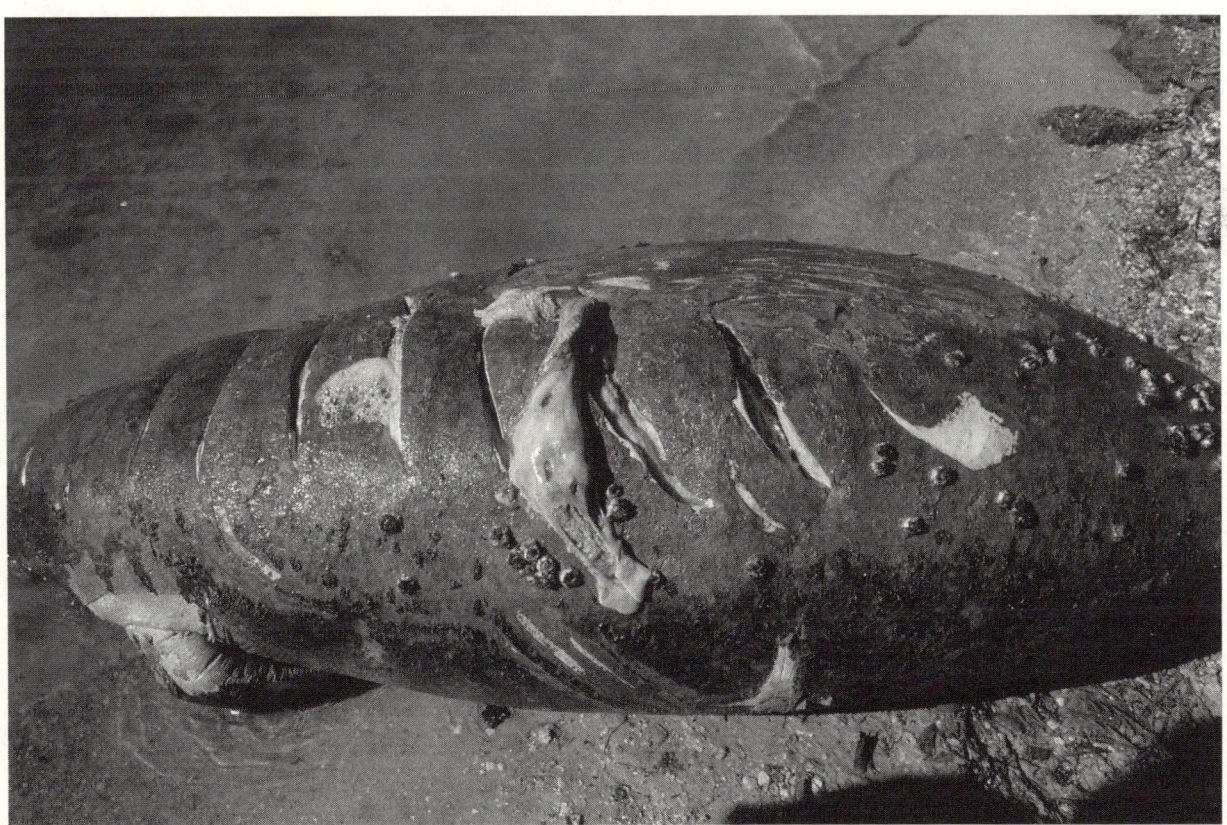

Figure 17.1. Fatally injured West Indian manatee in Florida with characteristic propeller lesions on dorsum. (Courtesy of U.S. Geological Survey.)

enough for the animal to succumb to shock or drowning, and death is rapid. In chronic cases some individuals develop bone lesions that can become systemic and eventually cause death[7].

Another form of human-related death in Florida is attributed to entrapment in the gates of canal locks or flood control structures resulting in crushing or drowning[8]. Poor nutritional condition in manatees can also be anthropogenic in nature, as it is often related to habitat loss and possibly high contaminant exposure levels[9].

Entanglement in fishing gear or debris is usually not life threatening but can lead to severe tissue damage and sometimes self-amputation of one or both flippers as blood flow is restricted. Entanglement can involve several types of abandoned fishing gear, but commonly, monofilament fishing lines and thicker nylon ropes are implicated. Sirenians can be bound or restricted when the lines become wrapped around their flippers or body. If detected early, the lesions often can be treated by removal of the constricting material and debridement of necrotic tissue. Conservation education can inform fishers of the potential damage caused by reckless discarding of fishing gear. Ingestion of debris, hunting, and vandalism are also of major concern in sirenian conservation throughout the world[10].

Trauma

Categories of traumatic injuries are based on historic criteria established in Florida[11] and may be a result of human-inflicted injury, including sharp penetrating trauma from boat propellers or blunt trauma from the impact of a boat hull or outdrive skeg (figure 17.2). It also may include penetrating wounds produced by firearms, spear guns, or harpoons. Based on gross and microscopic findings, death by trauma can be further subdivided into the categories of acute (i.e., injury considered severe enough to have caused death immediately or within a few hours with no pathologic evidence of preexisting disease) and chronic (i.e., injury that was not immediately fatal but resulted in secondary inflammatory disease and death).

Most often, trauma is associated with internal wounds, hemorrhage, blood clots, and severe damage to tissues and organ systems. Care should be taken to assess and determine whether the trauma in question is post- or antemortem in nature. Samples should be collected and submitted for histopathological analyses. Trauma from shark, alligator, or crocodile predation would fall into the natural category but should be distinguished from postmortem scavenging of a carcass that may have died of other causes.

Drowning

By itself, drowning does not have consistent clinical signs, and often there may not be any associated pathology to identify drowning as the specific cause of death. Drowning is therefore usually a diagnosis of exclusion. Just prior to death, agonal (labored, irregular) breathing

Figure 17.2. Injured West Indian manatee in Florida with severe propeller lesions on tail stock. (Courtesy of Kit Curtin.)

is present and aspiration of foreign bodies (e.g., mud, sand, plant material) may be apparent. Drowning in a marine mammal is often secondary to some other process or etiology.

Toxins

Sirenian mortality may be associated with toxins and chemical pollution from biotoxins, pharmaceuticals, and industrial discharge or spills[12]. Suspected cases of anthropogenic toxins impacting sirenians have been documented[13], but to date no direct related morbidity or mortality has been verified. Some suspect cases were reported during the Iran/Iraq War in the Persian Gulf during the 1980s, where dugongs were exposed to large quantities of spilled petroleum products[14] that may have contributed to their death. During this die-off there were also rumors of potentially fatal algal blooms in the area that may have contributed to the dugong mortality. Under these circumstances, the examiner can directly detect the caustic substance on the animal, but cause and effect in a fatality may be very difficult to prove[15]. In subtle cases, where small quantities of these products might have been ingested, a necropsy is needed to examine stomach contents, and tissue samples should be collected for contaminant analyses. Other pollutants directly affecting sirenians may include pesticides and herbicides. Impacts from exposure to these toxins could affect changes in reproductive, metabolic, and immune functions without killing the animal and may be more detrimental to overall population health and recovery. Causes for these biological stressors are difficult to identify, and in cases where toxins are suspected, blood, brain, liver, kidney, muscle, and blubber samples should be taken and frozen in chemically clean glass containers with Teflon lids (available from scientific supply houses; clean aluminum foil can be used for organic contaminants if such containers are unavailable). These samples should then be submitted to an appropriate toxicology laboratory for analyses.

Natural Causes of Mortality

Disease

Based on clinical findings, West Indian manatees appear to be remarkably resistant to disease and the sublethal effects of traumatic injury[16]. Their disease-resistant traits may result partially from a highly efficient and responsive immune system[17], which in some cases may take the manatee to a weakened state, even to the extent of cachexia (severe malnutrition), over a long period of time (figure 17.3). Notable exceptions to nontraumatic deaths in manatees from Florida are found with mortality associated with prolonged cold-water exposure and the inhalation and/or ingestion of red tide toxins (see discussion to follow)[18]. However, the general pathologic aspects of disease associated with mortality in other manatee species and the dugong have not been well characterized.

Verminous and bacterial pneumonia and enteritis are the most common diseases found in manatees from Florida and Puerto Rico[19]. Pneumatosis intestinalis (gas-filled areas in the bowel wall of the gastrointestinal tract) has been detected in manatee calves from both Florida and Puerto Rico[20].

Over the last 15 years field biologists have observed papillomatous lesions on some captive manatees[21] and papilloma-suspect dermal lesions on wild manatees in northwest Florida[22]. These lesions were not present decades ago during detailed surveillance of manatees in Crystal River as part of the photo-identification program[23]; research efforts are under way to ascertain whether they are the result of environmental and/or physical changes or stressors in the habitat or due to a compromise of the manatee's immune system function.

Preliminary studies suggest that unlike manatees from Florida, West Indian manatees throughout the rest of their range do not have pathologic findings consistent with either cold stress syndrome (CSS) or brevetoxicosis. This is not surprising as the prolonged exposure to low water temperatures necessary to induce CSS or the frequent red tide blooms consisting of the brevetoxin-producing dinoflagellates are rarely found in the Antillean manatees' habitat.

Recently it has been postulated that sirenians may be good sentinels for ocean and human health[24]. In this context, the characterization of sirenian mortality factors could provide early warning indicators of stressors, contaminants, or habitat changes in the aquatic environment. Disease characterization among sirenians would potentially permit us to manage related impacts on human and animal health associated with our coastal ecosystems. Thus as we indentify environmental degradation affecting sirenian health, we may also be identifying factors affecting human health.

Harmful Algal Blooms

Recent epizootics (animal epidemics) have been associated with potent marine neurotoxins known as brevetoxins, which are produced in Florida by the "red tide" dinoflagellate *Karenia brevis*[25]. Brevetoxins are known to kill large numbers of fish and to cause illness in humans who ingest filter-feeding shellfish contaminated with the brevetoxin (neurotoxic shellfish poisoning) or who

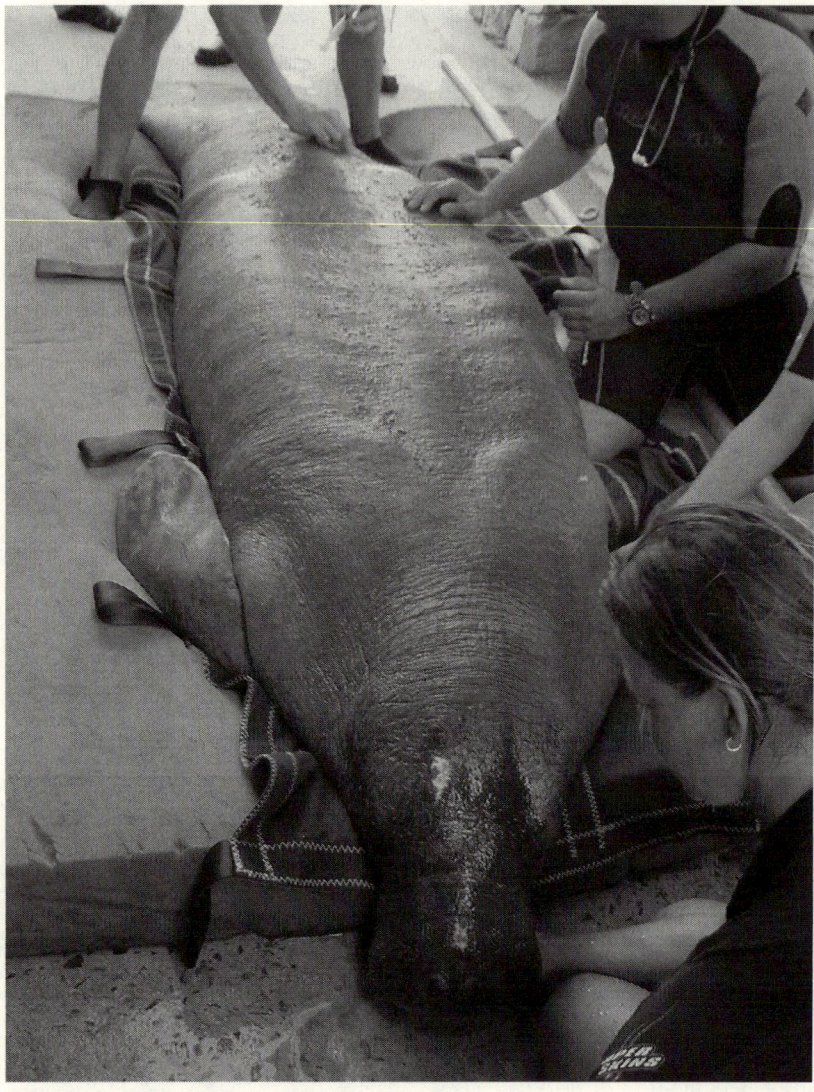

Figure 17.3. Chronically sick West Indian manatee rescued in the British Virgin Islands in a severe state of cachexia and debilitation. (Courtesy of Puerto Rico Manatee Conservation Center.)

inhale the toxic aerosols. The pathogenesis of manatee brevetoxicosis is suspected to involve direct inhalation and/or ingestion of toxins from the environment. Important new data indicate that brevetoxin vectors such as epiphytes on seagrasses or incidentally ingested invertebrates can result in delayed or remote manatee exposure causing intoxication in the absence of active toxin-producing dinoflagellates[26]. Thus, unexpected toxin vectors may account for manatee deaths long after, or remote from, a dinoflagellate bloom.

Diagnosis of brevetoxicosis in manatees is typically by exclusion and may be based on pathologic findings and postmortem demonstration of the toxins in fluids and tissues. Gross findings of inhalational brevetoxicosis in manatees include irritation of the upper respiratory tract and excessive congestion and edema in the lungs. Present data suggest that manatee mortality resulting from brevetoxicosis may not necessarily be acute but rather occurs after chronic inhalation and/or ingestion[27]. The inhalational route of brevetoxin exposure appears to be unique among marine mammals and humans. Increases in human pulmonary emergency room diagnoses often are temporally related to "red tide" occurrences, which may be increasing in frequency along the Florida coastline[28].

Neurotoxic signs of clinical brevetoxicosis include seizure, disorientation, ataxia, hyperflexion, muscle fasciculations, flaccid paralysis, and dyspnea. Manatees with brevetoxicosis may be treated symptomatically with corticosteroids and nonsteroidal anti-inflammatory drugs. Supportive care includes removal from toxic waters, providing fluids, nutritional supplementation, and providing water buoyancy devices to prevent submersion and subsequent drowning. It is essential that all findings be discussed with an experienced veterinarian and pathologist.

Cold Stress Syndrome

Chronic exposure to cold water produces a cascade of clinical signs and disease processes termed manatee cold stress syndrome (CSS)[29]. All age and sex categories are affected by CSS; however fewer cases are detected among the perinatal age category. Additionally, large adults tend to be affected by CSS less frequently than small adults and subadults, owing to their greater experience at utilizing known warm water sites, their increased competence at heeding the signs of approaching cold weather, or the ability to decrease body heat loss due to a reduced surface area to volume ratio. Pathologic features of CSS include emaciation, fat store depletion, serous fat atrophy, lymphoid depletion, epidermal hyperplasia, pustular dermatitis, enterocolitis, and degeneration of heart muscle. The data indicate that CSS is a complex disease process that involves compromise to metabolic, nutritional, and immunologic balances and culminates in secondary diseases. The pathogenesis of manatee CSS appears to involve a series of events that initially involves chronic exposure to water temperatures well below 20ºC. This exposure, in turn, results in lethargy, decreased food intake, dehydration, and constipation, which further compromise nutritional, metabolic, and immune balances. The latter would ultimately result in additional immunologic compromise, predisposing CSS manatees to opportunistic infections and other unusual lesions that may have infectious, nutritional, and/or metabolic components. Therefore, treatment for rescued manatees with CSS should address these specific factors with special emphasis on reestablishing normal gastrointestinal function and fluid/nutritional status.

The long-term sublethal effects of CSS may be more insidious and involve increased susceptibility to disease and impacts on fecundity and calf survival. The preliminary evidence of the combined suppressive immunologic effects of CSS and exposure to red tide toxins needs further investigation. Additionally, understanding the pathophysiologic mechanisms of manatee CSS is becoming critically important for developing future management strategies. The availability of a network of warm water refugia may be one of the most important and challenging long-term needs for manatees[30]. Most Florida manatees rely on natural or artificial warm water refuges to survive cold winters and typically return to the same refuges year after year. Over the past 30 years in Florida, warm water effluent sources at electric power plants have provided life-sustaining refugia for many manatees during the winter. These refugia become particularly significant as winter manatee counts at a single power plant warm water refuge may exceed 500 animals or approximately 15% of the remaining population[31]. Serious concern exists about the inevitable shutdown and/or deregulation of aging power plants on which manatees have become dependent during cold weather[32]. Because manatees are unable to adapt quickly to changes in the availability of warm water, elimination of these warm water refugia could have profound effects on increasing mortality and altering population distributions in this already vulnerable species[33].

Parasites

Heavy parasitic loads in manatees are common, but generally these loads are not of pathologic concern. Parasites have been studied in detail in manatees from Florida[34], the Dominican Republic[35], and Puerto Rico[36], and in dugongs[37]. The most common parasite in Florida manatees is the trematode *Chirochis fabaceus*, whereas *C. groschafti* is found in manatees from the Caribbean. Both are flukes inhabiting the lower gastrointestinal tract. Another fluke common in Florida and Antillean manatees is *Pulmonicola cochleotrema*, located in the nasal passages, which has been implicated in rare cases of verminous pneumonia[38]. An ascarid nematode, *Heterochelius tunicatus*, is often present in the mucosa of the stomach and duodenum or free within the lumen[39]. Additionally, manatees in Florida, Belize, and Puerto Rico may have up to five species of barnacles on their dermis[40], and their skin is often encrusted with algae and other epiphytes. Recently a tanaid crustacean, *Hexapleomera robusta*, was discovered imbedded in the skin of manatees in Mexico[41] and Belize[42] (figure 17.4), and a new species of nematode has been identified, yet undescribed, in the urine of manatees from Belize[43]. A copepod, *Harpacticus pulex*, was isolated on the skin of a captive manatee in Florida[44] and recently from wild captured manatees from Puerto Rico and Mexico[45]. In dugongs, one species of protozoan, a nematode, and 19 trematode species[46] have been found. Most of these species only occur in the dugong and not other animals. Sharksucker species (*Echeneis naucrates* and *E. neucratoides*) are common associates with West Indian manatees and dugongs in marine environments[47].

Perinatal

The social structure of all sirenians entails a strong bond between the cow and calf, which can last as long as three years in some pairs. If for some reason a mother is separated from her offspring, the nutritionally and socially dependent calf usually dies, though there is some evidence that orphaned calves have been adopted by other lactating females. Calves can be separated from their

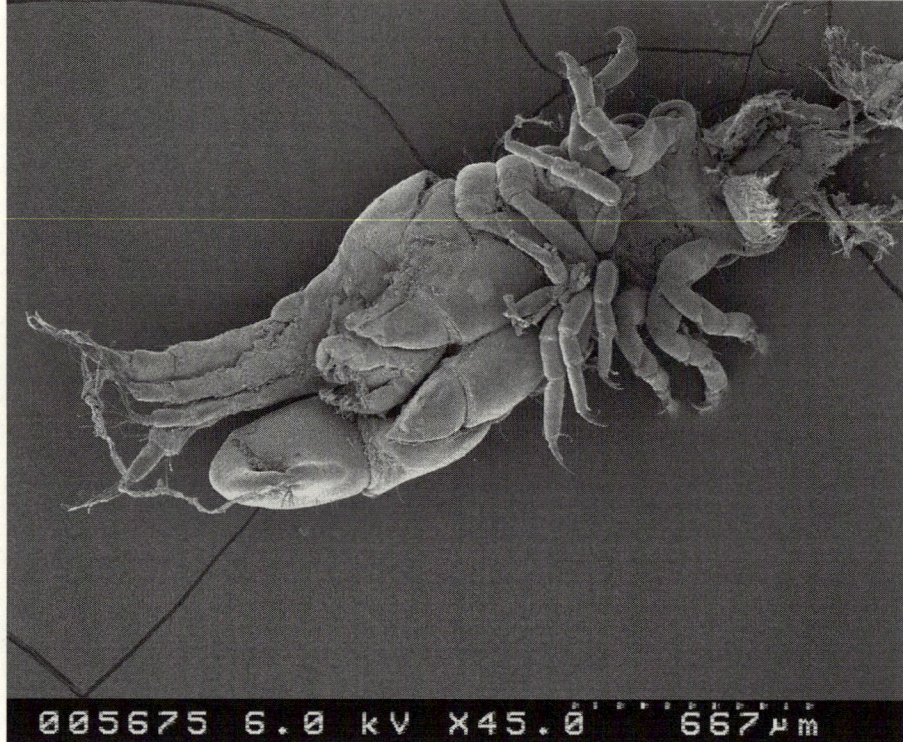

Figure 17.4. A tanaid (*Hexapleomera robusta*), an epibiont found embedded in the skin of a West Indian manatee from Belize. (Courtesy of U.S. Geological Survey.)

mothers for several reasons. The mother may have died, the two could have been separated by human or other curious manatee disturbance resulting in flight avoidance, the cows or calves may not be behaviorally compatible and were separated, or they could be genetically unfit and die in the natural culling process. From 1990 to 2006, 35.5% of the manatee carcasses recovered from Puerto Rico were calves[48]. Deaths in this group are generally attributed to cachexia and pathologic lesions consistent with prolonged protein-caloric deficiency[49]. The clinicopathologic features are similar to those often seen in orphaned manatees rescued and presented to rehabilitation facilities for medical care[50].

Quantitatively, this grouping of dependent calf deaths is deemed important and could have a direct impact on the growth rate of the overall population. Dependent calves that die generally do so in their first year. In Florida, these are manatees that are often shorter than 175 cm in total length. By process of elimination, the proximate cause of death in these cases is not likely to be human-related[51].

Predation

Sirenians are presumed to be opportunistically attacked and sometimes consumed by large predators, although documentation of this interaction is very rare. Dugongs are preyed upon by sharks, including tiger sharks (*Galeocerdo cuvier*), killer whales (*Orcinus orca*), probably by salt-water crocodiles (*Crocodylus porosus*), and hammerhead sharks (*Sphyrina* spp.)[52]. Amazonian manatees are said to be occasionally preyed upon by sharks, jaguars (*Panthera onca*), and caimans[53]. No natural predation on West African manatees has been documented[54], and it has been reported that the West Indian manatee has no natural predators[55]. However, Falcón-Matos et al.[56] documented the first case of an antemortem predatory attack on a manatee in Puerto Rico, probably by a large tiger shark. Recently, shark predation events have been recorded from Florida and Belize[57], and now West Indian manatees are suspected to be opportunistically preyed upon as well by the American crocodile (*Crocodylus acutus*) and American alligators (*Alligator mississippiensis*).

Stochastic Events

Stochastic or unpredictable events such as hurricanes, also can result in mortality[58]. During storms animals may be swept from their normal distributional range into inappropriate or unsuitable habitat. One such case has been documented where a manatee was displaced from its natural Florida habitat to waters around an island in the Bahamas, hundreds of kilometers away. Hurricane Georges off Puerto Rico in September 1998 was associated with a manatee mother and calf separation, resulting in the need to rescue the calf. In September 1996 a manatee calf death in Puerto Rico was directly related to Hurricane Hortense. At present, the extent of storm-induced mortality and the consequences of global warming affecting range dispersal on sirenian populations are not well understood.

Mortality Documentation

Recovery and History

If there is a report of a carcass, it should be examined as soon as possible. The examiner should obtain as much information as possible, including the location, circumstances, date, and time of events and the name and contact information for the initial observer or informer. Most marine mammals, and particularly sirenians, even dead ones, are protected by local and national laws and regulations. Make sure you are familiar with applicable laws and understand the implications of recovering a carcass. Obtain proper permits prior to conducting research on any marine mammal. When recovering a carcass, observe and note the weather and environmental conditions where the animal was found, as this may help in determining the cause of death. In some cases these factors may be associated with the demise of the animal (e.g., red tide, other dead wildlife, signs of water contamination, recent passage of a hurricane or storm, etc.). Take full body photographs, with appropriate reference scales, of each side of the animal and its ventral and dorsal surfaces before moving the carcass. Transfer the animal to the examination site, taking care not to damage the carcass, and note especially signs of disease or trauma that may be altered by the ropes, nets, stretchers, or cranes used during recovery. If the animal is transported, if possible apply bags of ice around the carcass to reduce the rate of decomposition until it can be examined. Carcasses which are going to be examined in the near future may be better if refrigerated rather than frozen. Freezing artifact or burn will damage cells and complicate the interpretation of tissues collected at necropsy.

Necropsy Examination

Although there is no set standard for necropsy examination of a sirenian carcass, some useful guides have been produced[59]. Experience and a thorough, consistent approach are important in a necropsy examination, especially when dealing with sirenians and their unusual morphological aquatic adaptations. Try to determine abnormal conditions even though this may be difficult if you are not familiar with normal sirenian or mammal anatomy and pathology. The initial examiner should take detailed notes and photographs, which, along with submitted tissues, can be examined later by a pathologist to attempt to provide a definitive cause of death. One should carefully examine the carcass

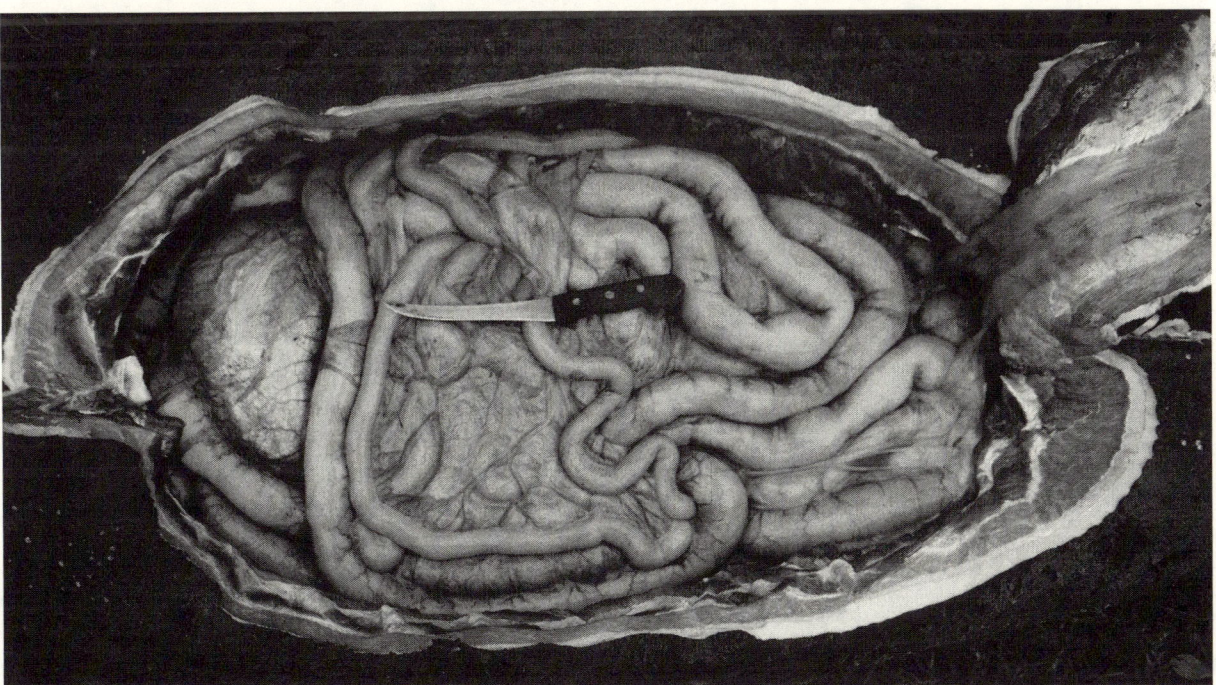

Figure 17.5. Necropsy of a West Indian manatee, showing dorsal recumbency position used for examination of organs in situ. (Courtesy of U.S. Geological Survey.)

for unusual marks, lesions, or trauma. Complete morphometrics, photographs, and video documentation should be taken as well. Place the carcass on its back so that it can be opened ventrally, exposing all organ systems to the examiner (figure 17.5). Tissue samples from each organ should be collected and properly preserved. For pathology purposes, a sample should be collected from each major organ (heart, lungs, liver, spleen, stomach, duodenum, small intestine, large intestine, testes or ovaries, kidneys, urinary bladder, lymph nodes, and brain) as well as from any suspect tissue. Samples should measure about 2 cm by 2 cm by 0.5 cm thick and should be preserved in 10% neutral buffered formalin. The volume ratio of tissue to preservative should be approximately 1:10. Note tissue color, size, shape, consistency, and smell. Be cautious when interpreting color and wetness of tissues since lividity can create artifactual changes by redistributing fluids. Search for, and collect in ≥70% ethanol, ectoparasites and epibionts (barnacles, copepods, algae, etc.) as well as endoparasites found in the airways, stomach, and intestines[60]. Collect a small piece of skin for genetic analyses and preserve it in a tissue buffered DMSO solution or ≥70% ethanol[61]. Practice proper sanitary hygiene and safety at all times throughout the examination[62].

Conclusions

Understanding the cause and effect of mortality processes is a first step in better understanding the population dynamics of the studied species. Mortality assessment programs have been important aspects of acquiring basic life-history information on the species and useful for monitoring conservation efforts in Florida, Puerto Rico, Mexico, Belize, Brazil, and Australia. Mitigation efforts have resulted in substantial reductions in sirenian mortality over the last few decades in certain portions of their range. In some areas, these conservation efforts to protect sirenians—such as net bans, boat access and speed restrictions, changes in flood gate operations, habitat protection, and establishment of sanctuaries—have already shown measurable success. The continuation of these diligent safeguards, coupled with monitoring of mortality to identify and detect potential threats to populations of sirenians, will help ensure persistence and population viability.

18

Delineating and Assessing Habitats for Sirenians

EDUARDO MORAES-ARRAUT, ALEJANDRO ORTEGA-ARGUETA,
LEON D. OLIVERA-GÓMEZ, AND JAMES K. SHEPPARD

Habitat has been defined as the physiographic conditions and resources (e.g., shelter, food, water, temperature) present in an area that allow the occupancy, survival, and reproduction of a given organism[1]. The physiographic conditions and resources of a habitat delimit the distribution and abundance of the various organisms within it.

Habitat assessments are based upon the knowledge and measurement of ecological resources. Each sirenian species has specific habitat requirements, and the maximum distribution and density of sirenians in any given area is determined by the availability of those resources. Various techniques are used to measure the availability of ecological resources as a proxy for habitat components. Selection of methods depends on the research objectives, the ecology of the habitat, the species' habitat requirements, and the parameters to be analyzed.

Habitat assessment requires sound ecological knowledge of the species concerned. Unfortunately biological and ecological data for sirenians are limited, available from only a few areas of the world. Ecological and habitat research has been conducted mostly for the Florida manatee, *Trichechus manatus latirostris*[2]; the Amazonian manatee, *T. inunguis*[3], and the dugong in Australia, *Dugong dugon*[4]. Ecological research that includes habitat assessments for the Antillean manatee (*T. manatus manatus*) has also been conducted in Mexico[5] and Central and South America[6]. Ecological information on sirenians is relatively scarce for the West African manatee and the Antillean manatee in the Caribbean region. Basic information is often extrapolated from the United States and Australia to studies in other regions.

In this chapter we discuss the habitat requirements for sirenians; explain methods and techniques potentially applicable for habitat assessment, showing their advantages and limitations; and illustrate practical applications through four case studies (presented in boxes). Information on ecological models for habitats of sirenians is relatively scarce. We do not intend to provide an exhaustive analysis of methods and techniques for habitat ecological modeling, but we provide examples of practical applications of habitat assessments. Guisan and Zimmermann and Franklin[7] offer a useful review of methods and statistical tools on ecological habitat modeling. Resources based on marine mammal habitat modeling workshops held at the Society for Marine Mammalogy biennial conferences since 1999 can be consulted at http://www.whoi.edu/sbl/liteSite.do?litesiteid=7272.

Sirenian Habitat Requirements

Ecological resources widely recognized as critical components of sirenians habitats follow[8]:

- Manatees in marine habitats (*T. m. manatus*, *T. m. latirostris*, *T. senegalensis*): shallow water (~3m deep), proximity to deeper waters to escape from danger (boats or predators), availability of freshwater sources, aquatic vegetation (mostly submerged), warm water (17°C minimum temperature), shelter from storms, waves, strong winds and currents; and travel corridors between habitat areas.
- Manatees in freshwater habitats (*T. m. manatus*, *T. m. latirostris*, *T. inunguis*, *T. senegalensis*): aquatic macrophytes (submerged, emergent, rooted, floating), calm waters, travel corridors between habitat areas, and zones free of predation risk by caimans, jaguars and/or humans.
- Dugongs (*Dugong dugon*): coastal areas, shallow to medium deep waters (typically 0.5 to 60 m, although large-scale moves across water 2–3 km deep do occur), warm water (17°C minimum), seagrass beds containing high-nutrient (starch and nitrogen), low-fiber species such as *Halophila ovalis* and *Halodule uninervis*, and protected sites such as shallow bays, which provide enhanced protection during calving from rough seas and sharks.

Habitat conditions may vary in different temporal scales. Sirenians follow different behavior patterns as they adapt to daily, seasonal, and annual changes in habitat conditions. The availability of food and freshwater resources may change as determined by annual hydrological cycles. An example of these temporal changes is the migration of Florida manatees southward in winter because of cooler water temperatures. Such temporal scales are important elements when planning and conducting habitat research.

Human intervention is also a crucial consideration. Because of their preference for riverine and coastal areas, sirenians have long been in close contact with human settlements. In some Florida freshwater springs manatees are accustomed to human contact. However, in other regions such as Mexico and Central and South America, manatees tend to be afraid of human interactions and avoid contact. Researchers must distinguish between changes caused by human activities and changes that occur naturally in ecosystems[9]. This distinction requires detailed knowledge of sirenian habitat and baseline information at appropriate spatial and temporal scales.

Habitat Assessment Procedures

There are two methods generally used to identify a sirenian population and the extent of the area from which to collect data. The first, reconnaissance sampling, can be used for preliminary investigations where little information is available. During a reconnaissance survey, the study area is surveyed by characterizing the landscape and gaining an overview of its geographical and ecological characteristics[10]. Information sources and tools may include aerial and orbital photographs, topographic maps, and geographic information systems (GIS). The second method, intensive sampling, is used to obtain specific data from measurements from within a smaller habitat area[11]. The intensive sampling technique needs more staff, resources and time. Depending on the type of ecosystem (marine, estuarine, river or lagoon), important habitat parameters to measure might include vegetation cover, bathymetry, water salinity, and temperature.

Once the extent of the study area has been established, the next step is to identify variables thought to influence species distribution and abundance. The habitat can be assessed by recording the occurrence or abundance patterns of the sirenian being studied and relating these to environmental variables by applying statistical methods[12]. A basic knowledge of the species' ecology is crucial for the researcher to select carefully the most important habitat variables to sample. Table 18.1 shows habitat variables commonly measured and the instruments and tools used for data collection.

Data collection may combine sampling of both the aquatic and terrestrial ecosystems that surround nearshore areas. Manatees, for example, not only consume submerged aquatic vegetation but also forage near mangroves, along riverbanks, and at lagoon margins.

Table 18.1. Variables and instruments for sirenian habitat research.

Variables to measure	Instruments, techniques and sources of complementary information
1. Sirenian biological information: spatial and temporal distribution, abundance, home range; breeding and feeding behavior	Interviews, boat or aerial surveys; stranding or hunting records, focal observations; Global position system (GPS)
2. Characterization of landscape: type of ecosystem, mapping and measuring geographical features	Topographic maps, aerial photographs, satellite imagery, geographical information systems (GIS)
3. Water depth	Sonar, cord with marked measurements, depth sounder
4. Fluctuation of water level through time scale	Measures of water depth during various seasons (or same season sampled each year)
5. Aquatic vegetation: distribution, composition, density, cover, biomass	Sampling by hand-pulling, plots, SCUBA diving, trawl, mechanical digger
6. Salinity and distance to freshwater sources	Salinometer, electronic instruments, GIS
7. Temperature	Thermometer, electronic instruments, thermal imaging satellite
8. Turbidity	Secchi disk
9. Currents	Mechanical and electronic instruments
10. Anthropogenic features: settlements, infrastructure, transportation routes, high-use areas; indicators of disturbance, threat-influenced areas, land tenure, protected areas	Aerial photographs, digital maps, cartographic maps of different scales, settlements and socioeconomic censusing inventories, regional environmental management plans, field trips, GPS and GIS

The Habitat Suitability Index

The Habitat Suitability Index (HSI) is a method developed to assess the condition of a habitat area based on the sum of indicators of site quality for wildlife[13]. The method consists of measuring a series of environmental variables in selected sites. Then it uses correlation analysis to detect the most significant variables determining the absence or presence of the species (based on records from sightings, strandings, scats, browsed plants, and trapped or hunted animals). Researchers can then evaluate sirenian habitats by the presence or absence of key habitat attributes.

The use of a ranking system is complementary to the HSI. Assessment of habitat is based on a ranking that utilizes a combination of biological assessment and rating criteria. The value of a habitat area can be calculated by analyzing the availability of habitat requirements for the species of interest[14]. Habitat attributes are displayed as a habitat quality index with scores from 1 (lowest) to 10 (highest). The value of a given segment of land is proportional to the product of the habitat quality index and the size of habitat involved[15]. The total area can then be ranked into three habitat categories—optimum, suitable, or marginal.

Geographic Information Systems

A geographic information system (GIS) is a valuable tool that allows one to collect, store, search, transform and visualize spatial data of the real world[16]. A GIS provides a computer-based platform for overlaying detailed habitat information displayed on georeferenced digital maps. When availability of food and other key resources are indicators of habitat quality, a GIS map could show where these habitat qualities are and model how they vary in space and time. Then a ranking procedure can be performed through the GIS and a final map generated to depict habitat quality. A GIS also allows for the discovery of unknown potential habitats by incorporating and analyzing habitat variables and showing areas that sirenians could occupy. The ability of GIS to incorporate and project large spatial datasets as separate map layers allows multiple habitat variables to be analyzed simultaneously. A GIS can also map sirenians' movement data obtained from telemetry that can be stored, projected in a GIS, and analyzed by overlapping movement tracks with underlying habitat variables, such as vegetation cover, water depth, temperature, and distance to the shore. These data can then be transferred to statistical software to quantify the patterns of sirenian resource selection and to create predictive habitat models.

Remote Sensing

Remote sensing is a powerful tool for expanding our visual limits into landscape and regional scales and areas of the electromagnetic spectrum (EMS) that we normally would not be able to perceive. It can be an important means of obtaining data in a cost-effective way. It allows the analysis of large areas and over varied time periods; for example, the monitoring of aquatic vegetation banks over multiple seasons. Through remote sensing analysis, researchers can assess whether the spatial distributions of habitat characteristics influence sirenian locations obtained through radio-tracking, aerial, or boat survey techniques. It is especially useful when the study area is too large or difficult to access, making fieldwork expensive and complicated. Moreover, remote sensing can assist in correcting biased sampling caused by varied access to areas that might otherwise result in a nonrandom spatial distribution of sampling. In such situations, remote sensing may support unbiased periodic and (practically) simultaneous sampling over large areas.

Remote sensing data useful for studying larger areas can be acquired by either airborne or orbital sensors. Some commonly used satellite sensors and their spectral bands are shown in table 18.2. The selection of a sensor depends on several criteria, ranging from research objectives and data needed to financial resources.

Airplane sensors allow greater flexibility of planning, including the date and precise area to be sampled. Altitude can be determined so that cloud cover can be minimized. Airplanes fly at lower altitudes than satellites, so the spatial resolution of an image can be higher, though high resolution satellite sensors can now achieve a spatial resolution that is comparable to that of airborne sensors. However, images acquired by airborne sensors are more susceptible to geometric errors and distortion caused by the plane's movement than are those acquired from satellites. It is also considerably more expensive to survey using airborne sensors than satellites. Orbital sensors are discussed in more detail as they cover a wide variety of remote sensing possibilities and are generally more readily available to researchers in developing countries.

Optical sensors are distinguished by four different types of resolutions[17]:

1. Spatial resolution, or the ability to discriminate objects; the higher the resolution, the smaller the features that can be differentiated.
2. Temporal resolution, the time it takes to obtain images of the same area again.

Table 18.2. Examples of satellite sensors with different characteristics that can be used in habitat assessments.

Satellite	Sensor	Resolutions				Swath (km)
		Spatial (m)	Temporal (days)	Radiometric (bits)	Spectral Bands (µm)	
Landsat	TM	MS 30	16	8	B, G, R, 1 NIR, 2 MIR, 1 TIR	185
	ETM+	Pan 10 MS 30	16	8	B, G, R, 1 NIR, 2 MIR, 1 TIR, 1 Pan	185
EOS Terra and Aqua	MODIS	250–1,000	1–2	12	36 (visible to TIR)	2330
EOS Terra	ASTER	15 (Bands 1–3) 30 (Bands 4–9) 90 (Bands 10–14)	16	8	14 (visible to TIR)	60
EOS Terra	MISR	275–1,100	9	?	R, G, B, NIR	360
CBERS-2	CCD	20	26	8	R, G, B, NIR	120
SPOT 4	HRVIR Vegetation	Pan 10 MS 20	261	88	G, R, NIR, MIR, Pan	602250
OrbView-3		Pan 1 MS 4	>3	11	R, G, B, NIR, Pan	8
Quickbird-2	Quickbird	Pan 0.61 MS 2.44	1–5	11	R, G, B, NIR, Pan	20 to 40
IKONOS-2	IKONOS	Pan 1 MS 4	>3	11	R, G, B, NIR, Pan	11
EROS Series		Pan 1.8		11	Pan	13.5
KOMPSAT-2		Pan 1 MS 4		11	R, G, B, NIR, Pan	15

Note: MS = Multi-spectral imagery, Pan = Panchromatic imagery. Color bands and their respective ranges in light spectrum (µm) are B = Blue (0.41–0.5), G = Green (0.51–0.6), R = Red (0.61–0.7), NIR = Near Infrared (0.71–1.3), MIR = Middle infrared (1.55–2.5), TIR = Thermal infrared (10–30).

3. Spectral resolution, which is the ability of a sensor to discriminate between adjacent wavelengths (or band frequencies) of electromagnetic radiation (EMR): the more bands in an image, the higher the spectral resolution.
4. Radiometric resolution, the ability to differentiate intensities of the incoming EMR; images with higher radiometric resolution are able to discern more subtle differences in light intensity.

There need to be compromises between the differing resolutions of a sensor. For example, although a detector in a high spatial resolution sensor will discriminate smaller targets than a low spatial resolution sensor, its spectral and/or radiometric resolutions will be lower[18].

A sensor's image can be translated into useful tools for learning about sirenian habitat. Criteria for selecting the appropriate sensor include the area, size, and spatial context of the aquatic vegetation to be monitored. Monitoring a historical set of images can show changes in seagrass areas over time. Combining satellite-derived aquatic vegetation cover images with water-surface temperature and salinity data in a GIS could illustrate seasonal displacements of seagrass stands due to temperature/salinity variation. If seagrass areas are reasonably homogeneous in species composition, and the study area has water that is shallow and clear enough to observe underwater vegetation, a sensor of moderate spatial resolution (15 to 30 m) and moderate temporal resolution (15 to 30 days) might be adequate, such as Landsat Thematic Mapper, CCD/CBERS-2, or SPOT. The selection of sensors depends on cost and the availability of good images (e.g., few or no clouds, no black stripes) for the relevant dates (e.g., date close to that of an aerial or boat survey). The Thematic Mapper (TM) sensors have the longest historical set of images, since 1982, and these products have been widely used. The CCD/CBERS-2 sensor has collected images only since 2002, but its specifications are similar to those of TM. Images from both sensors can be downloaded at no cost for many areas of the globe (see table 18.3). The SPOT-4 sensor has similar specifications. Its images are more

Table 18.3. Web sites with satellite imagery and computer program tutorials.

NASA	http://www.ghcc.msfc.nasa.gov/sparcle/sparcle_tutorial.html
	Detailed online tutorial available at http://rst.gsfc.nasa.gov/.
ESRI	http://www.esri.com
	Free tutorials and grant opportunities for GIS training and software packages.
Dundee Satellite Receiving Station	http://www.sat.dundee.ac.uk/
	http://www.sat.dundee.ac.uk/freeimages.html
	Up-to-date archive of images from NOAA, SeaStar, Terra and Aqua polar satellites. Images from geostationary satellites covering the whole earth are also available.
China-Brazil Earth Resource Satellite—CBERS-2	http://www.cbers.inpe.br/
	http://www.cbers.inpe.br/en/programas/p_pedidos.htm
	Web pages to search and request satellite imagery (available from downloading or CD-ROM). Information can be accessed in English, but the image download page is in Portuguese.
Global Land Cover Facility—Landsat GeoCover	http://glcf.umiacs.umd.edu/portal/geocover/
	https://zulu.ssc.nasa.gov/mrsid/
	Satellite images derived from Landsat TM scenes. GeoCover-LC (Land Cover) products are medium-resolution land cover images. Both sites provide Landsat images that were orthorectified by NASA.
ResMap Earth Image Source	http://www.resmap.com/index.html
	Provides free access to GIS-ready satellite data. Global imagery, with resolutions from 1km to 14.25m for most areas, and 1m in selected regions.
Georeferenced Information Processing System—SPRING National Institute for Space Research (INPE), Brazil	http://www.dpi.inpe.br/spring/
	GIS and remote sensing image processing system which provides integration of raster and vector data representations in a single environment.
Terralib	http://www.terralib.org/
	A GIS class and functions library, available from the Internet as open source. A collaborative environment for the development of multiple GIS tools.
GPS Trackmaker	http://www.gpstm.com/index.php
	Useful tools for working with GPS. A free program for GPS devices; compatible with more than 160 GPS models; technical support for Garmin, Magellan and other brands.
Australia's Spatial Industry Portal	http://www.xyz.au.com/public/general_info/listings.cfm?category_id=25&sub_category_id=84
	Good online database for landscape data and GIS information for dugong habitat assessment in Australia.
Coastal Habitat Resources Information System (CHRIS), Australia	http://chrisweb.dpi.qld.gov.au/chris/
	Resource center for Australia's coastal fish habitat, fisheries resources and environmental datasets developed by the Department of Fisheries. The integration of CHRIS thematic maps facilitates monitoring of coastal habitats.
Geoscience Australia–Australian Centre for Remote Sensing	http://www.ga.gov.au/
	Link to satellite and data processing resources; offers free online MODIS and NOAA satellite data and a technical introduction to the use of remote sensing.

expensive, but it has the capacity to acquire images at intervals of one to five days in case there is cloud cover.

On the other hand, if the seagrass areas are highly heterogeneous, it might be better to use a high spatial resolution (0.5 to 5 m) sensor such as IKONOS or Quickbird. In this case, although spatial resolution is enhanced, more images are needed to cover the same area because the IKONOS satellite has an 11 km swath in contrast to the 185 km swath of the TM sensor.

When there is interest in a more detailed temporal picture of vegetation cover throughout a larger region, and less precise estimates of area are needed, a low spatial (>150 m)/high temporal (0.5 to 2 days) resolution sensor like the free images from MODIS/Terra and/or Aqua might be adequate. Its swath of 2,330 km results in a temporal resolution of two days, or one day when images from the MODIS sensors on board both Terra and Aqua satellites are used.

Among the active sensors, Radar is currently used for environmental applications of remote sensing[19]. This technology is changing quickly. Light Detecting and Ranging Sensors (Lidar) are active sensors that emit laser beams and use the delay in the time of arrival of the different beams to estimate target distances. Lidar use is increasing, especially Shoals Lidar for intertidal and coastal mapping.

There is no best sensor *per se*. Each sensor is best for a particular application, and it is important to note that in some situations remote sensing might not be appropriate at all. For example, it is not applicable when studying dugong habitats off the coast of Australia in sparse tropical seagrasses and turbid waters (see the case study in box 18.1). However, satellite imagery that captures sea surface temperatures is useful for determining the role of water temperature in limiting the range of dugongs. Dugongs at the higher latitudes of their thermal tolerance can be limited from foraging in quality seagrass habitats during winter by water below 18°C. It is important for the researcher to take all aspects of habitat use into account before using remote sensing.

While remote sensing can be a useful tool in the delineation and assessment of sirenian habitat (see box 18.2), after the acquisition of an image it is necessary to process it digitally. The reader interested in using remote sensing is advised to work with experienced researchers and consult other resources[20].

Quantitative Habitat Modeling

Owing to difficulties in conducting site-scale field surveys on extensive and highly modified landscapes, the response of sirenians to large-scale environmental changes has not been studied in detail. Locally, research can estimate the distribution and abundance of sirenian species based on habitat modeling. This strategy may assist habitat assessment where gathering actual distribution and abundance data is problematic. This happens where murky and hyacinth-covered waters make it impossible to observe manatees or dugongs. In those circumstances GIS and habitat modeling could be adequate.

For habitat modeling, selected habitat attributes can be measured *in situ* and/or by means of a remote sensor, and then incorporated into a computer GIS database for spatial display and analysis. An explicit spatial model can then be created in the GIS, and the configuration of the predictive model can be quantitatively analyzed by various statistical programs.

There is a broad range of modeling methods useful for sirenian research. The choice depends on the objectives of the study, the availability of computer software, and local expertise. However, owing to the complexity of ecological processes occurring at local scales, generalizing habitat models is not recommended, unless similarities between habitats in the different regions can be shown (e.g., see box 18.2). Nonetheless caution is necessary because simplistic assumptions about ecosystem variability and dynamics reduce accuracy and could have conservation and management implications. We also strongly recommend that habitat models be used in conjunction with fieldwork data, when available, to validate model assumptions.

The most widely used modeling methods include ANUCLIM, Generalized Linear Models (GLM), Generalized Additive Models (GAM) and Bioclimate Models (BIOCLIM)[21].

ANUCLIM is a climate-oriented program that incorporates data as point locations on maps. It stores data on elevation, climatic surfaces, long-term rainfall, temperature, and radiation. Other types of data used depend on the profile of the species. The process produces ranked predictions for a particular site based on the habitat needs of the species[22].

GLMs are statistical models that include ordinary regression and analysis of variance. All GLMs have a random component (the response variable), systematic components (predictor or explanatory variables), and a link function that describes the relationship between the expected value of the response and the predictors[23]. The GLMs used to estimate species distributions are logistic regressions for presence-absence data and Poisson regressions for abundance data[24]. Those methods estimate the probability of species presence, which may then be used as an index of habitat quality. A case study describ-

Case Study: Videography, Near-Infrared Spectroscopy, and GIS for Habitat Assessment
James K. Sheppard

Seagrass meadows exhibit high spatial and temporal heterogeneity and dugongs appear to prefer some seagrass pastures and avoid others. Hence understanding the species composition, nutrient profile, and spatial dynamics of seagrass communities is essential for predicting patterns of habitat use by foraging dugongs and for the effective management of seagrass resources.

Dugong seagrass habitat at Burrum Heads off the coast of Queensland, Australia, was identified and delineated from the spatial patterns of dugongs that were tagged and GPS-tracked. Dugong selection for seagrass food resources was then estimated by comparing an individual animal's patterns of space-use with the available seagrass patches within its habitat. Kernel home ranges of seven animals were generated from GPS location fixes and overlaid in a GIS to create a single 24 km^2 survey area. This survey area was assumed to represent available seagrass habitat for all dugongs in the region. A sampling grid was generated within the survey area to cover the habitat most frequented by foraging dugongs (Sheppard et al. 2006).

Remote sensing is of limited use in evaluating the biomass and species composition of tropical seagrasses occurring at low density. It is further limited in deep or turbid water. Therefore point sampling and spatial analysis using a GIS was used to map the seagrass habitat. Seagrass species and percentage cover was estimated visually at each sampling site within the survey area. Samples of seagrass material were taken from a random subset of the sampling sites for nutrient analysis. Sites external to the survey area were also randomly selected and sampled to compare the seagrasses targeted by the tracked dugongs with those less used.

The intertidal seagrass habitat available to dugongs within the Burrum Heads habitat was accessed and evaluated on foot using a handheld GPS. Subtidal seagrasses were located from a vessel using a marine GPS/Sonar plotter and were point-sampled using a portable marine video camera. Videography techniques can sample subtidally without the need for SCUBA and its associated time and costs. Linear estimations of percent seagrass cover relative to the substratum were calculated at each sample site. A steel benthic grab (Van Veen type) was used to confirm the species composition of seagrass viewed on the video monitor, collect subtidal samples for nutrient analysis, and assess sediment type. The relationship between percentage cover and above- and below-ground seagrass biomass was calibrated. Because dugongs extract the entire plant during feeding, above- and below-ground seagrass components were combined into a whole-plant value for each seagrass species.

Near-infrared reflectance spectroscopy (NIRS) was used to determine the nutrient content of the seagrass samples. This technique can identify the composition of organic samples in a rapid, cost-effective, and repeatable manner. Raster surfaces of bathymetry, seagrass cover, and nutrient profiles were interpolated from the sample point data within a GIS. The seagrass meadows in the Burrum Heads habitat were able to be effectively interpolated into a two-dimensional surface using the point data because the seagrass formed continuous patches with gradual gradients and very low (<5 cm) canopy height. Water depths at each subtidal sample point were matched with the tide height at the time the sample was recorded and were adjusted to give the water depth at mean sea level. These corrected depth values were then interpolated in a GIS to create a bathymetric surface for the survey area.

Nutrient masses for each species were combined to provide an estimate of mean nutrient g/m^2 at each sample point. The points were then interpolated into maps of nitrogen and starch mass to create a map of definitive dugong habitat quality. Resource selection functions (RSFs) were used to relate a probabilistic measure of each individual dugong's space-use to the spatial landscapes of the resource variables. The RSF models indicated that dugong space-use within the Burrum Heads habitat was consistently centered over seagrass patches with high nitrogen concentrations, except during the day at low tides, when their space-use was centered over high seagrass biomass and away from seagrass with high starch concentration. Dugong association with seagrass high in starch was positive during both day and night high tides, when dugongs could access intertidal areas where the seagrass biomass was generally low.

The Burrum Heads seagrass meadow has recently been legislated as a Habitat Protection Zone within the Great Sandy Marine Park on the basis of its importance as dugong habitat as identified by this study. The meadow has also been designated a "go-slow" zone for boaters. (Web link: http://www.derm.qld.gov.au/parks/great-sandy-marine/faq.html).

ing an application of multivariate statistical methods is in box 18.2.

GAMs are a nonparametric extension of GLMs. They are considered a useful tool in modeling biological systems because the response is not limited to a parametric function. This means that the fitted response surface may be a more realistic representation of the true response shape. The resulting modeled probability surface may be mapped and interpreted as an estimate of habitat suitability[25].

BIOCLIM modeling can be applied where only species presence data is available (with latitude, longitude, and elevation parameters). The procedure uses the computer program BIOCLIM to generate global estimates

---

BOX 18.2

Case Study: Seasonal Migrations of Amazonian Manatees

Eduardo Moraes Arraut and Miriam Marmontel

Migration is an adaptation to environments in which habitat quality changes asynchronously in space and/or time (Dingle and Drake 2007). This implies that in a particular season, habitat quality in the destination must be better than at the starting point, but not necessarily that it must be good. Amazonian manatees that live in the mid-River Solimões region (Western Amazon) spend the high-water season (see later description) in *várzea* lakes, and during the low-water season they are subjected to difficult habitat conditions and migrate to Ria Amanã. The flood pulse of River Solimões varies seasonally up to 16 m in water level, which results in annual flooding and drying up of extensive regions of the floodplain. *Várzea* lakes are lakes within the floodplains and are characterized by high-sediment and nutrient-rich waters (called "white" waters), while a *ria* is a long narrow lake formed by the partial submergence of a river valley.

Manatee habitat was characterized by mapping the river boundaries and macrophyte coverage dynamics associated with the annual flood pulse cycle of the River Solimões. Manatee movements (daily and seasonal) were studied by tracking ten males with VHF telemetry between 1994 and 2006. The locations were used to estimate seasonal home ranges to determine migration patterns. Because the Amazon is an immense and complex area where it is often difficult to reach manatee habitat, we chose to use a combination of remote sensing, GIS, and fieldwork.

Habitat information came from: (1) classifications of Landsat-TM/ETM+ images acquired for dates that represented different flood pulse phases of River Solimões (high, lowering, low, and rising water); (2) water level variation measured daily using two hydrographs positioned in two seasons where manatees are found; (3) a three-dimensional model of the water bodies; and (4) fieldwork, which included data on the density, height, and diversity of macrophyte stands and bathymetric mapping of the main lakes and migration routes of the manatees.

A major question was whether manatees were using certain classes of habitats (macrophyte-covered waters, flooded forest, and open water) evenly. This was done with a compositional analysis of log-ratios (Aebischer et al. 1993), in which habitat areas used by manatees were compared to other areas in the study region. During high water, macrophyte-covered waters were used by male manatees in a larger proportion than were other habitat classes.

Macrophyte cover percentages within várzea and other habitat areas were compared to see if the spatial distribution of macrophytes explained where manatees migrated to during high water. The analysis, using an analysis of variance (ANOVA) and a generalized linear model (GLM), showed that during high-water season (mid-May to end June), when manatees had access to all water bodies, they remained in várzea lakes where macrophytes were more abundant.

The next question was why manatees did not spend the low-water season (October and November) in várzea lakes? Different seasonal home ranges were compared using the proportional reduction in the flooded area as the response variable. The analysis showed that the flooded area within home ranges in várzea lakes is reduced to less than 10% during low water, while home ranges in Ria Amanã retain more than 90% of their area. Moreover, caimans, jaguars, and humans visit várzea lakes more often during the low-water season, mainly in search of the large quantities of fish that aggregate in what is left of those lakes. Thus during the low-water season, lakes become more dangerous for manatees, and they migrate to Ria Amanã. In Ria Amanã, however, manatees have no access to food (which is not present in the várzea lakes at this time either), so they may fast during this season, though they are not as exposed to predators.

in the form of climate surfaces[26]. Climate surfaces may include precipitation and temperature data arranged in a spatially referenced grid. Thus, in BIOCLIM, we can estimate a species profile from the climatic conditions where the species has been recorded. The next step identifies other areas that have similar climatic conditions and can predict new potential distributions for the species[27]. However, the predicted distribution of the species of interest may be restricted by limitation of resources, competition, or disturbance.

Quantitative habitat assessment is increasingly useful in applied natural resource management for assessing the impacts of human activities, restoring perturbed systems, designing protected areas, identifying land units for regional planning, developing recovery strategies for threatened ecosystems and species, and setting priorities for conservation[28]. Habitat models have recently been put to greater use for predicting the movement of species in alternative impact scenarios for predicting global climate change.

Other parameters such as the spatial-temporal distribution, abundance, or movements of sirenians may need to be measured to understand how a habitat is being utilized. Data from complementary research techniques such as aerial surveys, telemetry, and interviews can be incorporated into habitat assessments to make them more robust[29].

The effects of human-caused threats and current impacts on sirenians also need to be considered in habitat assessments. Threats such as hunting, gillnet entanglements, chemical pollutants, boat strikes, and human harassment might be included as major human variables of a habitat assessment. Human impact mapping is an important step toward the zoning of management units to facilitate the assessment of threats and to formulate appropriate management measures for their abatement.

Case studies showing how habitat assessment has been used to define critical habitat and to set priority areas for conservation and management are provided in boxes 18.3 and 18.4. Because sirenians are cryptic

BOX 18.3

Case Study: Using Generalized Linear Models for Antillean Manatee Habitat in Bahia de Chetumal

Leon D. Olivera-Gómez

In habitat models an area that supports more individuals than another may be considered richer. In these models the relative importance of habitat features can be explored to find those which assist scientists build more complete and realistic predictive models. The main objective of such modeling is to recognize the most important features and predict the probability of the species occurring. Research on habitat modeling for the Antillean manatee is limited. A multivariate analysis test was used to determine direct and indirect effects of selected habitat features on manatee sightings in Bahia de Chetumal, Mexico. Bahia de Chetumal is a large estuary on Mexico's Caribbean coast. This area is a coastal protected area and manatee sanctuary, with the largest manatee population in the Yucatán Peninsula. Distance to freshwater sources and nature of vegetation cover, depth, slope, salinity, and shelter were sampled concurrently during 17 manatee aerial surveys between 1998 and 2000. Using predictive modeling, researchers found that distance to freshwater sources and water depth were the habitat features that contributed most to model variance and were assessed as the most important variables (Olivera-Gómez and Mellink 2005).

The procedure consisted of combining knowledge of the manatee's habitat requirements with the mapped habitat features mentioned. During the aerial surveys, manatee presence and relative abundance were recorded as the response variables and habitat features as independent variables. Then a multivariate regression using a generalized linear model (GLM) was performed. This allowed the researchers to include categorical or numerical variables as independent variables and use a particular link function to produce the kind of response modeled (i.e., a binary response: presence/absence used in logistic regression and average number of sighted manatees in Poisson regression). By using forward, backward, or stepward procedures, researchers could select those variables that produced significant changes in model deviance (a measure of variance).

For the statistical analysis any mathematical or statistical software that includes GLMs can be used (e.g., R, MATLAB, SPSS, NTSS, MINITAB). These methods are practical for developing countries, and the results could be considered in association with other approaches to delineate habitat and in planning management strategies.

species that are difficult to track in the wild, spatial modeling of ecological resources can be a useful tool to help locate potential habitats for protection and conservation. In some countries, environmental legislation requires the identification of critical habitats of threatened species.

Possible Biases

Habitat was previously defined as the presence of an animal correlated with a group of selected environmental variables. This definition has been criticized as it considers only the presence and, at best, the abundance of

---

BOX 18.4

Case Study: Evaluating Antillean Manatee Habitat in the Alvarado Lagoon System, Mexico
Alejandro Ortega-Argueta

This research was conducted in the Alvarado Lagoon System (ALS), a coastal wetland in Veracruz, in the southern Gulf of Mexico. The study area is a wetland system of 300,000 hectares formed by about 100 estuarine lagoons interconnected by ten rivers. Pristine mangrove forest covers around 15% of the study area. The ALS has a high economic importance due to agriculture, fisheries, and oil and gas industries.

The main objectives of the study were: (1) evaluation of manatee habitat to estimate critical areas for conservation; (2) identification of main threats to manatees and their habitat; and (3) providing management recommendations for manatee protection and conservation (Ortega-Argueta 2002).

Before this study, only scarce manatee distribution data in the form of interviews and anecdotal records were available. Muddy waters and floating aquatic vegetation blocked sightings of manatees during three aerial surveys (9 hours effort) and boat surveys (15 days effort) conducted between 1999 and 2000. Manatees are under pressure in the region from human activities such as poaching, entanglement in fishing gear, and degradation of habitats by unregulated agricultural and urban development. Habitat degradation is caused by mangrove deforestation, industrial waste pollution, and agrochemical run-off.

To estimate manatee habitat, a map of the study area was created in a geographic information system (GIS) by combining fieldwork data, aerial photography, and 1:50,000 digitized topographic maps. Data on manatee distribution obtained from previous research and interviews were also incorporated into the GIS database. To cross-check the manatee distributional data with habitat parameters, complementary information on habitat resources was incorporated into a habitat model. Published information from the region was used to select the parameters or variables to be sampled in the field as indicators of manatee habitat. Three indicators of critical habitat were selected: availability of food resources for manatees, depth of and accessibility to bodies of water, and potential human impacts. Each of these indicators was represented as a digital map layer in the GIS. Then a map of good quality habitat derived from an overlay of those layers was used to denote critical manatee habitat areas. The map of food resources incorporated information from sampling river-bank vegetation and macro-scale analysis of data from aerial photography and digitized vegetation maps. The water depth or bathymetric map was created by depth sampling along the main bodies of water, including rivers and estuaries. Depth was measured at 680 points by an electronic echo-sounder and referenced in Universal Transverse Mercator (UTM) coordinates with a GPS. The map of potential human impacts incorporated socioeconomic data obtained from digital settlement censuses that included main towns, commercial fishing areas, land tenure, and navigation and fishing routes. Major threats affecting manatees and their habitat were identified in a workshop held with members of the Manatee Advisory Committee of Mexico. Because manatee poaching and entanglement in fishing gear were identified as current severe threats in the ALS, areas with higher density of human settlements and fishing activities were considered to indicate areas with higher risk of impacts. This information was also incorporated into the potential human impact map.

Once the three indicator maps were produced, they were combined using GIS overlay commands. Maps of food resources availability and bathymetry were used to show suitable areas of habitat. The human impact map illustrated conditions that would limit or affect the habitat condition. Considering the relatively large area of the ALS, one of the biggest achievements of the study was the identification of geographic regions where conservation efforts should be focused with higher priority. Recommendations for management and protection were also generated for areas where manatee habitats were not yet protected. A habitat assessment of this type can be applied to estimate sirenian habitat in areas where distributional data are limited.

organisms. However, habitat defined in this way says nothing about the ecological relationships or interactions between species and the physical and biological variables that govern them, or about the environment's effect on survival or reproduction[30]. It says nothing about the potential habitats that are not detected when the temporal or spatial limits of a survey, or its physical constraints, result in an organism's presence not being detected[31]. We can only select those variables apparent to us and measurable by today's instruments. There is a danger that the assessment of habitat may reflect a researcher's subjective judgment.

Another disadvantage is the lack of detailed biological and ecological knowledge of sirenians in developing countries. It has been a common practice to use research conducted in developed countries and apply it elsewhere. As variables may be temporally and spatially different, important factors in one region or year would not necessarily be applicable in other circumstances.

Assumptions based on habitat models may not consider the temporal variation of ecological resources and processes. Habitat models are difficult to validate because they are too general to allow researchers to make precise and testable predictions[32]. Accurate landscape-scale model predictions depend on the accuracy of the ecological and geographical data incorporated, and the assumptions and structure of the model itself, and hence predictive habitat models should be used carefully when making management recommendations. Continued monitoring of ecological variables through different scales over time is necessary to define more reliable habitat characteristics, dynamics, and patterns.

Summary

Limitations and Advantages of Habitat Assessments

Wide-ranging species such as sirenians may undertake large-scale movements (~1,000 km) in response to seasonal changes in environmental variables and available resources[33]. Sirenians may have large ranges of distribution and use different environments within the landscape at varying temporal scales. Consequently, habitat modeling over a large area can be very time-consuming and expensive.

Adequate fieldwork can be extensive in large, intricate habitat areas. Satellite imagery and aerial photography may not always be available, and the hardware, software, and skilled personnel to develop spatially explicit models may also be lacking. Addressing such limitations call for international cooperation to share information and finance basic equipment and materials such as GIS software, satellite imagery, and aerial photography. Training in the use of GIS and spatial image analysis should be provided to local researchers and managers in developing countries through regional workshops. Cooperation among several organizations that are working within the same region may allow sharing expenses for equipment, materials, and expertise.

Habitat assessment can be relatively expensive because hardware, software, and skilled personnel are necessary, although it is noteworthy that free sources of data (e.g., satellite images) and free software for GIS analysis are becoming more common and readily available for any user. Such is the case with the R-Project (http://www.r-project.org/), a powerful open-source software with packages that can carry out several types of analyses, such as statistical, deterministic, and spatial. Once these initial limitations are resolved, assessment becomes cost-effective because the information gathered and analyzed can be used in both short- and long-term applications. Valuable sets of data such as digital maps, aerial and spatial photography and imagery, natural resources inventories, and sirenian survey data can be stored in computers, allowing the updating of data as they become available from monitoring or new studies.

In summary, habitat assessment methods are valuable tools for understanding the environment that drives habitat use and thus governs sirenian distribution, movement, and abundance. Such methods can be applied to sirenian conservation and management to address environmental impacts, identify and protect critical habitats, predict potential effects of human activities or other sources of disturbance, and model scenarios at varied spatial and temporal scales. With the information gathered, managers and conservationists can make better predictions for the protection and management of sirenians and their habitats.

19

Sirenian Genetics and Demography

LESLEE PARR, FABRÍCIO R. SANTOS, MICHELLE WAYCOTT,
JULIANA A. VIANNA, BRENDA MCDONALD, SUSANA CABALLERO,
AND MARIA JOSÉ DE SOUZA LOPES

As previous chapters in this book make clear, the long-term survival of the four extant species of Sirenia is in peril due to many confounding factors, the majority of which are caused, directly or indirectly, by human activity. One of the most critical effects, along with habitat fragmentation and a reduction in manatee and dugong numbers, is a possible loss of genetic diversity. Genetic diversity is the fundamental level of biodiversity. Therefore, a critical first step in developing management programs for endangered or threatened species is the determination of existing genetic variability within and between management units. The accurate delineation of distinct management units and the ability to detect changes in genetic diversity within these units is critical. Box 19.1 gives steps for gathering and preserving samples for genetic analysis. Box 19.2 is a glossary of selected terms in genetics.

Overview of Molecular Techniques

Natural variations at the level of DNA can be used for investigating genetic relationships within and between populations and for monitoring genetic fluctuations of populations over time and across the range of their natural habitat. The authors of this chapter have successfully employed each of the following classes of DNA for studying the genetic relationships and population dynamics of manatees and dugongs.

Mitochondrial DNA

Direct sequencing of mitochondrial DNA (mtDNA) has been used extensively as a tool for inferring demography, evolutionary past, and geographic distribution of genetic lineages[1]. MtDNA is also one of the molecular markers of choice for studies directed at the application of genetic techniques for conservation of endangered species[2].

Several characteristics of mtDNA make it useful for these studies. MtDNA is small in size—it is about 1/10,000th the size of the smallest animal nuclear genome[3] and is therefore easy to distinguish. Mammalian mitochondrial DNA is estimated to evolve at a rate about a five to nine times higher than does nuclear DNA[4]. This creates easily detectable variability between individuals within populations. The mitochondrial ge-

---

BOX 19.1

Handling Animal Tissue for Genetic Analysis

Ann Marie Clark

- Obtain CITES and/or all relevant regional permits before collection and shipment.
- When possible, it is best to collect samples using sterile instruments (tubes, new scalpel blades for each sample) and wearing latex gloves to prevent contamination of samples and cross-contamination between samples. However, when field conditions make this impossible, careful handling of samples during collection and in the genetics lab can mitigate many of the field contamination issues. Inform the lab of the collection conditions so that necessary precautions can be taken when working with the samples.
- Mark each sample tube or bag with all the available information (date of collection, species, location, gender, sample id#, etc.) using indelible ink on the outside of the container and/or in pencil on waterproof paper, and place the label inside the sample container.
- Keep duplicate log sheets with all sample information.
- Maintain samples at a cool (ambient) temperature and out of direct sun.
- Ship to a cooperating genetics lab as soon as possible (any of the chapter authors would be willing to assist).

Collection vials should be made of high impact, chemically resistant polyethylene (HDPE) and have screw-on caps. These vials are resistant to breakage and impervious to alcohol and buffers such as the SED or blood lysis buffer, and will ensure safe transport of samples. Double bag all samples before shipping.

Collecting Tissue without Refrigeration

SED Buffer for Skin, Muscle, Heart, or Liver Tissue

1. Prepare SED buffer (Saturated NaCl; 250 mM EDTA pH 7.5; 20% DMSO); see preparation instructions following.
2. A tissue sample the size of a large marble is generally sufficient. Remove sample using a sterile or clean scalpel or knife. Biopsy punch samples can also be stored in SED buffer.
3. Cut larger tissue samples a few times to increase penetration of buffer.
4. Add tissue to a pre-labeled tube containing SED buffer.
5. Samples can be stored at room temperature for up to a year or in a refrigerator indefinitely. Avoid extended exposure to heat or sunlight.
6. Prior to shipping, reseal the tubes carefully and double wrap in an airtight plastic bag (Ziploc or equivalent) to prevent leakage.
7. Ship samples by air freight or express mail.

Note: SED buffer is nontoxic, nonflammable, and noncorrosive and can be stored indefinitely at room temperature. Since this buffer is saturated with salt (NaCl), a white precipitate may form in some tubes. This does not affect the ability of the buffer to preserve tissue.

To make SED buffer:
- Dissolve 95 g tetrasodium EDTA in 700 ml distilled water.
- pH to 7.5 with glacial acetic acid.
- Saturate the solution with about 200 g NaCl. Allow salt to dissolve completely.
- Add 200 ml DMSO. Bring buffer to 1 liter with distilled water.

(Protocol modified from Amos and Hoelzel 1991 and Proebstel et al. 1993.)

Desiccant Storage Method for Skin and Muscle

1. Excise a small amount of tissue (~10 g) from each animal. Use a scraping tool or biopsy punch for skin if the animal is living, or cut ~10 g of skin or muscle during necropsy of dead animals.
2. Cut tissue sections to ~0.5 cm cubes or very thin slices.
3. Place each tissue sample in a labeled container (small Ziploc bags or screw-cap tubes work best) and add desiccant. Be sure to cover tissue sample completely. If using 1.5 ml tubes, add ~1.0–1.5 ml desiccant/0.5 cm cube of tissue. Camera and lens desiccant or anhydrous calcium sulfate (Drierite) both work well.

Preservation of Fecal Material

- Fecal samples can be stored using 70–100% ethanol or they can be frozen. It is best to collect as much as possible. Most feces extractions require at least 1 ml of feces. Be sure to use a large enough container to collect an adequate amount of fecal material or take multiple samples from each individual. Label vials accordingly.

Collection and Storage of Blood Samples

- Blood samples can be collected using a vacuum tube (Vacutainer) treated with EDTA, an untreated tube, or a syringe. Three ml of whole blood are sufficient for DNA extractions. Blood samples in EDTA must be stored in the refrigerator. Alternatively, an EDTA-preserved blood sample can be mixed with a blood lysis solution of 10 mM NaCl, 100 mM EDTA, 100 mM Tris (pH 8), and 1% (w/v) SDS, in a 1:10 ratio (blood:lysis buffer) and kept at room temperature.

1. Draw 1–3 ml of blood using an untreated syringe or Vacutainer tube.
2. Add blood immediately to a pre-labeled tube, or multiple tubes, containing blood lysis buffer at a 1:10 ratio blood to lysis buffer. Do not add too much blood to the tube!
3. Immediately but gently invert or rock the tube several times to mix.
4. Samples can be stored at room temperature for at least 1 year and indefinitely in a refrigerator. Avoid extended exposure to heat or sunlight.
5. Ship samples by air freight or express mail.

Note: SDS (sodium dodecyl sulfate or sodium lauryl sulfate) may form a precipitate in cool conditions. Warm the vial to get the SDS back into solution before using if possible; however, the precipitant will not affect the effectiveness of the buffer. Blood lysis buffer is nontoxic, nonflammable, and noncorrosive and can be stored for an extended period at room temperature.

(Protocol modified from White and Densmore 1992.)

Collection and Preparation of Bone Samples

- Bone samples can work well for DNA extractions. Sirenian bones do not have a medullary cavity but those bones involved in the production of red and white blood cells (i.e., ribs and sternum) can still be used for DNA isolations. The highest quality and quantity of DNA is obtained from bones that have not been cooked, treated, or lacquered, although all will generally yield some DNA. Bone fragments can be transported in dry plastic bags preferably containing some desiccant. About 20 mg of powered bone is required for DNA isolations; however, bone DNA extractions are not 100% successful, so it is highly recommended that enough bone is collected for at least three separate DNA extractions. See Tuross (1994) and Holland et al. (2003).

---

nome is usually maternally inherited (though there is some evidence of "paternal leakage" and contribution during fertilization in some taxa) as a single unit that does not recombine with the paternal genome[5]. This makes mtDNA the preferred molecular marker for descriptions of maternal lineage, population structure, and genetic diversity[6].

Microsatellites

Microsatellites are short nucleotide sequence repeats (SSRs)[7] that are distributed throughout the nuclear genome[8]. These repeats, consisting of two, three, or four nucleotides, show high levels of polymorphism[9]. Microsatellites are regarded as some of the most useful molecular markers for the study of population genetic structure and dynamics[10]. Assessing microsatellite profiles or "genotypes" allows researchers to assign individuals to particular populations within the species' range[11].

Molecular Sexing

Sex-specific regions of the mammalian genome have been relatively well studied. Thompson[12] utilized a portion of the genes on the X and Y chromosomes to develop a sex-specific molecular assay for the dugong that may be applicable in other Sirenia.

Molecular Aging

Recent advances in our understanding of mammalian chromosome structure have led to the development of potential methods for aging individuals using a DNA assay based on the shortening of telomeres during an organism's lifespan. Telomeres are located at the end of nearly all animal chromosomes. In mammals, these long repeats of TTAGGG are between 10,000 and 150,000 base pairs (bp) long at birth. A correlation between age and the rate of telomere shortening per year (loss of bp/yr) has been established in both birds and mammals[13].

BOX 19.2

Useful Terms and Definitions

Allele: A portion of DNA that codes for a functional protein.

Basal: A species, taxon, or clade that is located closest to the root of a phylogenetic tree, indicating it is the ancestral group.

Base pairs: Number of repeating pairs of nucleotides making up the portion of DNA being considered.

Bootstrap values: Technique for estimating the statistical error when the sampling distribution is unknown.

Bottleneck: A sudden, large reduction in population size.

Cluster: In phylogenetic analysis, a group of closely related individuals that appears "clustered" on branches of a phylogenetic tree.

Control region: Highly variable sequence of mitochondrial DNA, also referred sometimes as D-loop.

Diploid (2n): The condition in which a cell or individual has two copies of every chromosome.

Evolutionary Significant Unit (ESU): Genetically distinct populations that are considered to require management as separate units.

Exon: The coding region of a gene.
Founder effect: A loss of genetic variation in a population that was established by a small number of individuals carrying only a fraction of the genetic diversity of the larger population.
Genetic diversity: The extent of genetic variation in a population or species or across a group of species. It can be measured as heterozygosity, haplotype or nucleotide diversity, allelic diversity, or heritability.
Genome: The full complement of genes present in a haploid set of chromosomes in an organism.
Genotype: The genetic constitution of an organism at one, many, or all of the genetic loci.
Haploid (1N): The condition in which a cell or individual has one copy of every chromosome.
Haplotype: Unique mitochondrial DNA sequences/lineages and/or allelic composition for several different loci on a chromosome.
Homoplasy: Two alleles or characters that are identical in state yet have different evolutionary origins.
Inbreeding: The mating of organisms related by descent.
Introgression: Diffusion of alleles from one population or species into another as a result of interbreeding or hybridization between them.
Mantel test: A statistical test relating geographical distance of samples taken to their relative genetic distance from one another.
Monophyletic: A group of organisms that contains the group's most common ancestor and all of its descendants.
Mitochondrial DNA (mtDNA): Haploid, double stranded circular DNA molecule located in the mitochondria.
Nucleotides: Molecular subunits of DNA.
Panmixia: Random mating within a breeding population.
Paraphyly: A group of organisms that contains the group's most recent common ancestor but does not contain all of the descendants of that ancestor.
Philopatry: A condition of reproductive behavior where individuals faithfully home to natal sites.
Phylogenetics: The relationship of evolutionary lineages among organisms. Phylogenetic relationships are usually represented in a phylogenetic tree.
Phylogenetic tree: A branching diagram representing the evolutionary relationships of the taxa or individuals analyzed.
Phylogeography: The study of the principles and processes involved in the geographical distribution of genealogical or genetic lineages.
Polymorphism: The percentage of the loci (portion of DNA of interest) that is variable.
Primer: A short nucleotide sequence that pairs with one strand of DNA and provides a free end at which the *Taq* polymerase enzyme begins synthesis of a complimentary segment of DNA.
Single nucleotide polymorphism (SNP): The occurrence of alleles with different nucleotide bases at a specific point of a DNA sequence.
Sympatric: Occupying the same geographic areas.
Telomeres: The terminal regions of chromosomes; in mammals these consist of the repeating nucleotide series, such as TTAGGG.
Vicariance: The separation or division of a group of organisms by a geographic barrier, such as a mountain or a body of water, resulting in differentiation of the original group into new varieties or species.
ZFX/ZFY: Zinc finger chromosomal proteins; genes located in the Y and X chromosome of mammals.

Insights Gained on the Genetics and Demography of Manatees

Subspecies Designation, West Indian and Amazonian Manatees

In 1998 Garcia-Rodriguez et al.[14] presented the first population genetic and phylogeographic study of West Indian and Amazonian manatees. The study was based on mtDNA sequence of 86 manatees from eight countries. The phylogenetic tree of mtDNA haplotypes identified three distinct, genetically related clusters of West Indian manatees (*Trichechus manatus*) compared to only a single cluster in Amazonian manatees (*T. inunguis*). The division of West Indian manatees into three clusters did not agree with previous morphological analysis (based on cranial characters), which divided this species into two subspecies: the Florida manatee (*T. manatus latirostris*) and the Antillean manatee (*T.*

m. manatus)[15]. None of the three genetic clusters detected was made up exclusively of the Florida lineage, as would be expected under the hypothesis of a separate Florida subspecies. Instead, Florida mtDNA haplotypes were grouped into shared clusters with Puerto Rico and the Dominican Republic manatees. In a more recent study, Florida haplotypes were also detected in Mexico[16].

Parr[17] reported a similar level of population structure in West African manatees (*T. senegalensis*). As West African manatee tissue samples have been difficult to obtain, the DNA sequence was analyzed for only 17 individuals. However, the phylogenetic tree of West African manatee mtDNA haplotypes, like that for West Indian manatees, showed three distinct clusters. One cluster consisted solely of animals from Guinea Bissau, a second cluster was derived from Cameroon-Gabon-Ghana in the south, and a third cluster was composed of inland manatees from the lake region of Chad (now landlocked due to recent construction of dams). The Guinea Bissau cluster displayed a marked genetic diversity and was identified as an important region in which to focus conservation efforts.

Cantanhede et al.[18] focused their genetic study on Amazonian manatees (*T. inunguis*), using mtDNA sequence of 68 individuals. They suggested the occurrence of unrestricted gene flow (breeding) and long-distance dispersal throughout the entirety of the Amazon basin. In this case, all Amazon manatees would behave as a single, random mating population. This hypothesis of panmixia was supported by a Mantel test, which did not show any significant correlation between genetics and geographic distances.

Recently, an extensive and international effort to sample and analyze DNA made it possible to do the first comparative study involving phylogeography and phylogeny of all three manatee species based on two separate mitochondrial genes of 189 West Indian manatees, 93 Amazonian manatees, and 6 West African manatees[19]. The phylogeny derived in this study suggested the monophyly (shared, common ancestry) of the trichechids, with the Amazonian manatee in position as the basal or ancestral species. This agrees with the morphological analyses of Domning[20], who proposed the monophyly of the marine species (the West Indian and West African species, *T. manatus* and *T. senegalensis*) and a long separation time for the Amazonian manatee, *T. inunguis*, which he suggests is the only surviving species of an ancient lineage adapted to the Amazon freshwater environment.

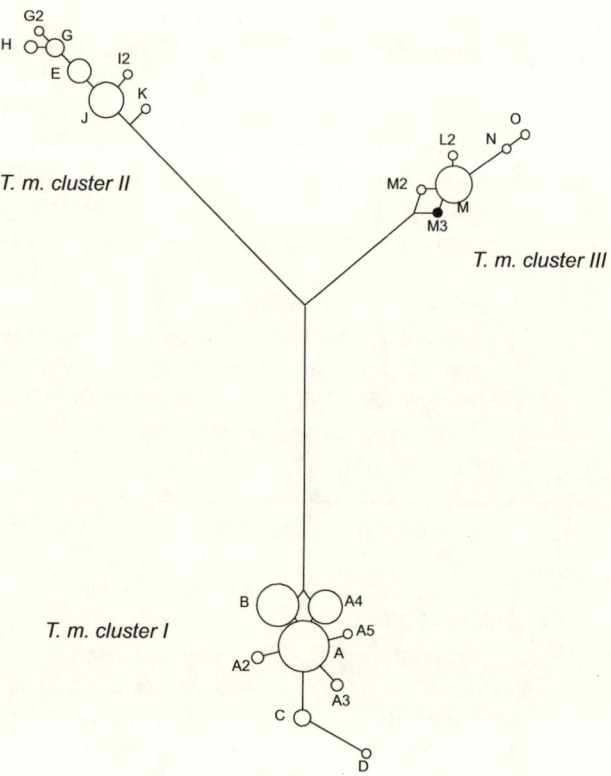

Figure 19.1. Median neighbor joining network showing a three-haplotype cluster pattern identified in mtDNA analysis of 189 West Indian manatees. (Courtesy of Fabrício R. Santos and Juliana A. Vianna.)

Spatial Distribution and Gene Flow, West Indian Manatees

The analysis of mtDNA from 189 West Indian manatees originating from ten countries allowed the resolution of a highly structured population in this species. A positive correlation between genetic and coastline geographic distances supported the idea that manatees migrate along the coast. The three-haplotype cluster pattern identified by Garcia-Rodriguez et al.[21] was also found in this sample set (figure 19.1), and the expansions of each cluster were dated back to the Pleistocene. A discontinuity in the *T. manatus* genetic structure was detected and was regarded as a historical break in gene flow, promoted by a geographic barrier (most likely the continuous chain of islands extending from the Lesser Antilles through Trinidad, near the mouth of the Orinoco River in Venezuela). This historical barrier appears to have isolated the Guyanas-Brazil population from other populations of manatees. The resulting bipartite structure in populations east and west of the Lesser Antilles indicates the existence of at least two independent evolutionary significant units (ESUs), or two subspecies, in the West Indian manatee.

West African Manatee Population Structure

Although only six *T. senegalensis* samples were analyzed in the Vianna et al.[22] study, two different mtDNA clusters were inferred: (1) inland samples from Lake Tchad, which spans the border between Chad and Niger, form a monophyletic group with coastal samples from Ghana (a small, isolated population of manatees that inhabit the lake and the upper reaches of the Benue River, a tributary of the Niger River, likely isolated there after dams were constructed on the Benue); and (2) Guinea-Bissau. Cluster separation was suggested to occur between hydrographic basins, with coastal occupation expanding from each river mouth. However, larger population surveys are needed to properly evaluate the remaining population structure of this species.

Geographical and Genetic Distances Association, Amazonian Manatees

Molecular demographic analysis in the Vianna et al. study revealed a strong bottleneck followed by population expansion in the recent past (Pleistocene). In agreement with Cantanhede et al.[23], all of the 31 different Amazonian haplotypes identified are closely related, forming a single cluster (figure 19.2), despite the fact that the individuals analyzed originated from different Amazon countries and separate regions within Brazil. Moderate population structure was observed (three to four times larger than that detected by Cantanhede et al[24]). This could be explained by the larger sample size over a greater geographic distribution and also by the fact that a larger portion of mtDNA sequence was analyzed by Vianna et al.[25]. However, the genetic correlation with geography is much weaker in Amazonian manatees than in West Indian manatees, which could be associated with a relatively recent expansion in Amazonia.

Hybridization between West Indian and Amazonian Manatees

The existence of possible *T. manatus* × *T. inunguis* hybrids had been previously suggested by morphological examinations[26] and mtDNA analysis[27]. Vianna et al.[28] presented unequivocal evidence of the occurrence of these interspecies hybrids using mtDNA, autosomal microsatellites, and cytogenetic analyses. Initially, seven individuals identified as West Indian (from the coasts of Guyana, French Guyana, and north Brazil) possessed mtDNA haplotypes related most closely to Amazonian

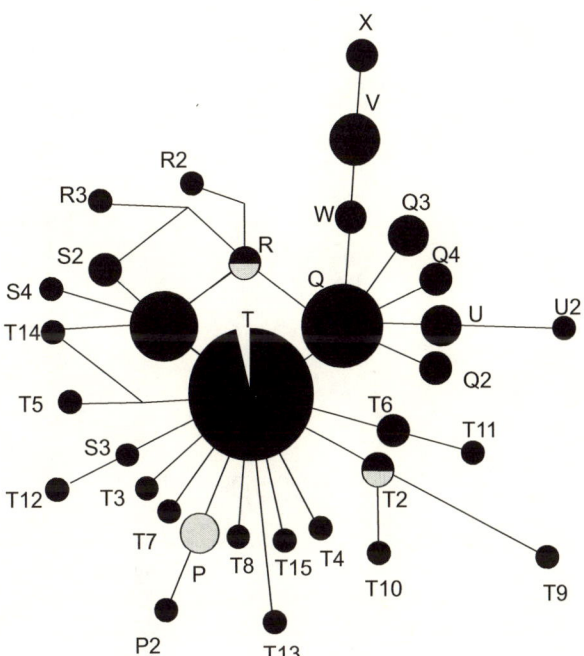

Figure 19.2. Median neighbor joining network showing a single-cluster pattern identified in the mtDNA analysis of 93 Amazonian manatees. The star shape pattern of the cluster indicates a recent expansion following a bottleneck. (Courtesy of Fabrício R. Santos and Juliana A. Vianna.)

sequences. Also, an Amazonian manatee found near the mouth of the Amazon presented a West Indian mtDNA haplotype. Microsatellite loci, used for the first time in this study, allowed the identification of species-specific alleles (making it possible to identify alleles from one or both species) in the eight likely hybrids. The microsatellite data also suggested the occurrence of F_2 (second generation) or further generation backcrosses, meaning some F_1 (first generation) hybrids may be able to interbreed with one of the parental species. One of the likely hybrids identified is a captive animal and has been submitted to a detailed karyotype (chromosome visualization) analysis. This hybrid manatee from the northern Brazilian coast presented an intermediate number of chromosomes (the diploid number of chromosomes, $2n = 50$, figure 19.3) between Amazonian ($2n = 56$) and West Indian ($2n = 48$) as well as microsatellite alleles specific to both parental species. All detected hybrids were from the region around the mouth of the Amazon where both species are sympatric, occupying the same habitat (figure 19.4).

Implications for Conservation and Management

The marked genetic structure and geographic subdivision of *T. manatus* should be considered in its manage-

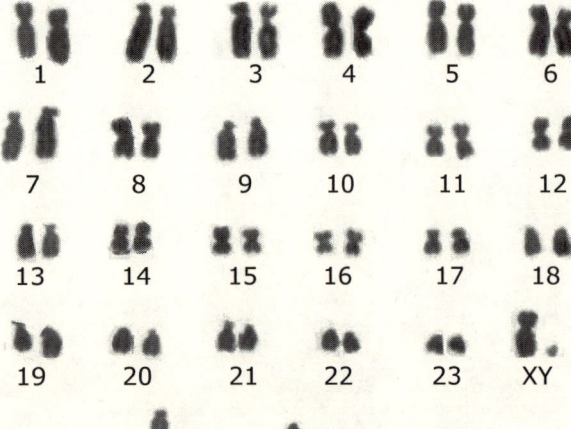

Figure 19.3. Karyotype of the hybrid manatee from the northern Brazilian coast presented an intermediate number of chromosomes. The diploid number of chromosomes, $2n = 50$. (Courtesy of Maria José de Souza Lopes.)

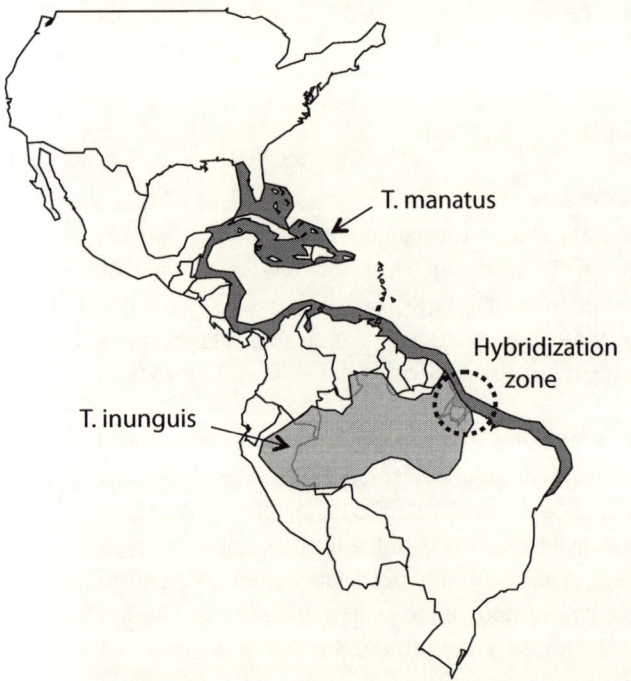

Figure 19.4. All detected hybrids between West Indian and Amazonian manatees were from samples obtained from the region around the mouth of the Amazon (hybridization zone), where both species are sympatric. (Courtesy of Fabrício R. Santos, Juliana A. Vianna, and Maria José de Souza Lopes.)

ment and conservation. The two different ESUs (or perhaps subspecies) identified in *T. manatus* indicate the need for separate management and conservation strategies for each.

There is a special need for careful management of both coastal and Amazonian manatees in Brazil, where the population is under serious threat due to its small size and low genetic diversity. The finding that the ten West Indian populations studied by Vianna et al.[29] are highly structured indicates a need for a population-level approach for future management.

Hybridization can be a very important conservation problem[30], particularly when it involves populations consisting of a few individuals, like the *T. manatus* from the Brazilian coast. Animals recovered from the mouth of the Amazon in Brazil or nearby regions (Guyanas) should not be translocated to areas where hybrids were not detected, such as the northeastern coast of Brazil and the interior of the Amazon basin.

A genotype/phenotype approach will be important in Puerto Rico also, where the two haplotypes identified were geographically separated (haplotype A occurs on the north coast, haplotype B on the south coast, and both on the east and west coast)[31]. This separation of genotypes could reflect adaptive selection to specific habitats and may indicate that translocation between these areas could fail.

It will be important to expand these phylogeographic studies (especially at the population level, using microsatellite) to include manatees from countries and regions not included in the original analyses, such as Cuba, Jamaica, Honduras, Nicaragua, Costa Rica, and Panama.

The same management attention should be considered in the Panama Canal System, where nine *T. manatus* and one *T. inunguis* from Peru were reintroduced in 1964[32]. Hybrids could be caused by anthropogenic activities in the area; however, little is known about this population and the survival of the translocated animals. Genetics studies are needed in the area to detect possible hybrids and genetic diversity of this population.

The observed diversity in the small sample set of West African manatees indicates higher geographic differentiation than the observed population structure in Amazonian manatees, which could possibly be equal to or greater than that of the West Indian manatee. Although larger surveys are needed for a more complete understanding, the two or three clusters of West African manatees should also be managed separately, at least between different hydrographic basins. This will require cross-border cooperation, which creates a special challenge because of the evolving state of economic, political, and social considerations faced on the African continent.

Insights Gained on the Genetics and Demography of Dugongs

Approaches and Techniques

Studies to date focus on the Australian region, where the largest known living population of the dugong occurs in Torres Strait and the northern Great Barrier Reef[33]. However, Palmer[34] analyzed mtDNA sequence of dugongs from the Andaman Sea and the Gulf of Thailand. The analysis of broad-scale population genetic structure and phylogeography utilizing mtDNA and microsatellite markers has provided significant insight into the large spatial scale dugongs inhabit across tropical and subtropical Australia[35].

Molecular Sexing of Dugongs

Thompson[36] utilized exon 11 of the ZFX/ZFY genes to develop a sex-specific molecular assay for the dugong that may be applicable in other sirenians. A fragment in exon 11 of the ZFX/ZFY genes was used in this analysis. Within this gene an *Rsa*I restriction site (a site that can be cut by the RsaI enzyme) is present in ZFY copy of the gene region but not in the ZFX. Thus dugong males (being XY), have both the ZFX and the ZFY genotype, but females (being XX) have only the ZFX sequence (figure 19.5). Preliminary analysis of the utility of this DNA segment for sex determination in manatees awaits verification. The advantage of this technique is that it may be applied to a small amount of DNA and is useful for screening of animals for their gender based on skin samples alone.

Molecular Aging of Dugongs

Dunshea[37] tested the utility of a telomere assay on dugongs with some success; the test involved comparing the age of dugongs established using age determined by tusk growth layer group analysis[38] with telomere region fragment length. Dunshea discovered a significant relationship between age assigned by tusk analysis and age determined using telomere length in dugongs from Torres Strait. However, the number of samples available where both tusk age and sufficient DNA quantity could be obtained was small, so that a usable assay has not been reliably confirmed[39]. Future technical developments in this area hold considerable promise for adding to our ability to assess sirenian population age structure without the need for destructive sampling.

Dugong Population Structure in the Australian Region

Tikel[40] presented the first evidence of phylogeographic divisions in the dugong. Analyzing sequence data of the mtDNA control region from 103 individuals, two distinct lineages were observed within Australia that overlapped geographically in the Great Barrier Reef region. McDonald[41] sequenced a longer segment of the control region from a geographically more representative collection of samples, including many from northern and western populations of Australian dugongs. This more recent study included a larger sample set (115 samples) and supported the existence of two distinct lineages around Australia, one geographically widespread lineage and one more geographically restricted lineage not found in the west coast populations (figure 19.6). In addition, limited samples from outside Australia indicated that additional lineages occur in other countries.

The maternal lineages observed among Australian dugongs are most likely the signature of a series of vicariance events where changes in sea level created isolated populations for significant periods of time. This could be due to the emergence of the Torres Strait land bridge for extended periods of the Pleistocene, and its recent inundation[42]. The lack of subsequent mixing (interbreeding) of these lineages implies some female philopatry, although the geographic scale of this would be regional rather than local[43]. These findings indicate regional-scale differences in haplotype frequency and demonstrate that historical patterns of habitat connectivity/disconnectivity have had a major impact upon the population structuring of dugongs.

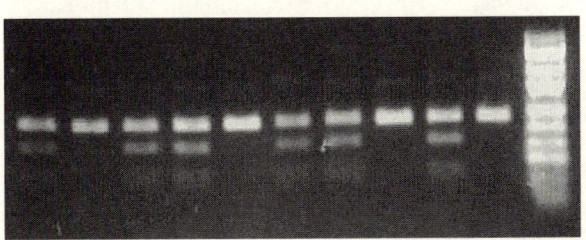

Figure 19.5. PCR products (amplified using paenungulate specific primers) from exon 11 of ZFX/ZFY from known male (lanes 1, 3, 4, 6, 7, 9) and female (lanes 2, 5, 8, 10) dugongs, digested with *Rsa*I and fragments separated on a 3% agarose gel. Bands of sizes 236 bp, 171 bp, and 65 bp are seen in samples from males, while only a single 236 bp band is seen in samples from females. Dugong males (being XY) have both the ZFX and the ZFY genotype, but females (being XX) have only the ZFX sequence. (Courtesy of Michelle Waycott and Brenda McDonald.)

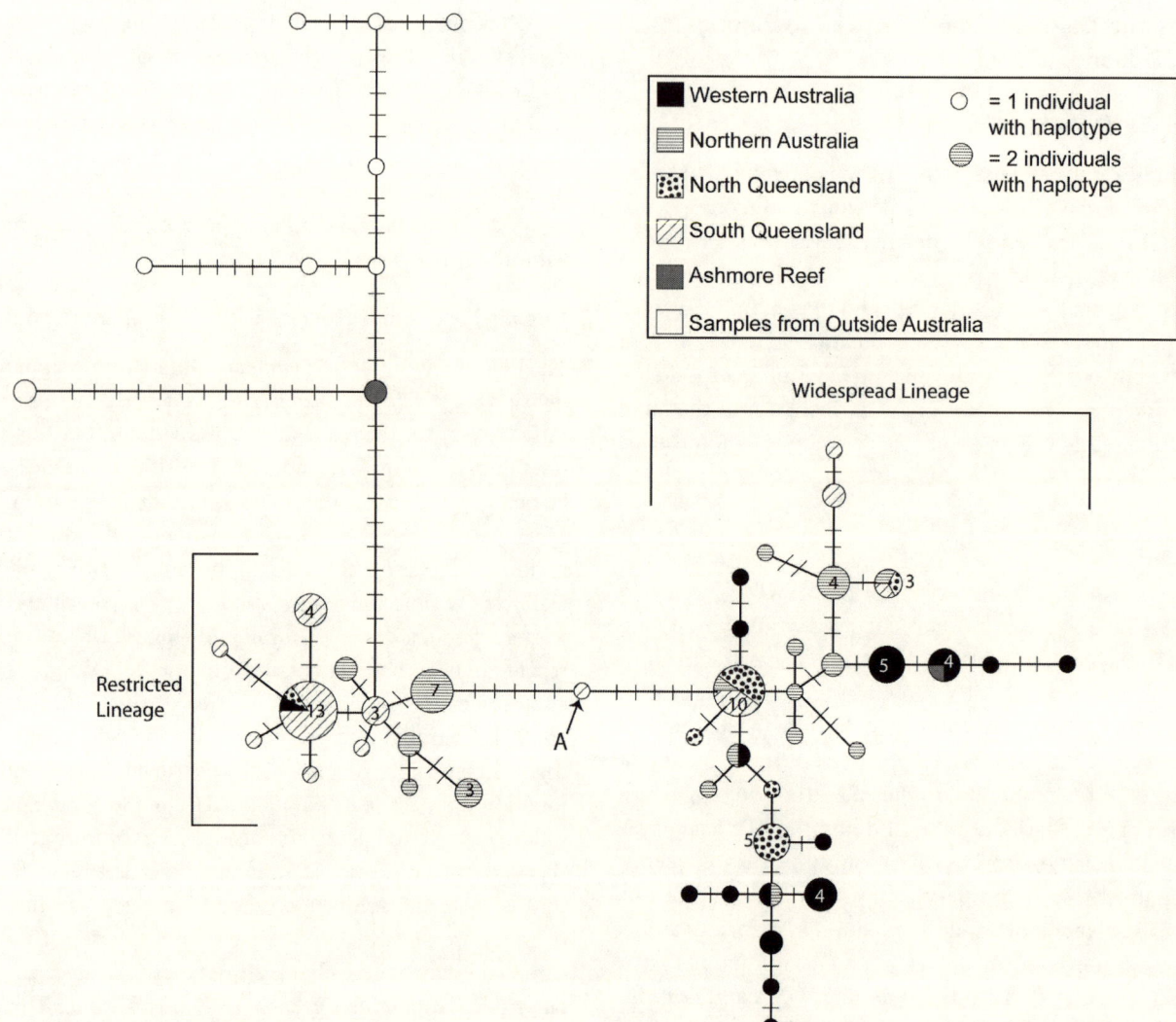

Figure 19.6. Minimum spanning tree showing the relationships between the dugong long haplotypes (492 bp; 115 individuals). Circles indicate the location of samples containing that haplotype. The size of each circle and the number within it indicate the number of individuals with that haplotype. Dashes indicate single base pair differences between haplotypes. The two Australian lineages are identified. (Courtesy of Michelle Waycott and Brenda McDonald.)

MtDNA Phylogeographic Analysis of the Dugong in Thailand

Palmer[44] sequenced samples of 40 individual dugongs from Thailand. The genetic diversity observed was lower than that reported by McDonald[45] for Australian dugongs. Mean interpopulation diversity and mean genetic distance between the Gulf of Thailand and the Andaman Sea populations were small, suggesting little differentiation between the dugongs of the east and west coasts of Thailand. Phylogenetic analysis reveals the existence of two maternal lineages within the population of Thailand dugongs.

Though the sample size of this study was small, it is estimated that approximately 200 dugongs remain along the Andaman Sea, while estimates for Gulf of Thailand are thought to be even smaller[46].

Microsatellite Analysis Reveals High Level of Migration and Interbreeding

To date, only one study has published microsatellite loci in sirenians[47]. This initial screening of three dugongs identified nine of the 14 loci to be polymorphic. However, McDonald[48] found that only six of the nine microsatellites were variable, amplified consistently, and were easy to score reliably in the dugong. She screened 452 dugong samples with these six microsatellite loci. These samples included 417 from Australian waters, 31 from Asia (Thailand, Indonesia, Philippines, Sabah, and Japan), and four from the Pacific (New Caledonia and Palau).

The microsatellites developed for the Florida manatee are highly variable in the dugong[49] and have a greater allelic diversity in the dugong than in the manatee (table 19.1). The results of these tests suggest that the dugong population has not undergone an extensive bottleneck or founder effect. The high allelic diversity of dugongs is also an indication of the larger geographic area and larger effective population size of the dugong compared with the manatee[50]. The microsatellite loci used indicate that dugongs most likely engage in nonrandom mating facilitated by a variety of mating systems around Australia and by an asynchronous breeding season.

McDonald[51] found a lack of population differentiation over a large geographic scale for dugongs around Australia and between Australia and overseas. This lack of structure indicates that there is a high level of gene flow and migration occurring[52]. More important, it indicates that a percentage of dugongs that make long-distance journeys are mating at their destination site[53]. Isolation-by-distance is observed over the Australian scale, which is not surprising considering the vagility of the dugong and the geographic scale of sampling[54].

Limited Concordance between mtDNA and Microsatellite Data

The significant haplotypic divergence observed with mtDNA (which is inherited maternally) contrasts with the lack of structure from microsatellite DNA (which is inherited from both parents). It is tempting to invoke the explanation that there is sex-biased dispersal and/or gene flow[55]. This interpretation is in conflict with satellite tracking evidence, which shows that both sexes can move long distances[56]. However, Sheppard's study is based on a relatively small sample size, and dugongs were tracked for periods ranging from 15 to 551 days, which is a small proportion of their lifespan. In addition, the geographic scale of gender-biased dispersal may be very large (a large proportion of the Queensland coastline, for example), and thus tracking studies will be limited in their applicability[57].

These two datasets (on an overlapping sample set) indicate that representatives of the different mtDNA lineages in Australia are interbreeding where sympatric[58]. This result suggests that the two refugia at times of low sea level were not separated for sufficient time to cause a recognizable difference in appearance or behavior of the two matrilines, thus facilitating interbreeding between the lineages when reunited. The lineages therefore cannot be termed ESUs but may be broken into management units based on regional geographic boundaries[59].

Implications for Conservation and Management

Owing to the very large spatial scales dugongs appear to inhabit, breed in, and move in and out of, the scale of habitat management that is required spans political boundaries, posing ongoing challenges in this area.

Historical patterns of habitat connectivity have had a major impact upon the population structuring of dugongs. Currently, the distribution of seagrass beds in the coastal waters of northern Australia is naturally fragmented. It is therefore likely that further fragmentation of seagrass beds around coastal northern Australia as a result of anthropogenic impacts will also have a significant effect on the genetic structuring of the dugong population in the longer term.

Application of Genetic Techniques in Developing Countries

DNA is a powerful tool when used to resolve the taxonomy, biology, and ecology of organisms. Maintaining genetic diversity is an important issue in conservation

Table 19.1 Allelic diversity, as indicated by the number of alleles in dugongs compared with the manatee.

Species	Microsatellite Locus						
	n	TmaA01	TmaA02	TmaA04	TmaE08	TmaE26	TmaM79
Dugong	372	6	25	27	8	17	18
Florida manatee	223	1	3	1	3	2	3
Antillean manatee	21	2	3	3	4	8	3
Amazonian manatee	7	2	5	1	2	1	3

Sources: Garcia-Rodriguez et al. 2000.
Note: Dugong (*Dugong dugon*); Florida manatee (*Trichechus manatus latirostris*); Antillean manatee (*T. m. manatus*); Amazonian manatee (*T. inunguis*); n = number of samples.

management. At its best, molecular analysis can provide vital information relevant to the management of species of concern, and it can do so quickly and without intrusive or lethal means. However, molecular reagents and especially the equipment required to process such information are often prohibitively expensive tools for scientists in developing countries.

Hope resides in the fact that reagent and equipment prices are decreasing with the development of new technologies. Also, the formation of new national genome research programs (for example, in Brazil) has allowed many laboratories to acquire expensive sequencing equipment to be shared cooperatively by many research groups, allowing molecular techniques to be applied in conservation studies.

The most important solution may be international collaboration. Collaborative efforts have been paramount to the success of the genetic studies reported in this chapter. The authors have enjoyed the personal and professional benefits of joining forces (sharing samples, sequence data, funding procurement, and reporting efforts) in an attempt to understand manatee and dugong biology better. We look forward to our continual collaboration and offer our collective assistance to readers seeking to undertake genetic research applied to conservation efforts in their own countries.

20

Boat- and Land-Based Surveys for Sirenians

LEMNUEL V. ARAGONES, KATHERINE S. LACOMMARE, SARITA KENDALL, NATALY CASTELBLANCO-MARTINEZ, AND DANIEL GONZALEZ-SOCOLOSKE

Observers taking part in boat and land-based surveys of cetaceans and sirenians scan and collect data from a particular vantage point. They study the distribution, abundance, behavior, feeding ecology, and migration of a wide variety of species, including dolphins[1], sperm whales[2] and dugongs[3]. Although underutilized, such surveys do have broad applicability to manatee and dugong research, especially in developing countries[4].

But such methods are not effective in determining the general presence or absence of animals over a large area. In fact, it is hard to find sirenians even in areas where they are abundant, as their physical, behavioral, and habitat characteristics make sirenians inconspicuous and difficult to detect and observe. Yet, once their presence has been established, usually from interviews with local residents[5], land or boat-based surveys can address a broad range of research questions. In areas such as the Amazon and Orinoco basins, where forest canopy and extreme seasonal water level changes make strategies such as aerial surveys ineffective[6], a combination of boat and land-based surveys is the only means of monitoring manatee distribution and abundance.

Boat and land-based methods have several general advantages over other protocols. Researchers can directly observe animals in their natural environment and become familiar with their behavior. Boat and land-based surveys are cheaper than deploying technologically advanced devices such as satellite and radiotelemetry or conducting aerial surveys. In developing countries, where funding can be extremely limited, it is important to find cost-effective monitoring strategies that can address multiple research objectives simultaneously. Boat surveys can be used to determine distribution and conduct habitat monitoring, or collect count or presence-absence data in conjunction with photo-identification.

Research from land or boats is not applicable to broad spatial extents, such as distribution studies along a regional portion of coastline or river. It would be inefficient and expensive.

Boat or land-based surveys can be labor intensive and require a longer term approach than other techniques, but combined with analysis using statistical sampling techniques, when repeated annually[7], they can provide an index of abundance within a limited area.

Although this high labor input requires time, energy, and money to recruit, train, and pay assistants, these costs can be offset by encouraging local involvement. Local stakeholders such as fishers or tour guides have experience in the local environment. Fishers, highly experienced observers of the marine and river environment, require little training to notice subtle changes in water conditions that may indicate the presence of animals. In the Amazon, fishers between the ages of 35 and 55 years are the best observers; they are experienced hunters with good eyesight. Training programs create a participatory atmosphere that leads to better awareness and enhances conservation. For instance, locals employed as co-researchers and volunteers in the Amazon basin stopped hunting Amazonian manatees and became involved in habitat preservation[8].

Boat-Based Surveys

Boats are used to traverse a particular area to search for and record encounters with manatees or dugongs. Surveys can be conducted while the boat is moving; however, because sirenians can have long dive times when resting—an average of 16 minutes for West Indian manatees and 8 minutes for dugongs[9]—searching for animals while the boat is anchored in predetermined places is more effective. Side-scan sonar can also be used during boat-based surveys to detect sirenians[10]. In tannin-stained water this method is an alternative to visual observation (see box 20.2).

BOX 20.1

Counting Manatees for Their Own Protection

Sarita Kendall

Amazonian manatees are notoriously difficult to observe in the wild, rarely showing more than a black snout at the surface of turbid rivers or blackwater lakes. Because of this, data from direct observations are very limited. In the Puerto Nariño area of the Colombian Amazon, to take advantage of people experienced in manatee sightings, we established a network of fishers. They reported sightings, feeding areas, and hunting events, and from these data and with their assistance, we were able to survey key sites. Some of the fishers had been manatee hunters, but as they worked to decipher manatee migrations and answer research questions, they became more interested in the animals' behavior and in ensuring manatee survival.

We used both a small aluminum boat with a 4HP motor and a canoe for these surveys. As we never saw manatees when we had the motor running, we would circle around a target site until well upstream and then cut the motor and drift. We were able to approach the manatees more directly in the canoe. If we sighted manatees, we would anchor for up to four hours. We nearly always had two observers aboard: a researcher and a fisherman. We would position the boat to maximize visibility and minimize interference with the animals. Sometimes we also placed an observer on a nearby beach.

We collected data on the number and approximate size of manatees, breathing intervals, behavior, presence/absence of other animals, human activities, proximity to feeding areas, and environmental factors including depth and current. Gradually, the fishers became adept at explaining why manatees were found in certain locations and at certain times during the hydrological cycle, and we charted migrations by mapping the sightings. By watching exactly where animals surfaced and keeping track of their breathing patterns, we were able to estimate numbers for the sites where animals seemed to occur most frequently. Between 2003 and 2005, our numbers rose from 8 individuals to 14 at one site and 10 individuals to 16 at another. Although the survey forms completed by fishers usually had less detail than those filled in by researchers, the numbers of manatees observed were similar.

While the mere fact of observing Amazonian manatees was significant, the surveys had even greater importance: the fishers/co-researchers became known as guardians of the manatees, and this reinforced our anti-hunting campaign (see Aragones et al., this volume, chapter 24). Other fishers would paddle by the co-researchers, joking that they must have a harpoon hidden in the canoe, but the co-researchers would explain that they were looking after the manatees. The combination of learning about manatees, monitoring presence, and involving local people in the surveys became the key to gradually eliminating hunting along the Colombian Amazon River until, during 2005 and 2006, no manatees were taken.

BOX 20.2

Using Side-Scan Sonar to Find Manatees

Daniel Gonzalez-Socoloske

New technologies are being developed every year to study sirenians. Side-scan sonar is a recent use of technology that helps biologists detect manatees in turbid and tannin-stained waters.

Between June and August of 2005 I conducted over 170 boat-based stationary surveys in the rivers and coastal lagoons of a small protected area in northern Honduras that reportedly had a relatively high abundance of manatees (Gonzalez-Socoloske 2007). During these 20-minute surveys in turbid waters, manatees were detected in only 7% of the surveys, and each observation lasted only a few seconds. In 57 hours of observation I was able to observe manatees for less than five minutes.

After returning from this field season I came across a new fish-finder that boasted a side imaging feature. It was the first time that a commercial quality side-scan sonar was integrated into a personal fish-finder at a consumer price.

The idea of detecting manatees with sound navigation and ranging (SONAR) devices is not new. In the 1980s and 1990s several types of sonar were tested with the aim of detecting manatees in Florida to prevent channel locks from killing them. None of these efforts proved successful. The difference was that these units used stationary sonar (echo sounders) that usually point downward. Side-scan sonar uses narrow lateral (side) beams to create slices of an acoustic picture-like image off both sides of the boat, so that passing next to an object, not over it, allows detection. Side-scan sonar, limited to boat surveys, is ideal for determining manatee presence/absence in areas where they are difficult to detect due to water turbidity.

With the assistance of local scientists I tested the device, a Humminbird 987c (Johnson Outdoors, Racine, Wisconsin) in Crystal River, Florida, and Villahermosa, Mexico. The clear water at Crystal River was ideal for detecting manatees visually. Compared to visual detection, we were able to detect between 70 and 95% of the animals using side-scan sonar. In addition, the resulting images provided some information about animal body orientation and relative size (if there were multiple manatees in the same screenshot). We next tested the sonar in a land-locked lagoon in Tabasco, Mexico, which contains at least 18 manatees. Just as in Florida, we were able to detect 93% of the manatees (figure 20.1).

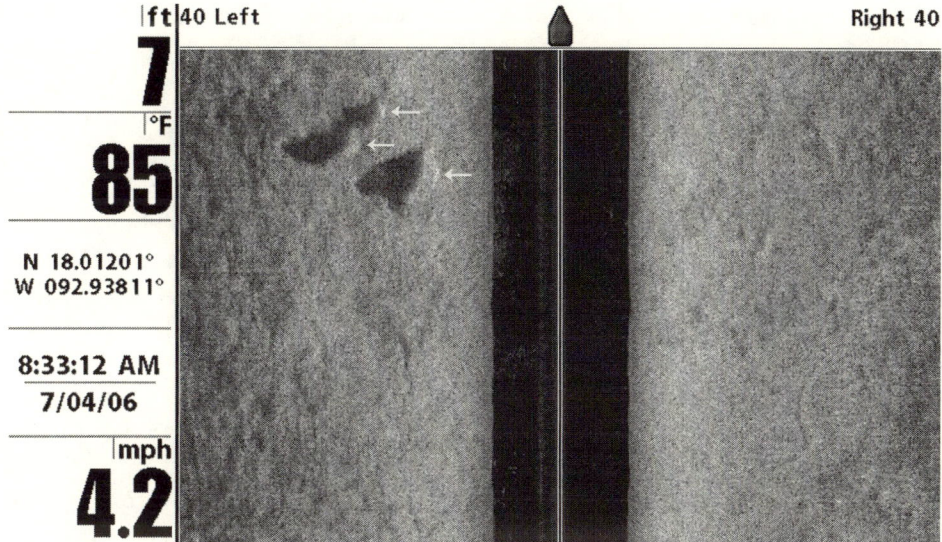

Figure 20.1. Side-scan sonar image of manatees in Mexico. (Courtesy of Daniel Gonzalez-Socoloske.)

This tool is particularly helpful for those working in developing countries because of its relative affordability (less than the cost of several hours of aerial surveys). Sonar is reliable in various environmental conditions (i.e., clear or turbid water, marine or fresh water, day or night). In addition, the unit provides additional information such as water surface temperature, habitat data (i.e., bottom substrate texture, depth, substrate type), and location (built-in GPS).

The side-scan sonar technique is particularly useful where it is almost impossible to detect and monitor manatees visually. Thus far we have trained six groups of scientists and managers of protected areas in various countries throughout the Americas (e.g., Mexico, Belize, Costa Rica, Panama, and Honduras). We are currently developing a census methodology using this detection technique. Our hope is that this new technology will give us a better glimpse into the secret lives of sirenians so that we can continue to learn about and protect them.

There are currently three Humminbird models with side-scan sonar, ranging in price from U.S. $1,000 to $3,000 depending on output screen size. For more information see Gonzalez-Socoloske et al. 2009.

The number of observers on a boat should be sufficient so that when searching for animals on all sides of the boat, there is some redundancy. Observers should be rotated among positions and given breaks to maintain efficiency and reduce fatigue.

Exactly how and what data are collected is dependent on the experimental design, the research goals, and the inherent characteristics of the study area. Nearly all studies record the number of sirenians observed. Other data may include time and location of sightings, tidal state, feeding sites, aggregation sites, number of groups, occurrence of cow-calf pairs, salinity, temperature, turbidity, and sighting conditions. Recording factors that may impact sighting conditions—such as weather (e.g., sunny, cloudy, glare, and rain) and Beaufort sea state (see table 20.1), a measure of the effect of wind on the water's surface—are important for examining variability in detection probability and possible detection bias.

There are specific techniques that observers can use to determine and record the number of sirenians encountered. A preformatted data sheet, with compass directions and notation instructions, can be used to keep track of when and where individual animals surface (figure 20.2). This helps observers note the exact location of each manatee or dugong in relation to the boat, one another, or surrounding landscape features. Observers may also record the time intervals of respiration. Sirenians often have regular breathing patterns when they are resting, but individual patterns can vary slightly. Keeping track of individual breathing patterns can help determine the number of animals.

Even survey craft can have a negative impact on sirenians. If an area is repeatedly visited by motorized boats, the animals may leave. Castelblanco-Martínez[11] specifically noted this impact on Antillean manatees in the Orinoco basin of Colombia during the dry season when water levels were low. Kendall et al.[12] found a similar impact on Amazonian manatees. In the Orinoco basin this was resolved by combining a boat survey with a land-based survey on a seasonal basis so that the most sensitive areas were surveyed with minimum interference during critical times. To minimize speed and noise, in Belize poles are used to maneuver both research and ecotourism boats (25- to 30-foot, fiberglass) through areas regularly occupied by manatees[13].

Watercraft types range from small canoes to large motor-powered vessels. The appropriate boat depends on the characteristics of the water system, the experimental design, and the extent of the study area. Important considerations when choosing a craft include transport efficiency and maneuverability. A canoe allows a silent approach with smaller coverage, while a motorized boat gives greater mobility, provides a higher observation platform, and can traverse a larger area. In the Philippines some motorized outrigger boats (*bancas*) have been modified by locals to provide elevated platforms for whale watching by tourists. These can also be used for sirenian surveys. A higher vantage point is especially useful when water clarity allows observers to see animals underwater. In blackwater river or lake systems, where the water is turbid, a higher vantage point is a disadvantage. A lower position, such as that from a canoe, provides a better chance for the observer to spot a snout breaking the water's surface.

Other tools include a handheld global positioning system (GPS) for recording locations, devices for recording environmental conditions (e.g., refractometers, thermometers), and binoculars. Although binoculars have a limited field of view (table 20.2) and can often be difficult to use on a boat, they can be useful for observing from a distance and can help researchers determine or confirm behavior. For instance, if animals are 100 m or more away and they appear to be feeding (e.g., based on breathing cycles and dive patterns), binoculars can confirm this by helping the researcher observe seagrass in their mouths or on the water surface.

Boat-Based Survey Techniques

Dedicated Boat Surveys

In dedicated boat surveys the researcher can plan the survey tracks so that data are collected according to a specific experimental design. The researcher can study specific applications such as occupancy, abundance, and behavior.

Table 20.1. Description of Beaufort Scale and accompanying wind speed, wind description, and sea state.

Beaufort Number	Wind Speed (in knots)	Wave Height (in feet)	Wind Description	Sea State
0	< 1	0	Calm	Calm, like a mirror
1	1–3	0.25	Light air	Ripples with appearance of scales, no foam crests
2	4–6	0.5–1	Light breeze	Small wavelets, crests of glassy appearance, not breaking
3	7–10	2–3	Gentle breeze	Large wavelets, crests begin to break, scattered whitecaps
4	11–16	3.5–5	Moderate breeze	Small waves, becoming longer, numerous whitecaps

Source: http://www.spc.noaa.gov/faq/tornado/beaufort.html.

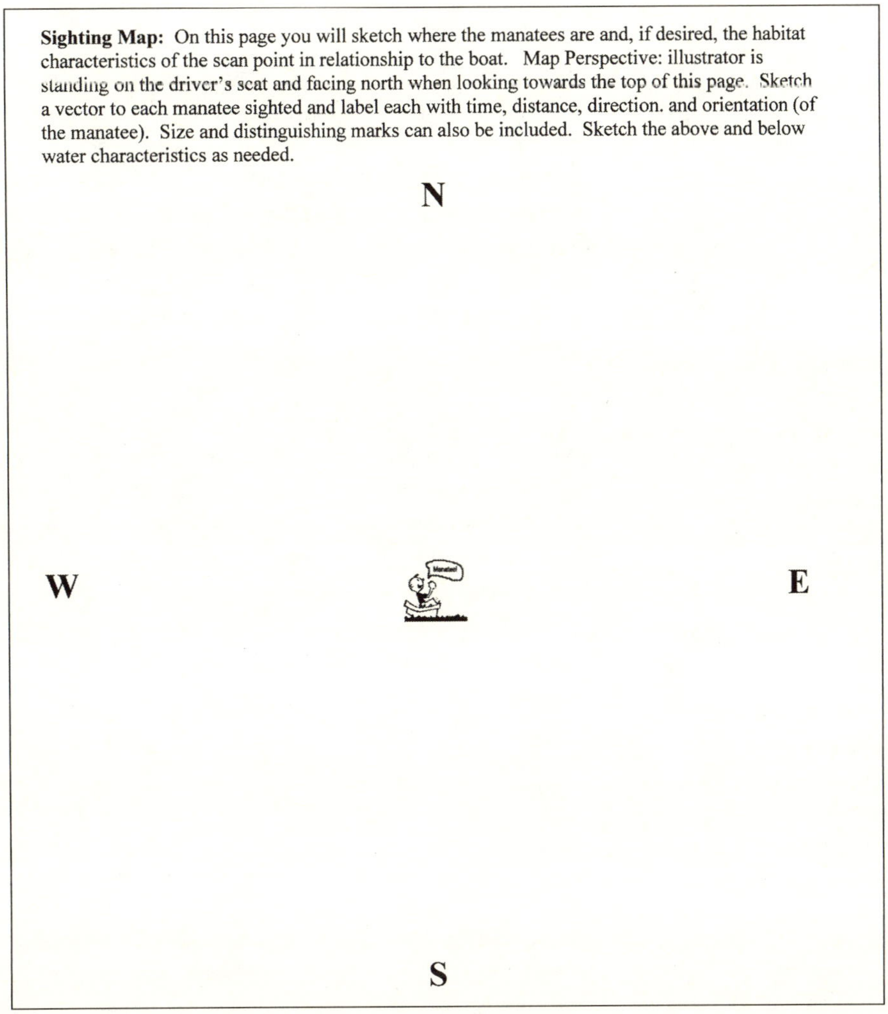

Sighting Map: On this page you will sketch where the manatees are and, if desired, the habitat characteristics of the scan point in relationship to the boat. Map Perspective: illustrator is standing on the driver's seat and facing north when looking towards the top of this page. Sketch a vector to each manatee sighted and label each with time, distance, direction. and orientation (of the manatee). Size and distinguishing marks can also be included. Sketch the above and below water characteristics as needed.

N

W E

S

Figure 20.2. Sighting map for boat-based surveys. (Courtesy of Katherine S. LaCommare and Caryn Self-Sullivan.)

Table 20.2. Magnification devices for sirenian surveys.

Tool	Magnification[a]	Field of View[a]	Possible Features	Comments[b]
Binoculars	4x–20x	350'–170' at 1,000 yards	· Night vision · Image stabilization · Waterproof · Wide angle	· Some manufacturers offer wide angle models that provide a small increase in field of view for the same magnification. · The width of the objective lens determines how much light is allowed into the binocular and is an important feature.
Reticled Binoculars	7x[c]	350' at 1,000 yards		· Binoculars with reticles can be used to determine distances. · There is a limited selection of this style of binocular.
Spotting Scopes	15x–60x	150'–50' at 1,000 yards	· Night vision · Image stabilization · Waterproof	· The width of the objective lens is an important feature.
Range Finders	4–8x	Not published		· Range of distance determination and accuracy varies from model to model.

[a]Measurements are approximations and vary widely depending on the specific features of particular products.
[b]Generally, field of view decreases as magnification increases.
[c]Limited availability.

Occupancy, which is measured as the fraction of sampling units used by a species in a landscape, is an important measurement for examining and monitoring distribution and habitat use[14]. Sampling units can be either arbitrary spatial units, such as grid cells of a specific size, or natural units, such as patches of habitat[15]. In occupancy studies, researchers must consider the possibility of false absences, when an animal is present but not seen. Properly designing the survey and recording changes in sighting conditions can allow researchers to examine variability in detection probability and to account properly for variation through modeling techniques[16].

Assessing the absolute (a count of the number of individuals per unit area) or relative (an estimation of population size) abundance[17] of sirenians using boat-based surveys is difficult but possible. Scale and challenging survey conditions make it difficult to determine the abundance of dugongs by using boats, but in certain instances, such as for manatees on the Amazon River, this may be the only way of collecting data on relative abundance. Through line transect sampling along a predetermined track, a researcher can determine the density of a population by counting objects (individual, group, or cue) and measuring their distance from the observer. The density measurement is then based on the determination of the detection function, defined as the probability of detecting an object, given that the object is at a specific distance from a random line or point. Once density is measured, estimates of population size can be determined and monitored[18].

Photo-identification can be used to analyze movement, residency patterns, and abundance. By cataloguing individual animals based on scarring patterns, repeated photographs of an animal along a coastline can establish animal movement along a stretch of water[19]. In addition, a minimum count can be established based on the number of individuals that can be identified from photographs. Through the use of mark-recapture statistics, population size can be estimated and population demographics monitored[20].

Individual studies of behavior using dedicated boat-based surveys are conducted primarily through focal animal sampling, a standard technique in animal behavior studies, in which an individual or group is followed for a specified time frame and behavior is recorded. Some sample behaviors can include feeding, resting, or traveling[21]. Focal animal sampling should be conducted with the motor turned off, using a pole or drifting with the current. Amazonian manatees rarely show themselves near a motorized boat with its engine running.

Opportunistic Surveys

In opportunistic surveys, data are collected outside the framework of a rigorous experimental design. Researchers hitch a ride on boats that have other purposes and data are collected by chance. Typical vessels include regularly scheduled ferry boats or fishing boats. Research objectives are limited, but relevant applications include pilot studies and long-term monitoring. Pilot or preliminary studies provide an opportunity for training as well as for testing procedures and equipment[22].

Opportunistic surveys can be used to collect preliminary information that can be used to determine where and when to sample and to plan for further, more concentrated research. Sample size, expected variance[23], and statistical power needed to test a particular hypothesis on distribution and population size can all be determined through preliminary surveys[24].

Opportunistic data can be collected by providing fishers, tour guides, ferry boat personnel, and other vessel operators with preformatted data sheets. In areas where literacy is an obstacle, data sheets can be designed with pictures, or volunteers can make verbal reports.

Although opportunistic surveys are ideal for pilot studies, they can be designed to conduct long-term monitoring studies over the course of several years or decades, examining trends in abundance and/or habitat use patterns. For instance, Kendall et al.[25] were able to show how Amazonian manatee habitat use shifted over the course of four years in response to river beach shape changes and changes in water level. With this information, local researchers were able to define priority conservation areas and show how Amazonian manatees adapt to various river conditions. By recording the number of new calves born each year, they were able to suggest that there was an increase in the population after the cessation of hunting. In a specific area of the Orinoco River, visual sightings were used to monitor the seasonal activity of Antillean manatees from 2001 to 2005[26].

Land-Based Surveys

Land- or shore-based surveys use stationary elevated platforms such as hilltops, cliffs, or tall buildings[27]. Land-based protocols can address the same applications as dedicated boat surveys, but at a smaller scale. They have two major advantages over boat-based protocols. First, the presence of observers on land will not affect animal behavior. Second, land-based surveys are cheaper. The only costs are building materials, binoculars, training, and paying observers. However, the observer is stationary, and observations may be limited to certain times of the day as a result of either sun glare or tidal state.

To design an effective land-based study, the researcher must have previous knowledge of sites regularly frequented by sirenians. Depending on the research objectives, several sighting stations should be established along a coastline, a portion of river, an island, or around a lake. If accurate counts can be made, then relative abundance can be calculated and seasonal and annual abundance patterns can be examined[28]. Experimental design should incorporate methods that allow for the measurement of perception bias—the bias in a count because an animal is present but not seen. Ideally there should be some overlap in viewing area between stations. Simultaneous observations at multiple sighting stations can ensure that animals are not double counted or that double counts are easily recognized[29]. Multiple independent observers can be used on each station[30] to obtain a measure of perception bias. As with boat surveys, observer fatigue should be reduced by limiting the amount of time any one observer scans and searches for animals.

In the Orinoco River, Castelblanco-Martinez[31] established five imaginary quadrants for monitoring Antillean manatees during the dry season (January to May). Each quadrant, dimensions of approximately 300 m x 300 m, was sampled for two hours by one observer scanning the area looking for manatees from a fixed sighting station. The number of sightings per unit time (N°s/h) and maximum number of simultaneous sightings (MNSS) were used as relative indices of occurrence. A Kruskal-Wallis analysis of variance showed that the N°s/h was statistically different between areas and months. The MNSS was statistically different between areas but not months.

The principal tool for land-based surveys is the observation platform itself. If a study area does not have a naturally occurring accessible elevated platform, then observation towers should be built. In the Philippines, Aragones (1994) constructed watch towers on treetops to observe and count dugongs in their feeding sites. Platforms of long bamboo sticks set on top of seagrass beds served as sighting stations for lightweight observers. In the Amazon, anchored boats have been used as permanent observation stations.

The stability of land stations makes it easier to use binoculars, spotting scopes, or range finders. Some binoculars are reticulated and allow for the calculation of the distance of the animals from shore. Range finders use lasers to determine the distance from the viewer to the object, but they have a limited magnification. Spotting scopes have a high level of magnification but a greatly reduced field of view, making them useful for observing distant behavior but not for spotting animals (table 20.2).

Conclusion

Boat and land-based survey protocols can be a cost-effective means for addressing a wide range of research applications at medium and small spatial extents[32] (table 20.3). Whether using a rigorous experimental design or opportunistic data collection, boat-based surveys can be used to collect preliminary data and for habitat use, abundance, behavioral, or photo-identification studies. Land-based surveys address similar research objectives but at a smaller scale. Although these survey protocols are limited by their intensive labor requirements and their long-term approach, these limitations can be offset by conservation gains obtained by including local stakeholders as research assistants, technicians, and volunteers in data collection.

Table 20.3. Applications and limitations of boat-based and land-based survey methods applicable to sirenians.

Survey type	Applications	Limitations
Dedicated boat-based	· Distribution over a small area · Absolute or relative abundance (population size) · Population trends (long-term) · Occupancy · Behavior · Residency patterns · Photo-identification studies	Regional and large scale distribution and habitat use
Opportunistic boat-based	· For pilot studies to determine potential sites (and for training observers) · Preliminary data · Relative abundance (if long-term monitoring)	Population size and trends (absolute abundance)
Land-based	Similar to dedicated boat survey but on a much smaller, cheaper scale, does not disturb animals	Regional and large-scale distribution, and absolute abundance

21

Utility and Design of Aerial Surveys for Sirenians

JOHN E. REYNOLDS III, BENJAMÍN MORALES-VELA,
IVAN LAWLER, AND HOLLY H. EDWARDS

Aerial surveys have been used as a tool to assess aspects of sirenian biology for three decades. Although aerial surveys can be a useful method of assessing sirenian population distribution and abundance, they can be logistically difficult and expensive and may not always be the appropriate method. Budget and the availability of reliable aircraft, skilled pilots, and trained staff must be considered before deciding to use aerial surveys. Equally important is the feasibility of detecting an animal from an aircraft, especially if habitat characteristics conceal animals. Aerial survey practitioners have learned a number of lessons over the years. Here we provide an overview to help others decide whether they should adopt aerial survey as a technique, and if so, how best to ensure that the surveys meet their objectives.

The goals of this chapter include:

- providing general guidance to investigators who are considering using aerial surveys to assess aspects of sirenian biology;
- describing the types of surveys that are typically used for sirenians;
- assessing the types of bias that can reduce the utility of aerial surveys;
- recommending appropriate survey design features to reduce survey bias;
- providing guidance regarding enhanced safety measures; and
- assessing how aerial surveys can fit into multifaceted programs.

Contributions to Science and Management

The value of such surveys is in identifying the distribution and abundance of a species or population in a rapid time frame and over a relatively large area. The high vantage point allows most animals close to the surface to be seen. Usually, trained observers can easily distinguish sirenians from other large vertebrates.

Unfortunately, many of the current aerial survey methods are inadequate and unreliable. Often the end-users (e.g., management agencies) of the data attribute too much validity to aerial survey results. Lefebvre et al.[1] discussed problems that have prevented aerial surveys from providing accurate indices of abundance and trends or valid population size estimates. This is particularly relevant if the goal of the project is to identify population trends in a management or political context. In addition, where populations are small, surveys are unlikely to have sufficient statistical power to identify changes in population size[2]. Thus reliance on some surveys may result in inappropriate management responses, or important measures may be deferred while the problem worsens.

Before investing in aerial surveys, consider the objectives and explicitly address the ability of the survey to meet them. The physical scale, personnel, location, and other factors all determine the cost. Despite their frequent use, aerial surveys do not always answer the relevant questions. The reasons for choosing this methodology may relate more to tradition or to misperceptions of what questions such surveys can answer than to good science. Below we provide a framework for making these decisions.

Effective Aerial Survey Design

Importance of Asking Appropriate Questions

The first and most crucial question is: "What questions are we trying to answer?" Aerial surveys can address a few simple questions:

- Where are the animals (in what habitats or locations within the study area)?
- Is the distribution of animals in this area different from that in other survey areas?
- How many animals are there?

- Does the number of animals in the study area differ (a) over time and (b) from one place to another?

If the research question is consistent with these, then more specific questions about the particular circumstances will determine whether an aerial survey can be useful. The most fundamental questions are:

- Are animals likely to be visible to an aerial observer? Certain habitats occupied by sirenians, and especially manatees (e.g., overgrown rivers and lagoons; extremely turbid waters) may make such surveys unsuitable.
- If they are not all likely to be available to observers, then is the level of this bias (availability) constant across the survey or can it be adjusted? We return to this issue later.
- In cases where aerial surveys are intended to provide an estimate of population size or trend, is there likely sufficient statistical precision in the estimates to enable the desired comparisons to be made? For example, for a given level of statistical power, what is the smallest population decline likely to be detectable?
- Is an aerial survey cost efficient compared with alternative methods, such as boat-based surveys, questionnaire surveys of local water users, etc.?

Once the research questions have been defined and the applicability of aerial surveys has been determined, a survey needs to be designed to facilitate the acquisition of data. Regardless of the type survey envisaged, all successful ones have certain protocols in common. To prevent the introduction of unnecessary variables, surveys should ensure consistent methods (altitude, air speed, route, and frequency), weather, sea conditions, and personnel (pilot and observers).

Methods

Since the major objective of an aerial survey is to observe and record animals visually, surveys should meet the following criteria:

- The aircraft should be high-winged (figure 21.1).
- Altitude should be sufficient to allow maximum coverage of the target area while reducing the likelihood of misidentifying the subject species. Whereas greater height increases transect width, at some point it becomes difficult to tell a manatee or dugong from a dolphin or large shark. Reducing altitude reduces survey coverage. Survey heights of 750–1,000 feet are common. A related issue here is safety—when flying low, there is little time to make adjustments if the plane malfunctions.
- Aircraft speed should be as slow as is safe. Ideally the aircraft should be able to maintain altitude at a speed of between 70 and 100 knots.

Conditions

Environmental factors including turbidity, cloud cover, glare, and sea state (based on wind intensity and direction) may hinder observations. Turbidity is difficult to control and is unlikely to be reduced by standardizing survey methods. It is best dealt with as a survey bias, which we address later.

The influence of clouds, glare, and sea state can be

Figure 21.1. A Cessna 172 high-winged aircraft is an ideal platform from which to conduct surveys. The high wings allow a clear view of the water; it is economical to run; and it can be flown safely at slow speeds. (Courtesy of John E. Reynolds III.)

minimized by standardizing the times, conditions, and directions under which surveys are conducted. The most effective approach to reduce these effects is to set a threshold level for each one, above which the survey is postponed. Confronted with very heavy cloud cover or significant white caps, observers could miss a significant number of sightings.

The effects of glare and, to a lesser extent, wind can also be reduced by standardizing flight time and direction. Very early in the morning and late in the afternoon, the sun is low to the horizon and much of the water's surface may be obscured by glare. Similarly, at midday there is direct reflection off the water into the observers' eyes. The earlier part of the day often has less wind, as sea breezes develop in the afternoon. Flight times should be planned to minimize these effects. Glare can also be reduced by setting the transect direction to be predominantly east-west and by using polarizing sunglasses.

It is important to note the effect of standardizing conditions on budgeting of both time and expense. For example, for dugong surveys conducted by Marsh and her team in Australia a general rule of thumb is that the total survey effort (and costs) from start to finish will be about three times the actual flying time. This includes transit time, significant time spent waiting for poor weather to abate, and other delays.

Personnel

The pilot is fundamental to a safe and effective aerial survey, and yet his or her contribution is often not acknowledged. The requirements of flying aerial surveys are unlike the day-to-day flying that most pilots do. When conducting a survey that has parallel transects several miles long and within half a mile of each other, a deviation of two or three degrees from the designated course may cause the transects to overlap, resulting in some areas being surveyed twice and other areas skipped. And the altitude must be constant. If it is 100 feet above the desired survey altitude of 500 feet, the survey results may be 20 percent higher than intended (thus overestimating abundance). Similarly, the tendency for the plane to roll slightly from side to side may be insignificant in general transit but can greatly expand or reduce the survey area for observers on either side of the aircraft. Discuss the survey plans and constraints in advance with the pilot. If available, use a global positioning system (GPS) to track a route during the first few surveys to show the pilot in real time how closely the flight path matches the planned route.

The observer's job also requires specific skills. Obviously the first is to be able to identify the animals and distinguish them from other large marine animals (figure 21.2). This is best learned via training flights (if resources allow) but video and photographs from other surveys can also serve well. Ideally one should use the same observers across all surveys, both to capitalize on their experience and to minimize the effect of inherent variability among observers. This latter difference can be described as a component of "perception bias," which we address in the next section.

Observer fatigue is a significant concern. As sirenians

Figure 21.2. Experienced observers are essential to good survey success. A large group of manatees aggregated at a warm-water discharge requires an experienced surveyor to make an accurate count. (Courtesy of John E. Reynolds III and Florida Power and Light Company.)

typically have tropical distribution and the survey altitude is low, the aircraft can be hot and noisy. Under these conditions, and especially where wildlife abundance is low, observers tend to lose focus and may fail to see animals that are present. A good general rule of thumb is that observers take a break at least every two to three hours to help them stay alert. However, the survey leader should regularly ask the observers how they feel as this may vary from day to day and person to person. As long as it does not significantly detract from the amount of time an observer watches the water, it can be useful to have the observers formally record other sightings (sea turtles, dolphins, rays, cover vegetation, etc.); even if these are not used in analysis, such other recording simply helps keep observers stimulated and alert.

Questions, Biases, and Costs vs. Benefits

There are three fundamental types of aerial surveys that are routinely conducted to assess sirenian populations: distributional surveys, intensive search surveys, and transect surveys. The strengths and weaknesses of each survey type appear in table 21.1. Some methodological aspects are common to all the surveys. In all cases data must be recorded, coordinate position at any given time must be known, and observers must be able to communicate with one another while in flight. Older survey methods relied on each observer having a map and noting on it the location of both observer and sightings with reference to geographic features. In some cases this is still necessary (especially in manatee surveys in which animals are located in narrow, small, or irregularly shaped bodies of water). If available, a handheld GPS receiver allows researchers surveying large or open water areas to collect more accurate and precise data.

Distributional Surveys

Distributional surveys are conducted to assess where sirenians are found, both in general terms and in relation to specific habitat features. These surveys do not generally provide data suitable for rigorous estimation of population size or trend. In locations where there is little available information on numbers or distribution of sirenians, distributional surveys can represent a particularly useful and cost-effective early means of assessment, especially when combined with community interviews[3].

Distribution surveys are usually flown several times over a given time period so that data can be compared over time (e.g., the Florida Fish and Wildlife Conservation Commission flies manatee distribution surveys twice a month for two years). Distributional surveys have been conducted frequently for sirenians[4] and results can be mapped and analyzed using geographic information systems (GIS)[5]. Flamm et al.[6] used a creative application of GIS technology (variable-shaped spatial filters) to map the relative abundance of manatees in a survey area—an approach that managers in Florida have found to be useful.

To develop effective methods for flying distribution surveys that cover a wide area, investigators should attempt to take the following steps:

- Assess the area (e.g., a particular embayment or coastline) to determine if the target species is likely to be present and if an aircraft can be used to survey that area safely and effectively.
- Consider a flight pattern that permits coverage of the inshore areas as well as other locations likely to be attractive to sirenians (e.g., offshore shallow seagrass meadows). Often scientists employ a "race track pattern" for the surveys, in which multiple elongated circles are conducted along the shoreline (figure 21.3). The planned survey route should not last more than four to six hours (taking breaks at least every three hours).
- Prepare large-scale, detailed maps of the survey area on which to record sightings as accurately as possible. The maps should include information regarding bathymetry and bottom type. On each map, or

Table 21.1. Summary of strengths and weaknesses of different survey designs for sirenians.

Survey type	What it can answer	What it cannot answer
Distributional	Distribution, habitat use, detection of discrete manatee habitats; good first assessment tool	Population size and trends
Intensive Search	Numbers and in some cases trends for specific locations	Regional distribution; large-scale habitat use
Transect	Population size and trend (if assumptions regarding random distribution are met)	May miss local high-use spots

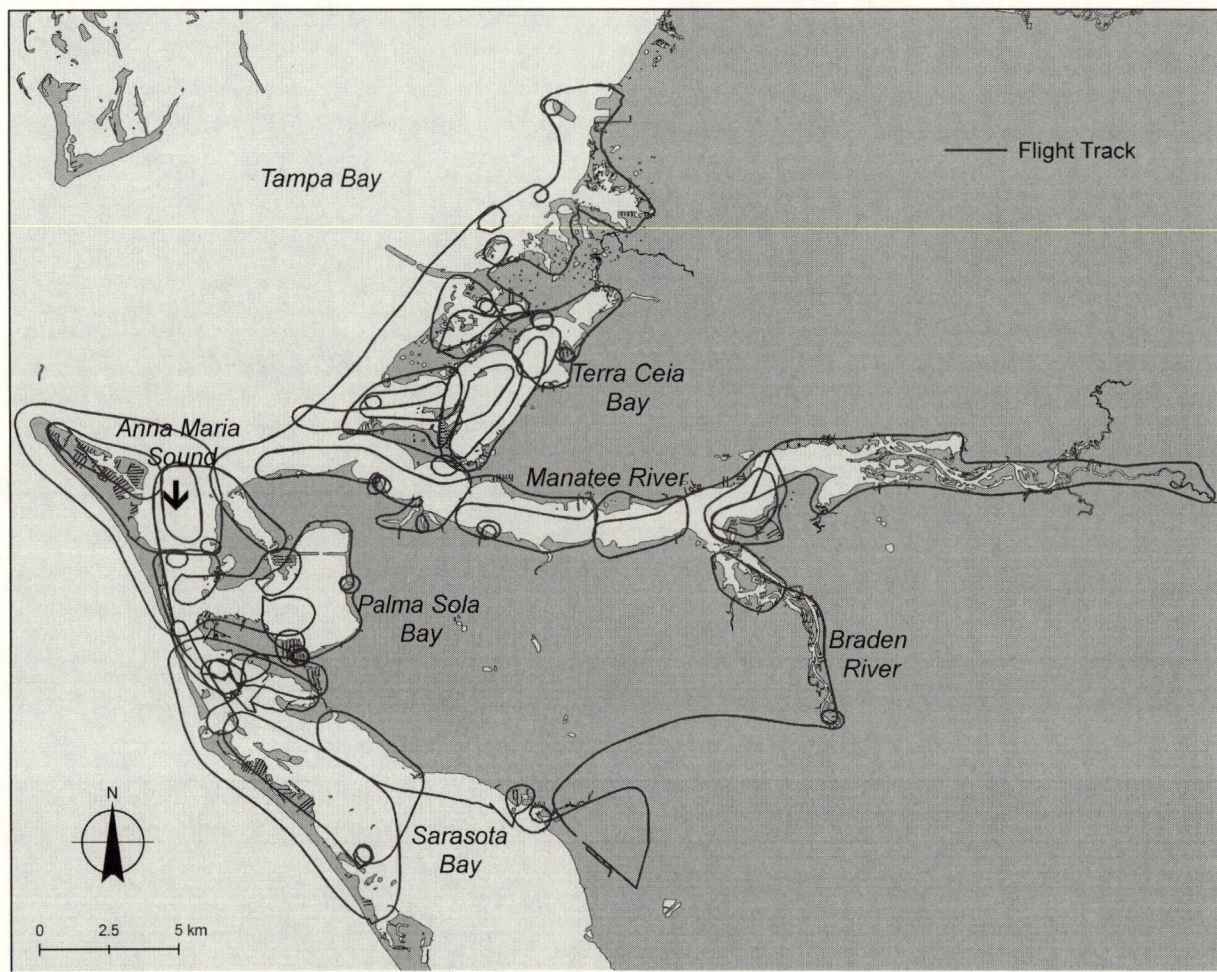

Figure 21.3. The "race track pattern" used to conduct many distributional surveys. The use of a GPS allows the precise flight path as well as locations of sightings to be recorded. (Courtesy of Holly Edwards, Florida Wildlife Research Institute.)

on a separate data sheet, the investigator should include blank spaces in which to record name of the observer(s), date, time, and location of the survey, sighting conditions (cloud cover, wind direction and speed, water clarity, and temperature), and general animal behavior and general habitat characteristics.

· Conduct surveys with a handheld GPS receiver to record the flight path and sighting locations and to keep track of survey effort, or time spent searching for animals.

Intensive Search Surveys

Intensive searches involve repeated counts of sirenians occupying particular locations[7]. A goal of such surveys is to generate indices of abundance or trends at locations of interest for conservation and management[8]. For example, the surveys of power plants conducted by Reynolds since 1982[9] represent extended, intensive search counts. The technique is valuable in providing insight to sirenian use of particular locations of management importance, but the value of the data is reduced unless efforts to assess animal detectability are incorporated[10] or plausible assumptions about detectability are made[11]. The Florida manatee synoptic (that is, general or large-scale) surveys conducted each year by the Florida Fish and Wildlife Conservation Commission (FWCC) to obtain a general count of manatees statewide represents a modified intensive search survey. However, these surveys do not include efforts to assess the detectability of animals, which—as in all surveys that do not account for bias—reduces their value as a tool to achieve their goal of censusing manatees (discussed in more detail later). Intensive search techniques provide considerable insight into manatee use of discrete areas but do not generally provide data that lead to regional population estimates or regional habitat use patterns; a notable exception that does provide population estimates and trends is seen in Craig and Reynolds[12], involving the development of a sophisticated Bayesian model that incorporated data from well over 100 separate, virtually identical surveys conducted over three decades.

Investigators conducting intensive search surveys follow many of the same guidelines that apply to distributional surveys. The main difference is that effort in intensive search surveys is deliberately "stratified" such that some areas receive extensive searching; others areas receive modest attention; and still other areas are ignored. A scientist organizing an intensive search survey would likely have some prior knowledge of where the sirenians are located or likely to be found. The scientist then creates a survey in which those selected areas are circled multiple times to get as complete a count as possible. Ideally, the survey effort (e.g., number of circles) in each location would be standardized to ensure consistency[13].

Transect Surveys

Transect surveys are conducted to assess animal distribution and abundance along predetermined survey pathways perpendicular to shore. They generally run parallel to each other at prescribed distances (e.g., 500 m), based on time allotted to the survey and sighting conditions, or to assess sirenian distribution as a function of habitat characteristics[14].

One alternative transect design includes a zigzag pattern[15]. This has both advantages and disadvantages. It requires an experienced transect survey pilot and navigator and expert use of a GPS tracking device. Over large survey regions the parallel line pattern has a serious disadvantage because there is significant off-transect effort as the aircraft moves from one line to the next. In these

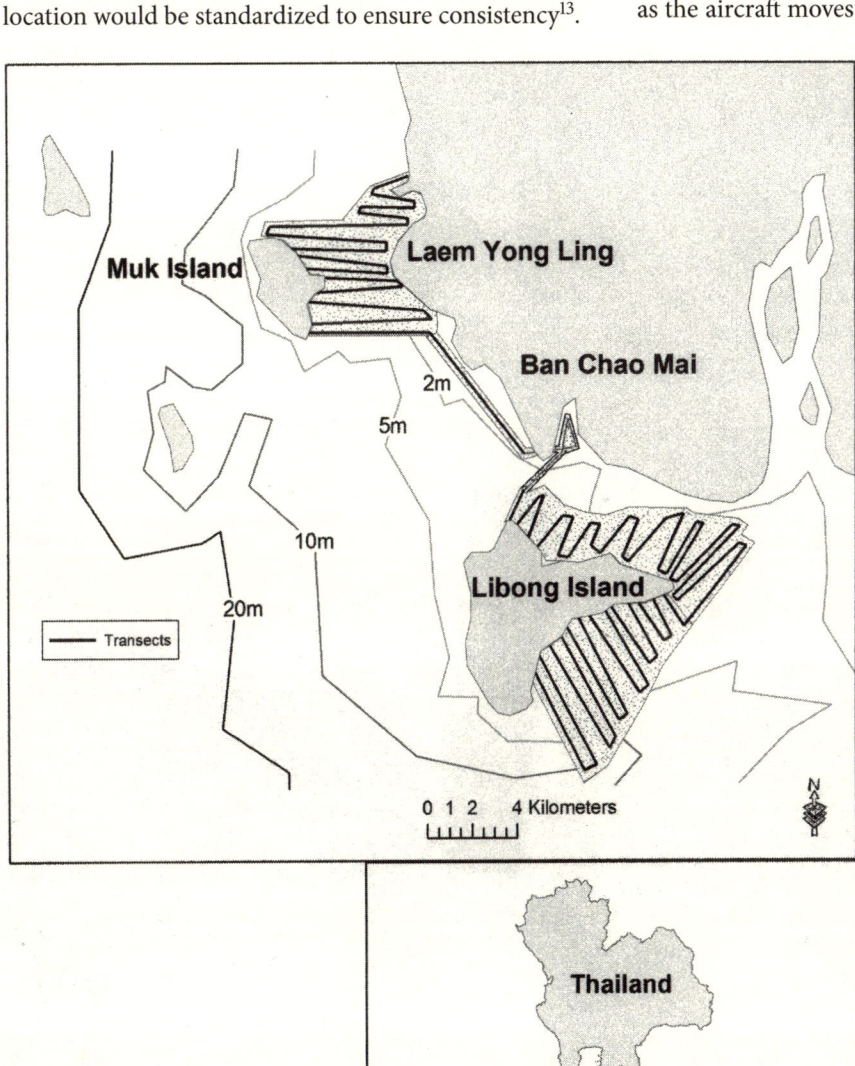

Figure 21.4. A transect survey may be done when certain assumptions about animal distribution and detectability are met. (Courtesy of Ellen Hines.)

cases the zigzag survey should be considered to improve overall survey efficiency. On the other hand, the breaks between parallel-line surveys can offer a short rest for the observers[16] (figure 21.4).

If the distribution of the sirenian population is random or uniform, and visibility of the animals is unobstructed, transect surveys may be extremely useful in determining population size; this is the case for some dugong populations[17]. However, the approach seems less suited to estimating manatee population size because of uncertainty about the extent to which assumptions about the distribution and detectability of the animals are valid, especially in areas where vegetation obstructs the view.

Transect surveys follow the same general rules and guidelines as do distributional surveys, except that the pilot and navigator must be extremely attentive to the position of the aircraft. The distance between transect lines is an important criterion, and it must be maintained throughout the survey. If the transect lines are close together, one risks double counting; if they are too widely spaced, one risks missing large numbers of animals, especially if habitat type and use are not homogeneous[18]. Hines et al.[19] provide an excellent example of application of zigzag strip-transect survey and analysis for population estimation of dugongs in a developing country.

Bias in Aerial Surveys

Historically, aerial surveys have been used to try to develop indices of abundance that reflect temporal trends in populations or provide methods of estimating population size that would allow for comparisons between or among locations and years[20]. However, biases in aerial survey methods result in these surveys not yielding valid indices or accurate population estimates and therefore having limited use. In some cases such biases can foster a misleading perception of scientists' ability to monitor sirenian populations.

While biases can limit the survey's usefulness as a monitoring tool, if biases are recognized and accommodated for, results can provide statistically reliable means for assessing populations. New methodologies are being developed to improve on the current aerial survey methods[21].

Generally, biases in aerial surveys occur when: (1) only part of the area is sampled; (2) an area is not sampled in a random or stratified-random manner, making it impossible to extrapolate results to areas not covered; and (3) counts obtained from surveys are not adjusted to account for the animals not observed.

Researchers have named three fundamental types of biases: perception and availability biases[22] and absence bias[23]. Perception or observer bias results when animals are detectable in the survey area but are simply not counted[24]. Environmental factors, behavior of the animals, observer experience, observer fatigue, and choice of flight path all contribute to it. Ways to reduce perception bias include standardization of the survey procedures, such as the flight path and amount of circling; using consistent and experienced observers; flying in good weather; and clearly defining sighting phenomena, including what constitutes an adult vs. a calf. Within these constraints, one way to estimate remaining perception bias is to use at least two independent observers during surveys[25]. Having two observers on each side of the plane (four total) is optimal. Thus independent observers survey the same area, enabling each participant's observations to be checked against another's and to quantify the observers' ability to detect animals[26].

Availability bias occurs when animals are present in the survey area but are not available to be counted. For example, animals may be submerged in turbid water[27], obscured in narrow tropical canals by dense overhanging tree branches[28], or simply invisible due to glare. Availability bias is more difficult to control than perception bias, although developing a survey route that potentially includes all areas where sirenians are likely to be found and conducting surveys when conditions are optimal for counting (light winds; sunny) can reduce the bias. In addition, using double sampling approaches (i.e., ground surveys concurrently with aerial surveys, using highly detectable animals that are visibly marked or radio-tagged[29]; or multiple counts of specific areas of interest[30]) help to reduce availability bias.

Together, perception bias and availability bias constitute visibility bias. Packard et al.[31] addressed visibility bias by doing multiple counts of particular index areas (the unit-recount method). Craig et al. and Craig and Reynolds[32] developed plausible estimations of population size and trends associated with repeated winter surveys of manatees at index locations (warm-water discharges of power plants) using a Bayesian approach, a method of statistical analysis that incorporates both current and previous data. Edwards et al.[33] estimated detection probability of manatees at a particular warm-water discharge using distinctly marked animals and using multiple observers/aircraft as a means by which to calibrate survey counts at that index location.

Scientists studying dugongs in Australia have recently devised an important method to address availability bias and estimate absolute abundance for dugong aerial surveys[34]. They collected information on diving behavior, via time-depth recorders attached to free-ranging dugongs, and on visibility of dugongs under different water and depth conditions, using artificial dugong models. Together these data were used to determine the proportion of time that a dugong is available to an aerial survey observer under a range of conditions. Observers now record not only the sighting but the conditions of the sighting (turbidity level, whether the bottom is visible). The absolute estimates of dugong numbers are important as they enable sustainable mortality levels to be estimated based on population size and reproductive capacity[35] and hence allow for potential biological removal levels to be calculated and adopted[36].

Absence bias reflects animals not physically present at the time of the survey. Thus this type of bias reflects survey-related factors more than environmental or behavioral ones. A way to minimize absence bias is to focus surveys at times when manatees or dugongs are likely to be present[37].

Attempts to develop survey protocols that minimize these biases have not been entirely satisfactory, especially for manatees. Lefebvre et al.[38] provide useful general guidance, including using independent observers (either in a single aircraft or in two aircraft) to record sightings, estimating correction factors, and calibrating a population index.

In Florida, FWC staff are working to develop protocols to improve the accuracy of their statewide synoptic survey, including a plot sampling approach[39], dual observers, removal sampling[40], and stochastic simulation for Bayesian inference to obtain an estimate of the statewide manatee population.

Staff from the U.S. Geological Survey and U.S. Fish and Wildlife Service are also working to improve aerial surveys by conducting occupancy surveys[41] in the Ten Thousand Island region in Collier County, Florida. These methods use the number of occupied sampling units, rather than counts of individuals, as the observation unit, and use the probability of occupancy, rather than population size, as the variable of interest. The advantage of this approach is that not all individuals need to be counted, and models based on this approach have been developed that estimate abundance. This method of survey is particularly useful for large-scale surveys with limited resources. However, models for calculating abundance estimates require repeat visits to sampling units and assume closure of the population (i.e., no gains or losses to the population) between visits. This assumption is clearly problematic[42].

Enhanced Safety during Aerial Surveys

The challenge for aerial surveys has been to reach a balance where safety is promoted strongly without making survey costs prohibitively expensive. Strict guidelines are now used in the United States (especially in those surveys conducted through the federal government), but they may not be entirely practical in some other countries where aerial surveys might be useful. Since some scientists may not be able to assure the highest possible safety standards at an affordable cost, limitations on aircraft availability may simply mean that aircraft of optimal safety are unavailable. Scientists need to make a careful and conscious decision about whether they feel comfortable doing surveys[43]. In all cases, some general guidelines should be followed:

- Hire aircraft from reputable vendors only, and hire trustworthy and experienced pilots.
- Communicate well and often with the pilot; discuss the mission thoroughly with all crew members prior to take-off.
- Insist that pilots tell you if any requested procedure makes them uncomfortable in terms of safety.
- File a flight plan.
- Discuss responses to emergencies prior to take-off to be sure all observers/passengers know the appropriate procedures.
- Ensure that life preservers and a raft are present and that passengers know how and when to use them.
- Establish a system for tracking the survey. Appoint a ground contact with knowledge of all details of the flight (times, routes, planned stops, etc.), who will be responsible for proper notification of authorities if the survey aircraft is overdue.
- Consider purchasing an emergency position indicating radio beacon (EPIRB) to alert rescue authorities to your location. Costs are presently between US$200 and $1,500 and units are becoming less expensive.
- Err on the side of safety. If anything associated with the operation of the aircraft or the competence of the pilot causes concern for anyone, stop the survey. Do not conduct surveys when weather conditions make flying unsafe or when weather conditions change in ways that reduce safety (e.g., low clouds; high winds).
- Accidents can happen due to aircraft malfunction

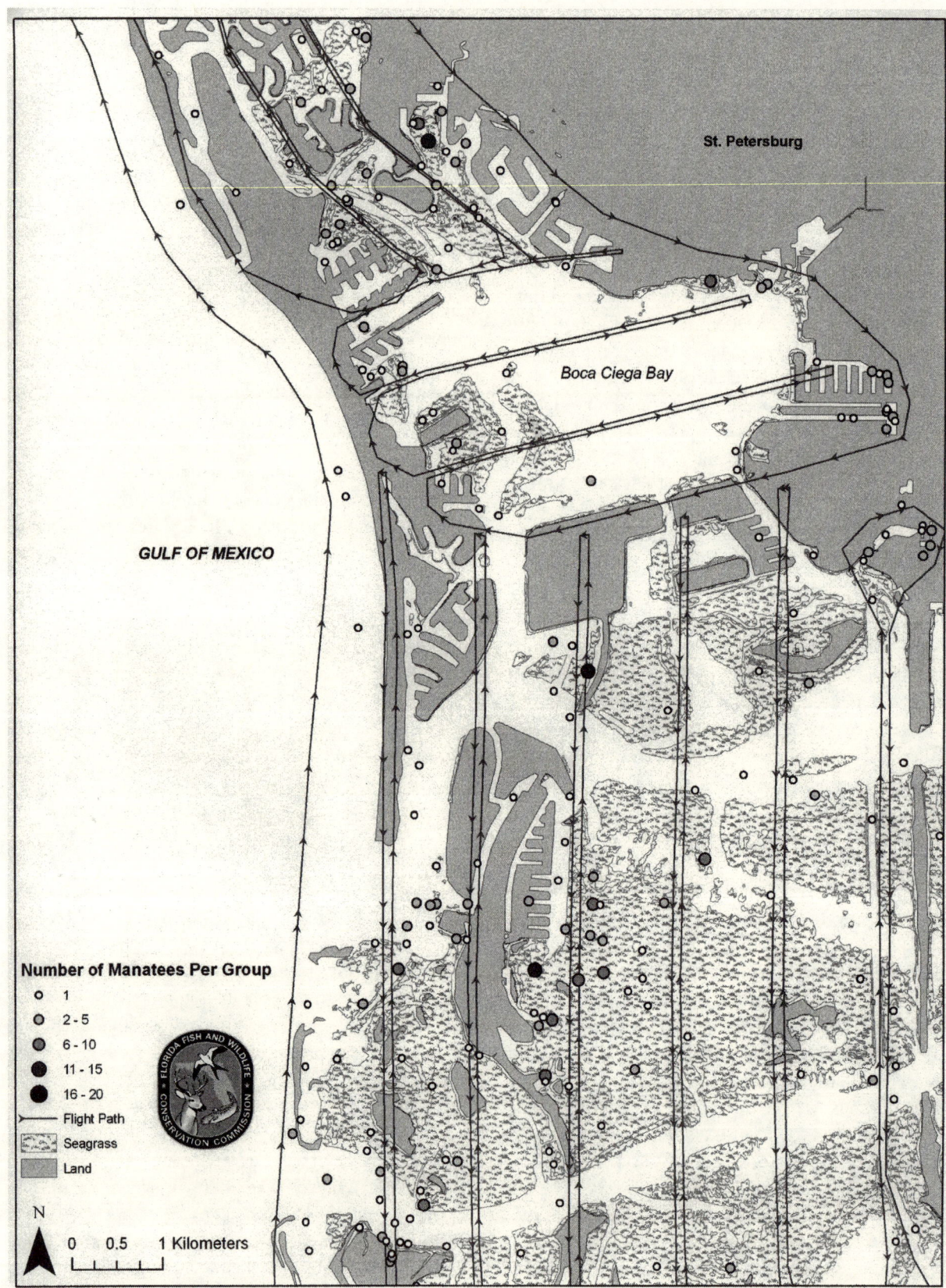

Figure 21.5. Use of geographic information systems (GIS) allows simultaneous overlays of manatee sightings, habitat types, and human activities to be made. Such information is especially useful to managers. (Courtesy of Stacie Koslovsky, Florida Wildlife Research Institute.)

rather than pilot error (or may result from a combination of both). Make sure that all survey planes are routinely maintained and serviced. If possible, use twin engine planes, especially if going significant distances offshore.

Conclusions

Carefully designed aerial surveys can be useful in developing countries to provide important insights regarding population size and trends, habitat use, and general distribution. The key is to develop a clear understanding of the questions to be answered and to develop surveys that provide high quality data, with as few biases as possible. When aerial surveys are not feasible, interviews, habitat studies, and boat/land surveys are other cost-effective ways by which information needed for conservation and management planning can be acquired[44]. Carefully designing a survey prior to conducting it pays great benefits by providing data that are likely to be useful in answering specific research questions.

Scientists wishing to design optimal surveys for their particular location can benefit from collaborations with statisticians, modelers, and spatial analysts (GIS experts)[45] (figure 21.5). Thanks to the work of the scientists referenced in this chapter, aerial survey design is improving by addressing the issues we have discussed.

Acknowledgments

The authors thank Kerri Scolardi, Ellen Hines, Ron Murphy, and Ester Quintana-Rizzo for their valuable comments on drafts of this chapter.

22

Organic Contaminants and Sirenians

DANA L. WETZEL, ERIN PULSTER, AND JOHN E. REYNOLDS III

Most programs that have assessed the status of marine mammals have used two primary approaches: counting individuals or estimating population size, and documenting mortality. A more complete approach[1] involves at least two additional factors: health of individuals and populations, and demography of the population. With such information available, managers are better able to: (1) make more informed decisions regarding current and future threats to sirenian populations and subpopulations, (2) initiate appropriate mitigation for those threats, and (3) clarify status of impacted populations and subpopulations. In fact, studies of contaminants in sirenians have implications for understanding manatee and dugong health, health of ecosystems and habitats used by sirenians, health of other organisms including humans that use those same habitats, and optimal approaches for mitigation.

A host of studies have identified contaminant levels in tissues of marine mammals[2], although contaminant studies of sirenians have been rare. However, participants at a Marine Mammal Commission–sponsored workshop[3] noted that an assessment of contaminant body burdens is not very informative unless it is accompanied by some assessment of the effects those contaminants may be having at the cellular, tissular, and molecular levels. For studies of sirenians, the optimal goals are to: (1) assess a wide range of organic contaminant levels from different geographic locations (and presumably different exposure levels), (2) conduct a suite of biomarker assays to demonstrate exposures to and significant sublethal effects of those contaminants, and (3) inform decision makers of the levels and effects, in order to promote appropriate conservation actions.

Why is an assessment of chemical contamination vital? Although exposure to chemical contaminants may not kill manatees and dugongs outright, there can be more insidious effects on reproduction, immune function, and endocrine function. Especially in light of the persistence of organic contaminants and their potential for bioaccumulation in fat of long-lived species like sirenians, it makes sense to develop a fuller understanding of levels and effects as soon as possible. It is also important to realize that humans use many of the same preferred sirenian habitats for swimming, fishing, and other activities that could expose people to the same harmful chemicals. Thus the sirenians, like other marine mammals, may be excellent "sentinel species" for which health problems could signal potential concerns for human and ecosystem health[4].

Priority Organic Contaminants in the Environment

In 1995 the United Nations Environmental Programme (UNEP) formally declared a need for global action on particular organic pollutants. The Governing Council of UNEP recognized that a suite of organic pollutants called persistent organic pollutants (POPs) possessed toxic properties, resisted degradation, and bioaccumulated through the food web, posing threats to human and environmental health[5]. The council called on the United Nations to develop recommendations and information on international action and possible international legal mechanisms for controlling the use of these chemicals. The list of 12 contaminants identified included several classes of compounds: organochlorine pesticides (e.g., aldrin, chlordane, DDT, dieldrin, endrin, heptachlor, mirex, and toxaphene), industrial compounds such as hexachlorobenzene and polychlorinated biphenyls (PCBs), and industrial by-products (including dioxin and furan). The negotiations for this initiative, known as the Stockholm Convention, were completed in 2001 and put into action by 2004.

In 1998 the United States Environmental Protection Agency (EPA) began a program that serves as a national companion strategy to the Stockholm Convention. These contaminants of concern were named "Priority Persistent, Bioaccumulative and Toxic Pollutants" (PBTs). The strategy was derived to reduce risk of exposure to priority pollutants, which included most of the same contaminants as those noted by the Stockholm Convention. The EPA list, however, did not include endrin or heptachlor, but it added to the list four additional compounds: benzo(a)pyrene (a type of polycyclic aromatic hydrocarbon or PAH), mercury, octachlorostyrene, and alkyl-lead. Additional pollutants have been identified as potential contaminant risks, such as other carcinogenic PAHs, brominated flame retardants, polybrominated diphenyl ethers (PBDEs), and tributyltin (TBT). In this chapter, persistent pollutants identified by both the Stockholm Convention and the EPA combined are considered as one group of contaminants called POPs/PBTs.

POPs/PBTs are among the most persistent, ubiquitous, and toxic pollutants in estuarine and marine ecosystems. Many, but not all, contain halogens (i.e., chlorine, bromine, fluorine, or iodine); however, they are all characterized by their lipophilic, hydrophobic, and semi-volatile nature. These compounds include substances ranging from low-molecular-weight volatile compounds, which have become common components of the atmosphere and surface waters of the ocean, to higher-molecular-weight compounds, which are widely distributed in estuarine and coastal marine waters[6]. In contrast to the low-molecular-weight compounds, the higher-molecular-weight lipophilic compounds accumulate in the lipid-rich tissues of animals and subsequently are detected in most biota worldwide. Toxicity and environmental impacts of POPs/PBTs have been primarily associated with damage to the nervous and reproductive systems of animals and recently with cancer and developmental abnormalities[7]. Responses of organisms to these contaminants can manifest at four levels of biological organization: (1) biochemical, cellular, and tissular; (2) organismal; (3) population; and (4) community.

Halogenated organic contaminants are not the only organic contaminants that require careful environmental monitoring. Despite urgent regional concerns about the effects of oil and gas development, toxicant studies of marine mammals to date have generally not focused on body burdens of PAHs[8]. For many sirenian species, oil and gas exploration and development constitute a serious environmental issue.

The National Research Council[9] estimated that over 1.3 million metric tons of oil (more than 1.3 billion liters) are released annually into the marine environment. There appears to be a correlation between high levels of PAHs and cytotoxic, genotoxic, immunotoxic, and carcinogenic effects on aquatic wildlife[10].

Because marine mammals have the enzymes (e.g., mixed function oxidase systems) necessary for detoxification and elimination of petroleum hydrocarbons and other organic contaminants, compounds of petroleum hydrocarbons are not often accumulated and sequestered in tissues, as occurs with chlorinated hydrocarbons. However when they are found, it may be indicative of a mixed function oxidase system overload. Additionally, compounds produced by metabolism of PAHs may accumulate and induce toxic effects[11].

Persistent organic pollutants accumulate in estuaries and coastal marine environments[12], which are essential habitats for many species (e.g., as maturation zones, spawning grounds, or egg laying areas for birds and reptiles, as birthing areas for oviparous fishes, and as feeding areas, particularly for early life history stages of other marine species). The susceptibility of these habitats to POP/PBT contamination is dependent on the physical and chemical properties of the contaminants and their transformation products; concentrations entering the ecosystem; input duration; ecosystem properties (e.g., flushing time); and ecosystem location in relation to point and nonpoint sources[13].

These compounds can be transported over long distances to remote areas of the world and persist in the environment for many years. Although it has been suggested that some contaminant concentrations are decreasing in sediments[14] and in a few marine mammal populations[15], there has been a shift toward increasing concentrations of "new" or emerging chemicals, such polybrominated diphenyl ethers (PBDEs), polychlorinated dibenzodioxins (PCDDs), and perfluorooctane sulfonate (PFOS). These compounds are also characterized by their persistence, tendency to bioaccumulate, and toxic potential.

The Cast of Characters

The contaminants identified for inclusion by the Stockholm Convention and the EPA's PBT program have many common characteristics. As noted, these compounds are mainly lipophilic in nature and bioaccumulate in animal tissue through biomagnification in the food chain. They also appear to be globally ubiquitous due to the ease of long-range transport, and because of their chemical nature, they resist degradation and can persist in the environment for lengthy time periods, sometimes as long as several generations. Finally and most significant, they can cause serious damage to the environment and the ecological health of countless species. However, understanding the backgrounds of and historic uses for these

POP/PBTs may prove valuable in evaluating potential impacts in specific areas of exposure. Most of the following information on the organic contaminants of highest concern is available through the Web sites of EPA[16] and the UNEP priority organic pollutant programme[17]. With the exception of a newer group of contaminants of concern, the perfluorooctane sulfonates, all the POP/PBTs have been classified for human carcinogenicity by the International Agency for Research on Cancer (IARC), part of the World Health Organization. The IARC's mission is to coordinate and conduct research on the causes of human cancer and the mechanisms of carcinogenesis, and to develop sound scientific strategies for cancer control[18]. The IARC classification scheme groups chemical compounds based on several possible levels of human carcinogen exposure and risk[19], as follows:

1. Group 1 compounds are known carcinogens. This category is used when there is sufficient evidence of carcinogenicity in either humans or animals.
2. Group 2A compounds are probable carcinogens. If there is limited human exposure but sufficient experimental animal exposure, this classification is applied.
3. Group 2B compounds are considered possible carcinogens. There is a slight difference between Groups 2A and 2B. In 2B, the evidence for human and animal carcinogenicity is less strong than in 2A but sufficient to warrant concern for human exposure.
4. Group 3 compounds are not considered carcinogenic. These compounds, while possibly carcinogenic in animals, do not appear to have similar mechanisms for carcinogenicity in humans.
5. Group 4 compounds are probably not carcinogenic. If there is no evidence for carcinogenicity in experimental animals or humans, compounds are classified into this group.

The IARC classification scheme considers many of the priority pollutants that can affect marine mammals, including sirenians. In order to begin to evaluate contaminant risks associated with particular chemicals in specific parts of the world, it is useful to understand when and why particular anthropogenic chemicals were produced and used. The following manufacturing and period-of-use information is for the United States only. Although many countries have agreed to follow the priority pollutant ban initiated by the Stockholm Convention, there are probably stockpiles of these banned chemicals that may be available and may therefore be used in some countries. Monitoring use of priority pollutants globally becomes very difficult, particularly if the use is not reported to any international agency.

- Aldrin/dieldrin—Aldrin and dieldrin (a by-product of aldrin) are organochlorine pesticides used from 1950 to 1972 as broad spectrum insecticides for crops and for termite, locust, ant, and mosquito control. In 1972 the EPA restricted their use to subsurface termite control, dipping of nonfood plant root and tops, and moth-proofing only. These chemicals were finally withdrawn from production by the manufacturer in 1974, and their use in the United States has been completely banned since 1987. These compounds are classified into Group 3 by the IARC.
- Endrin—is a stereoisomer of dieldrin, and like aldrin and dieldrin, it was used beginning in 1950 as a pesticide applied to field crops, mainly cotton, and for the controlling of mice. Although it was once widely used in the United States, most uses were canceled in 1980. Endrin has also been classified as a Group 3 compound.
- Chlordane—was used as a fumigating agent for the control of ants and termites in buildings, crops, nurseries, and lawns from 1948 to 1978. From 1978 to 1988 chlordane's only approved use was for termite control around the foundations of homes, and it was officially banned in the United States in 1988. This is a Group 2B compound.
- Heptachlor—was a constituent of technical grade chlordane, which began its use in 1953. The use of this pesticide was the same as for chlordane, namely controlling ants and termites in buildings and crops. All uses of heptachlor were canceled in 1988 with the exception of commercial control of fire ants in power transformers. Heptachlor is classified as a Group 2B compound.
- DDT—along with its metabolic products (DDD and DDE), DDT is probably one of the most famous of the persistent organic pollutants. Prior to its 1972 United States ban, this chemical was commonly used as a mosquito control pesticide, specifically targeting the malaria-carrying mosquitoes and tsetse flies. Although no longer used in most countries, it is still being used in places, such as Africa, for malaria-control programs. DDT and its metabolites are classified as Group 2B compounds.
- Mirex—is another pesticide used from 1962 to 1978 for the control of fire ants and as a flame retardant. It was later found to be very toxic to crustaceans, particularly shrimp and crabs, and rapidly fell out of fa-

vor after a series of public hearings. This compound is a Group 2B chemical.
- Toxaphene—was commonly used as an insecticide on cotton crops from 1947 to 1980. After 1980, use was severely limited and only allowed in case of extreme agricultural emergency. However, toxaphene is routinely used in Puerto Rico and the Virgin Islands for banana and pineapple crops. Toxaphene is a Group 2B contaminant.
- Hexachlorobenzene—is an industrial compound that was originally used as a fungicide for wheat seed. Now, this compound is used as a solvent in pesticides and it is a created as a by-product in the synthesis of other compounds. It is classified as a Group 2B compound.
- Dioxins and furans—are two families of chemicals with similar structures. Dioxins are polychlorinated dibenzodioxins (PCDDs), and furans are polychlorinated dibenzofurans (PCDFs). These families are made up of many congeners that are by-products of industrial processes such as incineration of waste, metal smelting, and chlorine bleaching of wood pulp. They are not commercially produced. One of the dioxins has been classified as a Group 1 compound, whereas the rest of the dioxins and furans are considered Group 2B.
- Octachlorostyrene (OCS)—is not manufactured but is formed under comparable conditions to other highly chlorinated compounds like hexachlorobenzene, dioxins, and furans. This by-product is a result of combining carbon and chlorine at high temperatures. There is no definitive toxicity available for OCS; however, since it is very similar to the structure of hexachlorobenzene, the EPA assumes that there would be a similar toxicological profile, making this a probable Group 2B compound.
- Polychlorinated biphenyls (PCBs)—are another of the well-known classes of persistent organic contaminants. They have been used in the past as coolants and lubricants, especially in electric transformers. PCBs have also been used as additives in paint, plastics, and sealants, and like dioxins and furans, they can be produced as a by-product in industrial processes. Commercial production of PCBs stopped in 1977. This group of contaminants is categorized as Group 2A compounds.
- Benzo(a)pyrene (B(a)P)—is one of many compounds in the polycyclic aromatic hydrocarbon (PAH) family. Whereas several of the PAHs can be toxic, B(a)P is one of the most toxic of the family. This compound occurs naturally in petroleum and can be found in tar and asphalt. It is released into the environment through incomplete combustion of petroleum, forest fires, industrial processes, waste burning, and even food preparation. As with many PAHs, B(a)P is considered to cause cancer in humans and is therefore a Group 1 contaminant.
- Alkyl lead—is an anthropogenically derived group of compounds with organic carbon groups attached to inorganic lead. These chemicals were manufactured first in the early 1920s as additives to gasoline in order to increase the octane rating in gasoline inexpensively. These additives have gradually been phased out over a 23-year period starting in 1973. The alkylated lead compounds are Group 3 contaminants.
- Methylmercury—is a contaminant which is formed by the addition of organic carbon groups to inorganic mercury. In the past, methylmercury was produced directly and indirectly as part of industrial processes. However, many of those industrial practices have ceased. Now, the sources of methylmercury include the burning of fossil fuels, in particular coal, and the mining and processing of some metal ores. As with other POPs/PBTs, methylmercury is transported atmospherically and can circulate there for many years before depositing in the environment. This contaminant is considered a Group 2B compound.

Other Compounds of Concern

There is discussion among regulatory/monitoring agencies such as the EPA and UNEP about adding additional chemicals of environmental concern to the existing POP/PBT lists. Two of these classes of compounds are the polybrominated diphenyl ethers (PBDEs) and perfluorooctane sulfonate (PFOS).

- Polybrominated diphenyl ethers (PBDEs)—are used as flame retardants in everyday products such as furniture foam, draperies, upholstery, consumer electronics, wire insulation, personal computers, and small appliances. These chemicals are able to slow ignition and rate of fire growth and have helped to save lives. However, PBDEs have been associated with liver, thyroid, and neurodevelopmental toxicity and are being found in human breast milk, fish, aquatic birds, and elsewhere in the environment[20]. These flame retardants are classified as Group 2A.
- Perfluorooctane sulfonate (PFOS)—is one of a group of related chemicals used for a wide variety of industrial, commercial, and consumer applications.

For example, PFOS is a component of certain soil and stain-resistant coatings for fabrics, leather, furniture, and carpets, fire-fighting foams, commercial and consumer floor polishes, and cleaning products; PFOS is also used as a surfactant and in pesticides and food packaging products. PFOS has been detected in a number of wildlife species and appears to be associated with hepatotoxicity, bladder cancer, and thyroid follicular cell adenomas. At this time, no carcinogen classification has been determined.

Why Study Contaminants in Sirenians?

Determining the biomagnification of POP/PBT contaminants is necessary to evaluate potential exposure and risks to human and wildlife populations[21]. It is increasingly recognized that marine mammals may suffer both directly and indirectly from diseases associated with chemical pollutants[22]. Dolphin mass stranding events[23], reproduction abnormalities[24], liver and kidney abnormalities[25], and immune suppression[26] have all been linked to high concentrations of POPs/PBTs. Complex mixtures of environmental contaminants may be linked with immunosuppresion in marine mammals in highly populated areas[27].

Sirenians are herbivorous marine mammals inhabiting rivers, estuaries, coastal marine waters, swamps, and marine wetlands. Since sirenians are restricted to areas that tend to accumulate POPs/PBTs, and because manatees and dugongs ingest sediments and plant epiphytes where POPs tend to be adsorbed, these animals could be subjected to a higher risk of exposures and adverse effects than would be predicted based on their trophic level. There is limited evidence of direct impacts of these contaminants on sirenian populations. Nevertheless, because sirenians are long-lived, have slow reproductive rates, and require high adult survival to maintain stable or increasing populations, any added impacts of toxic substances on reproduction or mortality of these animals could have serious consequences for population recovery and would be cause for concern[28].

The Importance of Assessing Biomarkers

The use of clinical diagnostic markers (often called biomarkers) is important because (a) marine mammals may be exposed and respond to chemical contaminants without necessarily having measurable body burdens, and (b) it is actually more important to understand effects of contaminants and biotoxins than simply to record levels within tissues. Therefore, when possible, a range of established biomarker assays should be performed[29], including but not limited to assays indicative of:

- DNA alterations (e.g., adducts, breakages);
- protein responses, such as esterases, mixed function oxidases (e.g., EROD), and stress proteins;
- metabolic products, including porphyrins; and
- immune system alterations.

The various biomarker assays involve collection and analysis of a range of tissues or matrices, but blood and skin are commonly used and easily acquired. Analyses should follow well-established protocols[30] with proper positive and negative controls.

Studies of Contaminants in Sirenians

O'Shea et al. and O'Shea[31] provide detailed reviews of contaminants in sirenians. Currently there are very few documented studies on organochlorines (OCs) in either dugong or manatee populations. OCs were not detected in muscle tissues of Indonesian dugongs[32], but it is important to note that OCs tend to sequester in lipid rich tissue (e.g., blubber). Thus it is reasonable to assume that tissues with relatively low levels of lipids (e.g., muscle) may not have detectable levels of OCs. Australian dugongs have PCB levels ranging from nondetectable in muscle and liver to 209 ppb lipid weight (lw) in their blubber[33]. These levels are the same order of magnitude as those found in bowhead whales and ringed and bearded seals in the Beaufort-Chukchi Sea[34]. However, they are considerably lower than those reported for most marine mammal species in the northern hemisphere. Toxic threshold levels, resulting in adverse health effects such as immunosuppression and reproductive failure, have been derived for cetaceans at 14–17 ppm lw[35]. Congener-specific profiles observed by Haynes et al.[36] and Vetter et al.[37] were characteristically different from those reported for other marine mammals. The prominent congeners (PCB 153, 138, 180) typically found in marine mammals globally were only minor constituents in dugongs.

Organic contaminant concentrations can vary between genders, with higher concentrations generally found in male marine mammals. Contrary to this, Vetter et al.[38] detected higher concentrations of PCPs and OCPs in female dugongs than in males. Profile differences and concentration variability among species may suggest variation in metabolic capacity among marine mammals or differences in exposure. In addition, naturally occurring heptachlorobipyrrole (Q1) and unknown brominated compounds were among the most prominent congeners in the dugongs. Interestingly, the concentration of Q1 in one animal (160 ppb lw) was similar to that of DDE (161 ppb lw).[39]

Polychlorinated dibenzo-p-dioxins (PCDDs) and dibenzofurans(PCDFs) have recently been reported in the blubber of dugongs with levels (260–390 ppt ww ΣPCDD/F) exceeding those found in any other marine mammal[40]. The dominant congener was OCDD (170–250 ppt ww), which is generally a minor constituent in other species.

Organochlorine pesticides (OCPs) in the blubber of dugongs found along the coast of Queensland, Australia, tend to be limited to dieldrin, DDT, and DDT metabolites. Detectable concentrations showed ranges of 1.2–66 ppb lw for DDT, 0.9–161 ppb lw for DDE, 4.1–5.4 ppb lw for DDD, and 1–43 ppb lw for dieldrin[41].

Baseline OC data are also limited for the three species of manatees, with most studies being restricted to the West Indian manatee (*Trichechus manatus*). PCB levels in the blubber of Florida manatees (*T. m. latirostris*) ranged from nondetectable (ND)[42] to 4.6 ppm ww[43]. Wetzel et al.[44] found levels of 1.07 ppm lw for PCBs in Florida manatee blubber. These levels are similar to those reported for beluga whales in the Beaufort Sea[45] and narwhals in the Canadian Arctic[46]. Threshold concentrations of 14.8 ppm lw[47] and 17 ppm lw[48] were recently derived for adverse health effects (e.g., immunosuppression, reproductive failure) from PCB exposure in blubber of some other marine mammals.

Data from samples collected from free-ranging manatees in Chetumal Bay, Mexico, during 2006–2007 suggest that they have contaminant levels comparable to those of Florida manatees reported by O'Shea et al.[49] prior to regulations banning use in the United States of some especially toxic OCPs and PCBs. That being said, the Mexican manatees had high PCB levels for herbivores, with a range of 0.38 to 5.68 ppm lw[50]. The maximum concentration quantified is below the threshold concentrations (14–17 ppm lw) mentioned earlier for cetaceans; however, toxic threshold concentrations for sirenians are unknown. In addition, Wetzel et al. report that PCB concentrations in the blood (0.039 ppm ww) of manatees sampled in Chetumal Bay were considerably higher than blood PCB thresholds derived for dolphins (0.026 ppm ww) and harbor seals (0.020 ppm ww[51]), indicating a potential health risk for manatees. Dieldrin (ND–0.36 ppm ww) and DDT (ND–0.28 ppm ww) were the predominant OCPs detected in manatee blubber sampled in Florida[52]. Samples collected during 2003 in Florida suggested decreasing trends in both mean levels of dieldrin (0.01 ppm ww) and EDDT (0.02 ppm ww)[53]. Endosulfan I and lindanes were the dominant OCPs detected in the 2006–2007 blubber samples. The dominant OCPs in the blubber of manatees sampled in Chetumal Bay were heptachlor, dieldrin, and mirex[54]. The temporal and spatial variation observed in OCP concentrations and patterns in both Florida and Mexico manatees could suggest usage and exposure differences.

There have been no studies quantifying other organic contaminants (e.g., PAHs, PBDEs, PCDD/PCDFs) in manatees. An investigation of PAHs in manatees sampled in both Florida and Mexico resulted in no detectable levels found[55].

In most cases the reported levels in sirenians are comparatively low; nevertheless, the susceptibility of mammalian species to PCBs is variable, and some species have very low sensitivity[56]. Thus, although levels have been assessed for certain contaminants in certain sirenian populations, effects are completely unknown, underscoring the need for biomarker assays to accompany analyses of contaminant levels.

In addition, toxic equivalency factors (TEFs) have been developed for specific PCB congeners that are structurally similar to PCDDs and elicit dioxin-like toxic effects. In studies where these dioxin-like PCB congeners have been quantified, a toxic equivalency quotient (TEQ) can be determined using TEFs. Some species-specific TEQ values have been determined for species of pinniped and cetacean but not for any sirenians. However, TEQs developed for other marine mammals may be used as surrogates for comparisons, although an uncertainty factor exists owing to interspecies differences in toxic response sensitivity. The blubber samples collected from manatees in Chetumal Bay, Mexico, had PCB TEQ values (1,980 pg TEQ/g lw) more than an order of magnitude higher than TEQ thresholds (160 pg TEQ/g lw) for seals[57], warranting further research and health effects monitoring. The PCB TEQ values for Florida manatees were much less at 1.18 pg TEQ/g lw.

Recommended Sampling Protocols and Procedures

Contaminant research can be expensive, and as is the case for all science, careful thought needs to go into experimental design, tissue selection, sample size, collection protocols, instrumentation, and other factors prior to initiating studies. Biologists may devote considerable time and effort to sampling for contaminant studies, only to find that the tissues collected are not optimal for specific analyses, that the collection protocols have created inadvertent contamination of the samples, or that preservation techniques have been inappropriate. Furthermore, once the appropriate samples are properly collected and archived, laboratory analyses must be done following rigorous guidelines for quality control, using highly specialized instrumentation. Assessments of the levels and effects of chemical contamination are very important to understanding risks for particular species and environments, but such assessments must be undertaken carefully, using appropriate protocols and instrumentation, and with an awareness of the costs involved.

The following protocols and suggestions apply only to the organic contaminants, including pesticides, PCBs, PAHs, PBDEs, PCDDs, and PFOS. For analyses of elements (inorganic contaminants) that are not considered here, different protocols would be used.

An important preliminary step prior to initiating a study of contaminants is either to develop a collaborative relationship with scientists already doing such work (to benefit from their experience) or to conduct literature reviews to become familiar with methodology. Experimental design should consider both chemical and physical factors that may influence tissue accumulation (e.g., gender, age, tissue type). Sampling protocols and tissue selection can also be analysis specific and require rigorous sampling procedures. Knowledge of where the target analyte will tend to accumulate should guide tissue collections. For example, the kidney may accumulate trace metals, whereas lipid rich tissues, such as blubber, sequester lipophilic compounds (e.g.,

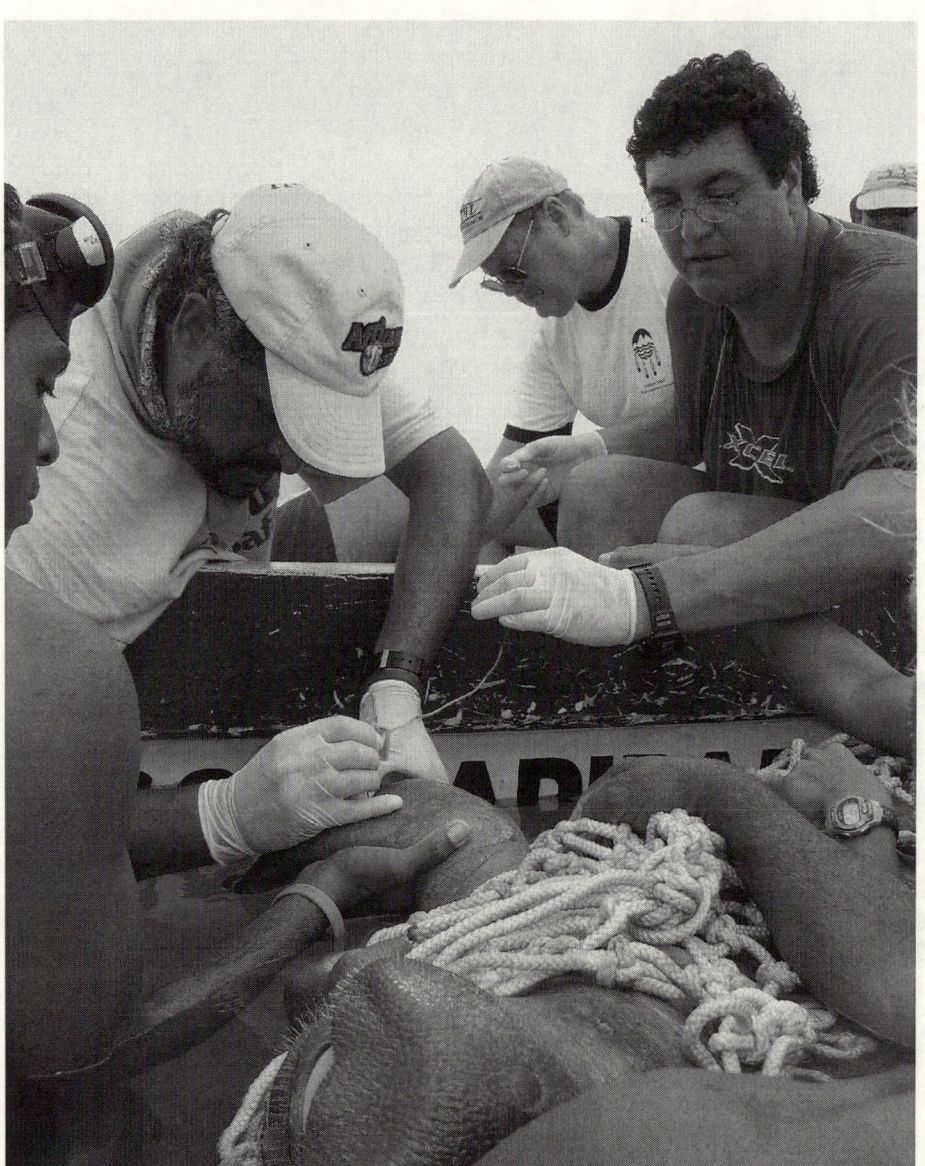

Figure 22.1. Using proper capture techniques, samples can be collected from manatees even while the animals remain in the water. Here veterinarians Dr. Marco Benitez (left) and Dr. Alonso Aguirre take samples from a manatee captured in the Yucatán Peninsula as part of a research program coordinated by Dr. Benjamín Morales. (Courtesy of Humberto Bahena.)

POPs/PBTs). Even among the various organic compounds listed earlier in this chapter, some are strongly lipophilic (e.g., DDT), whereas others are much less so (e.g., methylmercury). In addition, proper instruments, collection vials, and storage need to be employed to reduce degradation and inadvertent contamination. As noted earlier, the proper and complete analysis of samples for organic contaminants requires specialized instrumentation and careful laboratory technique using established methods.

Sirenian tissue samples can be obtained both from deceased animals and from biopsies of free-ranging animals. The collection of samples from deceased animals is somewhat easier than acquiring biopsies, but investigators must be aware of certain constraints: for example, samples must be collected within 2–4 hours of death in order to prevent loss of contaminants as decomposition occurs[58].

In addition, it will be useful to attempt to correlate what is found in the tissues of sirenians with levels of contaminants in the environment. To do so, we recommend sampling and analysis of sediments, which are repositories for hydrophobic organic contaminants. As such, sediment-associated POPs/PBTs are bioavailable for resuspension into the overlying waters inhabited by sirenians or the chemicals could be ingested directly by foraging sirenians.

With a carefully designed approach, it becomes possible to (a) create baselines against which to assess future impacts, (b) determine areas where POPs/PBTs may be having critical effects on individuals and populations, and (c) direct mitigation efforts in optimal ways. We encourage such studies, but given their costs relative to some other approaches, we reiterate our recommendation that careful thought go into experimental design, sampling locations, and other factors to ensure that optimal results occur. In some areas within the ranges of the various sirenian species, the effects of exposure to contaminants (e.g., reproductive impairment, immunological dysfunction) may constitute one of the greatest single threats to conservation of sirenians and other species; effective management, including mitigation, will likely not occur without the results of careful scientific studies to substantiate the problem.

23

Manatee Rescue, Rehabilitation, and Release Efforts as a Tool for Species Conservation

NICOLE ADIMEY, ANTONIO A. MIGNUCCI-GIANNONI, NICOLE E. AUIL-GOMEZ,
VERA M. F. DA SILVA, CAROLINA MATTOSINHO DE CARVALHO ALVITE, BENJAMÍN
MORALES-VELA, REGIS PINTO DE LIMA, AND FERNANDO C. WEBER ROSAS

Wildlife rehabilitation programs have been used on numerous species to augment conservation and management efforts. The rescue, rehabilitation, and release of injured or sick animals have become a widespread practice among wildlife management programs[1]. These programs can make a significant contribution, especially to threatened and endangered species or when specific populations are at risk of extinction. Sirenians are no exception (figure 23.1). Several countries, including the United States, Puerto Rico, Mexico, Belize, and Brazil, have established extensive manatee rehabilitation programs, consisting of four basic components: rescue, rehabilitation, release, and post-release monitoring. Rescue and rehabilitation of dugongs have also been conducted by Sea World–Gold Coast in Australia, Toba Aquarium in Japan, and Underwater World in Singapore. In this chapter we outline the basic components of manatee rehabilitation programs and detail those existing in North, Central, and South America.

Goals of Rehabilitation Programs

Rehabilitation programs may be established for a variety of reasons, including conserving species, increasing public awareness, supporting local economies, and satisfying governmental regulations or political concerns. Some programs focus on the humane, seeking to provide care for those animals affected by natural or anthropogenic impacts. Although these programs have merit, rehabilitation has greater worth when it contributes to species conservation and population growth.

Historically, rehabilitation programs have offered opportunities to educate the public about threats to wildlife and the environment while promoting conservation[2]. Rehabilitation and release programs can also provide platforms to develop and test the release of captive-bred threatened and endangered species to the wild[3], and to increase our knowledge and ability to treat wildlife diseases[4].

Rehabilitation programs are often initiated to protect animal populations at risk of extinction. Such programs intervene with injured or distressed wildlife, providing animals with a second chance to survive in the wild and contribute to the population's gene pool.

Program Structure

Rehabilitation programs may be developed in different ways, depending on available resources, infrastructure of the lead organization or agency, and the purpose of the program. A successful program depends on rapid response, proximity of adequate facilities, available resources, including funding and personnel, and an experienced rescue team[5]. A rehabilitation program typically has the following components: verifiers, rescuers, transporters, rehabilitation facilities, and biologists who conduct post-release monitoring.

Verifiers are used to determine if an animal is in distress. Their role typically does not involve hands-on work but rather a site visit and verification of reported sightings. Verifiers need to know the signs of distress that determine if assistance is necessary; these may include buoyancy problems including listing or inability to submerge, irregular breathing, lethargy, disorientation, and in cooler climates, the suite of symptoms termed "cold stress." Abandoned calves and severe injuries, such as those caused by people (e.g., boat strike, entanglement), are easier to verify. Once an animal is confirmed as being in need of assistance, verifiers monitor the animal until the rescue team arrives.

Rescuers and transporters require special training in particular species handling techniques. Protocols should be strictly followed to ensure that the health and welfare of the animal are not compromised. Typically, the

Figure 23.1. West Indian manatee in rehabilitation at Centro Mamíferos Aquáticos in Itamaracá, Brazil. (Courtesy of Luciano Candisani.)

individuals who rescue sirenians are also authorized to conduct transport.

Rehabilitation facilities require the most extensive understanding of sirenian biology and medicine, and caregivers should be experienced in current husbandry techniques. The attending veterinarian should possess training in wildlife medicine, especially marine mammal health and disease processes.

Once the attending veterinarian has given medical clearance, rehabilitated animals can be released, some through an acclimation process (e.g., naive orphaned animals) and others directly (e.g., animals brought in as injured adults). Prior to release, a final health assessment should be conducted on all animals. Distinguishing marks should be documented, and all individuals should be tagged using a passive integrated transponder (PIT) tag[6]; animals without distinguishing marks may be freeze branded for future identification[7]. Blood serum and tissue samples for genetics assessment should be collected and archived[8].

Monitoring is conducted on all manatees that have been released in Puerto Rico, Belize, and Brazil and for selected animals in the United States. The intensity of monitoring efforts depends on available resources, the release candidate, monitoring goals, and the risk associated with the release of the individual. Monitoring typically includes radio-tracking to obtain location data, visual sightings, and planned capture for full health assessments[9]. Researchers conducting the post-release monitoring must possess specific training in the various capture, tagging, and tracking techniques[10].

Those responsible for the development and implementation of a rehabilitation program should clearly delineate its structure and goals, define protocols, and identify partners with designated roles. Program success relies on effective communication among participants and on timely reporting. Periodic review of rehabilitation protocols is also recommended to determine if modifications are necessary.

Partnerships

A successful program requires extensive resources, and expertise and partnerships are essential. Partners can leverage limited resources and bring stability and longevity to a program. They can be drawn from national, state, local, and tribal governments, nongovernmental organizations (NGOs), aquariums and zoos, academia, or the private sector. Partners will have various reasons for participating, and common goals or objectives should be defined initially and agreed upon by all.

Partners play a variety of roles depending on the needs of the program and personal interests. Some individuals or organizations may serve on an executive committee that makes decisions for the program, while others may serve in an advisory capacity when needed. Partners may be asked to provide expertise on issues regarding medical treatment, husbandry care, rescue and release logistics, or field monitoring. Others may contribute monetary resources, in-kind services, or other donations, such as field equipment. Rehabilitation programs may also offer local communities an opportunity to be involved in wildlife management, promote the ecological value of rehabilitating wildlife, and increase environmental awareness[11].

Management and Science

A critical component of any rehabilitation program is the cooperation among scientists, the rehabilitators, and the managers who rely on the supply of biological data acquired through research. Similarly, scientists need managers and rehabilitators for support and guidance to identify species needs, support protection measures, and drive conservation efforts.

Efficient rehabilitation programs possess a close working relationship among all the players. Scientists answer the biological questions, while managers make conservation decisions, and rehabilitators implement appropriate actions to save individual sirenians. A lack of cooperation between management and scientists can result in managers making biological decisions without supporting scientific evidence. Conversely, scientists may not conduct the critical research necessary to manage a species if they are not conversant with the conservation issues.

Assessing Rehabilitation Program Success

One of the more challenging tasks of animal rehabilitation is assessing success. Success may be difficult to determine, and assessment can vary greatly. It can be defined in many ways: increases in the numbers of animals released, births, thriving generations, improvements in population survival rates, overall population numbers, or successful medical treatments. Other programs may base initial success on increased funding contributions, improved cost-effectiveness, benefits to the local community, or advancement in science. In some instances the evaluation of success and the effectiveness of a rescue and rehabilitation program may require knowledge of population structure[12].

Educational benefits may also define program success, especially in local communities where hunting exists. Although difficult to measure, educational benefits can contribute significantly to rehabilitation programs. The persistence of a viable population does not depend solely on financial contributions and conservation-minded expertise; it also depends on the attitudes and actions of people who share the animals' habitat.

The measure of success for any rehabilitation program can be arduous, especially when resources are limited, baseline data are lacking, sample sizes are small, or program longevity is not yet established[13]. Although rehabilitation is acknowledged as a means for conserving and managing species, it remains controversial because the expense and labor may not match the overall success of the program's contribution to the population[14].

Manatee Rehabilitation and Captive Programs

West Indian manatee (*Trichechus manatus*) and Amazonian manatee (*T. inunguis*) rehabilitation programs exist in the United States, Mexico, Belize, Puerto Rico, Peru, and Brazil (table 23.1). In addition, manatees are sporadically kept captive at facilities for rehabilitation in Colombia, the Dominican Republic, Guyana, Jamaica, and Venezuela (table 23.1).

West Indian Manatee

United States

The United States has a long-standing rescue, rehabilitation, and release program assisting injured or distressed manatees and, when necessary, providing supplemental captive care. The program's goal is to release manatees to the wild and ensure their greatest chance of survival.

The U.S. Fish and Wildlife Service (USFWS) provides management oversight and is ultimately responsible for the animals under the authority of the U.S. Endangered Species Act and Marine Mammal Protection Act.

The program was formalized in 1973, and in 1991 the Interagency/Oceanaria (I/O) Working Group was created to support and assist in its implementation. Partners represent national, state, and local agencies, oceanaria, academia, and NGOs.

Table 23.1. Summary of facilities holding West Indian manatees (*Trichechus manatus*) or Amazonian manatees (*T. inunguis*) for rehabilitation or display in the Americas as of August 2009.

Facility	Location	Year established*	Manatees		Volume	Water	Tank system	Staff	
			Rehab	Captivity				Vets	Caretakers
West Indian manatee (*Trichechus manatus*)									
Acuario de Veracruz	Veracruz, MEX	1998	0	6	40,250	Salt	Closed	2	3
Acuario Nacional	Santo Domingo, DOM	1995	0	0	108,300	Salt	Open	2	2
Belize Manatee Rehabilitation Centre	Sarteneja, BLZ	1999	1	0	10,640	Brackish	Open	2	2
Caleta de Xel-Há	Quintana Roo, MEX	1999	0	3	-	Fresh	Open	1	2
Centro de Convivencia Infantil	Tabasco, MEX	1981	0	3	-	Fresh	Enclosed lake	-	-
Centro Mamíferos Aquáticos	Pernambuco, BRA	1991	17	10	1,079,750	Salt	Open	1	13
Cincinnati Zoo and Botanical Garden	Ohio, USA	1999	2	0	456,000	Fresh	Closed	2	3
Colombus Zoo and Aquarium	Ohio, USA	1999	2	0	950,000	Brackish	Closed	1	3
CVS/Fundación Omacha	Córdoba, COL	1990	1	3	-	Fresh	Enclosed lake	1	1
Dallas World Aquarium	Texas, USA	2000	2	0	839,000	Fresh	Closed	2	1
Disney's Living Seas	Florida, USA	1988	2	0	608,000	Salt	Closed	2	6
Dolphin Discovery's Cozumel	Quintana Roo, MEX	2007	0	3		Salt	Open	4	4
Dolphin Discovery's Isla Mujeres	Quintana Roo, MEX	2007	0	3		Salt	Open	4	4
Dolphin Discovery's Puerto Aventuras	Quintana Roo, MEX	2001	0	4	1,145,000	Salt	Open	4	4
El Colegio de la Frontera Sur	Quintana Roo, MEX	2003	0	1	690,000	Brackish	Open	1	2
Fundación Ecológica Amigos del Manatí	Bolivar, COL	1986	0	33	-	Fresh	Enclosed lake	0	1
Fundacion Zoológico Metropolitano del Zulia	Maracaibo, VEN	1998	0	1	80,000	Fresh	Closed	3	2
Guyana Zoological Park	Georgetown, GUY	1895	0	13	-	Fresh	Closed	1	9
Homossasa Springs Wildlife State Park	Florida, USA	1980	5	1	456,000	Fresh	Enclosed river	3	9
Tampa's Lowry Park Zoo	Florida, USA	1990	11	0	962,000	Fresh	Closed	1	7
Miami Seaquarium	Florida, USA	1954	7	2	950,000	Salt	Closed	3	8
Mote Marine Laboratory	Florida, USA	1996	2	0	266,000	Salt	Closed	1	3
Natural Resources Conservation Authority	Clarendon, JAM	1981	0	3	-	Fresh	Open	0	1
Parker Manatee Aquarium	Florida, USA	1949	2	1	245,000	Fresh	Closed	1	4
Parque Zoológico y Botánico Bararida	Barquisimeto, VEN	1994	0	3	-	Fresh	Closed	2	1
Puerto Rico Manatee Conservation Center	Bayamón, PRI	1990	2	0	160,000	Fresh	Closed	2	10
Puerto Rico Zoo	Mayagüez, PRI	2005	0	0	-	Fresh	Closed	1	2

continued

Table 23.1—*continued*

Facility	Location	Year established*	Manatees		Volume	Water	Tank system	Staff	
			Rehab	Captivity				Vets	Caretakers
Sea World of Florida	Florida, USA	1985	13	0	1,712,000	Fresh	Closed	4	4
Xcaret	Quintana Roo, MEX	1999	0	2	413,000	Fresh	Open	1	2
Yumká	Tabasco, MEX	1993	0	4	2,460,194	Fresh	Open	1	2
Zoológico de Barranquilla	Atlántico, COL	1988	0	2	-	Fresh	Closed	1	-
Total			69	101					
Amazonian manatee (*Trichechus inunguis*)									
Centro de Proteção e Pesquisa de Mamíferos Aquáticos	Amazonas, BRA	1992	9	35	850,000	Fresh	Open	2	8
Centro de Rescate Amazónico	Iquitos, PER	2007	9	0	409,000	Fresh	Open/closed	2	4
INPA Laboratório de Mamíferos Aquáticos	Amazonas, BRA	1974	8	30	650,000	Fresh	Open	1	6
Museu Paraense Emílio Goeldi	Para, BRA	1955	0	1	160,000	Fresh	Open	1	1
Total			26	66					

* Year that the manatee program was established. Rehab = at present in rehabilitation, Captivity = at present in permanent captivity or semi-captivity, Volume = lite of water, Vets = veterinarians, BLZ = Belize, BRA = Brazil, COL = Colombia, DOM = Dominican Republic, GUY = Guyana, JAM = Jamaica, MEX = Mexico, PER = Peru, PR = Puerto Rico, USA = United States of America, VEN = Venezuela.

The core of the rehabilitation program consists of eleven facilities: seven in Florida, two in Ohio, and two in Puerto Rico (table 23.1). Five of these—Sea World of Florida, Tampa's Lowry Park Zoo, Miami Seaquarium, Puerto Rico Zoo, and the Puerto Rico Manatee Conservation Center—are authorized for critical care. Additional facilities and organizations are authorized to verify, rescue, and transport injured or distressed manatees.

Causes of distress include watercraft injuries, entanglement, exposure to cold or red tide, entrapment or crushing in water control structures, orphaned calves, and other natural causes such as disease or reproductive complications. As of 2008, the program has rescued over 1,051 manatees and has released 351[15]. The longevity of the program has enabled significant global contributions to the advancement of manatee biology and medicine (figure 23.2).

In 1992 the USFWS and the I/O Working Group developed release criteria for the program, based on medical history, the circumstances of birth (e.g., wild-born adult, wild-born orphan, captive-born, inbred, foster-reared, human-reared) and length of time in captivity.

Five release categories were defined: <1 year, 1 to 5 years, 5 to 10 years, 10 to 15 years, and >15 years. Initially, animals rescued as adults, or those in captivity for the shortest period of time, were given highest priority for release. Over the years, the program has progressed to releasing younger animals and individuals that have been in captivity for longer periods of time.

The most challenging release candidates are those captive-born orphans with minimal wild experience or animals with over 15 years in captivity. These high-risk animals are monitored after release via radio transmitters. Although expensive and time-consuming, these efforts have allowed managers and biologists to develop a better understanding of habitat use, distribution patterns, behavior, health, and the capacity for adaptation to the wild. With over 107 manatees tagged, the program has further refined protocols and criteria that have enhanced survival rates.

Puerto Rico

Rescue and rehabilitation efforts began in Puerto Rico in 1990[16] and are at present conducted by two rescue and rehabilitation facilities. The Puerto Rico Manatee Con-

Figure 23.2. Rescue and transport of a West Indian manatee in Crystal River, Florida. (Courtesy of Antonio A. Mignucci-Giannoni.)

servation Center (PRMCC) is operated by the NGO Red Caribeña de Varamientos (Caribbean Stranding Network) and the Inter American University of Puerto Rico under special permits from the U.S. and Puerto Rican governments (table 23.1). PRMCC staff consists of caretakers, a curator, an attending veterinarian, and an alternate veterinarian. Volunteers assist in daily duties and an extensive educational outreach program. The PRMCC has also provided expertise and assistance to other Latin American countries, Africa and China.

Since 1990, the program has cared for 27 manatees. The majority of animals rescued (85%) were calves that had been orphaned or separated from their mothers. Adults and juveniles brought in for rehabilitation generally suffer from pneumonia or long-term malnutrition, including severe cachexia (extreme loss of weight and muscle mass). Calves typically are prematurely born and malnourished, with colic, enteritis, colitis, and pneumatosis instestinalis as medical complications (figure 23.3).

The rehabilitation approach involves intensive 24-hour supervision during the first week, hydration through a calculated and balanced formula of electrolytes and elemental peptide-based milk formula (Nestle's Peptamen Junior or Enfamil's Nutramigen), and antibiotics based on bacteriology and sensitivity. If necessary, animals are hydrated intravenously or tube-fed to secure nutrition and electrolyte balance. Feeding is then transitioned to a soy or milk-based diet (Similac's Isomil Advance, Nestle's Nutren Junior, Enfamil's Kindercal) and a bitch-replacement milk (PetAg's Zoologic Milk Matrix 33/40) with vitamins (multivitamin, taurine, and vitamins E and C), and canola oil as a source of fat (figure 23.4). Animals are started on vegetables and fruits after six months of age until they are progressively weaned at 1.5 years. After weaning, diets become completely solid, consisting of romaine and iceberg lettuce, spinach, broccoli, cabbage and a variety of fruits and tuberous roots, including cantaloupe and honeydew melons, bananas, papayas, carrots, pumpkin, cucumbers, apples, pears,

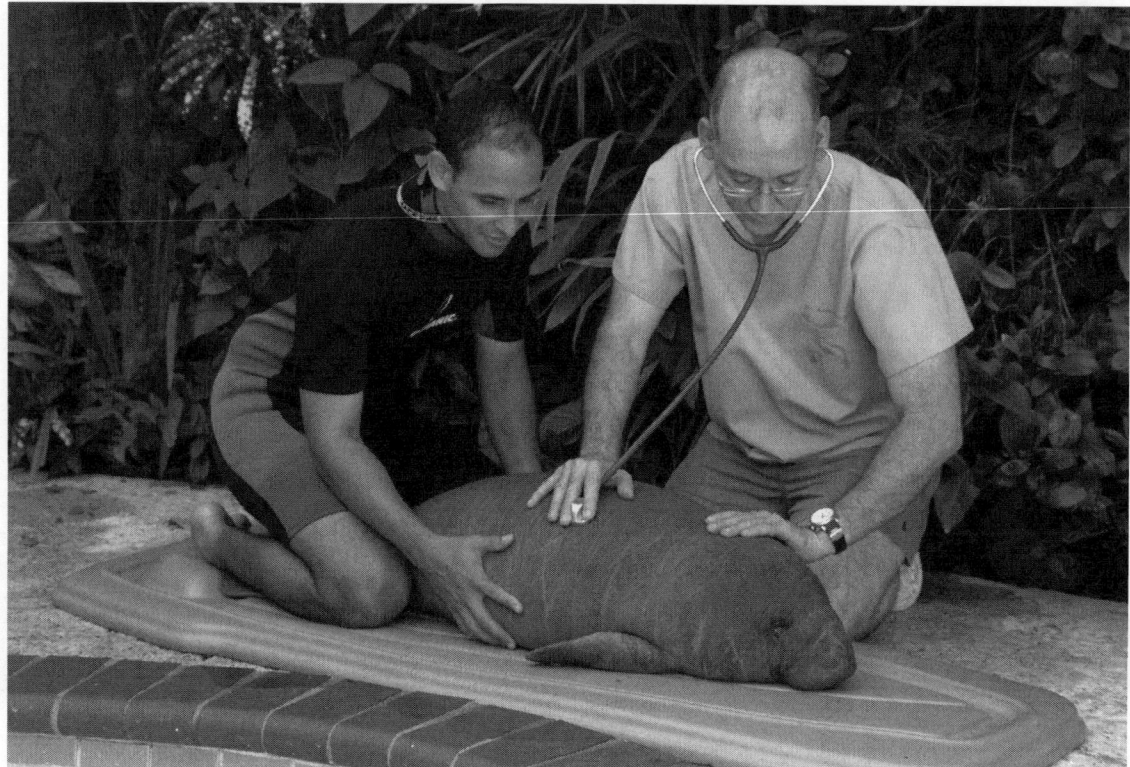

Figure 23.3. Routine medical examination of a West Indian manatee calf in Puerto Rico. (Courtesy of Antonio A. Mignucci-Giannoni.)

yams, and sweet potatoes. Diets are often supplemented with "manatee" biscuits consisting of alfalfa, soybean meal and hulls, kelp, wheat, and a vitamin and mineral mixture, with a nutrient composition similar to that of romaine lettuce.

Successful rehabilitation protocols used at PRMCC include periodic health assessments, first at weekly intervals and then monthly. Morphometric measurements are taken to document developmental progress, and health parameters are documented on an extensive assessment form. Hematology and blood chemistry history of all patients allows the staff to detect and treat medical problems early, comparing values with those for a clinically healthy Antillean manatee. The program has also pioneered the use of a subdermal PIT tag system that incorporates temperature-sensing capabilities (Destron Fearing's LifeChip with Bio-Thermo technology), allowing caretakers to take multiple temperature readings using a hand-held reader (Destron Fearing's DTR4) without having to capture or restrain the manatee.

Puerto Rico's approach to rehabilitated manatee release includes weaning animals from milk to a herbivorous diet through the use of bottom PVC feeders, presentation of seagrasses (*Thalassia testudinum* and *Syringodium fili-*

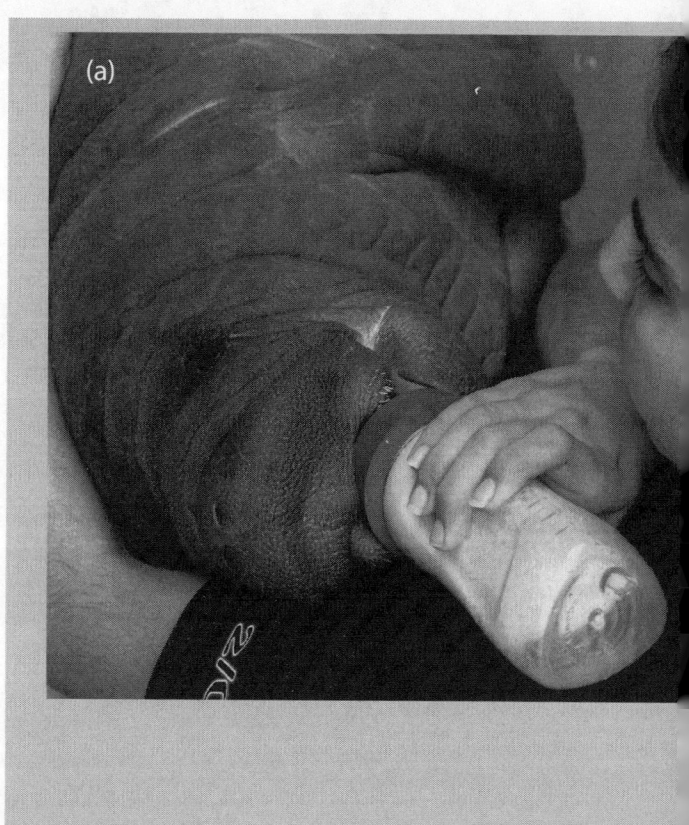

(a)

Figure 23.4a–e (*facing and above*). Bottle-feeding of orphaned West Indian and Amazonian manatees at different rehabilitation facilities in Puerto Rico, Brazil, Mexico, and Peru. (Courtesy of Antonio A. Mignucci-Giannoni, Geraldo Falcão, Benjamín Morales-Vela, and INPA.)

forme) and water hyacinths (*Eichhoria crassipes*) one year prior to release, progressive saltwater acclimation in captivity three months prior to release, and a three- to six-month soft release using a shore-based 15 km² sea-pen with seagrasses to allow for acclimation. In the sea-pen, manatees are weaned from lettuce onto seagrass and offered fresh water from a hose at different intervals during the day. Following release from the sea-pen, manatees are monitored for one year via radio-tracking (figure 23.5) with periodic health assessments, mostly through trained medical behaviors (e.g., blood and urine sampling, physical exams)[17].

A release is considered successful when the manatee is observed feeding on wild vegetation and drinking fresh water from a natural source, such as a river; interacting with other manatees; avoiding watercraft and other human-related hazards; and traveling out of the sea-pen and into adjacent areas; and when it is repeatedly found medically stable and healthy and survives for a year after release. A release is considered unsuccessful if the manatee exhibits excessive weight loss (30–40%), does not meet the preceding criteria, or shows signs of stress or illness.

Three animals have been released under this program and others are scheduled. Moisés, the first successful rehabilitated manatee of the program and considered a symbol for manatee conservation in Puerto Rico, was rescued in 1991 and released in 1994[18]. After 17 years, he is still thriving in the wild. Rafael, released in 2003, survived for just over a year; unfortunately, when found, his body was too decomposed to determine the cause of death. Tuque, released in 2010 is still being monitored through radio-telemetry.

Dominican Republic

A rehabilitation program has been run by the Acuario Nacional in Santo Domingo since 1995, using protocols from Puerto Rico. The Acuario Nacional has rescued two orphaned calves and two ill adults[19]. One of the calves was kept captive for over 12 years and was featured in a long-standing education campaign in the Dominican Republic. A major limitation to this program is the lack of funding to expand facilities and train volunteers, veterinarians, and biologists in current methods of manatee care and husbandry. Future plans include the enhancement of community outreach, partnerships with local and municipal NGOs in rescue efforts, and development of conservation-oriented research projects that should aid in manatee conservation throughout Hispaniola.

Jamaica

Manatees are highly endangered in Jamaica owing to severe poaching and habitat destruction, with a population of fewer than 30 animals[20]. Around 1980 the Natural Resources Conservation Authority initiated a project to manage manatees and hold a small captive population for display, education, and breeding[21]. Four female manatees were introduced into the fenced-off Alligator Hole River in Clarendon; however, by 1984 funding ceased. Repeated unsuccessful attempts were made to manage or release the animals with radio-transmitters. One of the animals died, and three are still trapped in the river[22].

Figure 23.5. Recently released West Indian manatee with satellite transmitter in Puerto Rico, part of the post-release monitoring program. (Courtesy of Marlene Colón.)

Mexico

A rescue and rehabilitation program was initiated in 1995 with the relocation of 17 manatees isolated in a drying lake in Chiapas to a nearby lake with a small manatee population. Under the supervision of the National Subcommittee for Manatee Conservation, partnerships were established between the federal and state governments, oceanaria, zoos, and university programs.

The Acuario de Veracruz was the first to provide care for two orphaned calves in 1998, and since then has rehabilitated another five. These manatees, along with an additional two born in captivity, are on permanent exhibit. In 2001, Xcaret and Dolphin Discovery, two wildlife recreational parks in Quintana Roo, assisted in the rescue of six manatees isolated in a small lagoon at the Centro de Convivencia Infantil in Jonuta, Tabasco. Two of the animals were placed in semi-captivity in the same lagoon and are now cared for by the Centro under the auspices of the municipal government. The remaining manatees were split among the two facilities in Quintana Roo, initially for rehabilitation, and later for exhibition, research breeding, and a "swim with manatee program." In 2001 another young manatee was received in the Centro in Jonuta. In 2002 Dolphin Discovery received a manatee stranded in a lagoon in Tabasco, and Xcaret received in 2005 an additional calf from Jonuta. Four manatees rescued from fishers' nets are exhibited in a lake at Yumká, a park in Villahermosa, Tabasco.

In 2003 El Colegio de la Frontera Sur (ECOSUR) and Africam Safari rescued an orphaned calf in Quintana Roo and transferred it to improvised facilities in Chetumal. The calf was bottle-fed a milk-based formula (PetAg's Multi-Milk) with canola oil and a taurine supplement. After failed attempts to release the calf into the wild it was kept in semi-captivity to increase public education and species conservation.

A total of 26 manatees reside in captivity or semi-captivity, exhausting the current capacity of Mexican rescue and rehabilitation facilities. A new facility dedicated for rescue, rehabilitation, and release is needed.

Belize

Manatee rescue and rehabilitation in Belize is conducted as part of the Belize Marine Mammal Stranding Network, established under the government's Coastal Zone Management Institute (CZMAI) and in partnership with the NGOs Wildtracks and Wildlife Trust. Rehabilitation activities began in 1999 with the rescue of an orphaned calf. The rescue of a second calf led to the formal beginning of Belize's Manatee Rehabilitation Program in 1999.

The majority of the animals rescued are orphaned calves; however, two injured adults have also been rehabilitated. The husbandry protocol includes continual observation until animals are roughly two years old and routine medical checkups. The feeding protocol begins with a milk replacement formula and later introduction of and feeding with local aquatic vegetation (i.e., purslane [*Portulaca* spp.]), water hyacinths, water spinach (*Ipomoea aquatica*), and shoal grass (*Halodule beaudettei*). Once rehabilitated, manatees are transferred to a national protected area, where they are tagged, released, and monitored for an additional two years. Success is achieved when the animals are observed interacting with conspecifics, grazing, gaining weight, and avoiding watercraft and human interactions. If a released animal does not adapt, it is brought back to the rehabilitation facility or kept in a protected sea-pen.

The first rehabilitated manatee was released in 2001 at Gales Point (Manatee) Wildlife Sanctuary, chosen because it is a semi-enclosed coastal lagoon used by manatees year-round[23] and a site for an ongoing tagging project. Two additional calves have been successfully rehabilitated and released.

The program relies on the public to report abandoned or stranded animals to the stranding network and a centralized coordinator. Additionally, the program incorporates a public awareness component targeted at schools in key manatee areas. One limitation has been the lack of specialized veterinarians and limited training for caretakers. Partnerships and liaisons between CZMAI, Wildtracks, Wildlife Trust, the Forest Department, and the Belize Agriculture Health Authority are an invaluable asset. Operating funds are scarce, but the program survives with support from local private sector entities and a dedicated group of volunteers.

The existence of the program has led to increased interest and awareness among the public, a rise in manatee reporting, and an observed decrease in manatee hunting. These factors, together with increased experience, have enhanced the efficacy and success of manatee rehabilitation in Belize.

Colombia

Manatees, threatened by poachers, have been rescued informally in Colombia since the late 1980s. Montoya-Ospina et al.[24] documented a total of 33 manatees in captivity or semi-captivity, including four captive-born. Manatees are also kept in artificial lakes (currently 40 individuals) along the Magdalena, Cauca, Meta, Sinú, and San Jorge river beds. These animals have access to natural forage with limited human contact. In Magangué, manatees are cared for by the NGO Fundación Ecológica Amigos del Manatí, which also provides educational programs to reduce poaching. Captive animals are also held by the Fundación Yamato, the Zoológico de Baranquilla, and Corporación Autónoma Regional de los Valles del Sinú y San Jorge (CVS), under the guidance of the NGO Fundación Omacha.

Many manatees, illegally captured for meat, have been confiscated by the government, including several orphans, and some injured or sick (e.g., cachexia, septicemia) individuals. These cases have provided valuable baseline data on manatee biology in Colombia, including disease processes[25], hematology[26] and population genetics[27].

At present all rehabilitation efforts are coordinated by the Colombian Environmental Ministry and the environmental public corporations in each region, in partnership with NGOs, and under guidelines set by the National Program for the Conservation and Management of Manatees in Colombia[28]. Regular monitoring programs for captive and semi-captive manatees have been established, and a release program with post-release radio-telemetry monitoring has been implemented in the Sinú River by the CVS and Fundación Omacha since 2008.

Venezuela

Manatee rescue and rehabilitation has been conducted since 1985, when a calf was rescued where the Portuguesa and Apure rivers meet[29]. Since then, a few animals have been rescued from poachers, and in collaboration with the Dallas World Aquarium, two females were transported to the United States until a formal rescue and rehabilitation program can be established in Venezuela. In 2005 a calf was rescued at Lake Maracaibo and it is exhibited at the Parque Zoológico Sur. The calf was bottle-fed using a goat milk and Multi-Milk formula and weaned onto iceberg lettuce, chard (*Beta vulgaris*), papaya, and bananas. In 2007 a calf was born to the manatee pair at the Parque Zoológico y Botánico Bararida. The two facilities now holding manatees in Venezuela are both remodeling and expanding their manatee exhibits.

Guyana

Manatees have been kept captive at the Guyana Zoological Park and Botanical Gardens in Georgetown since 1895[30]. They were originally kept to help maintain the irrigation canals, keeping them clear of aquatic vegetation, but rescued animals have been introduced into the wild population. Their reproduction has been very successful; manatees have been exported to zoos and aquariums in Denmark, France, Germany, Japan, Netherlands, Portugal, and Singapore.

Brazil

Field research by the Projeto Peixe-Boi and Fundação Mamíferos Aquáticos to study West Indian manatees on the northeastern Brazilian coast discovered that many of the dead animals were orphaned calves. In response, the Manatee Rescue and Rehabilitation Facility at the Centro Mamíferos Aquáticos, a unit of Instituto Brasileiro do Meio Ambiente e dos Recursos Naturais Renováveis (IBAMA), was created in 1991 on Itamaracá Island, Pernambuco (figure 23.6). Partnerships with members of the Rede de Encalhe de Mamíferos Aquáticos do Nordeste (Northeastern Stranding Network) have allowed for rapid and efficient responses to live strandings, resulting in increased survival rates.

Several adults and 48 orphaned calves have been transported to this facility. Ten resident manatees are housed in three large interconnected pools; the remaining captives will eventually be released. Orphaned calves, housed in eleven pools in a separate area isolated from public viewing, are cared for over approximately 30 months with a soymilk formula and shoal grass. After two years they are fed only seagrass and algae from bottom feeders used for encouraging benthic feeding.

The established release protocol includes general guidelines and criteria for candidates, release sites, the translocation process, public education campaigns, acclimation, and post-release monitoring. The reintroduction of youngsters along the coast of Alagoas, the southernmost known extent of the West Indian manatee's range, began in 1994 with two manatees (Astro and Lua). Animals at this location are of critical concern due to their geographic isolation from the remaining Brazilian manatee population. The desire is for future releases to restock this area to historical numbers. Since 2006 there have been eight reintroductions, totaling 15 animals. All animals are radio-tagged and their health is regularly monitored.

Results from the reintroduction and post-release monitoring have been used to modify and improve captivity care. The conservation strategy developed by the Centro Mamíferos Aquáticos has been successful in minimizing mortality through rescue, rehabilitation, and release. The goal is to increase manatee numbers throughout their historical range along the northeastern coast of Brazil.

Figure 23.6. West Indian manatee rehabilitation facility at Centro Mamíferos Aquáticos in Itamaracá, Brazil. (Courtesy of Geraldo Falcão.)

Amazonian Manatees

Amazonian manatees are traditionally hunted with harpoons. However, they are also hunted by using calves as bait to attract their mothers. Many orphaned calves are kept alive in small tanks, backyard ponds, or bound with rope in shallow water and inadequately fed.

Brazil

There are currently two Amazonian manatee rehabilitation centers in Brazil: the Robin C. Best Aquatic Center at the Laboratório de Mamíferos Aquáticos of the Instituto Nacional de Pesquisas da Amazônia (INPA) in Manaus (Amazonas), and the Eletronorte's Centro de Preservação e Pesquisa de Mamíferos Aquáticos (CPPMA) in the city of Presidente Figueiredo (Amazonas).

INPA pioneered rehabilitation of and scientific research on Amazonian manatees in captivity. Since 1974 INPA, and more recently CPPMA, have rescued more than 250 Amazonian manatees. Most of these were orphans, their mothers having been victims of illegal hunting, the early orphans arriving emaciated and with severe cachexia, dying within days. However, an increase in trained technicians and financial support has substantially improved the survival success of rescued manatees[31].

Young orphaned Amazonian manatees are typically easy to raise if they are not seriously dehydrated, malnourished, stressed, or suffering acute harpoon wounds. Upon rescue, orphans are fed an artificial formula consisting of whole-fat powdered cow milk, water, canola oil, and the supplement Aminomix[32]. This formula is offered every two hours during the daytime, giving a total volume of 2–4 liters/day, depending on the age of the animal. Newborn calves and those in poor health are fed with lactose-free milk, to avoid complications with diarrhea, flatulence, and colic, until at least two months of age (figure 23.7). Calves are also exposed to aquatic plants and vegetables to initiate familiarity with different types of food items and are weaned when they reach 60 kg of body weight. Captive Amazonian manatees are fed over 23 different species of cultivated vegetables, such as cabbage, kale, lettuce, pumpkin, cucumber, tomatoes, carrots, and several other fruits and roots. Floating pellets specially developed for manatees are being tested at INPA/Manaus for acceptance, palatability, and nutritional requirements to reduce the costs of maintenance of Amazonian manatees in captivity and improve their diet quality. Routine health examinations are conducted to monitor captive animals, including biometry and blood (hematology, biochemistry, and serology) and urine analysis[33]. The success of the rehabilitation program of INPA can be measured by the first birth of an Amazonian manatee in captivity in 1998. The mother of the first calf conceived and born in captivity arrived in INPA in 1974, when she was about six months old. She was raised with an artificial milk formula and since 1998 she has been reproducing at a rate of about one calf every three years. Today captive manatees reproduce regularly at INPA and CPPMA.

Although releasing rehabilitated animals is also among the main goals of INPA's Amazonian manatee conservation program, it has been avoided for many years for various reasons. First, manatee slaughter is a common practice, and as manatees raised in captivity are habituated to human contact, released manatees may approach coastal communities and boats and be harpooned. Second, Amazonian manatees travel long distances, at times over 250 km from flooded areas during the high-water period to lakes or to main river channels during receding and low-water periods. These movement patterns require learning that naive captive-raised

Figure 23.7. Amazonian manatee rehabilitation facility at INPA's Laboratório de Mamíferos Aquáticos in Manaus, Brazil. (Courtesy of INPA.)

manatees do not possess, making them susceptible to stranding and hunting. Third, financial limitations have precluded implementation of releases.

However, in March 2008 INPA, together with the Instituto de Pesquisas Ecológicas (IPÊ), started the first phase of a project to release Amazonian manatees raised in captivity. Genetic flow of this species in the Amazon is high, and consequently the populations are genetically well mixed[34], so releasing animals in areas different from their original locality is not a major concern. The first phase of the project aimed to explore potential areas where manatees could be safely released by characterizing habitats used by resident manatees, determining food availability, and identifying local human perception regarding manatees. The second phase of the project focused on an intensive environmental education program within riverine communities, along with the completion of health assessments of possible release candidates. The criteria adopted to choose the animals to be released were being male, subadult, and presenting good health conditions and higher haplotypic similarity with wild manatees of the area. Animals have been released in small groups at different intervals and tracked by radiotelemetry. This is an expensive project, as both trackers and educators must be in the field full-time. Nevertheless, thanks to financial support from Petrobras S.A., to date four captive-raised Amazonian manatees have been released back in the wild, two in March 2008 and two in April 2009.

Colombia

Amazonian manatee calves have been rescued in Colombia after their mothers were butchered. One calf was kept at the Jardín Zoológico de Leticia from 1992 until its death in 2006. In 1998 Fundación Omacha rescued a calf in Puerto Nariño, which was successfully rehabilitated and released with a transmitter in 2002. The Indigenous Ticuna community rescued a calf in 2004; however, it died while receiving medical treatment.

Peru

In the Loreto region of Peru, poaching activities have resulted in orphaned calves, which have been housed in private ponds as pets or in aquaculture stations to control aquatic plants. In 2007 the Ministerio de la Producción (PRODUCE) found a calf and a subadult in the Marañón River and turned them over to local NGOs for rehabilitation. These rescues prompted the creation of the Centro de Rescate Amazónico in conjunction with the Dallas World Aquarium, where nine manatee calves are now in rehabilitation and five have been released. Through this initiative, the Centro Peruano and the regional government jointly manage orphaned or confiscated Amazonian manatees at the same time that an aggressive outreach community effort is made to educate people about the need for conserving this species in this part of the Amazon region.

Conclusions

As the primary threats to sirenians are increasingly human-related, many countries are supporting local populations through various recovery schemes. The rescue and rehabilitation of orphans and injured or ill individuals is a significant tool that supports conservation of sirenians, both locally and regionally. Partnerships between management and science and the incorporation of education and public awareness are critical. Rehabilitation programs around the world continue to evolve and to collaborate with one another, advancing general biological knowledge, improving medical treatments, enhancing protocols for release and adaptation to the wild, and assisting in promoting protection measures to ensure population viability and species conservation.

Acknowledgments

We would like to thank our colleagues for providing information regarding rescue and rehabilitation efforts in their respective countries: L. Añez, J. Bolaños, D. Caicedo, A. Delgado, H. Domínguez, M. Espinoza, L. Figueroa, D. de Freitas, R. Guillén, D. Jiménez, A. Manzanilla, S. Millán, M. Montiel, R. Montoya, D. Morast, E. Mujica, J. Padilla, C. M. Perea, D. Pirela, E. Pugibet, R. Sánchez, M. Silva, J. Truda, F. Trujillo, F. Vanoye, M. Vega, J. Vergara, L. J. Velázquez, Z. Walker, and R. Yalan. We appreciate the assistance from partners within the entire USA Facility Management Team and other individuals working with the federal and state governments, NGOs, and academic institutions. We also appreciate the support, guidance and encouragement offered by C. Beck, R. Bonde, G. Bossart, L. Lefebvre, D. Murphy, J. Powell, J. Reid, R. Turner, J. Valade, and M. Walsh in running, establishing, and providing guidance to many of the programs in Latin America. Our heartfelt gratitude goes to all caretakers, rehabilitators, veterinarians, biologists, resource managers, volunteers, and sponsors who have made the success of manatee rescue and rehabilitation efforts possible in each of these programs.

SECTION III

Strategies for Conservation-Oriented Science

24

Working with Communities for Sirenian Conservation

LEMNUEL V. ARAGONES, MIRIAM MARMONTEL, AND SARITA KENDALL

If manatees and dugongs are to survive, people living in communities where sirenian populations still thrive need to be involved in protecting them. However, among these communities are some of the poorest and most marginalized members of society. And some have traditional, exploitive links to sirenians: for example, Indigenous groups in Amazon communities have been hunting manatees for thousands of years[1]. Most remaining dugong populations are only found in remote areas because these regions have been least exposed to anthropogenic disturbances and thus offer the best conditions for the animals' survival[2].

Historically, people living in remote areas are often socially and economically marginalized and may never have had a voice in major decisions that directly and indirectly affect their lives[3]. As a result, they have been denied resources and rarely earn above a subsistence level. Thus a researcher from outside may have to face an understandable level of bitterness or feelings of discontent when entering communities to work toward sirenian conservation.

Today, in most areas of the world, sirenian hunting has already been banned or at least regulated, but the practice continues in places such as the Torres Strait Islands of Australia and the Amazon basin[4]. Hunting in these areas is important both as a cultural practice and for subsistence.

When it comes to managing natural resources, there are big differences in the financial and organizational capacities of nations to tackle problems and offer solutions. A management strategy involving payments to fishers who capture sirenians incidentally in nets and release them is simply not an option for a developing country, partly because of the lack of financial resources and also because the ability to enforce the law adequately varies from one part of the country to another: some countries have long coastlines (e.g., Thailand, India), others have many islands (e.g., Philippines, Indonesia), and still others have a huge riverine systems (e.g., Brazil, Colombia).

The difficulty of effective patrolling is often exacerbated by poor governmental support for mandated enforcement agencies.

We believe that it is imperative to involve local people and to adopt a grassroots or bottom-up approach to conserving sirenians. There is a social dimension inherent in any conservation effort, and those most likely to be affected by regulatory or management measures should take the lead in developing management plans. Participatory conservation or management establishes a sense of ownership for all interest groups with regard to a specific action, be it a program, a project, or an act of law. This approach provides for consensus building, political sustainability of decisions that influence the lives and interests of various people and entities[5], and social acceptability.

The other common resource management strategy is the top-down approach, which is often difficult to implement. Usually such management intervention requires the banning of certain activities as required by the national or regional governments. A classic example is enacting a national law prohibiting the killing or taking of sirenians, but without adequate consultations with the appropriate stakeholders. In such cases, the implementation or enforcement of laws is usually unsuccessful. Locals may disagree with a prohibitive law, either because it affects their livelihood directly or because of indirect effects due, for example, to bans on setting nets in traditional fishing areas. In some cases, people may not be aware of nearshore conservation issues or, threatened by poverty and a lack of alternative livelihoods, are forced to rely on nonsustainable resource extractions.

Laws that deny access to a traditional and important resource can also breed corruption, with enforcers demanding money or favors in exchange for ignoring an offense. Enforcers such as local police or judges may even pity the fisher or hunter, usually the main breadwinner of the family, and let the offender go free rather than jeopardize the survival of his family. These individuals and the corruptible nature of most systems in a community are reasons why the depletion of coastal resources (including sirenians) continues unabated in most coastal and marine areas[6].

This situation can be changed, especially if the community actively supports hunting controls, becomes involved in the formulation and monitoring of management plans, and invests in becoming stewards of sirenians and other wildlife. In this chapter we show how researchers and conservationists can work with communities to avoid endangering the resource and can facilitate participatory conservation and/or management.

Working in Communities

Communities are one of the most important sources of information on local animals and their habitats. For some time, scientists have acknowledged the importance of local knowledge[7], yet it is often one of the least tapped sources. Local people are a rich source of information on the animals and their habitat and can make important contributions to research and diagnostic studies. A fisher may not know the length of the sirenian gestation period but probably knows where and when mothers with calves can be found.

The importance of interviewing fishers, hunters and those who have local knowledge cannot be overemphasized. In some regions this knowledge is shared freely; in others it may be guarded jealously, especially if people feel their heritage is being exploited by outside professionals with high salaries. Local people should be integrated into conservation processes as early as possible so that they contribute to decisions instead of merely supplying data to others[8].

Once you have enlisted the support of concerned stakeholders such as fishers, other locals, and associated politicians, a conservation program specifically based on their capabilities and cultural context can be developed. Any conservation/management plan will be far more effective if local people are responsible for carrying it through, whether it consists of monitoring populations and habitats, with long-term funding[9], or creating awareness within the community of the threats faced by sirenians.

There is no single formula for ensuring the success of any conservation project. What we describe here are some fundamental ideas and procedures; they may require modification depending on the community. Solutions to most conservation-related problems can be facilitated through a participatory process that engages the community in a specific program, such as a conservation or management plan. Establishing a good rapport with politicians and community or tribal leaders is fundamental, so it may be advantageous to employ stakeholder analysis—this is an analysis tool that considers the principal stakeholders and their interests, perceptions, and expectations[10]. Interview surveys[11] and information found in censuses of the local population can assist in identifying these stakeholders. Singh and Hegde[12] outline important questions used to familiarize every stakeholder with the problems the project is addressing or its stated objectives. The following questions should be considered in any sirenian conservation project:

- Who are the potential beneficiaries of this project?
- Who might be adversely affected?
- Who are the susceptible groups (e.g., often marginalized or easily neglected)?
- Who would be the supporters and opponents of the project?
- What are the relationships among these stakeholders?
- What are the expectations of the different stakeholders of this project?
- What stakeholder interests conflict with the project's goals?

The next step is to find out each stakeholder's influence and importance. Influence refers to how powerful a stakeholder is, while importance refers to those stakeholders whose problems, needs, and interests are being addressed by the project[13]. It is important to know the local political system, who has power over whom, and who has control over resources and the flow of information. This is especially relevant in many tribal areas. Some training materials are available to enhance stakeholder analysis among NGOs and others working with local communities[14].

Researchers should also learn about the perceptions of different stakeholders, especially regarding sirenian conservation or other related project goals. Are stakeholders concerned with declining sirenian populations or deteriorating environments? This can be determined by conducting focal group discussions, or gathering a small group of locals and facilitating a discussion of relevant issues. Educational workshops also can teach locals about the vulnerabilities of the sirenians and the nearshore environment[15] and the relevant legal and economic implications inherent in sirenian conservation[16]. Sometimes conflicts between stakeholders or opposition to a sirenian conservation project are unavoidable, but these conflicts can be resolved by leveling the playing field among the various stakeholders through empowerment of local populations via focal group discussions and education workshops. Good facilitators, who possess the appropriate skills and temperament for resolving conflicts, are critical.

Once there is an understanding of the local key stakeholders and their expectations, it is easier to involve them as active participants. At this stage, consensus building should be pursued through educational workshops and/or focal group discussions, focusing on the importance of protecting sirenians and how this will benefit local communities over the long term.

One of the best ways to obtain information on local perceptions and incorporate people into conservation efforts is a semi-structured interview built around biological, cultural, and conservation themes[17]. This is also a way of getting to know key players such as hunters and local leaders.

A possible sequence could work as follows:

1. Contact people in the community (by walking around, using the radio, calling a meeting, or talking to elders and community leaders) to inform them of the purpose of the research, explaining that some people will be interviewed. Ask for suggestions as to who knows about sirenians.
2. Carry out interviews with hunters, fishers, and leaders and suggest to the interviewees that they join a network of informants to help provide data and work for the conservation of manatees/dugongs. The role of women in sirenian knowledge and conservation should not be underestimated. Although rare, there are cases of female manatee hunters. Women often take part in some of the activities related to hunting, such as flensing and preparing or selling the meat.
3. Invite those interviewed to a workshop to hear the results and identify and discuss the main issues. Set up an information network involving all those interested in collaborating on a voluntary basis. Give each person a data sheet, or a notebook and pencil, even a T-shirt or hat if funds are sufficient, and arrange for them to report in regularly.
4. Keep the network functioning as a source of data and forum for debate, with nonmonetary incentives or meetings to view videos, listen to manatee or dugong sounds, etc., in order to encourage participation. This could lead to choosing the most valuable informants as co-investigators and guardians of the species. Clearly, there can be many variations on this process depending on the local context, but the important thing is that much can be achieved with relatively little funding.

The Cultural Context

Few communities actually depend on sirenians for their income, but a significant number of people living within the distribution range of sirenians have strong cultural ties to the species and derive at least some economic benefit from occasional hunting[18] or tourist activities[19].

Perhaps the most important point to establish is whether the species is seen as a source of food: in most developing countries manatees and dugongs were eaten in the recent past and may still be hunted for food. In some places the hunt has strong cultural connotations; for example, among the Yanyuwa of northern Australia, dugong hunters still have high social status[20]; and some Amazon groups have served manatee meat at girls' puberty ceremonies within the last 20 years[21]. In these cases protection measures leading toward the elimination of hunting must be discussed with respect for local traditions and transition agreements (for example, a hunting quota for special ceremonies). In the Indo-Malay region the dugong, referred to as *duyong*, meaning sea pig, is desecrated but not hunted by the Muslim fishers. Unfortunately, some Christian settlers changed this perspective by highlighting that *duyong* means sea cow and not sea pig.

Other uses of manatee and dugong parts are likely to be secondary to food but may involve the exploitation of animals caught incidentally in nets, for medical purposes[22] or as practical tools (the skin for belts, the shoulder blade for stirring, etc.) Where such uses are based on local belief systems, understanding, tact, and patience are needed in searching for substitute options.

Language and stories can provide insights into the cultural importance of sirenians in a community; for example, there may be vegetation known as "manatee grass" or "manatee flour." Local story themes may include references to dugong hunter ancestors[23], the creation of manatees[24], and star constellations named after the spray thrown up by the thrust of the manatee's tail (Orinoco).

Large manatees in murky water can be intimidating: fishers in Amazon communities often refer to frightening situations when they have seen a "big black thing" like an anaconda. Some identify the "thing" as a manatee, and others paddle off in panic. However, as manatees become more familiar through education and awareness campaigns, people see them as tame. This can foster positive attitudes for conservation by taking away the prestige associated with hunting a fierce animal.

The dangers of sirenian interaction with boats and

fishing nets also need to be understood in terms of local culture as a prelude to finding acceptable solutions. In some areas the animals have become a tourist attraction, a development that may initially be seen as a local income option but that in the longer term could bring even more serious conservation problems unless carefully managed.

The outcomes of local initiatives are often unpredictable, and it is essential to be alert to changing perceptions: for example, an Amazonian community that cared for a manatee juvenile in need of rehabilitation became so attached to the manatee that when it died they wanted to find another; by maintaining close contact with the community it was possible to prevent this (box 24.1). In some areas of Colombia, manatees have been kept in lakes as curiosities or pets, creating a market for young animals. Where legal measures are ineffective, such practices can only be stopped through education to change attitudes.

Education in Communities

A research and conservation process involving a community becomes in actuality an education process[25]. Almost all decisions affecting the future of manatees and dugongs, from the location of a pier to regulations covering fishing nets, have a significant local component. Educational processes can motivate local people to participate in these decisions; if enough are committed to environmental welfare, political leaders and professionals will have to take their views into account.

Flagship species are species that can serve as the representative of environmental conservation in educational processes[26] (see box 24.2). If sirenians are singled out as flagship species or given special status, it is essential to be armed with clear, convincing, and culturally appropriate answers to basic questions such as: Why should I protect manatees/dugongs?

A well-designed education program targeting young people and schools can be a powerful tool in helping to forge conservation values. Teachers in remote areas are usually pleased to have extra materials for science, nature, or environmental education classes and may be willing to negotiate a permanent opening in the curriculum for an educator. This is a long-term commitment best carried out by a local nongovernmental organization (NGO).

Nearly everyone in a community has a child or close relation in school, and pro-conservation attitudes and behavior developed in class will carry over into the home. But educational programs should not be restricted to school children. They should also be customized to reach different segments within a community, especially fishers and hunters. Most of the educational materials (such as booklets) produced with a playful emphasis please children and adults alike and can be spread throughout the community. Well-produced materials, such as calendars or posters with sirenian photos, or including drawings by local inhabitants, will likely be given a special place in a house and will remind people daily of sirenian concerns and issues.

When planning an education campaign, it is important to work with locally appropriate forms of communication and information transmission as well as written materials. In communities with a high percentage of illiteracy, priority can be given to visual and oral communication strategies. As a conservation program develops, meetings and agreements need to be documented and materials produced to support the decision-making process. Ensuring that research results are fed back is an im-

BOX 24.1

Thailand

Kanjana Adulyanukosol, Phuket Marine Biological Center

In Thailand the dugong became a well-known conservation issue soon after a baby dugong was found in the Chao Mai river mouth in Trang Province in southern Thailand in 1993. People came to see the tamed calf and learn about dugongs and seagrass beds. The communities realized that they could increase their income with ecotourism programs involving dugongs and seagrass beds. They also learned how dugongs play an important role in a seagrass ecosystem and consequently used the dugong as a flagship species symbolizing the prohibition of fishing gear that destroyed seagrass. The livelihood of the communities soon began to improve because they earned more income from the local fishery inside the now protected seagrass beds. The communities valued the dugongs because of the success of the community-based seagrass conservation.

BOX 24.2

Communities in the Colombian Amazon

Sarita Kendall

The Manatee Conservation Program (MCP) in Puerto Nariño, Colombia, started with broad-based education in 1998. We used interview surveys as a way to identify and enlist the support of a major stakeholder group, the manatee hunters, in establishing an information and conservation network. MCP gathered information on local knowledge and perceptions of manatees, including threats. At the same time we carried out surveys of feeding areas and collected plant materials that fishers identified as being eaten by manatees. We also rehabilitated an injured calf, named Airuwe (meaning manatee in the Ticuna Indian language), apparently orphaned and caught in a fishing net. Airuwe's feeding time drew and fascinated local crowds, and the experience helped challenge the local perception of manatee as only meat.

This led to a series of community workshops with former hunters and fishers where we discussed the status of manatees in their area. We revealed one crucial fact: that the Amazonian manatee gives birth to one calf approximately every three years. Learning this was enlightening and proved the key to securing a community agreement to stop manatee hunting. The fishers realized that the manatee population had been declining within memory. Only a few even knew of the legislation protecting the species. We also listened to fascinating manatee stories from the Indian fishers. This showed that manatees are deeply embedded in local culture. One story told of trees where grubs grew fat on the leaves and, during a violent thunder storm, broke free and rolled down to a lake, transforming into manatees as they reached the water. This implied an endless supply of manatees. However, they agreed that these trees were almost impossible to find nowadays and that the animals themselves actually reproduce.

We printed anti-hunting bulletins that quoted the laws protecting manatees in Colombia, Brazil, and Peru (this being a frontier area) and distributed the bulletins during workshops to local authorities in more than 30 communities. Whenever an animal was captured, we would interview the fisher concerned, explaining the need to cease hunting and enlisting people to join the network to supply information and look after manatees. A few fishers still continued to hunt. The majority of the fishers agreed that these hunters should be denounced to the authorities, although they believed it was unfair to send them to jail as mandated by law.

When Airuwe celebrated his third birthday we threw a community party. Biscuits were baked in the shape of manatees and everyone shared a huge cake. Other activities included painting and story-writing competitions, a procession through the village with a life-size manatee, and theatre and dance presentations on conservation themes related to the aquatic world. Airuwe's release was planned in consultation with the community fishers. Four of them took turns following him with the aid of VHF radio-telemetry. Everyone in the region asked about his progress, and the sale of manatee wood carvings boomed (Kendall and Orozco 2003).

We lost track of Airuwe after four months, but his role as a manatee ambassador was indispensable. The fishers began to work as co-researchers in the manatee observation/protection program, and other former hunters joined. A total of nine fishers were involved. None earned full-time wages because of the dangers of paying people not to hunt and creating dependence on the program, but most received recognition in kind or in subsistence for the days worked. This program helped convince others, and no manatees were hunted along the Colombian Amazon in 2005. Interestingly, fishers began to insist that there were already more manatees in the area. Using posters and booklets, we disseminated the techniques and results of the research and conservation programs. This reached dozens of schools and communities, including the Indian Reserve Authorities and the Regional Environmental Authority, which became a supporter of the MCP.

---

portant part of this process[27]. Maps made by local people are also useful: the drawing of the map brings everyone into the discussion, and the map itself can provide information on areas where conflicts between sirenians and humans occur as well as basic data on distribution and feeding and breeding zones.

The best way to develop appropriate materials and activities is to involve local teachers, students, and stakeholders in creating culturally appropriate conservation messages, designing posters, and choosing illustrations. Some of the following materials and activities can be useful for raising awareness:

- creating posters, videos, flyers, booklets, postcards
- taking advantage of local festivals to present songs, puppets, drama, dance, story telling
- holding special days devoted to sirenians with a parade, games, and activities for children
- developing local crafts including wood carvings, paintings, jewelry
- making sirenian-shaped biscuits, chocolates
- building a statue or mural dedicated to the local sirenian species

In Brazil and Colombia, NGOs and government organizations have sponsored and carried out manatee education and awareness-building campaigns. Some of these are long-term, permanent programs involving local people and schools; some are one-time campaigns linked to a particular phase of research. The manatee program in Puerto Nariño, Colombia, has made community education a key element for conservation: special aquatic days are celebrated, and education materials include manatee booklets, posters, and videos as well as an Interpretation Center where a statue of a full-size manatee is hung. Campaigns cover some schools in Leticia and other Colombian cities and also include workshops in communities along the Colombia-Peru border.

Likewise, manatee programs in Brazil—the NGO Associação dos Amigos para Proteção ao Peixe-boi da Amazônia (AMPA), Mamirauá Institute, and the rehabilitation facility Centro de Preservação e Pesquisa de Mamíferos Aquáticos (CPPMA)—have employed awareness-building and education strategies as part of overall conservation efforts, with education work in schools and communities and the diffusion of information through booklets and posters. Mamirauá has produced two educational booklets about manatees, one including drawings by local school children. These have provided very good feedback, as the children see their work and their art depicted and help spread the word about conservation. Mamirauá has also included manatees (and other water creatures) in theatrical productions performed by community and urban youth involved in the Environmental Education Group, staging plays in several communities and towns in the zone surrounding the Mamirauá Sustainable Development Reserve. Manatees have also been depicted in handcraft articles made by local inhabitants, becoming a new source of nonconsumptive income.

Conflicts

A conservation or management plan forged through community agreements is likely to be robust and long-lasting[28]. However, if there is a serious short-term risk to sirenians, immediate action may be needed: for example, if one hunter is illegally killing several animals a year, it may be necessary to report him to the authorities. This kind of action can make an outside researcher very unpopular; support from other hunters or former hunters should be sought so that the "outsider" does not stand alone and jeopardize the whole program.

Another problem the researcher may face is how to obtain samples and other sirenian material in the con-

---

BOX 24.3

When Communities Are Not Consulted

Miriam Marmontel

Between 1980 and 1984, 42 manatees from the Amanã region (upper Solimões River, Amazonas state, Brazil) were captured by local inhabitants of the Lake Amanã, transported several hundred kilometers downriver, and introduced into a reservoir created by one of the smallest (86 km^2) hydroelectric dams in the world (Curuá Una, 70 km from the city of Santarém in the eastern part of the Amazon basin). The reason for the operation was to use the animals as aquatic-weed-control agents, as plants were proliferating and creating problems with the dam's turbines. Curuá Una was also considered a safe place, since locals had no tradition of hunting manatees. Those animals were radio-tagged and monitored for approximately two years uninterruptedly, until the project was terminated.

At the time of the operation, communication with the local communities was not common practice, so contacts were made with only a few individuals. Conversations were not held with the communities on the purpose of the project and its implications, nor were follow-up visits conducted to provide feedback on what happened to the animals. This created mixed feelings among the people in Amanã, involving those who were hired and not hired to help in the process. Locals also were skeptical about what happened to the animals.

BOX 24.4

Volunteer Wardens Return Manatee Calves to the Natural Environment

Miriam Marmontel

The Brazilian Institute for the Environment and Renewable Natural Resources (IBAMA) has instituted the position of volunteer wardens. By offering capacity-building courses and empowering individuals from local communities to approach, educate, and write notifications to people conducting illegal acts within the boundaries of the Mamirauá and Amanã sustainable development reserves, several community members have been implementing the law locally. The reserves are large areas where law enforcement agencies cannot be present at all times, or at the time of an urgent necessity.

Two of the volunteer wardens have demonstrated commitment to manatee conservation by releasing manatee calves back to the wild. In late July of 2006, an agent from the Aranapu-Barroso sector of the Mamirauá Reserve learned about a manatee calf that had been entangled in a fishing net in a nearby lake and brought back to the community. As only a short time had elapsed, and the animal was not hurt, the warden took it back to where it had been caught and waited for two hours until the animal found its mother. In early September another warden, from Jubará community, also released a small manatee calf close to an island on the Japurá River, where it had become entangled.

---

text of a conservation program. Local people will be only too aware of mixed messages, such as "we would prefer you not to hunt any animals, but if you do, then please give us the organs/bones/tissue samples, etcetera." Paying for such materials is even more problematic and could seriously undermine conservation efforts. However, if paying for samples is unavoidable, make sure that the parties involved understand the necessity and importance of collecting some samples—that is, for scientific examination (e.g., genetic analysis).

When working with communities, a researcher should expect to be met with skepticism. Often local communities in the Amazon show some reservations toward foreigners or anyone who is not from the region, a legacy from past projects that created much expectation but delivered very little. A significant amount of time and effort will probably be necessary to build trust and confidence. Skepticism can be overcome with time, especially if one is attentive to important details (box 24.3).

Some things to remember: do not make promises you cannot keep, do ask permission to take pictures in the community, and bring back photos to give to people. Contribute food to communal meetings, and most important, become a part of people's lives by sharing your experiences with them. Furthermore, remember to come back and give the community some return on what you have learned and accomplished. Working with a community involves a commitment. Do not expect to obtain very strong and positive results and gather reliable information simply by visiting a community once.

When discussing long-term goals in a community, difficult questions are likely to come up. For example, if one of the goals is the recovery or stabilization of a sirenian population, hunters may ask when they will be able to hunt again. Honesty and tact are needed here: one approach would be to explain that this is a continuing process which must respond to changes along the way and that the community will have to decide whether a renewal of hunting can be considered in the future.

As mentioned earlier, the introduction of new legal measures is frequently a conflict. One of the most commonly used management strategies is the creation of nature reserves or parks, often without taking into account the views of communities. If local people lose control of part of their territory and resources, they are likely to oppose such reserves. On the other hand, if they are consulted and offered alternative income options, such as employment as guides, rangers, or co-researchers, they may support the reserve (box 24.4).

Summary

Despite the difficulties, working with communities can also be very satisfying. When a sense of common purpose develops and local people take pride in the conservation process, the rewards are great. Perhaps the most important guidelines are to listen patiently and to work with humility instead of imposing outside values.

25

Guidelines for Developing Protected Areas for Sirenians

HELENE MARSH AND BENJAMÍN MORALES-VELA

Why We Need Protected Areas for Sirenians

The range of sirenians spans almost 90 subtropical and tropical countries and territories on five continents. Most of these countries are classified as less developed. The purpose of this chapter is to assist managers and scientists with their responsibilities in these countries to work with stakeholders to design protected areas that will reverse the declines in sirenian populations.

Because of their high cultural value and political profile, sirenians can be of great value as flagship species for more broadly based conservation initiatives including protected areas that aim to conserve biodiversity in general rather than sirenians specifically. Flagship species are "charismatic species which serve as a symbol and rallying point to stimulate conservation awareness and action"[1]. In Japan, for example, a sirenian was used as a flagship species to prevent an offshore landing facility being built in dugong habitat[2].

Sirenians can also serve as umbrella species ("a species whose conservation confers protection on a large number of naturally occurring co-species"[3]). For example, the Chetumal Bay Manatee Protected Area in Mexico consists of 281,000 hectares, of which 101,000 hectares of wetlands, mangroves, savannas, and tropical forests protect many aquatic and terrestrial species in addition to manatees.

The use of flagship or umbrella species as shortcuts to designing protected areas for biodiversity conservation is controversial[4], and the overall conservation outcomes are likely to be stronger if sirenian conservation is nested into more broadly based biodiversity conservation initiatives. In the Yucatán Peninsula in Mexico, the UNESCO biosphere reserve of Sian Ka'an is a good model of biodiversity conservation that has strong community participation and support. This reserve protects aquatic mammals including manatees in Ascension and Espiritu Santo bays and is within Chetumal Bay, a natural wetland corridor in the south of Quintana Roo (box 25.1).

BOX 25.1

Chetumal Bay Manatee Protected Area in Mexico

Chetumal-Corozal Bay provides an example of the challenge of using protected areas to conserve sirenians in developing countries. This bay is the natural border between Mexico and Belize (see figure 4.1). It is an important area for manatee conservation (Morales-Vela et al. 2000), with the highest concentration of manatees in the Yucatán Peninsula (Morales-Vela et al. 2003). Chetumal Bay Manatee Protected Area (CHMPA) was created in 1996 by the state government of Quintana Roo, Mexico, as the first protected area dedicated to manatee conservation in the country. The CHMPA includes over 101,000 hectares of mangroves, wetland, savannas, and hydrological basins adjacent to the bay. Two years later, in 1998, the Belize government declared the southern part of the bay a manatee sanctuary.

By the time of this writing, budgetary and management constraints have compromised the effectiveness of this conservation attempt. There are strong pressures to develop economic activities inside and around the CHMPA, and the few attempts to coordinate conservation activities between Belize and Mexico have failed. The government administrative arrangements limit both enforcement and the participation of local communities (Morales-Vela 2004). In addition, nongovernmental organizations (NGOs) no longer have a local presence in the south of Quintana Roo. The Mexican federal academic and research institution ECOSUR and the NGO Sian Ka'an are currently interested in evaluating the potential of a co-management process for conservation with the state government of Quintana Roo.

Although protected areas are certainly not the complete answer to sirenian conservation[5], they are a significant tool in the conservation toolbox that has been adopted by many countries. In their reviews of dugong conservation, Marsh et al.[6] documented protected areas with the potential to conserve dugongs in 14 countries plus plans for additional protected areas (and their list is not complete). Four countries had protected areas specifically designed for dugongs. Quintana-Rizzo and Reynolds[7] documented at least 46 protected areas with the potential to conserve Antillean manatees in 13 countries in the Caribbean region.

But not all of these protected areas are effective; too many are "paper parks"; protected areas that exist in name only, without having a measurable impact on conservation. Aquatic reserves are of limited value without the backup of firm management guidelines. As Hooker and Gerber[8] have pointed out, scientists and managers need to become less accepting of having areas designated as sanctuaries without tangible protection.

Types of Protected Areas

The World Conservation Union's Guidelines for Protected Area Management Categories[9] defines a protected area as "an area of land and/or sea especially dedicated to the protection and maintenance of biological diversity, and of natural and associated cultural resources, and managed through legal or other effective means." Under the IUCN definition, there are six categories of protected areas ranging from strict nature reserves or wilderness areas to managed resource protected areas ("protected areas managed mainly for the sustainable use of natural ecosystems"). Ecosystem-scale networks of protected areas are increasingly favored over small, isolated reserves. Such networks are vital for sirenians because individuals routinely move over distances of hundreds of kilometers and occasionally more[10].

Because sirenians variously use coastal, estuarine, and riverine environments, protected areas for sirenians are collectively classified as aquatic protected areas. Protected areas for dugongs and some populations of Antillean and West African manatees also come under the more specialized category of marine protected areas, about which there is much theoretical literature[11] as well as a body of publications offering practical advice[12].

For an area to be considered as an aquatic protected area, protective management arrangements must be consistent with one of the six categories of protected areas defined by the World Conservation Union. Not all protected area agencies or other organizations have assigned IUCN categories to their sites. Indeed, the 34,036 protected areas without IUCN categories cover 3.6 million km^2 and represent a significant proportion of the global conservation estate[13].

Aquatic ecosystems may also receive some protection under management arrangements such as nature reserves, water catchment zones, conservation agreements, protective covenants, forest reserves, or international designations such as World Heritage or Ramsar Wetland sites. Whether the protection afforded by such arrangements is adequate to conserve sirenians must be evaluated on a case by case basis. For example, Refugio de Vida Silvestre Bocas del Polochic in Guatemala is a Ramsar site that provides protection to numerous wetlands and wildlife species, including the Antillean manatee, but the potential development of mines in the northeastern corner of the Lago de Izabal near the town of El Esto is of concern. Two mining companies propose to deforest an area of more than 300 km^2. The wastewater from one operation is to be dumped directly into the protected area. Though the owners of that company argue that the project will not have a significant effect on manatees and their habitats, there is great concern among environmental agencies and scientists about the effects of the mine, especially from sediment run-off after heavy storms[14].

It is not necessary for a protected area to be established specifically to protect sirenians. Grech et al.[15] showed that the network of ecosystem-scale marine protected areas and other management arrangements in the Great Barrier Reef World Heritage Area since 2003 protects a high proportion of high density dugong habitats, much more than the dedicated Dugong Protection Areas established in part of the region in 1997[16]. An important proportion of high density manatee habitats along the coast of Yucatán Peninsula in Mexico is protected by a network of state and federal protected areas (including biosphere reserves)[17].

In the following section we outline the steps required to develop an effective protected area to conserve dugongs or manatees. These steps are not presented in strict order of implementation, and some will proceed simultaneously.

Steps to Developing an Effective Protected Area to Conserve Dugongs or Manatees

Review the Relevant Background Information

Aquatic protected areas are typically established to increase the likelihood of sustainable fisheries, biodiversity conservation, species conservation, and the preservation of cultural values or some combination of these factors[18]. The required background information will, of course, depend on whether manatee or dugong conservation is the major rationale for, part of the rationale for, or a serendipitous outcome of the establishment (or upgrading) of a protected area.

The background information required to establish an effective protected area must include:

1. Ecological information on the distribution and abundance of the target sirenian and its habitat (especially on critical habitats, such as breeding areas or movement corridors).
2. Information on the nature, distribution, and relative importance of threats to the sirenian population, such as incidental take (e.g., drowning in gillnets, vessel strikes); directed take for meat, oil, or amulets; damage to habitat (e.g., from bottom trawling, land reclamation, or pollution, including land-based pollution).
3. Social, cultural, and economic information about the people causing the threats and others who will be affected by the establishment of the protected area (especially those living in the area).
4. Knowledge of the relevant geopolitical boundaries, such as the boundaries between waters under federal and state jurisdiction and the clan boundaries of local and Indigenous peoples.
5. The long-term economic and development aspirations of relevant governments; such aspirations are typically incompatible with local community conservation actions.

It is also important to review information on the legal protection afforded to manatees or dugongs in the area of interest, the legal status of the protected area if one already exists, and whether the country is signatory to relevant international conventions, such as the Convention on Biological Diversity, the Protocol on Specially Protected Areas and Wildlife (SPAW Protocol) in the Wider Caribbean Region, and the Convention on Migratory Species (Bonn Convention), or is already listed under the Ramsar Convention on Wetlands or the World Heritage Convention[19]. The protection of a species or site by an international convention may increase the potential for funding from international NGOs.

Both independent experts and local people can be extremely valuable in gathering this information. As Preen[20] points out, in countries with limited financial resources but extensive artisanal fisheries, useful information on the distribution of dugongs or manatees can be obtained by interviewing coastal peoples, especially local fishers. Hines et al.[21] provide a practical example of this approach for dugongs in Thailand. Aragones et al. and Ortega-Argueta et al.[22] outline techniques for interview surveys. Marsh and co-workers[23] are using large satellite photographs downloaded from Google Earth and color-coded stick-on dots to record information provided by Indigenous community members in northern Australia about the distribution and relative abundance of dugongs and seagrass. If funding is available, interview surveys can be supplemented by aerial surveys for a more comprehensive and unbiased picture[24]. A community GIS can be used to store the community information along with the western science information obtained from aerial surveys.

Technical experts are notoriously reluctant to provide an expert opinion not based on robust science, but they can often be persuaded to provide relevant advice if the confidence associated with the information on which their advice is based is also recorded on an agreed scale[25]. Involving stakeholders can be an effective method of garnering community support for the protected area, especially if the way in which this input is used is made explicit in follow-up meetings[26]. Because protected areas are spatial constructs, it is particularly useful if all this information can be stored for analysis and visualization in a geographical information system.

The information available will inevitably be incomplete, even for well-studied systems. It is important to proceed without perfect knowledge. Arguments to postpone action to gather further information will inevitably be used as a delaying tactic by those stakeholders who consider their interest best served by not establishing a protected area[27].

Work with Local Communities so That the Perspectives of All Stakeholders Are Understood

Protected areas are usually established as part of a precautionary approach to protecting biodiversity. The Rio Declaration[28] endorsed the need for this approach to environmental protection, recognizing that when threats of serious or irreversible damage exist, a lack of full scientific certainty should not be not used as a reason to postpone cost-effective measures that prevent environmental degradation. Nonetheless, it is not sufficient for threats to be recognized by scientists and planners. Local people need to be educated about existing and potential threats to the dugongs or manatees and their ecosystem, including information about risks and uncertainty. Community outreach about the threats

Table 25.1. Major motivations of key stakeholders involved in the development of a protected area.

Stakeholder	Major motivation
Protected area management agency	Addressing their public mandate
State and federal government	Addressing effective governance
Commercial sector	Economic profit
NGOs	Conserving public goods
Researchers	Scientific robustness of protected area allowing for uncertainty in the data
Local community members	Continued sustainability of their livelihoods and lifestyles, economic profit

Source: McNeely 2001.

that are prompting the management intervention is a vital part of the protected area planning process that is often neglected. If the risks are not widely understood by the local people, the need for action will not be appreciated, and the initiative to establish a protected area may be resisted.

Local problems and proposed solutions have to be owned by many people in both the community and managing agencies, not just a few champions. An initiative must survive changes in personnel, management authorities, and the local NGO presence. For example, the Maza Wildlife Management Area in the Western Province of Papua New Guinea was one of the most successful early examples of working with local people to conserve dugongs. Unfortunately, this initiative lapsed after funding ceased and its champion (Brydget Hudson) left Papua New Guinea. However, a workshop held in 2009 demonstrated community enthusiasm for reconstituting the Maza Wildlife Management Area, even though it had not been actively managed for some 25 years[29].

It is important to understand the situation from the perspectives of the relevant stakeholders, whose priorities are almost certainly very different from those of the scientists, managers, and NGOs (table 25.1). Local people may be worried about their livelihoods and perhaps their cultural identity and/or food security if hunting dugongs or manatees is still a significant part of their culture. Because local people often distrust government officials, involving researchers who are perceived by the local community as independent helps considerably. Researchers who have worked in the region for a long time and are trusted by the locals can be particularly effective[30].

Involve Local Communities in Negotiating Clear Goals and Objectives

It will be impossible to evaluate the effectiveness of the protected area (see later discussion) if the management goals and objectives are not clear and transparent. A goal is a broad statement about what the protected area is trying to achieve, whereas an objective is a more specific measurable statement about what must be accomplished to attain a related goal. Objectives (and preferably agreed targets) need to be specific. It is critical to disaggregate broad, high-level goals and to divide them into clear, measurable objectives. For example, the goal "to conserve manatees" is imprecise. Is the objective population maintenance or recovery? If recovery, to what historical population level and over what time frame?

Given the practical difficulties and expense of monitoring the population sizes of sirenians using techniques such as tagging and aerial surveys, it may be more practical to frame conservation objectives in terms of the proportion of high quality habitat in a country that is to be protected by various management arrangements[31].

Goals and objectives should be developed in a participatory manner to reflect a balance of the needs and priorities of all the stakeholders. The goals should not be limited to conservation outcomes. If the protected area is to be viable in the long term, then social, economic, cultural, and management feasibility goals are as important as ecological and conservation goals and objectives.

Negotiate Ecologically, Culturally, and Socially Relevant Boundaries

Dugongs and manatees operate at ecological scales of hundreds of kilometers[32]. In many localities, resident sirenians cross jurisdictional boundaries every day, so it is highly desirable to coordinate management across jurisdictions at both an ecological scale relevant to the species and a cultural scale relevant to stakeholders. Community-based management operates on a local scale, reflecting the interests of the community. For example, Indigenous stakeholders in Australia are primarily interested in dugongs in the sea country of their clan group, and most community-based management plans are being developed at that scale[33]. Management, on the other hand, usually functions at geopolitical scales, which are determined by the boundaries of nations and/or their component states or provinces.

There have been very few attempts to co-ordinate management across these different scales, particularly within national waters. The Convention on Migratory Species offers a structure for negotiating transboundary coordination. Some of the dugong's range states negotiated a memorandum of understanding under this Convention in 2007[34]. Transboundary protected areas have the potential to be effective conservation tools in many parts of the ranges of dugongs and manatees and should be considered if appropriate and practicable.

In the Caribbean region, the Mesoamerican Barrier Reef System Project was funded by the Global Environment Facility and the governments of Belize, Guatemala, Honduras, and Mexico to enhance protection and coordinate regional policies for the conservation and sustainable use of this reef system. One of its four components concerns planning, management, and monitoring of the constituent marine protected areas. This project has the potential to be an effective regional transboundary coordination initiative to conserve the manatee population and the coastal ecosystems in the Caribbean.

Develop Robust Design Principles

The design principles for each protected area should be developed to address its goals and objectives explicitly. Operational principles that address agreed biophysical, social, cultural, and management feasibility criteria should be developed and customized for each area and weighted as to their relative importance with stakeholder input. Stakeholder agreement on a final design is more likely to be reached if the design principles are negotiated first and released for stakeholder comment before the planning process; that is, including at least a two-stage public participation program is important. The reaction of individual stakeholders to the detailed plan will be governed by the extent to which it threatens their livelihoods or otherwise restricts their activities (table 25.1).

Fernandes et al.[35] list the operational principles that were developed for the 2003 rezoning of the 344,400 km² Great Barrier Reef Marine Park. Dugong protection was considered as part of the biophysical operational principle to "ensure that no-take areas represent identified dugong habitat areas summing to about 50% of all high-priority dugong habitat." The actual high priority dugong habitat chosen for the no-take areas was selected in conjunction with the other biophysical operating principles, such as to "protect uniqueness: include biophysically special unique places," and social, economic, and cultural operating principles, including "consider all costs and benefits: ensure that the final selection of no-take areas recognizes social costs and benefits." The fact that the overall area being planned was very large enabled such choices to be made. In a plan developed for a small area there will be fewer choices.

The final plan should aim to be ecologically robust and socially, culturally, and economically viable. This goal is more likely to be achieved if the design principles integrate the biophysical, socioeconomic, and cultural elements, rather than emphasizing the biophysical principles, as was done in the Great Barrier Reef Representative Areas Program[36].

It may not be feasible to achieve all the desired goals and objectives in the first plan. The aim is to "win the war not the battle." If the protected area is seen to be successful by local stakeholders, it can be upgraded later. When the Great Barrier Reef Marine Park was first zoned in the 1980s, only 4.5% of the marine park was protected in no-take areas, and more than 80% of this area protected only one habitat type in the ecosystem—coral reefs. In contrast, the 2003 zoning plan protected 33% of the park in no-take areas, and the network contained at least 20% of each of the park's bioregions[37].

Reserve design software is available to assist in decision making[38]. The software allows multiple data sets and multiple objectives and social costs to be considered simultaneously to derive various relatively optimal reserve designs. The applicability of this approach depends on the size of the planned protected area and the amount of required data available in digital format.

Build Community Capacity and Alternative Livelihoods

Local people whose homes and livelihoods are threatened by a protected area typically have nowhere to go. An effective protected area needs to provide sufficient resources for community consultation and education to enable park managers to understand community aspirations[39]. When such resources are not available, the consequences can be serious. The history of violent conflict between park rangers and fishers in Komodo National Park in Indonesia indicated that the initial management plan did not adequately reflect the needs of local communities. The situation was exacerbated by poor communication between the park authority and local communities. The fishers were so poor that they had few alternatives but to opt for destructive fishing, and their plight was not recognized by the authorities[40].

Obtain Funding and Expertise for Implementation and Enforcement

Planning a protected area is much easier than implementing the plan; implementation requires resources and community capacity. The resources required for long-term implementation should ideally be available before planning is completed to capitalize on the momentum generated during the planning phase and as an incentive during the negotiation process.

In many developing countries, the effectiveness of a protected area is seriously compromised by the lack of funding available for enforcement of the rules and the prevention of illegal activities such as drug dealing. Quintana-Rizzo[41] reported that drug dealers are appropriating land for housing in aquatic protected areas in Guatemala and that some local people in Costa Rica and Nicaragua alternate between hunting manatees and selling drugs.

Effective enforcement of the rules of a protected area is essential to ensure stakeholder compliance. Local people may see working as rangers for the protected area as an attractive (but limited) employment option. The benefits of offering such employment have to be weighed against the cultural challenges of requiring a local person to police the actions of neighbors. Appropriate training and capacity building are essential.

Develop and Implement an Interactive and Culturally Relevant Education Plan

It is logistically impossible to enforce all the management arrangements for a protected area, and education is the most important tool for ensuring stakeholder compliance. As iconic megafauna with considerable public appeal in most cultures, dugongs and manatees are eye-catching features of outreach programs for any area in which they occur.

It is important to identify the audiences critical to the success of the protected area and to develop a plan for communicating with each of them (and to measure the effectiveness of this communication). The audience will include local fishers and their families, including school-age children, responsible environmental agencies, NGOs, and other donors. These audiences need to be prioritized as a basis for rationalizing the resources available for education. For each audience, consider its preferred method of receiving information, which will depend on their technical capacity and access to appropriate infrastructure. Does the target audience prefer to read information or listen to radio or television? Do they have access to the Internet? Do they gather at meetings and when are these meetings scheduled? Well-targeted products and media mechanisms are required. Those involved in outreach programs need to be capable of engendering public respect due to their skills in listening to, discussing, and communicating ideas, concepts, and concerns and translating these communications into action.

Measure the Effectiveness of the Protected Area

Attention is increasingly focused on measuring the effectiveness of conservation initiatives, including protected areas, and the IUCN has developed a useful management effectiveness framework[42]. The Conference of the Parties of the Convention on Biological Diversity[43] calls for signatories to develop and adopt methods, standards, criteria, and indicators for evaluating management effectiveness and governance. "Ensuring Effective Management" was a theme at the First International Marine Protected Areas Congress in October 2005. At the second such meeting in 2009, a workshop attended by sirenian experts identified features of protected areas with the potential to reduce the risk to sirenians in developing countries (see box 25.2).

Pomeroy et al.[44] have written a guidebook for managers and other conservation practitioners that outlines a process and methods for evaluating the effectiveness of marine protected areas. This guidebook is full of practical ideas that have been field-tested. The evaluation is based on social and ecological indicators that allow managers to measure effectiveness of management in attaining the goals and objectives. The flexible approach can be used in many types of aquatic protected areas, including multiple use areas and no-take zones.

Effective evaluation of management requires the careful selection of ecological, socioeconomic, and cultural indicators of success. Stakeholders as well as managers need to be involved in identifying what should be monitored and evaluated. Marsh et al.[45] discuss some of the problems in identifying robust ecological indicators of management effectiveness for dugongs. However, the approach they outline may be too expensive for developing countries. Regular interviews of fishers, asking carefully designed questions about where and when they last saw manatees or dugongs might be more appropriate. Such questions should be designed with the assistance of an experienced social scientist. If such an approach is used, it is vital that information is transferred back to the community in an accessible format.

A necropsy program potentially allows managers to evaluate their initiatives by tracking the relative importance of the various sources of mortality (assuming that the carcasses are equally available[46]). Marsh et al.[47] have pointed out that anthropogenic mortality targets that are

> **BOX 25.2**
>
> ### Key Features for Protected Areas
>
> A four-day workshop (with between 25 and 35 participants from 16 countries) at the International Marine Conservation Conference held in Washington, D.C., in May 2009 identified the following features of protected areas with the potential to reduce the risk to sirenians in developing countries:
>
> 1. Community involvement that incorporates local knowledge.
> 2. Management planning that reflects the legal framework and includes goals specific to sirenians.
> 3. Legal frameworks with political will to implement the protected area.
> 4. Strong education and outreach programs.
> 5. Protected area networks large enough to protect ecological processes and include a high proportion of the sirenian population throughout the year.
> 6. Long-term funding adequate to implement management planning.
> 7. Co-management involving government, NGOs, local communities, and researchers.
> 8. Effective enforcement of management plans.
> 9. Capacity building, including succession planning for all partners in the co-management arrangement: government, NGOS, community, and researchers.
> 10. Management informed by active research programs.
> 11. Alternative livelihoods for those community members affected by the implementation of the management plan.

low enough for a population to recover may be more feasible to estimate and monitor than recovery targets.

Practice Adaptive and Collaborative Management

Adaptive management is iterative—learning by doing, systematically trying new initiatives, evaluating the results, and further improving management practices in response to the evaluation process[48]. In a protected area context, adaptive management results in improved effectiveness and increased progress toward achieving the goals and objectives. Adaptive management has been criticised as being government-led and bureaucratic[49], but collaborative adaptive management actively engages all key stakeholders in the processes of goal setting, planning, management, enforcement, and evaluation[50].

Conclusions

Protected areas will make a significant difference to sirenian conservation efforts if they are based on the best available information, are culturally appropriate, and are developed together by the key stakeholders, NGOs, and managing agencies. Most successful initiatives are an iterative mixture of approaches variously initiated by governments, NGOs, and the community. Managing agencies and NGOs have an important role in providing statutory support, capacity building, and resources, but community initiatives are an essential prerequisite for community ownership and cooperation. Effective intergovernmental collaboration in transborder protected areas will be important in promoting efficient regional conservation actions for sirenians.

Acknowledgments

This chapter was written while the senior author was a visiting scientist in John Reynolds's group at Mote Marine Laboratory, Sarasota, Florida. We thank John Reynolds and Ester Quintana-Rizzo for useful discussions and James Cook University for providing study leave.

26

The Role of Law in Protecting Sirenians and Their Habitat in Developing Nations

WYNDYLYN M. VON ZHAREN

As seen throughout this book, challenges to sirenian conservation are formidable and complex. Unfortunately, legal regimes have not kept pace with the increasing need to conserve and protect marine ecosystems. Since developing nations have within their jurisdiction over 90% of the coastal waters that lie within international 200-nautical-mile exclusive economic zones (EEZs), it is imperative that their environmental laws and enforcement thereof ensure effective management strategies to protect living marine species[1].

The legal system plays a key role in addressing conservation of these species. International environmental law is the principal means by which the community of nations builds and expresses international consensus on environmental and development challenges. Thus, the role of law from an international perspective must be based on the obligations of members of the international community. International law provides the framework upon which a nation can build its own environmental protection regime.

National environmental law is the most effective instrument for translating environmental and development policies into action. Statutes, regulations, and the judiciary are key mechanisms for ensuring legal effectiveness of conservation strategies. Analysis must be made of the role of law in defining norms for a society and assisting developing nations to be cohesive in solving their environmental problems and protecting sirenians. This is particularly challenging when many developing nations traditionally have not had a culture of utilizing legal systems, the law, and public advocacy to resolve disputes.

Because international law can be an effective template from which nations may promulgate their own national strategy, this chapter begins with an overview of a representative sampling of the major international legal regimes that aim, among other goals, to protect the integrity of the marine environment in general and living marine species in particular. Following this is a discussion of the role of law in the management and lessening of anthropogenic threats to sirenians and their habitat in those nations that have less developed legal protection strategies.

Representative Samplings of Existing International Legal Regimes

International attempts at protecting living marine species are embodied in a prodigious number of international, regional, and nation-state regimes. In general, most of these regimes have proved ineffective in slowing the clear-cutting of the world's oceans and in restoring the rich fabric of the ocean and coastal marine environment. Few legal regimes focus on the ocean's ecosystem as an interconnected biotic circle. Still, the following international laws represent legal regimes that address ocean stewardship principles as well as protection of living marine species in particular. The legal regimes noted in the first part of this section, "hard law," represent norms that command a high level of compliance by international and national bodies[2]. Typically, hard laws would include binding treaties, for example, and are created through formal diplomatic processes.

Soft law has been defined as "guidelines, policy declarations, or codes of conduct that set standards of conduct but are not directly enforceable"[3]. In other words, soft law may include legal guides and model rules that, although not binding, may have a significant practical application. These laws are becoming increasingly important in protection of marine species because such laws may be conducive to embracing the needs of multiple stakeholders and may provide greater adaptability, flexibility, and harmonization in reaching goals and setting norms[4]. Nongovernmental organizations (NGOs), individuals, and other non-nation-state participants often influence soft law. Ultimately, soft law can significantly influence the development of hard law[5].

Hard Law

United Nations Law of the Sea Convention (UNCLOS III), 1982, 1994

The provisions of UNCLOS III emphasize forcefully the need for a renewed focus on the deleterious impacts on the marine environment by anthropogenic stressors. UNCLOS III is the international community's most ambitious attempt to protect the oceans and coastal waters from anthropogenic stressors. As such, it is potentially the most influential marine treaty. The UNCLOS III represents a clarion call to delineate clearly the rights and duties of coastal and flag states toward living marine species. The management and protection thrust of UNCLOS III is one of a holistic or ecosystem approach. Marine pollution must be prevented, reduced, or controlled in order to protect and preserve rare or fragile ecosystems as well as the habitat of depleted, threatened, or endangered species and other forms of marine life. In particular, Article 65 indicates that marine mammals deserve special attention in each country's EEZ:

> Nothing in this Part restricts the right of a coastal State or the competence of an international organization, as appropriate, to prohibit, limit or regulate the exploitation of marine mammals more strictly than provided for in this Part. States shall cooperate with a view to the conservation of marine mammals....

As noted in other chapters, pollution from multiple anthropogenic activities is a major threat to sirenians and their habitat[6]. Article 207 requires both coastal and landlocked nations to take measures to prevent the pollution of the marine environment, including the adoption of marine protection law. One source of pollutants in sirenian habitats is vessel source pollution, for example, from cruise ships; UNCLOS III prohibits vessel-source pollution. As well, coastal states must adopt measures to prevent and limit pollution. In addition to vessel-source pollution, five other sources of ocean pollution are addressed in the convention—land-based and coastal activities; continental shelf drilling; potential seabed mining; ocean dumping; and pollution from or through the atmosphere—all of which may have a significant impact on sirenian populations. However, the impacts may come from outside the jurisdiction of the coastal state.

One of the strengths of the UNCLOS III lies in its role as the framework on which to develop and implement nation-specific and regional protection strategies. These provisions have generated a number of regional seas agreements, including the Convention for the Protection and Development of the Marine Environment of the Wider Caribbean Region (Cartagena Convention), a primary component of which is the Protocol on Specially Protected Areas and Wildlife (SPAW), the goal of which is to protect, among others, the West Indian manatee.

Unfortunately, several of the major provisions in the application of UNCLOS III are vague. For example, in Article 194, the parties "shall" take all measures necessary to prevent, reduce, and control marine pollution from any sources. This statement, however, is weakened in Article 194(1): the efforts of parties shall be made "in accordance with their abilities." As well, there is no enforcement mechanism as the duties are not binding on a party, and conservation is described only in general terms (von Zharen 1998). Unless actual transboundary damage is triggered, a nation cannot legally object to the internal, domestic environmental policies of another nation.

Convention on International Trade in Endangered Species of Wild Fauna and Flora (CITES), 1973, 1975

CITES is a multilateral convention that seeks to protect certain species of wild fauna and flora against overexploitation in international trade. It addresses the export, import, and transit of these wild species. The goal of CITES is to prevent the overexploitation of listed species for which survival is in jeopardy. Parties may not trade in species listed in the appendices, except in accordance with the convention. CITES has over 170 member nations and governs 30,000 species[7]. CITES represents a compromise between the profits in wildlife trade and the need to protect endangered species. According to its preamble, CITES recognizes the "ever-growing value of wild fauna and flora from aesthetic, scientific, cultural, recreational and economic points of view" and the need to protect biodiversity as an "irreplaceable part of the natural systems of the earth which must be protected for this and generations to come."

Trade in species listed under CITES is restricted. Trade is defined as an introduction from the sea, export, import, and re-export. "Introduction from the sea" refers to the "transportation into a State of specimens of any species which were taken in the marine environment not under the jurisdiction of any state"[8]. Species are listed in one of three appendices to the treaty. Appendix I lists species that are the most endangered and bans all commercial trade in those species. Appendix II lists species that are not presently threatened with extinction but may become so unless trade is closely controlled; therefore, trade is allowed only if the species will not be harmed and the trade is carefully monitored. Appendix III is a list of species included at the request of a party (or ratifying nation) to CITES that already regulates trade in the species and that needs the cooperation of other countries to prevent unsustainable or illegal exploitation.

CITES is one of two international treaties to address sirenians specifically[9]. (The other is the Convention on Migratory Species, discussed in the following section.) Manatees and dugongs are listed as Appendix I species under CITES which means that international trade is subject to "particularly strict regulation." International trade in sirenians is permitted only if such trade is conducted in accordance with CITES provisions. No commercial trade is allowed; however, movement of manatees from one country to another, for example, would be permitted in the case of zoos.

Unfortunately, CITES addresses only international trade of sirenian populations, not domestic issues. For example, CITES does not address conservation of habitat or the creation of regional protected areas or hunting of these species within a country.

Even with CITES restrictions, however, CITES is often ineffectual because of inadequate enforcement provisions. The differences among domestic laws of the parties to CITES further complicate the issue and may result in trading among those nations whose own domestic protection laws are inadequate in substance and/or enforcement. Because the provisions of CITES focus exclusively on international trade rather than nation-specific law, these provisions have no application for trade that does not cross international borders[10].

Convention on the Conservation of Migratory Species of Wild Animals (CMS, Bonn Convention), 1980

The mandate of the CMS is the conservation of migratory wildlife on a global scale. This intergovernmental treaty concluded under the aegis of the United Nations Environmental Programme (UNEP) seeks to conserve terrestrial, marine, and avian wildlife. There are 109 parties to the convention from Africa, Central and South America, Asia, Europe, and Oceania. Migratory species threatened with extinction are listed on Appendix I. The parties attempt to strictly protect these species, including conserving and/or restoring their habitat and "mitigating obstacles to migration and controlling other factors that might endanger them. Besides establishing obligations for each State joining the Convention, CMS promotes concerted action among the Range States of many of these species"[11]. Species that "need or would significantly benefit from international co-operation" are listed in Appendix II. For this reason, the convention encourages the range states to create global or regional agreements. The agreements may range from legally binding treaties (called Agreements) to less formal instruments, such as memoranda of understanding (MOU), and can be adapted to the requirements of particular regions. The development of models tailored according to the conservation needs throughout the migratory range is a unique feature of the CMS[12]. Of particular significance for sirenian protection efforts are the MOUs aimed at conserving dugongs and the West African manatee. The CMS lists both animals in its Appendix II, which means that the conservation of the species would benefit from international cooperative activities organized across their migratory range.

For the dugong, intergovernmental meetings by participants from approximately 20 countries spanning the distribution of the dugong resulted in an MOU signed in 2007 that designed a conservation management plan (CMP) to facilitate national-level and transboundary actions that will lead to the conservation of dugong populations and their habitats. There are currently 11 signatories to the MOU.

> The CMP provides the basis for focused species and habitat-specific activities coordinated across the dugong's migratory range. Together, the MOU and CMP would be the primary platform for conservation actions on behalf of the species in all of the waters of coastal and archipelagic States of the Indian Ocean, East Asia, and western Pacific Ocean, as well as their adjacent seas[13].

In October of 2008, fifteen countries and three non-governmental collaborating organizations signed a new CMS Memorandum of Understanding Concerning the Conservation of the Manatee and Small Cetaceans of Western Africa and Macronesia. This MOU includes an Action Plan for Conservation of the West African manatee, with a goal:

> To significantly improve the conservation status of the west African manatee across its range through the implementation of strategic policy, research, conservation and awareness actions[14].

Convention on Biological Diversity (CBD), 1992

The goal of the CBD is to conserve biological diversity, defined as a "composite of genetic information, species, and ecosystems... [that] provides material wealth in the form of food, fiber, medicine, and inputs into industrial processes"[15]. The preamble of the CBD recognizes:

> the close and traditional dependence of many Indigenous and local communities embodying traditional lifestyles on biological resources, and the desirability of sharing equitably benefits arising from the use of traditional knowledge, innovations and practices relevant to the conservation of biological diversity and the sustainable use of its components.

Important for protecting sirenian populations, the CBD attempts to "place marine biodiversity issues . . . on the same footing as more widely understood terrestrial problems"[16]. The CBD explicitly includes within the definition of biological diversity the "marine and other aquatic ecosystems and the ecological complexes of which they are part"[17]. The CBD also states that "contracting Parties shall implement the Convention with respect to the marine environment consistently with the rights and obligations of States under the law of the sea"[18].

There has been some success in incorporating the tenets of the CBD into a nation's law. Using the West Indian manatee of the Wider Caribbean as an example, manatee populations exist in the waters of approximately 19 countries in this area. The CBD has been signed and ratified by all but a few of the manatee-range states in this geographical region.

In 2008, at the Convention of Parties (COP)–Meeting of the Parties (MOP), a specific program to address threats to marine species was developed. The plan included scientific criteria for identifying and selecting ecologically or biologically significant and representative areas in need of protection, and to implement conservation and management measures, including the establishment of marine protected areas.

International Convention for the Prevention of Pollution from Ships 1973, as Modified by the Protocol of 1978 and Its Annexes (MARPOL)

In 1948 the United Nations developed the International Maritime Organization (IMO) to address marine issues and to provide guidance. The IMO promulgated an important marine environmental protection document, MARPOL, which was subsequently modified by a further protocol in 1978. MARPOL's objective is to "create a verifiable, enforceable regime to prevent" ship pollution. It attempts to accomplish this through six annexes. Only the first two are mandatory for all signature parties. The pollutants addressed include: Annex I—oil; Annex II—noxious liquid substances; Annex III—harmful substances in packaged form; Annex IV—sewage; Annex V—garbage; and Annex VI—air pollution from ships[19].

As discussed in other chapters, degradation of sirenian habitat poses a significant threat to the species. Degradation includes discharges of substances targeted in MARPOL's annexes. For example, Annex V establishes international regulations for prohibiting or otherwise restricting discharges into the oceans of all types of garbage generated during the normal operation of vessels. This annex could significantly reduce the amount of plastic garbage and other debris entering sirenian habitat. Adherence to the provisions of the other annexes may provide critical habitat protection as well.

Coastal nations can serve as an integrity check on the enforcement of MARPOL requirements. Because each nation may enact laws to protect its own waters, a coastal state, for example, may choose to enact laws to regulate cruise line pollution, often a critical anthropogenic stressor on sirenians and their habitat. However, while some domestic laws regulate cruise line pollution, they are often weak and inadequate[20].

Soft Law

Stockholm Declaration on the Human Environment (Stockholm Declaration), 1972

The Stockholm Declaration, with its 26 principles and 109 recommendations, cemented the recognition that international environmental law should be given preference and represented a powerful force for increasing public awareness of the fragility of the environment. Its aspirational language enjoined states to "ensure that international organizations play a coordinated, efficient and dynamic role for the protection and improvement of the environment"[21].

The Stockholm Declaration emphasizes the importance of improving the environment for future generations; for example, "The natural resources of this earth, including the air, water, land, flora and fauna . . . must be safeguarded for the benefit of present and future generations"[22]. Principle 6 asserts that "States shall take all possible steps to prevent pollution of the seas by substances that are liable to create hazards to human health, to harm living resources and marine life, to damage amenities, or to interfere with other legitimate uses of the sea[23]."

An important concept emerging from the Stockholm Declaration is the basis for the precautionary approach (or principle), a policy-making device that defines obligations concerning environmental protection (see UNCED, next section). The Stockholm Declaration,

Principle 21, provides that nations have the "sovereign right to exploit their own resources pursuant to their own environmental policies" as well as the "responsibility to ensure that activities within their jurisdiction or control do not cause damage to the environment of other States or areas beyond the limits of national jurisdiction." Thus, all nations have both rights and responsibilities toward the environment: the right of equal enjoyment as well as the responsibility to protect and improve the environment. This notion of states anticipating responsibility should play a major role in achieving protection of sirenian populations and their habitat.

United Nations Conference on Environment and Development (UNCED): Rio Declaration and Agenda 21

Delegates from 176 nations met in Rio de Janeiro, Brazil, in 1992, for the United Nations Conference on Environment and Development (UNCED), resulting in the Rio Declaration and Agenda 21. The Rio Declaration produced 27 principles on environmental protection and the precautionary principle: "In order to protect the environment, the precautionary approach shall be widely applied by States according to their capabilities. Where there are threats of serious or irreversible damage, lack of full scientific certainty shall not be used as a reason for postponing cost-effective measures to prevent environmental degradation"[24]. The Rio Declaration asserts that all people "are entitled to a healthy and productive life in harmony with nature"[25] and to exploit their own resources. Concomitant with these rights come responsibility: economic development should "equitably meet developmental and environmental needs of present and future generations"[26]. The Rio Declaration pronounces the right to consume and develop. This approach is critical to the developing coastal nations that need to fast-track traditional development but at the same time encourage the development of, for instance, marine ecotourism, which in turn requires the protection of the inhabitants of the marine environment, such as sirenian populations. However, the Rio Declaration's call for a precautionary approach is tempered by inclusion of the term "cost-effective." In other words, measures are implemented only if they are cost-effective.

Agenda 21 outlines an agreement of what nations and international organizations will do to protect the environment and promote sustainable development in the developing world and acts as a roadmap for sustainable development. Chapter 17 of Agenda 21 is a blueprint for protection of the oceans and coastal areas and their resources. It focuses exclusively on marine resources and acknowledges that the UNCLOS III lays the foundation for the environmental law of the sea[27]. The chapter recognizes needs for an integrated approach to marine environmental protection if we are to protect and restore endangered marine species and to preserve habitats and other ecologically sensitive areas. Unfortunately, the provisions of chapter 17 have not as yet translated specifically into protection measures for sirenians. What is important is that the blueprint has been developed, and nations can look to this document when developing legal and management strategies for sirenians and their habitat.

Marine Protected Areas (MPAs)/Regional Seas Program/Other Regional Plans

Coastal nations generally have legal authority to manage their ocean territories out to 200 nautical miles from shore (EEZs) to protect marine ecosystems. Nations with substantial coastlines, as well as islands, have implemented national systems of marine protected areas (MPAs). Although definitions can vary from one area to another, MPAs refer to any area of the ocean protected from at least some uses, and the term can apply to reserves, sanctuaries, refuges, parks, and marine biospheres. Identifying and managing these underwater ecosystems (and closing off sections of ocean to all commercial use in the case of no-take reserves) are increasingly becoming a method of choice for protecting specific marine species and are recognized as effective in preserving and restoring marine species[28]. MPAs have been promoted as "insurance zones" to negate the impacts of the uncertainties in science and management[29].

The United Nations Environment Programme's (UNEP) Regional Seas Program (RSP), launched in 1974, recognized the need for special protection for specific geographical areas of oceans and enclosed and semi-enclosed seas. It provides a template for crafting a regional approach to protecting the environment and managing natural resources. More than 140 countries participate in 13 Regional Seas Programs, which function through an action plan. In most cases, the action plan is underpinned with a strong legal framework in the form of a regional convention and associated protocols on specific problems[30].

Although RSP agreements have been negotiated under the UNEP, the framework provisions of the UNCLOS III have inspired the most comprehensive set of marine protection measures. These plans often represent a shift to a marine ecosystem approach: management focuses not only on a particular species but also on all species and their habitat in a specific region. As well, an ecosystem approach recognizes the interconnectivity and interdependency of the marine environment through which some species migrate. This recognition is particularly important when the geographical range of sirenian populations crosses jurisdictional boundaries, further complicating their protection.

A regional cooperative under the RSP, and one that crystallized Caribbean environmental cooperation, is the Convention for the Protection and Development of the Marine Environment of the Wider Caribbean Region (Cartagena Convention), which was adopted in 1983 and entered into force in 1986. This convention is a regional framework convention that sets out general obligations to protect the wider Caribbean environment and is the only legally binding regional environmental treaty for the region. Article 10 requires parties to take "all appropriate measures" to protect and preserve "rare or fragile ecosystems" as well as the "habitats of depleted, threatened or endangered species," and to this end, to establish specially protected areas. In response, the governments of the region adopted a Protocol on Specially Protected Areas and Wildlife (SPAW) in 1990; in 1991, the species requiring protection were listed. The West Indian manatee was included because it "is rapidly disappearing with a few numbers left in most of the countries where it exists"[31]. (The impact of the Cartagena Convention and SPAW on the West Indian manatee is further discussed in the second section of this chapter.)

Neither Soft nor Hard Law: International Union for the Conservation of Nature (IUCN)

Although it is neither hard nor soft law, mention should also be made of one of the oldest and largest global environmental networks, the International Union for the Conservation of Nature (IUCN). This organization maintains a Red List of critically endangered, endangered, and vulnerable species, similar to the CITES appendices for threatened and endangered species. The IUCN's Species Survival Commission is made up of some 10,000 volunteer scientists, field researchers, natural resource managers, government officials, and conservation leaders from around the world who identify these at-risk species within different taxonomic categories. The Red List of Threatened Species remains a key information tool, for example, for the Convention on Migratory Species (CMS). The assessment of the status of species on a global scale highlights "taxa threatened with extinction, and therefore promotes their conservation."[32] Science-based assessments of the vulnerability of sirenians, their conservation status, and distribution provides the foundation for making informed decisions about conserving biodiversity from local to global levels. All sirenians are classified as vulnerable or considered to be facing a high threat of extinction in the wild[33].

Role of Law in Protecting Sirenians in Developing Nations

International treaties can provide the essential framework on which to build nation-specific laws and regional programs to protect the marine ecosystem. The importance of developing nations in the protection of sirenians is illustrated by dugong distribution: although dugongs occur in the waters of thirty-nine countries, nearly all these countries are developing nations[34].

At the same time, the role of developing nations in conserving sirenian populations and their habitat may pale in light of the essential economic outcomes. These developing nations may lack financial and technical resources, and what scarce funding there is may not be allocated to environmental, let alone sirenian, protection. Because of these challenges, the importance of species and habitat protection laws in developing nations becomes more apparent. In varying degrees, protective legislation has been enacted in most countries in which sirenians are found[35].

Assessing the role of law in developing nations is understandably complex; there is no single formula to use as a reference. One question, however, needs to be answered as a starting point for any exploration of the role of law: How can a country reform its legal system? Economic, cultural, societal, political, environmental, institutional, geographical, and historical factors all figure into the equation. The complexity increases when, as with sirenians, a species may cross multiple jurisdictions. An example of this can be found in the Wider Caribbean Region as defined by the Cartagena Convention. The area includes all of the insular and coastal states and territories bordering the Caribbean Sea and the Gulf of Mexico, from the U.S. Gulf Coast states to the Central and South American countries bordering the Caribbean Sea south to the Department of French Guiana in South America[36].

Although knowledge about the role of law in developing nations is still emerging, there remain a number of ideological building blocks. The most critical would be creating a legal consciousness. This term evokes multiple layers required in the process of actually achieving legal consciousness and improving the legal culture. The primary layer is the development of a respect for the rules of law. To develop this sense of respect, to inculcate the idea that laws are needed and therefore should be respected, the laws must reflect specific characteristics that create or improve an individual's and a community's legal consciousness to make it more amenable to change.

Often in developing nations, environmental laws designed to protect sirenians are not well defined, or if they are, enforcement mechanisms are lacking or nonexistent[37]. Implementing effective legal regimes to protect sirenians and their habitat requires this legal consciousness. For those nations with scant or nonexistent legal regimes, the process may begin with recognition by all stakeholders that unregulated development is degrading coastal areas and causing resources to become scarce; that people do indeed depend on a healthy environment for their own economic well-being.

Developing a legal consciousness requires an active, public-spirited citizenry founded on egalitarian relations that foster social trust and cooperation. In many countries there are political, class, and economic realities acting as barriers to civic involvement. However difficult to achieve, education and civic engagement form the cornerstones for the realization of the need for conservation that supports the enforcement of laws[38]. Laws will fail unless the role and functions of law and its appropriate application are understood. One of the challenges in rural areas is that people may be unaware that their governments have laws in place designed to protect manatees.

Thus the primary role of law is serving the community. In doing so, the law must suit the needs of a particular nation's unique priorities[39]. To accomplish this, laws must include specific provisions regarding participation by citizenry in conservation efforts through public comment and review of environmental protection policies. Many developing nations have implemented these provisions[40]. The ultimate goal is to have clear and relevant input from all stakeholders. There is also an onus on scientists and participating agencies to ensure that observations are based on credible information and studies.

The structure of education and civic engagement should lend itself to being responsive to state and regional needs to tap local knowledge and build upon specific, unique strengths of particular regions. This includes protecting the knowledge and practices of Indigenous and local peoples and their economic, social, and cultural systems that depend on the sustainable use of natural resources to support their long-term survival[41].

A co-management regime is created from a mandate, such as a memorandum of understanding among parties, in order to establish its legitimacy. Stakeholders formally recognized as parties to the co-management regime could be signatories to an agreement or those identified in legislation[42].

Co-management aids in the enforcement of law when the geographical area is inaccessible. A case in point is the Amazonian manatee: although it is protected throughout its range, enforcement of these laws is all but impossible in the inaccessible areas of the interior jungles of these countries[43].

Legislation must include flexibility that allows for changes in the environmental, economic, and societal impacts. Thus adaptive management is required. The strategy should be one that tests theories and adapts to the results of these tests[44].

Laws that protect sirenians must be based on an ethical foundation, an integral part of the collective and legal consciousness. The role of law in sirenian conservation must rest on something deeper, something that pulls humans beyond the narrow focus of human utilization of these species[45].

An inspirational example may be emerging in Belize in the Swallow Caye and the Drowned Cayes areas near Belize City, where grassroots and co-management efforts have resulted in protected areas for Antillean manatees (*Trichechus manatus manatus*)[46]. As background, Belize endorsed the Cartagena Convention and its subsequent Protocol Concerning Specially Protected Areas and Wildlife[47]. These encouraged the protection of both endangered species and their ecosystems, with the SPAW Protocol being the driving force behind establishment of MPAs and a focus on conservation of manatees as a species of priority concern[48].

Historically, manatees have had legally protected status in Belize since the 1930s and they are listed as endangered under Belize's Wildlife Protection Act of 1981. However, with the increase in the number of cruise vessels and other tourist water activities, among additional anthropogenic stressors, the manatee population became more frequently subjected to habitat encroachment and injury/death from boat propellers.

Since endorsement of the Cartagena Convention and SPAW, Belize has implemented several types of MPAs, including marine reserves, national parks, natural monuments, wildlife sanctuaries, and World Heritage sites, encompassing 26 coastal and marine protected areas[49]. One of the factors contributing to this success was Belize's Coastal Zone Management Authority and Institute (CZMA&I), a quasi-governmental organization. The CZMA&I played a vital leadership role in coordinating and integrating species protection and ecosystem protection during this period, including development of a National Manatee Recovery Plan in 1998, a National Integrated Coastal Zone Management Strategy in 2003, and the Belize National Protected Areas System Plan in 2005[50].

However, the governmental agencies charged with managing protected species and protected areas in Belize are relatively small and understaffed[51]. A solution to the problem of limited resources is being sought through a variety of mechanisms, including a Protected Areas Conservation Trust (PACT) and co-management agreements in which the enforcement agencies—the Forestry Department and the Fisheries Department—work with NGOs to manage protected areas. PACT is well funded by a conservation tax levied on every traveler who leaves Belize. PACT does not engage directly in conservation activities but awards grants to governmental agencies and NGOs based on proposals to implement conservation of protected areas policy[52].

In the case of Swallow Caye Wildlife Sanctuary, a co-management agreement has been established between the Belize Forestry Department and Friends of Swallow Caye, a nonprofit organization of manatee tour operators and other interested stakeholders. One measure of the successful aspects of this strategy is co-management among government agencies and NGOs[53]. Other reasons for this success include key individuals being motivated and informed, availability of funding to ensure communication and coordination, and the fact that there are jobs available and thus tangible value is apparent to stakeholders. These conditions are crucial to the importance of developing a legal consciousness within which citizenry and other stakeholders can respect the role and rule of law.

Conclusion

The role of law in the conservation of sirenians is varied and complex. The variety of issues surrounding sirenian conservation and the evolution of multiple anthropogenic stressors requires that laws be multifaceted, integrated, and adaptive. The challenges of sirenian conservation are global, regional, and nation-state specific and, as such, require cooperative solutions. To protect sirenian populations and to return their fragile ecosystem to stability and health, much more remains to be done, not only in pragmatic aspects, such as information access, compliance, and enforcement, but also in management strategies, all of which may need retooling.

More precisely, the role of law will have a significant impact on the livelihood of many. The impact for humans and sirenians will be affected by whether sirenians are seen as part of an ecosystem as well as whether the seas will be acknowledged as an integral part of a larger ecological phenomenon. Ultimately, basic to effective legislation is a thoughtful analysis of how sirenians and their conservation are perceived by humans.

27

The Role of Scientists in Sirenian Conservation in Developing Countries

ELLEN M. HINES, DARYL DOMNING, LEMNUEL V. ARAGONES, MIRIAM MARMONTEL, ANTONIO A. MIGNUCCI-GIANNONI, AND JOHN E. REYNOLDS III

Based on the increasing impact of humans on a species' habitat and that species' small and/or decreasing population, at a certain point in scientific research, a project has to shift its priorities from biological assessment to conservation. While research to establish baseline information about a species is rarely complete, plans for conservation and management of an endangered species and its habitat are too crucial to delay pending further data. As we have seen numerous times in previous chapters, this plan must consider the ecological, social, cultural and economic influences both inside and outside protected areas[1]. More important than planning and policy is the need to implement action that is embraceable by stakeholders, realistically enforceable, and ultimately sustainable[2].

Pressures from the rapidly rising human population in coastal, marine, and fluvial regions in developing countries have had a significant impact on resources[3]. Sirenians are threatened by incidental takes in fishing operations and recreation activities, habitat loss, pollution, direct take (legal and illegal), dams, and coastal development. The cumulative impact of these activities is largely unknown[4].

To assess these impacts accurately, the complicated and intertwined events, both modern and historic, that cause wildlife extinctions cannot be ignored. Fossil records show extinctions going back millions of years, but many of the extinctions over the last 12,000 years were caused primarily by humans. At present, unprecedented rates of extinction are occurring, and it is projected that they will accelerate over the next 25–30 years[5]. The collective environmental conscience about species extinctions has grown over the last century[6]. The demise of Atlantic gray whales in the seventeenth and eighteenth centuries was noted only long after the fact[7]. Domning[8] found warnings of species depletion in government reports on Steller's sea cows and Amazonian manatees in the late 1700s, though these kinds of concerns were not considered important enough to change policies or activities until much later.

Though endangered species legislation and policy exist today in most countries, they alone will not prevent extinctions. To create conservation-oriented strategies, many researchers maintain that awareness of the social, economic, and political causes needs to become integrated with knowledge of the natural and life history of these animals[9]. Strategies need to address not only traditional biological and ethological research but also the realities of economic and cultural limitations, inadequate resources, the frustrations and insecurity of politics, agency complexities and conflicts, the sluggishness of social change, and the ambiguities of communication[10].

Accounts by scientists, who have become involved with conservation as their subjects have become endangered, show how they have been thrust into the center of these issues[11]. The survival of sirenians is jeopardized by the depletion and degradation of aquatic resources, economic insecurity, complicated government jurisdictions, uncertain funding for research and the implementation of conservation measures, a rapidly increasing human population, and consequential changes in social and economic roles within coastal communities.

Sirenians are perfect examples of species caught in the middle of this anthropogenic maelstrom. Dugongs originally had a huge range throughout the tropics and subtropics of most of the Eastern Hemisphere. But outside of Australia, the country with the largest estimated dugong population today, dugongs now survive only in fragmented populations. Neither the number of dugongs remaining in most of these local populations nor the extent of their remaining habitat is known except for incidental sightings and the reports of fishers[12]. How many populations of dugongs have grown isolated from each other as a result of anthropogenic influences and have already become extirpated?

Similar declines of numbers and increasing patchiness of distribution are reasonably well documented for the Antillean subspecies of the West Indian manatee[13] and suspected for West African and Amazonian manatees[14].

A further role for scientists is to be involved in the conservation, natural resources management, and environmental planning stages. We emphasize the importance of collaborating with scientists from various pertinent fields to encompass an interdisciplinary approach: not just biologists, but sociologists, geographers, economists, and anthropologists, to mention a few. The role of scientists is easily overlooked in developing countries; they are often approached by governments only when environmental problems are already irreversible or populations of threatened or endangered species are already in serious decline. The reality in developing countries is that most mandated government agencies do not have the technical, economic, social, and/or political capacity to perform their functions. This handicap is worsened by the corruption found in many governments and agencies. Fortunately, capacity building programs are now getting a lot of attention with funding from institutions such as the United States Agency for International Development (USAID) and World Bank[15].

After the planning stage, an important role for scientists is to be a friendly supporter of the concerned agency and/or local government unit. The conservation solution in most cases often depends less on science and more on the political realm (i.e., developing appropriate policies and implementing them). This is where scientists could remind local governments of the importance of having sustainable practices, including in regard to population growth.

Another role of scientists in conserving sirenians in developing countries is to encourage the training, professional development, and retention of more local researchers. The scientist should also be teaching and training students in the fields of sirenian biology and conservation biology. Sirenian distribution ranges are extensive, and there are roles for many more field scientists conducting research and supporting conservation. Often students are attracted to remote regions where sirenians occur (such as the Amazon), but rarely do they stay long enough to implement long-term research projects or conservation initiatives. When one analyzes a map of sirenian research and conservation actions along the Amazon, it is clear that most actions are concentrated in or near medium-sized to large urban centers, especially the state capitals. It is extremely important not only to build in-country capacity but to establish professionals in the region. Researchers should start expanding their field efforts to radiate out from the interior towns closer to where sirenians are actually found. Scientists in developing countries should also publicize the results of their work widely, both through papers in international journals and by producing materials for the national and local public and media. Material that is easily accessed by national students and local communities encourages interest and involvement in conservation actions. These materials can now be placed in Web sites, where they can be accessed by a wider range of interested students.

Ultimately, scientific information on endangered species, including modules on conservation beginning in primary education and reinforced throughout, is the most crucial medium- to long-term solution to saving endangered species. Without proper integration of conservation issues in various levels of education in developing countries, environmental threats will not be understood nor acted upon.

Yet another role for sirenian scientists in developing countries is to involve the local population in all steps of research and conservation planning. By turning local inhabitants into collaborators and co-investigators, scientists can share and exchange knowledge with the people who most closely interact with the species and increase the probability of sensitizing the population to the conservation issues related to sirenians.

Sirenian scientists should strive for what coral reef biologists and ecologists achieved through the Coastal Resource Management Programs (CRMP), a series of ten regional workshops organized in the 1980s by the Association of Southeast Asian Nations (ASEAN, an organization of ten southeast Asian countries). The CRMP provided technical assistance and training to local government units and nongovernmental organizations, and even to concerned national government agencies, to promote sustainable management of coastal resources, particularly coral reefs, seagrass communities, and mangrove forests. The workshops eventually resulted in building a consensus on the need to standardize methods and compare results. Resulting data[16] were essential to the continuing development of the CRMP throughout the ASEAN region. Similar results have been obtained for sea turtles through the Wider Caribbean Sea Turtle Network (WIDECAST).

Cultural attitudes, languages and dialects, philosophies, religions, and other belief systems are often relevant and sometimes critical in wildlife conservation, and must not be ignored by scientists or policymakers[17].

Any conservation approach that neglects the perceptions, culture, or experience of local community members will never work. Local people have created their own knowledge of ecological complexity, sometimes based on generations of experience[18]. Whether dealing with bureaucracies, mass media, key decision or opinion makers, or the public in general, scientists must keep in mind both the pitfalls and the possibilities presented by these attitudes.

In various periods and places, such attitudes have ranged from denial that biological extinction is possible to conviction that preventing it is a moral obligation. We must work with this conviction and encourage it. In every society there are divisions—urban-rural, rich-poor, ethnic and religious rivalries—and support for conservation can be found on any side of such divisions, often in surprising places. Indigenous peoples, for example, often have both the motivation and the know-how to protect the biodiversity of their lands and waters against encroaching development; they can be the conservationists' best allies. In another place, however, an educated urban middle class may be the readiest source of environmental awareness. Conservationists must be alert to the social realities of where they work and tailor their tactics accordingly.

Even multinational corporations will become environmentally responsible as soon as they are convinced that doing so is more profitable. Governments, however undemocratic, can likewise come to realize the economic and even security threats posed by environmental damage. As living creatures molded by natural selection, humans have no deeper nor more ancient drive than self-interest. As intelligent creatures, humans can and must learn that species conservation is in their enlightened self-interest; and it is our job as scientists to provide the enlightenment.

Arguments for species preservation will differ, depending on the circumstances. Domning[19] presented a spectrum of reasons for saving manatees, most of which apply equally to dugongs. They range from the plainly utilitarian (the animals' value for tourism, weed control, health of aquatic ecosystems, or as potential genetic resources) to the less tangible (the aesthetic, psychological, and health benefits we derive from wilderness and wildlife) to the moral reasons (extermination of species is intrinsically wrong).

The utilitarian arguments will usually be the first ones used in any local situation: people naturally want to know what is in it for them if they avoid harming sirenians or their habitat. But all such arguments, based as they are on what other species might do for us, potentially falter on the fact that if our practical need for a species ends, so does the justification for preserving it. Or the species' utility may remain, but government or voters may decide it is outweighed by some more compelling human need or desire. For example, ecotourism is nice, but power boating may generate more jobs and revenue.

Therefore, we must also be prepared to make a moral case for conservation, and to argue for a species' survival on the basis of a principle that transcends human needs and desires—whether couched in terms of animal rights or of human responsibilities, either to posterity or to a higher power[20]. Obviously, not all cultures and individuals are equally receptive to such an argument; and as the global human population and its material demands continue to explode, there will be less and less willingness to set aside space or resources for nonhuman species. Yet most cultures and spiritual traditions do acknowledge some sense in which humans are accountable to some entity beyond themselves, whether natural or supernatural. It behooves conservationists to be sensitive to the cultures in which they work, and if necessary to seek appropriate guidance and assistance in presenting such moral arguments.

Even if the conservationist does not share these beliefs, or agree that moral arguments are appropriate, respect for the other people involved demands attention. It is, after all, people who cause the conflicts with wildlife that we seek to resolve. Unless we persuade people to reconsider their actions, we as scientists will not succeed.

28

A Framework for Sirenian Conservation in Developing Countries

ELLEN M. HINES

Sirenians are in danger of extinction because of factors common not only to other marine mammals but to endangered species worldwide: habitat degradation and destruction, and directed or incidental killing. Specific circumstances may change, but the results are the same. As seen in this volume, and as stated in figure 28.1, which introduces the concepts underpinning the framework I present in this chapter, the problems behind endangered species habitat and population decline are derived from human values, beliefs, and practices. The methods and issues discussed in previous chapters are designed to create an example of the foundation for a practical toolbox for the inclusion of sound scientific inquiry into an integrated conservation and management process for sirenians and other endangered species.

The reasons for endangerment discussed in this volume combine to form a net of factors intricately tangled into the structure of modern human society. Therefore, to be preoccupied with biological assessments and dependent on biological solutions ignores the risks to these animals associated with social, economic, and political factors[1]. In figure 28.1 the consideration of social, economic, and other related issues is as important as animal biology in sirenian conservation planning. Michael Soulé, who argued for the creation of the discipline of conservation biology in the 1980s, thought of conservation-oriented biology as a crisis science, a mixture of sci-

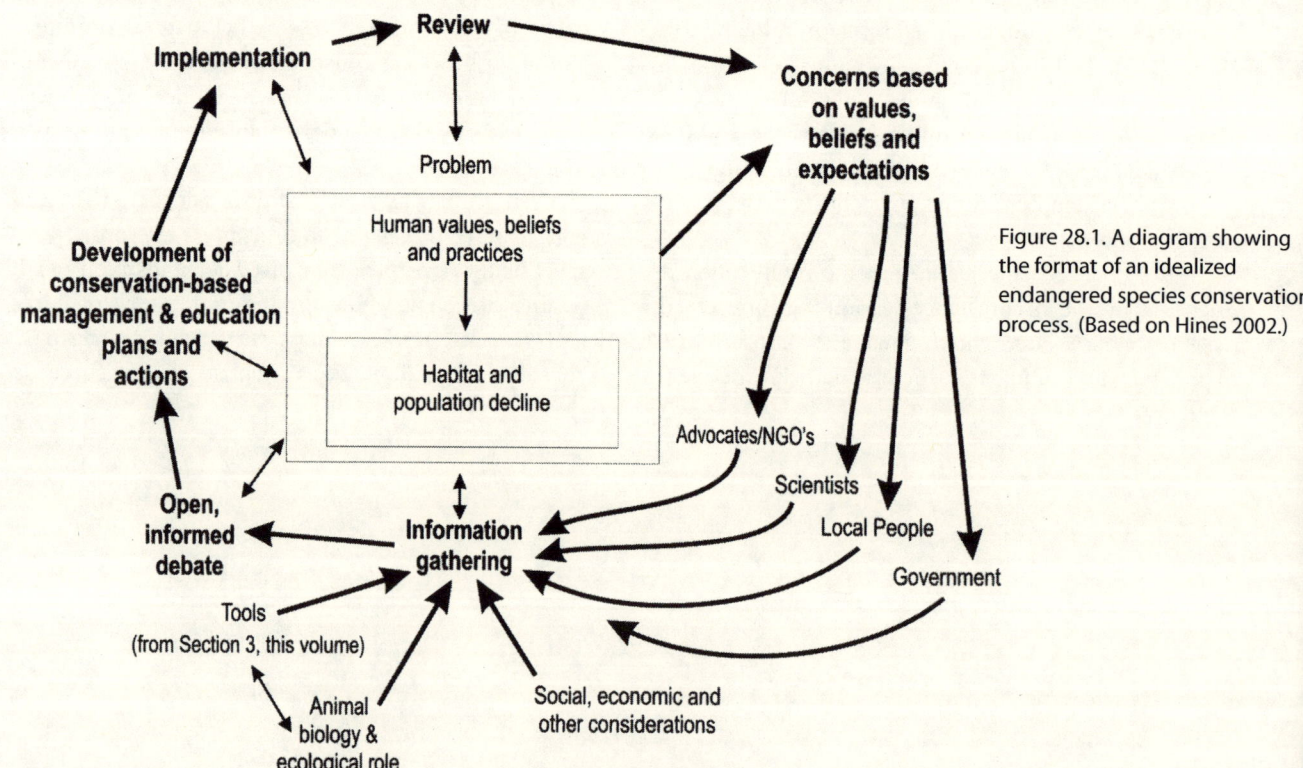

Figure 28.1. A diagram showing the format of an idealized endangered species conservation process. (Based on Hines 2002.)

ence and art, requiring intuition as well as information, and the integration of biological and social sciences[2]. In his 1991 paper entitled "Conservation: Tactics for a Crisis Science," Soulé stated:

> Reappraisal (of conservation's goals and tactics) would be more fruitful if there were a deeper appreciation of the biological and social contexts of conservation actions, particularly how both biogeography and political geography dictate different conservation tactics in different situations[3].

In addition, without the context of history, conservation problems cannot be fully understood, nor can effective conservation planning be developed. In this chapter I incorporate these contexts and the issues and strategies presented throughout this volume and then introduce a further tool into an overall framework that can be a guide to sirenian conservation planning. I believe this framework to be generally useful in most if not all situations and at all scales (local to national to regional).

I highlight three concepts, bolded and underlined in the framework shown in figure 28.2, that are the most crucial ingredients in conservation planning. The first two already have chapters that address them in detail.

Chapter 24, on working with communities, demonstrates that it is critical for conservation-oriented scientists to understand the social context behind actions that deplete wildlife and degrade natural systems. To achieve conservation goals, the results of scientific inquiry need to be communicated to all people affected by or involved with management planning. The concept of collaboration between scientists and government, management, educators, and the community is an important step in increasing communication and education for conservation.

Chapter 25, on guidelines for developing protected areas for sirenians, introduces the concept of the designation of reserves to protect marine resources. Some protected areas have already been allocated and more have been suggested[4]. However, marine protected areas are dynamic and complicated, and as discussed by Marsh and Morales-Vela[5], lack of attention to management, the community, and local ecology has limited their success[6].

The third concept that I introduce here, focal species, is a tool for discerning the significance of the interactions or the ecological role of animals within their biotic and abiotic environments. One focal species concept, the flagship species, relies on the symbol or image

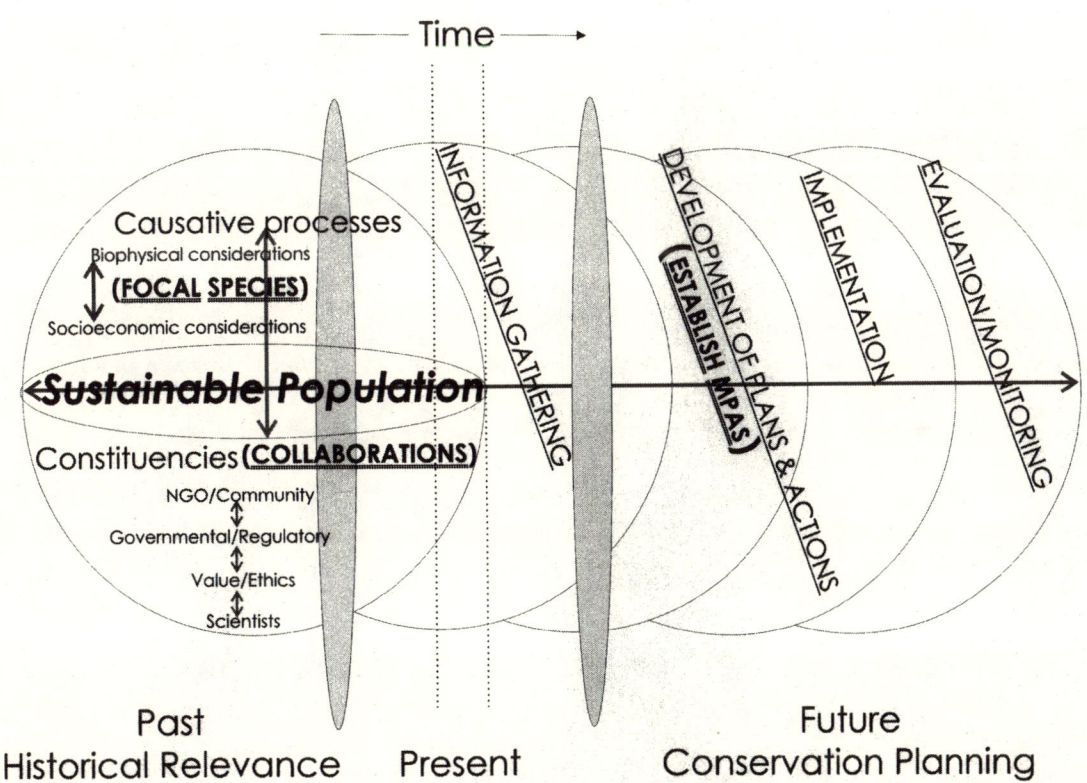

Figure 28.2. An example of an integrated framework for sirenian conservation planning. The three concepts discussed in this chapter are bolded and underlined where they fit into the planning process. (Based on Hines 2002.)

of an animal as a way to generate support for conservation[7]. Other focal species theories, such as umbrella, keystone, and indicator species, which attempt to explain and categorize the ecological interaction between an animal and its biological and physical surroundings[8], can have specific relevance to conservation planning. A concept that I do not discuss further here is that of sentinel species, which is specifically focused on animal health conditions as "indicators" of negative anthropogenic impacts on the environment and their effects on both humans and animals[9]. This concept illustrates a type of conditional indicator species, defined later.

Focal Species Concepts and Their Relevance to Sirenian Conservation

In figure 28.1 the ecological role of an animal is paired with animal biology as inputs into the information gathering process. Focal species patterns of abundance or simply presence are thought of as tools for understanding the relationships of species with their habitats and communities[10]. Simberloff[11] talks of focal species concepts as "shortcuts . . . whereby we monitor and protect single species." Focal species concepts can be considered tools for the understanding, management, and conservation of environments as well[12].

Focal concepts such as flagship, indicator, keystone, and umbrella species have potential in sirenian conservation strategies. A flagship species is not an ecological concept but a social one, for it focuses on a charismatic animal that can arouse public interest in conservation[13]. Indicator species are those for which presence or absence suggests the presence or condition of a particular habitat or community. A keystone species is critical to the ecological functioning of a community. The significance of that role is beyond what is expected in relation to the animals' biomass and abundance. Umbrella species need such a large habitat area that other species dependent on that habitat will be protected[14].

There are roles for focal species concepts in determining areas for marine reserves, habitat characterization and monitoring, identifying and monitoring biological communities, and integrated coastal zone management[15]. However, the use of focal species concepts depends on an understanding of species' interactions with their environment. Aragones et al.[16] discuss the importance of feeding ecology in the role or influence of sirenians on the structure of the marine environment. Bowen states that knowledge of the functional significance of marine mammals is central to conservation, as it provides a context through which to evaluate the potential impact of their predations on prey populations and community structure, and the impact of variation in prey populations, of harvesting by humans, and environmental change on the dynamics of marine mammals[17].

While this understanding is important, it is difficult to measure system properties with such variable temporal and spatial scales[18]. Food webs, trophic levels, and landscapes are complex and dynamic in the marine environment, so the ability to determine if any given species represents the structure or functioning of a community may be challenging[19].

Flagship Species

Community awareness of the significance of threats to the environment can be triggered by the presence of a species for which existence or habitat is in danger. Knowledge of an endangered species can enhance perception of the environment and the effects of continued deleterious use. A flagship species can serve as the representative of environmental conservation in educational processes[20]. There are well-known precedents in both popular and academic literature for the value of a flagship species in drawing attention to problems of resource exploitation[21]. Flagship species can also publicly represent their own depletion and threats from fishing or hunting, pollution, and loss of habitat, and they have been shown to contribute to the successful conservation of natural systems[22]. The manatee (*Trichechus manatus*) in Florida and the dugong (*Dugong dugon*) in Australia are recognized as flagship species representing coastal conservation efforts[23]. In Thailand, dugongs on the Andaman coast can be considered a flagship species based on their place in the cultures of the residents of nearby coastal settlements and on the concern of an international community[24].

The use of flagship species as an advocacy tool for the preservation of habitat has drawbacks. The notion of flagship species is more a means for advocating public support than an ecological concept. The animal's popularity can be based more on political or management strategies than on a scientific foundation of information about the species' needs and vulnerabilities[25]. Flagship conservation can also be expensive and, if not well planned, can de-emphasize the inherent importance of the ecological systems and other species it should represent[26]. In the case of the dugong in southern Thailand, its use as a flagship species is already starting to bring tourists to an area without the infrastructure to prevent environmental degradation. Dugong watching by boat and microlight aircraft has begun without consideration of (1) the futility of attempting to see dugongs by boat, (2) the extent and effects of disturbance to dugongs from noise and the shadows of both boats and microlights, (3) damage to and pollution of seagrass from the boats, and (4) increased danger of boat strikes.

Simberloff has asked "But what happens when the flagship sinks? . . . Will public emotional investment in this species turn to despair and disenchantment with conservation in general?[27]" There is a real possibility that a sirenian could go extinct while being "watched." Again using the example of southern Thailand, there may be up to 200 animals remaining in Trang province. However, increasing development and tourism alone are enough to destroy local seagrass beds. The construction of a pier over seagrass in a nearby village is an indication of the importance placed on short-term economic development over careful expansion that considers the long-term well-being of the coastal environment. Most local people, even those who belong to conservation groups, welcome the pier as a boom to the local economy. Use of the dugong as a flagship will not overcome the effects of ongoing poverty or unrestrained development.

When a flagship species becomes the basis for a recreational experience from which a local population expects to benefit economically, there is a potential for both the animal and its habitat to be seriously disturbed[28]. For example, the question of long-term disturbance from recreational whale watching has been a concern of both the whale-watching public and researchers[29]. It is difficult to establish cause and effect relationships or to ascertain long-term biological significance based on measurable behavioral parameters[30].

There are numerous examples of marine mammals as flagship species, but even with comprehensive education programs and enforceable management planning, changing human perceptions and attitudes is difficult, especially as wildlife conservation is usually pitted against the interests of economic development and resource exploitation. Any management effort will be inadequate without public interest acting on behalf of an endangered species and its habitat[31].

Keystone Species

The keystone species concept is often explained using the example of the sea otter (*Enhydra lutris*)[32]. Sea otters forage on sea urchins. Urchins usually graze on kelp forests, but when otters come into a community, the larger urchins decline in abundance, and kelp forests increase in abundance. Fish species that inhabit kelp forests then increase, and the community changes. Recent research is finding, however, that outside influences such as storms, currents, or temperature changes can also have strong influences on the growth of kelp forests. Recently, killer whale predation on sea otters in Alaska has caused a decline in otter population abundance and has reduced or eliminated the keystone role of the sea otter[33].

Zacharias and Roff[34] argue that: (1) complex communities are rarely controlled by a single species, (2) all species are keystones to some degree, (3) identifying true keystones is difficult, (4) keystone species are only keystones in specific situations, (5) conservation centered around a keystone species does not guarantee that conservation objectives are met, especially in the variable and complex marine environment, and (6) most important, the presence or absence of a keystone species changes relative abundance in a community, not the community structure itself. Sirenians, as obligate herbivores in seagrass, and possibly as cultivation grazers, do have an influence on the species distribution within the seagrass beds[35]. However, as sirenian grazing changes the relative abundance of species only temporarily, and is not a strong enough influence to create a change in community structure, the keystone species concept is not the most relevant for sirenians.

Umbrella Species

Marsh et al.[36] identify the dugong as an umbrella species, because the large extent of reserve area required for dugong conservation will bring other species under protection. Characteristics of umbrella species have been described by Zacharias and Roff[37], identifying them as animals that:

· demonstrate fidelity to particular types of habitats,
· are nonmigratory,
· are specialists rather than generalists,
· decline in disturbed habitats,
· require large areas of relatively natural habitat, and
· will affect community and habitat structure if they disappear from an area.

Sirenians fit these criteria perfectly[38]. The problem with using the present distribution of sirenians as a decisive factor in the selection of protected areas is that in developing countries especially, sirenians are often found in groups that are remnants of their former distribution, and we have little if any knowledge of current population viability[39] or the true spatial extent of habitat use[40]. For example, little is known of historic or current dugong movement and distribution outside Australian waters. As conservation ideally considers past, present, and future habitat areas, in such cases the umbrella species should be seagrass beds that contain species of seagrass suitable for sirenian foraging[41].

Indicator Species

The indicator species concept in application can be further delineated as either composition or condition indicators. Composition indicators are representative of the presence of a habitat or community. A condition indicator can be used to monitor the condition of, or the environmental change in, a habitat or community resulting from either anthropogenic or natural disturbances[42]. The concept of composition indicator is relevant for sirenians as it is independent of spatial scale and relatively independent of sample size. It demands that the species demonstrate a definable range of ecological tolerances and show fidelity to specific community and habitat types. This concept also corresponds to research directions and methodology to determine the nature and possible predictability of sirenian use of habitat. In terms of applicability for conservation, the habitat use of a composition indicator species can demarcate a community type or habitat area that can be mapped. Examples of critical habitat areas could include distinct areas based on courting, mating, nursing, or foraging behaviors[43].

A condition indicator species is the only one of these concepts that is focused on monitoring the effects of natural and anthropogenic stress on the habitat and the animal. Also independent of spatial scale and sample size, this concept is a tool for measuring ecologically significant change. The presence, absence, abundance, or behavior of a condition indicator can be considered representative of specific environmental factors. Condition indicators can also be used to evaluate conservation efforts once habitat areas have been identified[44]. As sirenians have specialized foraging needs, habitat areas used for grazing are usually identifiable. Continued research characterizing, modeling, or predicting the specialized foraging habitats of the manatee or dugong will more firmly establish their importance as conditional indicators and further establish the significance of sirenians within a coastal ecological system.

Indicator concepts have the most utility of all focal species concepts as ingredients in a framework for sirenian conservation planning, management, and monitoring. As focal species tools based on testable ecological theory, determination of both composition and condition indicator properties can answer basic questions about species ecology and behavior that are necessary both for conservation and for scientific inquiry. Examples of such questions include the species' behavioral correlation with measurable habitat variables, or how the presence of an animal or its absence from its historic range indicates anthropogenic stress.

The Role of Collaboration

The role and reason for scientific collaboration with government, management, community, and educational organizations is communication. A definition of communication in this context is "bridging understanding within a human community, exchanging messages to create meaning and enrich common knowledge, often in order to face change[45]." Scientific findings are not the only knowledge basis for management decisions. In both the developed and developing world people have local knowledge systems. These systems are not based on scientific method and do not necessarily rely on an understanding of scientific concepts[46]. The extent of discrepancies between scientific models and the perspective of resource users can be a major determinant of local acceptance of scientific information and the success of subsequent management strategies. Other factors that influence local user approval include (1) perceptions of the relationship between humans and nature—for example, small-scale fishers see coastal resources primarily from a utilitarian standpoint rather than a scientific perspective focused on ecological processes; (2) the magnitude of changes that communities will be expected to make, and how those changes will affect them politically, culturally, and economically; and (3) the social relationship and amount of trust between users and authorities. This last relationship can be complicated by a history of corruption or a lack of enforcement on the part of government representatives[47]. A history of such interactions can further alienate people who are already politically and economically marginalized.

Efforts at effective communication can be empowering, promoting social solidarity and, importantly, collaboration with conservation strategies. Orr[48] believes that the failure of scientists to communicate to societies comes from inadequate efforts by scientists to talk to the public or government in understandable terms. In his opinion, efforts of scientists to remain reasonable and objective have by default led to continuing environmental degradation and have damaged the standing of science as a source of common sense. There are, however, examples of individuals who have communicated widely the importance of the implications of their research and have become catalysts for social change. Sirenian scientists in developing countries, such as Kanjana Adulyanukosol in Thailand, Benjamín Morales-Vela in Mexico, and the co-editors of this volume, have brought a wider awareness of critical environmental issues to the public as a whole and have influenced the directions of natural and social sciences as well as attitudes toward conservation.

The extent and details of involvement of each scientist depend, of course, on the nature of the circumstances. To be an effective catalyst, a conservation-oriented scientist, working with people with widely differing views, must acknowledge the validity of a diversity of values in order to be successful.

Research results must be communicated even where the fundamental values of essential collaborators differ, and conservation plans must be negotiated to meet the needs of all constituencies[49]. The quality of conservation science should be judged not only by the empirical work but also by "a thoughtful evaluation of the research in the context of the social-scientific community in which it was carried out"[50].

By this criterion, one of the most important avenues of communication is with the local community[51]. Local nongovernmental organizations (NGOs) have increasingly been the impetus for community organization, mobilization, and education[52]. This applies both in developed and in developing countries. The Save the Manatee Club in Florida, a vast organization built around manatee conservation, also generates public support to fund much applied and basic research[53]. According to Perrin, "NGOs help keep us as scientists accountable and focused in the right direction[54]."

Environmental NGOs in developing countries are largely dedicated to alleviating poverty and empowering villagers as well as supporting long-term conservation strategies. They have created partnerships that have benefited villagers and can present suggestions in a culturally appropriate manner.

I feel strongly that for a conservation process to be effective in a developing country, the role of scientific advisor should fall to local scientists. This process can include the cooperation of the outside scientific community, who may have skills or technology that can augment local scientific work that is limited by economic or political realities. Unfortunately, governments sometimes listen to the recommendations of outside scientists or give projects more credibility once they have attracted outside researchers or funding. Therefore, collaboration between scientists from abroad and local scientists should be done carefully.

Data and specimens from developing countries still flow for the most part to the developed nations, though the days of the worst exploitation are largely over. Some scientists still do their research, publish in academic publications, and leave[55]. Research results are then not disseminated locally, leaving the local scientists who assisted them feeling exploited. Such research has little if any conservation value beyond broad recommendations in a scientific publication. Conservation-oriented scientists must establish rapport in the communities, both scientific and local, where they work. It can take time and effort to learn how to cope in a country where tasks are approached very differently.

The extent of collaboration with governments, NGOs, local scientists, educators, and communities in both native and foreign countries depends on many factors, personal and political. Long-term, multinational, collaborative research projects are needed that train native scientists and work closely with local NGOs. While challenging, such collaborations are necessary to increase sensitivity and achieve effective communication within the social parameters surrounding conservation needs.

Protected Areas for Marine Mammals

In their chapter on protected areas in this volume, Marsh and Morales-Vela[56] quote the IUCN's definition of a protected area as "an area . . . especially dedicated to the protection and maintenance of biological diversity, and of natural and associated cultural resources, and managed through legal or other effective means." This definition includes an important point: "managed through legal . . . means" implies that the protected area has the committed support of and enforcement by the government[57]. As stated by Perrin, "Laws without the will and resources to enforce them are worse than no laws at all[58]."

However, the opposite is not effective either. Without legislation, there is no backbone to enforcement, and people have no guidelines with which to defend common resources or elucidated goals to which planners aspire[59]. If a conservation ethic is needed to protect both endangered species and local communities, and many say it is[60], then stakeholders, especially marginalized groups such as artisanal fishing communities in developing countries[61], need the inclusion of integrated planning, and need protection under an ethically mandated authority of regional, national, or international legislation.

Summary

In any conservation or management planning process, it is necessary to take a detailed view of the historical and socioeconomic perspective of the issues that have been influencing the interactions between people and nature[62]. In many developing areas, a rapidly increasing human population has resulted in the degradation of coastal resources that were historically sustainable.

Every region has unique issues owing to its distinctive geography, biological resources, political structure, and social concerns. Thorough analysis, awareness, and consideration of all these parameters can reveal the necessities and constraints necessary for developing successful conservation and management strategies[63].

The use of focal species concepts and marine protected areas for the conservation of sirenians demands an integrated approach that combines biological assessment and an awareness of socioeconomic context. Further research is needed to define sirenian behavior, life history, and genetics in relation to habitat distribution and oceanographic parameters.

Scientists need to collaborate with agencies, users, educators, and other research institutions. The roles of each need to be clearly defined and, by necessity, integrated. Science is only one part of sirenian conservation; its function is the investigation and objective description of specific phenomena and processes. Effective conservation entails "interactive, reciprocal, and continuous" communication and education of scientific findings to the public and decision makers"[64].

The objective of this chapter has been to create a general framework to integrate the many issues surrounding sirenian conservation in the developing world into a template for cross-cultural application. The elements and relationships for this framework are derived from both the elements discussed in the volume and the issues discussed in this chapter.

A major component of figure 28.2 is that the elements are adapted to fit along a timeline. The vertical dotted lines in the middle of the diagram show the present. Conservation-based management and education planning decisions made in the present need to be filtered through lenses (the gray ellipses) of both the past events that have created the current situation and the realistic desired goals for the future. In each concentric circle, the goal of a sustainable population remains, accompanied by the elements comprising causative processes and constituencies. The vertical arrows connecting these elements stand for the need to connect knowledge of biophysical and socioeconomic considerations to all stakeholders through education and collaboration. The horizontal arrow with arrowheads in both directions represents the necessity for an ongoing adaptive process of conservation planning and implementation based on continual information gathering, evaluation, and monitoring.

The three concepts of focal species, collaboration, and marine protected areas fit into the framework implicitly. Focal species concepts are included in causative processes. A flagship species is related to both socioeconomic and biophysical considerations, as knowledge of cultural roles as well as habitat requirements is pertinent. Exploration of a sirenian's role as an umbrella or indicator species can be a guide to research questions and management decisions throughout present and future planning. The collaboration between constituencies, including a realization of cultural values and ethics, is addressed here and, in this framework, is ongoing throughout each stage. If a marine protected area (MPA) is prescribed during the development of plans and actions, the protected area should be planned and implemented using the information gathered considering the combined causative processes: past, present, and anticipated. This MPA would also address the concerns arrived at as a result of the collaboration of all constituencies. The MPA will, ideally, be continually evaluated by a succession of monitoring and information gathering actions.

This framework is a tool to help organize and guide research and conservation planning for an endangered marine mammal, especially when incorporating the element of time. For example, beyond research on the animals themselves across time, which is a requirement for most ecological-process-based research, research conducted within this framework will include exploration of past and present socioeconomic considerations that may have caused destructive fishing practices or incidental catch: factors that have degraded habitat or depleted a population. The key is that both ecological and social research look to history and toward the future in tandem. At each stage in the past, both of these domains have interacted to produce the conditions of endangerment.

If future conservation planning is to be successful, it too should function by linking ecological and social factors. Future research on causative processes based on this framework could be directed at gathering specific data to test hypotheses regarding the ecological role of a sirenian through a more detailed investigation of the relationship between manatees and dugongs and their habitat. The information gathering as outlined in the framework is ongoing, as are the management and education plans and actions to which the information contributes, which are in turn continually adjusted by evaluation and monitoring.

Perhaps a key to the framework I present here is the idea that the research methods are open to local knowledge and continual review. Of course, the population and habitat issues are best studied by scientific methods. But science can be informed and supported by local knowledge to greater or lesser degrees depending on the setting. Social research can be carried on under a wide variety of methodological approaches. In one instance an open interview can be conducted; in other area a statistical sample or an attitude survey may better reveal the required information.

A final point is the role of the researcher as catalyst. In this arena there is no single method per se. Each individual engaging in conservation-oriented science has to build a suite of skills and develop his or her judgment and sensitivity as to how to approach the various stakeholders. As scientists we contribute to understanding causative processes, but in the processes of doing so, information is created that is used by many parties, some of whom have competing goals. In fact, some of the users may have goals that directly compete with conservation-oriented goals for the species and its habitat. Thus conservation biologists are faced with a conundrum. While gathering information, one enters into the interactive social sphere of conservation: attends meetings, cajoles with government figures, and builds relationships with local communities and scientists.

Long-term planning requires long-term research. Collaboration between constituencies is crucial for future conservation planning. I would be remiss in not mentioning the threat of climate change to sirenians. While the effects of sea-level rise and a rapidly changing physical environment (predictions for significant changes are on the decadal time scale) on sirenians and their habitat are complex, and are only beginning to be addressed, paradigms for conserving nearshore species, communities, and ecosystems as we know them will need to shift dynamically[65]. Without sound conservation planning and effort, I believe several remnant populations of sirenians around the globe will be extirpated before the end of the twenty-first century.

Notes

Chapter 1. The Role of Sirenians in Aquatic Ecosystems

1. Blanshard 2001.
2. Reynolds and Odell 1991.
3. Reeves et al. 2002.
4. Lanyon 1991; Preen 1992; Aragones 1996.
5. Lefebvre and Powell 1990; Provancha and Hall 1991.
6. Packard 1981; Thayer et al. 1984; De Iongh et al. 1995; Preen 1995a; Aragones and Marsh 2000; Aragones et al. 2006.
7. Jackson et al. 2001.
8. Hartman 1979; Best 1981; Zieman 1982; Etheridge et al. 1985; Reynolds and Odell 1991.
9. Preen 1992; Aragones 1994.
10. Preen 1992.
11. Coles et al. 2002.
12. Marsh et al. 2005.
13. Provancha and Hall 1991.
14. Preen 1992.
15. Lefebvre and Powell 1990; Lefebvre et al. 2000.
16. Domning 2001.
17. Ibid.
18. Marsh et al. 1982a.
19. Hartman 1979; Best 1981; Reeves et al. 2002.
20. Hartman 1979; Reynolds and Odell 1991.
21. Best 1981; Colares and Colares 2002.
22. Domning 1977, 1980.
23. Best 1981; Domning 1982a; Colares and Colares 2002; Marshall et al. 2003.
24. Marsh et al. 1999a.
25. Reynolds 1981; Shane 1983.
26. Domning 1978.
27. Lanyon and Sanson 2006.
28. Domning and Hayek 1984.
29. Marsh et al. 1999a.
30. Ibid.
31. Domning 1982a.
32. Green and Short 2003.
33. Lanyon 1986; Mukai 1993.
34. Marsh et al. 1982a; Lanyon 1991; Preen 1992; André et al. 2005.
35. Smith 1993.
36. Aragones and Marsh 2000; McMahon 2005.
37. E.g., Lanyon 1991; Aragones et al. 2006.
38. Heinsohn et al. 1977; Preen 1995a.
39. Anderson 1982.
40. André et al. 2005.
41. Domning and Beatty 2007.
42. Bengtson 1983.
43. Lefebvre and Powell 1990.
44. Hartman 1979; Smith 1993.
45. E.g., Provancha and Hall 1991.
46. Hartman 1979; Baugh et al. 1989.
47. Anderson 1989; Preen 1995b.
48. Marsh et al. 1982b; Preen 1992.
49. O'Shea and Rathbun 1982; O'Shea and Kochman 1990.
50. Hurst and Beck 1988.
51. Powell 1978.
52. Marsh et al. 1982b.
53. Heinsohn and Spain 1974.
54. Marsh et al. 1982b.
55. Whiting 2002.
56. Domning 1977.
57. Domning 1978.
58. Best 1981.
59. Bengtson 1983; Reeves et al. 2002.
60. Timm et al. 1986.
61. Colares and Colares 2002.
62. Best 1981; Reeves et al. 2002.
63. Reynolds and Odell 1991.
64. Reeves et al. 2002.
65. Hartman 1979.
66. Etheridge et al. 1985.
67. Hurst and Beck 1988.
68. O'Shea 1986.
69. E.g., McNaughton 1979, 1983; Dyer et al. 1982.
70. E.g., Hay et al. 1983, 1987; Hixon and Brostoff 1996.
71. Preen 1992.
72. Aragones 1996.
73. Aragones and Marsh 2000.
74. Aragones et al. 2006.
75. Aragones and Marsh 2000.
76. Marsh et al. 1982b.
77. Wake 1975; Anderson and Birtles 1978; Preen 1992; Aragones 1994, 1996; Supanwanid 1996.
78. Lanyon 1991; Aragones 1996.
79. Aragones and Marsh 2000.
80. Preen 1992.

81. Aragones and Marsh 2000.
82. Perry and Dennison 1999.
83. Preen 1995a.
84. Perry and Dennison 1999.
85. Preen 1995a.
86. Anderson and Birtles 1978.
87. Aragones et al. 2006.
88. Perry and Dennison 1999.
89. Preen 1995a.
90. McNaughton 1979; Hilbert et al. 1981; Dyer et al. 1982.
91. Aragones et al. 2006.
92. Perry and Dennison 1999.
93. Aragones and Marsh 2000.
94. Ibid.
95. Ibid.
96. E.g., Aragones 1994; Aragones and Marsh 2000; Supanwanid 1996.

Chapter 2. Vulnerability of Sirenians

1. Reynolds and Rommel 1999.
2. Glaser and Reynolds 2003.
3. Reviewed by Pabst et al. 1999; Marshall 2002.
4. Pabst et al. 1999; Marshall 2002.
5. Rommel et al. 2001; Rommel and Caplan 2003.
6. Ricklefs 1990, p. 815.
7. Glaser and Reynolds 2003.
8. Ricklefs 1990.
9. Boyd et al. 1999; Wells et al. 1999.
10. Reynolds et al. 2004.
11. In Boyd et al. 1999.
12. Ibid.
13. Marsh and Kwan 2008.
14. Kwan 2002.
15. Boyd et al. 1999.
16. Glaser and Reynolds 2003.
17. U.S. Marine Mammal Commission 2008.
18. Dayton et al. 1998.
19. Reynolds et al. 2009.
20. Costa and Williams 1999.
21. Reynolds and Odell 1991.
22. UNEP 2008a.
23. Kwan 2002; Marsh et al. 2002; Heinsohn et al. 2004; Daley et al. 2008.
24. Domning 1982a.
25. Read 2005.
26. Marsh et al. 2002.
27. Deutsch and Reynolds, this volume, chap. 3.
28. Sargent et al. 1995.
29. Dawes et al. 1997.
30. See Aragones et al., this volume, chap. 1.
31. Haynes et al. 1999.
32. McLachlan et al. 2001.
33. Ames and Van Vleet 1996.
34. O'Shea et al. 1984.
35. Wetzel et al., this volume, chap. 22.
36. O'Shea 1999.
37. Glaser and Reynolds 2003; Miksis-Olds 2006.
38. Buckingham et al. 1999.
39. Reeves et al. 1988.
40. Reviewed by Pabst et al. 1999; Marshall 2002.
41. Sarko et al. 2007a, 2007b.
42. Cohen et al. 1982; Griebel and Schmid 1996, 1997; Ahnelt and Kolb 2000.
43. Walls 1942.
44. Mass et al. 1997; Hatfield et al. 2003; Harper et al. 2005; Natiello et al. 2005.
45. Reep and Bonde 2006.
46. Hartman 1979; Gerstein 1994; Bauer et al. 2003.
47. G. B. Bauer, pers. comm.
48. Reep et al. 2002.
49. Ibid.
50. Gerstein et al. 1999.
51. Ketten et al. 1992.
52. Bullock et al. 1980, 1982; Klishin et al. 1990; Mann et al. 2005.
53. E.g., Hartman 1979.
54. Wright et al. 1995.
55. Nowacek et al. 2004.
56. Glaser and Reynolds 2003.
57. Ames et al. 2002.
58. G. B. Bauer, pers. comm.
59. Domning and Buffrenil 1991.
60. Domning 1980.
61. Reynolds et al. 2002; Rommel et al. 2003.
62. Rommel and Reynolds 2002.
63. Domning and Buffrenil 1991; Taylor 2000.
64. Kipps et al. 2002.
65. Domning and Buffrenil 1991.
66. Clifton et al. 2008a, 2008b.
67. Clifton et al. 2008a, 2008b.
68. Marshall et al. 2000.
69. Marshall et al. 1998a.
70. Marshall et al. 2007.
71. Reep et al. 1998.
72. Marshall et al. 2003.
73. Marshall et al. 2007; Sarko et al. 2007c.
74. Marshall et al. 1998b, 2003.
75. Bachteler and Dehnhardt 1999.
76. Marsh 1980.
77. Marsh et al. 1999a.
78. Domning 1999b.
79. Domning 1982b.
80. Domning and Hayek 1984.
81. Hartman 1979.
82. Janis 1976; Parra 1976; Reynolds and Rommel 1996.
83. Reynolds and Rommel 1996.
84. Rommel et al. 2003.
85. E.g., Craig and Reynolds 2004.
86. Reynolds et al. 2005; Reynolds et al. 2009.

Chapter 3. Florida Manatee Status and Conservation Issues: A Primer

1. Hartman 1979; Reynolds and Odell 1991; Glaser and Reynolds 2003; Reep and Bonde 2006; USFWS 2001, the federal Florida Manatee Recovery Plan; and FWC 2007, the state Florida Manatee Management Plan.
2. Linnaeus 1758.
3. Domning and Hayek 1986; Garcia-Rodriguez et al. 1998.
4. Vianna et al. 2006.
5. Caughley and Gunn 1996.
6. FWC 2002; MPSWG 2005; Haubold et al. 2006; USFWS 2007.
7. Lefebvre et al. 2001.
8. Alvarez-Alemán et al. 2007.
9. Rathbun et al. 1982; Schwartz 1995.
10. Deutsch et al. 2003.
11. Beck 2006.
12. Powell and Rathbun 1984; Fertl et al. 2005.
13. R. Bonde, pers. comm., 2007.
14. Weigle et al. 2001; Deutsch et al. 2003.
15. Reid et al. 1991; Koelsch 1997; Deutsch et al. 2003.
16. Best 1981; Smith 1993.
17. Reynolds and Wilcox 1994; USFWS 2000; Laist and Reynolds 2005a, 2005b.
18. Irvine 1983.
19. Laist and Reynolds 2005b.
20. Ibid.
21. Ibid.
22. O'Shea 1988.
23. Laist and Reynolds 2005b.
24. O'Shea 1988; FWC 2002.
25. USFWS 2001; MPSWG 2005.
26. IUCN 2001, p. 10.
27. Bengtson 1981; Rathbun et al. 1990; Reid et al. 1991; Weigle et al. 2001; Deutsch et al. 2003.
28. FWC 2007; USFWS 2007.
29. Garcia-Rodriguez et al. 1998; Vianna et al. 2006; Hunter et al. 2010; Nourisson et al. 2011.
30. Garcia-Rodriguez et al. 2000; Pause 2007; Tringali et al. 2008.
31. Garcia-Rodriquez et al. 1998; See Parr et al., this volume, chap. 19.
32. Packard et al. 1985; Lefebvre et al. 1995; Edwards et al. 2007; Reynolds et al., this volume, chap. 21.
33. Ackerman 1995.
34. Florida Fish and Wildlife Conservation Commission, unpublished data.
35. Eberhardt et al. 1999.
36. Runge et al. 2004.
37. W. L. Kendall et al. 2004; Langtimm et al. 2004.
38. Beck and Reid 1995, this volume, box 3.3.
39. Ackerman 1995; Eberhardt and O'Shea 1995; Runge et al. 2004.
40. Runge et al. 2007b.
41. Runge et al. 2004.
42. Craig and Reynolds 2004.
43. Runge et al. 2004.
44. Langtimm et al. 2004.
45. See Reynolds and Marshall, this volume, chap. 2.
46. MPSWG 2005.
47. Eberhardt and O'Shea 1995; Marmontel et al. 1997; Runge et al. 2004.
48. Ackerman et al. 1995; Wright et al. 1995; MPSWG 2005.
49. Runge et al. 2007b.
50. FWC 2006.
51. Florida Fish and Wildlife Conservation Commission, unpublished data.
52. Wright et al. 1995.
53. Beck and Barros 1991; Ackerman et al. 1995.
54. FWC 2007.
55. Ackerman et al. 1995.
56. Beck and Barros 1991.
57. Spellman 1999.
58. USFWS 2000, 2001.
59. Runge et al. 2007b.
60. Deutsch 2000; Deutsch et al. 2003.
61. Ackerman et al. 1995; Packard et al. 1989; Deutsch et al. 2000; Laist and Reynolds 2005a.
62. Taylor 2006.
63. Florida Springs Task Force 2006.
64. Perry and Mackun 2001; Mackun and Wilson 2011; GeoPlan Center 2006.
65. Sargent et al. 1995; Fonseca et al. 1998.
66. Kurz et al. 2000.
67. Robblee et al. 1991; Preen and Marsh 1995; Preen et al. 1995.
68. Langtimm and Beck 2003; Langtimm et al. 2006.
69. O'Shea et al. 1985; Bossart et al. 2002b.
70. Harwood and Hall 1990; Bossart et al. 2002a; Woodruff et al. 2005.
71. Flewelling et al. 2005.
72. Wetzel et al., this volume, chap 22.
73. King and Heinen 2004.
74. Munns 2006.
75. Walsh et al. 2005.
76. O'Shea et al. 1991; Bossart et al. 1998; Landsberg and Steidinger 1998.
77. Flewelling et al. 2005.
78. Bossart et al. 1998.
79. Florida Fish and Wildlife Conservation Commission, unpublished data.
80. Landsberg and Steidinger 1998.
81. Steidinger et al. 2004.
82. Boyce 1992; Beissinger and Westphal 1998.
83. Harwood 2000; Morris and Doak 2003.
84. FWC 2002; Haubold et al. 2006; Runge et al. 2007a.
85. Generation time ~20 years; Haubold et al. 2006; Runge et al. 2007a.
86. Runge et al. 2007b.

87. Runge et al. 2007a.
88. See FWC 2007; USFWS 2007.
89. Gosliner 1999.
90. Reynolds and Gluckman 1988; Glaser and Reynolds 2003.
91. USFWS 2007.
92. Deutsch et al. 2007.
93. FWC 2002; Haubold et al. 2006.
94. O'Shea et al. 2001; FWC 2007.
95. Reynolds and Gluckman 1988; Wallace 1994; Reynolds 1999; USFWS 2001; Glaser and Reynolds 2003; FWC 2007.
96. Wallace 1994.
97. Adimey et al., this volume, chap. 23.
98. USFWS 2001; now in its 4th version.
99. Forrer et al. 2005.
100. Reynolds et al. 2005.
101. Ibid.
102. Wallace 1994.
103. Reynolds 1995, 1999; USFWS 2001; FWC 2007.
104. Beck and Reid 1995; Langtimm et al. 1998, 2004; Beck and Clark, this volume, chap. 15.
105. Garrott et al. 1994; Reynolds and Wilcox 1994; Ackerman 1995; Craig and Reynolds 2004; Reynolds et al., this volume, chap. 21.
106. Ackerman et al. 1995; Lightsey et al. 2006; Rommel et al. 2007; Bonde and Bossart, this volume, chap. 17.
107. Eberhardt and O'Shea 1995; Runge et al. 2004, 2007a.
108. King and Heinen 2004.
109. Nowacek et al. 2004.
110. Hauxwell et al. 2004a, 2004b.
111. Deutsch et al. 1998, 2003; Weigle et al. 2001.
112. Irvine 1983; Ortiz et al. 1998.
113. Reynolds and Rommel 1996; Rommel and Reynolds 2000; Rommel and Caplan 2003.
114. Marshall et al. 1998a, b; Gerstein et al. 1999; Reep et al. 2002; Bauer et al. 2003.
115. Garcia-Rodriguez et al. 1998.
116. O'Shea et al. 1999.
117. FWC 2007.
118. Roux et al. 2006.
119. Deutsch et al. 2003.
120. See O'Shea 1988.
121. Ibid., p. 192.
122. Laist and Reynolds 2005a.
123. O'Shea 1995.
124. Runge et al. 2004.

Chapter 4. West Indian Manatees (*Trichechus manatus*) in the Wider Caribbean Region

1. Self-Sullivan and Mignucci-Giannoni 2008.
2. See Deutsch and Reynolds, this volume, chap. 3.
3. Reid 2001; R. Bonde, pers. comm., 2009.
4. Garcia-Rodriguez et al. 1998; Vianna et al. 2006; Parr et al., this volume, chap 19.
5. Deutsch et al. 2003; Debrot et al. 2006; B. Morales-Vela and N. E. Auil-Gomez, pers. comm.; B. M. Riggs, pers. comm., 2005.
6. Lefebvre et al. 2001.
7. McKillop 1985; Mercado 1990; Riviera and Rodriguez 1991; Wing and Scudder 1991.
8. Newsom and Wing 2004.
9. McKillop 2002.
10. McKillop 1984.
11. Morison 1942.
12. Cuní 1918.
13. Whitehead 1977, 1978.
14. Domning 1982b.
15. Quintana-Rizzo and Reynolds 2010.
16. Durand 1983; Lefebvre et al. 2001.
17. Bertram and Ricardo Bertram 1964.
18. Bertram 2002.
19. E.g., Bertram and Ricardo Bertram 1963, 1964, 1973; Wilson 1974; Duplaix and Reichart 1978; Klein 1979; Belitsky and Belitsky 1980; Domning 1981; O'Donnell 1981; Rathbun et al. 1985b; O'Shea 1986; Estrada and Ferrer 1987; Boyle and Khan 1993; Auil 1998; Ottenwalder and León 1999; Montoya-Ospina et al. 2001; Lima et al. 1992.
20. Powell et al. 1981; Rathbun et al. 1985a.
21. Fairbairn and Haynes 1982.
22. Belitsky and Belitsky 1980; Ottenwalder 1995.
23. Rathbun et al. 1985b.
24. Estrada and Ferrer 1993.
25. Campbell and Gicca 1978; Morales-Vela et al. 2000, 2003.
26. Charnock-Wilson 1968, 1970; Bengtson and Magor 1979; O'Shea and Salisbury 1991; Morales-Vela et al. 2000; Auil 2004.
27. Quintana-Rizzo 1993.
28. Rathbun et al. 1983a.
29. Carr 1994.
30. Reynolds et al. 1995.
31. Mou Sue and Chen 1990.
32. O'Shea 1986.
33. See Reynolds et al., this volume, chap. 21.
34. Bengtson and Magor 1979; O'Shea and Salisbury 1991; Gibson 1995; Morales-Vela et al. 2000, 2003; Auil 2004; Reynolds et al., this volume, chap. 21.
35. B. Morales-Vela, J. A. Powell, N. E. Auil-Gomez, and R. Bonde, pers. comm., 2007.
36. Auil 2004; Self-Sullivan et al. 2003; LaCommare et al. 2008; Self-Sullivan 2008.
37. O'Shea 2009.
38. Reynolds 2009.
39. Deutsch et al. 2008.
40. Quintana-Rizzo and Reynolds 2010.
41. Self-Sullivan and Mignucci-Giannoni 2008.
42. Quintana-Rizzo and Reynolds 2010.
43. Lefebvre et al. 2001; Quintana-Rizzo and Reynolds 2010.
44. Freestone 1991; Sheehy 2004.
45. See von Zharen, this volume, chap. 26.
46. Ramsar 2009.
47. Sheehy 2004.

48. Pomeroy et al. 2004a.
49. Domning 1982b.
50. Deutsch et al. 2008.
51. Lefebvre et al. 2001; Quintana-Rizzo and Reynolds 2010; Deutsch et al. 2008; Self-Sullivan and Mignucci-Giannoni 2008.
52. Quintana-Rizzo and Reynolds 2010.
53. Self-Sullivan and Mignucci-Giannoni 2008.
54. Quintana-Rizzo and Reynolds 2010.
55. O'Shea and Salisbury 1991.
56. Auil and Valentine 2003, 2006.
57. Belize Tourism Board 2006.
58. Self-Sullivan 2008.
59. Self-Sullivan et al. 2003; Self-Sullivan 2008.
60. See Deutsch and Reynolds, box 5.3, this volume.
61. Parente et al. 2004.
62. Bonnelly de Calventi and Lancho-Dieguez 2005.
63. Ottenwalder 1995; Pugibet and Vega 2000; Bonelly de Calventi and Lancho-Dieguez 2005.
64. Santos Mariño 2006.
65. Janson 1980.
66. Jiménez Pérez 2002.
67. Lima 1997.
68. De Thoisy et al. 2003.
69. O'Shea et al. 1988.
70. Castelblanco-Martínez et al. 2003; Castelblanco-Martínez and Bermudez 2004.
71. Arzoumanian et al. 2005.
72. Quintana-Rizzo and Reynolds 2010.

Chapter 5. The Amazonian Manatee

1. Domning 1982a.
2. Sioli 1984.
3. Rosas and Pimentel 2001.
4. Domning 1982b.
5. Tirira 2001.
6. Ibid.
7. Soini et al. 1996.
8. Sioli 1984.
9. Domning 1982b.
10. Ibid.
11. Husar 1977.
12. Marsh et al. 1984; Packard 1985.
13. Marmontel et al. 1992; Reynolds and Marshall, this volume, chap 2.
14. Garcia-Rodriguez et al. 1998; Vianna et al. 2002; Caballero and Giraldo 2004.
15. Cantanhede et al. 2005; Vianna et al. 2006.
16. Vianna et al. 2006.
17. IBAMA 2001.
18. Tirira 2000.
19. Domning 1982b.
20. C. Castro, pers. comm., 2005.
21. Utreras and Zapata, pers. comm., 2005.
22. Reeves et al. 1996; Kendall and Orozco 2003; Ulloa Gómez 2004, personal observation.
23. Lima et al. 2001.
24. Kendall and Orozco 2003.
25. Ulloa Gómez 2004.
26. Lazzarini et al. 1998.
27. Lazzarini et al. 2000.
28. Wallace 1853, repr. 1972; Goeldi 1893.
29. S. M. Lazzarini and M. C. L. Picanço, pers. comm., 2005.
30. Reeves et al. 1996; Ulloa Gómez 2004.
31. Ulloa Gómez 2004.
32. Reeves et al. 1996; Ulloa Gómez 2004.
33. Picanço and Lazzarini, unpublished data, 2005.
34. F. C. W. Rosas and V. M. F. da Silva, pers. comm., 2005.
35. Ibid.
36. Fundación Omacha and Ministerio de Ambiente 2005.
37. Lazzarini and Picanço, pers. comm., 2005.
38. Ulloa Gómez 2004; Kendall et al. 2005.
39. Kendall 2001; Orozco 2001; Kendall et al. 2005.
40. Sartor et al. 2004.
41. Kendall 2001; S. Kendall et al. 2004.
42. Fearnside 1990.
43. Rosas 1994.
44. F. Sartor, pers. comm., 2005.
45. C. Castro, pers. comm., 2005; F. Sartor, pers. comm., 2005.
46. Kendall 2001.
47. Tirira 2001.
48. S. Lazzarini, M. Picanço, F. Luna, F. Sartor, and M. Alves, pers. comm., 2005.
49. Sartor, pers. comm., 2005.
50. Lima et al. 2001; Luna et al. 2004.
51. Castro, pers. comm., 2005.
52. Lazzarini, Picanço, Hage, and Sartor, pers. comm., 2005; Lima et al. 2001; M. Marmontel, personal observation.
53. Hage, pers. comm., 2005; Marmontel, personal observation.
54. Lazzarini and Picanço, pers. comm., 2005; Lima et al. 2001.
55. Lima et al. 2001.
56. Lazzarini and Picanço, pers. comm., 2005.
57. S. Kendall, pers. comm., 2005.
58. C. Castro, pers. comm., 2005.
59. Kendall and Marmontel, in prep.
60. Adimay et al., this volume, chap. 23.
61. Kendall 2001.
62. Orozco 2001.
63. Kendall 2001; Ulloa Gómez 2004; Lazzarini and Picanço, pers. comm., 2005.
64. Ulloa Gómez 2004.
65. Lazzarini and Picanço, pers. comm., 2005.
66. C. Bassi, pers. comm., 2005.
67. R. E. Bodmer, pers. comm., 2005.
68. Lazzarini and Picanço, pers. comm., 2005.
69. Kendall et al. 2005.
70. S. Kendall, pers. comm., 2005.
71. Timm et al. 1989.

72. C. Castro, pers. comm., 2005.
73. Ulloa Gómez 2004.
74. Bodmer et al. 1996.
75. Bodmer, pers. comm., 2005.
76. Kendall and Orozco 2003.
77. Ibid.
78. Kendall 2001.
79. Ibid.
80. Ibid.
81. Kendall and Orozco 2003.
82. Kendall 2001.
83. Orozco 2001.
84. Best 1982a.
85. Reeves et al. 1996.
86. Tirira 2001.
87. Vianna et al. 2006.

Chapter 6. The West African Manatee

1. Nishiwaki et al. 1982.
2. Reeves et al. 1988.
3. Roth and Waitkuwait 1986.
4. Powell 1996.
5. Kouadio 2002, 2004.
6. L. Keith, pers. comm., 2009.
7. Roth and Waitkuwait 1986; Powell 1996; Kouadio 2004.
8. Hatt 1934; Husar 1978a; Nishiwaki et al. 1982; Haltenorth and Diller 1986; UNEP 2008b.
9. Powell 1996; Kouadio 2004.
10. Roth and Waitkuwait 1986.
11. S. Louembet, WWF unpublished report, 2008.
12. Reeves et al. 1988; Kouadio 2004.
13. Johnson 1937.
14. Powell 1996.
15. L. Keith, pers. comm., 2009.
16. Powell 1996.
17. A. Kouadio, personal observation, 2009.
18. Grigione 1996.
19. Kouadio, personal observation, 2009.
20. IUCN 2009.
21. Robinson 1971; Nishiwaki et al. 1982; Reeves et al. 1988; Sykes 1974; Kienta 1985; Kouadio 1994; Mbina 2001; Silva and Araújo 2001; Kouadio 2002; Marchais 2006.
22. Reynolds and Odell 1991.

Chapter 7. Dugongs in Asia

1. Chua and Garces 1994.
2. Kirkman and Kirkman 2000.
3. Pauly 2006a.
4. Mathew 2003; Pomeroy and Viswanathan 2003.
5. Reynolds and Marshall, this volume, chap. 2.
6. Marsh et al. 2002.
7. Roberts and Hawkins 1999.
8. UNESCAP 2009.
9. Hines et al. 2005a; Hines et al. 2008a.
10. Marsh et al. 2002.
11. Hines 2002; Hines et al. 2005b.
12. Sae Aueng et al. 1993.
13. Adulyanukosol 1995.
14. Adulyanukosol 1999; Adulyanukosol et al. 1997, 1999.
15. Chansang and Poovachiranon 1994; Poovachiranon and Chansang 1994.
16. Adulyanukosol 2004; Hines 2002; Hines et al. 2003, 2004, 2005a, 2005b; Intongcome et al. 2005; Poovachiranon et al. 2006.
17. Adulyanukosol 2004; Hines et al. 2005b.
18. Hines et al. 2003, 2004.
19. Adulyanukosol 2004; Intongcome et al. 2005.
20. Adulyanukosol 1999; 2000.
21. Intongcome et al. 2005.
22. Hines et al. 2005a.
23. Adulyanukosol and Thongsukdee 2005.
24. Hines 2002; Hines et al. 2005a.
25. Hines et al. 2003, 2004, 2008b, 2009.
26. Adulyanukosol 1999, 2004; Intongcome et al. 2005.
27. Humphrey and Bain 1990.
28. Saranakomkul 2002.
29. Hines et al., in revision.
30. Adulyanukosol et al. 2005, National News Bureau of Thailand 2011.
31. Chansang and Poovachiranon 1994.
32. Pauly 2006a.
33. Thai Department of Fisheries 2000.
34. Flaherty and Karnjanakesorn 1995.
35. Hines et al., in revision; Hines et al. 2005b.
36. Pauly 1997; Mathew 2003.
37. Hines et al. 2005a.
38. Hines et al., in revision.
39. Adulyanukosol and Poochaviranon 2006.
40. Hines et al. 2003, 2004.
41. Nelson 1999, as cited in Marsh et al. 2002.
42. Beasley et al. 2002.
43. Hines et al. 2008a.
44. Ibid.
45. Ibid.
46. Ibid.
47. Ibid.
48. See von Zharen, this volume, chap. 26.
49. Hines et al. 2004, 2008a.
50. Van Bree and Gallagher 1977; Marsh et al. 2002; Hoa 2001.
51. Cox 2004.
52. Hines et al. 2008a.
53. Cox 2004.
54. Ibid.
55. Cox et al. 2003.
56. Cox 2004.
57. Hines et al. 2008a.
58. WWF Indochina Dugong Action Plan 2006.
59. Chiêm 2003.
60. Symington, pers. comm., 2006; Hines et al. 2008a.

61. Tuấn 2003.
62. WWF Indochina Dugong Action Plan 2006.
63. Cox et al. 2003.
64. WWF Indochina Dugong Action Plan 2006.
65. Ibid.
66. Hines et al. 2008a.
67. Mason 1882.
68. *Guardian* (U.K.), 4 November 1966; Yin 1971.
69. Tun and Ilangakoon 2006; Ilangakoon and Tun 2007.
70. Hines et al. 2007.
71. Ilangakoon and Tun 2007.
72. Tun and Ilangakoon 2006.
73. Tun and Ilangakoon 2006; Ilangakoon and Tun 2007.
74. See Reynolds et al., this volume, chap. 21.
75. SeagrassNet.org; Novak et al. 2009.
76. Hines et al. 2007.
77. CIA 2007.
78. Piestch 1991.
79. Allen et al. 1976; Hendrokusumo et al. 1976; Erftemeijer et al. 1993; De Iongh et al. 2007.
80. De Iongh et al. 2007.
81. De Iongh et al. 1995.
82. Brownell et al. 1981.
83. Marsh et al. 1984.
84. Trono 1995.
85. De Iongh et al. 1998.
86. Preen 1995a.
87. Marsh et al. 2002.
88. Salm 1984.
89. Nishiwaki and Marsh 1985.
90. De Iongh et al. 2009.
91. De Iongh et al. 1997; Marsh et al. 2002.
92. Marsh et al. 2002.
93. De Iongh et al. 2007.
94. Kreb and Budiono 2005.
95. De Iongh et al. 2006b.
96. De Iongh et al. 1995.
97. Hendrokusumo et al. 1976; Tas'an et al. 1979.
98. Ibu Mega, pers. comm., 2009.
99. ISC 2003.
100. De Iongh et al. 2009.
101. De Iongh et al. 2007.
102. Marsh et al. 2002; De Iongh 1997.
103. De Iongh 1996; De Iongh et al. 2007.
104. De Iongh et al. 2009.
105. Marsh et al. 2002; De Iongh et al. 2006a.
106. Novaczek et al. 2001.
107. De Iongh and Persoon 1991.
108. Marsh et al. 2002; Hendrokusumo et al. 1976.
109. DeIongh and Persoon 1991; Hendrokusumo et al. 1976.
110. Persoon et al. 1996.
111. Aragones 1990.
112. Aragones 1994.
113. Kataoka et al. 1995.
114. Marsh et al. 2002; Perrin et al. 2005.
115. Kataoka et al. 1995.
116. Aragones 1998; Baltazar and Yaptinchay 1998.
117. Dolar et al. 2005.
118. Aragones, unpublished data.
119. Kataoka et al. 1995.
120. Marsh et al. 2002.
121. Aragones, unpublished data.
122. Aragones et al. 2010.
123. Uri et al. 1998.
124. Marsh et al. 2002.
125. Allen 1938.
126. Shou 1958.
127. As cited by Shou 1958.
128. Wang and Sun 1986.
129. Dong et al. 1992.
130. Zhou et al. 2003.
131. Ibid.
132. Sun 1999.
133. Deng and Lian 2002, 2004.
134. Wang and Sun 1986.
135. Deng 2002.
136. Marsh et al. 2002.
137. Zhou et al. 2003.
138. Deng 2002.
139. Shou 1958.
140. Deng 2002.
141. Ibid.
142. Wang 2008.
143. Ibid.
144. Tennent 1859.
145. Haley 1884; Phillips 1927; Norris 1960.
146. Jonklass 1961; Deraniyagala 1965; Bertram and Ricardo Bertram 1970; Jones 1980.
147. Leatherwood and Reeves 1989; Ilangakoon et al. 2004.
148. Leatherwood and Reeves 1989.
149. Leatherwood and Reeves 1989; Ilangakoon et al. 2008.
150. Ilangakoon et al. 2004, 2008.
151. Tennent 1859; Haley 1884; Neville 1885; Phillips 1927.
152. Neville 1885.
153. Haley 1884.
154. Bertram and Ricardo Bertram 1970; Leatherwood and Reeves 1989; Ilangakoon et al. 2008.
155. Ilangakoon et al. 2004, 2008.
156. Ilangakoon et al. 2008.
157. Ibid.
158. Haley 1884.
159. Norris 1960.
160. Ilangakoon 1989, 2002.
161. Leatherwood and Reeves 1989.
162. Ilangakoon et al. 2008.
163. Ibid.
164. Ibid.
165. Ibid.
166. Annandale 1905.
167. Jones 1959, 1967; Lal Mohan 1976.

168. Mani 1960; Silas 1961.
169. Lal Mohan 1963, 1976.
170. James 1974; James and Mohan 1987.
171. Leatherwood and Reeves 1989.
172. Ilangakoon et al. 2008.
173. Anon. 1909; Jones 1980; James 1988.
174. Das and Dey 1999.
175. D'souza and Patankar 2009; D'souza 2008.
176. Annandale 1905; James 1974; Jones 1959, 1980; Jonklass 1961; Lal Mohan 1963, 1976; Mani 1960; Nair et al. 1975; Prater 1928; Silas 1961; Silas and Fernando 1985.
177. Nishiwaki and Marsh 1985.
178. Yin 1971.
179. Jerdon 1874.
180. Anon. 1909.
181. Husar 1975a; Jethva and Solanki 2007.
182. Jethva and Solanki 2007.
183. Frazier and Mundkur 1990.
184. Lal Mohan 1963; Frazier and Mundkur 1990; Singh et al. 2004.
185. Sutaria and Jefferson 2004.
186. Singh et al. 2004; Jethva and Solanki 2007.
187. Annandale 1905.
188. Ilangakoon et al. 2008.
189. Das and Dey 1999.
190. Ibid.
191. D'souza and Patankar 2008; D'souza 2009; Jethva and Solanki 2007.
192. Lal Mohan 1994.
193. Silas and Fernando 1985.
194. Nair et al. 1975.
195. Jones 1980.
196. Ilangakoon et al. 2008.
197. Singh et al. 2004.
198. Frazier and Mundkur 1990; Jethva and Solanki 2007.
199. Ilangakoon et al. 2008.
200. Das and Dey 1999.
201. Das 2000.
202. Das 1996.
203. Das and Dey 1999; Das 2000.
204. R. Arthur, pers comm., 2001.
205. Jones 1967.
206. Kulkarni et al. 2008; Ramachandran et al. 2005; Sankaran et al. 2005.
207. Ilangakoon et al. 2008.
208. T. M. Koya, pers. comm, 1988.
209. Aragones et al. 1997; Reynolds et al., this volume, chap. 21.

Chapter 8. Dugongs in Japan

1. Kasuya et al. 1999.
2. Defense Agency of Japan 2001.
3. Ministry of the Environment 2006a, 2006b.
4. Ministry of the Environment 2002.
5. Ministry of the Environment 2002, 2003, 2004a, 2004b.
6. Ministry of the Environment 2005, 2006a, 2006b.
7. Ministry of the Environment 2006b.
8. Ministry of the Environment 2003, 2004a.
9. Ministry of the Environment 2003, 2004a.
10. Aketa 2003; Ministry of the Environment 2003; 2004a.
11. Wakai et al. 2002.
12. Aketa et al. 2003; Goto et al. 2004a.
13. Goto et al. 2004b.
14. Ikeda 2006.
15. Ibid.
16. Ogura et al. 2005; Mukai et al., unpublished data.
17. Ohtaishi 2005.
18. Yoshida et al. 2003.
19. Ministry of the Environment 2003, 2004b.
20. Uni 2003.
21. Uchida 1994.
22. Ministry of the Environment 2004b.
23. Ministry of the Environment 1997.
24. Kuo et al. 2006; Mukai et al., unpublished data.
25. Toma 1999.
26. Aketa 2003; Ministry of the Environment 2003, 2004a.
27. Ministry of the Environment 2004b.
28. Ministry of the Environment 2006b; Uchida 1994.
29. Kasuya et al. 1999.
30. Defense Agency of Japan 2001.
31. Ministry of the Environment 2002, 2003, 2004a, 2005.
32. Ministry of the Environment 2004c.
33. Kasuya et al. 2000.
34. Ogura et al. 2005; Mukai et al., unpublished data.
35. Mammalogical Society of Japan 1997.
36. Ecological Society of Japan 2000.
37. Ministry of the Environment 2007.
38. National parks and quasi-national parks have the same management policies and restrictions but differ in the designation process and in management authority. National parks are designated by the minister of the environment and managed by the national government, while quasi-national parks are designated by the minister of the environment at the request of prefectures and are managed by prefectures. Prefectural national parks are representative landscapes of local importance with natural scenic beauty approaching that of national parks and quasi-national parks and are also managed by prefectures.
39. Ministry of the Environment 2006b.
40. Maeda 2000b.
41. Kamiya 1989.
42. Maeda 2000a.
43. Morimoto 2004; Maeda 2000a.
44. Takara 1984.
45. Ibid.
46. *Utaki* are holy shrines distributed all over on the Ryukyu Archipelago (more than 900 have been counted). Local people believe that the land of the gods, Nirai Kanai, is located far to the east at the end of the sea. In this sense an *utaki*, as a representation of Nirai Kanai, is a cultural landscape closely associated with religious beliefs unique to Ryukyuan nature worship,

a living religious tradition still flourishing in the contemporary rituals and festivals of this region.

47. Ministry of the Environment 2004c.

Chapter 9. Eastern African Dugongs

1. Marsh et al. 2002; WWF EAME 2004; Kiszka et al. 2007.
2. Stoddart 1971.
3. Heinsohn et al. 1979; Anderson 1981; WWF EAME 2004.
4. Sosovele 2000.
5. Kemp 2000; IUCN 2000a, 2011.
6. Korrubel and Cockcroft 1997; Marsh et al. 2002; WWF EAME 2004.
7. Marsh et al. 2002.
8. WWF EAME 2004.
9. Husar 1975b; Muir et al. 2003.
10. Kemp 2000.
11. Husar 1975b.
12. Wamukoya et al. 1997.
13. Ibid.
14. Omar Sherman, pers. comm., 2005.
15. Sheppard et al. 2006.
16. Muir 2005, 2007.
17. Omar Ali Amir, pers. comm., 2005.
18. Cockcroft et al. 2008.
19. A. Guissamulo, pers. comm., 2005.
20. WWF EAME 2004.
21. R. von Brandis et al., pers. comm., 2005.
22. Beudard and Ciccione 2008.
23. Kiszka et al. 2007.
24. WWF EAME 2004.
25. Muir et al. 2003.
26. Kiszka et al. 2007, 2009.
27. Muir 2007; C. Muir, unpublished data.
28. Amir et al. 2002; WWF EAME 2004.
29. Reynolds and Marshall, this volume, chap. 2.
30. Marsh 1999.
31. Marsh et al. 2002.
32. Muir 2004.
33. Guissamulo 2004.
34. WWF EAME 2004.
35. Muir et al. 2003; WWF EAME 2004.
36. C. Muir, unpublished data.
37. von Brandis et al. 2005.
38. Ortega-Argueta et al., this volume, chap 12.
39. Reynolds et al., this volume, chap. 21.
40. Hines et al. 2005a.
41. Muir 2005.
42. Beck and Clementz, Bonde et al., and Adimay et al., this volume, chaps. 14, 17, and 23.
43. Moraes-Arraut et al., this volume, chap. 18.
44. Marmontel et al., this volume, chap. 13.
45. Parr et al., this volume, chap. 19.
46. Marsh and Morales-Vela, this volume, chap. 25.
47. Kiszka et al. 2007.

Chapter 10. Dugongs in Arabia

1. Preen 1989; Gohar 1957.
2. Bibby 1970.
3. Thesiger 1959; Carp 1976; Gallagher 1976; Dean and Dean 1981; Price 1982.
4. Bertram and Ricardo Bertram 1973; Husar 1978b; Nishiwaki et al. 1979.
5. Gohar 1957.
6. MEPA 1985.
7. Preen 1989.
8. A. Farmer, pers. comm. to A. Preen, 1987.
9. Preen 1989.
10. WWF 1983; Begley et al. 1983; Anon. 1983a, 1983b; Vousden 1985.
11. Preen, unpublished data.
12. Preen 1989.
13. Ibid.
14. Preen 2004.
15. Hodgson 2009.
16. Preen 1989.
17. Ibid.
18. Ibid.
19. Sheppard et al. 2006; Whiting 1999.
20. Preen 1989.
21. Ibid.
22. Jolly 1969; Norton-Griffiths 1978.
23. Preen 1989, 1992.
24. Preen 1989.
25. Preen 2004.
26. Ibid.
27. Hodgson 2009.
28. Ibid.
29. Ibid.
30. Preen 1989; Phillips et al. 2004.
31. Al Zayani et al. 2009.
32. Phillips et al. 2004.
33. Preen 1989.
34. Preen et al. 2004.
35. Baldwin and Cockcroft 1995.
36. Marsh et al. 1984.
37. Hodgson 2009.
38. Ibid.
39. Preen 1989.
40. Preen, unpublished data.
41. Zainal et al. 2009.
42. Abdulqadar 2006.
43. Ibid.
44. WCMC 1991.
45. Preen, unpublished data.
46. Domingo et al. 1990; Duignan et al. 1996.
47. Sheppard et al. 1992.
48. Preen et al. 1989.
49. Preen et al. 2000.
50. Bibby 1970.
51. Jousse 1999.

52. Hellyer 2000.
53. Preen 1989.
54. Ibid.
55. Preen 1989.
56. Anon. 1977; Harris and Bertram 1977.
57. Dr. R. M. Ali, pers. comm., 1986.
58. Harris and Bertram 1977.
59. Thesiger 1959.
60. Preen 1989.
61. Nishiwaki and Marsh 1985.
62. Preen 1989.
63. Preen et al. 1989.

Chapter 11. Dugongs in Australia and the Pacific

1. Marsh et al. 2002.
2. Aragones et al., this volume, chap. 1.
3. Hudson 1977.
4. Kwan 2005.
5. Marsh et al. 2002.
6. Hudson 1977.
7. Kwan 2005.
8. Ibid.
9. Heinsohn et al. 2004; Marsh et al. 2004.
10. Marsh et al. 2002.
11. Hudson 1986b.
12. Smyth 2006.
13. In Australia, management and monitoring of both dugongs and turtles, usually green turtles, is necessary because both species can be hunted using the same equipment in the same habitats.
14. See Ross et al. 2004.
15. For example, Kwan 2002; Hamann et al. 2005; Nursey-Bray 2006; Ross et al. 2004.
16. Sheppard et al. 2006.
17. Reynolds et al., this volume, chap. 21.
18. Heinsohn et al. 1977, 1978.
19. Marsh and Sinclair 1989a, 1989b.
20. Queensland coast (Marsh and Lawler 2001, 2002; Marsh et al. 2004); Shark Bay, Western Australia (Preen et al. 1997); Northern Territory (Saafeld 2000); and beyond—New Caledonia (Garrigue and Patenaude 2004) and the Persian Gulf (Preen 2004).
21. Chilvers et al. 2004.
22. Pollock et al. 2006.
23. Marsh 1995b.
24. Wade 1998; Marsh et al. 2004.
25. Marsh et al. 2005.
26. Wade 1998.
27. Heinsohn et al. 2004; Marsh et al. 2004.
28. E.g., Aragones et al. 1997; Hines et al. 2005a, 2005b; Reynolds et al., this volume, chap 21.
29. Marsh and Lawler 2006.
30. E.g., Marsh 1995b.
31. Marsh and Saafeld 1990.
32. Marsh et al. 1996.
33. Marsh and Lawler 2001.
34. Ibid.
35. Gales et al. 2004; Holley et al. 2006.
36. Marsh et al. 1997, 2004.
37. Lawler 2002; Chilvers et al. 2005.
38. Sheppard et al. 2006.
39. Ibid.
40. Weigle et al. 2001; Deutsch et al. 2003.
41. Sheppard et al. 2006.
42. Tikel 1997.
43. McDonald 2005.
44. Parr et al., this volume, chap. 19.
45. Aragones et al., this volume, chap. 1.
46. Sheppard et al. 2007.
47. Welsby 1905.
48. Jackson et al. 2001.
49. Marsh et al. 2005.
50. Ibid.
51. Marsh and Lawler 2006.
52. Grech and Marsh 2007.
53. Garrigue et al. 2008.

Chapter 12. Using Interviews in Sirenian Research

1. Aragones et al., this volume, chap. 24.
2. Hines et al. 2005a, 2005b; Calvimontes 2009.
3. Silva and Araújo 2001; Marsh and Lefebvre 1994; Chambers et al. 1989.
4. Reynolds et al., this volume, chap. 21.
5. Aragones et al., this volume, chap. 20.
6. Marsh and Lefebvre 1994; Hudson 1981.
7. Kahn and Cannell 1958, as cited by Fowler and Mangione 1990, p. 11.
8. Fowler and Mangione 1990.
9. Backstrom and Hursh-César 1981; Fowler and Mangione 1990; Alreck and Settle 1995; Pole and Burgess 2000; Ember and Ember 2001; Drew et al. 2006.
10. See Hines 2002 for an example of a questionnaire.
11. Drew et al. 2006.
12. Calvimontes 2009.
13. Bernard 1988.
14. Calvimontes 2009.
15. Ibid.
16. Ibid.
17. Chambers et al. 1989; Hines 2002; Hines et al. 2005a, b, 2008a, b; Rajamani et al. 2006.
18. Calvimontes 2009; Kwan 2002; Kwan et al. 2006; Orozco 2001.
19. Biernacki and Waldorf 1981.
20. Taylor et al. 2006.
21. Bradburn 1983.
22. Ibid.
23. Verhoeven 2000.
24. Broadfoot 2000.
25. Fontana and Frey 2000.
26. Fontana and Frey 2000, p. 660.

27. McNeill and Chapman 2005.
28. Ibid.
29. Aragones et al., this volume, chap. 24.

Chapter 13. Tagging and Movement of Sirenians

1. Reid et al. 1995; Deutsch et al. 1998.
2. Marmontel, unpublished data.
3. Weigle et al. 2001.
4. Deutsch et al. 1998.
5. Reeves et al. 1988.
6. Morales-Vela et al. 1995.
7. Ibid.
8. Marsh and Rathbun 1990; Lanyon et al. 2006.
9. See Stamper and Bonde, this volume, chap. 16.
10. See Beck and Clark, this volume, chap. 15.
11. Rathbun et al. 1987a.
12. Ibid.
13. Kenward 1987.
14. Bengtson 1981.
15. Rosas et al. 1984.
16. Bengtson 1981.
17. Rathbun et al. 1987b; Marsh and Rathbun 1990.
18. Mech and Barber 2002.
19. Mech 1983.
20. Mech 1983; White and Garrott 1980.
21. White and Garrott 1980.
22. Marmontel, unpublished data.
23. See White and Garrott 1980.
24. O'Shea and Kochman 1990; Deutsch et al. 1998.
25. See www.ecostats.com.
26. Preen 2001.
27. Morales-Vela 2000.
28. Fancy et al. 1988.
29. Mate et al. 1985; Weigle et al. 2001.
30. Moen et al. 1997.
31. Mech and Barber 2002.
32. James Reid, pers. comm., 1999.
33. See http://www.telonics.com/.
34. Sheppard et al. 2006.
35. Ibid.
36. Sheppard et al. 2009.
37. http://www.nationalgeographic.com/crittercam/index.html.
38. Johnson and Tyack 2003.
39. Sheppard et al. 2006.
40. Sheppard et al. 2007.
41. Morales-Vela et al. 2007.
42. Castelblanco-Martínez 2007.
43. Morales-Vela 2000.
44. Ramirez-Jimenez 2008.
45. Http://www.epa.qld.gov.au/projects/park/index.cgi?park id=247.

Chapter 14. Techniques for Determining the Food Habits of Sirenians

1. Burn 1986; Langer 1988; Murray et al. 1977; Snipes 1984.
2. Lanyon and Sanson 2006; Marsh et al. 1999a; Snipes 1984.
3. Lanyon 1991; Marsh et al. 1982b.
4. Anderson 1979.
5. Anderson 1989; Preen 1995b.
6. Best 1981; Baugh et al. 1989; Hurst and Beck 1988; Ledder 1986; O'Shea 1986; Powell 1978.
7. Anderson 1986, 1994.
8. Best 1981, 1982b, 1983.
9. Ledder 1986.
10. Vavra and Holechek 1980; Hurst and Beck 1988.
11. Metcalf and Chalk 1950; Tomlinson 1980; Channels and Morrissey 1981; Kuo and den Hartog 2006; Guterres et al. 2008.
12. Best 1981.
13. Hurst and Beck 1988.
14. Channels and Morrissey 1981; Hurst and Beck 1988.
15. Hurst and Beck 1988.
16. Ames et al. 1996; Hobson et al. 1997; Burton and Koch 1999; Clementz and Koch 2000.
17. Estep and Hoering 1980; Ambrose and Norr 1993; Tieszen and Fagre 1993.
18. Dansgaard 1964; Craig and Gordon 1965; Boon and Bunn 1994; Hemminga and Matteo 1996; Raven et al. 2002.
19. Tieszen et al. 1983; Hobson and Clark 1992; Jim et al. 2004.
20. Tieszen et al. 1983; Koch et al. 1994; Hobson et al. 1996; Hobson et al. 1997.
21. Clementz 2002; MacFadden et al. 2004.
22. Clementz 2002.
23. Ames et al. 1996; Yamamuro et al. 2004.
24. Cerling and Harris 1998.
25. Yamamuro et al. 2004; Reich and Worthy 2006; Clementz et al. 2007.
26. Richards et al. 2003.
27. Kaehler and Pakhomov 2001.
28. O'Leary 1988; Farquhar et al. 1989.
29. Hemminga and Mateo 1996; Raven et al. 2002.
30. André and Lawler 2003.
31. Lawler et al. 2006.
32. Foley et al. 1998.
33. André and Lawler 2003.

Chapter 15. Individual Identification of Sirenians

1. Irvine and Scott 1984; Wright et al. 1998; Lander et al. 2001; Lanyon et al. 2002.
2. Irvine and Scott 1984; Marmontel 1994.
3. Irvine and Scott 1984.
4. Ibid.
5. Wright et al. 1998.
6. Lanyon et al. 2002.
7. Ibid.
8. See Marmontel et al., this volume, chap. 13.
9. Beck and Reid 1995; Langtimm et al. 2004.
10. See text box 3.3 in Deutsch and Reynolds, this volume, chap. 3.

11. W. L. Kendall et al. 2004; Langtimm and Beck 2003; Langtimm et al. 1998, 2004, 2006; Runge et al. 2004.

12. See Parr et al., this volume, chap. 19.

13. See Stamper and Bonde, this volume, chap. 16; Walsh and Bossart 1999; Harr et al. 2006.

14. See Parr et al., this volume, chap. 19.

15. See box 19.1 in Parr et al., this volume, chap. 19, modified from White and Densmore 1992.

16. See box 19.1 in Parr et al., this volume, chap. 19, modified from Amos and Hoelzel 1991; Proebstel et al. 1993.

17. R. Bonde, USGS, pers. comm., 2007.

18. O'Brien et al. 1983; Menotti-Raymond and O'Brien 1993; Weber et al. 2000.

19. Hedrick 1995; Crnokrak and Roff 1999.

20. O'Shea et al. 1991; Bossart et al. 1998.

Chapter 16. Health Assessment of Captive and Wild-Caught West Indian Manatees (*Trichechus manatus*)

1. Bonde et al. 2004; Bossart 2006a.
2. Geraci and Lounsbury 1993.
3. Ward-Geiger 1997.
4. See Beck and Clark, this volume, chap. 15.
5. Wright et al. 1998.
6. Walsh and Bossart 1999; Wong 2008.
7. Siegal-Willott et al. 2006.
8. Irvine 1983.
9. Bossart et al. 2001.
10. Pratt 1985.
11. Bayer Corporation 1992.
12. Tripp et al. 2008.
13. Bowman 1999.
14. Harvey et al. 2009.
15. Willard et al. 1999.
16. Harvey et al. 2007, 2009.
17. Montoya-Ospina 1994.
18. Walsh and Bossart 1999.
19. Bossart 2001.
20. Forrester 1992a.
21. Bossart et al. 2002b; Rector et al. 2004; Woodruff et al. 2005; Wellehan et al. 2008.

Chapter 17. Sirenian Pathology and Mortality Assessment

1. See Ortega-Argueta et al., this volume, chap. 12.
2. Reynolds and Odell 1991; Marsh and Lefebvre 1994; Reep and Bonde 2006.
3. Deutsch and Reynolds, this volume, chap. 3.
4. Mignucci-Giannoni et al. 2000; Mignucci-Giannoni, unpublished data.
5. Eros et al. 2002.
6. Buergelt et al. 1984; Bossart et al. 2004; Lightsey et al. 2006.
7. Walsh and Bossart 1999; Bossart 2001; Bossart et al. 2001.
8. O'Shea et al. 1985; Ackerman et al. 1995.
9. Stavros et al. 2008.
10. O'Shea et al. 1985; Beck and Barros 1991; Ackerman et al. 1995.
11. Beck et al. 1982; Bonde et al. 1983; Buergelt et al. 1984; Wright et al. 1995; Lightsey et al. 2006; Rommel et al. 2007.
12. O'Hara et al. 2003.
13. Stavros et al. 2008.
14. Loritz 1991; Preen 1989; see Preen et al., this volume, chap. 10.
15. Geraci and Lounsbury 2005.
16. Buergelt et al. 1984; Buergelt and Bonde 1983; Bossart et al. 2002a; Falcón-Matos et al. 2003; Varela and Bossart 2005.
17. Bossart 1995, 1999.
18. O'Shea et al. 1985; O'Shea 1988; O'Shea et al. 1991; Bossart et al. 1998; Bossart 2001; Bossart et al. 2003.
19. Buergelt et al. 1984; Forrester 1992b; Bossart et al. 2004.
20. Bossart 2001.
21. Bossart et al. 2002b; Rector et al. 2004.
22. R. Bonde, personal observation; Woodruff et al. 2005.
23. See Deutsch and Reynolds, this volume, chap. 3.
24. Bonde et al. 2004; Bossart 2006a; Moore 2008.
25. O'Shea et al. 1991; Bossart et al. 1998; Bossart 2006b.
26. Flewelling et al. 2005.
27. Bossart et al. 2002b; Bossart 2006b.
28. Kirkpatrick et al. 2004.
29. Bossart et al. 2003.
30. U.S. Marine Mammal Commission 2001; Laist and Reynolds 2005b.
31. U.S. Marine Mammal Commission 2001.
32. Laist and Reynolds 2005b.
33. See Deutsch and Reynolds, this volume, chap. 3.
34. Beck and Forrester 1988; Dailey et al. 1988; Forrester 1992b.
35. Mignucci-Giannoni et al. 1999a.
36. Mignucci-Giannoni et al. 1999b; Mora-Pinto 2000; Colón-Llavina et al. 2009.
37. Blair 1979, 1981, 2005.
38. Forrester 1992b; Blair 2005.
39. Sprent 1981; Beck and Forrester 1988.
40. Cintrón de Jesús 2001.
41. Morales-Vela et al. 2008.
42. R. Bonde, pers. comm., 2007.
43. R. Bonde, unpublished data.
44. Humes 1964.
45. Mignucci-Giannoni, unpublished data.
46. Blair 1981; Eros et al. 2000.
47. Mignucci-Giannoni et al. 1999b; Williams et al. 2003.
48. Mignucci-Giannoni et al. 2000; Mignucci-Giannoni, unpublished data.
49. Bossart et al. 2004.
50. Bossart 2001.
51. O'Shea et al. 1985.
52. Macmillan 1955; Jarman 1966; Kingdon 1971; Husar 1975a; Anderson and Prince 1985.
53. Pereira 1947.

54. Cadenat 1957; Husar 1978a; Reeves et al. 1992.
55. Hartman 1979.
56. Falcón-Matos et al. 2003.
57. Ibid.
58. Marsh 1989; Langtimm and Beck 2003; Langtimm et al. 2006.
59. See Bonde et al. 1983 (available in English and in Spanish); Eros et al. 2000; Geraci and Lounsbury 2005.
60. See Beck and Forrester 1988; Mignucci-Giannoni et al. 1999b.
61. See Parr et al., this volume, chap. 19.
62. Mazet et al. 2004.

Chapter 18. Delineating and Assessing Habitats for Sirenians

1. Hall et al. 1997.
2. Hartman 1979; Packard and Wetterqvist 1986; Smith 1993; Ward and Weigle 1993; Lefebvre et al. 2000.
3. Rosas 1994; Arraut et al. 2010.
4. Aragones et al. 2006; Sheppard et al. 2006, 2007.
5. Axis-Arroyo et al. 1998; Morales-Vela et al. 2000; Olivera-Gómez and Mellink 2005.
6. Jiménez Pérez 2005a; Spiegelberger and Ganslosser 2005.
7. Guisan and Zimmerman 2000; Franklin 2010.
8. E.g., Hartman 1979; Reynolds and Odell 1991; Reynolds 1999.
9. Ragen 2005.
10. Gysel and Lyon 1980.
11. Ibid.
12. Nicholls 1989; Axis-Arroyo et al. 1998; Jiménez Pérez 2005a; Olivera-Gómez and Mellink 2005; Redfern et al. 2006.
13. Gysel and Lyon 1980.
14. Ibid.
15. Gysel and Lyon 1980.
16. Burrough and McDonnell 1998.
17. Jensen 2007.
18. Ibid.
19. Jensen 2007.
20. Raney 1998; Mather 1999; Lillesand et al. 2004; Martin 2006; Jensen 2007.
21. Elith 2000; Lindenmayer and Burgman 2005; Redfern et al. 2006.
22. Elith 2000.
23. Ibid.
24. McCullagh and Nelder 1989.
25. Elith 2000.
26. Nix 1986; Lindenmayer and Burgman 2005.
27. Lindenmayer and Burgman 2005.
28. Beatley 1994; Hooker et al. 1999; Meffe et al. 2002; Ragen 2005.
29. Morales-Vela et al. 2000; Olivera-Gómez and Mellink 2002, 2005; Jiménez Pérez 2005a; Reynolds et al., this volume, chap. 21; Marmontel et al., this volume, chap. 13; Ortega-Argueta et al., this volume, chap. 12.
30. Armstrong 2005.
31. Mitchell 2005.
32. Ibid.
33. Deutsch et al. 2003; Sheppard et al. 2006.

Chapter 19. Sirenian Genetics and Demography

1. Kocher et al. 1989; Ballard and Whitlock 2004.
2. Avise et al. 1987; Ballard and Whitlock 2004; Frankham et al. 2002.
3. Ballard and Whitlock 2004.
4. Ballard and Whitlock 2004; Hoelzel et al. 1991.
5. Springer et al. 2001.
6. Lin and Danforth 2004.
7. Tautz 1989.
8. Beebee and Rowe 2004.
9. Ballard and Whitlock 2004.
10. Bruford and Wayne 1993; Zhang and Hewitt 2003.
11. Valsecchi and Amos 1996; Pritchard et al. 2000.
12. Thompson 2002.
13. Haussmann et al. 2003.
14. Garcia-Rodriguez et al. 1998.
15. Domning and Hayek 1986.
16. Vianna et al. 2006.
17. Parr 2000.
18. Cantanhede et al. 2005.
19. Vianna et al. 2006.
20. Domning 1994.
21. Garcia-Rodriguez et al. 1998.
22. Vianna et al. 2006.
23. Cantanhede et al. 2005.
24. Ibid.
25. Vianna et al. 2006.
26. Domning and Hayek 1986.
27. Garcia-Rodriguez et al. 1998; Parr 2000.
28. Vianna et al. 2006.
29. Ibid.
30. Allendorf et al. 2001.
31. Rodríguez-López 2004.
32. MacLaren 1967.
33. Marsh et al. 2002.
34. Palmer 2004.
35. McDonald 2005.
36. Thompson 2002.
37. Dunshea 2003.
38. Kwan 2002.
39. Dunshea 2003.
40. Tikel 1997.
41. McDonald 2005.
42. Ibid.
43. Ibid.
44. Palmer 2004.
45. McDonald 2005.
46. Hines, this volume, chap. 7.
47. Garcia-Rodriguez et al. 2000.
48. McDonald 2005.
49. McDonald 2005.

50. Ibid.
51. Ibid.
52. Ibid.
53. Ibid.
54. Ibid.
55. Ibid.
56. Sheppard et al. 2006.
57. Marmontel et al., this volume, chap. 13.
58. McDonald 2005.
59. Ibid.

Chapter 20. Boat- and Land-Based Surveys for Sirenians

1. Wells 1991; Lusseau 2006; Lemon et al. 2006.
2. Whitehead 2003.
3. Anderson and Birtles 1978.
4. Aragones et al. 1997.
5. See Ortega-Argueta et al., this volume, chap 12.
6. Vasquez and Wilbert 1992; O'Shea et al. 1995.
7. Buckland et al. 2001; Thompson 2004.
8. Kendall and Orozco 2003.
9. Irving 1939; Jefferson et al. 1993; Nishiwaki and Marsh 1985.
10. Gonzalez-Socoloske et al. 2009; Gonzalez-Socoloske and Olivera-Gomez in press.
11. Castelblanco-Martínez 2004a.
12. Kendall et al. 2005.
13. K. S. LaCommare, personal observation.
14. MacKenzie 2005; MacKenzie and Royle 2005.
15. Thompson 2004.
16. MacKenzie 2005, 2006; MacKenzie and Royle 2005.
17. Gibbs 2000.
18. Buckland et al. 2001.
19. Self-Sullivan et al. 2003.
20. For more information, see Murray and Fuller 2000.
21. See Altman 1974.
22. Buckland et al. 2001.
23. Ibid.
24. Underwood 1997.
25. Kendall et al. 2005.
26. Castelblanco-Martínez et al. 2009.
27. Aragones et al. 1997.
28. Aragones 1994.
29. Ibid.
30. Aragones et al. 1997.
31. Castelblanco-Martínez 2004b.
32. Dawson et al. 2008.

Chapter 21. Utility and Design of Aerial Surveys for Sirenians

1. Lefebvre et al. 1995.
2. Marsh 1995b.
3. Ortega-Argueta et al., this volume, chap. 12; Morales-Vela et al. 2003.
4. Rathbun et al. 1983b; Colmenero and Zarate-Becerra 1990; Mou Sue and Chen 1990; Morales-Vela et al. 2000, 2003; Wright et al. 2002.
5. Wright et al. 2002; Gannon et al. 2007.
6. Flamm et al. 2001.
7. Packard 1985.
8. Packard et al. 1986.
9. Garrott et al. 1994; Reynolds and Wilcox 1994; Craig et al. 1997; Craig and Reynolds 2004.
10. Edwards et al. 2007.
11. Craig and Reynolds 2004.
12. Ibid.
13. Edwards et al. 2007.
14. Morales-Vela and Olivera-Gómez 1994; Marsh 1995a; Olivera-Gomez and Mellink 2002, 2005; Marsh et al. 2004.
15. Strindberg and Buckland 2004.
16. Ibid.
17. E.g., Marsh 1995a; Gales et al. 2004; Marsh et al. 2004; Holley et al. 2006; Pollock et al. 2006.
18. Buckland et al. 2001.
19. Hines et al. 1995a.
20. Pollock and Kendall 1987.
21. Fonnesbeck et al. 2009; Pollock et al. 2006.
22. Marsh and Sinclair 1989a; Pollock et al. 2006.
23. Lefebvre et al. 1995.
24. Marsh and Sinclair 1989a.
25. Marsh and Sinclair 1989a; Pollock et al. 2006; Edwards et al. 2007.
26. Marsh and Sinclair 1989a; Pollock et al. 2006.
27. Ibid.
28. Reynolds et al. 1995.
29. Edwards et al. 2007.
30. I.e., index areas; Packard 1985; Packard et al. 1986.
31. Packard et al. 1985, 1986.
32. Craig et al. 1997; Craig and Reynolds 2004.
33. Edwards et al. 2007.
34. Pollock et al. 2006.
35. Wade 1998.
36. Marsh et al. 2004.
37. E.g., surveys of Florida manatees at warm-water refugia in winter: Garrott et al. 1994; Craig et al. 1997; Craig and Reynolds 2004.
38. Lefebvre et al. 1995.
39. Williams et al. 2002.
40. Dorazio et al. 2005.
41. MacKenzie et al. 2006.
42. Sheppard et al. 2006.
43. Lefebvre 1995.
44. Ortega-Argueta et al., Moraes-Arraut et al., and Aragones et al., this volume, chaps. 12, 18, and 20.
45. Flamm et al. 2001.

Chapter 22. Organic Contaminants and Sirenians

1. Ragen et al. 2002.
2. O'Shea 1999.
3. O'Shea et al. 1999.

4. Wells et al. 2004.
5. Http://www.pops.int/.
6. Kennish 1997.
7. E.g., Ritter et al. 1995; Moore et al. 2002; UNEP 2002.
8. O'Shea 1999.
9. NRC 2003.
10. NRCC 1983.
11. Brunström et al. 1991.
12. Sericano et al. 1990; Loganathan et al. 2001.
13. Rand and Petrocelli 1985.
14. Luoma 1996.
15. Helle and Stenman 1984; Addison et al. 1984, 1986.
16. Www.epa.gov.
17. Http://www.pops.int/.
18. Http://www.iarc.fr/ENG/General/index.php.
19. Http://www.iarc.fr/.
20. Http://www.epa.gov/oppt/pbde/.
21. Hoekstra et al. 2003.
22. Busbee et al. 1999.
23. Marcovecchio et al. 1990; Aguilar and Borrell 1994; Kuehl and Haebler 1995; Beck et al. 1997; Law et al. 2001.
24. Reddy et al. 2001.
25. Beck et al. 1997; Storelli and Marcotrigiano 2002.
26. Aguilar and Borrell 1994.
27. Ross et al. 1996.
28. O'Shea 2003.
29. Fossi and Marsili 1997; Fossi et al. 1997.
30. Fossi and Marsili 1997; Fossi et al. 1997.
31. O'Shea et al. 1999; O'Shea 2003.
32. Miyazaki et al. 1979.
33. Haynes et al. 1999; Vetter et al. 2001.
34. Kucklick et al. 2002; Hoekstra et al. 2003.
35. Kannan et al. 2000; Schwacke et al. 2002.
36. Haynes et al. 1999.
37. Vetter et al. 2001.
38. Ibid.
39. Abbreviations commonly used in contaminant studies include: lw—lipid weight; ww—wet weight; ppb—parts per billion (ng/g—nanogram/gram); ppm—parts per million (μg/g—microgram/gram); ppt—parts per thousand (pg/g—picogram/gram). Note that the use of different units of measurement (e.g., lw and ww) makes comparisons among studies difficult.
40. Haynes et al. 1999.
41. Vetter et al. 2001; Haynes et al. 2005.
42. O'Shea et al. 1984; O'Shea et al. 1991; Forrester et al. 1975.
43. O'Shea et al. 1984.
44. D. L. Wetzel et al., unpublished data.
45. Stern et al. 2005.
46. Muir et al. 1992.
47. Schwacke et al. 2002.
48. Kannan et al. 2000.
49. O'Shea et al. 1984.
50. D. L. Wetzel et al., unpublished data.
51. Kannan et al. 2000.
52. O'Shea et al. 1984.
53. Wetzel et al., unpublished data.
54. Ibid.
55. Ibid.
56. O'Shea 1999.
57. Kannan et al. 2000.
58. Borrell and Aguilar 1990.

Chapter 23. Manatee Rescue, Rehabilitation, and Release Efforts as a Tool for Species Conservation

1. Lander et al. 2002.
2. Measures 2004.
3. Brill and Friedl 1993.
4. Measures 2004.
5. Ibid.
6. Marmontel et al., this volume, chap. 13.
7. Beck and Clark, this volume, chap. 15.
8. Parr et al., this volume, chap. 19.
9. Stamper and Bonde, this volume, chap. 16.
10. Marmontel et al., this volume, chap. 13.
11. Estes 1998; Lunney et al. 2004.
12. See Parr et al., this volume, chap. 19.
13. St. Aubin et al. 1996.
14. Lander et al. 2002.
15. USFWS, unpublished data, 2009.
16. Mignucci-Giannoni 1996, 2001, 2003; Valade et al. 1999; Mignucci-Giannoni et al. 2000.
17. Martínez-Díaz et al. 2001.
18. Moore and Mignucci-Giannoni 1993; Marsh and Lefebvre 1994; Jiménez-Marrero et al. 1995; Mignucci-Giannoni 1998.
19. Mignucci-Giannoni et al. 1999a.
20. Self-Sullivan and Mignucci-Giannoni, this volume, chap. 4.
21. Mignucci-Giannoni et al. 2003.
22. Ibid.
23. Auil 1998.
24. Montoya-Ospina et al. 2001.
25. Millán-Sánchez 1999.
26. Montoya-Ospina 1994; Jiménez-Marrero et al. 1998.
27. Garcia-Rodriguez et al. 1998; Caballero and Giraldo 2004; Vianna et al. 2006.
28. Fundación Omacha and Ministerio de Ambiente 2005.
29. Boede and Mujica 1995.
30. Converse et al. 1994.
31. d'Affonseca Neto et al. 2002; Pantoja 2004.
32. Rodriguez et al. 1999; Rosas et al. 2001.
33. Colares 1991; Rosas et al. 1999; Rosas and Pimentel 2001.
34. Cantanhede et al. 2005.

Chapter 24. Working with Communities for Sirenian Conservation

1. Marmontel et al., this volume, chap. 5.
2. E.g., Ilangakoon and Tun 2007.
3. Grimble and Chan 1995.
4. Dobbs et al., this volume, chap. 11; Sharp 2002; Rosas 1994.

5. Schmandt and Ward 2000.
6. E.g., White and Vogt 2001.
7. E.g., Johannes 1981.
8. Escobar 1995; Kendall and Orozco 2003.
9. White et al. 2002.
10. Grimble and Chan 1995.
11. See Ortega-Arhueta et al., this volume, chap. 12.
12. Singh and Hegde 2004.
13. Ibid.
14. E.g., MacArthur 1997; IIRR 1998.
15. See Reynolds and Marshall, this volume, chap. 2.
16. See von Zharen, this volume, chap. 26.
17. Ortega-Argueta et al., this volume, chap. 12.
18. Marmontel et al. and Dobbs et al., this volume, chaps. 5 and 11.
19. Belize, C. Self-Sullivan and N. E. Auil-Gomez, pers. comm., 2008.
20. Sharp 2002.
21. S. Kendall, unpublished data.
22. Hines 2002.
23. Northern Australia, Sharp 2002.
24. Amazon, Kendall 1999.
25. Jacobson 1995.
26. Simberloff 1998.
27. Shanley and Laird 2002.
28. Hall 1997.

Chapter 25. Guidelines for Developing Protected Areas for Sirenians

1. Caro et al. 2004, p. 63.
2. See Marsh et al. 2002; Ikeda and Mukai, this volume, chap. 8.
3. Roberge and Angelstam 2004, p. 77.
4. Simberloff 1998; Caro 2003; Caro et al. 2004; Roberge and Angelstam 2004.
5. Hines et al. 2005b.
6. Marsh et al. 2002, 2003.
7. Quintana-Rizzo and Reynolds 2010.
8. Hooker and Gerber 2004.
9. IUCN 1994, p. 1.
10. Deutsch et al. 2003; Sheppard et al. 2006.
11. See the journal *Ecological Applications*, Supplement: Marine Reserves, vol. 13, 2003.
12. E.g., see Kelleher 1999; Salm et al. 2000.
13. See United Nations 2003.
14. Quintana-Rizzo and Reynolds 2010.
15. Grech et al. 2008.
16. Marsh 2000.
17. Morales-Vela 2000; Morales-Vela et al. 2000.
18. See Kelleher et al. 1995, regarding marine protected areas.
19. See von Zharen, this volume, chap. 26.
20. Preen 1998.
21. Hines et al. 2005b.
22. Aragones et al. 1997; Ortega-Argueta et al., this volume, chap. 12.
23. Marsh et al. 2010.
24. Reynolds et al., this volume, chap. 21.
25. Marsh et al. 2007.
26. Aragones et al., this volume, chap. 24.
27. Fernandes et al. 2005.
28. United Nations 1992.
29. See Hudson 1986b on the defunct project; H. Marsh, personal observation, 2009.
30. See Aragones et al., this volume, chap. 24.
31. On tagging and aerial surveys, see Marmontel et al. and Reynolds et al., this volume, chaps. 13 and 21. On habitat emphasis, see Marsh 2000; Fernandes et al. 2005; Grech et al. 2008; Ortega-Argueta et al., this volume, chap. 12.
32. Deutsch et al. 2003; Sheppard et al. 2006.
33. Havemann et al. 2005.
34. Convention on Migratory Species 2008.
35. Fernandes et al. 2005, pp. 1735–38.
36. Fernandes et al. 2005.
37. Ibid.
38. E.g., Ball and Possingham 2000; Possingham et al. 2000; Vreugdenhil 2003.
39. Kelleher and Kenchington 1992.
40. Mustika 2006.
41. Qintana-Rizzo, pers. comm., 2006.
42. Hocking et al. 2000.
43. Convention on Biological Diversity 2004.
44. Pomeroy et al. 2004b.
45. Marsh et al. 2005.
46. See Bonde et al. and Adimey et al., this volume, chaps. 17 and 23.
47. Marsh et al. 2005.
48. Pomeroy et al. 2004b.
49. Lee 2001.
50. See Buck et al. 2001 for ideas and useful case studies.

Chapter 26. The Role of Law in Protecting Sirenians and Their Habitat in Developing Nations

1. Blank 1996.
2. Toman 1992.
3. Garner 1999.
4. Sokol 2007; Mistelis 2000.
5. Lakhani 2006.
6. See Reynolds and Marshall, and Wetzel et al., this volume, chaps. 2 and 22.
7. CITES 2011.
8. CITES 2011, Article 1[c].
9. von Zharen 1998.
10. Batchelor 1988.
11. Convention on the Conservation of Migratory Species of Wild Animals 2011.
12. Ibid.
13. Ibid.
14. Ibid.
15. World Bank 1992.
16. Hanson 1993.

17. Convention on Biological Diversity, Article 2.
18. Convention on Biological Diversity, Article 22.
19. MARPOL 1973.
20. Cruise ship waste 2008.
21. Stockholm Declaration, Principle 25.
22. Stockholm Declaration, Principle 2.
23. Stockholm Declaration, Principle 6.
24. Rio Declaration Agenda 21, Principle 15.
25. Rio Declaration Agenda 21, Principle 1.
26. Rio Declaration Agenda 21, Principle 3.
27. Sitarz 1993.
28. Palumbi 2002; Marsh and Morales-Vela, this volume, chap. 25.
29. Pitcher 2001.
30. UNEP/Regional Seas Program 2008.
31. Vanzella-Khouri 2008.
32. IUCN 2009.
33. Ibid.
34. Marsh et al. 2002.
35. Zeiller 1992; Marsh et al. 2002; this volume, chaps. 3–11.
36. Cartagena Convention, Article 2, 2009.
37. McCutcheon 1998.
38. See Aragones et al., this volume, chap. 24.
39. Wilson 1991.
40. Bruch et al. 2001.
41. see Dobbs et al., this volume, chap. 11.
42. von Zharen 1998.
43. Cote 1994.
44. Cundill and Fabricius 2009.
45. von Zharen 1998; Reynolds et al. 2009.
46. Self-Sullivan 2008.
47. See Vanzella-Khouri 2008.
48. Self-Sullivan 2008.
49. Ibid.
50. Ibid.
51. Ibid.
52. Ibid.
53. Ibid.

Chapter 27. The Role of Scientists in Sirenian Conservation in Developing Countries

1. Schaller 1993; Jaramillo-Legorreta et al. 2007; Turvey et al. 2007.
2. Aragones et al., this volume, chap. 24; Bearzi 2007.
3. Aragones et al. 1997; Hinrichsen 1998.
4. Aragones et al. 1997.
5. Holdgate 1994; Domning 1999a; IUCN 2000a, 2011; Groom et al. 2005.
6. Domning 1999a.
7. Mead and Mitchell 1984.
8. Domning 1978, 1982b.
9. Richter and Redford 1999; Orr 2001; Ehrlich 2002; Robinson 2006; Noss 2007; Scott et al. 2007.
10. Wallace 1994; Ralls 1997.
11. Marsh et al. 1980–81; Schaller 1993; Rabinowitz 1991; Katona and Kraus 1999; Oates 1999; Perrin 1999; Reynolds 1999; Reeves et al. 2003.
12. Marsh et al. 1999b.
13. Lefebvre et al. 2001.
14. See Marmontel et al. and Kouadio, this volume, chaps. 5 and 6.
15. E.g., White et al. 2002.
16. E.g., Alcala et al. 1991; Ming and Wilkinson 1992.
17. Domning 1999a.
18. Gomez-Pompa and Kaus 1992.
19. Domning 1991.
20. Reynolds et al. 2009.

Chapter 28. A Framework for Sirenian Conservation in Developing Countries

1. Kellert 1986.
2. Soulé 1985; Coleman et al. 1996.
3. Soulé 1991, p. 744.
4. Blane 1997.
5. Marsh and Morales-Vela, this volume, chap. 25.
6. Alder 1996; Christie et al. 2009.
7. Simberloff 1998.
8. Zacharias and Roff 2000.
9. Bossart 2006a.
10. Zacharias and Roff 2001.
11. Simberloff 1998, p. 247.
12. Zacharias and Roff 2001.
13. Simberloff 1998.
14. Zacharias and Roff 2001; Simberloff 1998.
15. Zacharias and Roff 2001.
16. Aragones et al., this volume, chap. 1.
17. Bowen 1997, p. 267.
18. Bowen 1997.
19. Lindenmayer et al. 2008.
20. Aragones et al., this volume, chap. 24; Marsh and Morales-Vela, this volume, chap. 25.
21. Panwar 1987; Dietz et al. 1994; Johnsingh and Joshua 1994; Downer 1996; Durbin et al. 1996; Simberloff 1998.
22. Dietz et al. 1994; Simberloff 1998.
23. Marsh and Lefebvre 1994.
24. Hines 2002; Hines et al., in prep.
25. Simberloff 1998; Zacharias and Roff 2001; Bowen-Jones and Entwistle 2002.
26. Simberloff 1998; Williams et al. 2000.
27. Simberloff 1998, p. 250.
28. Duffus and Dearden 1990.
29. Duffus 1988; Corkeron 1994; Duffus 1996; Bass 2000; Hoyt 2005; Scarpaci et al. 2008, Wiley et al. 2008.
30. Corkeron 1994; Duffus 1996; Bass 2000; Hoyt and Iñíquez 2008; Stockin et al. 2008.
31. Kellert 1986; Simberloff 1998; Dietz et al. 1994; Bowen-Jones and Entwistle 2002.
32. Bowen 1997; Zacharias and Roff 2001; Lindenmayer et al. 2008.
33. Estes et al. 1998; Chapin et al. 2000; Estes et al. 2007.

34. Zacharias and Roff 2001.
35. Peterkin and Conacher 1997; Aragones 1996; Preen 1992.
36. Marsh et al. 1999b.
37. Zacharias and Roff 2001.
38. Marsh and Morales-Vela, this volume, chap. 25.
39. Roberge and Angelstam 2004.
40. Caro 2003.
41. Ryti 1992; Zacharias and Roff 2001.
42. Zacharias and Roff 2001.
43. Ibid.
44. Ibid.
45. Borrini-Feyerabend et al. 2000, p. 11.
46. Johannes 1981.
47. Weeks and Packard 1997.
48. Orr 1991.
49. Maguire 1996.
50. Meffe and Viederman 1995; Maguire 1996, p. 915.
51. Aragones et al., this volume, chap. 24.
52. Rivera and Newkirk 1997.
53. Domning 1999.
54. Perrin 1999, p. 306.
55. Colvin 1992.
56. Marsh and Morales-Vela, this volume, chap. 25.
57. Hooker et al. 1999; Reeves 2000.
58. Perrin 1999, p. 305.
59. von Zharen, this volume, chap. 26.
60. Chazdon et al. 2009; Cundill and Fabricius 2009; Reynolds et al. 2009; Millenium Ecosystem Assessment 2005; Tilman 2000; Lélé and Norgaard 1996; Sagoff 1996; Commoner 1971; Leopold 1936.
61. Pauly 2006b.
62. Srichai et al. 1994.
63. Schelhas 1992.
64. Meffe et al. 1999, p. 451.
65. Short and Neckles 1999; Hannah et al. 2002; Millenium Ecosystem Assessment 2005; Baker et al. 2006; IPCC 2007; Waycott et al. 2009.

References

Abdulqadar, E.A.A. 2006. "National fisheries resources survey: An extension of MARGIS II." Unpublished report. Manama, Bahrain: Geomatec and Bahrain Centre for Studies and Research.

Ackerman, B.B. 1995. "Aerial surveys of manatees: A summary and progress report." In *Population Biology of the Florida Manatee*, ed. T.J. O'Shea, B.B. Ackerman, and H.F. Percival, 13–33. Washington, D.C.: National Biological Service Information and Technology Report 1.

Ackerman, B.B., S.D. Wright, R.K. Bonde, D.K. Odell, and D.J. Banowetz. 1995. "Trends and patterns in the mortality of manatees in Florida, 1974–1992." In *Population Biology of the Florida Manatee*, ed. T.J. O'Shea, B.B. Ackerman, and H.F. Percival, 223–58. Washington, D.C.: National Biological Service Information and Technology Report 1.

Addison, R.F., P.F. Brodie, M.E. Zinck, and D.E. Sergeant. 1984. "DDT has declined more than PCBs in eastern Canadian seals during the 1970's." *Environmental Science and Technology* 18:935–37.

Addison, R.F., M.E. Zinck, and T.G. Smith. 1986. "PCBs have declined more than DDT-group residues in Arctic ringed seals (*Phoca hispida*) between 1972 and 1981." *Environmental Science and Technology* 20:253–55.

Adulyanukosol, K. 1995. "The status and tendency of declination of dugong population in Thailand." In *Proceedings of the Seminar on Fisheries, Department of Fisheries 1995*, Bangkok, Thailand, 385–92 (in Thai).

———. 1999. "Dugongs, dolphins and whale in Thai waters." In *Proceedings of the First Korea-Thailand Joint Workshop on Comparison of Coastal Environment: Korea-Thailand*, 9–10 September 1999, Seoul, Korea.

———. 2000. "Dugong surveys in Thailand." *Biologia Marina Mediterranea* 7:191–94.

———. 2004. "Dugong and Dugong Conservation in Thailand." *Technical Paper no. 5, Phuket Marine Biological Center* (in Thai).

Adulyanukosol, K., S. Chantrapornsyl, and S. Poovachiranon. 1997. "Aerial survey of dugong (*Dugong dugon*) in the Andaman coast, Thailand." *Thai Fisheries Gazette* 50:359–74 (in Thai).

Adulyanukosol, K., S. Chantrapornsyl, S. Poovachiranon, and K. Kittiwattanawong. 1999. "Report on aerial surveys of dugong along the Andaman Coast in 1997 and 1999 using the Royal Thai Navy Aircraft." *Technical Paper, Phuket Marine Biological Center* (in Thai).

Adulyanukosol, K., S. Poovachiranon, M. Charuchida, P. Manopawitr, and S. Sathummanatpun. 2005. *Dugong and Seagrass and Action Plan for Thailand*. First Meeting on Dugong Conservation in the Indian Ocean and South-East Asia Region, 23–25 August 2005, Bangkok, Thailand.

Adulyanukosol, K., and S. Thongsukdee. 2005. "Report of the results of the survey on dugongs, dolphins, sea turtles, and seagrass in Trang Province." Phuket Marine Biological Center, Department of Marine and Coastal Resources. March 2005.

Adulyanukosol, K., and S. Poovachiranon. 2006. "Dugong (*Dugong dugon*) and seagrass in Thailand: Present status and future challenges." In *Proceedings of the 7th SEASTAR Workshop*, 12–14 December 2006, Bangkok.

Aebischer, N.J., P.A. Robertson, and R.E. Kenward. 1993. "Compositional analysis of habitat use from animal radio-tracking data." *Ecology* 74:1313–25.

Aguilar, A., and A. Borrell. 1994. "Abnormally high polychlorinated biphenyl levels in striped dolphins (*Stenella coeruleoalba*) affected by the 1990–1992 Mediterranean epizootic." *Science of the Total Environment* 154:237–47.

Ahnelt, P.K., and H. Kolb. 2000. "The mammalian photoreceptor mosaic-adaptive design." *Progress in Retinal and Eye Research* 19:711–77.

Aketa, K. 2003. "Kaigyurui no setsujitokusei to shoukakikou ni kansuru kenkyu (Study of feeding habits and digestion of sirenians)." Ph.D. diss., Mie University, Tsu City, Japan.

Aketa K., S. Asano, Y. Wakai, and A. Kawamura. 2003. "Apparent digestibility of eelgrass *Zostera marina* by captive dugongs *Dugong dugon* in relation to the nutritional content of eelgrass and dugong feeding parameters." *Mammal Study* 28:23–30.

Alcala, A., C.L. Ming, W. Kastoro, M. Fortes, G. Wooi-Khoon, A. Sasekumar, R. Bina, and S. Tridech, eds. 1991. *Proceedings of the Regional Symposium on Living Resources in Coastal Areas*. Diliman, Quezon City: University of the Philippines Printery.

Alder, J. 1996. "Have tropical marine protected areas worked? An initial analysis of their success." *Coastal Management* 24:97–114.

Allen, G.M. 1938. *The Mammals of China and Mongolia*. New York: American Museum of Natural History.

Allen, J.F., M.M. Lepes, I.T. Budiarso, A. Sumitro, and D. Hammond. 1976. "Some observations on the biology of the dugong (*Dugong dugon*) from the waters of south Sulawesi." *Aquatic Mammals* 4:33–48.

Allendorf, F.W., R.F. Leary, P. Spruell, and J.K. Wenburg. 2001. "The problem with hybrids: Conservation guidelines." *Trends in Ecology and Evolution* 16:613–22.

Alreck, P.L., and R.B. Settle. 1995. *The Survey Research Handbook*. New York: Irwin Press.

Altman, J. 1974. "Observational study of behavior: Sampling methods." *Behavior* 49:227–65.

Alvarez-Alemán, A., J.A. Powell, and C.A. Beck. 2007. "First report of a Florida manatee documented on the north coast of Cuba." *Sirenews* (IUCN/SSC Sirenia Specialist Group) 47:9–10.

Al Zayani, A.K., A.J.M. Zainal, and P.R. Choudhury. 2009. "An overview of the marine habitats of Bahrain, the classification and distribution." In *Marine Atlas of Bahrain*, ed. R.A. Loughland and A.J.M. Zainal, 67–84. Manama, Bahrain: Geomatec.

Ambrose, S.H., and L. Norr. 1993. "Experimental evidence for the carbon isotope ratios of whole diet and dietary protein to those of bone collagen and carbonate." In *Prehistoric Human Bone: Archaeology at the Molecular Level*, ed. J.B. Lambert and G. Grupe, 1–37. New York: Springer.

Ames, A.L., and E.S. Van Vleet. 1996. "Organochlorine residues in the Florida manatee, *Trichechus manatus latirostris*." *Marine Pollution Bulletin* 32:374–77.

Ames, A.L., E.S. Van Vleet, and W.M. Sackett. 1996. "The use of stable carbon isotope analysis for determining dietary habits of the Florida manatee, *Trichechus manatus latirostris*." *Marine Mammal Science* 12:555–63.

Ames, A.L., E.S. van Vleet, and J.E. Reynolds III. 2002. "Comparison of lipids in selected tissues of the Florida manatee (Order Sirenia) and bottlenose dolphin (Order Cetacea; Suborder Odontoceti)." *Comparative Biochemistry and Physiology* Part B 132:625–34.

Amir, O., P. Berggren, and N. Jiddawi. 2002. "Incidental catch of dolphins in gillnet fisheries in Zanzibar, Tanzania." *Western Indian Ocean Journal of Marine Science* 1:155–62.

Amos, B., and A.R. Hoelzel. 1991. "Long-term preservation of whale skin for DNA analysis." *Reports of the International Whaling Commission,* Special Issue 13:99–103.

Anderson, P.K. 1979. "Dugong behavior: On being a marine mammal grazer." *Biologist* 61:113–44.

———. 1981. "The behaviour of the dugong (*Dugong dugon*) in relation to conservation and management." *Bulletin of Marine Science* 31:640–47.

———. 1982. "Studies of Dugongs at Shark Bay, Western Australia. II. Surface and Subsurface Observations." *Australian Wildlife Research* 9:85–99

———. 1986. "Dugongs of Shark Bay, Australia: Seasonal migration, water temperature, and forage." *National Geographic Research* 2:473–90.

———. 1989. "Deliberate foraging on macroinvertebrates by dugongs." *National Geographic Research* 5:4–6.

———. 1994. "Dugong distribution, the seagrass *Halophila spinulosa*, and thermal environment in winter in deeper waters of eastern Shark Bay, Western Australia." *Wildlife Research* 21:381–88.

Anderson, P.K., and A. Birtles. 1978. "Behavior and ecology of the dugong, *Dugong dugon* (Sirenia): Observations in Shoalwater and Cleveland bays, Queensland." *Australian Wildlife Research* 5:1–23.

Anderson, P.K., and R.I.T. Prince. 1985. "Predation on dugongs: Attacks by killer whales." *Journal of Mammalogy* 66:554–56.

André, J., and I.R. Lawler. 2003. "Near infrared spectroscopy as a rapid and inexpensive means of dietary analysis for a marine herbivore, dugong *Dugong dugon*." *Marine Ecology Progress Series* 257:259–66.

André, J., E. Gyuris, and I.R. Lawler. 2005. "Comparison of the diets of sympatric dugongs and green turtles on the Orman Reefs, Torres Strait, Australia." *Wildlife Research* 32:53–62.

Annandale, N. 1905. "Notes on the species, external characteristics and the habits of the Dugong." *Journal of the Asiatic Society of Bengal* 1:238–43.

Anon. 1909. *The Imperial Gazetteer of India*, vol. 1: *The Indian Empire, Descriptive*. Oxford: Clarendon.

Anon. 1977. "Sea cows." *Journal of the Emirates Natural History Group*, pp. 3–4.

Anon. 1983a. "Oil spill slaughters sea cows." *New Scientist* 21 July: 180.

Anon. 1983b. "Oil spill killing sea animals." *Arab News,* 25 July.

Aragones, L.V. 1990. The status, distribution and basic feeding ecology of the dugong, *Dugong dugon* (Müller) [Mammalia: Sirenia] at Calauit island, Busuanga. M.Sc. thesis, Marine Science Institute, University of the Philippines, Diliman.

———. 1994. "Observations on dugongs at Calauit Island, Busuanga, Palawan, Philippines." *Wildlife Research* 21:709–17.

———. 1996. "Dugongs and green turtles: Grazers in the tropical seagrass system." Ph.D. diss., James Cook University, Townsville, Australia.

———. 1998. "The fate of the charismatic dugong in the Philippines." Abstract. First National Dugong Seminar Workshop, 6–8 November, Davao City, Philippines. WWF-Philippines and DENR-PAWB, Philippines.

Aragones, L.V., T.A. Jefferson, and H. Marsh. 1997. "Marine mammal survey techniques applicable in developing countries." *Asian Marine Biology* 14:15–39.

Aragones, L.V., and H. Marsh. 2000. "Impact of dugong grazing and turtle cropping on tropical seagrass communities." *Pacific Conservation Biology* 5:277–88.

Aragones, L.V., I.R. Lawler, W.J. Foley, and H. Marsh. 2006. "Dugong grazing and turtle cropping: Grazing optimization in tropical seagrass systems?" *Oecologia* 149:635–47.

Aragones, L.V., M.A. Roque, M.B. Flores, R.P. Encomienda, G.E. Laule, B.G. Espinos, F.E. Maniago, G. Diaz, E.B Alesna, and R.C. Braun. 2010. "The Philippine marine mammal strandings from 1998 to 2009: Animals in the Philippines in peril? *Aquatic Mammals* 36, no. 3:219–33.

Armstrong, D.P. 2005. "Integrating the metapopulation and

habitat paradigms for understanding broad-scale declines of species." *Conservation Biology* 19:1402–10.

Arraut, E.M., M. Marmontel, J.E. Mantovani, E.M.L.M. Novo, D.W. Macdonald, and R.E. Kenward. 2010. "The lesser of two evils: Seasonal migrations of Amazonian manatees in the Western Amazon." *Journal of Zoology* 280:247–56.

Arzoumanian, Z., J. Holmberg, and B. Norman. 2005. "An astronomical pattern-matching algorithm for computer-aided identification of whale sharks *Rhincodon typus*." *Journal of Applied Ecology* 42:999–1011.

Auil, N.E. 1998. *Belize Manatee Recovery Plan*. UNDP/GEF Coastal Zone Management Project, Belize (BZE/92/G31). Kingston, Jamaica: UNEP Caribbean Environmental Programme.

———. 2004. "Abundance and distribution trends of the West Indian manatee in the coastal zone of Belize: Implications for conservation." M.S. thesis, Department of Wildlife and Fisheries Sciences, Texas A&M University, College Station.

Auil, N.E., and A. Valentine. 2003. "Manatee stranding report 1996–2003." Belize City, Belize: Coastal Zone Management Institute.

———. 2006. "Manatee strandings along the coastal zone of Belize 1996–2003." Extended abstract. National Marine Science Symposium, 18–20 January 2006, Belize City, Belize.

Avise, J.C., J. Arnold, R.M. Ball Jr., E. Bermingham, T. Lamb, J.E. Neigel, C.A. Reeb, and N.C. Saunders. 1987. "Intraspecific phylogeography: The mitochondrial DNA bridge between population genetics and systematics." *Annual Review of Ecology and Systematics* 18:489–522.

Axis-Arroyo, J., B. Morales-Vela, D. Torruco-Gómez, and M.E. Vega-Cendejas. 1998. "Variables asociadas al uso del hábitat del manatí del Caribe (*Trichechus manatus*), en Quintana Roo, México (Mammalia)." *Revista de Biologia Tropical* 46:791–803.

Bachteler, D., and G. Dehnhardt. 1999. "Active touch performance in the Antillean manatee: Evidence for a functional differentiation of facial tactile hairs." *Zoology* 102:61–69.

Backstrom, C.H., and G. Hursh-César. 1981. *Survey Research*. 2nd ed. New York: Macmillan.

Baker, J.D., C.L. Littnan, and D.W. Johnston. 2006. "Potential effects of sea level rise on the terrestrial habitats of endangered and endemic megafauna in the northwestern Hawaiian Islands." *Endangered Species Research* 4:1–10.

Baldwin, R., and V.G. Cockcroft. 1995. "Is the world's second-largest population of dugongs safe?" Sirenews (IUCN/SSC Sirenia Specialist Group) 24:11–13.

Ball, I., and H. Possingham. 2000. "Marxan, Version 1.2: Marine reserve design software using spatially explicit annealing: A manual." Brisbane, Australia: University of Queensland.

Ballard, J.W.O., and M.C. Whitlock. 2004. "The incomplete natural history of mitochondria." *Molecular Ecology* 13:729–44.

Baltazar, R., and A.A. Yaptinchay. 1998. "Current knowledge on dugong status and distribution in the Philippines based on hearing and aerial surveys, sighting and capture reports." Abstract. First National Dugong Seminar Workshop, 6–8 November, Davao City, Philippines. WWF-Philippines and DENR-PAWB, Philippines.

Bass, J. 2000. "Variations in gray whale feeding behaviour in the presence of whale-watching vessels in Clayoquot Sound, 1993–1995." Ph.D. diss., Department of Geography, University of Victoria, British Columbia, Canada.

Batchelor, A. 1988. "The preservation of wildlife habitat in ecosystems: Towards a direction under international law to prevent species' extinction." *Florida Journal of International Law* 3:331.

Bauer, G.B., D.E. Colbert, J.C. Gaspard III, B. Littlefield, and W. Fellner. 2003. "Underwater visual acuity of Florida manatees (*Trichechus manatus latirostris*)." *International Journal of Comparative Psychology* 16:130–42.

Baugh, T.M., J.A. Valade, and B. Zoodsma. 1989. "Manatee use of *Spartina alterniflora* in Cumberland Sound." *Marine Mammal Science* 5:88–90.

Bayer Corporation, Elkhart, Indiana. 1992. Package insert for BAYER Multistix (10SG, 9, 9 SG, 8 SG, 7), N-Multistix (SG), and Bili-Labstix Reagent Strips.

Bearzi, G. 2007. "Marine conservation on paper." *Conservation Biology* 21:1–3.

Beasley, I., P. Davidson, P. Somany, and L. Sam Ath. 2002. "Abundance, distribution and conservation management of marine mammals in Cambodia's coastal waters." Final unpublished report. Cambodia: Wildlife Conservation Society.

Beatley, T. 1994. *Habitat Conservation Planning: Endangered Species and Urban Growth*. Austin: University of Texas Press.

Beck, C.A. 2006. "Florida manatee travels to Cape Cod, Massachusetts!" Sirenews (IUCN/SSC Sirenia Specialist Group) 46:15–16.

Beck, C.A., R.K. Bonde, and G.B. Rathbun. 1982. "Analyses of propeller wounds on manatees in Florida." *Journal of Wildlife Management* 46:531–35.

Beck, C.A., and D.J. Forrester. 1988. "Helminths of the Florida manatee, *Trichechus manatus latirostris*, with a discussion and summary of the parasites of sirenians." *Journal of Parasitology* 74:628–37.

Beck, C.A., and N.B. Barros. 1991. "The impact of debris on the Florida manatee." *Marine Pollution Bulletin* 22:508–10.

Beck, C.A., and J.P. Reid. 1995. "An automated photo-identification catalog for studies of the life history of the Florida manatee." In *Population Biology of the Florida Manatee*, ed. T.J. O'Shea, B.B. Ackerman, and H.F. Percival, 120–34. Washington, D.C.: National Biological Service Information and Technology Report 1.

Beck, K.M., P. Fair, W. McFee, and D. Wolf. 1997. "Heavy metals in livers of bottlenose dolphins stranded along the South Carolina coast." *Marine Pollution Bulletin* 34:734–39.

Beebee, T., and G. Rowe. 2004. *An Introduction to Molecular Ecology*. Oxford: Oxford University Press.

Begley, S., J. Carey, and J. Callcott. 1983. "The tragic death of the Gulf." *Newsweek,* 25 July:46–46.

Beissinger, S.R., and M.I. Westphal. 1998. "On the use of demographic models of population viability analysis in endangered species management." *Journal of Wildlife Management* 62:821–41.

Belitsky, D.W., and C.L. Belitsky. 1980. "Distribution and abundance of manatees *Trichechus manatus* in the Dominican Republic." *Biological Conservation* 17:313–19.

Belize Tourism Board. 2006. "Cruise arrivals by month 1998–2005." http://www.belizetourism.org.

Bell, I. 2001. "A preliminary assessment of the turtle and dugong populations of Bahrain and the Hawar Islands." Ministry of Housing, Municipalities and Environment, Bahrain.

Bengtson, J.L. 1981. "Ecology of manatees (*Trichechus manatus*) in the St. Johns River, Florida." Ph.D. diss., University of Minnesota, Minneapolis.

———. 1983. "Estimating food consumption of free-ranging manatees in Florida." *Journal of Wildlife Management* 47:1186–92.

Bengtson, J.L., and D. Magor. 1979. "A survey of manatees in Belize." *Journal of Mammalogy* 60:230–32.

Bernard, H.R. 1988. *Research Methods in Cultural Anthropology.* Lanham, Md.: Altamira Press.

Bertram, B. 2002. "George Colin Lawder Bertram, 11 January 2001, at Graffham, Sussex, England." *Marine Mammal Science* 18:304.

Bertram, G.C.L., and C.K. Ricardo Bertram. 1963. "The status of manatees in the Guianas." *Oryx* 7:90–93.

———. 1964. "Manatees in the Guianas." *Zoologica* 49:115–20.

———. 1970. "The dugongs of Ceylon." *Loris* 12:53–55.

———. 1973. "The modern Sirenia: Their distribution and status." *Biological Journal of the Linnean Society* 5:297–338.

Best, R.C. 1981. "Foods and feeding habits of wild and captive Sirenia." *Mammal Review* 11:3–29.

———. 1982a. "A salvação de uma espécie: novas perspectivas para o peixe-boi da Amazônia." *Revista IBM* 14:1–8.

———. 1982b. "Seasonal breeding in the Amazonian manatee, *Trichechus inunguis* (Mammalia: Sirenia)." *Biotropica* 14:76–78.

———. 1983. "Apparent dry-season fasting in Amazonian manatees (Mammalia: Sirenia)." *Biotropica* 15:61–64.

———. 1984. "The aquatic mammals and reptiles of the Amazon." In *The Amazon: Limnology and Landscape Ecology of a Mighty Tropical River and Its Basin*, ed. H. Sioli, 371–412. Dordrecht, Netherlands: Dr. W. Junk Publishers.

Beudard, F., and S. Ciccione. 2008. "Dugong survival around Mohéli island." *Sirenews* (IUCN/SSC Sirenia Specialist Group) 49:13–16.

Bibby, G. 1970. *Looking for Dilmun*. Middlesex, England: Penguin.

Biernacki, P., and D. Waldorf. 1981. "Snowball sampling: Problems and techniques of chain referral sampling." *Sociological Methods and Research* 10:141–63.

Blair, D. 1979. "A new family of monostome flukes (Platyhelminthes: Digenea) from the dugong, *Dugong dugon* (Müller)." *Annales de Parasitologie* 54:519–26.

———. 1981. "The monostome flukes (Digenea: Families Opisthotrematidae Poche and Rhabdiopoeidae Poche) parasitic in sirenians (Mammalia: Sirenia)." *Australian Journal of Zoology*, Supplement Series, 81:1–54.

———. 2005. "Family Opisthotrematidae Poche, 1926." In *Keys to Trematoda*, vol. 2, ed. A. Jones, R.A. Bray, and D.I. Gibson, 401–6. London: CABI International and Natural History Museum.

Blane, J.M. 1997. *Marine Protected Areas as a Tool for Cetacean Conservation: An Evaluation of Application in the Northwest Atlantic and the St. Lawrence Estuary.* Halifax, Nova Scotia, Canada: Marine Affairs Program, Dalhousie University.

Blank, D.P. 1996. "Target based environmental trade measures: A proposal for the new WTO committee on trade and environment." *Stanford Environmental Law Journal* 15:61–96.

Blanshard, W.H. 2001. "Dugong strandings," 26 pp. In *Notes for the Marine Mammal Stranding Workshop held on 1 July 2001*, preceding Veterinary Conservation Biology: Wildlife Health and Management in Australasia. Joint Conference of the AAVCB, WAWV, WDA and NZWS, 2–6 July 2001, Taronga Zoo, Sydney, New South Wales.

Bodmer, R.E., J.F. Eisenberg, and K.H. Redford. 1996. Hunting and the likelihood of extinction of Amazonian mammals. *Conservation Biology* 11:460–66.

Boede, E.O., and E. Mujica. 1995. "Experiencias en el manejo en cautiverio y observaciones en el ambiente natural del manatí (*Trichechus manatus*) en Venezuela." In *Delfines y otros mamíferos acuáticos de Venezuela: Una política para su conservación*. Caracas, Venezuela: FUDECI.

Bonde, R.K., T.J. O'Shea, and C.A. Beck. 1983. "A manual of procedures for the salvage and necropsy of carcasses of the West Indian manatee (*Trichechus manatus*)." National Technical Information Service, PB83-255273, Springfield, Virginia.

Bonde, R.K., A.A. Aguirre, and J. Powell. 2004. "Manatees as sentinels of marine ecosystem health: Are they the 2000-pound canaries?" *EcoHealth* 1: 255–62.

Bonnelly de Calventi, I., and P. Lancho-Dieguez. 2005. "El manatí en la Republica Dominicana: Taller situación actual del manatí en la Republica Dominicana." Unpublished report. Santo Domingo, Dominican Republic, December.

Boon, P.I., and S.E. Bunn. 1994. "Variations in the stable isotope composition of aquatic plants and their implications for food web analysis." *Aquatic Botany* 48:99–108.

Borrell, A., and A. Aguilar 1990. "Loss of organochlorine compounds in the tissues of a decomposing stranded dolphin." *Bulletin of Environmental Contamination and Toxicology* 45:46–53.

Borrini-Feyerabend, G., M.T. Farvar, J.C. Nguinhuiri, and V.A. Ndangang. 2000. *Co-management of Natural Resources: Organising, Negotiating and Learning-by-Doing.* Heidelberg, Germany: GTZ and IUCN, Kasparek Verlag.

Bossart, G.D. 1995. "Immunocytes of the Atlantic bottlenose dolphin (*Tursiops truncatus*) and West Indian manatee (*Trichechus manatus latirostris*): A morphological characterization with correlations between healthy and disease states under free-ranging and captive conditions." Ph.D. diss., Florida International University, Miami.

———. 1999. "The Florida manatee: On the verge of extinction?" *Journal of the American Veterinary Medical Association* 214:10–15.

———. 2001. "Manatees." In *Marine Mammal Medicine*, ed. L. Dierauf and F. Gulland, 939–60, Boca Raton, Florida: CRC Press.

———. 2006a. "Marine mammals as sentinel species for oceans and human health." *Oceanography* 19:44–47.

———. 2006b. "Red tides and sirens: Brevetoxicosis and the endangered Florida manatee." Session on Marine Mammals on the Frontline: Indicators for Ocean and Human Health. American Association for the Advancement of Science, 16–20 February, St. Louis, Missouri.

Bossart, G.D., D.G. Baden, R.Y. Ewing, B. Roberts, and S.D. Wright. 1998. "Brevetoxicosis in manatees (*Trichechus manatus latirostris*) from the 1996 epizootic: Gross, histologic and immunohistochemical features." *Toxicologic Pathology* 26:276–82.

Bossart, G.D., T. Reiderson, L. Dierauf, and D. Duffield. 2001. "Clinical Pathology." In *Marine Mammal Medicine*, ed. L. Dierauf and F. Gulland, 383–436. Boca Raton, Florida: CRC Press.

Bossart, G.D., D.G. Baden, R.Y. Ewing, and S.D. Wright. 2002a. "Manatees and brevetoxicosis." In *Molecular and Cell Biology of Marine Mammals*, ed. C. Pfeiffer, 205–12. Melbourne, Fla.: Krieger Publishing.

Bossart, G.D., R.Y. Ewing, M. Lowe, M. Sweat, S.J. Decker, C.J. Walsh, S. Ghim, and A.B. Jenson. 2002b. "Viral papillomatosis in Florida manatees (*Trichechus manatus latirostris*)." *Experimental and Molecular Pathology* 72:37–48.

Bossart, G.D., R.A. Meisner, S.A. Rommel, S. Ghim, and A.B. Jenson. 2003. "Pathological features of the Florida manatee cold stress syndrome." *Aquatic Mammals* 29: 9–17.

Bossart, G.D., R. Meisner, S.A. Rommel, J.A. Lightsey, R.A. Varela, and R.H. Defran. 2004. "Pathologic findings in Florida manatees (*Trichechus manatus latirostris*)." *Aquatic Mammals* 30:434–40.

Bowen, W.D. 1997. "Role of marine mammals in aquatic ecosystems." *Marine Ecology Progress Series* 158:267–74.

Bowen-Jones, E., and A. Entwistle. 2002. "Identifying appropriate flagship species: The importance of culture and local contexts." *Oryx* 36:189–95.

Bowman, D. 1999. *Georgis' Parasitology for Veterinarians*, 7th ed. Philadelphia: W.B. Saunders Company.

Boyce, M.S. 1992. "Population viability analysis." *Annual Review of Ecology and Systematics* 23:481–506.

Boyd, I.L., C. Lockyer, and H. Marsh. 1999. "Reproduction in marine mammals." In *Biology of Marine Mammals*, ed. J.E. Reynolds III, and S.A. Rommel, 218–86. Washington, D.C.: Smithsonian Institution Press.

Boyle, C., and J. Khan. 1993. "National report on the status of the West Indian manatee population in Trinidad and Tobago." Unpublished report.

Bradburn, N. M. 1983. "Response effects." In *Handbook of Survey Research*, ed. P.H. Rossi, J.D. Wright, and A.B. Anderson, 289–328. New York: Academic Press.

Brill, R.L., and W.A. Friedl. 1993. "Reintroduction to the wild as an option for managing navy marine mammals." RDT&E Division Technical Report 1549. San Diego, Calif.: Naval Command Control and Ocean Surveillance Center.

Broadfoot, P. 2000. "Interviewing in a cross-cultural context: Some issues for comparative research." In *Cross-Cultural Case Study*, ed. C.J. Pole and R.G. Burgess, 53–66. New York: Elsevier Science.

Brownell, R.L. Jr., P.K. Anderson, R.P. Owen, and K. Ralls. 1981. "The status of dugongs at Palau, an isolated island group." In *The Dugong*, ed. H. Marsh, 11–23. Proceedings of seminar/workshop, 8–13 May 1979, James Cook University of North Queensland, Townsend, Australia.

Bruch, C., W. Coker, and C. VanArsdale. 2001. "Constitutional environmental law: Giving force to fundamental principles in Africa." *Columbia Journal of Environmental Law* 26:131–79.

Bruford, M.W., and R.K. Wayne. 1993. "Microsatellites and their application to population genetic studies." *Current Opinions in Genetics and Development* 3:939–43.

Brunström, B., D. Broman, and C. Näf. 1991. "Toxicity and EROD-inducing potentcy of 24 polycyclic aromatic hydrocarbons (PAHs) in chick embryos." *Archives in Toxicology* 65:485–89.

Buck, L.E., C.G. Geisler, J. Schelhas, and E. Wollenburg, E. 2001. *Biological Diversity: Balancing Interests through Adaptive Collaborative Management*. Boca Raton, Fla.: CRC Press.

Buckingham, C. A., L.W. Lefebvre, J.M. Schaefer, and H.I. Kochman. 1999. "Manatee response to boating activity in a thermal refuge." *Wildlife Society Bulletin* 27:514–22.

Buckland, S.T., D.R. Anderson, K.P. Burnham, J.L. Laake, D.L. Borchers, and L. Thomas. 2001. *Introduction to Distance Sampling: Estimating Abundance of Biological Populations*. Oxford: Oxford University Press.

Buergelt, C.D., and R.K. Bonde. 1983. "Toxoplasmic meningoencephalitis in a West Indian manatee." *Journal of the American Veterinary Medical Association* 183:1294–96.

Buergelt, C.D., R.K. Bonde, C.A. Beck, and T.J. O'Shea. 1984. "Pathologic findings in manatees in Florida." *Journal of the American Veterinary Medical Association* 185:1331–34.

Bullock, T.H., D.P. Domning, and R.C. Best. 1980. "Evoked brain potentials demonstrate hearing in a manatee (*Trichechus inunguis*)." *Journal of Mammalogy* 61:130–33.

Bullock, T.H., T.J. O'Shea, and M.C. McClune. 1982. "Auditory evoked potentials in the West Indian manatee (Sirenia: *Trichechus manatus*)." *Journal of Comparative Physiology* 148:547–54.

Burn, D.M. 1986. "The digestive strategy and efficiency of the West Indian manatee, *Trichechus manatus*." *Comparative Biochemistry and Physiology* 85:139–42.

Burrough, P.A., and R.A. McDonnell. 1998. *Principles of Geographical Information Systems*. Oxford: Oxford University Press.

Burton, R.K., and P.L. Koch. 1999. "Isotopic tracking of foraging and long distance migration in northeastern Pacific pinnipeds." *Oecologia* 119:578–85.

Busbee, D., I. Tizard, J. Stott, D. Ferrick, and E. Ott-Reeves. 1999. "Environmental pollutants and marine mammal health: The potential impact of hydrocarbons and halogenated hydrocarbons on immune system dysfunction." *Journal of Cetacean Research Management* 1:223–48.

Caballero, S., and J.P. Giraldo. 2004. "Filogeografía del manatí antillano (*Trichechus manatus*) y del manatí amazónico (*Trichechus inunguis*) en Colombia." In *Programa nacional de manejo y conservación de manatíes en Colombia*, 159–63. Bogotá, Colombia: Ministerio de Ambiente, Vivienda y Desarrollo Territorial, Fundación Omacha.

Cadenat, J. 1957. "Observations de cétaces, siréniens, cheloniens et sauriens en 1955–1956." *Bulletin de l'Institut Française d'Afrique Noire*, Série A 19:1358–83.

Caicedo-Herrera, D. 2004. "Manatíes *Trichechus manauts* y *Trichechus inunguis* em cautiverio y semicautiverio em Colômbia." In *Programa Nacional de Manejo y Conservación de Manatíes en Colombia*, 164–69. Bogotá, Colombia: Ministerio de Ambiente, Vivienda y Desarrollo Territorial, Fundación Omacha.

Calleson, C.S., and R.K. Frohlich. 2007. "Slower boat speeds reduce risks to manatees." *Endangered Species Research* 3:295–304.

Calvimontes, J. 2009. "Etnoconocimiento, Uso y Conservación del manatí amazónico (*Trichechus inunguis*) en la Reserva de Desarrollo Sostenible Amanã, Brasil." Masters thesis, Universidad Nacional Agraria La Molina, Lima, Peru.

Campbell, H.W., and D. Gicca. 1978. "Reseña preliminar del estado actual y distribución del manatí (*Trichechus manatus*) en México." Anales del Instituto de Biología, Universidad Nacional Autónoma de México, *Serie Zoología* 1:257–64.

Cantanhede, A.M., V.M.F. da Silva, I.P. Farias, T. Hrbek, S.M. Lazzarini, and J. Alves-Gomes. 2005. "Phylogeography and population genetics of the endangered Amazonian manatee, *Trichechus inunguis* Natterer 1883 (Mammalia, Sirenia)." *Molecular Ecology* 14:401–13.

Caro, T.M. 2003. "Umbrella species: Critique and lessons from East Africa." *Animal Conservation* 6:171–81.

Caro, T.M., A. Englis Jr., E. Fitzherbert, and T. Gardner. 2004. "Preliminary assessment of the flagship species concept at a small scale." *Animal Conservation* 7:63–70.

Carp, E. 1976. "United Arab Emirates: Report of survey of marine habitats carried out during 3–15 February 1975." In *Promotion of the Establishment of Marine Parks and Reserves in the Northern Indian Ocean Including the Red Sea and Persian Gulf*. IUCN Publications, New Series no. 35:107–14.

Carr, T. 1994. "The manatees and dolphins of the Miskito Coast Protected Area, Nicaragua." Final report to U.S. Marine Mammal Commission, contract T94070376. NTIS PB94-170354. Bethesda, Maryland.

Cartagena Convention. 2009. http://www.cep.unep.org/cartagena-convention.

Castelblanco-Martínez, D.N. 2004a. "Estudio del comportamiento en vida silvestre del manatí del Orinoco (*Trichechus manatus*)." In *Estudios de fauna silvestre en ecosistemas acuáticos en la Orinoquia Colombiana*, ed. M.C. Diazgranados and T. Trujillo-González, 113–32. Bogotá, Colombia: Fundación Cultural Javeriana de Artes Gráficas.

———. 2004b. "Peixe boi *Trichechus manatus manatus* na Orinoquia Colombiana: Status de conservação e uso de habitat na época seca." Masters thesis, Instituto Nacional de Pesquisas da Amazônia/INPA, Universidade do Amazonas, Manaus, Brazil.

———. 2007. "Ecology and habitat use of manatees in the Chetumal Bay, Quintana Roo, Mexico." Ph.D. protocol, ECOSUR, Chetumal, Quintana Roo, Mexico.

Castelblanco-Martínez, D.N., F.C.W. Rosas, A. Bermudez, and T. Trujillo-Gonzales. 2003. "Conservation status of the West Indian manatee, *Trichechus manatus manatus*, in the Middle Orinoco (Vichada, Colombia)." Abstract. 15th Biennial Conference of the Biology of Marine Mammals, 14–19 December, Greensboro, North Carolina.

Castelblanco-Martínez, D.N., and L. Bermudez. 2004. "Manatíes del Orinoco: Factores de riesgo y consecuencias para su conservación." In *Estudios de fauna silvestre en ecosistemas acuáticos en la Orinoquia Colombiana*, ed. M.C. Diazgranados and F. Trujillo-González, 159–74. Bogotá: Fundación Cultural Javeriana de Artes Gráficas.

Castelblanco-Martínez, D.N., A.L. Bermudez-Romero, I. Gómez-Camelo, F.C.W. Rosas, F. Trujillo, and E. Zerda-Ordoñez. 2009. "Seasonality of habitat use, mortality and reproduction of the vulnerable Antillean manatee *Trichechus manatus manatus* in the Orinoco River, Colombia: Implications for conservation." *Oryx* 43:235–42.

Caughley, G., and A. Gunn. 1996. *Conservation Biology in Theory and Practice*. Cambridge, Ma.: Blackwell Science.

Cerling, T.E., and J.M. Harris. 1998. "Carbon isotopes in bioapatite of ungulate mammals: Implications for ecological and paleoecological studies." *Journal of Vertebrate Paleontology* 18:33A.

Chacón, E. 2000. "Estado de conservación del manatíen la zona sur de la Bahía de Bluefields. Lic. thesis, Escuela de Ecología, Universidad Centroamericana, Managua, Nicaragua.

Chambers, M.R., E. Bani, and B.E.T. Barker-Hudson. 1989. "The status of the dugongs (*Dugong dugon*) in Vanuatu." South Pacific Regional Environmental Programme Topic Review no. 37. South Pacific Commission, Noumea, New Caledonia.

Chambers, R. 1994. "Participatory rural appraisal (PRA): Analysis of experience." *World Development* 22, no. 9:1253–68.

Channels, P., and J. Morrissey. 1981. "Technique for analysis of seagrass genera present in dugong stomachs, including a key to North Queensland seagrasses based on cell details." In *The Dugong*, ed. H. Marsh, 303–9. Proceedings of a seminar/workshop, 8–13 May 1979, James Cook University of North Queensland, Australia.

Chansang, H., and S. Poovachiranon. 1994. "The distribution and species composition of seagrass beds along the Andaman Sea, coast of Thailand." *Phuket Marine Biological Center Research Bulletin* 59:43–52.

Chapin, F.S. III, E.S. Zevaleta, V.T. Eviner, R.L. Naylor, P.M. Vitousek, J.L. Renolds, D.U. Hooper, S. Lavorel, O.E. Sala, S.E. Hobbie, M.C. Mack, and S. Diaz. 2000. "Consequences of changing biodiversity." *Nature* 405:234–42.

Charnock-Wilson, J. 1968. "The manatee in British Honduras." *Oryx* 9:293–94.

———. 1970. "Manatees and crocodiles." *Oryx* 10:236–38.

Chazdon, R.L., C.A. Harvey, O. Komar, D.M. Griffith, B.G. Ferguson, M. Martinez-Ramos, H. Morales, R. Nigh, L. Soto-Pinto, M. van Breugel, and S.M. Philpott. 2009. "Beyond reserves: A research agenda for conserving biodiversity in human-modified tropical landscapes." *Biotropica* 41:142–53.

Chiêm, N.V. 2003. "The system of law relating to dugong protection in Viet Nam." In *Proceedings of the Workshop on the Conservation of the Dugong and Seagrass Habitats in Vietnam,* ed. N. Cox, T.C. Khuong, and E. Hines, 20–21 January 2003, Hanoi, Vietnam. World Wildlife Fund Indochina Programme.

Chilvers, B.L., S. Delean, N. Gales, D. Holley, I.R. Lawler, H. Marsh, and A.R. Preen. 2004 "Diving behavior of dugongs, *Dugong dugon.*" *Journal of Experimental Marine Biology and Ecology* 304:203–24.

Chilvers, B.L., I.R. Lawler, F. MacKnight, H. Marsh, M. Noad, and R. Patterson. 2005. "Moreton Bay, Queensland, Australia: An example of the co-existence of significant marine mammal populations and large-scale coastal development." *Biological Conservation* 122:559–71.

Christie, P., R.B. Pollnac, D.L. Fluharty, M.A. Hixon, G.K. Lowry, R. Mahon, D. Pietri, B.N. Tissot, A.T. White, N. Armada, and R-L Eisma-Osorio. 2009. "Tropical marine EBM feasibility: A synthesis of case studies and comparative analysis." *Coastal Management* 37:374–85.

Chua, T-E., and L.R. Garces. 1994. "Marine living resources management in the ASEAN Region: Lessons learned and the integrated management approach." In *Ecology and Conservation of Southeast Asian Marine and Freshwater Environments Including Wetlands,* ed. A. Sasekumar, N. Marshall, and D. J. MacIntosh, 257–70. Belgium: Kluwer Academic Publishers.

CIA. 2007. "The World Factbook." www.cia.gov/library/publications/the-world-factbook.

Cintrón de Jesús, J. 2001. "Barnacles associated with marine vertebrates in Puerto Rico and Florida." Masters thesis, University of Puerto Rico, Mayagüez, Puerto Rico.

CITES, Convention on International Trade in Endangered Species of Wild Fauna and Flora. 2011. http://cites.org, http://www.cites.org/eng/disc/parties/alphabet.shtml.

Clementz, M.T. 2002. "Sea cows, seagrasses, and stable isotopes: Biogeochemical evaluation of the evolution and ecology of the Sirenia and Desmostylia." Ph.D. diss., University of California, Santa Cruz.

Clementz, M.T., and P.L. Koch. 2000. "Differentiating aquatic mammal foraging ecology with stable isotopes in tooth enamel." *Oecologia* 129:461–72.

Clementz, M.T., P.L. Koch, and C.A. Beck. 2007. "Diet induced differences in carbon isotope fractionation between sirenians and terrestrial ungulates." *Marine Biology* 151:1773–84.

Clifton, K.B., R.L. Reep, and J.J. Mecholsky. 2008a. "Quantitative fractography for estimating whole bone properties of manatee rib bones." *Journal of Material Science* 43:2026–34.

Clifton, K.B., J. Yan, J.J. Mecholsky, and R.L. Reep. 2008b. "Material properties of manatee rib bone." *Journal of Zoology* 274:150–59.

Cockcroft, V.G., A. Guissamulo, and K. Findlay. 2008. "Dugongs of the Bazaruto archipelago, Mozambique." Center for Dolphin Studies, Plettenberg Bay, South Africa.

Cohen, J.L, G.S. Tucker, and D.K. Odell. 1982. "The photoreceptors of the West Indian manatee." *Journal of Morphology* 173:197–202.

Colares, I.G. 1991. "Hábitos alimentares do peixe-boi da Amazônia (*Trichechus inunguis*, Mammalia: Sirenia)." Masters thesis, Instituto Nacional de Pesquisas da Amazônia/INPA, Universidade do Amazonas, Manaus, Brazil.

Colares, I.G., and E.P. Colares. 2002. "Food plants eaten by Amazonian manatees (*Trichechus inunguis*, Mammalia: Sirenia)." *Brazilian Archives of Biology and Technology* 45:67–72.

Coleman, W.G., J. Mattice, and R.W. Brocksen. 1996. "Soulé's conservation biology as a foundation for econometric ecosystem management." *Conservation Biology* 10:1494–99.

Coles, R.W., L. Lee Long, L.J. McKenzie, and C. A. Roder. 2002. *Seagrass and Marine Resources in the Dugong Protection Areas of Upstart Bay, Newry Region, Sand Bay, Lllewellyn Bay, Ince Bay and the Clairview Region, April/May and October 1999.* Research Publication no. 72. Townsville, Australia: Great Barrier Reef Marine Park Authority.

Colmenero R., L.C., and M.E. Hoz Z. 1986. "Distribución de los manatíes, situación y su conservación en México." *Anales del Instituto de Biología, Universidad Nacional Autónoma de México, Serie Zoología* 56:955–1020.

Colmenero R., L.C., and E. Zarate-Becerra. 1990. "Distribution, status and conservation of West Indian manatee in Quintana Roo, Mexico." *Biological Conservation* 52:27–35.

Colón-Llavina, M.M., A.A. Mignucci-Giannoni, S. Mattiucci, M. Paoletti, G. Nascetti, and E.H. Williams Jr. 2009. "Additional records of metazoan parasites from Caribbean marine mammals, including genetically identified anisakid nematodes." *Parasitology Research*, DOI 10.1007/s00436-009-1544-4.

Colvin, J.G. 1992. "A code of ethics for research in the third world." *Conservation Biology* 6:309–11.

Commoner, B. 1971. *The Closing Circle: Nature, Man and Technology,* New York: Alfred Knopf.

Convention on Biological Diversity. http://www.cbd.int/.

Convention on Biodiversity. 2004. Seventh meeting of the conference of the parties to the Convention on Biological Diversity (COP 7). February 2004, Kuala Lumpar, Malaysia.

Decision vii/28 protected areas, articles 8(a) to (e). http://www.biodiv.org/decisions/default.aspx?dec=vii/28.

Convention on the Conservation of Migratory Species of Wild Animals (CMS). 2011. http://www.cms.int/about/intro.htm, http://www.cms.int/species/dugong/index.htm.

Convention on Migratory Species. 2008. Dugong Memorandum of Understanding. http://www.cms.int/bodies/meetings/regional/dugong/pdf/docs_mtg3/Inf_05_Dugong_MoU_E.pdf.

Converse, L.J., P.J. Fernandes, P.S. MacWilliams, and G.D. Bossart. 1994. "Hematology, serum chemistry and morphometric reference values for Antillean manatees (*Trichehus manatus manatus*)." *Journal of Zoo and Wildlife Medicine* 25:423–31.

Corkeron, P. 1994. "Humpback whales (*Megaptera novaeangliae*) in Hervey Bay, Queensland: Behaviour and responses to whale-watching vessels." *Canadian Journal of Zoology* 73:1290–99.

Costa, D.P., and T.M. Williams. 1999. "Marine mammal energetics." In *Biology of Marine Mammals*, ed. J.E. Reynolds III and S.A. Rommel, 176–217. Washington, D.C.: Smithsonian Institution Press.

Cote, S. M. 1994. "Note: The manatee: Facing imminent extinction." *Florida Journal of International Law* 9:189–97.

Cox, N. 2004. "The current status of dugongs in Vietnam." Unpublished report to World Wildlife Fund Indochina Programme. Hanoi, Vietnam.

Cox, N., T.C. Khuong, and E. Hines, eds. 2003. *Proceedings of the Workshop on the Conservation of the Dugong and Seagrass Habitats of Vietnam*, 20–21 January 2003, Hanoi, Vietnam. World Wildlife Fund Indochina Programme.

Craig, B.A., M.A. Newton, R.A. Garrott, J.E. Reynolds III, and J.R. Wilcox. 1997. "Analysis of aerial survey data on Florida manatees using Markov chain Monte Carlo." *Biometrics* 53:524–41.

Craig, B.A., and J.E. Reynolds III. 2004. "Determination of manatee population trends along the Atlantic coast of Florida using a Bayesian approach with temperature-adjusted aerial survey data." *Marine Mammal Science* 20:386–400.

Craig, H., and L.I. Gordon. 1965. "Deuterium and oxygen-18 variations in ocean and the marine atmosphere." In *Stable Isotopes in Oceanographic Studies and Paleotemperatures*, ed. E. Tongiorgi, 9–130. Consiglio Nazionale delle Ricerche Laboratorio di Geologia Nucleare, Pisa, Italy. http://climate.colorado.edu/research/CG/CraigGordon1965_Noone_small3.pdf.

Crnokrak, P., and D.A. Roff. 1999. "Inbreeding depression in the wild." *Heredity* 83:260.

"Cruise ship waste, laws and regulations." Oceana: Laws. June 2008. http://www.oceana.org/uploads/!Cruise_Ship_Waste-Laws&Regs.pdf.

Cundill, G., and C. Fabricius. 2009. "Monitoring in adaptive management: Toward a learning based approach." *Journal of Environmental Management* 90:3205–11.

Cuní, L.A. 1918. "Contribución al estudio de los mamíferos acuáticos observados en las costa de Cuba." *Memorias de las Sociedad Cubana de Histria Natural "Felipe Poey"* 3:83–126.

d'Affonseca Neto, J.A., S.M. Lazzarini, V.M.F. da Silva, R.S. Sousa-Lima, M.C.L. Picanço, F.C.W. Rosas, and G.E. de Mattos. 2002. "Health history of captive Amazonian manatees in Brazil." Abstract. Florida Marine Mammal Health Conference, 4–7 April 2002, Gainesville, Florida.

Dailey, M.D., W. Vogelbein, and D.J. Forrester. 1988. "*Moniligerium blairii* new genus, new species and *Nudacotyle undicola* new species (Trematoda: Digenea) from the West Indian manatee, *Trichechus manatus* L." *Systematic Parasitology* 11:159–63.

Daley, B., B. Griggs, and H. Marsh. 2008. "Exploiting marine wildlife in Queensland: The commercial dugong and marine turtle fisheries, 1847–1969." *Australian Economic History Review* 48:227–65.

Dampier, Capt. W. 1699. A new voyage around the world. 4th ed., corrected. London: James Knapton.

Dansgaard, W. 1964. "Stable isotopes in precipitation." *Tellus* 16:436–68.

Das, H.S. 1996. "The vanishing mermaids of Andaman and Nicobar islands." *Sirenews* (IUCN/SSC Sirenia Specialist Group) 26:5–6.

———. 2000. "Onges and their vanishing mermaids." *Hornbill, Bombay Natural History Society*, January–March: 4–8.

Das, H.S., and S.C. Dey. 1999. "Observations on the dugong, *Dugong dugon* (Müller), in the Andaman and Nicobar Islands, India." *Journal of the Bombay Natural History Society* 96:195–98.

Dawes, C.J., J. Andorfer, C. Rose, C. Uranowski, and N. Ehringer. 1997. "Regrowth of the sea grass *Thalassia testudinum* into propeller scars." *Aquatic Botany* 59:139–55.

Dawson, S.M., Wade, P., Slooten, E. and J. Barlow. 2008. "Design and field methods for sighting surveys of cetaceans in coastal and riverine habitats." *Mammal Review* 8:19–49.

Dayton, P.K., M.J. Tegner, P.B. Edwards, and K.L. Riser. 1998. "Sliding baselines, ghosts, and reduced expectations in kelp forest communities." *Ecological Applications* 8:309–22.

Dean, C.G., and L.J. Dean. 1981. "The occurrence of the sea cow, *Dugong dugon* Müller (Sirenia: Dugongidae) in the Arabian Gulf." In *5th Symposium on the Biological Aspects of Saudi Arabia*, 13–16 April 1981, King Saud University, Abha. Saudi Biological Society.

Debrot, A.O., G. Van Buurt, A. Caballero, and A.A. Antczak 2006. "A historical review of records of the West Indian manatee and the American crocodile in the Dutch Antilles." *Caribbean Journal of Science* 42:272–80.

Defense Agency of Japan. 2001. "Jugon no seisokujoukyou ni kakaru yobiteki chousa (Report of preliminary survey on dugongs in FY 2000)." Defense Agency of Japan, Tokyo.

De Iongh, H.H. 1996. "Plant-herbivore interactions between seagrasses and dugongs in a tropical small island ecosystem." Ph.D. Diss., Catholic University, Nijmegen, Netherlands.

———. 1997. "Current status of dugongs in Indonesia." In *The Ecology of the Indonesian Seas: Part II,* ed. T. Tomascik,

A.J. Mali, A. Nontji, and M.K. Moosa, 1158–66. Singapore: Periplus Editions.

De Iongh, H.H., and G. Persoon. 1991. "Dugong management and conservation project." Final report to the Environmental Study Center, Pattimura University (PPLH), Ambon, Indonesia, and aid Environment, Amsterdam.

De Iongh, H.H., R. Wenno, B. Bierhuizen, and B. van Orden. 1995. "Aerial survey of the dugong (*Dugong dugon* Müller 1776) in coastal waters of the Lease Islands, East Indonesia." *Marine and Freshwater Research* 46:759–61.

De Iongh, H., B. Bierhuizen, and B. van Orden. 1997. "Observations on the behavior of the dugong (*Dugong dugon* Müller, 1776) from waters of the Lease Islands, eastern Indonesia." *Contributions to Zoology* 67:71–77.

De Iongh, H.H., P. Langeveld, and M. van der Wal. 1998. "Movement and home ranges of dugongs around the Lease Islands, East Indonesia." *Marine Ecology* 19:179–93.

De Iongh, H.H., W. Kiswara, and W. Kustiawan. 2006a. "Dugong grazing patterns and interaction with traditional conservation (Sasi Laout) Indonesia: A review." *Journal of Natural and Life Sciences* 1:1–10.

De Iongh, H., M. Moraal, and C. Souffreau. 2006b. "Dugong survey of Derawan Island and Adang Bay, East Kalimantan, Indonesia." *Sirenews* (IUCN/SSC Sirenia Specialist Group) 46:8.

De Iongh, H.H., W. Kiswara and W. Kustiawan. 2007. "A review of fifteen years research on the interaction between dugongs (*Dugong dugon* Müller 1776) and intertidal seagrass beds in Indonesia." *Hydrobiologia* 4:23.

De Iongh, H.H., M. Moraal, M. Hutomo, and W. Kiswara. 2009. *National Conservation Strategy and Action Plan for the Dugong in Indonesia.* Parts I and II. Research Centre for Oceanography (RCO-LIPI) Jl. Pasir Putih No. 1, Ancol Timur No. 1. Jakarta Utara, Indonesia.

Deng, C. 2002. *Biodiversity of Dugongs and Marine Life in Beibu Gulf.* Nanjing: Guangxi Press of Science and Technology.

Deng, C., and X. Lian. 2002. "Conservation and management of marine mammals in the Beibu Gulf in Guangxi." *Research and Development in South China Sea* 2:53–57.

———. 2004. "Conservation and management of rare and endangered marine mammals in the Beibu Gulf in Guangxi." *Journal of Guangxi Academy of Sciences* 20:123–26.

Deraniyagala, P.E.P. 1965. "A sanctuary for turtles, the dugong, whales and dolphins in the Indian and Southern oceans." *Loris* 10:246–50.

de Thoisy, B., T. Spiegelberger, S. Rousseau, G. Talvy, I. Viguel, and J-C. Vié. 2003. "Distribution, habitat, and conservation status of the West Indian manatee *Trichechus manatus* in French Guiana." *Oryx* 37:431–36.

Deutsch, C.J. 2000. "Winter movements and use of warm-water refugia by radio-tagged West Indian manatees along the Atlantic coast of the United States." Final report prepared for Florida Power and Light Company and U.S. Geological Survey, Gainesville, Fla.

Deutsch, C.J., R.K. Bonde, and J.P. Reid. 1998. "Radio-tracking manatees from land and space: Tag design, implementation, and lessons learned from long-term study." *Marine Technology Society Journal* 32:18–29.

Deutsch, C.J., J.P. Reid, L.W. Lefebvre, D.E. Easton, and B.J. Zoodsma. 2000. "Manatee response to elimination of a thermal refuge in northeastern Florida: A preliminary report of results." In *Florida Manatees and Warm Water: Proceedings of the Warm-Water Workshop,* 24–25 August 1999, Jupiter, Florida, 71–73. U.S. Fish and Wildlife Service.

Deutsch, C.J., J.P. Reid, R.K. Bonde, D.E. Easton, H.I. Kochman, and T.J. O'Shea. 2003. "Seasonal movements, migratory behavior and site fidelity of West Indian manatees along the Atlantic Coast of the United States." *Wildlife Monographs* 151:1–77.

Deutsch, C.J., C. Self-Sullivan, and A.A. Mignucci-Giannoni. 2007. "*Trichechus manatus.*" 2007 IUCN Red List of Threatened Species. www.iucnredlist.org.

Deutsch, C.J., C. Self-Sullivan, and A. Mignucci-Giannoni. 2008. "*Trichechus manatus.*" 2009 IUCN Red List of Threatened Species. www.iucnredlist.org.

Dietz, J.M., L.A. Dietz, and E.Y. Nagagata. 1994. "The effective use of flagship species for conservation of biodiversity: The example of lion tamarins in Brazil." In *Creative Conservation: Interactive Management of Wild and Captive Animals,* ed. P.J.S. Olney, G.M. Mace, and A.T.C. Feistner, 32–49. London: Chapman and Hall.

Dingle, H., and V. Drake. 2007. "What Is Migration?" *Bioscience* 57:113–21.

Dolar, M.L.L., H.P. Calumpong, W.F. Perrin, and J. Estacion. 2005. Rediscovery of a dugong in the southern Visayan Sea. Poster presented at the 16th Biennial Conference on the Biology of Marine Mammals, 12–16 December 2005, San Diego, Calif.

Domingo, M., L. Ferrer, M. Pumarola, A. Marco, J. Plana, S. Kennedy, M. McAliskey, and B.K. Rima. 1990. "Morbillivirus in dolphins." *Nature* 348:21.

Domínguez, H.M. 2006. "Evaluaciones preliminares de áreas con registros previos de presencia de manatíes." Unpublished report. Fundemar. Informe Final Proyecto Talleres y Censos Acuáticos para la Conservación de los Mamíferos Marinos para The Nature Conservancy.

———. 2007. "Estudio preliminar sobre el manatí Antillano *Trichechus manatus manatus* en el Santuario de Mamíferos Marinos de Estero Hondo, República Dominicana." Reporte Final a la Secretaría de Estado de Educación Superior, Ciencia y Tecnología.

Domínguez, E., K. Grasela, and F. Núñez. 2008. "Análisis de vacíos de representación del Sistema Nacional de Áreas Protegidas (SINAP) de la República Dominicana." Informe Técnico Secretaría de Estado de Medio Ambiente y Recursos Naturales.

Domning, D.P. 1977. "An ecological model for Late Tertiary sirenian evolution in the North Pacific Ocean." *Systematic Zoology* 25:352–62.

———. 1978. *Sirenian Evolution in the North Pacific Ocean.* University of California Publications in Geological Science 118.

---. 1980. "Feeding position preference in manatees (*Trichechus*)." *Journal of Mammalogy* 61:544–47.

---. 1981. "Distribution and status of manatees *Trichechus* spp. near the mouth of the Amazon River, Brazil." *Biological Conservation* 19:85–97.

---. 1982a. "Evolution of manatees: A speculative history." *Journal of Paleontology* 56:599–619.

---. 1982b. "Commercial exploitation of manatees *Trichechus* in Brazil c. 1785–1973." *Biological Conservation* 22:101–26.

---. 1991. "Why save the manatee?" In *Manatees and Dugongs*, ed. J.E. Reynolds III and D.K. Odell, 167–73. New York: Facts on File.

---. 1994. "A phylogenetic analysis of the Sirenia." In *Contributions in Marine Mammal Paleontology Honoring Frank C. Whitmore, Jr.*, ed. A. Berta and T.A. Deméré, 177–89. Proceedings of San Diego Society of Natural History 29.

---. 1999a. "Endangered species: The common denominator." In *Conservation and Management of Marine Mammals*, ed. J.R. Twiss and R.R. Reeves, 332–41. Washington D.C.: Smithsonian Institution Press.

---. 1999b. "Fossils explained 24: Sirenians (seacows)." *Geology Today* 15:75–79.

---. 2001. "Sirenians, seagrasses, and Cenozoic ecological change in the Caribbean." *Palaeogeography Palaeoclimatology Palaeoecology* 166:27–50.

Domning, D.P., and L.A.C. Hayek. 1984. "Horizontal tooth replacement in the Amazonian manatee (*Trichechus inunguis*)." *Mammalia* 48:105–27.

---. 1986. "Interspecific and intraspecific morphological variation in manatees (Sirenia: *Trichechus*)." *Marine Mammal Science* 2:87–144.

Domning, D.P., and V. Buffrenil. 1991. "Hydrostasis in the Sirenia: Quantitative data and functional interpretations." *Marine Mammal Science* 7:331–68.

Domning, D.P., and B.L. Beatty. 2007. "The use of tusks in feeding by dugongid sirenians: Observations and tests of hypotheses." *Anatomical Record* 290:523–38.

Dong, J., G. Song, and G. Wang. 1992. "Preliminary study on anatomy and histology of larynx, trachea and lung of *Dugong dugon*." *Oceanologia et Limnologia Sinica* 23:433–36.

Dorazio, R.M., H.L. Jelks, and F. Jordan. 2005. "Improving removal-based estimates of abundance by sampling a population of spatially distinct subpopulations." *Biometrics* 61:1093–1101.

Downer, C.C. 1996. "The mountain tapir, endangered 'flagship' species of the high Andes." *Oryx* 30:45–58.

Drew, P., G. Raymond, and D. Weinberg. 2006. *Talk and Interaction in Social Research Methods*. Thousand Oaks, Calif.: Sage Publications.

D'souza, E. 2008. "Out of the blue." *Sanctuary Asia* (Mumbai, India) 28:40–45.

D'souza, E., and V. Patankar. 2009. "First underwater sighting and preliminary behavioural observations of dugongs (*Dugong dugon*) in the wild from Indian waters, Andaman Islands." *Journal of Threatened Taxa* 1:49–53.

Duignan, P.J., C. House, D.K. Odell, R.S. Wells, L.J. Hansen, M.T. Walsh, D.J. St Aubin, B.K. Rima, and J.R. Geraci. 1996. "Morbillivirus infection in bottlenose dolphins: Evidence of recurrent epizootics in the western Atlantic and Gulf of Mexico." *Marine Mammal Science* 12:499–515.

Duffus, D.A. 1988. "Non-consumptive use and management of cetaceans in British Columbia coastal waters." Ph.D. diss., Department of Geography, University of Victoria, British Columbia, Canada.

---. 1996. "The recreational use of grey whales in southern Clayoquot Sound, Canada." *Applied Geography* 16:179–90.

Duffus, D.A., and P. Dearden. 1990. "Non-consumptive wildlife-oriented recreation: A conceptual framework." *Biological Conservation* 53:213–31.

Dunshea, G.J. 2003. "Telomere biology and dynamics in the sirenian *Dugong dugon*: Investigation of a possible new age estimation technique." Honors thesis, James Cook University, Townsville, Australia.

Duplaix, N., and H.A. Reichart. 1978. "History, status and protection of the Caribbean manatee *Trichechus m. manatus* in Suriname." Unpublished report. Rare Animal Relief Effort and U.S. Fish and Wildlife Service.

Durand, J., 1983. *Ocaso de sirenas, esplendor de manatíes*. Mexico City: Fondo de Cultura Económica. 239 pp.

Durbin, J., V. Rajafetra, D. Reid, and D. Razandriznakanirina. 1996. "Local people and Project Angonoka: Conservation of the ploughshare tortoise in north-western Madagascar." *Oryx* 30:113–20.

Dyer, M.I., J.K. Detling, D.C. Coleman, and D.W. Hilbert. 1982. "The role of herbivores in grasslands." In *Grasses and Grasslands*, ed. J.R. Estes, R.J. Tyrl, and J.N. Brunken, 255–95. Norman: University of Oklahoma Press.

Eberhardt, L.L., and T.J. O'Shea. 1995. "Integration of manatee life-history data and population modeling." In *Population Biology of the Florida Manatee*, ed. T.J. O'Shea, B.B. Ackerman, and H.F. Percival, 269–79. Washington, D.C.: National Biological Service Information and Technology Report 1.

Eberhardt, L.L., R.A. Garrott, and B.L. Becker. 1999. "Using trend indices for endangered species." *Marine Mammal Science* 15:766–85.

Ecological Society of Japan. 2000. "Decisions of the 47th annual meeting of the ecological society of Japan." http://www.esj.ne.jp/esj/ESJ_NConsv/2000Jugon.html.

Edwards, H.H., K.H. Pollock, B.B. Ackerman, J.E. Reynolds III, and J.A. Powell. 2007. "Estimation of detection probability in manatee aerial surveys at a winter aggregation site." *Journal of Wildlife Management* 71:2052–60.

Ehrlich, P.R. 2002. "Human nature, nature conservation, and environmental ethics." *BioScience* 52:31–43.

Eletronorte. 1991. *Centro de Preservação e Pesquisa de Mamíferos Aquáticos*. Brasília: UHE Balbina.

---. N.d. *Linhas de Ação e Operação do Centro de Preservação e Pesquisa de Mamíferos Aquáticos–CPPMA*. Brasília: UHE Balbina.

Elith, J. 2000. "Quantitative methods for modeling species habitat: Comparative performance and an application to Australian plants." In *Quantitative Methods for Conservation Biology*, ed. S. Ferson and M. Burgman, 39–58. New York: Springer-Verlag.

Ember, C.R., and M. Ember. 2001. *Cross-Cultural Research Methods.* Walnut Creek, Calif.: Altamira Press.

Eros, C., H. Marsh, R. Bonde, T. O'Shea, C. Beck, C. Recchia, and K. Dobbs. 2000. *Procedures for the Salvage and Necropsy of the Dugong* Dugong dugon. Research Publication no. 64. Townsville, Australia: Great Barrier Reef Marine Park Authority.

Erftemeijer, P.L.A, W. Djunarli, and W. Moka. 1993. "Stomach content analysis of a dugong (*Dugong dugon*) from South Sulawesi, Indonesia." *Australian Journal of Marine and Freshwater Research* 44:229–33.

Escobar, A. 1995 *Encountering Development*, Princeton, N.J.: Princeton University Press.

Espinoza Marin, C. 2004. "El manatí Antillano (*Trichechus manatus L.*) en el territorio Misquito: Historia, cultura, y economia en el Caribe Nicaraguense." Tesis de maestria, Universidad Nacional de Costa Rica, San Pedro. 158 pp.

Estep, M.F., and T.C. Hoering. 1980. "Biogeochemistry of stable hydrogen isotopes." *Geochimica et Cosmochimica Acta* 44:1197–1206.

Estes, J.A. 1998. "Concerns about rehabilitation of oiled wildlife." *Conservation Biology* 12:1156–57.

Estes, J.A., M.T. Tinker, T.M. Williams, and D.F. Doak. 1998. "Killer whale predation on sea otters linking oceanic and nearshore ecosystems." *Science* 282:473–76.

Estes, J.A., D.P. DeMaster, D.F. Doak, T.M. Williams, and R.L. Brownell Jr. 2007. *Whales, Whaling and Ocean Ecosystems.* Berkeley: University of California Press.

Estrada, A.R., and L.T. Ferrer. 1987. "Distribución del manatí antillano, *Trichechus manatus* (Mammalia: Sirenia), en Cuba. I. Región occidental." *Poeyana* 354:1–12.

———. 1993. "Informe sobre el estado del manatí antillano en Cuba." Unpublished report prepared for United Nations Environment Programme.

Etheridge, K., G.B. Rathbun, J.A. Powell, and H.I. Kochman. 1985. "Consumption of aquatic plants by the West Indian manatee." *Journal of Aquatic Plant Management* 23:21–25.

Fairbairn, P.W., and A.M. Haynes. 1982. "Jamaican surveys of the West Indian manatee (*Trichechus manatus*), dolphin (*Tursiops truncatus*), sea turtles (Families Cheloniidae and Dermochelydae) and booby terns (Family Laridae)." *United Nations Food and Agriculture Organization Fisheries Report* 278:289–95.

Falcón-Matos, L., A.A. Mignucci-Giannoni, G.M. Toyos-Gonzalez, G.D. Bossart, R.A. Meisner, and R.A. Varela. 2003. "Evidence of a shark attack on a West Indian manatee (*Trichechus manatus*) in Puerto Rico." *Journal of Neotropical Mammalogy* 10:161–66.

Fancy, S.G., L.F. Pank, D.C. Douglas, C.H. Curbvy, G.W. Garner, S.C. Amstrup, and W.L. Regelin. 1988. "Satellite telemetry: A new tool for wildlife research and management." U.S. Fish and Wildlife Service, Resource Publication 172.

Farquhar, G.D., J.R. Ehleringer, and K.T. Hubick. 1989. "Carbon isotope discrimination and photosynthesis." *Annual Review of Plant Physiology and Plant Molecular Biology* 40:503–37.

Fearnside, P.M. 1990. "A hidrelétrica de Balbina : O faraonismo irreversível versus o meio ambiente na Amazônia." Estudos IAMÁ 1. Instituto de Antropologia e Meio Ambiente, São Paulo, Brazil.

Fernandes, L., J. Day, A. Lewis, S. Slegers, B. Kerriga, D. Breen, D. Cameron, B. Jago, J. Hall, D. Lowe, J. Innes, J. Tanzer, V. Chadwick, L. Thompson, K. Gorman, M. Simmons, B. Barnett, K. Sampson, G. De'ath, B. Mapstone, H. Marsh, H. Possingham, I. Ball, T. Ward, K. Dobbs, J. Zumen, D. Slater, and K. Stapleton. 2005. "Establishing representative no-take areas in the Great Barrier Reef: Large-scale implementation of theory on marine protected areas." *Conservation Biology* 19:1733–44.

Fertl, D., A.J. Schiro, G.T. Regan, C.A. Beck, N. Adimey, L. Price-May, A. Amos, G.A.J. Worthy, and R. Crossland. 2005. "Manatee occurrence in the northern Gulf of Mexico, west of Florida." *Gulf and Caribbean Research* 17:69–74.

Ferreira, A.R. 1903. "Memoria sobre o peixe boy e do uso que lhe dão no Estado do Grão Pará." *Archivos do Museu Nacional do Rio de Janeiro* 12:169–74.

Flaherty, M., and C. Karnjanakesorn. 1995. "Marine shrimp aquaculture and natural resource degradation in Thailand." *Environmental Management* 19:27–37.

Flamm, R.O., L.I. Ward, and B.L. Weigle. 2001. "Applying a variable-shape spatial filter to map relative abundance of manatees (*Trichechus manatus latirostris*)." *Landscape Ecology* 16:279–88.

Flewelling, L.J., J.P. Naar, J.P. Abbott, D.G. Baden, N.B. Barros, G.D. Bossart, M.Y. Bottein, D.G. Hammond, E.M. Haubold, C.A. Heil, M.S. Henry, H.M. Jacocks, T.A. Leighfield, R.H. Pierce, T.D. Pitchford, S.A. Rommel, P.S. Scott, K.A. Steidinger, E.W. Truby, F.M. Van Dolah, and J.H. Landsberg. 2005. "Brevetoxicosis: Red tides and marine mammal mortalities." *Nature* 435:755–56.

Florida Springs Task Force. 2006. "Florida's springs: Strategies for protection and restoration." Prepared for Florida Department of Environmental Protection, Tallahassee.

Foley, W.J., A. McIlwee, I. Lawler, L. Aragones, A.P. Woolnough, and N. Berding. 1998. "Ecological applications of near infrared reflectance spectroscopy: A tool for rapid, cost-effective predication of the composition of plant and animal tissues and aspects of animal performance." *Oecologia* 116:293–305.

Fonnesbeck, C.J., H.H. Edwards, and J.E. Reynolds III. 2009. "A hierarchical covariate model for detection, availability and abundance of Florida manatees at a warm water aggregation site." In *Modeling Demographic Processes in Marked Populations*, ed. D.L. Thomson, E.G. Cooch, and M.J. Conroy, 562–78. Environmental and Ecological Statistics Series vol. 3. New York: Springer Publishing.

Fonseca, M.S., W.J. Kenworthy, and G.W. Thayer. 1998. "Guidelines for the conservation and restoration of seagrasses in the United States and adjacent waters." NOAA Coastal

Ocean Program Decision Analysis Series no. 12. NOAA Coastal Ocean Office, Silver Spring, Maryland.

Fontana, A., and J.H. Frey. 2000. "The interview: From structured questions to negotiated text." In *Handbook of Qualitative Research*, 2nd edition, ed. N.K. Denzin and Y.S. Lincoln, 645–72. Thousand Oaks, Calif.: Sage Publications.

Forrer, D.A., L. Jackson, J. McBride, E.R. Kruse, R. Goby, S. Goby, J. Cull, and M.K. Benson. 2005. "The manatee vs. the local economy: The Cape Coral, Florida, experience, an integrated case study." Lincoln, Ne.: iUniverse.

Forrester, D.J. 1992a. *Parasites and Diseases of Wild Mammals in Florida*. Gainesville: University Press of Florida.

———. 1992b. "Manatees." In *Parasites and Diseases of Wild Mammals in Florida*, 255–74. Gainesville: University Press of Florida.

Forrester, D.J., F.H. White, J.C. Woodard, and N.P. Thompson. 1975. "Intussusception in a Florida manatee." *Journal of Wildlife Diseases* 11:566–68.

Fossi, M.C., and L. Marsili. 1997. "The use of non-destructive biomarkers in the study of marine mammals." *Biomarkers* 2:205–16.

Fossi, M.C., L. Marsili, M. Junini, H. Castello, J.A. Lorenzani, S. Casini, C. Savelli, and C. Leonzio. 1997. "Use of nondestructive biomarkers and residue analysis to assess the health status of endangered species of pinnipeds in the south-west Atlantic." *Marine Pollution Bulletin* 34:157–62.

Fowler, F.J., and T.W. Mangione. 1990. "Standardized Survey Interviewing: Minimizing interviewer-related error." Applied Social Research Methods Series vol. 18. Thousand Oaks, Calif.: Sage Publications.

Frankham, R., J.D. Ballou, and D.A. Briscoe. 2002. *Introduction to Conservation Genetics*. Cambridge, U.K.: Cambridge University Press.

Franklin, J. 2010. *Mapping Species Distributions: Spatial Inference and Prediction*. Cambridge, U.K.: Cambridge University Press.

Frazier, J.G., and T. Mundkur. 1990. "Dugong, *Dugong dugon* (Müller) in the Gulf of Kutch, Gujarat." *Journal of the Bombay Natural History Society* 87:368–79.

Freestone, D. 1991. "Laws of the sea—protection of marine species and ecosystems in the Wider Caribbean: The Protocol on Specially Protected Areas and Wildlife." *Marine Pollution Bulletin* 22:579–81.

Fundación Omacha and Ministerio de Ambiente. 2005. *Programa nacional de manejo y conservación de manatíes en Colombia*. Bogotá, Colombia: Ministerio de Ambiente, Vivienda y Desarrollo Territorial, Fundación Omacha.

FWC, Florida Wildlife Commission. 2002. "Final biological status review of the Florida Manatee (*Trichechus manatus latirostris*)." St. Petersburg: Florida Fish and Wildlife Conservation Commission's Florida Marine Research Institute.

———. 2006. "Boating accidents 2005: Statistical report." Florida Fish and Wildlife Conservation Commission's Division of Law Enforcement. http://myfwc.com/law/boating.

———. 2007. "Florida manatee management plan, *Trichechus manatus latirostris*." Tallahassee: Florida Fish and Wildlife Conservation Commission.

Gales, N., R. McCauley, J.M. Lanyon, and D. Holley. 2004 "Change in abundance of dugongs in Shark Bay, Ningaloo and Exmouth Gulf, Western Australia: Evidence of large scale migration." *Wildlife Research* 31:1–8.

Gallagher, M.D., 1976. "The dugong *Dugong dugon* (Sirenia) at Bahrain, Persian (Arabian) Gulf." *Journal of the Bombay Natural History Society* 73:211–12.

Gannon, J.G., K.M. Scolardi, J.E. Reynolds III, J.K. Koelsch, and T.J. Kessenich. 2007. "Habitat selection by manatees in Sarasota Bay, Florida." *Marine Mammal Science* 23:133–43.

Garcia-Rodriguez, A.I., B.W. Bowen, D. Domning, A.A. Mignucci-Giannoni, M. Marmontel, R.A. Montoya-Ospina, B. Morales-Vela, M. Rudin, R.K. Bonde, and P.M. McGuire. 1998. "Phylogeography of the West Indian manatee (*Trichechus manatus*): How many populations and how many taxa?" *Molecular Ecology* 7:1137–49.

Garcia-Rodriguez, A.I., D. Moraga-Amador, W. Farmerie, P. McGuire, and T.L. King. 2000. "Isolation and characterization of microsatellite DNA markers in the Florida manatee (*Trichechus manatus latirostris*) and their application in selected sirenian species." *Molecular Ecology* 9:2155–34.

Garner, B.A. 1999. *Black's Law Dictionary*. 7th ed. St. Paul, Minn.: West Publishing Company.

Garrigue, C., and N. Patenaude. 2004. "Etude du statut de la population de dugongs en Provinces Nord et Sud." Rapport Final. Zoneco-WWF.

Garrigue, C., N. Patenaude, and H. Marsh. 2008. "The third worldwide largest population of dugong identified in New Caledonia: A challenge for conservation. Distribution and abundance of the dugong in New Caledonia, southwest Pacific." *Marine Mammal Science* 24:81–90.

Garrott, R.A., B.B. Ackerman, J.R. Cary, D.M. Heisey, J.E. Reynolds III, P.M. Rose, and J.R. Wilcox. 1994. "Trends in counts of Florida manatees at winter aggregation sites." *Journal of Wildlife Management* 58:642–54.

GeoPlan Center at the University of Florida. 2006. Florida 2060: A population distribution scenario for the State of Florida. Research project prepared for 1000 Friends of Florida.

Geraci, J.R., and V.J. Lounsbury. 1993. *Marine Mammal Ashore: A Field Guide for Strandings*. Galveston: Texas A&M Sea Grant Publication.

———. 2005. *Marine Mammals Ashore: A Field Guide for Strandings*. 2nd ed. Baltimore: National Aquarium.

Gerstein, E.R. 1994. "The manatee mind: Discrimination training for sensory perception testing of West Indian manatees (*Trichechus manatus*). *Marine Mammals: Public Display and Research* 1:10–21.

Gerstein, E.R., L. Gerstein, S. Forsythe, and J. Blue 1999. "The underwater audiogram of the West Indian manatee (*Trichechus manatus*)." *Journal of the Acoustic Society of America* 105:3575–83.

Giannecchini, J. 1993. "Ecotourism: New partners, new relationships." *Conservation Biology* 7:429–32.

Gibbs, J.P. 2000. "Monitoring Populations." In *Research Techniques in Animal Ecology*, ed. L. Boitani and T.K. Fuller, 213–52. New York: Columbia University Press.

Gibson, J. 1995. "Managing manatees in Belize." M.S. thesis, Department of Marine Sciences and Coastal Management, University of Newcastle upon Tyne, Newcastle, United Kingdom.

Glaser, K.S. (photographs) and J.E. Reynolds III (text). 2003. *Mysterious Manatees*. Gainesville: University Press of Florida.

Goeldi, A. 1893. *Os mammiferos do Brasil*. Monographias Brasileiras. Rio de Janeiro: Livraria Clássica de Alves.

Gohar, H.A.F. 1957. "The Red Sea dugong." *Publications of the Marine Biological Station Al Ghardaqa (Red Sea)* 9:3–49.

Gomez-Pompa, A., and A. Kaus. 1992. "Taming the wilderness myth." *BioScience* 42:271–79.

Gonzalez-Socoloske, D. 2007. "Status and distribution of manatees in Honduras and the use of side-scan sonar." M.S. thesis, Loma Linda University, Loma Linda, Calif.

Gonzalez-Socoloske, D., and L.D. Olivera-Gomez, and R. E. Ford. 2009. "Detection of free-ranging West Indian manatees *Trichechus manatus* using side-scan sonar." *Endangered Species Research* 8:249–57.

Gonzalez-Socoloske, D., and L.D. Olivera-Gomez, in press. "Gentle giants in dark water: Using side-scan sonar for manatee research." *The Open Remote Sensing Journal*.

Gorzelany, J. 2004. "Evaluation of boater compliance with manatee speed zones along the Gulf coast of Florida." *Coastal Management* 32:215–26.

Gosliner, M.L. 1999. "The laws governing marine mammal conservation in the United States." In *Conservation and Management of Marine Mammals*, ed. J.R. Twiss Jr. and R.R. Reeves, 48–86. Washington, D.C.: Smithsonian Institution Press.

Goto, M., C. Ito, S.M. Yahaya, K. Wakamura, S. Asano, Y. Wakai, Y. Oka, M. Furuta, and T. Kataoka. 2004a. "Effect of age, body size and season on food consumption and digestion of captive dugongs (*Dugong dugon*)." *Marine and Freshwater Behaviour and Physiology* 37:89–97.

Goto, M., C. Ito, S.M. Yahaya, Y. Wakai, S. Asano, Y. Oka, S. Ogawa, M. Furuta and T. Kataoka. 2004b. "Characteristics of microbial fermentation and potential digestibility of fiber in the hindgut of dugong (*Dugong dugon*)." *Marine and Freshwater Behaviour and Physiology* 37:99–107.

Grech, A., and H. Marsh. 2007. "Prioritising areas for dugong conservation in a marine protected area using a spatially explicit population model." *Applied GIS* 3:1–14.

Grech, A., H. Marsh, and R. Coles, R. 2008. "A spatial assessment of the risk to a mobile marine mammal from bycatch." *Aquatic Conservation: Marine and Freshwater Ecosystems* 18:1127–39.

Green, E.P., and F.T. Short, eds. 2003. *World Atlas of Seagrasses*. United Nations Environment Programme and World Conservation Monitoring Centre. Berkeley: University of California Press.

Griebel, U., and A. Schmid. 1996. "Color vision in the manatee (*Trichechus manatus*)." *Vision Research* 36:2747–57.

———. 1997. "Brightness discrimination ability in the West Indian manatee (*Trichechus manatus*)." *Journal of Experimental Biology* 200:1587–92.

Grigione, M.M. 1996. "Observations on the status and distribution of the West African manatee in Cameroon." *African Journal of Ecology* 34:189–95.

Grimble, R., and Chan, M.K. 1995. "Stakeholder analysis for natural resource management in developing countries: Some practical guidelines for making management more participatory and effective." *Natural Resources Forum* 19:113–24.

Groom, M.J., G.K. Meffe, and C.R. Carroll. 2005. *Principles of Conservation Biology*, 3rd ed. Sunderland, Mass.: Sinauer Associates.

Guisan, A., and N. E. Zimmermann. 2000. Predictive habitat distribution models in ecology. *Ecological Modeling* 135:147–86.

Guissamulo, A.T. 2004. "The status of dugongs in Mozambique." In *Towards a Western Indian Ocean Dugong Conservation Strategy*, ed. C. Muir, A. Ngusaru, and L. Mwakanema, 30–39. WWF East African Marine Ecoregion.

Guterres, M.G., M. Marmontel, D. M. Ayub, R.F. Singer, and R.B. Singer. 2008. "Anatomia e morfologia de plantas aquáticas da Amazônia: Utilizadas como potencial alimento por peixe-boi amazônico." Instituto de Desenvolvimento Sustentável, Mamirauá (IDSM).

Gysel, L.W., and L.J. Lyon. 1980. "Habitat analysis and evaluation." In *Wildlife Management Techniques Manual*, 4th edition, ed. S.D. Schemnitz, 305–27. Washington, D.C.: Wildlife Society.

Haley, A. 1884. "Administration Report of the Director of the Colombo Museum for 1883." National Museum of Sri Lanka, Colombo. 18 pp.

Hall, A. 1997. *Sustaining Amazonia: Grassroots Action for Productive Conservation*. Manchester, U.K.: Manchester University Press.

Hall, L.S., P.R. Krausman, and M.L. Morrison. 1997. "The habitat concept and a plea for standard terminology." *Wildlife Society Bulletin* 25:173–82.

Haltenorth, T., and H. Diller. 1986. *Mammals of Africa*. London: William Collins.

Hamann, M., J. Grayson, and H. Marsh. 2005. "Raising indigenous community awareness and promoting on-ground recovery activities for marine turtle and dugong in Torres Strait." Unpublished report to the Australian Department of the Environment and Heritage, Canberra.

Hannah, L., G.F. Midgley, T. Lovejoy, W.J. Bond, M. Bush, J.C. Lovett, D. Scott, and F.J. Woodward. 2002. "Conservation of biodiversity in a changing climate." *Conservation Biology* 16:264–68.

Hanson, A.J. 1993. "Sustainable development and the oceans." *Ocean and Coastal Management* 39:167–77.

Harper, J.Y., D.A. Samuelson, and R.L. Reep. 2005. "Corneal

vascularization in the Florida manatee (*Trichechus manatus latirostris*) and three-dimensional reconstruction of vessels." *Veterinary Ophthalmology* 8:89–99.

Harr, K., J. Harvey, R. Bonde, D. Murphy, M. Lowe, M. Menchaca, E. Haubold, and R. Francis-Floyd. 2006. "Comparison of methods used to diagnose generalized inflammatory disease in manatees (*Trichechus manatus latirostris*)." *Journal of Zoo and Wildlife Medicine* 37:151–59.

Harris, T., and W. Bertram, W. 1977. "Dugongs in Abu Dhabi waters." *Bulletin of the Emirates Natural History Group* (Abu Dhabi), no. 1 (March): 5–6.

Hartman, D.S. 1979. *Ecology and Behavior of the Manatee (Trichechus manatus) in Florida*. Special Publication 5. American Society of Mammalogy. 153 pp.

Harvey, J.W., K.E. Harr, D. Murphy, M.T. Walsh, E.J. Chittick, R.K. Bonde, E.M. Haubold, C. Deutsch, M. Menchaca, and M.A. Stamper. 2007. "Clinical biochemistry in healthy manatees (*Trichechus manatus latirostris*)." *Journal of Zoo and Wildlife Medicine* 38:269–79.

Harvey, J.W., K.E. Harr, D. Murphy, M.T. Walsh, E.C. Nolan, R.K. Bonde, M.G. Pate, C.J. Deutsch, H.H. Edwards, and W.L. Clapp. 2009. "Hematology of healthy manatees (*Trichechus manatus*)." *Veterinary Clinical Pathology* 38:183–93.

Harwood, J. 2000. "Risk assessment and decision analysis in conservation." *Biological Conservation* 95:219–26.

Harwood, J., and A. Hall. 1990. "Mass mortality in marine mammals: Its implications for population dynamics and genetics." *Trends in Ecology and Evolution* 5:254–57.

Hatfield, J.R., D.A. Samuelson, P.A. Lewis, and M. Chisholm. 2003. "Structure and presumptive function of the iridocorneal angle of the West Indian manatee (*Trichechus manatus*), short-finned pilot whale (*Globicephala macrorhynchus*), hippopotamus (*Hippopotamus amphibious*), and African elephant (*Loxodonta africana*)." *Veterinary Ophthalmology* 6:35–43.

Hatt, R. 1934. "A manatee collected by the American Museum Congo Expedition, with observations on the recent manatees." *Bulletin of the American Museum of Natural History* 66:533–66.

Haubold, E.M., C.J. Deutsch, and C. Fonnesbeck. 2006. "Final biological status review of the Florida manatee (*Trichechus manatus latirostris*)." Final report. Florida Fish and Wildlife Conservation Commission, St. Petersburg.

Haussmann, M.F., D.W. Winkler, K.M. O'Reilly, C.E. Huntington, I.C.T. Nisbet, and C.M. Vleck. 2003. "Telomeres shorten more slowly in long-lived birds and mammals than in short-lived ones." *Proceedings of the Royal Society of London, Series B*, 270:1387–92.

Hauxwell, J., T.K. Frazer, and C.W. Osenberg. 2004a. "Grazing by manatees excludes both new and established wild celery transplants: Implications for restoration in Kings Bay, Florida, USA." *Journal of Aquatic Plant Management* 42:49–53.

Hauxwell, J., C.W. Osenberg, and T.K. Frazer. 2004b. "Conflicting management goals: Manatees and invasive competitors inhibit restoration of a native macrophyte." *Ecological Applications* 14:571–86.

Havemann, P., D. Thiriet, H. Marsh, and C. Jones. 2005. "Decolonising conservation? Traditional use of marine resources agreements and dugong hunting in the Great Barrier Reef World Heritage Area." *Environmental and Planning Law Journal* 22:258–80.

Hay, M.E., T. Coburn, and D. Downing. 1983. "Spatial and temporal patterns in herbivory on a Caribbean fringing reef: The effects on plant distribution." *Oecologia* 58:299–308.

Hay, M.E., W. Fenical, and K. Gustafson. 1987. "Chemical defense against diverse coral-reef herbivores." *Ecology* 68:1581–91.

Haynes, D., J.F. Müller, and M.S. McLachlan. 1999. "Polychlorinated dibenzo-p-dioxins and dibenzofurans in Great Barrier Reef (Australia) dugongs (*Dugong dugon*)." *Chemosphere* 38:255–62.

Haynes, D., S. Carter, C. Gaus, J. Müller, and W. Dennison. 2005. "Organochlorine and heavy metal concentrations in blubber and liver tissue collected from Queensland (Australia) dugong (*Dugong dugon*)." *Marine Pollution Bulletin* 51:361–69.

Hedrick, P.W. 1995. "Gene flow and restoration: The Florida panther as a case study." *Conservation Biology* 9:996–1007.

Heinsohn, G.E., and A.V. Spain. 1974. "Effects of a tropical cyclone on littoral and sub-littoral biotic communities and on a population of dugongs (*Dugong dugon* (Müller))." *Biological Conservation* 6:143–52.

Heinsohn, G.E., J. Wake, H. Marsh, and A.V. Spain. 1977. "The dugong (*Dugong dugon* (Müller)) in the seagrass system." *Aquaculture* 12:235–48.

Heinsohn, G.E., R.J. Lear, M.M. Bryden, H. Marsh, and B.R. Gardner. 1978. "Discovery of a large population of dugongs off Brisbane, Australia." *Environmental Conservation* 5:91–92.

Heinsohn, G.E., H. Marsh, and P.K. Anderson. 1979. "Australian dugong." *Oceans* 12:48–52.

Heinsohn, R., R.C. Lacy, D.B. Lindenmayer, H. Marsh, D. Kwan, and I.R. Lawler. 2004. "Unsustainable harvest of dugongs in Torres Strait and Cape York (Australia) waters: Two case studies using population viability analysis." *Animal Conservation* 7:417–25.

Helle, E., and O. Stenman. 1984. "Recent trends in levels of PCB and DDT compounds in seals from the Finnish waters of the Baltic Sea." Council Meeting of the International Council for the Exploration of the Sea (ICES).

Hellyer, P. 2000. "Coastal habitats and national heritage: A view from the southern Arabian Gulf." In *Second Arab International Conference and Exhibition on Environmental Biotechnology: Coastal Habitats*, April 2000, Abu Dhabi, United Arab Emirates.

Hemminga, M.A., and M.A. Mateo. 1996. "Stable carbon isotopes in seagrasses: Variability in ratios and use in ecological studies." *Marine Ecology Progress Series* 140:285–98.

Hendrokusumo, S., A. Soemetro, and I. Tas'an. 1976. "The distribution of the *Dugong dugon* in Indonesian waters and report regarding the care of these animals in the Jaya Ancol Oceanarium Jakarta." Jakarta, Indonesia: Jaya Ancol Oceanarium.

Hilbert, D.W., D.M. Swift, J.K. Detling, and M.I. Dyer. 1981. "Relative growth rates and grazing optimization hypothesis." *Oecologia* 51:14–18.

Hines, E. 2002. "Conservation of the dugong (*Dugong dugon*) along the Andaman coast of Thailand: An example of the integration of conservation and biology in endangered species research." Ph.D. diss., University of Victoria, British Columbia, Canada.

Hines, E., K. Adulyanukosol, and M. Charuchinda. 2003. "Conservation of the dugong (*Dugong dugon*) on the eastern coast of the Gulf of Thailand." Report to Ocean Park Conservation Foundation, Hong Kong.

Hines, E., K. Adulyanukosol, M. Charuchinda, P. Somany, and L. Sam Ath. 2004. "Conservation of dugongs (*Dugong dugon*) along the eastern Gulf of Thailand in Thailand and Cambodia." Report to Ocean Park Conservation Foundation, Hong Kong, and Project Aware, Australia.

Hines, E., K. Adulyanukosol, and D.A. Duffus. 2005a. "Dugong abundance along the Andaman coast of Thailand." *Marine Mammal Science* 21:536–49.

Hines, E., K. Adulyanukosol, D.A. Duffus, and P. Dearden. 2005b. "Community perspectives and conservation needs for dugongs along the Andaman Coast of Thailand." *Environmental Management* 36:654–64.

Hines, E., M. Than Tun, L. Parr, D. Kwan, and A. Novak. 2007. "Status and conservation of dugongs and coastal cetaceans in the Myeik Archipelago of Myanmar." Report to Ocean Park Conservation Foundation, Hong Kong.

Hines, E., K. Adulyanukosol, P. Somany, L. Sam Ath, N. Cox, P. Boonyanate, and N. Hoa. 2008a. "Community interviews to assess conservation needs of the dugong (*Dugong dugon*) in Cambodia and Phu Quoc, Vietnam." *Oryx* 42:113–21.

Hines, E., Charuchinda, M., Manansap, S., Ilangakoon, A., and L. Ponnampalam. 2008b. "Irrawaddy Dolphins (*Orcaella brevirostris*) in Trat Province, Eastern Thailand (2007-2008)." Report to Ocean Park Conservation Foundation, Hong Kong.

Hines, E., Manansap, S., Ilangakoon, A., Ponnampalam, L., and L. Morse. 2009. "Coastal cetaceans in Trat Province, Eastern Thailand." Report to Ocean Park Conservation Foundation, Hong Kong.

Hines, E., K. Adulyanukosol, and P. Boonyanate. "The cultural significance of dugongs to Thai villagers: Implications for conservation" (in revision).

Hinrichsen, D. 1998. *Coastal Waters of the World: Trends, Threats, and Strategies*. Washington D.C.: Island Press.

Hixon, M.A., and W.N. Brostoff. 1996. "Succession and herbivory: Effects of differential fish grazing on Hawaiian coral-reef algae." *Ecological Monographs* 66:67–90.

Hoa, N.Y. 2001. "The status of seagrass beds and dugong population in Con Dao National Park." April 2001. Nha Trang Oceanography Institute, Nha Trang, Vietnam.

Hobson, K.A., and R.G. Clark. 1992. "Assessing avian diets using stable isotopes. I: Turnover of carbon-13 in tissues." *Condor* 94:181–88.

Hobson, K.A., D.M. Schell, D. Renouf, and E. Noseworthy. 1996. "Stable carbon and nitrogen isotopic fractionation between diet and tissues of captive seals: Implications for dietary reconstructions involving marine mammals." *Canadian Journal of Fisheries and Aquatic Sciences* 53:528–33.

Hobson, K.A., J.L. Sease, R.L. Merrick, and J.F. Piatt. 1997. "Investigation of trophic relationships of pinnipeds in Alaska and Washington using stable isotope ratios of nitrogen and carbon." *Marine Mammal Science* 13:114–32.

Hocking, M., S. Stolton, and N. Dudley. 2000. "Evaluating effectiveness: A framework for assessing the management of protected areas." Gland, Switzerland: IUCN.

Hodgson, A. 2009. "Marine Mammals." In *Marine Atlas of Bahrain*, ed. R.A. Loughland and A.J.M. Zainal, 232–61. Manama, Bahrain: Geomatec.

Hoekstra, P.F., T.M O'Hara, A.T. Fisk, K. Borgå, K.R. Solomon, and D.C.G. Muir. 2003. "Trophic transfer of persistent organochlorine contaminants (OCs) within an arctic marine food web from the southern Beaufort-Chukchi Seas." *Environmental Pollution* 124:509–22.

Hoelzel, A.R., J.M. Hancock, and G.A. Dover. 1991. "Evolution of the cetacean mitochondrial D-loop region." *Molecular Biology and Evolution* 8:475–93.

Holdgate, M.W. 1994. "Ecology, development and global policy." *Journal of Applied Policy* 31:201–11.

Holland, M. M., C. A. Cave, C. A. Holland, and T. W. Bille. 2003. "Development of a quality, high throughput DNA analysis procedure for skeletal samples to assist with the identification of victims from the World Trade Center Attacks." *Forensic Sciences* 44:264–72.

Holley, D., I.R. Lawler, and N. Gales. 2006. "Summer survey of dugong distribution and abundance in Shark Bay reveals additional key habitat area." *Wildlife Research* 33:243–50.

Hooker, S.K., H. Whitehead, and S. Gowans. 1999. "Marine protected area design and the spatial and temporal distribution of cetaceans in a submarine canyon." *Conservation Biology* 13:592–602.

Hooker, S.K., and L.R. Gerber. 2004. "Marine reserves as a tool for ecosystem-based management: The potential importance of megafauna." *BioScience* 54:27–39.

Hoyt, E. 2005. *Marine Protected Areas for Whales, Dolphins and Porpoises*. London: Earthscan.

Hoyt, E., and M. Iñíguez. 2008. *The State of Whale Watching in Latin America*. WDCS, Chippenham, U.K.; IFAW, Yarmouth Port, U.S.A.; and Global Ocean, London. http://www.wdcs.org/submissions_bin/WW_Latinamerica_English.pdf.

Hudson, B.E.T, 1977. "Dugong: Distribution, hunting, protective legislation and cultural significance in Papua New Guinea." Wildlife in Papua New Guinea. Wildlife Division, Department of Lands and Environment, Konedobu, Papua New Guinea.

———. 1981. "Interview and aerial survey data in relation to resource management of the dugong in Manus province, Papua New Guinea." *Bulletin of Marine Science* 31:662–72.

———. 1986a. "Dugongs and people." *Oceanus* 29:100–6.

———. 1986b. "The hunting of dugong in Daru, Papua New Guinea, during 1978–82: Community management and education initiatives." In *Torres Strait Fisheries Seminar, Port Moresby, 11–14 February 1985*, ed. A.K. Haines, G.C. Williams, and C. Coates, 77–94. Canberra: Australian Government Printing Service.

Humes, A.G. 1964. "*Harpacticus pulex*, a new species of copepod from the skin of a porpoise and a manatee in Florida." *Bulletin Marine Science Gulf and Caribbean* 14:517–28.

Humphrey, S.R., and J.R. Bain. 1990. *Endangered Animals of Thailand*. Gainesville, Florida: Sandhill Crane Press.

Hunter, M.E., N.E. Auil-Gomez, K.P. Tucker, R.K. Bonde, J. Powell, and P.M. McGuire. 2010. "Low genetic variation and evidence of limited dispersal in the regionally important Belize manatee." *Animal Conservation* 13:592–602.

Hurst, L.A., and C.A. Beck. 1988. "Microhistological characteristics of selected aquatic plants of Florida with techniques for the study of manatee food habits." U.S. Fish and Wildlife Service, Biological Report no. 88(18).

Husar, S.L. 1975a. "A review of the literature of the dugong (*Dugong dugon*)." U.S. Fish and Wildlife Service, Wildlife Research Report 4. Washington, D.C. 30 pp.

———. 1975b. "The dugong: Endangered siren of the South Seas." *National Parks and Conservation Magazine* (National Parks and Conservation Association), February, pp. 15–18.

———. 1977. "The West Indian manatee (*Trichechus manatus*)." U.S. Fish and Wildlife Service, Wildlife Research Report 7. Washington, D.C. 22 pp.

———. 1978a. "*Trichechus senegalensis*." *Mammalian Species* 89:1–3.

———. 1978b. "*Dugong dugon*." *Mammalian Species* 88:1–7.

IBAMA, Instituto Brasileiro do Meio Ambiente e dos Recursos Naturais Renováveis. 1996. *I Workshop interno do Projeto Peixe-boi: Histórico, organização e atuação*. Maceió, Alagoas, Brazil.

———. 1997. *Reunião de trabalho sobre pesquisa para a conservação do peixe-boi no Brasil*. Barra de Mamanguape, Paraiba, Brazil.

———. 1998. *Oficina para elaboração do Plano de ações integradas para a conservação do peixe-boi da Amazônia*. Manaus, Brazil.

———. 2001. *Mamíferos aquáticos do Brasil: Plano de ação, versão II*. Brasília, Brazil: Instituto Brasileiro do Meio Ambiente e dos Recursos Naturais Renováveis.

IIRR, International Institute of Rural Reconstruction. 1998. *Participatory Methods in Community-Based Coastal Resource Management*. 3 vols. 1:15–16. Silang, Cavite, Philippines: International Institute of Rural Reconstruction.

Ikeda K. 2006. "Study on dugong (*Dugong dugon*) grazing and seagrass in Okinawa, Japan." Masters thesis, Kyushu University, Fukuoka, Japan.

Ilangakoon, A.D., 1989. "A socio-economic study of cetacean harvesting in Sri Lanka." In *Marine Mammal Research and Conservation in Sri Lanka 1985–1986*, ed. S. Leatherwood and R.R. Reeves, 54–67. Marine Mammal Technical Report no. 1. Nairobi, Kenya: United Nations Environment Program, Oceans and Coastal Areas.

———. 2002. *Whales and Dolphins, Sri Lanka*. Colombo, Sri Lanka: WHT Publications.

Ilangakoon, A.D., D. Sutaria, R. Raghavan, and E. Hines. 2004. "Interview survey on dugongs (*Dugong dugon*) in the Gulf of Mannar area, Sri Lanka and India." Unpublished report to Sirenian International, U.S.A.

Ilangakoon, A.D., and T. Tun. 2007. "Rediscovering the dugong (*Dugong dugon*) in Myanmar and capacity building for research and conservation." *Raffles Bulletin of Zoology* 55:195–99.

Ilangakoon, A.D., D. Sutaria, E. Hines, and R. Raghavan. 2008. "Community interviews on the status of the dugong (*Dugong dugon*) in the Gulf of Mannar (India and Sri Lanka)." *Marine Mammal Science* 24:704–10.

Intongcome, A., T. Thrapsomboon, and R. Tongnak. 2005. "Preliminary aerial survey on marine endangered species at Suratthani Province in 2004." *Technical Paper no. 4/2005*. Phuket Marine Biological Center (in Thai).

IPCC, Intergovernmental Panel on Climate Change. 2007. "Summary for Policymakers." In *Climate Change 2007: Impacts, Adaptation and Vulnerability. Contribution of Working Group II to the Fourth Assessment Report of the Intergovernmental Panel on Climate Change*, ed M.L. Parry, O.F. Canziani, J.P. Palutikof, P.J. van der Linden, and C.E. Hanson, 7–22. Cambridge, U.K.: Cambridge University Press.

Irvine, A.B. 1983. "Manatee metabolism and its influence on distribution in Florida." *Biological Conservation* 25:315–34.

Irvine, A.B., and M.D. Scott. 1984. "Development and use of marking techniques to study manatees in Florida." *Biological Sciences* 47:12–26.

Irving, L. 1939. "Respiration of diving mammals." *Physiological Review* 19:112–34.

ISC, Indonesian Seagrass Committee. 2003. *Policy, Strategy and Action Plan for Management of Seagrass Ecosystems in Indonesia*. UNEP-GEF project: Revising environmental degradation in South China Sea and Gulf of Thailand. Jakarta, Indonesia: UNEP-GEF.

IUCN, International Union for Conservation of Nature. 1994. "Guidelines for protected area management categories." IUCN, Cambridge, U.K. and Gland, Switzerland. http://www.unep-wcmc.org/protected_areas/categories/index.html.

———. 2000a. *The 2000 Red List of Threatened Species*. Gland, Switzerland: IUCN

———. 2000b. The World Conservation Union. http://www.iucn.org/redlist/2000/background.html.

———. 2001. "IUCN Red List categories and criteria." Prepared by the IUCN Species Survival Commission, 9 February 2000, Gland, Switzerland.

———. 2009. "IUCN Red List of Threatened Species." Version 2009.2. www.iucnredlist.org.

———. 2011. "IUCN Red List of Threatened Species." Version 2011.1. www.iucnredlist.org.

Jackson, J.B.C., M.X. Kirby, W.H. Berger, K.A. Bjorndal, L.W. Botsford, B.J. Bourque, R.H. Bradbury, R. Cooke, J. Erlandson, J.A. Estes, T.P. Hughes, S. Kidwell, C.B. Lange, H.S. Lenihan, J.M. Pandolfi, C.H. Peterson, R.S. Steneck, M.J. Tegner, and R.R. Warner. 2001. "Historical overfishing and the recent collapse of coastal ecosystems." *Science* 293:629–38.

Jacobson, S. 1995. *Conserving Wildlife: International Education and Communication Approaches.* New York: Columbia University Press.

James, D.B. 1988. "Some observations and remarks on the endangered marine animals of Andaman and Nicobar Islands." In *Proceedings of the Symposium on Endangered Marine Animals and Marine Parks,* 12–16 January 1985, Cochin, India, 337–40. Marine Biological Association of India.

James, P.S.B.R. 1974. "An osteological study of the dugong *Dugong dugon* (Sirenia) from India." *Marine Biology* 27:173–84.

James, P.S.B.R., and R.S.L. Mohan. 1987. "The marine mammals of India." *Marine Fisheries Information Service Technical and Extension Series* 71:1–13.

Janis, C. 1976. "The evolutionary strategy of the Equidae and the origins of rumen and cecal digestion." *Evolution* 30:757–74.

Janson, T. 1980. "Discovering the mermaids." *Oryx* 5:373–79.

Jaramillo-Legorreta, A., L. Rojas-Bracho, R.L. Brownell Jr., A.J. Read, R.R. Reeves, K. Ralls, and B.L. Taylor. 2007. "Saving the vaquita: Immediate action, not more data" *Conservation Biology* 21:1653–55.

Jarman, P.J. 1966. "The status of the dugong (*Dugong dugon* Müller): Kenya, 1961." *East African Wildlife Journal* 4:82–88.

Jefferson, T.A., S. Leatherwood, and M.A. Webber. 1993. *FAO Species Identification Guide: Marine Mammals of the World.* Rome, Italy: Food and Agricultural Organization.

Jensen, J.R. 2007. *Remote Sensing of the Environment: An Earth Resource Perspective.* 2nd ed. Upper Saddle River, N.J.: Pearson Prentice Hall.

Jerdon, T.C. 1874. *The Mammals of India: A Natural History of All Animals Known to Inhabit Continental India.* London: J. Wheldon.

Jethva, B., and P. Solanki. 2007. "Population status and distribution of dugongs (*Dugong dugon*) in India." Gandhinagar, India: GEER Foundation, Ministry of Environment and Forests, Government of India.

Jim, S., S.H. Ambrose, and R.P. Evershed. 2004. "Stable carbon isotopic evidence for differences in the dietary origin of bone cholesterol, collagen and apatite: Implications for their use in palaeodietary reconstruction." *Geochimica et Cosmochimica Acta* 68:61–72.

Jiménez-Marrero, N.M., A.A. Mignucci-Giannoni, J.P. Reid, R.K. Bonde, N.M. Lee, and E.H. Williams. 1995. "First successful release of a captive-raised orphaned Antillean manatee in the Caribbean." In *Abstracts, Eleventh Biennial Conference on the Biology of Marine Mammals,* Orlando, Florida, December 1995, 59.

Jiménez-Marrero, N.M., I. Méndez-Matos, R.A. Montoya-Ospina, E.H. Williams, L. Bunkley, and A.A. Mignucci-Giannoni. 1998. "Rangos de referencia de inmunoglobulina G en individuos de tres poblaciones del manatí (*Trichechus manatus*)." *Caribbean Journal of Science* 34:313–15.

Jiménez Pérez, I. 1999. "Estado de conservación, ecologia, y conocimiento popular del manatí (*Trichechus manatus*) en Costa Rica." *Vida Silvestre Neotropical* 8:18–30.

———. 2002. "Heavy poaching in prime habitat: The conservation status of the West Indian manatee in Nicaragua." *Oryx* 36:1–7.

———. 2003. *Los manatíes de Río San Juan y los Canales de tortugueros: ecología y Conservación.* Managua: Araucaria. 87 pp.

———. 2005a. "Development of predictive models to explain the distribution of the West Indian manatee (*Trichechus manatus*) in tropical watercourses." *Biological Conservation* 125:491–503.

———. 2005b. "Actualizacion del estado de conservacion del manati en el noreste de Costa Rica: Distribución, abundancia, amenazas y acciones de conservación (1996–2005)." Technical report. Fundacion Salvemos al Manati de Costa Rica/FUNDAR. http://www.eco-index.org/search/pdfs/727 report_1.pdf.

Johannes, R.E. 1981. "Working with fishermen to improve coastal tropical fisheries and resource management." *Bulletin of Marine Science* 31:673–80.

Johnsingh, A.J.T., and J. Joshua. 1994. "Conserving Rajaji and Corbett National Parks: The elephant as a flagship species." *Oryx* 28:135–40.

Johnson, E. 1937. "List of vanishing Gambian mammals." *Society for the Preservation of the Fauna of the Empire* 31:63–64.

Johnson, M.P., and P.L. Tyack. 2003. "A digital acoustic recording tag for measuring the response of wild marine mammals to sound." *IEEE Journal of Oceanic Engineering* 28:3–12.

Jolly, G.M. 1969. "Sampling methods for aerial censuses of wildlife populations." *East African Forestry Journal* 34:46–9.

Jones, S. 1959. "On a pair of captive dugongs." *Loris (Journal of Ceylon Wildlife Protection Society),* December: 83–87.

———. 1967. "The dugong *Dugong dugon* (Müller): Its present status in the seas around India with observations on its behaviour in captivity." *International Zoo Yearbook* 7:215–20.

———. 1980. "The dugong or the so-called mermaid, *Dugong dugon* (Müller) of the Indo-Sri Lanka waters: Problems of research and conservation." *Spolia Zeylanica* 35:22–260.

Jonklass, R. 1961. "Some observations on dugongs (*Dugong dugon* Erxleben)." *Loris* 9:1–8.

Jousse, H. 1999. "The fossil dugongs of Akab Island (Umm al-Qaiwain, UAE)." Ph.D. diss., Centre des Sciences de la Terre, Université Claude Bernard, Lyon, France.

Kaehler, S., and E.A. Pakhomov. 2001. "Effects of storage and preservation on the $d^{13}C$ and $d^{15}N$ signatures of selected marine organisms." *Marine Ecology Progress Series* 219:299–304.

Kamiya, T. 1989. *Ningyo no Hakubutu-shi: Kaiju-gaku jishi* (Natural history of mermaids: Study of sirenians). Tokyo, Japan: Shisakusha.

Kannan, K., A.L. Blankenship, P.D. Jones, and J.P. Giesy. 2000. "Toxicity reference values for the toxic effects of polychlorinated biphenyls to aquatic mammals." *Human and Ecological Risk Assessment* 6:181–201.

Kasuya, K., M. Shirakihara, H. Yoshida, H. Ogawa, H. Yokochi, S. Uchida, and K. Shirakihara. 1999. "Nihonsan Jugon no genjou to hogo (Status and protection of dugong in Japan)." *Report of 8th Pro Natura Fund.* 8:6–13.

Kasuya, K., H. Ogawa, H. Yokochi, T. Hosokawa, M. Shirakihara, and N. Higashi. 2000. "Nihonsan Jugon no genjou to hogo (Status and protection of dugong in Japan)." *Report of 9th Pro Natura Fund.* 9:29–36.

Kataoka, T., Mori, T., Wakai, Y., Palma, J.A.M., Yaptinchay, A. A.S.P., DeVeyra, R.R., and R.B. Trono. 1995. *Dugongs of the Philippines: A Report of the Joint Dugong Research and Conservation Program May 1995.* Shin-Nihon Kogyo Company. 167 pp.

Katona, S.K., and S.D. Kraus. 1999. "Efforts to conserve the North Atlantic right whale." In *Conservation and Management of Marine Mammals*, ed J.R. Twiss and R.R. Reeves, 311–31. Washington D.C.: Smithsonian Institution Press.

Kelleher, G. 1999. *Guidelines for Marine Protected Areas.* Gland, Switzerland: IUCN.

Kelleher, G., and R. Kenchington. 1992. *Guidelines for Establishing Marine Protected Areas.* Marine Conservation and Development Report. Gland, Switzerland: IUCN.

Kelleher, G., C. Bleakley, and S. Wells. 1995. *A Global Representative System of Marine Protected Areas*, vol. 1: Antarctic, Arctic, Mediterranean, Northwest Atlantic, Northeast Atlantic and Baltic. Washington, D.C.: Great Barrier Reef Marine Park Authority, World Bank, and World Conservation Union.

Kellert, S.R. 1986. "Social and perceptual factors in the preservation of animal species." In *The Preservation of Species: The Value of Biological Diversity*, ed. B.G. Norton. Princeton, N.J.: Princeton University Press.

Kemp, J. 2000. *WWF-Eastern Africa Marine Ecoregion: Biological Reconnaissance.* Final Report. World Wildlife Fund.

Kendall, S. 1999. "Dolphins as people, manatees as maggots: Incorporating indigenous knowledge and story into environmental education in the Colombian Amazon." In *Indigenous Knowledge in/as Environmental Education Processes*, ed. R. O'Donoghue, L. Masuku, E. Janse van Rensburg, and M. Ward. Howick, South Africa: Environmental Education Association of Southern Africa.

———. 2001. "Distribution and conservation of the Amazonian manatee (*Trichechus inunguis*) in the area of Puerto Nariño, Colombia." Final Report to Fauna & Flora Intl., Proj. Ref. 99/54/4.

Kendall, S., and D.L. Orozco. 2003. "El árbol de los manatíes: Caza, concertación y conservación en el Amazonas colombiano" (The manatee tree: Hunting, conciliation and conservation in the Colombian Amazon). In *Fauna socializada: Tendencias de manejo de fauna con comunidades locales en America Latina* (Fauna and people: Tendencies in the management of fauna with local communities in Latin America), ed. C. Campos-Rozo and A. Ulloa, 215–37. Bogotá, Colombia: Fundación Natural/ICANH.

Kendall, S., D.L. Orozco, C. Ahué, and D. Silva. 2004. "Uso de hábitat y conservación del manati *Trichechus inunguis* en la Amazonia Colombiana." Informe final, Proyecto Fondo para Acción Ambiental, Fundación Omacha, Bogotá.

Kendall, S., D.L. Orozco, and C. Ahué. 2005. "Ecology, hunting and conservation of the manatee (*Trichechus inunguis*) in the Colombian Amazon." In *Programa nacional de manejo y conservación de manatíes en Colombia*, 143–58. Bogotá, Colombia: Ministerio de Medio Ambiente, Vivienda y Desarrollo Territorial, Fundación Omacha.

Kendall, W.L., J.E. Hines, and J.D. Nichols. 2003. "Adjusting multistate capture-recapture models for misclassification bias: Manatee breeding proportions." *Ecology* 84:1058–66.

Kendall, W.L., C.A. Langtimm, C.A. Beck, and M.C. Runge. 2004. "Capture-recapture analysis for estimating manatee reproductive rates." *Marine Mammal Science* 20:424–37.

Kennish, M.J. 1997. *Practical Handbook of Estuarine and Marine Pollution.* Boca Raton, Fla.: CRC Press.

Kenward, R. 1987. *Wildlife Radio Tagging: Equipment, Field Techniques, and Data Analysis.* London: Academic Press.

Ketten, D.R., D.K. Odell, and D.P. Domning. 1992. "Structure, function, and adaptation of the manatee ear." In *Marine Mammal Sensory Systems*, ed. J. Thomas, 77–95. New York: Plenum Press.

Kienta, M. 1985. "Preliminary investigation on the manatee (*Trichechus senegalensis*) at Lac Debo, Bamaoko, West Africa." Unpublished report for Wildlife Conservation International.

Kimmell, J.R. 1999. "Ecotourism as environmental learning." *Journal of Environmental Education* 30:40–44.

King, J.M., and J.T. Heinen. 2004. "An assessment of the behaviors of overwintering manatees as influenced by interactions with tourists at two sites in central Florida." *Biological Conservation* 117:227–34.

Kingdon, J. 1971. *East African Mammals: An Atlas of Evolution in Africa.* Vol. 1. New York: Academic Press.

Kipps, E.K., W.A. McLellan, S.A. Rommel, and D.A. Pabst. 2002. "Skin density and its influence on buoyancy in the manatee (*Trichechus manatus latirostris*), harbor porpoise (*Phocoena phocoena*), and bottlenose dolphin (*Tursiops truncatus*)." *Marine Mammal Science* 18:765–78.

Kirkman, H., and J. A. Kirkman. 2000. "The management of seagrasses in South East Asia and Australia." *Biologica Marina Mediterranea* 7:305–19.

Kirkpatrick, B., L.E. Fleming, D. Squicciarini, L.C. Backer, R. Clark, W. Abraham, J. Benson, Y.S. Cheng, D. Johnson, R. Pierce, J. Zaias, G.D. Bossart, and D.G. Baden. 2004. "Literature review of Florida red tide: Implications for human health effects." *Harmful Algae* 3:99–115.

Kiszka, J., A. Jamon, and C.E. Muir. 2007. "Status of a marginal dugong (*Dugong dugon*) population in the lagoon of Mayotte (Mozambique Channel), in the western Indian Ocean. *Western Indian Ocean Journal of Marine Science* 6:111–16.

Kiszka, J., C.E. Muir, C. Poonian, T.M. Cox, O.A. Amir, J. Bourjea, Y. Razafindrakoto, N. Wambiji, and N. Bristol. 2009. "Marine mammal bycatch in the southwest Indian Ocean:

Review and need for a comprehensive assessment." *Western Indian Ocean Journal of Marine Science* 7(2):119–36.

Klammer, G., 1984. "The relief of the extra-Andean Amazon basin." In *The Amazon*, ed. H. Sioli, 47–84. Dordrecht, Netherlands: Dr. W. Junk Publishers.

Klein, E.H. 1979. "Review of the status of manatee (*Trichechus manatus*) in Honduras, Central America." *Ceiba* 23:21–28.

Klishin, V.O., R. Pezo Diaz, V.V. Popov, and A. Ya. Supin. 1990. "Some characteristics of hearing of the Brazilian manatee, *Trichechus inunguis*." *Aquatic Mammals* 16:139–44.

Koch P.L., M.L. Fogel, and N. Tuross. 1994. "Tracing the diets of fossil animals using stable isotopes." In *Stable Isotopes in Ecology and Environmental Science*, ed. K. Lajtha and R.H. Michener, 63–92. Boston: Blackwell.

Kocher, T.D., W.K. Thomas, A. Meyer, S.V. Edwards, S. Pääbo, F. X. Villablanca, and A.C. Wilson. 1989. "Dynamics of mitochondrial DNA evolution in animals: Amplification and sequencing with conserved primers." *Proceedings of the National Academy of Sciences of the USA* 86:6196–6200.

Koelsch, J.K. 1997. "The seasonal occurrence and ecology of Florida manatees (*Trichechus manatus latirostris*) in coastal waters near Sarasota, Florida." Masters thesis, University of South Florida, Tampa.

———. 2001. "Reproduction in female manatees observed in Sarasota Bay, Florida." *Marine Mammal Science* 17:331–42.

Korrubel, J., and V. Cockcroft. 1997. "Dire days for dugongs." *Africa-Environment and Wildlife* 5:28–33.

Kouadio, Akoi. 1994. "Une enquête préliminaire sur les lamantins dans les eaux de la Réserve de la Conkouati au sud du Congo." *Canopée* 4:10.

———. 2002. In *Commitments of the Heart: Odysseys in West African Conservation*, by T.T. Cable. Urbana, Ill.: Sagamore Publishing.

———. 2004. "Evaluation du projet d'éducation et de conservation du lamantin ouest Africain en Côte d'Ivoire." Status report, Wildlife Conservation Society.

Kreb, D., and Budiono. 2005. "Cetacean diversity and habitat preference in tropical waters of east Kalimantan, Indonesia." *Raffles Bulletin of Zoology* 53:149–55.

Kucklick, J.R., W.D.J. Struntz, P.R. Becker, G.W. York, T.M. O'Hara, and J.E. Bohonowych. 2002. "Persistent organochlorine pollutants in ringed seals and polar bears collected from northern Alaska." *Science of the Total Environment* 287:45–59.

Kuehl, D.W., and R. Haebler. 1995. "Organochlorine, organobromine, metal, and selenium residues in bottlenose dolphins (*T. truncatus*) collected during an unusual mortality event in the Gulf of Mexico, 1990." *Archives of Environmental Contamination and Toxicology* 28:494–99.

Kulkarni, S., V. Patankar, and E. D'souza. 2008. "Status of earthquake and tsunami affected coral reefs in the Andaman and Nicobar islands, India." In *Ten Years after Bleaching: Facing the Consequences of Climate Change in the Indian Ocean*, ed. D.O. Obura, J. Tamelander, and O. Linden, 173–83. CORDIO Status Report 2008. CORDIO (Coastal Oceans Research and Development, Indian Ocean)/Sida-SAREC, Mombasa. http://www.cordioea.org. 493 pp.

Kuo, J., and C. den Hartog. 2006. "Morphology, anatomy, and ultrastructure." In *Seagrasses: Biology, Ecology and Conservation*, ed. A.W.D. Larkum, R.J. Orth, and C.M. Duarte, 51–88. Berlin: Springer Verlag.

Kuo, J., Z. Kanamoto, H. Iizumi, K. Aioi and H. Mukai. 2006. "Seagrasses from the Nansei Islands, Southern Japanese Archipelago: Species composition, distribution and biogeography." *Marine Ecology* 27:290–98.

Kurz, R.C., D.A. Tomasko, D. Burdick, T.F. Ries, K. Patterson, and R. Finck. 2000. "Recent trends in seagrass distributions in southwest Florida coastal waters." In *Seagrasses: Monitoring, Ecology, Physiology, and Management*, ed. S.A. Bortone, 157–66. Boca Raton, Fla.: CRC Press.

Kwan, D. 2002. "Towards a sustainable indigenous fishery for dugongs in Torres Strait: A contribution of empirical data analysis and process." Ph.D. diss., James Cook University, Townsville, Australia.

———. 2005. "Traditional use in contemporary Ailan (island) Ways: The management challenge of a sustainable dugong fishery in Torres Strait." In *Indigenous Use and Management of Marine Resources*, ed. N. Kishigami and J.M. Savelle. Osaka Japan: Senri Ethnological Studies 67.

Kwan, D., H. Marsh and S. Delean. 2006. "Factors influencing the sustainability of customary dugong hunting by a remote indigenous community." *Environmental Conservation* 33:164–71.

LaCommare, K.S., C. Self-Sullivan, and S. Brault. 2008. "Distribution and habitat use of Antillean Manatees (*Trichechus manatus manatus*) in the Drowned Cayes area of Belize, Central America." *Aquatic Mammals* 34:34–43.

Laist, D.W., and J.E. Reynolds III. 2005a. "Florida manatees, warm-water refuges, and an uncertain future." *Coastal Management* 33:279–95.

———. 2005b. "Influence of power plants and other warm-water refuges on Florida manatees." *Marine Mammal Science* 21:739–64.

Laist, D.W., and C. Shaw. 2006. "Preliminary evidence that boat speed restrictions reduce deaths of Florida manatees." *Marine Mammal Science* 22:472–79.

Lakhani, A. 2006. "The role of citizens and the future of international law: A paradigm for a changing world." *Cardozo Journal of Conflict Resolution* 8:159.

Lal Mohan, R.S. 1963. "On the occurrence of *Dugong dugon* (Müller) in the Gulf of Cutch." *Journal of the Marine Biological Association of India* 5:152–53.

———. 1976. "Some observations on the sea cow, *Dugong dugon* from the Gulf of Mannar and Palk Bay during 1971–1975." *Journal of the Marine Biological Association of India* 18:391–97.

———. 1994. "Review of gillnet fisheries and cetacean bycatches in the northeastern Indian Ocean." *Reports of the International Whaling Commission* 15: 329–43.

Lander, M., A. Westgate, R.K. Bonde, and M. Murray. 2001. "Tagging and telemetry." In *Handbook of Marine Mammal Medicine*, 2nd edition, ed. L.A. Dierauf and F.M.D. Gulland, 851–80. Florida: CRC Press.

Lander, M.E., J.T. Harvey, K.D. Hanni, and L.E. Morgan. 2002. "Behavior, movements and apparent survival of rehabilitated and free-ranging harbor seal pups." *Journal of Wildlife Management* 66:19–28.

Landsberg, J.H., and K.A. Steidinger. 1998. "A historical review of *Gymnodinium breve* red tides implicated in mass mortality of the manatee (*Trichechus manatus latirostris*) in Florida, USA." In *Harmful Algae*, ed. B. Reguera, J. Blanco, M.L. Fernandez, and T. Wyatt, 97–100. Xunta de Galicia and Intergovernmental Oceanographic Commission of UNESCO.

Langer, P. 1988. *The Mammalian Herbivore Stomach: Comparative Anatomy, Function, and Evolution*. Stuttgart: Gustav Fischer.

Langtimm, C.A., T.J. O'Shea, R. Pradel, and C.A. Beck. 1998. "Estimates of annual survival probabilities for adult Florida manatees (*Trichechus manatus latirostris*)." *Ecology* 79:981–97.

Langtimm, C.A., and C.A. Beck. 2003. "Lower survival probabilities for adult Florida manatees in years with intense coastal storms." *Ecological Applications* 13:257–68.

Langtimm, C.A., C.A. Beck, H.H. Edwards, B.B. Ackerman, K.J. Fick-Child, S.L. Barton, and W.C. Hartley. 2004. "Survival estimates for Florida manatees from the photo-identification of individuals." *Marine Mammal Science* 20:438–63.

Langtimm, C.A., M.D. Krohn, J.P. Reid, B.M. Stith, and C.A. Beck. 2006. "Possible effects of the 2004 and 2005 hurricanes on manatee survival rates and movement." *Estuaries and Coasts* 29:1026–32.

Lanyon, J.M. 1986. *Seagrasses of the Great Barrier Reef*. Special Publication Series no. 3. Townsville, Australia: Great Barrier Reef Marine Park Authority.

———. 1991. "The nutritional ecology of the dugong (*Dugong dugon*) in tropical North Queensland." Ph.D. diss., Monash University, Melbourne, Australia.

Lanyon, J.M., H.L. Sneath, J.M. Kirkwood, and R.W. Slade. 2002. "Establishing a mark-recapture program for dugongs in Moreton Bay, south-east Queensland." *Australian Mammalogy* 24:51–56.

Lanyon, J.M, and G.D. Sanson 2006. "Degenerate dentition of the dugong (*Dugong dugon*), or why a grazer does not need teeth: Morphology, occlusion and wear of mouthparts." *Journal of Zoology* 268:133–52.

Lanyon J.M., R.W. Slade, H.L. Sneath, D. Broderick, J.M. Kirkwood, D. Limpus, C.L. Limpus, and T. Jessop. 2006. "A method for capturing dugongs (*Dugong dugon*) in open water." *Aquatic Mammals* 32:196–201.

Law, R.J., M.E. Bennett, S.J. Blake, C.R. Allchin, B.R. Jones, and C.J.H. Spurrier. 2001. "Metals and organochlorines in pelagic cetaceans stranded on the coasts of England and Wales." *Marine Pollution Bulletin* 42:522–26.

Lawler, I.R. 2002. "Distribution and abundance of dugongs and other megafauna in Moreton Bay and Hervey Bay between December 2000 and November 2001." Queensland Parks and Wildlife Service, Brisbane.

Lawler, I.R., L. Aragones, N. Berding, H. Marsh and W. Foley. 2006. "Near-infrared reflectance spectroscopy is a rapid, cost-effective predictor of seagrass nutrients." *Journal of Chemical Ecology* 32:1353–65.

Lazzarini, S.M., J.L. Barroso, and A. Begrow. 1998. "Caça de subsistência e comercial do peixe-boi da Amazônia (*Trichechus inunguis*) no Estado do Amazonas, 1994 a 1997." In 8th *Reunião de Trabalho de Especialistas em Mamíferos Aquáticos,* 25–29 October, Olinda, Brazil, 105.

Lazzarini, S.M., M.C.L. Picanço, J.L. Barroso, and A. Begrow. 2000. "Caça comercial e de subsistência do peixe-boi da Amazônia (*Trichechus inunguis*) no Estado do Amazonas, 1998 a 2000." In 9th *Reunião de Trabalho de Especialistas em Mamíferos Aquáticos*, Buenos Aires, Argentina, 69.

Leatherwood, S., and R.R. Reeves, eds. 1989. *Marine Mammal Research and Conservation in Sri Lanka 1985–86*. Marine Mammal Technical Report no. 1. Nairobi, Kenya: United Nations Environmental Program, Oceans and Coastal Areas.

Ledder, D.A. 1986. "Food habits of the West Indian manatee, *Trichechus manatus latirostris*, in South Florida." M.S. thesis, University of Miami, Coral Gables, Florida.

Lee, K. 2001. "Appraising adaptive management." In *Biological Diversity: Balancing Interests through Adaptive Collaborative Management*, ed. L.E. Buck, C.G. Geisler, J. Schelhas, and E. Wollenburg, 3–26. Boca Raton, Florida: CRC Press.

Lefebvre, L.W. 1995. "Manatee aerial surveys safety rules." *Sirenews* (IUCN/SSC Sirenia Specialist Group) 24:2–3.

Lefebvre, L.W., T.J. O'Shea, G.B. Rathbun, and R.C. Best. 1989. "Distribution, status and biogeography of the West Indian manatee." *Biogeography of the West Indies,* 1989:567–610.

Lefebvre, L.W., and J.A. Powell. 1990. "Manatee grazing impacts on seagrasses in Hobe Sound and Jupiter Sound in southeast Florida during the winter of 1988–89." National Technical Information Service, #PB90–271883, Springfield, Virginia.

Lefebvre, L.W., B.B. Ackerman, K.M. Portier, and K.H. Pollock. 1995. "Aerial survey as a technique for estimating trends in manatee population size: Problems and prospects." In *Population Biology of the Florida Manatee*, ed. T.J. O'Shea, B.B. Ackerman, and H.F. Percival, 63–74. Washington, D.C.: National Biological Service Information and Technology Report 1.

Lefebvre, L.W., J.P. Reid, W.J. Kenworthy, and J.A. Powell. 2000. "Characterizing manatee habitat use and seagrass grazing in Florida and Puerto Rico: Implications for conservation and management." *Pacific Conservation Biology* 5:289–98.

Lefebvre, L.W., M. Marmontel, J.P. Reid, G.B. Rathbun, and D.P. Domning. 2001. "Status and biogeography of the West Indian manatee." In *Biogeography of the West Indies: New Patterns and Perspectives*, ed. C.A. Woods and F.E. Sergile, 425–74. Boca Raton, Fla.: CRC Press.

Lélé, S., and R.B. Norgaard. 1996. "Sustainability and the scientist's burden." *Conservation Biology* 10:354–65.

Lemon, M., T.P. Lynch, D.H. Cato, and R.G. Harcourt. 2006. "Response of travelling bottlenose dolphins (*Tursiops truncatus*) to experimental approaches by a powerboat in Jervis

Bay, New South Wales, Australia." *Biological Conservation* 127:363–72.

León, Y.M., and J.A. Ottenwalder. 1997. "Resultados de las entrevistas del proyecto Situación del Manatí en la República Dominicana." Unpublished report.

Leopold, A. 1936, published 1990. "Means and ends in wildlife management." *Environmental Ethics* 12:329–32.

Lightsey, J.D., S.A. Rommel, A.M. Costidis, and T. Pitchford. 2006. "Methods used during gross necropsy to determine watercraft-related mortality in the Florida manatee (*Trichechus manatus latirostris*)." *Journal of Zoo and Wildlife Medicine* 37:262–75.

Lillesand, T.M., R.W. Kiefer, and J.W. Chipman. 2004. *Remote Sensing and Image Interpretation*, 5th ed. New York: Wiley.

Lima, R.P. 1997. "Peixe-boi marinho (*Trichechus manatus*): Distribuição, status de conservação e aspectos tradicionais ao longo do litoral nordeste do Brasil." Ph.D. diss., Programa de Pósgraduação em Oceanografia, Universidade Federal de Pernambuco, Recife, Brazil.

Lima, R.P., D. Paludo, K.G. Silva, R.J. Soavinsk, and E.M.A. Oliveira. 1992. "Levantamento da distribuição, ocorrência e status de conservação do peixe-boi marinho (*Trichechus manatus*, Linnaeus, 1758) ao longo do litoral nordeste do Brasil." *Periódico Peixe-boi* 1:47–72.

Lima, R.P., F.O. Luna, D.F. Castro, and J.A. Vianna. 2001. "Levantamento da distribuição, status de conservação e campanhas conservacionistas do peixe-boi amazônico (*Trichechus inunguis*)." Relatório Final do Convênio IBAMA/CMA, FNMA e FMA–IBAMA/CMA.

Lin, C.P., and B.N. Danforth. 2004. "How do insect nuclear and mitochondrial gene substitution patterns differ? Insights from Bayesian analyses of combined datasets." *Molecular Phylogenetics and Evolution* 30:686–702.

Linares, O. 1998. *Mamíferos de Venezuela*. Caracas: Sociedad Conservacionista Audubon de Venezuela.

Lindenmayer, D., and M. Burgman. 2005. *Practical Conservation Biology*. Victoria, Australia: CSIRO Publishing.

Lindenmayer, D., R.J. Hobbs, R. Montague-Drake, J. Alexandra, A. Bennett, M. Burgman, P. Cale, A. Calhoun, V. Cramer, P. Cullen, D. Driscoll, L. Fahrig, J. Fischer, J. Franklin, Y. Haila, M. Hunter, P. Gibbons, S. Lake, G. Luck, C. MacGregor, S. McIntyre, R. Mac Nally, A. Manning, J. Miller, H. Mooney, R. Noss, H. Possingham, D. Saunders, F. Schmiegelow, M. Scott, D. Simberloff, T. Sisk, G. Tabor, B. Walker, J. Wiens, J. Woinarski, and E. Zavaleta. 2008. "A checklist for ecological management of landscapes for conservation." *Ecology Letters* 11:78–91.

Linnaeus, C. 1758. Tomus I. Systema naturae per regna tria naturae, secundum classes, ordines, genera, species, cum characteribus, differentiis, synonymis, locis. Editio decima, reformata. Holmiae. (Laurentii Salvii): 1–4. 824 pp. http://gdz.sub.uni-goettingen.de/dms/load/img/?PPN=PPN362053006.

Loganathan, B.G., K.S. Sajwan, J.P. Richardson, C.S. Chetty, and D.A. Owen. 2001. "Persistent organochlorine concentrations in sediment and fish from Atlantic coastal and brackish waters off Savannah, Georgia, USA." *Marine Pollution Bulletin* 42:246–50.

Loritz, J. 1991. "Animal victims of the Gulf war." *Physicians for Social Responsibility Quarterly* 1991:221–25.

Luna, F.O., R.P. Lima, D.F. Castro, and J.A. Vianna. 2001. "Capture and utilization of the Amazonian manatee (*Trichechus inunguis*) in the State of Amazonas, Brazil." 14th Biennial Conference on the Biology of Marine Mammals, 28 November–3 December, Vancouver, Canada.

Luna, F.O., L.Hage-Magalhães, R.P. Lima, L.C. Leite, and J.M.M. Schmiegelow. 2004. "Análise bioquímica de produtos comercializados como de origem biológica do peixe-boi amazônico (*Trichechus inunguis*)." 11ª [11th] Reunião de Trabalho de Especialistas em Mamíferos Aquáticos da América do Sul e 5º [5th] Congresso da Sociedade Latinoamericana de Especialistas em Mamíferos Aquáticos (SOLAMAC), 11–17 September, Quito, Ecuador.

Lunney, D., S.M. Gresser, P.S. Mahon, and A. Matthews. 2004. "Post-fire survival and reproduction of rehabilitated and unburnt koalas." *Biological Conservation* 120:567–75.

Luoma, S.N. 1996. "The developing framework of marine ecotoxicology: Pollutants as a variable in marine ecosystems?" *Journal of Experimental Marine Biology and Ecology* 200:29–55.

Lusseau, D. 2006. "Short-term behavioral reactions of bottlenose dolphins to interactions with boats in Doubtful Sound, New Zealand." *Marine Mammal Science* 22:802–18.

MacArthur, J. 1997. "Stakeholder analysis in project planning: Origins, applications and refinements of method." *Project Appraisal* 12:251–65.

MacFadden, B., P.L. Higgins, M.T. Clementz, and D. Jones. 2004. "Ancient diet, habitat preferences, and niche differentiation of Cenozoic sirenians from Florida: Evidence from stable isotopes." *Paleobiology* 30:824–27.

MacKenzie, D.I. 2005. "What are the issues with presence-absence data for wildlife managers?" *Journal of Wildlife Management* 69:849–60.

MacKenzie, D.I. 2006. "Modeling the probability of resource use: The effect of, and dealing with, detecting a species imperfectly." *Journal of Wildlife Management* 70:367–74.

MacKenzie, D.I., and J.A. Royle. 2005. "Designing occupancy studies: General advice and allocating survey effort." *Journal of Applied Ecology* 42:1105–14.

MacKenzie, D., J. Nichols, J. Royle, K. Pollock, L. Bailey, and J. Hines. 2006. *Occupancy Estimation and Modeling: Inferring Patterns of Dynamics and Species Occurrence*. London: Academic Press.

MacLaren, J.P. 1967. "Manatees as a naturalistic biological mosquito control method." *Mosquito News* 27:387–93.

Macmillan, L. 1955. "The dugong." *Walkabout* 21:17–20.

Mackun, P.J., and S. Wilson. 2011. Population Distribution and Change: 2000 to 2010. U.S. Census Bureau Report C2010BR-01, 12 pp. http://www.census.gov/prod/cen2010/briefs/c2010br-01.pdf.

Maeda, I. 2000a. "Niraikanai karakita Kaiju Jugon, 2: Kichouna niku ha Sinkouju (Dugong, a marine mammal from Niraikanai, 2: The importance of dugong meat)." *Okinawa Times*, 11 October.

———. 2000b. "Niraikanai karakita Kaiju Jugon, 4: Meishou de wakaru seitai (Dugong, a marine mammal from Niraikanai, 4: Ecology and name of dugong)." *Okinawa Times*, 17 October.

Maguire, L.A., 1996. "Making the role of values in conservation explicit: Values and conservation biology." *Conservation Biology* 10:914–16.

Mammalogical Society of Japan. 1997. *Red Data Nihon no honyurui* (Red Data Book of Japanese mammals). Tokyo: Bunichi sougou syuppann (in Japanese with English summary).

Mani, S.B. 1960. "Occurrence of the sea cow, *Halicore dugong* (Exrl.) off the Saurashtra coast." *Journal of the Bombay Natural History Society* 56:216–17.

Mann, D.A., D.E. Colbert, J.C. Gaspard, B.M. Casper, M.L.H. Cook, R.L. Reep, and G.B. Bauer. 2005. "Temporal resolution of the Florida manatee (*Trichechus manatus latirostris*) auditory system." *Journal of Comparative Physiology A* 191:903–8.

Marchais, J. 2006. "Rapport d'enquête sur les connaissances des pêcheurs du fleuve Sénégal à propos du lamantin d'Afrique de l'Ouest (*Trichechus senegalensis*)." Consultation pour Noé Conservation.

Marcovecchio, J.E., V.J. Moreno, R.O. Bastida, M.S. Gerpe, and D.H. Rodriguez. 1990. "Tissue distribution of heavy metals in small cetaceans from the southwestern Atlantic ocean." *Marine Pollution Bulletin* 21:299–304.

Marmontel, M. 1994. "Aerophotogrammetry and manatee size distribution: A feasibility study." Final Report to the University of Florida, Florida Cooperative Fish and Wildlife Research Unit and to the Sirenia Project, National Biological Survey. Cooperative Agreement No. 14-16-0009-1544.

Marmontel, M., D.K. Odell, and J.E. Reynolds III. 1992. "Reproductive biology of South American manatees." In *Reproductive Biology of South American Vertebrates*, ed. W.C. Hamlett, 295–312. New York: Springer-Verlag.

Marmontel, M., S.R. Humphrey, and T.J. O'Shea. 1997. "Population viability analysis of the Florida manatee (*Trichechus manatus latirostris*), 1976–1991." *Conservation Biology* 11:467–81.

MARPOL: International Convention for the Prevention of Pollution from Ships. 1973. http://www.imo.org/Conventions/contents.asp?doc_id=678&topic_id=258

Marsh, H. 1980. "Age determination of the dugong, *Dugong dugon*, (Müller) in northern Australia and its biological implications." *Reports of the International Whaling Commission*, Special Issue 3:181–201.

———. 1989. "Mass stranding of dugongs by a tropical cyclone in northern Australia." *Marine Mammal Science* 12:54–88.

———. 1995a. Fixed wing aerial transects for determining dugong population sizes and distribution patterns. In *Population Biology of the Florida Manatee*, ed. T.J. O'Shea, B.B. Ackerman, and H.F. Percival, 56–62. Washington, D.C.: National Biological Service Information and Technology Report 1.

———. 1995b. "Limits of detectable change." In *Conservation through Sustainable Use of Wildlife*, ed. G. Grigg, P. Hale, and D. Lunney, 122–30, Sydney: Surrey Beatty and Sons.

———. 1999. "Reproduction in sirenians." In *Reproduction of Marine Mammals*, ed. I.L. Boyd, C. Lockyer, and H.D. Marsh, 243–56. Washington, D.C.: Smithsonian Institution Press.

———. 2000. "Evaluating management initiatives aimed at reducing the mortality of dugongs in gill and mesh nets in the Great Barrier Reef World Heritage Area." *Marine Mammal Science* 16:684–94.

Marsh, H., A. Spain, and G. Heinsohn. 1978. "Minireview: Physiology of the dugong." *Comparative Biochemistry and Physiology* 61:159–68.

Marsh, H., B.R. Gardner, and G.E. Heinsohn. 1980–81. "Present-day hunting and distribution of dugongs in the Wellesley Islands (Queensland): Implications for conservation." *Biological Conservation* 19:255–67.

Marsh, H., G. Heinsohn, and L. Marsh. 1982a. "Breeding cycle, life history and population dynamics of the dugong, *Dugong dugon* (Sirenia: Dugongidae)." *Australian Journal of Zoology* 32:767–88.

Marsh, H., P.W. Channells, G.E. Heinsohn, and J. Morrissey. 1982b. "Analysis of stomach contents of dugongs from Queensland." *Australian Wildlife Research* 9:55–67.

Marsh, H., G.E. Heinsohn, and L.M. Marsh. 1984. "Breeding cycle, life history and population dynamics of the dugong, *Dugong dugon* (Sirenia: Dugongidae)." *Australian Journal of Zoology* 32:767–88.

Marsh H., and D.F. Sinclair. 1989a. "Correcting for visibility bias in strip transect aerial surveys of aquatic fauna." *Journal of Wildlife Management* 53:1017–24.

Marsh, H., and D.F. Sinclair. 1989b. "An experimental evaluation of dugong and sea turtle aerial survey techniques." *Australian Wildlife Research* 16:639–50.

Marsh, H., and G.B. Rathbun. 1990. "Development and application of conventional and satellite radio-tracking techniques for studying dugong movements and habitat usage." *Australian Wildlife Research* 17:83–100.

Marsh, H., and W.K. Saafeld. 1990. "Distribution and abundance of dugongs in the Great Barrier Reef Marine Park south of Cape Bedford." *Australian Wildlife Research* 17:511–24.

Marsh, H., and L.W. Lefebvre. 1994. "Sirenian status and conservation efforts." *Aquatic Mammals* 20:155–70.

Marsh H., P. Corkeron, I.R. Lawler, J.M. Lanyon, and A.R. Preen. 1996. *The Status of the Dugong in the Southern Great Barrier Reef Marine Park*. Research Publication no. 41. Townsville, Australia: Great Barrier Reef Marine Park Authority.

Marsh, H., A.N.M. Harris, and I.R. Lawler. 1997. "The sustainability of the Indigenous dugong fishery in Torres Strait, Australia/Papua New Guinea." *Conservation Biology* 11:1375–86.

Marsh, H., C.A. Beck, and T. Vargo. 1999a. "Comparison of the capabilities of dugongs and West Indian manatees to masticate seagrasses." *Marine Mammal Science* 15:250–55.

Marsh, H., C. Eros, P. Corkeron, and B. Breen. 1999b. "A conservation strategy for dugongs: Implications of Australian research." *Marine and Freshwater Research* 50:979–90.

Marsh, H., G. De'ath, N. Gribble, and B. Lane. 2001. *Shark Control Records Hindcast Serious Decline in Dugong Numbers off the Urban Coast of Queensland*. Research Publication no. 70. Townsville, Australia: Great Barrier Reef Marine Park Authority.

Marsh, H., and I.R. Lawler. 2001. *Dugong Distribution and Abundance in the Southern Great Barrier Reef Marine Park and Hervey Bay: Results of an Aerial Survey in October–December 1999*. Research Publication no. 70. Townsville, Australia: Great Barrier Reef Marine Park Authority.

———. 2002. *Dugong Distribution and Abundance in the Northern Great Barrier Reef Marine Park, November 2000*. Research Publication no. 77. Townsville, Australia: Great Barrier Reef Marine Park Authority.

Marsh, H., C. Eros, H. Penrose, and J. Hugues. 2002. *Dugong: Status Report and Action Plans for Countries and Territories*. UNEP/DEWA/RS. 02-1.

Marsh, H., H. Penrose, and C. Eros. 2003. "A future for the dugong." In *Marine Mammals: Fisheries, Tourism and Management Issues*, ed. N. Gales, M. Hindell, and R. Kirkwood, 383–99. Victoria, Australia: CSIRO Publishing.

Marsh H., I.R. Lawler, D. Kwan, S. Delean, K. Pollock, and M. Alldredge. 2004. "Aerial surveys and the potential biological removal technique indicate that the Torres Strait dugong fishery is unsustainable." *Animal Conservation* 7:435–43.

Marsh, H., G. De'ath, N. Gribble, and B. Lane. 2005. "Historical marine population estimates: Triggers or targets for conservation? The dugong case study." *Ecological Applications* 15:481–92.

Marsh, H., and I.R. Lawler. 2006. *Dugong Distribution and Abundance on the Urban Coast of Queensland: A Basis for Management*. Final report to Marine and Tropical Research Sciences facility Interim Projects 2005-6. James Cook University, Townsville, Australia.

Marsh, H., A. Dennis, H. Hines, A. Kutt, K. McDonald, E. Weber, S. Williams, and J. Winter. 2007. "Optimizing the allocation of management resources to species of wildlife." *Conservation Biology* 21:387–99.

Marsh, H., and D. Kwan. 2008. "Temporal variability in the life history and reproductive biology of female dugongs in Torres Strait: The likely role of sea grass dieback." *Continental Shelf Research* 28:2152–59.

Marsh, H., J. Bradley, G.J. Parra, A. Grech, S. Whiting, I. Beasley, S. Johnson, D. Barrett, N. Fitzpatrick, G. Friday, A. Johnston, F. Keighran, R. Miller, Laura Norman, Leonard Norman, D. Pracy, and the Yanyuwa families. 2010. *Yarrbanthawu ki-Miriyiyu: Looking for Dolphins. Developing a decision process based on expert knowledge to inform the management of dugongs and coastal dolphins in northern Australia: The Yanyuwa sea country in the Northern Territory as a case study*. Townsville, Queensland, Australia: School of Earth and Environmental Sciences, James Cook University.

Marshall, C.D. 2002. "Functional Morphology." In *Encyclopedia of Marine Mammals*, ed. W.F. Perrin, B. Wursig, and H.G.M. Thewissen. San Diego: Academic Press.

Marshall, C.D., L.A. Clark, and R.L. Reep. 1998a. "The muscular hydrostat of the Florida manatee (*Trichechus manatus latirostris*) and its role in the use of perioral bristles." *Marine Mammal Science* 14:290–303.

Marshall, C.D., G.D. Huth, V.M. Edmonds, D.L. Halin, and R.L. Reep. 1998b. "Prehensile use of perioral bristles during feeding and associated behaviors of the Florida manatee (*Trichechus manatus latirostris*)." *Marine Mammal Science* 14:274–89.

Marshall, C.D., G.D. Huth, V.M. Edmonds, D.L. Halin, and R.L. Reep. 2000. "Food-handling ability and feeding-cycle length of manatees feeding on several species of aquatic plants." *Journal of Mammalogy* 81:649–58.

Marshall, C.D., H. Maeda, M. Iwata, M. Furuta, S. Asano, F. Rosas, and R.L. Reep. 2003. "Orofacial morphology and feeding behaviour of the dugong, Amazonian, West African and Antillean manatees (Mammalia: Sirenia): Functional morphology of the muscular-vibrissal complex." *Journal of Zoology* (London) 259:245–60.

Marshall, C.D., S.D. Vaughn, D.K. Sarko, and R.L. Reep. 2007. "Topographical organization of the facial motor nucleus in Florida manatees (*Trichechus manatus latirostris*)." *Brain Behavior and Evolution* 70:164–73.

Marshall, N.T. 1998. *Searching for a Cure: Conservation of Medicinal Wildlife Resources in East and Southern Africa*. Cambridge, U.K.: TRAFFIC International.

Martin, S. 2006. *An Introduction to Ocean Remote Sensing*. Cambridge, U.K.: Cambridge University Press.

Martínez-Díaz, K., M. Pérez-Lewis, A. Quijano-Rossy, J.A. Valentín-Narváez, and A.A. Mignucci-Giannoni. 2001. "Training of medical behaviors in an orphan manatee to be re-introduced into wild in Puerto Rico." In *Abstracts, Fourteenth Biennial Conference on the Biology of Marine Mammals*, November 2001, Vancouver, Canada. 136.

Mason, F. 1882. *Burma, People and Productions: Notes on the Fauna, Flora and Minerals of Tenasserim, Pegu and Burma*. Hertford, U.K.: Stephen Austin and Sons.

Mass, A.M., D.K. Odell, D.R, Ketten, and A. Ya. Supin. 1997. "Ganglion layer topography and retinal resolution of the Caribbean manatee *Trichechus manatus latirostris*." *Doklady Biological Sciences* 355:392–94.

Mate, B.R., G.B. Rathbun, R. Merrick, and J.P. Reid. 1985. "Preliminary technical evaluation of an Argos-monitored radio tag for tracking manatees." In *Proceedings of the Argos Users Conference*. Kiel, West Germany: Service Argos.

Mather, P.M. 1999. *Computer Processing of Remotely-Sensed*

Images: An Introduction. Chichester, U.K.: John Wiley and Sons.

Mathew, S. 2003. "Small-scale fisheries perspectives on an ecosystem-based approach to fisheries management." In *Responsible Fisheries in the Marine Ecosystem,* ed. M. Sinclair and G. Valdimarsson, 47–63. Rome, Italy, and Wallingford, U.K.: FAO and CAB International.

Mazet, J.A.K., T.D. Hunt, and M.H. Ziccardi. 2004. "Assessment of the risk of zoonotic disease transmission to marine mammal workers and the public: Survey of occupational risks." Final Report K005486-01, Wildlife Health Center, School of Veterinary Medicine, University of California, Davis.

Mbina, C. 2001. "Evaluation and status of manatees (*Trichechus senegalensis*) of the Ogooue Basin in Gabon." Unpublished report for Wildlife Conservation Society.

McCullagh, P., and J.A. Nelder. 1989. *Generalized Linear Models*. 2nd ed. London: Chapman and Hall.

McCutcheon, E.D. 1998. "Think globally, (en)act locally: Promoting effective national environmental regulatory infrastructures in developing nations." *Cornell International Law Journal* 31:395–438.

McDonald, B. 2005. "Population genetics of dugongs around Australia: Implications of gene flow and migration." Ph.D. diss., James Cook University, Townsville, Australia.

McKillop, H.I. 1984. "Prehistoric Maya reliance on marine resources: Analysis of a midden from Moyo Caye, Belize." *Journal of Field Archaeology* 11:25–35.

———. 1985. "Prehistoric exploitation of the manatee in the Maya and circum-Caribbean areas." *World Archaeology* 16:337–53.

———. 2002. *Salt, White Gold of the Ancient Maya*. Gainesville: University Press of Florida.

McLachlan, M.S., D. Haynes, and J.F. Müller. 2001. "PCDDs in the water/sediment-sea grass-dugong (*Dugong dugon*) food chain on the Great Barrier Reef (Australia)." *Environmental Pollution* 113:129–34.

McMahon, K. 2005. "Growth and regeneration of seagrass after disturbance from dugong grazing." Ph.D. diss., University of Queensland, Brisbane, Australia.

McNaughton, S.J. 1979. "Grass-herbivore dynamics." In *Serengeti: Dynamics of an Ecosystem,* ed. A.R. Sinclair and M. Norton-Griffiths, 46–81. Chicago: Universsity of Chicago Press.

———. 1983. "Serengeti grassland ecology: The role of composite environmental factors and contingency in community organization." *Ecological Monographs* 53:291–320.

McNeely, J.A. 2001. "Roles for civil society in protected areas management: A global perspective on current trends in collaborative management." In *Biological Diversity: Balancing Interests through Adaptive Collaborative Management,* ed. L.E. Buck, C.G. Geisler, J. Schelhas, and E. Wollenburg, 27–50. Boca Raton, Fla.: CRC Press.

McNeill, P., and S. Chapman. 2005. *Research Methods*. 3rd ed. New York: Routledge.

Mead, J.B., and E.D. Mitchell. 1984. "Atlantic gray whales." In *The Gray Whale* Eschrichtius robustus, ed. M.L. Jones, S.L. Swartz, and S. Leatherwood, 33–53, Orlando, Fla.: Academic Press.

Meade, R.H., J.M. Rayol, S.C. da Conceição, and J.R.G. Natividade. 1991. "Backwater effects in the Amazon river basin of Brazil." *Environmental Geology and Water Sciences* 18:105–14.

Measures, L.N. 2004. "Marine mammals and wildlife rehabilitation programs." Canadian Science Advisory Secretariat, Research Document 2004/122, Department of Fisheries and Oceans Canada, Mont-Joli, Quebec, Canada.

Mech, L.D. 1983. *A Handbook of Animal Radio-Tracking*. Minneapolis: University of Minnesota Press.

Mech, L.D., and S.M. Barber. 2002. "A critique of wildlife radio-tracking and its use in national parks: A report to the U.S. National Park Service." U.S. Geological Survey, Northern Prairie Wildlife Research Center. Jamestown, N.D.: Northern Prairie Wildlife Research Center Online. http://www.npwrc.usgs.gov/resource/wildlife/radiotrk/index.htm.

Meffe, G.K., and S. Viederman. 1995. "Combining science and policy in conservation biology." *Wildlife Society Bulletin* 23:327–32.

Meffe, G.K., Perrin, W.F., and P.K. Dayton. 1999. Marine mammal conservation: Guiding principles and their implementation. In *Conservation and Management of Marine Mammals,* ed. J.R. Twiss and R.R. Reeves, 437–454. Washington, D.C.: Smithsonian Institution Press.

Meffe, G.K., L.A. Nielsen, R.L. Knight, and D.A. Schenborn. 2002. *Ecosystem Management: Adaptive, Community-Based Conservation*. Washington, D.C.: Island Press.

Menotti-Raymond, M., and S.J. O'Brien. 1993. "Dating the genetic bottleneck of the African cheetah." *Proceedings of the National Academy of Sciences* 90:3172–76.

MEPA, 1985. "The Nowruz oil spill: The Saudi Arabian response January 1983–January 1985." Meteorology and Environmental Protection Administration, Jeddah.

Mercado, M.C. 1990. "Estrategias de pesca de las poblaciones indígenas Antillanas en relación a la ecología del manatí." *Proceedings of the Eleventh Congress of the International Association for Caribbean Archaeology,* San Juan, Puerto Rico, 438–41.

Metcalf, C.R., and L. Chalk. 1950. *Anatomy of the Dicotyledons*. Vols. 1 and 2. Oxford, U.K.: Clarendon Press.

Mignucci-Giannoni, A.A. 1996. "Marine mammal strandings in Puerto Rico and the United States and British Virgin Islands." Ph.D. diss., University of Puerto Rico, Mayagüez, Puerto Rico.

———. 1998. "Marine mammal captivity in the northeastern Caribbean, with notes on the rehabilitation of stranded whales, dolphins and manatees." *Caribbean Journal of Science* 34:191–203.

———. 2001. "Status of manatees in Puerto Rico." In *International Sirenian Conservation Workshop, Fourteenth Biennial Conference on the Biology of Marine Mammals,* November 2001, Vancouver, Canada.

———. 2003. "Status of West Indian manatees (*Trichechus manatus*) in Puerto Rico: 2001–2003." In *International Sirenian*

Workshop: Exploring Issues Related to Sirenian Management, Research and Conservation, Fifteenth Biennial Conference on the Biology of Marine Mammals, Greensboro, North Carolina, December 2003.

Mignucci-Giannoni, A.A., E.H. Williams Jr., G.M. Toyos-González, J. Pérez-Padilla, M.A. Rodríguez-López, M.B. Vega-Guerra, and M. Ventura-González. 1999a. "Helminths from a stranded manatee in the Dominican Republic." *Veterinary Parasitology* 81:69–71.

Mignucci-Giannoni, A.A., C.A. Beck, R.A. Montoya-Ospina, and E.H. Williams Jr. 1999b. "Parasites and commensals of the West Indian manatee from Puerto Rico." *Journal of the Helminthological Society of Washington* 66:67–69.

Mignucci-Giannoni A.A., R.A. Montoya-Ospina, N.M. Jiménez-Marrero, M.A. Rodríguez-López, E.H. Williams Jr., and R.K. Bonde. 2000. "Manatee mortality in Puerto Rico." *Environmental Management* 25:189–98.

Mignucci-Giannoni, A.A., R.A. Montoya-Ospina, and M. Velasco-Escudero. 2003. "Status of semicaptive manatees in Jamaica." *Latin American Journal of Aquatic Mammals* 2:7–12.

Miksis-Olds, J. 2006. "Manatee response to environmental noise." Ph.D. diss., University of Rhode Island, Kingston.

Miksis-Olds, J.L., P.L. Donaghay, J.H. Miller, P.L. Tyack, and J.E. Reynolds III. 2007. "Simulated vessel approaches elicit differential responses from manatees." *Marine Mammal Science* 23:629–49.

Millán-Sánchez, S.L. 1999. "Estado de salud del manatí (*Trichechus* spp.) en Colombia." Masters thesis, University of Puerto Rico, Mayagüez, Puerto Rico.

Millennium Ecosystem Assessment. 2005. *Ecosystems and Human Well-being: Biodiversity Synthesis.* Washington, D.C.: World Resources Institute.

Miller, K.E., B.B. Ackerman, L.W. Lefebvre, and K.B. Clifton. 1998. "An evaluation of strip-transect aerial survey methods for monitoring manatee populations in Florida." *Wildlife Society Bulletin* 26:561–70.

Ming, C.L., and C.R. Wilkinson, eds. 1992. *Third ASEAN Science and Technology Week Conference Proceedings*, vol. 6: *Marine Science: Living Coastal Resources*. Singapore: Department of Zoology, National University of Singapore, and National Science and Technology Board.

Ministry of the Environment, Japan. 1997. *Nihon no higata moba sango-shou no genjou moba* (Status of tidal flats, seagrass beds, and coral reefs in Japan).

———. 2002. *Heisei 13 nendo jugon to moba no kouikiteki chousa* (Report of the survey on dugong and seagrass in Japan in FY 2001).

———. 2003. *Heisei 14 nendo jugon to moba no kouikiteki chousa* (Report of the survey on dugong and seagrass in Japan, FY 2002).

———. 2004a. *Heisei 15 nendo jugon to moba no kouikiteki chousa* (Report of the survey on dugong and seagrass in Japan, FY 2003).

———. 2004b. *Jugon to moba no kouikiteki chousa Heisei 13–15 nendo kekka gaiyou* (Comprehensive report of survey on dugong and seagrass in Japan, FY 2001–2003).

———. 2004c. *Heisei 15 nendo jugon no resukyu-taisei, houhou oyobi hyochaku kotaino shuuyouhouhou no gijutsu no fukyu itaku gyoumu* (Report of training and dissemination of the dugong rescue framework and rescue method in Okinawa, FY 2003).

———. 2005. *Heisei 16 nendo jugon to moba no kouikiteki chousa* (Report of the survey on dugong and seagrass in Japan, FY 2004).

———. 2006a. *Heisei 17 nendo jugon to moba no kouikiteki chousa* (Report of the survey on dugong and seagrass in Japan, FY 2005).

———. 2006b. *Jugon to moba no kouikiteki chousa Heisei 13–17nendo kekka gaiyou* (Comprehensive report of survey on dugong and seagrass in Japan, FY 2001–2006).

———. 2007. "Red List of Threatened Species in Japan." http://www.biodic.go.jp/rdb/rdb_f.html http://www.env.go.jp/press/press.php?serial=8648.

Mistelis, L. 2000. "Regulatory aspects: Globalization, harmonization, legal transplants and law reform—some fundamental observations." *International Lawyer* 34:1055.

Mitchell, S.C. 2005. "How useful is the concept of habitat?—A critique." *Oikos* 110:634–38.

Miyazaki, N., K. Itano, M. Fukushima, S.I. Kawai, and K. Honda. 1979. "Metals and organochlorine compounds in the muscle of dugong from Sulawesi Island." *Scientific Reports of the Whales Research Institute* 31:125–28.

Moen, R., J. Pastor, and E. Cohen. 1997. "Accuracy of GPS telemetry collar locations with differential correction." *Journal of Wildlife Management* 61:530–39.

Montoya Ospina, R.A. 1994. "Preliminary serum chemistry references ranges of the Antillean manatee (*Trichechus manatus manatus*) in Colombia and Puerto Rico." Masters thesis, University of Puerto Rico, Mayagüez, Puerto Rico.

Montoya-Ospina, R.A., D. Caicedo-Herrera, S.L. Millán-Sánchez, A.A. Mignucci-Giannoni, and L.W. Lefebvre. 2001. "Status and distribution of the West Indian manatee, *Trichechus manatus manatus*, in Colombia." *Biological Conservation* 102:117–29.

Moore, D.P., and A.A. Mignucci-Giannoni. 1993. "Unprecedented successful rescue of an orphaned Antillean manatee (*Trichechus manatus manatus*) in the northeastern Caribbean." In *Abstracts, Tenth Biennial Conference on the Biology of Marine Mammals*, Galveston, Texas, November 1993, 79.

Moore, M.R., W. Vetter, C. Gaus, G.R. Shaw, and J.F. Müller. 2002. "Trace organic compounds in the marine environment." *Marine Pollution Bulletin* 45:62–68.

Moore, S. 2008. "Marine mammals as ecosystem sentinels." *Journal of Mammalogy* 89:534–40.

Mora-Pinto, D.M. 2000. "Morphometric variation of the trematode *Chiorchis fabaceus* and *C. groschafti* parasitic in the West Indian manatee (*Trichechus manatus*)." Masters thesis, University of Puerto Rico, Mayagüez, Puerto Rico.

Morales-Vela, B. 2000. "Distribución, abundancia y uso de hábitat por el manatí en Quintana Roo y Belice, con observaciones sobre su biología en la Bahía de Chetumal." Ph.D. diss., Universidad Nacional Autónoma de México, Mexico City.

———. 2004. "Bahía de Chetumal-Corozal, un recurso costero compartido entre México y Belice." In *El Manejo Costero en Mexico*, ed. E. Rivera-Arriaga, G.J. Villalobos, I. Azuz-Adeath, and F. Rosado-May, 532–39. Campeche, México: Universidad de Quintana Roo, Universidad Autónoma de Campeche, SEMARNAT, CETYS-Universidad.

Morales-Vela, B., and D. Olivera-Gómez. 1994. "Distribución espacial y estimación poblacional de los manaties en la Bahia de Chetumal, Quintana Roo, Mexico." *Revista de Investigacion Cientifica* vol. 2 (No. Especial SOMEMMA 2), UABCS 2:27–32.

Morales-Vela, B., Rathbun, G.B., Olivera-Gómez, L.D., 1995. "Radiotagging manatees in Mexico." (IUCN/SSC Sirenia Specialist Group) 23:6.

Morales-Vela, B., D. Olivera-Gomez, J.E. Reynolds III, and G.B. Rathbun. 2000. "Distribution and habitat use by manatees (*Trichechus manatus manatus*) in Belize and Chetumal Bay, Mexico." *Biological Conservation* 95:67–75.

Morales-Vela, B., J.A. Padilla-Saldivar, and A.A. Mignucci-Giannoni. 2003. "Status of the manatee (*Trichechus manatus*) along the northern and western coasts of the Yucatán Peninsula, México." *Caribbean Journal of Science* 39:42–49.

Morales-Vela, B., J. Padilla-Saldivar, J. Reid, and S. Butler. 2007. "First records of long-distance manatee movements between Mexico and Belize." Sirenews (IUCN/SSC Sirenia Specialist Group) 47:12–13.

Morales-Vela, B., E. Suarez-Morales, J. Padilla-Saldivar, and R.W. Heard. 2008. "The tanaid *Hexapleomera robusta* (Crustacea: Peracardia) from the Caribbean manatee, with comments on other crustacean epibionts." *Journal of the Marine Biological Association of the United Kingdom* 88:591–96.

Morimoto, I. 2004. "Preliminary survey of excavated dugong bones." *Okinawa maibun kenkyu* (Bulletin of Okinawa archeological cultural studies) 2:23–42.

Morison, S.E. 1942. *Admiral of the Ocean Sea: A Life of Christopher Colombus*. Boston, Mass.: Little, Brown.

Morris, W.F., and D.F. Doak. 2003. *Quantitative Conservation Biology: Theory and Practice of Population Viability Analysis*. Sunderland, Mass.: Sinauer Associates.

Mouho, G.J. 1997. "Conservation biology and status of the African manatee in the Côte d'Ivoire." M.Sc. Thesis, University of Stockholm, Sweden.

Mou Sue, L.L., and D.H. Chen. 1990. "Distribution and status of manatees (*Trichechus manatus*) in Panama." *Marine Mammal Science* 6:234–41.

MPSWG, Manatee Population Status Working Group. 2005. "Biological population assessment of the Florida manatee." Jacksonville, Fla.: Report from the Manatee Population Status Working Group, Florida Manatee Recovery and Implementation Team to the U.S. Fish and Wildlife Service.

Muir, C.E. 2005. "Recent dugong captures in the Rufiji-Mafia area: Proof of their continued existence in Tanzania." Fourth Western Indian Ocean Marine Science Association (WIOMSA) Symposium. 30 August–1 September 2005, Grand Baie, Mauritius.

———. 2007. "Community-based endangered marine species conservation in Tanzania." Sea Sense Annual Report 2007, Dar es Salaam, Tanzania.

Muir, C.E., A. Sallema, O. Abdallah, D. De Luca, and T.R.B. Davenport. 2003. "The dugong in Tanzania: A national assessment of status, distribution and threat." Wildlife Conservation Society, Tanzania.

Muir, D.C., C.A. Ford, N.P. Grift, R.E. Stewart, and T.F. Bidleman. 1992. "Organochlorine contaminants in narwhal (*Monodon monoceros*) from the Canadian Arctic." *Environmental Pollution* 75:309–16.

Mukai, H. 1993. "Biogeography of the tropical seagrasses in the Western Pacific." *Australian Journal of Marine and Freshwater Research* 44:1–17.

Munns, W.R. Jr. 2006. "Assessing risks to wildlife populations from multiple stressors: Overview of the problem and research needs." *Ecology and Society* 11:23. http://www.ecologyandsociety.org/vol11/iss1/art23/.

Murray, D.L., and M.R. Fuller. 2000. "A critical review of the effects of marking on the biology of vertebrates." In *Research Techniques in Animal Ecology: Controversies and Consequences*, ed. L. Boitani and T.K. Fuller, 15–46. New York: Columbia University Press.

Murray, R.M., H. Marsh, G.E. Heinsohn, and A.V. Spain. 1977. "The role of the midgut caecum and large intestine in the digestion of seagrasses by the dugong (Mammalia: Sirenia)." *Comparative Biochemistry and Physiology* 56(A):7–10.

Mustika, P.L.K. 2006. "Marine mammals in the Savu Sea (Indonesia): Traditional knowledge, threat analysis and management options." Masters thesis, James Cook University, Townsville, Australia.

Nair, R., R.S. Lal Mohan, and K. Satyenarayana Rao. 1975. "The Dugong *Dugong dugon*." ICAR Bulletin of the Central Marine Fisheries Research Institute, Cochin, India.

Natiello, M., P. Lewis, and D. Samuelson. 2005. "Comparative anatomy of the ciliary body of the West Indian manatee (*Trichechus manatus*) and selected species." *Veterinary Ophthalmology* 8:375–85.

National News Bureau of Thailand. 2011. "Thailand signs MoU with UNEP on dugong conservation." http://thainews.prd.go.th/en/news.php?id=255406300020

Neville, H. 1885. "Aeolian's account of the dolphins of Taprobane." *Taprobanian* (London: Trubner) 2:1.

Newsom, L.A., and E.S. Wing. 2004. *On Land and Sea: Native American Uses of Biological Resources in the West Indies*. Tuscaloosa: University of Alabama Press.

Nicholls, A.O. 1989. "How to make biological surveys go further with generalized linear models." *Biological Conservation* 50:51–75.

Nishiwaki, M., T. Kasuya, N. Miyazaki, T. Tobayama, and T.

Kataoka. 1979. "Present distribution of the dugong in the world." *Scientific Reports of the Whales Research Institute* 31:133–41.

Nishiwaki, M., M. Yamaguchi, S. Shokita, S. Uchida, and T. Kataoka. 1982. "Recent survey on the distribution of the African manatee." *Scientific Reports of the Whales Research Institute* 34:137–47.

Nishiwaki, M., and H. Marsh. 1985. "The Dugong *Dugong dugon* (Müller, 1776)." In *Handbook of Marine Mammals*, ed. S.H. Ridgeway and R.J. Harrison, 1–31. London: Academic Press.

Nix, H.A. 1986. "Biogeographic analysis of Australian elapid snakes." In *Atlas of Elapid Snakes*, ed. R. Longmore, 4–15. Australian Flora and Fauna Series no. 7. Canberra: Australian Government Publishing Service.

Norris, C.E. 1960. "The dugong." *Loris* 8:296–300.

Norton-Griffiths, M., 1978. "Counting animals." Handbook no. 1. Serengeti Biological Monitoring Programme, African Wildlife Leadership Foundation, Kenya.

Noss, R.F. 2007. "Values are a good thing in conservation biology." *Conservation Biology* 21:18–20.

Nourisson, C., B. Morales-Vela, J. Padilla-Saldivar, K.P. Tucker, A. Clark, L.D. Olivera-Gómez, R. Bonde, and P. McGuire. 2011. "Evidence of two genetic clusters of manatees with low genetic diversity in Mexico and implications for their conservation." *Genetica* DOI 10.1007/s10709-011-9583-z.

Novaczek, I., J. Sopacua, and I. Harkes. 2001. "Fisheries management in central Maluku, Indonesia, 1997–1998." *Marine Policy* 25:239–49.

Novak, A.B, E. Hines, D. Kwan, L. Parr, M. Than Tun, and H. Wen. 2009. "Seagrasses of the Myeik Archipelago, Myanmar." *Aquatic Botany* 91:250–52.

Nowacek, S.M., R.S. Wells, E.C.G. Owen, T.R. Speakman, R.O. Flamm, and D.P. Nowacek. 2004. "Florida manatees, *Trichechus manatus latirostris*, respond to approaching vessels." *Biological Conservation* 119:517–23.

NRC, National Research Council. 2003. *Oil in the Sea III: Inputs, Fates and Effects*. Washington, D.C.: National Academies Press.

NRCC, National Research Council of Canada. 1983. "Polycyclic aromatic hydrocarbons in the aquatic environment: Formation, sources, fate and effects on aquatic biota." NRCC Associate Committee on Scientific Criteria for Environmental Quality, Publication no. NRCC 18981, Ottawa, Ontario.

Nursey-Bray, M. 2006. "Conflict to co-management—eating our words: Towards socially just conservation of green turtles and dugongs in the Great Barrier Reef, Australia." Ph.D. diss., James Cook University, Cairns, Australia.

Oates, J.F. 1999. *Myth and Reality in the Rain Forest: How Conservation Strategies Are Failing in West Africa*. Berkeley: University of California Press.

O'Brien, S.J., D.E. Wildt, D. Goldman, C.R. Merril, and M. Bush. 1983. "The cheetah is depauperate in genetic variation." *Science* 221:459–62.

O'Donnell, D.J. 1981. "Manatees and man in Central America." Ph.D. diss., Department of Geography, University of California, Los Angeles.

Ogura G., T. Hirayama, K. Sudo, N. Ohtaishi, H. Mukai, and Y. Kawashima. 2005. "Investigation of the northern limit of dugong habitat in the Tokara Islands and Amami-Oshima in the Ryukyu archipelago, Japan." *Wildlife Conservation Japan* 9:49–58 (abstract in English).

Ohtaishi, N. 2005. "Okinawa no jugon kotaigun to jugon-ryou no fukugen ni mukete (Restoration of dugong population and hunting of dugong in Okinawa Island)." *Ecosophia* 15:81–86.

O'Hara, T.M., Woshner, V.M., and Bratton, G., 2003. "Inorganic pollutants in arctic marine mammals." In *Toxicology of Marine Mammals*, ed. J.G. Vos, G.D. Bossart, M. Fournier, and T.J. O'Shea, 206–46. New York: Taylor and Francis.

O'Leary, M.H. 1988. "Carbon isotopes and photosynthesis." *BioScience* 38:328–36.

Oliver, J., and Berkelmans, R. 1999. *A Dugong Research Strategy for the Great Barrier Reef World Heritage Area and Hervey Bay*. Research Publication no. 58. Townsville, Australia: Great Barrier Reef Marine Park Authority.

Olivera-Gómez, L.D., and E. Mellink. 2002. "Spatial and temporal variation in counts of the Antillean manatee (*Trichechus manatus manatus*) during distribution surveys at Bahía de Chetumal, Mexico." *Aquatic Mammals* 28:285–93.

———. 2005. "Distribution of the Antillean manatee (*Trichechus manatus manatus*) as a function of habitat characteristics, in Bahía de Chetumal, Mexico." *Biological Conservation* 121:127–33.

Orozco, D.L. 2001. *Manati Trichechus inunguis: Caza, percepción y conocimiento de las comunidades del municipio de Puerto Nariño, Amazonas*. Tesis profesional, Fac. de Ciencias. Bogotá, Colombia: Pontificia Universidad Javeriana, Facultad de Estudios Ambientales y Rurales, Carrera de Ecologia.

Orr, D.W. 1991. "Politics, conservation, and public education." *Conservation Biology* 5:10–12.

———. 2001. "A literature of redemption." *Conservation Biology* 15:305–7.

Ortega-Argueta, A. 2002. Evaluación del hábitat del manatí (*Trichechus manatus*) en el sistema lagunar de Alvarado, Veracruz. Masters thesis, Programa de Manejo de Fauna Silvestre, Instituto de Ecología, Xalapa, Veracruz, Mexico.

Ortiz, R.M., G.A.J. Worthy, and D.S. MacKenzie. 1998. "Osmoregulation in wild and captive West Indian manatees (*Trichechus manatus*)." *Physiological Zoology* 71:449–57.

O'Shea, T.J. 1986. "Mast foraging by West Indian manatees (*Trichechus manatus*)." *Journal of Mammalogy* 67:183–85.

———. 1988. "The past, present and future of manatees in the southeastern United States: Realities, misunderstanding, and enigmas." In *Proceedings of the Third Southeastern Nongame and Endangered Wildlife Symposium*, ed. R.R. Odom, K.A. Riddleberger, and J.C. Ozier, 184–204. Social Circle: Georgia Department of Natural Resources, Game and Fish Division.

———. 1995. "Waterborne recreation and the Florida manatee." In *Wildlife and Recreationists: Coexistence through Management and Research*, ed. R.L. Knight and K.J. Gutzwiller, 297–311. Washington, D.C.: Island Press.

———. 1999. "Environmental contaminants and marine mammals." In *Biology of Marine Mammals*, ed. J.E. Reynolds III and S.A. Rommel, 485–563. Washington, D.C.: Smithsonian Institution Press.

———. 2003. "Toxicology of sirenians." In *Toxicology of Marine Mammals*, ed. J.G. Vos, G.D. Bossart, M. Fournier, and T.J. O'Shea, 270–87. Boca Raton, Fla.: CRC Press.

———. 2009. "Fifteen years further down the road: An armchair perspective on advances and challenges in sirenian biology and conservation." Abstract. Oral presentation, 2009 International Sirenian Conservation Conference, March 23–24, Atlanta, Georgia.

O'Shea, T.J., and G.B. Rathbun. 1982. "Summary report on a die-off of the West Indian manatee (*Trichechus manatus*) in Lee County, Florida, Spring, 1982." Sirenia Project, Gainesville Field Station, Gainesville, Florida.

O'Shea, T.J., J.F. Moore, and H.I Kochman. 1984. "Contaminant concentrations in manatees in Florida." *Journal of Wildlife Management* 48:741–48.

O'Shea, T.J., C.A. Beck, R.K. Bonde, H.I. Kochman, and D.K. Odell. 1985. "An analysis of manatee mortality patterns in Florida, 1976–81." *Journal of Wildlife Management* 49:1–11.

O'Shea, T.J., M. Correa-Viana, M.E. Ludlow, and J.G. Robinson. 1988. "Distribution, status, and traditional significance of the West Indian manatee *Trichechus manatus* in Venezuela." *Biological Conservation* 46:281–301.

O'Shea, T.J., and H.I. Kochman. 1990. "Florida manatees: Distribution, geographically referenced data sets, and ecological and behavioral aspects of habitat use." In *Report of the Workshop on Geographic Information Systems as an Aid to Managing Habitat for West Indian Manatees in Florida and Georgia*, ed. J.E. Reynolds III and K.D. Haddad. *Florida Marine Research Publication* 49:1–57.

O'Shea, T.J., G.B. Rathbun, R.K. Bonde, C.D. Buergelt, and D.K. Odell. 1991. "An epizootic of Florida manatees associated with a dinoflagellate bloom." *Marine Mammal Science* 7:165–79.

O'Shea, T.J., and C.A. Salisbury. 1991. "Belize: A last stronghold for manatees in the Caribbean." *Oryx* 25:156–64.

O'Shea, T.J., B.B. Ackerman, and H.F. Percival, eds. 1995. *Population Biology of the Florida Manatee*. Washington, D.C.: National Biological Service Information and Technology Report 1.

O'Shea, T.J., R.R. Reeves, and A.K. Long, eds.1999. *Marine Mammals and Persistent Ocean Contaminants: Proceedings of the Marine Mammal Commission Workshop*, 12–15 October 1998, Keystone, Colorado.

O'Shea, T.J., L.W. Lefebvre, and C.A. Beck. 2001. "Florida manatees: Perspectives on populations, pain, and protection." In *Handbook of Marine Mammal Medicine*, 2nd edition, ed. L.A. Dierauf and F.M.D. Gulland, 31–43. Boca Raton, Fla.: CRC Press.

Ottenwalder, J.A. 1995. "Situación del manatí en la República Dominicana." *Dominican Business* 32:41–44.

Ottenwalder, J.A., and Y. León. 1999. "Resultados del análisis inicial de los surveys (entrevistas) de manatí conducidas en la costa de República Dominicana entre 1994 y 1996." Unpublished report.

Pabst, D.A., S.A. Rommel, and W.A. McLellan. 1999. "The functional morphology of marine mammals." In *Biology of Marine Mammals*, ed.J.E. Reynolds III and S.A. Rommel, 15–72. Washington, D.C.: Smithsonian Institution Press.

Packard, J.M. 1981. "Abundance, distribution and feeding habits of manatees (*Trichechus manatus*) wintering between St. Lucie and Palm Beach Inlets, Florida." Report prepared for USFWS Contract no. 14-16-0004-80-105.

———. 1985. *Development of Manatee Aerial Survey Techniques*. Manatee Population Research Report 7. Technical Report 8-7. Gainesville: Florida Cooperative Fish and Wildlife Research Unit, University of Florida.

Packard, J.M., R.C. Summers, and L.B. Barnes. 1985. "Variation of visibility bias during aerial surveys of manatees." *Journal of Wildlife Management* 49:347–51.

Packard, J.M., D.B. Siniff, and J.A. Cornell. 1986. "Use of replicate counts to improve indices of trends in manatee abundance." *Wildlife Society Bulletin* 14:265–75.

Packard, J.M., and O.F. Wetterqvist. 1986. "Evaluation of manatee habitat systems on the Northwestern Florida Coast." *Coastal Zone Management Journal* 14:279–310.

Packard, J.M., R.K. Frohlich, J.E. Reynolds III, and J.R. Wilcox. 1989. "Manatee response to interruption of a thermal effluent." *Journal of Wildlife Management* 53:692–700.

Palmer, D.R. 2004. "Phylogeography and population genetic structure of the dugongs in Thailand." Masters thesis, San Jose State University, San Jose, California.

Palumbi, S.R. 2002. *Marine Reserves: A Tool for Ecosystem Management and Conservation*. Washington, D.C.: Pew Oceans Commission. http://www.pewtrusts.org/uploadedFiles/www.pewtrusts.org/Reports/Protecting_ocean_life/pew_oceans_marine_reserves.pdf.

Pantoja, T.M.A. 2004. "Análise física e química da urina de *Trichechus inunguis* (Mammalia, Sirenia): Valores-referência para o peixe-boi da Amazônia." Masters thesis, Instituto Nacional de Pesquisas da Amazônia/INPA, Universidade do Amazonas, Manaus, Brazil.

Panwar, H.S. 1987. "Project Tiger: The reserves, the tigers, and their future." In *Tigers of the World: The Biology, Biopolitics, Management and Conservation of an Endangered Species*, ed. R.A. Tilson and U.S. Seal, 110–17. Park Ridge, N.J.: Noyes Publications.

Parente, C.L., J.E. Vergara-Parente, and R.P. Lima. 2004. "Strandings of Antillean manatee (*Trichechus manatus manatus*) in northeastern Brazil." *Latin American Journal of Aquatic Mammals* 3:69–76.

Parr, L.A. 2000. "The position of sirenia within the Subungulates and comparison of intra- and inter-specific mitochondrial DNA variation in the extant species of manatee." Ph.D. diss., Portland State University, Portland, Oregon.

Parra, R. 1976. "Comparison of foregut and hindgut fermentation in herbivores." In *The Ecology of Arboreal Folivores*, ed. G.C. Montgomery, 205–29. Washington, D.C.: Smithsonian Institution Press.

Parsons, E.C.M., and A. Woods-Ballard. 2003. "Acceptance of voluntary whale-watching codes of conduct in west Scotland: The effectiveness of governmental versus industry-led guidelines." *Current Issues in Tourism* 6:172–83.

Pauly, D. 1997. "Small-scale fisheries in the tropics: Marginality, marginalization, and some implications for fisheries management." In *Conference on Global Trends in Fisheries Management*, ed. E.H. Pikitch, D.D. Huppert, and M.P. Sissenwine, 14–16 July, Seattle, Washington, American Fisheries Society Symposium, vol. 20.

———. 2006a. "Major trends in small-scale marine fisheries, with emphasis on developing countries, and some implications for the social sciences." *Maritime Studies* 4:7–22.

———. 2006b. "Rejoinder: Towards consilience in small-scale fisheries research." *Maritime Studies (MAST)* 4:47–51.

Pause, K.C. 2007. "Conservation genetics of the Florida manatee, *Trichechus manatus latirostris*." Ph.D. diss., University of Florida, Gainesville, Florida.

Pereira, N. 1947. "Peixe-boi da Amazônia." Técuico da Divisão de Caça e Pesca do Ministério da Agricultura. Imprensa Oficial, Manaus, Brasil.

———. 1954. *O Peixe-Boi da Amazônia*. Rio de Janeiro: Ministério da Agricultura, Divisão de Caça e Pesca.

Perrin, W.F. 1999. "Selected examples of small cetaceans at risk." In *Conservation and Management of Marine Mammals*, ed. J.R. Twiss and R.R. Reeves, 296–310. Washington D.C.: Smithsonian Institution Press.

Perrin, W.F., R.R. Reeves, M.L.L. Dolar, T.A. Jefferson, H. Marsh, J.Y.Wang, and J. Estacion. 2005. Report of the Second Workshop on the Biology and Conservation of Small Cetaceans and Dugongs of South-East Asia. Convention on Migratory Species. http://swfsc.noaa.gov/uploadedFiles/Divisions/PRD/Publications/Perrinetal.05%2889%29.pdf.

Perry, C.J., and W.C. Dennison. 1999. "Microbial nutrient cycling in seagrass sediments." *AGSO Journal of Australian Geology and Geophysics* 17:227–31.

Perry, M.J., and P.J. Mackun. 2001. Population Change and Distribution: 1990 to 2000. U.S. Census Bureau, Census 2000 Brief C2KBR/01-2, 7 pp. http://www.census.gov/prod/2001pubs/c2kbr01-2.pdf.

Persoon, G., H. De Iongh, and B. Wenno. 1996. "Exploitation, management and conservation of marine resources: The context of the Aru Tenggara Marine Reserve (Moluccas, Indonesia)." *Ocean and Coastal Management* 32:97–122.

Peterkin, C.J., and C.A. Conacher. 1997. "Seed germination and recolonisation of *Zostera capricorni* after grazing by dugongs." *Aquatic Botany* 59:333–40.

Phillips, R., R.A. Loughland, and A.M. Youssef. 2004. "The seagrass resources of Abu Dhabi Emirate." In *The Marine Atlas of Abu Dhabi*. Abu Dhabi: Emirates Heritage Club, 124–39.

Phillips, W.W.A. 1927. "Guide to the Mammals of Ceylon, part VII: Sirenia (the dugong)." *Spolia Zeylanica* 14:51–55.

Piestch, T.W. 1991. "Samuel Fallours and his "Sirene"from the Province of Ambon." *Archives of Natural History* 18:1–25.

Pitcher, T.J. 2001. "Fisheries managed to rebuild ecosystems? Reconstructing the past to salvage the future." *Ecological Applications* 11:601–17.

Pole, C.J., and R.G. Burgess. 2000. *Cross-Cultural Case Study*. New York: Elsevier Science.

Pollock, K.H., and W.L. Kendall. 1987. "Visibility bias in aerial surveys: A review of estimation procedures." *Journal of Wildlife Management* 51:502–10.

Pollock, K.H., H. Marsh, I. Lawler, and M.W. Alldredge. 2006. "Estimating animal abundance in heterogeneous environments: An application to aerial surveys of dugongs." *Journal of Wildlife Management* 70:255–62.

Pomeroy, R.S., and K. Viswanathan. 2003. "Fisheries comanagement developments in South-east Asia and Bangladesh." In *The Fisheries Co-Management Experience: Accomplishments, Challenges and Prospects*, ed. by D.G. Wilson, J. Raakjaer-Nielsen, and P. Degnbol, 99–118. Dordrecht, Netherlands: Kluwer Academic Publishers.

Pomeroy, R.S., P. McConney, and R. Mahon. 2004a. "Comparative analysis of coastal resource co-management in the Caribbean." *Ocean and Coastal Management* 47:429–47.

Pomeroy, R.S., J.E. Parks, and L.M. Watson. 2004b. "How is your MPA doing? A guidebook of natural and social indicators for evaluating marine protected area management effectiveness." IUCN–World Conservation Union. http://www.effectivempa.noaa.gov/guidebook/guidebook.html.

Poovachiranon, S., and H. Chansang. 1994. "Community structure and biomass of seagrass beds in the Andaman Sea. I: Mangrove-associated seagrass beds." *Phuket Marine Biological Center Research Bulletin* 59:53–64.

Poovachiranon, S., K. Adulyanukosol, P. Saelim, A. Charoenpornwattana, C. Yaem-arunchai, and C. Wutthivorawong. 2006. "Seagrasses in Thai waters." Phuket Marine Biological Center (in Thai).

Possingham, H., I. Ball., and S. Adelman. 2000. "Mathematical methods for identifying representative reserve networks." In *Quantitative Methods in Conservation Biology*, ed. S. Ferson and M.A. Burgman, 291–307. Berlin, Germany: Springer-Verlag.

Powell, J.A. 1978. "Evidence of carnivory in manatees (*Trichechus manatus*)." *Journal of Mammalogy* 59:442.

———. 1996. "The distribution and biology of the West African manatee (*Trichechus senegalensis* Link, 1975)." Nairobi, Kenya: United Nations Environment Program, Oceans and Coastal Areas.

Powell, J.A., D.W. Belitsky, and G.B. Rathbun 1981. "Status of the West Indian manatee (*Trichechus manatus*) in Puerto Rico." *Journal of Mammalogy* 62:642–46.

Powell, J.A., and G.B. Rathbun. 1984. "Distribution and abundance of manatees along the northern coast of the Gulf of Mexico." *Northeast Gulf Science* 7:1–28.

Prater, S.H. 1928. "The dugong or sea cow (*Halicore dugong*)." *Journal of the Bombay Natural History Society* 33:84–99.

Pratt, P. 1985. *Laboratory Procedures for Animal Health Technicians*. Goleta, Calif.: American Veterinary Publications.

Preen, A. R. 1989. "Dugongs: The status and conservation of dugongs in the Arabian Region." *MEPA Coastal and Marine Management Series*, Report no. 10, vol. 1: 200 pp. Meteorological and Environmental Protection Administration, Jeddah, Saudi Arabia.

———. 1992. "Interactions between dugongs and seagrasses in a subtropical environment." Ph.D. diss., James Cook University, Townsville, Australia.

———. 1995a. "Impacts of dugong foraging on seagrass habitats: Observational and experimental evidence for cultivation grazing." *Marine Ecology Progress Series* 124:201–13.

———. 1995b. "Diet of dugongs: Are they omnivores?" *Journal of Mammalogy* 76:163–71.

———. 1998. "Marine protected areas and dugong conservation along Australia's Indian Ocean coast." *Environmental Management* 22:173–81.

———. 2001. *Dugongs, Boats, Dolphins and Turtles in the Townsville-Cardwell Region and Recommendations for a Boat-Traffic Management Plan for the Hinchinbrook Dugong Protection Area*. Research Publication no. 67. Townsville, Australia: Great Barrier Reef Marine Park Authority.

———. 2004. "Distribution, abundance and conservation status of dugongs and dolphins in the southern and western Arabian Gulf." *Biological Conservation* 118:205–18.

Preen, A., H. Marsh, and G.E. Heinsohn. 1989. "Recommendations for the conservation of dugongs in the Arabian Region." *MEPA Coastal and Marine Management Series*, Report no. 10, vol. 2:43. Meteorology and Environmental Protection Administration, Jeddah, Saudi Arabia.

Preen, A.R., W.J. Lee Long, and R.G. Coles. 1995. "Flood and cyclone related loss, and partial recovery, of more than 1000 km^2 of seagrass in Hervey Bay, Queensland, Australia." *Aquatic Botany* 52:3–17.

Preen, A.R., and H. Marsh. 1995. "Response of dugongs to large-scale loss of seagrass from Hervey Bay, Queensland, Australia." *Wildlife Research* 22:507–19.

Preen A.R., H. Marsh, I.R. Lawler, R.I.T. Prince, and R. Shepherd. 1997. "Distribution and abundance of dugongs, turtles, dolphins and other megafauna in Shark Bay, Ningaloo Reef and Exmouth Gulf, Western Australia." *Wildlife Research* 24:185–208.

Preen, A., R. Loughland, A. Youssef, L. Al-Amri, F. Al-Hadrami, N. Shalhoub, B. Abu Shamalah, A. Al Atass, N. Al-Qadi, and H. Al-Adawi. 2000. "The distribution of dugongs, dolphins and turtles in Abu Dhabi, with recommendations for a marine protected area." In *Second Arab International Conference and Exhibition on Environmental Biotechnology: Coastal Habitats*, April 2000, Abu Dhabi, United Arab Emirates.

Preen, A., A. Loughland, A.M. Youssef, L. Al-Amri, F. Al-Hadrami, N. Shalhoub, Z. Daghastani, and A. Al Atass. 2004. "Marine mammals: Dugong, dolphins and porpoise." In *The Marine Atlas of Abu Dhabi*. Abu Dhabi: Emirates Heritage Club, 202–17.

Price, A.R.G. 1982. *Conservation and Sustainable Use of Natural Resources*, part 2: *Marine*. IUCN report to the Expert Meeting of the Gulf Co-ordinating Council to review environmental issues.

Pritchard, J.K., M. Stephens, and P. Donnelly. 2000. "Inference of population structure using multilocus genotype data." *Genetics* 155:945–59.

Proebstel, D.S., R.P. Evans, D.K. Shiozawa, and R.N. Williams. 1993. "Preservation of nonfrozen tissue samples from a salmonine fish *Brachymystax lenok* (Pallas) for DNA analysis." *Journal of Ichthyology* 9:9–17.

Provancha, J., and C. Hall. 1991. "Observations of association between seagrass beds and manatees in east central Florida." *Florida Scientist* 54:87–98.

Pugibet, E., and M. Vega. 2000. "Informe sobre el Manatí Antillano (*Trichechus manatus*) en la República Dominicana." Informe presentado al Secretario de Estado de Medio Ambiente y Recursos Naturales. Unpublished report.

Quintana-Rizzo, E. 1993. "Estimación de la distribución y el tamaño poblacional del manatí *Trichechus manatus* (Trichechidae—Sirenia) en Guatemala." M.Sc. thesis, Facultad de Ciencias Quimicas y Farmacia, Universidad de San Carlos de Guatemala, Guatemala.

Quintana-Rizzo, E., and J.E. Reynolds III. 2010. *Regional Management Plan for the West Indian Manatee (*Trichechus manatus*)*. CEP Technical Report No. 48, UNEP Caribbean Environment Programme, Kingston, Jamaica.

Rabinowitz, A. 1991. *Chasing the Dragon's Tail: The Struggle to Save Thailand's Wild Cats*. New York: Anchor Books.

Rafomanana, G., and H. Rasolojantovo. 2004. "The status of dugongs in Madagascar." In *Towards a Western Indian Ocean Dugong Conservation Strategy*, ed. C. Muir, A. Ngusaru, and L. Mwakanema, 40–44. WWF East African Marine Ecoregion.

Ragen, T.J. 2005. "Assessing and managing marine mammal habitat in the United States." In *Marine Mammal Research: Conservation beyond Crisis*, ed. J.E. Reynolds III, W.F. Perrin, R.R. Reeves, S. Montgomery, and T.J. Ragen, 125–34. Baltimore, Md.: Johns Hopkins University Press.

Ragen, T.J., J.E. Reynolds III, and M.L. Gosliner. 2002. "Assessment of marine mammal population status: A comparison of the mandates of federal laws and the requirements of good management." Proceedings of the Manatee Population Ecology and Management Workshop, 1–4 April 2002, Gainesville, Florida.

Rajamani, L., A.S. Cabanban, and R.A. Rahman. 2006. "Indigenous use and trade of Dugong (*Dugong dugon*) in Sabah, Malaysia." *Ambio* 35:266–68.

Ralls, K. 1997. "On becoming a conservation biologist: Autobiography and advice." In *Behavioral Approaches to Conservation in the Wild*, ed. J.R. Clemmons and R. Buchholz, 356–72. Cambridge, U.K.: Cambridge University Press.

Ramachandran, S., S. Anitha, V. Balamurugan, K. Dharanirajan, K. E. Vendhan, M.I.P. Divien, A.S. Vel, I.S. Hussain, and A. Udayaraj. 2005. "Ecological impact of tsunami on Nicobar Islands (Camorta, Katchal, Nancowry and Trinkat)." *Current Science* 89:195–200.

Ramirez-Jimenez H. 2008. "Uso de hábitat de manatíes (*Trichechus manatus*) aislados en la Laguna de las Iusiones, Tabasco, México." Masters thesis, El Colegio de la Frontera Sur (ECOSUR), Chetumal, Quintana Roo, Mexico.

Ramsar 2009. "The Ramsar Convention on Wetlands Website." http://www.ramsar.org.

Rand, G.M., and S.R. Petrocelli. 1985. *Fundamentals of Aquatic Toxicology: Methods and Applications*. Washington, D.C.: Hemisphere Publishing.

Raney, R.K. 1998. Radar fundamentals: Technical perspective. In *Principles and Applications of Imaging Radar (Manual of Remote Sensing*, 3rd ed., vol. 2), ed. F.M. Henderson and A.J. Lewis, 9–130. New York: John Wiley and Sons.

Rathbun, G.B., R.K. Bonde, and D. Clay. 1982. "The status of the West Indian manatee on the Atlantic Coast north of Florida." In *Proceedings of the Symposium on Nongame and Endangered Wildlife*, ed. R.R. Odom and J.W. Guthrie, 152–65. Georgia Department of Natural Resources, Game and Fish Division, Technical Bulletin WL5.

Rathbun, G.B., J.A. Powell, and G. Cruz 1983a. Status of the West Indian manatee in Honduras. *Biological Conservation* 26:301–8.

Rathbun, G.B., J.A. Powell, and J.P. Reid. 1983b. "Movements of manatees (*Trichechus manatus*) using power plant effluents in southern Florida." Prepared for the Florida Power and Light Company.

Rathbun, G.B., T. Carr, N.M. Carr, and C.A. Woods. 1985a. "The distribution of manatees and sea turtles in Puerto Rico." Springfield, Virginia: National Technical Information Service PB86–1518347AS.

Rathbun, G.B, C.A. Woods, and J.A. Ottenwalder 1985b. "The manatee in Haiti." *Oryx* 19:234–36.

Rathbun, G.B., J.P. Reid, and J.B. Bourassa. 1987a. Design and construction of a tethered, floating radiotag assembly for manatees. National Technical Information Service, #PB87-161345/AS, Springfield, VA. 49 pp.

———. 1987b. "Design and construction of a tethered, floating radio-tag assembly for dugongs." National Technical Information Service, #PB87–161345/AS, Springfield, Virginia.

Rathbun, G.B., J.P. Reid, and G. Carowan. 1990. "Distribution and movement patterns of manatees (*Trichechus manatus*) in northwestern peninsular Florida." *Florida Marine Research Institute Publication* 48:1–33.

Raven, J.A., A.M. Johnston, J.E. Kubler, R. Korb, S.G. McInroy, L.L. Handley, C.M. Scrimgeour, D.I. Walker, J. Beardall, M. Vanderklift, S. Fredriksen, and K.H. Dunton. 2002. "Mechanistic interpretation of carbon isotope discrimination by marine macroalgae and seagrass." *Functional Plant Biology* 29:355–78.

Read, A.J. 2005. "Bycatch and depredation." In *Marine Mammal Research: Beyond Crisis Management*, ed. J.E. Reynolds III, W.F. Perrin, R.R. Reeves, T.J. Ragen, and S. Montgomery, 5–18. Baltimore, Md.: Johns Hopkins University Press.

Rector, A., G.D. Bossart, S. Ghim, J.P. Sundberg, A.B. Jenson, and M. Van Ranst. 2004. "Characterization of a novel close-to-root papillomavirus from a Florida manatee by using multiply primed rolling-circle amplification: *Trichechus manatus latirostris* papilloma type 1." *Journal of Virology* 78:12698–702.

Reddy, M.L., J.S. Reif, A. Bachand, and S.H. Ridgway. 2001. "Opportunities for using navy marine mammals to explore associations between organochlorine contaminants and unfavorable effects on reproduction." *Science of the Total Environment* 274:171–82.

Redfern, J.V., M.C. Ferguson, E.A. Becker, K.D. Hyrenbach, C. Good, J. Barlow, K. Kaschner, M.F. Baumgartner, K.A. Forney, L.T. Balance, P. Fauchald, P. Halpin, T. Hamazaki, A.J. Pershing, S.S. Qian, A. Read, S.B. Reilly, L. Torres, and F. Werner. 2006. "Techniques for cetacean-habitat modeling." *Marine Ecology Progress Series* 310:271–95.

Reep, R.L., C.D. Marshall, M.L. Stoll, and D.M. Whitaker. 1998. "Distribution and innervation of facial bristles and hairs in the Florida manatee (*Trichechus manatus latirostris*). *Marine Mammal Science* 14:257–73.

Reep, R.L., C.D. Marshall, and M.L. Stoll. 2002. "Tactile hairs on the postcranial body in Florida manatees: A mammalian lateral line?" *Brain Behavior and Evolution* 59:141–54.

Reep, R.L., and R.K. Bonde. 2006. *The Florida Manatee: Biology and Conservation*. Gainesville: University Press of Florida.

Reeves, R.R. 2000. "The value of sanctuaries, parks, and reserves (protected areas) as tools for conserving marine mammals." Final report to U.S. Marine Mammal Commission, contract T74465385. Bethesda, Maryland.

Reeves, R.R., D. Tuboku-Mertzger, and R.A. Kapindi. 1988. "Distribution and exploitation of manatees in Sierra Leone." *Oryx* 12:75–84.

Reeves, R.R., B.S. Stewart, and S. Leatherwood. 1992. *The Sierra Club Handbook of Seals and Sirenians*. San Francisco, Calif.: Sierra Club Books.

Reeves, R.R., S. Leatherwood, T.A. Jefferson, B.E. Curry, and T. Henningsen. 1996. "Amazonian manatees, *Trichechus inunguis*, in Peru: Distribution, exploitation, and conservation status." *Interciencia* 21:246–54.

Reeves, R.R., B.S. Stewart, P.J. Clapham, and J.A. Powell. 2002. *Guide to Marine Mammals of the World*. Illus. Pieter Folkens. New York: Alfred A. Knopf.

Reeves, R.R., B.D. Smith, E.A. Crespo, and G. Notobartolo di Sciara (compilers). 2003. *Dolphins, Whales and Porpoises: 2002-2010 Conservation Action Plan for the World's Cetaceans*. Gland, Switzerland: IUCN/SSC Cetacean Specialist Group.

Reich, K., and Worthy, G. 2006. "An isotopic assessment of the feeding habits of free-ranging manatees." *Marine Ecology Progress Series* 322:303–9.

Reid, J.P. 2001. "Manatee birth in the Bahamas." *Sirenews* (IUCN/SSC Sirenia Specialist Group) 36.

Reid, J.P., G.B. Rathbun, and J.R. Wilcox. 1991. "Distribution patterns of individually identifiable West Indian manatees (*Trichechus manatus*) in Florida." *Marine Mammal Science* 7:180–90.

Reid, J.P., R.K. Bonde and T.J. O'Shea. 1995. "Reproduction and mortality of radio-tagged and recognizable manatees on the Atlantic Coast of Florida." In *Population Biology of the Florida Manatee*, ed. T.J. O'Shea, B.B. Ackerman, and H.F. Percival, 171–91. Washington, D.C.: National Biological Service Information and Technology Report 1.

Reynolds, J.E. III. 1981. "Behavior patterns in the West Indian manatee, with emphasis on feeding and diving." *Florida Scientist* 44:233–42.

———. 1995. "Florida manatee population biology: Research progress, infrastructure, and applications for conservation and management." In *Population Biology of the Florida Manatee*, ed. T.J. O'Shea, B.B. Ackerman, and H.F. Percival, 6–12. Washington, D.C.: National Biological Service Information and Technology Report 1.

———. 1999. "Efforts to conserve the manatees." In *Conservation and Management of Marine Mammals*, ed. J.R. Twiss Jr. and R.R. Reeves, 267–95. Washington, D.C.: Smithsonian Institution Press.

———. 2009. "Manatee research and conservation at Mote Marine Laboratory: Same vision, new directions." Abstract. Oral presentation at the 2009 International Sirenian Conservation Conference, March 23–24, Atlanta, Georgia.

Reynolds, J.E. III, and C.J. Gluckman. 1988. "Protection of the West Indian manatee (*Trichechus manatus*) in Florida. Final report to U.S. Marine Mammal Commission, Order MM4465868-3. NTIS Rept. no. PB88–222922. Bethesda, Maryland.

Reynolds, J.E. III, and D.K. Odell. 1991. *Manatees and Dugongs*. New York: Facts on File.

Reynolds, J.E. III, and J.R. Wilcox. 1994. "Observations of Florida manatees (*Trichechus manatus latirostris*) around selected power plants in winter." *Marine Mammal Science* 10:163–77.

Reynolds, J.E. III, W.A. Szelistowski, and M.A. León. 1995. "Status and conservation of manatees *Trichechus manatus manatus* in Costa Rica." *Biological Conservation* 71:193–96.

Reynolds, J.E. III, and S.A. Rommel. 1996. "Structure and function of the gastrointestinal tract of the Florida manatee, *Trichechus manatus latirostris*." *Anatomical Record* 245:539–58.

Reynolds, J.E. III, and S.A. Rommel, eds. 1999. *Biology of Marine Mammals*. Washington, D.C.: Smithsonian Institution Press.

Reynolds, J.E. III, S.A. Rommel, and M.E. Bolen. 2002. "Anatomical dissection: Thorax and abdomen." In *Encyclopedia of Marine Mammals*, ed. W.F. Perrin, B. Würsig, and H. Thewissen, 21–30. San Diego: Academic Press.

Reynolds, J.E. III, and R.S. Wells. 2003. *Dolphins, Whales, and Manatees of Florida: A Guide to Sharing Their World*. Gainesville: University Press of Florida.

Reynolds, J.E. III, S.A. Rommel, and M.E. Pitchford. 2004. "The likelihood of sperm competition in manatees: Explaining an apparent paradox." *Marine Mammal Science* 20(3):464–76.

Reynolds, J.E. III, W.F. Perrin, R.R. Reeves, T.J. Ragen, and S. Montgomery, eds. 2005. *Marine Mammal Research: Beyond Crisis Management*. Baltimore, Md.: Johns Hopkins University Press.

Reynolds, J.E. III, H. Marsh, and T.J. Ragen. 2009. "Marine Mammal Conservation." *Journal of Endangered Species Research* 7:23–28.

Richards, M.P., B.T. Fuller, M. Sponheimer, T. Robinson, and L. Ayliffe. 2003. "Sulphur isotopes in palaeodietary studies: A review and results from a controlled feeding experiment." *International Journal of Osteoarchaeology* 13:37–45.

Richter, B.D., and K.H. Redford. 1999. "The art (and science) of brokering deals between conservation and use." *Conservation Biology* 13:1235–37.

Ricklefs, R.E. 1990. *Ecology*, 3rd ed. New York: W.H. Freeman and Company.

Rio Declaration Agenda 21. 1992. http://habitat.igc.org/agenda21/rio-dec.htm.

Ritter, L., K.R. Solomon, and J. Forget. 1995. "Persistant organic pollutants: An assessment report on: DDTAldrin-Dieldrin-Endrin-Chlordane-Heptachlor-Hezachlorobenzene-Mirex-Toxaphene-Polychlorinated Biphenyl-Dioxins and Furans." International Programme on Chemical Safety, FAO.

Rivera, R., and G.F. Newkirk. 1997. "Power from the people: A documentation of non-governmental organizations' experience in community-based coastal resource management in the Philippines." *Ocean and Coastal Management* 36:73–95.

Riviera, V., and M. Rodriguez. 1991. "The Playa Blanca 5 site: A late prehistoric site in eastern Puerto Rico (A preliminary report)." In *Proceedings of the Thirteenth International Association for Caribbean Archeaology*, Curaçao, 541–58.

Robblee, M.B., T.R. Barber, P.R. Carlson Jr., M.J. Durako, J.W. Fourqurean, L.K. Muehlstein, D. Porter, L.A. Yarbro, R.T. Zieman, and J.C. Zieman. 1991. "Mass mortality of the tropical seagrass *Thalassia testudinum* in Florida Bay (USA)." *Marine Ecology Progress Series* 71:297–99.

Roberge, J-M., and P. Angelstam. 2004. "Usefulness of the umbrella species concept as a conservation tool." *Conservation Biology* 18:76–85.

Roberts, C.M., and J.P. Hawkins. 1999. "Extinction risk in the sea." *Trends in Ecology and Evolution* 14:241–46.

Robinson, J. 2006. "Conservation biology and real-world conservation." *Conservation Biology* 20:658–69.

Robinson, P.T. 1971. "Wildlife trends in Liberia and Sierra Leone." *Oryx* 11:117–22.

Rodríguez, J.P., and F. Rojas-Suarez. 2003. *Libro Rojo de la fauna venezolana*. 2nd ed. Caracas, Venezuela: Provita, Fundación Polar.

Rodriguez, Z.M., V.M.F. da Silva, and J.A. d'Affonseca Neto. 1999. "Teste de fórmula láctea na alimentação de filhotes órfãos de peixe-boi da Amazônia (*Trichechus inunguis*)." In *Manejo y conservación de fauna silvestre en América Latina*, ed. T.G. Fang, O.L. Montenegro, and R.E. Bodmer, 405–8. La Paz, Bolivia: Instituto de Ecologia.

Rodríguez-López, M.A. 2004. "Phylogeography of manatees (*Trichechus manatus*) in Puerto Rico: A management tool for species conservation." Master's thesis, Universidad Metropolitana, San Juan, Puerto Rico.

Rommel, S.A., and J.E. Reynolds III. 2000. "Diaphragm structure and function in the Florida manatee (*Trichechus manatus latirostris*)." *Anatomical Record* 259:41–51.

Rommel, S.A., D.A. Pabst, and W.A. McLellan. 2001. "Functional morphology of venous structures associated with the male and female reproductive systems in Florida manatees (*Trichechus manatus latirostris*)." *Anatomical Record* 264:339–47.

Rommel, S.A., and J.E. Reyznolds III. 2002. "Postcranial skeleton of marine mammals." In *Encyclopedia of Marine Mammals*, ed. W.F. Perrin, B. Würsig, and H. Thewissen, 1089–1103. San Diego: Academic Press.

Rommel, S.A., and H. Caplan. 2003. "Vascular adaptations for heat conservation in the tail of Florida manatees (*Trichechus manatus latirostris*)." *Journal of Anatomy* 202:343

Rommel, S.A., J.E. Reynolds III, and H.A. Lynch. 2003. "Adaptations of the herbivorous marine mammals." In *Matching Herbivore Nutrition to Ecosystems Biodiversity*, ed. L. Mannetje, T.L. Ramirez-Aviles, C. Sandoval-Castro, and J.C. Ku-Vera, 287–308. VI International Symposium on the Nutrition of Herbivores. Proceedings of an International Symposium held in Merida, Mexico, 19–24 October 2003, Universidad Autónoma de Yucatán.

Rommel, S.A., A.M. Costidis, T.D. Pitchford, J.D. Lightsey, R.H. Snyder, and E.M. Haubold. 2007. "Forensic methods for characterizing watercraft from watercraft-induced wounds on the Florida manatee (*Trichechus manatus latirostris*)." *Marine Mammal Science* 23:110–32.

Rosas, F.C.W. 1994. Biology, conservation and status of the Amazonian manatee *Trichechus inunguis*. *Mammal Review* 24:49–59.

Rosas, F.C.W., M. Marmontel, and R.C. Best. 1984. "Estudos do peixo-boi amazônico na Represa Hidrelétrica de Curuá Una." Resumos da I Renuião de Trabalho de Especialistas em Mamíferos Aquáticos da América do Sul, Buenos Aires.

Rosas, F.C.W., K.K. Lehti, and M. Marmontel. 1999. "Hematological indices and mineral content of serum in captive and wild Amazonian manatees, *Trichechus inunguis*." *Arquivos de Ciências Veterinárias e Zoologia da UNIPAR* 2:37–42.

Rosas, F.C.W., and T.L. Pimentel. 2001. "Order Sirenia (Manatees, dugongs, sea cows)." In *Biology, Medicine, and Surgery of South American Wild Animals*, ed. M.E. Fowler and Z.S. Cubas, 352–62. Ames: Iowa State University Press.

Rosas, F.C.W., V.M.F. da Silva, R.S. Sousa-Lima, G.E. de Mattos, and J.A. d'Affonseca Neto. 2001. "Adoption and growth of a captive Amazonian manatee (*Trichechus inunguis*) calf." In *Abstracts, Fourteenth Biennial Conference on the Biology of Marine Mammals*, 28 November–3 December 2001, Vancouver, Canada, 183.

Rosas, F.C.W., R.S. Sousa-Lima, and V.M.F. da Silva. 2003. "Avaliação preliminar dos mamíferos do baixo rio Purus." In *Piagaçu-Purus: Bases científicas para a criação de uma reserva de desenvolvimento sustentável*, ed. C.F. de Deus, R. da Silveira, and L.H.R. Py-Daniel, 49–59. Manaus: IDSM.

Ross, H., J. Innes, M. George, M. Gorman, and K. Gorman, eds. 2004. *Traditional Owner Aspirations towards Co-operative Management of the Great Barrier Reef World Heritage Area: Community Case Studies.* CRC Reef Research Centre Technical Report no. 56. Townsville, Australia: CRC Reef Research Centre.

Ross, P.S., R.L. De Swart, H.V. Loveren, A.D.M.E. Osterhaus, and J.G. Vos. 1996. "The immunotoxicity of environmental contaminants to marine wildlife: A review." *Annual Review of Fish Diseases* 6:151–65.

Roth, H.H., and E. Waitkuwait. 1986. "Repartition et statut des grandes espèces de mammifères en Côte d'Ivoire. III: Lamantins." *Mammalia* 50:227–42.

Roux, D.J., K.H. Rogers, H.C. Biggs, P.J. Ashton, and A. Sergeant. 2006. "Bridging the science-management divide: Moving from unidirectional knowledge transfer to knowledge interfacing and sharing." *Ecology and Society* 11:4. http://www.ecologyandsociety.org/vol11/iss1/art4/.

Runge, M.C., C.A. Langtimm, and W.L. Kendall. 2004. "A stage-based model of manatee population dynamics." *Marine Mammal Science* 20:361–85.

Runge M.C., C.A. Sanders-Reed, and C.J. Fonnesbeck. 2007a. "A core stochastic population projection model for Florida manatees (*Trichechus manatus latirostris*)." U.S. Geological Survey Open-File Report 2007-1082.

Runge M.C., C.A. Sanders-Reed, C.A. Langtimm, C.J. Fonnesbeck. 2007b. "A quantitative threats analysis for the Florida manatee (*Trichechus manatus latirostris*)." U.S. Geological Survey Open-File Report 2007-1086.

Ryti, R.T. 1992. "Effect of the focal taxon on the selection of nature reserves." *Ecological Applications* 2:404–10.

Saafeld, W.K. 2000. "Distribution and abundance of dugong in the coastal waters of the Northern Territory." Parks and Wildlife Commission of the Northern Territory, Darwin.

Sae Aueng (now Pitaksintorn), S., W. Witayasak, R. Lukanawakulra, W. Rearkwisaka, and P.S. O'Sullivan. 1993. "A survey of dugong in seagrass bed at Changwat Trang." 31st Technical Conference on Science Issues: Fisheries and Biology, Kasetsart University, Bangkok, Thailand.

Sagoff, M. 1996. "On the value of endangered and other species." *Environmental Management* 20:897–911.

Salm, R. 1984. *Marine Conservation Atlas of Indonesia.* IUCN/WWF Project 3108.

Salm, R.V., J. Clark, and E. Siirila. 2000. *Marine and Coastal Protected Areas: A Guide for Planners and Managers.* Washington D.C.: IUCN. www.iucn.org/themes/marine/pdf/mpaguid2.pdf.

Sankaran, R., H. Andrews, and A. Vaughan. 2005. *The Ground Beneath the Waves: Post-tsunami Impact Assessment of Wildlife and Their Habitats in India, Vol. 2: The Islands.* New Delhi: Wildlife Trust of India, International Fund for Animal Welfare and Sálim Ali Centre for Ornithology and Natural

History. 2:22–25. http://www.wildlifetrustofindia.org/publications/ground-beneath-the-waves-vol2.pdf.

Santos, E. 1984. "Entre o gambá e o macaco: Vida e costumes dos mamíferos do Brasil." In *Coleção Zoologia Brasília*, vol. 6. Belo Horizonte: Editora Itatiaia.

Santos Mariño, J.A. 2006. "Reporte sobre manatí antillano (*Trichechus manatus manatus*) en Cuba: Recopilación de información de diferentes fuentes." Unpublished report. Empresa Nacional para la Protección de la Flora y la Fauna.

Saranakomkul, K. 2002. "Laws of dugong and seagrass conservation." *Technical paper, Phuket Provincial Fishery Office*, 7. (in Thai).

Sargent, F.J., T.J. Leary, D.W. Crewz, and C.R. Kruer. 1995. "Scarring of Florida's seagrasses: Assessment and management options." FMRI Technical Report TR-1. Florida Marine Research Institute, St. Petersburg.

Sarko, D.K., and R.L. Reep. 2007a. "Somatosensory areas of manatee cerebral cortex: Histochemical characterization and functional implications." *Brain, Behavior and Evolution* 69:20–36.

Sarko, D.K., J.I. Johnson, R.C. Switzer III, W.I. Welker, and R.L. Reep. 2007b. "Somatosensory nuclei of the manatee brainstem and thalamus." *Anatomical Record* 290:1138–65.

Sarko, D.K., R.L. Reep, J.E. Mazurkiewicz, and F.L. Rice. 2007c. "Adaptations in the structure and innervation of folliclesinus complexes to an aquatic environment as seen in the Florida manatee (*Trichechus manatus latirostris*)." *Journal of Comparative Neurology* 504:217–37.

Sartor, F. 2004. *Aspectos da caça do peixe-boi amazônico Trichechus inunguis (Natterer, 1883) por populações ribeirinhas no rio Tapajós-PA*. Monografia de Conclusão do Curso de Ciências Biológicas. Brazil: Universidade Federal de Santa Catarina.

Sartor, F., F.O. Luna, P.C. Simões Lopes, R.P. Lima, D.F. Castro, and C.V. Aguilar. 2004. "Caça do peixe-boi amazônico (*Trichechus inunguis*) no rio Tapajós, Pará, Brasil." 11ª [11th] Reunião de Trabalho de Especialistas em Mamíferos Aquáticos da América do Sul e 5º [5th] Congresso da Sociedade Latinoamericana de Especialistas em Mamíferos Aquáticos (SOLAMAC), 11–17 September, Quito, Ecuador.

Sartor, F., F.O. Luna, and P.C. Simões-Lopes. "Peixe-boi amazônico: qual será o futuro da espécie?" (in prep.).

Scarpaci, C., E.C.M. Parsons, and M. Lück. 2008. "Recent advances in whale-watching research." *Tourism in Marine Environments* 5:55–66.

Schaller, G.B. 1993. *The Last Panda*. Chicago: University of Chicago Press.

Schelhas, J. 1992. "Socio-economic and biological analyses for buffer zone establishment." In *Science and the Management of Protected Areas*, ed. J.H.M. Willison, S. Bondrup-Nielsen, C. Drysdale, T.B. Herman, N.W.P. Munro, and T.L. Pollock, 163–69. Amsterdam, Netherlands: Elsevier.

Schlaepfer, M.A., M.C. Runge, and P.W. Sherman. 2002. "Ecological and evolutionary traps." *Trends in Ecology and Evolution* 17:474–80.

Schmandt, J., and Ward, C.H., eds. 2000. *Sustainable Development: The Challenge of Transition*. New York: Cambridge University Press.

Schwacke, L.H., E.O. Vorr, L.J. Hansen, R.S. Wells, G.B. Mitchum, A.A. Hohn, and P.A. Fair. 2002. "Probability risk assessment of reproductive effects of polychlorinated biphyenyls on bottlenose dolphins (*T. truncatus*) from the southeast United States coast." *Environmental Toxicology and Chemistry* 21:2752–64.

Schwartz, F.J. 1995. "Florida manatees, *Trichechus manatus* (Sirenia: Trichechidae), in North Carolina 1919–1994." *Brimleyana* 22:53–60.

Schwarz, L.K. 2007. "Survival rate estimates of Florida manatees (*Trichechus manatus latirostris*) using carcass recovery data." Ph.D. diss., Montana State University, Bozeman, Montana.

Scott, J.M., J.L. Rachlow, R.T. Lackey, A.B. Pidgorna, J.L. Aycrigg, G.R. Feldman, L.K. Svancara, D.A. Rupp, D.I. Stanish, and R.K. Steinhorst. 2007. "Policy advocacy in science: Prevalence, perspectives, and implications for conservation biologists." *Conservation Biology* 21:29–35.

SeagrassNet.org. http://www.seagrassnet.org/index.html.

Self-Sullivan, C. 2008. "Conservation of Antillean manatees in the Drowned Cayes area of Belize." Ph.D. diss., Department of Wildlife and Fisheries Sciences, Texas A&M University, College Station, Texas.

Self-Sullivan, C., and Mignucci-Giannoni, A. 2008. *Trichechus manatus* ssp. *manatus*. 2008 IUCN Red List of Threatened Species. www.iucnredlist.org.

Self-Sullivan, C., G.W. Smith, J.M. Packard, and K.S. LaCommare. 2003. "Seasonal occurrence of male Antillean manatees (*Trichechus manatus manatus*) on the Belize Barrier Reef." *Aquatic Mammals* 29:342–54.

Sericano, J.L., E.L. Atlas, T.L. Wade, and J.M. Brooks. 1990. "NOAA's status and trends mussel watch program: Chlorinated pesticides and PCBs in oysters (*Crassostrea virginica*) and sediments from the Gulf of Mexico, 1986–1987." *Marine Environmental Research* 29:161–203.

Shane, S.H. 1983. "Abundance, distribution, and movements of manatees (*Trichechus manatus*) in Brevard County, Florida." *Bulletin of Marine Science* 33:1–9.

Shanley, P., and S.A. Laird. 2002. "'Giving back': Making research results relevant to local groups and conservation." In *Biodiversity and Traditional Knowledge*, ed. S.A. Laird, 102–24, London, U.K.: Earthscan Publications.

Shapiro, S.L. 2001. "Assessing boater compliance with manatee speed zones in Florida." Final report to the U.S. Fish and Wildlife Service. St. Petersburg, Florida.

Sharp, N. 2002. *Saltwater People: The Waves of Memory*. Toronto, Ontario: University of Toronto Press.

Sheehy, B. 2004. "International marine environmental law: A case study in the Wider Caribbean Region." *Georgetown International Environmental Law Review* 16:441–72.

Sheppard, C., A. Price, and C. Roberts. 1992. *Marine ecology in the Arabian region: Patterns and Processes in Extreme Tropical Environments*. London: Academic Press.

Sheppard, J.K., A.R. Preen, H. Marsh, I.R. Lawler, S.D. Whiting, and R.E. Jones. 2006. "Movement heterogeneity of dugongs, *Dugong dugon* (Müller) over large spatial scales." *Journal of Experimental Marine Biology and Ecology* 334:64–83.

Sheppard, J.K., I.R. Lawler, and H. Marsh. 2007. "Seagrass as pasture for seacows: Landscape-level dugong habitat evaluation." *Estuarine, Coastal and Shelf Science* 71:117–32.

Sheppard, J.K., R.E. Jones, H. Marsh, and I.R. Lawler. 2009. "Effects of tidal and diel cycles on dugong habitat use." *Journal of Wildlife Management* 73:45–59.

Short, F.T., and H.A. Neckles. 1999. "The effects of global climate change on seagrass." *Aquatic Botany* 63:169–96.

Shou, Z.-H. 1958. "The dugong from Beibu Gulf." *Chinese Journal of Zoology* 2:146–52 (in Chinese).

Siegal-Willott, J., A. Estrada, R. Bonde, A. Wong, D.J. Estrada, and K. Harr. 2006. "Electrocardiography in two subspecies of manatee (*Trichechus manatus latirostris* and *T. m. manatus*)." *Journal of Zoo and Wildlife Medicine* 37:447–53.

Silas, E.G. 1961. "Occurrence of the sea cow, *Halicore dugong* (Exrl.) off the Saurashtra coast." *Journal of the Bombay Natural History Society* 58:263–66.

Silas, E. G., and B. Fernando. 1985. "The dugong in India: Is it going the way of the dodo?" Central Marine Fisheries Research Institute. Commission on Endangered Marine Animals and Marine Parks, Cochin, India.

Silva, M.A., and A. Araújo. 2001. "Distribution and current status of the West African manatee (*Trichechus senegalensis*) in Guinea-Bissau." *Marine Mammal Science* 17:418–24.

Simberloff, D. 1998. "Flagships, umbrellas, and keystones: Is single-species management passé in the landscape era?" *Biological Conservation* 83:247–57.

Singh H.S., C.N. Pandey, P. Yennawar, R.J. Asari, B.H. Patel, K. Tatu, and B.R. Raval. 2004. *The Marine National Park and Sanctuary in the Gulf of Kachchh: A Comprehensive Study of Biodiversity and Management Issues*. Gandhinagar, India: GEER Foundation. 370 pp.

Singh, T.P., and Hegde, R. 2004. "Stakeholder analysis in forest management in India: A case study of Haryana Shivaliks." In *Environmental Economics in Practice: Case Studies from India*, ed. G.K. Kodekodi, New Delhi: Oxford University Press.

Sioli, H. 1984. "The Amazon and its main affluents: Hydrography, morphology of the river courses, and river types." In *The Amazon: Limnology and Landscape Ecology of a Mighty River and Its Basin*, ed. H. Sioli, 127–65. Dordrecht, Netherlands: Dr. W. Junk Publishers.

Sitarz, D. 1993. *Agenda 21: The Earth Summit Strategy to Save Our Planet*. Boulder, Colo.: EarthPress.

Smith, K.N. 1993. "Manatee habitat and human-related threats to seagrass in Florida." Tallahassee, Florida: Department of Environmental Protection, Division of Marine Resources.

Smyth, D. 2006. "Dugong and marine turtle knowledge handbook: Indigenous and scientific knowledge of dugongs and marine turtles in northern Australia." Report to North Australian Indigenous Land and Sea Management Alliance, Darwin, Northern Territory.

Snipes, R. 1984. "Anatomy of the cecum of the West Indian manatee, *Trichechus manatus* (Mammalia, Sirenia)." *Zoomorphology* 104:67–78.

Soini, P. 1995. "Evaluación preliminar de la vaca marina (*Trichechus inunguis*)." In *Reporte Pacaya-Samiria, Informe no. 35. Investigaciones em Cahuana: 1980–1994*, ed. P. Soini, A. Tovar, and U. Valdez, 369–72. Lima: CDC-UNALM/FPCN/TNC.

Soini, P., L.A. Sicchar, G. Gil, A. Fachin, R. Pezo, and M. Chumbe. 1996. *Una evaluación de la fauna silvestre y su aprovechamiento de la Reserva Nacional Pacaya Samiria, Peru*. Documento Tecnico no. 24, IIAP.

Sokol, D. 2007. "Monopolists without borders: The institutional challenge of international antitrust in a global Gilded Age." *Berkeley Business Law Journal* 4:37.

Sorice, M.G., C.S. Shafer, and D. Scott. 2003. "Managing endangered species within the use/preservation paradox: Understanding and defining harassment of the West Indian Manatee (*Trichechus manatus*)." *Coastal Management* 31:319–38.

Sorice, M.G., C.S. Shafer, and R.B. Ditton. 2006. "Managing endangered species within the use-preservation paradox: The Florida manatee (*Trichechus manatus latirostris*) as a tourism attraction." *Environmental Management* 37:69–83.

Sorice, M.G., R.O. Flamm, and S. McDonald. 2007. "Factors influencing behavior in a boating speed zone." *Coastal Management* 35:357–74.

Sosovele, H., 2000. "East African Marine Ecoregion: Socioeconomic reconnaissance." WWF Tanzania Program Office, Dar es Salaam, Tanzania, Africa.

Soulé, M.E., 1985. "What is conservation biology?" *BioScience* 35:727–34.

———. 1991. "Conservation: Tactics for a Constant Crisis." *Science* 253:744–50.

Spellman, A.C. 1999. "Manatee entanglements in fishing gear and plastic debris." Abstract. 13th Biennial Conference on the Biology of Marine Mammals, Wailea, Hawaii.

Spiegelberger, T., and U. Ganslosser. 2005. "Habitat analysis and exclusive bank feeding of the Antillean manatee (*Trichechus manatus manatus* L. 1758) in the Coswine Swamps of French Guiana, South America." *Tropical Zoology* 18:1–12.

Sprent, J. 1981. "Ascaridoid nematodes of sirenians: The Heterocheilinae redefined." *Journal of Helminthology* 54:309–27.

Springer, M.S., R.W. DeBry, C. Douady, H. M. Amrine, O. Madsen, W. W. de Jong, and M. J. Stanhope. 2001. "Mitochondrial versus nuclear gene sequences in deep-level Mammalian phylogeny reconstruction." *Molecular Biology and Evolution* 18:132–43.

Srichai, N., S. Boromthanarat, and B. Chaijaroenwatana. 1994. "A historical perspective of the resources and issues of Pak Phanang Bay, southern Thailand." *Hydrobiologia* 285:283–85.

St. Aubin, D.J., J.R. Geraci, and V.J. Lounsbury. 1996. "Workshop summary and recommendations." In *Rescue, Rehabilitations and Release of Marine Mammals: An Analysis of Current Views and Practices*, ed. D.J. St. Aubin, J.R. Geraci, and V.J. Lounsbury, 1–24. NOAA Technical Memorandum NMFS-OPR-8.

Stavros, H-C.W., R.K. Bonde, and P.A. Fair. 2008. "Concentrations of trace elements in blood and skin tissue of the Florida manatee (*Trichechus manatus latirostris*)." *Marine Pollution Bulletin* 56:1221–25.

Steidinger, K.A., J.H. Landsberg, C.R. Tomas, and G.A. Vargo, eds. 2004. "Harmful algae 2002." Tallahassee: Florida Fish and Wildlife Conservation Commission, Florida Institute of Oceanography, and Intergovernmental Oceanographic Commission of UNESCO.

Stern, G.A., C.R. Macdonald, D. Armstrong, B. Dunn, C. Fuchs, L. Harwood, D.C.G. Muir, and B. Rosenberg. 2005. "Spatial trends and factors affecting variation of organochlorine contaminants levels in Canadian Arctic beluga (*Delphinapterus leucas*)." *Science of the Total Environment* 351–52:344–68.

Stockholm Declaration of the United Nations Conference on the Human Environment. http://www.unep.org/Documents.Multilingual/Default.asp?DocumentID=97&ArticleID=1503&l=en.

Stockin, K., D. Lusseau, V. Binedell, N. Wiseman, and M.B. Orams. 2008. "Tourism affects the behavioural budget of the common dolphin *Delphinus* sp. in the Hauraki Gulf, New Zealand. *Marine Ecology Progress Series* 355:287–95.

Stoddart, D.R. 1971. "Pinnipeds or sirenians at western Indian Ocean islands." *Journal of Zoology* 167:207–17.

Storelli, M.M., and G.O. Marcotrigiano. 2002. "Subcellular distribution of heavy metals in livers and kidneys of *Stenella coeruleoalba* and *T. truncatus* from the Mediterranean Sea." *Marine Pollution Bulletin* 44:71–79.

Strindberg, S., and S.T. Buckland. 2004. "Zigzag survey designs in line transect sampling." *Journal of Agricultural, Biological, and Environmental Statistics* 9:443–61.

Sun, J. 1999. "Marine mammals from the coastal waters of Guangxi, China." *Journal of Guangxi Academy of Sciences* 15:76–80.

Supanwanid, C. 1996. "Recovery of seagrass *Halophila ovalis* after grazing by dugong." In *Seagrass Biology: Proceedings of an International Workshop*, 25–29 January, Rottnest Island, Western Australia, ed. J. Kuo, R.C. Phillips, D.I. Walker, and H. Kirkman, 315–18. Nedlands: Faculty of Science, University of Western Australia.

Sutaria, D., and, and T. Jefferson. 2004. "Records of Indo-Pacific humpback dolphins (*Sousa chinensis*, Osbeck, 1765) along the coasts of India and Sri Lanka: An overview." *Aquatic Mammals* 30:125–36.

Sykes, S. 1974. "How to save the mermaids." *Oryx* 12: 465–70.

Takara, K. 1984. "Ningyo to ohsama (Mermaid and king)." In *Okinawa rekishi monogatari* (Okinawa history), ed. K. Takara, 45–46. Naha, Okinawa: Hirugisha.

Tas'an, I., A. Sumitro, and S. Hendrokusumo. 1979. "Some biological notes of two male dugongs in captivity at the Jaya Ancol Oceanarium, Jakarta." Jakarta, Jaya Ancol Oceanarium (Gelanggang Samudra Jaya Ancol). 30 pp.

Tautz, D. 1989. "Hypervariability of simple sequences as a general source for polymorphic DNA markers." *Nucleic Acid Research* 17:6463–71.

Taylor, C.R. 2006. "A survey of Florida springs to determine accessibility to Florida manatees (*Trichechus manatus latirostris*): Developing a sustainable thermal network." Final report to U.S. Marine Mammal Commission, Bethesda, Maryland. http://www.mmc.gov/reports/workshop/pdf/taylorFLspringsreport.pdf.

Taylor, C.R., J. Reynolds, and A. Brautigam. 2006. "Support of the SSG Sirenian Symposium and IUCN Red List Assessment, Ninth International Mammalogical Congress, Sapporo, Japan." Final report to Conservation International Foundation.

Taylor, M.A. 2000. "Functional significance of bone ballast in the evolution of buoyancy control strategies by aquatic tetrapods." *Historical Biology* 14:15–31.

Tennent, J.E. 1859. *Ceylon: An Account of the Island, Physical, Historical and Topographical with Notices of the Natural History, Antiquities and Productions*. Vol. 2. London: Longman, Green, Longman and Roberts.

Thai Department of Fisheries. 2000. http://www.fisheries.go.th/dof_eng/contents.htm.

Thayer, G.W., K.A. Bjorndal, J.C. Ogden, S.L. Williams, and J.C. Zieman. 1984. "Role of larger herbivores in seagrass communities." *Estuaries* 7:351–76.

Thesiger, W. 1959. *Arabian Sands*. Middlesex, U.K.: Penguin.

Thompson, K. 2002. "Molecular gender identification in Paenungulates: Same as other mammals?" Honors thesis, James Cook University, Townsville, Australia.

Thompson, W.L. 2004. *Sampling Rare or Elusive Species*. Washington, D.C.: Island Press.

Tieszen, L.L., T.W. Boutton, K.G. Tesdahl, and N.A. Slade. 1983. "Fractionation and turnover of stable carbon isotopes in animal tissues: Implications for d13C analysis of diet." *Oecologia* 57:32–37.

Tieszen, L.L., and T. Fagre. 1993. "Effects of diet quality and composition on the isotopic composition of respiratory CO_2, bone collagen, bioapatite, and soft tissues." In *Prehistoric Human Bone: Archaeology at the Molecular Level*, ed. J.B. Lambert and G. Grupe, 123–35. New York: Springer.

Tikel, D. 1997. "Using a genetic approach to optimize dugong (*Dugong dugon*) conservation management." Ph.D. diss., James Cook University, Townsville, Australia.

Tilman, D. 2000. "Causes, consequences and ethics of biodiversity." *Nature* 405:208–11.

Timm, R.M., V.L. Albuja, and B.L Clauson. 1986. "Ecology, distribution, harvest, and conservation of the Amazonian manatee *Trichechus inunguis* in Ecuador." *Biotropica* 18:150–56.

Timm, R.M., L. Albuja and B.L. Clauson. 1989. "Siona hunting techniques for the larger aquatic vertebrates in Amazonian Ecuador." *Studies on Neotropical Fauna and the Environment*, 24:1–7.

Tirira, D. 2000. *Libro Rojo de los mamíferos del Ecuador*. Quito, Ecuador: UICN.

———. 2001. *Libro Rojo de los mamíferos del Ecuador*. Serie Libros Rojos del Ecuador, tomo 1: Publicación Especial sobre los mamíferos del Ecuador 4. Quito: SIMBIOE/EcoCiencia/Min. Ambiente/UICN.

Toma, T. 1999. "Ryukyu rettou no umikusa: Shurui to bunpu. (Seagrasses of Ryukyu Archipelago: Species and distribution)." *Okinawa Seibutsu Gakkaishi* (Biological magazine of Okinawa) 37:75–92.

Toman, J. 1992. "Quasi-legal standards and guidelines for protecting human rights." In *Guide to International Human Rights Practice*, 2nd edition, ed. H. Hannum, 192. Leiden, Netherlands: Hotei Publishing.

Tomlinson, P.B. 1980. Leaf morphology and anatomy in seagrasses. In *A Handbook of Seagrass Biology*, ed. R.C. Phillips and C.P. McRoy, 7–28. New York: Garland STMP Press.

Tringali, M.D., S. Seyoum, S.L. Carney, M.C. Davis, M.A. Rodriguez-Lopez, J.E. Reynolds III, and E. Haubold. 2008. "Eighteen new polymorphic microsatellite markers for the endangered Florida manatee, *Trichechus manatus latirostris*." *Molecular Ecology Resources* 8:328–31.

Tripp, K.M., J.P. Verstegen, C.J. Deutsch, R.K. Bonde, M. Rodriguez, B. Morales, D.L. Schmitt, and K.E. Harr. 2008. "Validation of a serum immunoassay to measure progesterone and diagnose pregnancy in the West Indian manatee (*Trichechus manatus*)." *Theriogenology* 70:1030–40.

Trono, R.B. 1995. "Results of a dugong (*Dugong dugon*) survey in the Philippines." Proceedings of the Mermaid Symposium, 15–17 November, Toba, Japan.

Tuấn, P.N. 2003. "Dugong: The marine mammal remaining in Kien Giang Province, and listed in the Red Data Book of Vietnam." In *Proceedings of the Workshop on the Conservation of the Dugong and Seagrass Habitats of Vietnam*, ed N. Cox, T.C. Khuong, and E. Hines, 20–21 January 2003, Hanoi, Vietnam. World Wildlife Fund Indochina Programme.

Tun, T., and A.D. Ilangakoon. 2006. "Capacity building and preliminary assessment on dugong (*Dugong dugon*) occurrence off the Rakhine coast of Myanmar." Report to the Society for Marine Mammalogy.

Tuross, N. 1994. "The biochemistry of ancient DNA in bone." *Cellular and Molecular Life Sciences* 50:530–35.

Turvey, S.T., R.L. Pitman, B.L. Taylor, J. Barlow, T. Akamatsu, L.A. Barrett, X. Zhao, R.R. Reeves, B.S. Stewart, K. Wang, Z. Wei, X. Zhang, L.T. Pusser, M. Richlen, J.R. Brandon, and D. Wang. 2007. "First human-caused extinction of a cetacean species?" *Biological Letters* 3:537–40.

Uchida, S. 1994. "The dugong." In *Base Data of Japanese Rare Wild Aquatic Organisms*, ed. S. Odate, 569–83. Tokyo, Japan: Fisheries Agency and Japanese Association for Conservation of Aquatic Resources.

Ulloa Gómez, J.A. 2004. "Amazonian manatee (*Trichechus inunguis*) conservation in the Pacaya Samiria National Reserve, Peru: Implications for protected area management." M.Sc. thesis, Durrell Institute of Conservation and Ecology, University of Kent, Canterbury, U.K.

Underwood, A.J. 1997. *Experiments in Ecology: Their Logical Design and Interpretation Using Analysis of Variance*. Cambridge, U.K.: Cambridge University Press.

UNEP, United Nations Environment Programme. 2002. "Ridding the world from POPs." UNEP Chemicals, Geneva, Switzerland.

———. 2008a. "Action plan for the conservation of marine mammals in the Wider Caribbean Region." http://www.cep.unep.org/publications-and-resources/promotional-material/publications/spaw/mmap/at_download/file.

———. 2008b. "Memorandum of Understanding Concerning the Conservation of the Manatee and Small Cetaceans of Western Africa and Macronesia." Convention on the Conservation of Migratory Species of Wild Animals (CMS): http://www.ecolex.org/server2.php/libcat/docs/TRE/Multilateral/En/TRE146853.pdf.

———. 2009. "About the Cartagena Convention." http://www.cep.unep.org/cartagena-convention/.

UNEP/Regional Seas Program. 2008. "Regional Seas Programme." http://www.unep.org/regionalseas/.

UNESCAP, United Nations Economic and Social Commission for Asia and the Pacific. 2009. "Macroeconomic Update," 1 August 2009. http://www.unescap.org/publications/detail.asp?id=1341.

Uni, K. 2003. "Okinawa-ken no jugon hokaku toukei (Harvest report of dugong, *Dugong dugon*, in Okinawa prefecture)." *Bulletin of Nago Museum* 11:1–14.

United Nations. 1992. "The Rio Declaration on Environment and Development." Adopted 14 June 1992, United Nations Conference on Environment and Development, Rio de Janeiro, 3–14 June. UN Doc. A/CONF.151/5/Rev. 1.

———. 2003. *United Nations List of Protected Areas*. Gland, Switzerland: IUCN, and Cambridge, U.K.: UNEP World Conservation Monitoring Centre.

Uri, J., A.A. Yaptinchay, R.B. Trono, and N. Dumaup. 1998. "Monitoring of *Dugong dugon* in Dimakya Island, Palawan, Philippines." WWF Philippines Research Paper no. 8, Series of 1998. Quezon City: WWF-Philippines.

USFWS, U.S. Fish and Wildlife Service. 2000. "Florida manatees and warm water: Proceedings of the warm-water workshop, Jupiter, Florida, August 24–25, 1999." U.S. Fish and Wildlife Service, Jacksonville, Florida.

———. 2001. "Florida manatee recovery plan, *Trichechus manatus latirostris*, third revision." U.S. Fish and Wildlife Service. Atlanta, Georgia. http://northflorida.fws.gov/Manatee/manatees.htm.

———. 2007. "West Indian manatee (*Trichechus manatus*) 5-year review: Summary and evaluation." U.S. Fish and Wildlife Service. Jacksonville, Florida, and Boquerón, Puerto Rico.

U.S. Geological Survey. 2005. Sirenia Project files, Gainesville, Florida.

U.S. Marine Mammal Commission. 2001. "Annual report to Congress." U.S. Marine Mammal Commission, Bethesda, Maryland.

———. 2008. "Annual report to Congress 2007." U.S. Marine Mammal Commission, Bethesda, Maryland.

Utreras B., V., and V. Robushi. 1995. "Los últimos manatíes amazónicos." *El Observador Informativo* 7:1–3.

Valade, J.A., G. Bossart, K. Frohlich, L. Lefebvre, A.A. Mignucci-Giannoni, D. Murphy, J. Pearson, and J. Powell. 1999. "The manatee rescue, rehabilitation, and release program: An overview." In *Abstracts, Thirteenth Biennial Conference on the Biology of Marine Mammals*, November 1999, Maui, Hawaii, 191.

Valsecchi, E., and W. Amos. 1996. "Microsatellite markers for the study of cetacean populations." *Molecular Ecology* 5:151–56.

Van Bree, P.J., and M.D. Gallagher. 1977. "Catalogue de la collection des mammifères marin du Museum de Bordeaux." *Annales de la Societe des Sciences Naturelles de la Charente-Maritime* 6:289–307.

Vanzella-Khouri, A. 2008. "Protocol concerning specially protected areas and wildlife in the Wider Caribbean Region: A legal framework on biodiversity." SPAW Fact Sheet. http://www.cep.unep.org/cartagena-convention/spaw-protocol/spaw-factsheet-2008-e.pdf.

Varela R., and G.D. Bossart. 2005. "Evaluation of biochemical analytes in vitreous humor collected after death in West Indian manatees." *Journal of the American Veterinary Medical Association* 226:88–92.

Vasquez, E., and W. Wilbert. 1992. "The Orinoco: Physical, biological and cultural diversity of a major tropical alluvial river." In *The Rivers Handbook*, 1st edition, ed. P. Calow and G.E. Petts. London, U.K.: Blackwell Scientific Publications.

Vavra, M., and J.L. Holechek. 1980. "Factors influencing microhistological analysis of herbivore diets." *Journal of Range Management* 33:371–74.

Verhoeven, J.C. 2000. "Some reflections on cross-cultural interviewing." In *Cross-Cultural Case Study*, ed. C.J. Pole and R.G. Burgess, 1–20. New York: Elsevier Science.

Vetter, W., E. Scholz, C. Gaus, J.F. Müller, and D. Haynes. 2001. "Anthropogenic and natural organohalogen compounds in blubber of dolphins and dugongs (*Dugong dugon*) from northeastern Australia." *Archives of Environmental Contamination and Toxicology* 41:221–31.

Vianna, J.A., M. Marmontel, and F.R. Santos. 2002. "Filogeografia do peixe-boi marinho (*Trichechus manatus*) e peixe-boi amazônico (*Trichechus inunguis*)." 10ª [10th] Reunião de Trabalho de Especialistas em Mamíferos Aquáticos da América do Sul e 4º [4th] Congresso da Sociedade Latinoamericana de Especialistas em Mamíferos Aquáticos (SOLAMAC), 14–19 October, Valdívia, Chile.

Vianna, J.A., R.K. Bonde, S. Caballero, J.P. Giraldo, R.P. Lima, A.M. Clark, M. Marmontel, B. Morales-Vela, M.J. de Sousa, L. Parr, M. Rodríguez-Lopez, A.A. Mignucci-Giannoni, J. Powell, and F.R. Santos. 2006. "Phylogeography, phylogeny and hybridization in trichechid sirenians: Implications for manatee conservation." *Molecular Ecology* 15:433–47.

von Brandis, R., M. Aglae, S. Boniface, G. Esparon, S. Harryba, K. Isnard, A. Liljevic, D. Louang, M. Loustau-Lalanne, P. Lozé, T. Mahoune, O. Maurel, and U. Samedi. 2005. "Observations of dugong (*Dugong dugon*) at Aldabra atoll: Confirmation of Aldabra as a breeding site?" *Seychelles Island Foundation Newsletter* 7:7.

von Zharen, W.M. 1998. "Ocean ecosystem stewardship." *William & Mary Environmental Law & Policy Review* 1:23–24.

Vousden, D.H. 1985. "Dugong herd." *New Scientist* 1450:47.

Vreugdenhil, D. 2003. "Protected areas system planning and monitoring." http://library.wur.nl/wda/dissertations/dis3391.pdf.

Wade P.R. 1998. "Calculating limits to the allowable human-caused mortality of cetaceans and pinnipeds." *Marine Mammal Science* 14:1–37.

Wakai, Y., K. Hasegawa, S. Sakamoto, S. Asano, G. Watanabe, and K. Yaya. 2002. "Annual changes of urinary progesterone and estradiol-17β of the dugong (*Dugong dugon*) in captivity." *Zoological Science* 19:679–82.

Wake, J.A. 1975. "A study of the habitat requirements and feeding biology of the dugong, *Dugong dugon* (Müller)." Honours thesis, James Cook University, Townsville, Australia.

Wallace, A.R. 1972. *A Narrative of Travels on the Amazon and Rio Negro*. Orig. 1853; 2nd edition 1889; repr., New York: Dover Publications.

Wallace, R.L. 1994. "The Florida manatee recovery program: Organizational learning and a model for improving recovery programs." In *Endangered Species Recovery: Finding the Lessons, Improving the Process*, ed. T.W. Clark, R.P. Reading, and A.L. Clarke, 131–56. Washington, D.C.: Island Press.

Walls, G.L. 1942. *The Vertebrate Eye and Its Adaptive Radiation*. New York: Hafner.

Walsh, C.J., C.A. Luer, and D.R. Noyes. 2005. "Effects of environmental stressors on lymphocyte proliferation in Florida manatees, *Trichechus manatus latirostris*." *Veterinary Immunology and Immunopathology* 103:247–56.

Walsh, M.T., and G.D. Bossart. 1999. "Manatee medicine." In *Zoo and Wildlife Medicine*, ed. M.E. Fowler and R.E. Miller, 507–16. Philadelphia: W.B. Saunders.

Wamukoya, G.M., W.K. Ottichilo, and R.V. Salm. 1997. "Aerial surveys of dugongs in Ungwana Bay and the Lamu Archipelago, Kenya." Kenya Wildlife Service Technical Series Report no. 2. Kenya Wildlife Service, Mombasa.

Wang, H. 2008. "China funds protection of endangered sea cows. China View 10/13/2008." http://news.xinhuanet.com/english/2008-10/13/content_10188528.htm.

Wang, P., and J. Sun. 1986. "The distribution of dugong in coastal Chinese waters." *Acta Theriologica Sinica* 6:175–81 (in Chinese).

Ward, L.I., and B. Weigle. 1993. "To save a species: GIS for manatee research and management." *GIS World* 6:34–37.

Ward-Geiger, L.I. 1997. "Blubber depth and body condition indices in the Florida manatee (*Trichechus manatus latirostris*)." Masters thesis, University of South Florida, St. Petersburg.

Waycott, M., C.M. Duarte, T.J.B. Carruthers, R.J. Orth, W.C. Dennison, S. Olyarnik, A. Calladine, J.W. Fourqurean, K.L. Heck Jr., A.R. Hughes, G.A. Kendrick, W.J. Kenworthy, F.T.

Short, and S.L. Williams. 2009. "Accelerating loss of seagrasses across the globe threatens coastal ecosystems." *Proceedings of the National Academy of Sciences* 106:10377–81.

WCMC, World Conservation Monitoring Centre. 1991. "Gulf War impact on marine environment and species." http//scilib.ucsd.edu/sio/guide/zgulfwar.html.

Wearing, S., and J. Neil. 1999. *Ecotourism Impacts, Potentials, and Possibilities*. Oxford: Butterworth Heinemann.

Weber, D.S., B.S. Stewart, J.C. Garza, and N. Lehman. 2000. "An empirical genetic assessment of the severity of the northern elephant seal population bottleneck." *Current Biology* 10:1287–90.

Weeks, P., and J.M. Packard. 1997. "Acceptance of scientific management by natural resource dependent communities." *Conservation Biology* 11:236–45.

Weigle, B.L., I.E. Wright, M. Ross, and R. Flamm. 2001. "Movements of radio-tagged manatees in Tampa Bay and along Florida's west coast, 1991–1996." FMRI Technical Report TR-7. Florida Marine Research Institute, St. Petersburg.

Wellehan, J.F.X., A.J. Johnson, A.L. Childress, K.E. Harr, and R. Isaza. 2008. "Six novel gammaherpesviruses of Afrotheria provide insight into the early divergence of the Gammaherpesvirinae." *Veterinary Microbiology* 127:249–57.

Wells, R. 1991. "The role of long-term study in understanding the social structure of a bottlenose dolphin community." In *Dolphin Societies: Discoveries and Puzzles*, ed. K. Pryor and K.S. Norris, 199–225. Berkeley: University of California Press.

Wells, R.S., D.J. Boness, and G.B. Rathbun. 1999. "Behavior." In *Biology of Marine Mammals*, ed. J.E. Reynolds III and S.A. Rommel, 324–422. Washington, D.C.: Smithsonian Institution Press.

Wells, R.S., H.L. Rhinehart, L.J. Hansen, J.C. Sweeney, F.I. Townsend, R. Stone, D.R. Casper, M.D. Scott, A.A. Hohn, and T.K. Rowles. 2004. "Bottlenose dolphins as marine ecosystem sentinels: Developing a health monitoring system." *Ecohealth* 1:246–54.

Welsby T., 1905. *Schnappering and Fishing in the Brisbane River and Moreton Bay Waters*. Brisbane: Outridge Printing Company.

White, A., and H.P. Vogt. 2001. "Philippine coral reefs under threat: Lesson learned after 25 years of community-based reef conservation." *Marine Pollution Bulletin* 40:537–50.

White, A., C. Courtney, and A. Salamanca 2002. "Experience with marine protected area planning and management in the Philippines." *Coastal Management* 30:1–26.

White, G.C., and R.A. Garrott. 1980. *Analysis of Wildlife Radio-Tracking Data*. San Diego: Academic Press.

White, P.S., and L.D. Densmore. 1992. "Mitochondrial DNA isolation." In *Molecular Genetic Analysis of Populations: A Practical Approach*, ed. A.R. Hoelzel, 29–58. New York: IRL Press at Oxford University Press.

Whitehead, H. 2003. *Sperm Whales: Social Evolution in the Ocean*. Chicago: University of Chicago Press.

Whitehead, P.J.P. 1977. "The former southern distribution of New World manatees (*Trichechus* spp.)." *Biological Journal of the Linnean Society* 9:165–89.

———. 1978. "Registros antigos da presença do peixe-boi do Caribe (*Trichechus manatus*) no Brasil." *Acta Amazonica* 8:497–506.

Whiting, S.D. 1999. "Use of the remote Sahul Banks, northwestern Australia, by dugongs, including breeding females." *Marine Mammal Science* 15:609–15.

———. 2002. "Rocky reefs provide foraging habitat for dugongs in the Darwin region of northern Australia." *Australian Mammalogy* 24:147.

Whittington, M.W., C.M. António, M.S. Heasman, M. Meyers, and D. Stanwell-Smith. 1998. "Technical Report 6: Result Summary and Management Recommendations." *Marine Biological and Resource Use Surveys of the Quirimba Archipelago, Mozambique*. London: Society for Environmental Exploration, and Maputo: Ministry for the Coordination of Environmental Affairs.

Whyte, W.F. 1982. "Interviewing in field research." In *Field Research: A Sourcebook and Field Manual*, ed. R.G. Burgess, 111–22. London: Allen and Unwin.

Wiley, D.N., J.C. Moller, R.M. Pace, and C. Carlson. 2008. "Effectiveness of voluntary conservation agreements: Case study of endangered whales and commercial whale watching." *Conservation Biology* 22:450–57.

Willard, M., H. Tvedten, and G.H. Turnwald. 1999. *Small Animal Clinical Diagnosis by Laboratory Methods*. 3rd ed. Philadelphia: W.B. Saunders Company.

Williams, B., J. Nichols, and M. Conroy. 2002. *The Analysis and Management of Animal Populations*. San Diego, Calif.: Academic Press.

Williams, E.H. Jr., A.A. Mignucci-Giannoni, L. Bunkley-Williams, R.K. Bonde, C. Self-Sullivan, A. Preen, and V.G. Cockcroft. 2003. "Echeneid-sirenian associations, with information on sharksucker diet." *Journal of Fishery Biology* 63:1–8.

Williams, P.H., N.D. Burgess, and C. Rahbek. 2000. "Flagship species, ecological complementarity and conserving the diversity of mammals and birds in sub-Saharan Africa." *Animal Conservation* 3:249–60.

Wilson, A.R. 1991. *Environmental Risk: Identification and Management*, Boca Raton, Fla.: CRC Press.

Wilson, D.E. 1974. "Status report on manatees of Costa Rica." Unpublished report. U.S. Fish and Wildlife Service.

Wing, E.S., and S.J. Scudder. 1991. "The exploitation of animals." In *Cuello: An Early Maya Community*, ed. N. Hammond, 84–97. Cambridge, U.K.: Cambridge University Press.

Wong, A.W. 2008. "Monitoring oral temperature, heart rate, and respiration rate in field captured Florida and Antillean manatees (*Trichechus manatus latirostris* and *T. m. manatus*)." Masters thesis, University of Florida, Gainesville.

Woodruff, R.A., R.K. Bonde, J.A. Bonilla, and C.H. Romero. 2005. "Molecular identification of a papilloma virus from cutaneous lesions of captive and free-ranging Florida manatees." *Journal of Wildlife Diseases* 41:437–41.

World Bank. 1992. *World Development Report 1992: Development and The Environment.* Oxford: World Bank and Oxford University Press.

Wright, I.E., S.D. Wright, and J.M. Sweat. 1998. "Use of passive integrated transponder (PIT) tags to identify manatees (*Trichechus manatus latirostris*)." *Marine Mammal Science* 14:641–45.

Wright, I.E., J.E. Reynolds III, B.B. Ackerman, L.I. Ward, B.L. Weigle, and W.A. Szelistowski. 2002. "Trends in manatee counts and habitat use in Tampa Bay, 1987–1994: Implications for conservation." *Marine Mammal Science* 18:259–74.

Wright, S.D, B.B. Ackerman, R.K. Bonde, C.A. Beck, and D.J. Banowetz. 1995. "Analysis of watercraft-related mortality of manatees in Florida, 1979–1991." In *Population Biology of the Florida Manatee*, ed. T.J. O'Shea, B.B. Ackerman, and H.F. Percival. Washington, D.C.: National Biological Service Information and Technology Report 1.

WWF, World Wildlife Fund. 1983. "Dugongs, other marine life victims of Gulf oil spill." *WWF News* 24:1.

WWF EAME, Eastern African Marine Ecoregion Programme. 2004. "Towards a western Indian Ocean dugong conservation strategy: The status of dugongs in the western Indian Ocean region and priority conservation actions." Dar es Salam, Tanzania.

———. 2005. "Eastern African marine ecoregion conservation plan (2005–2009)." Dar es Salaam, Tanzania.

WWF Indochina. 2006. Dugong Action Plan. Hanoi, Vietnam.

Yamamuro, M., K. Aketa, and S. Uchida. 2004. "Carbon and nitrogen stable isotope ratios of the tissues and gut contents of a dugong from the temperate coast of Japan." *Mammal Study* 29:179–83.

Yin, T. 1971. "The dugong *Dugong dugon* (Müller) in Burmese waters." *Journal of the Bombay Natural History Society* 67 326–27.

Yoshida, M., N. Kouchi, and M. Nakaoka. 2003. "Shiminsanka niyoru Okinawa no umikusamoba no monitaringu chousa (Monitoring survey of seagrass bed by citizens in Okinawa)." *Japanese Journal of Conservation Ecology* 8:119–28.

Zacharias, M.A., and J.C. Roff. 2000. "An ecological framework for the conservation of marine biodiversity." *Conservation Biology* 14:1327–34.

———. 2001. "Use of focal species in marine conservation and management: A review and critique." *Aquatic Conservation: Marine and Freshwater Ecosystems* 2:59–76.

Zainal, A.J.M., F. Isa Al-Burshaid, P.R. Choudhury, and G.M.R. Abdulla. 2009. "Coastal development changes and the islands of Bahrain." In *Marine Atlas of Bahrain*, ed. R.A. Loughland and A.J.M. Zainal, 307–68. Manama, Bahrain: Geomatec.

Zeiller, W. 1992. *Introducing the Manatee.* Gainesville: University Press of Florida.

Zhang, D.X., and G.M. Hewitt. 2003. "Nuclear DNA analysis in genetic studies of populations: Practice, problems and prospects." *Molecular Ecology* 12:563–84.

Zhou K., X. Xu, and J. Tang. 2003. "Survey of the status of the dugong in the Beibu Gulf, China, with remarks on the Indian humpbacked dolphin (*Sousa plumbea*)." *Acta Theriologica Sinica* 23:21–26.

Zieman, J.C. 1982. "The ecology of the seagrasses of South Florida: A community profile." FWS/OBS-82/25, U.S. Fish and Wildlife Service, Washington, D.C.

Contributors

Nicole Adimey, a biologist with the U.S. Fish and Wildlife Service, currently manages the Manatee Rescue, Rehabilitation and Release Program.

Kanjana Adulyanukosol is senior marine biologist, Marine Endangered Species section, at the Marine and Coastal Resources Research Center (Upper Gulf), Samut Sakhon Province, Thailand. She has been researching dugongs since 1988.

Mohammed Al-Rumaidh is a researcher at the Bahrain Centre for Studies and Research.

Carolina Mattosinho de Carvalho Alvite works at the Centro Nacional de Pesquisa da Sociobiodiversidade Associada a Povos e Comunidades Tradicionais at the Instituto Chico Mendes de Conservação da Biodiversidade (ICMBio) in Brazil.

Lemnuel V. Aragones is associate professor at the University of the Philippines' Institute of Environmental Science and Meteorology in Diliman, Quezon City. He has more than 20 years' experience studying dugongs and cetaceans, primarily around the Philippine islands.

Nicole E. Auil-Gomez, an associate scientist for the Sea2Shore Alliance, has researched manatees in Belize since 1996. She has an M.S. in wildlife and fisheries sciences from Texas A&M University.

Sheri L. Barton is a senior biologist in the Manatee Research Program at Mote Marine Lab in Sarasota, Florida.

Cathy A. Beck, a wildlife biologist with the U.S. Geological Survey, Sirenia Project, has been conducting research on manatees since 1978. She is the project manager for the USGS-Manatee Individual Photo-identification System (MIPS).

Robert K. Bonde, research biologist with the U.S. Geological Survey, Sirenia Project, has been conducting research on the manatee for more than 30 years. He holds a courtesy professorship at the University of Florida, College of Veterinary Medicine, in Gainesville, Florida.

Gregory D. Bossart has spent the last 29 years working in clinical domestic, marine mammal, and avian medicine and wildlife pathology on a national and international basis. He is senior vice president and chief veterinary officer at the Georgia Aquarium in Atlanta, Georgia, where he oversees the animal care, pathology, research, and conservation programs.

Jim Brown has worked in conservation law enforcement for 30 years. He directs the Florida Fish and Wildlife Conservation Commission's Division of Law Enforcement.

Susana Caballero is assistant professor at the Laboratorio de Ecología Molecular de Vertebrados Acuáticos (LEMVA) in the Departamento de Ciencias Biológicas at the Universidad de los Andes, Bogotá, Colombia.

Jorge Calvimontes is a Ph.D. candidate at the Center for Environmental Studies and Research (NEPAM) at the University of Campinas (UNICAMP), São Paulo, Brazil, and a member of the Research Group of Amazonian Aquatic Mammals at Mamirauá Institute for Sustainable Development, Brazil.

Nataly Castelblanco-Martínez completed her Ph.D. in ecology and sustainable development in 2010 at El Colegio de la Frontera Sur, Mexico. She has been involved in aquatic mammal research in Latin America for more than 12 years.

Ann Marie Clark is scientific research manager at the Genetic Analysis Lab, Interdisciplinary Center for Biotechnology Research, at the University of Florida, Gainesville.

Mark T. Clementz, assistant professor at the University of Wyoming, is an expert in paleoecology and paleobiology through stable isotope analysis (i.e. C, N, O, Ca, and Sr).

Nick Cox lived and worked in Con Dao National Park in Vietnam between 2000 and 2002, developing conservation programs for marine turtles and dugongs. He currently coordinates the World Wildlife Fund's regional dry forests program and is based in Vientiane, Laos.

Himansu S. Das is a scientist in the Marine Endangered Species program at the Environment Agency–Abu Dhabi, United Arab Emirates.

Hans H. de Iongh is associate professor of conservation biology at the Institute of Environmental Sciences at Leiden University in the Netherlands, where he has worked since 1990. He has been guest professor with the research group for ecology and evolutionary biology at the University of Antwerp in Belgium since 2009.

Charles J. (Chip) Deutsch is an associate research scientist with the Florida Fish and Wildlife Conservation Commission. He has been actively engaged in applied research on the Florida manatee since 1994 and since 2002 has led FWC's Fish and Wildlife Research Institute program on the behavioral ecology of the Florida manatee.

Kirstin Dobbs is director of Strategic Advice in the Communications and Policy Coordination Branch at the Great Barrier Reef Marine Park Authority.

Haydée Domínguez Tejo is a scientific researcher at the Centro de Investigaciones de Biología Marina of the Universidad Autónoma de Santo Domingo. She is currently a Ph.D. student at Duke University, Durham, North Carolina, focusing on manatee research in the Dominican Republic.

Daryl P. Domning is professor of anatomy at Howard University, Washington, D.C. His research focuses on the evolution of sirenians.

Elrika D'souza is affiliated with the Nature Conservation Foundation in Mysore, India.

Holly Edwards received her doctorate in zoology from the University of Oklahoma in 1999. She has led the Florida Fish and Wildlife Conservation Commission's manatee aerial survey program since 2004.

Daniel Gonzalez-Socoloske is a Ph.D. candidate in ecology at Duke University. He has been working with manatees throughout North and Central America since 2004.

Ellen M. Hines is associate professor in the Department of Geography and Human Environmental Studies and director of the Marine and Coastal Conservation and Spatial Planning Center at San Francisco State University.

Amanda Hodgson is a postdoctoral research fellow in the Murdoch University Cetacean Research Unit in Western Australia. She is currently investigating new aerial survey technology.

Kazuko Ikeda is a research scientist at the Japan Wildlife Research Center. She has an M.Sc. in nature conservation biology from Kyushu University, Fukuoka, Japan.

Anouk Ilangakoon has been researching cetaceans and dugongs in Sri Lanka since the mid-1980s and is a member of the IUCN Cetacean Specialist Group. She is currently working on cetaceans in Sri Lanka and Southeast Asia.

Bharat Jethva (Ph.D.) is working with Green Support Services, Gujarat, India, as an ecologist. He specializes in endangered species conservation in India.

Ignacio Jiménez Pérez works as coordinator for endangered species recovery with the Conservation Land Trust in Argentina.

Sarita Kendall, a Brazilian-born geographer with master's degrees in economics and environmental education, has been working in Colombian Amazon communities since 1989.

Jeremy J. Kiszka completed his Ph.D. in marine biology in 2010; his doctoral work focused on the ecology and social structure of tropical delphinids. Since 2003 he has been involved in sirenian projects, particularly on endangered dugongs from eastern Africa. He currently works on the ecology, behavior, and conservation of top marine predators (including cetaceans and sharks), especially in the Indian Ocean.

Akoi Kouadio, West African manatee scientist and conservationist, coordinated the Wildlife Conservation Society's Coastal Wetland and Biodiversity Conservation Projects in Côte d'Ivoire. Dr. Kouadio died on 13 August 2009.

Donna Kwan is dugong program officer at the Abu Dhabi office of the UNEP/CMS Secretariat (United Nations Environmental Programme, Convention on Migratory Species) hosted by the Environment Agency Abu Dhabi (EAD).

Katherine S. LaCommare has studied manatees in Belize since 1998. She has a Ph.D. from the University of Massachusetts in Boston and is co-founder of Sirenian International, Inc.

Ivan Lawler is an assistant director in the Species Listing Section for the Department of the Environment, Water, Heritage and the Arts in Canberra, Australia. He is adjunct lecturer in the School of Earth and Environmental Science, James Cook University, Queensland Australia.

Regis Pinto de Lima is the marine protected area chief at the Tamoios Ecological Station, Paraty/RJ, in Brazil. He was the Peixe-Boi Project coordinator and Brazilian National Aquatic Mammals Center chief between 1996 and 2007.

Miriam Marmontel is a senior researcher with the Mamirauá Institute for Sustainable Development in western Brazil, where she leads the Aquatic Mammal Research Group.

Helene Marsh is dean of graduate research studies and distinguished professor of environmental science at James Cook University, Queensland, Australia. She has been studying dugongs for more than 30 years, is currently co-chair of the IUCN Sirenia Specialist Group, and is author of some 200 publications, including the UNEP status report on dugongs and a book on the ecology and conservation of the Sirenia published by Cambridge University Press in 2011.

Christopher D. Marshall is associate professor of marine biology and wildlife and fisheries science at Texas A&M University. He is interested in the ecological morphology, natural history, and evolutionary aspects of marine vertebrate foraging.

Brenda McDonald is affiliated with the School of Veterinary Science at the University of Queensland, Australia.

Antonio A. Mignucci-Giannoni is a biological oceanographer specializing in the biology, ecology, management, and conservation of marine mammals, particularly manatees, in the Caribbean. He is director of the Puerto Rico Manatee Conservation Center and research professor at the Inter American University of Puerto Rico, Bayamon Campus.

Eduardo Moraes-Arraut is a researcher at the Earth System Science Center of the National Institute for Space Research, Remote Sensing Division, in São José dos Campos, São Paulo, Brazil. He has worked with humpback whale bioacoustics and for the past 11 years has been working with the Amazonian manatee and its habitat through fieldwork and remote sensing.

Benjamín Morales-Vela is a senior scientist in the Department of Aquatic Ecology at ECOSUR research institute in Mexico. He has more than eighteen years' experience working with manatees in Mexico.

Catharine E. Muir has over 20 years' experience with species and habitat conservation, management, and environmental education in eastern Africa and is director of Sea Sense, an NGO focused on protecting turtles and dugongs in Tanzania.

Hiroshi Mukai is professor and division head at the Division of Integrated Coastal Management, Field Science Education and Research Center at Kyoto University in Japan.

Leon D. Olivera-Gómez, researcher and professor with the Biological Sciences Division of the State University of Tabasco (UJAT), Mexico, has been working with manatees in Mexico since 1990.

Alejandro Ortega-Argueta is based at the Instituto de Ecologia, AC, in Veracruz, Mexico. He has 15 years' experience working on marine mammal research and management in the Gulf of Mexico and the Caribbean Sea. He is a member of the Advisory Committee for Manatee Recovery in Mexico.

Leslee Parr is associate professor in the Department of Biological Sciences at San Jose State University in San Jose, California, where she teaches courses in conservation, evolution, and evolutionary genetics.

Vardhan Patankar is affiliated with the Nature Conservation Foundation in Mysore, India.

Sombat Poochaviranon is director of the Marine and Coastal Resources Research Center in the northern Gulf of Thailand.

Anthony Preen has been studying dugongs and cetaceans for over 20 years, mainly in Australia and in the Middle East. More recently he has worked for a government agency concerned with natural resource management in Australia.

Erin Pulster is a senior chemist at Mote Marine Laboratory, Sarasota, Florida.

James Reid is a biologist with the Sirenia Project at the Southeast Ecological Science Center, U.S. Geological Survey, in Gainesville, Florida.

John E. Reynolds III is the senior scientist and director of the Center for Marine Mammal and Sea Turtle Research at Mote Marine Laboratory, Sarasota, Florida.

Kari A. Rood is a research associate with the Florida Fish and Wildlife Conservation Commission. She has managed the Manatee Photo-identification Program within the FWC Research Institute since 2002.

Fernando C. Weber Rosas is a senior researcher at the Instituto Nacional de Pesquisas da Amazônia (INPA), Laboratório de Mamíferos Aquáticos, Brazil.

Leng Sam Ath trained in marine mammal research at the Phuket Marine Biological Center and works with the Cambodian Mekong Dolphin Conservation Project.

Fabrício R. Santos is professor and researcher in the Department of General Biology, Universidade Federal de Minas Gerais, Belo Horizonte, Brazil.

Caryn Self-Sullivan is president and co-founder of Sirenian International and adjunct faculty at Nova Southeastern University, Fort Lauderdale-Davie, Florida.

Shaoyong Lu is associate professor at the Chinese Research Academy of Environmental Sciences. He received a Ph.D. (2005) in environmental science and engineering from Tsinghua University.

James K. Sheppard is a conservation biologist at the San Diego Zoo Institute for Conservation Research. He has used GPS telemetry to research the spatial behaviors and habitat use of dugongs in Australia to inform conservation management.

Vera M. F. da Silva is a biologist specializing in the biology, ecology, management, and conservation of aquatic mammals in the Amazon. She is a senior researcher at the Laboratório de Mamíferos Aquáticos of the Instituto Nacional de Pesquisas da Amazônia (INPA) in Brazil and was president of the Associação Amigos do Peixe-boi (AMPA) between 2007 and 2011.

Parimal Solanki, research fellow at the Gujarat Ecological Education and Research Foundation, is investigating the status of dugongs in India as part of a project sponsored by the Ministry of Environment and Forests, Government of India.

Phay Somany trained in marine mammal research at the Phuket Marine Biological Center in Thailand and works with the Cambodian Mekong Dolphin Conservation Project.

Michael G. Sorice is assistant professor of natural resources recreation and human dimensions with the Department of Forest Resources and Environmental Conservation at Virginia Tech in Blacksburg.

Maria José de Souza Lopes is adjunct professor and researcher in the Department of Genetics, Universidade Federal de Pernambuco, Recife, Brazil.

M. Andrew Stamper is a veterinarian, board certified by the American College of Zoological Medicine with a specialty in aquatic animal medicine. He currently works in Florida at Epcot's The Seas as a research biologist and clinical veterinarian.

Dipani Sutaria just completed her doctorate on Irrawaddy dolphins in Chilika Lake, India, at James Cook University in Townsville, Australia.

Keith Symington is bycatch strategy leader for the World Wildlife Fund's Coral Triangle Programme. He worked previously with WWF's Greater Mekong Programme.

Tint Tun is a marine biologist and chairman of the Marine Science Association of Myanmar (MSAM).

Juliana A. Vianna is professor in the Departamento Ecología y Biodiversidad, Facultad de Ecología y Recursos Naturales, Universidad Andrés Bello in Santiago, Chile.

Wyndylyn M. von Zharen is professor of marine science at Texas A&M University, Galveston (TAMUG), holding graduate appointments in marine biology (TAMUG) and in wildlife and fisheries sciences and oceanography at Texas A&M University (TAMU).

Michelle Waycott is professor in the School of Earth and Environmental Sciences at the University of Adelaide and chief botanist at the State Herbarium of South Australia.

Dana L. Wetzel is a senior scientist and manager of the Aquatic Toxicology Program at Mote Marine Laboratory, Sarasota, Florida.

Xia Jiang is associate professor in the Lake Environmental Research Center at the Chinese Research Academy of Environmental Science.

Xin Jing is deputy director of the Department of Nature and Ecology Conservation at the Ministry of Environmental Protection of the Peoples' Republic of China.

Index

Page numbers in italics refer to illustrations; page numbers marked with "T" refer to tables.

Abundance, 4–5, 25, 102, 104
Accidental captures in gillnets, 49, 75, 81, 86, *88*, 96
Activity and mortality sensors, 123
Adimey, Nicole, 204
Adulyanukosol, Kanjana, 58, 224
Aerial surveys: aircraft and methods, 187, *187*; Arabia dugongs, 92, 93, *94*, 95; Australia and Pacific dugongs, 103; bias in, 192–93; conclusions, 195; contributions of, 186; design, 186–87; distributional, 189–90; Eastern African dugongs, 90; enhanced safety during, 193, 195; GIS for, *194*, 195; intensive search, 190–91; Japan dugongs, 77, 79; personnel, 188–89; race track pattern, 190; strengths and weaknesses, *189T*; Thailand dugongs, 60; transect, 191–92, *192*; utility and design, 186–95; West Indian manatees, 38, 44
Aguirre, Alonso, *202*
Aketa, K., 77
Algal blooms, 27, 29, 151–52
Al-Rumaidh, Mohammed, 91
Alvite, Carolina Mattosinho de Carvalho, 42–43, 204
Amazonian manatees (*Trichechus inunguis*), 115; accidental captures in gillnets, 49; captivity issues, 50–51; carrying capacity, 48; conservation, 52–53; cultural beliefs about, 51; diet, 5, 7; distribution, *7*, *47*, 48; in freshwater environment, 8; future outlook, 53; geographical and genetic distances associations, 173; grazing, 9; habitat, *7*, 48, 49–50; household and medicinal uses, 50; hunting, 48–49, 50; IUCN status, 7; legal status, 48; local, national, international uses, 50; manatee rehabilitation and captive programs, 215–17; overview, 47–48; with peduncle tagging equipment, *118*; population dynamics, 48; reproductive rates, 48; research, 51–53; rostral deflection, 5–6; seasonal migrations, 164; subspecies designation, 171–72; threats to, 48–51; value, 50; as vulnerable species, 48; West Indian manatees hybridization, 173, *174*
Ames, A. L., 15
Andaman Natural Resource Rehabilitation Project, 61
André, J. E., 132
Anthropogenic mortality, 26–27, 148–51, *149T*
Antillean manatee, *37*
"Antillean Manatees in Brazil," 42–43
Aquatic ecosystems, 4–11
Arabia dugongs: accidental captures in gillnets, 96; aerial surveys, 92, 93, *94*, 95; Arabian Gulf, 93–95, *95T*; awareness about, 98; climate change and, 96; conclusion, 98; conservation, 98; deliberate capture, 96; distribution, 92–94; habitat, *91*, 95–96; harvesting, 91; history and attitudes toward, 97; hunting, 97; legal status, 97–97; logistical constraints, 95; meat, 97; overview, 91–92; political boundaries, 95; pollution and, 96; protected area status, 97; Red Sea, 92–93, 95–96; research, 92, 98; research impediments, 94–95; restrictions, 94–95; threats to, 96–97; war and, 94
Arabian Gulf, 93–94, *95T*
Aragones, Lemnuel V., 1, 4, 58, 69, 221, 230
Argos system, 121
Asian dugongs: Cambodia, 62–63; China, 70–71; distribution, 58, *59*; future of, 76; India, 74–76; Indonesia, 66–68; Japan, 77–83; Myanmar, 65–66; Philippines, 68–70; Sri Lanka, 72–74; Thailand, 59–62; threats to, 58–59; Vietnam, 63–65
Ath, Leng Sam, 58
Auil-Gomez, Nicole E., 204
Australia and Pacific dugongs: abundance, 102, 104; aerial surveys, 103; cultural significance, 100–101; distribution, 102; habitat, 99; hunting, 100; indigenous peoples and, 100–101; legal protection, 101–2; live stranding or mortality causes, *105T*; movements, 102–3; overview, 99; research, 102–5; response to declines, 103; summary, 105

Bachteler, D., 18
Bacteriology, 146
Bahrain Centre for Studies and Research (BCSR), 92
Baltazar, R., 69
Barton, Sheri L., 32
Bauer, G. B., 16
BCSR. *See* Bahrain Centre for Studies and Research
Beasley, I., 62
Beaufort Scale, *182T*
Beck, Cathy A., 32, 126, 133
Becton-Dickinson's anaerobic specimen collector, 146
Behavioral plasticity, 35
Belitsky, D. W., 39
Belize, 38, 213
Benitez, Marco, *202*
Benjamin, S., 65
Bertram, Colin, 37
Bertram, Kate Ricardo, 37
Bioclimate Models (BIOCLIM), 162, 164–65
Biomarker assessment, 200
Blood samples, *144T*, *145*, 145–46
Boat-based surveys: applications and limitations, *185T*; conclusion, 185; crafts and procedures, 179, 181–82; dedicated boat, 182–83; magnification devices, *183T*; opportunistic, 184; overview, 179; sighting map, *183*; techniques, 182–84. *See also* Land-based surveys
Bonde, R. K., *134*
Bones: dugongs, 15, 86, 87; manatees, 15, 42, 45, 57
Bossart, G. D., 146
Brazil, 42–43, 50–53; manatee rehabilitation and captive programs, *211*, 214–17, *215*, *216*

Brazilian Institute for the Environment and Renewable Natural Resources (IBAMA), 43, 50–52
Brevetoxicosis, *148T*, 151–52
Brown, Jim, 30
Budiono, 67

Caballero, Susana, 168
Calvimontes, Jorge, 109, 115
Cambodia, 62–63
Captivity, xiii, 10; Amazonian manatees, 50–51; manatees, 17, 52. *See also* Manatee rehabilitation and captive programs
Caribbean-wide Marine Mammal Action Plan, 15
Carr, T., 44
Carrying capacity, 14, 33, *34T*, 35, 48
"Case Study: Evaluating Antillean Manatee Habitat in the Alvarado Lagoon System, Mexico," 166
"Case Study: Seasonal Migrations of Amazonian Manatees," 164
"Case Study: Using Generalized Linear Models for Antillean Manatee Habitat in Bahia de Chetumal," 165
"Case Study: Videography, Near-Infrared Spectroscopy and GIS for Habitat Assessment," 163
Castelblanco-Martinez, Nataly, 179
Cantanhede, 172, 173
CBD. *See* Convention on Biological Diversity
Centro de Pesquisa e Preservaçao de Mamíferos Aquáticos (CPPMA), 49, 51
Chambers, M. R., 111
"Chetumal Bay Manatee Protected Area in Mexico," 228
China, 70–72
CIBIMA-UASD. *See* Marine Biology Research Center of the Autonomous University of Santo Domingo
CITES. *See* Convention on International Trade of Endangered Species
Clark, Marie, 33
Clean Water Act, 27
Clementz, Mark T., 126
Climate change, xiii, 96
CMS, Bonn Convention. *See* Convention on the Conservation of Migratory Species of Wild Animals
CMS. *See* Convention of Migratory Species
Cold stress syndrome (CSS), 151, 153
Collaboration, in conservation, 250–51
Colombia, 53, 225; manatee rehabilitation and captive programs, 213–314

"Communities in the Colombian Amazon," 225
Community conservation: conflicts in, 226–27; cultural context, 223–24; education in, 224–26; overview, 221–22; summary, 227; working in communities, 222–23; work sequence, 223
Conservation: Amazonian manatees, 52–53; Arabia dugongs, 98; collaboration in, 250–51; in developing countries, 246–53; Eastern African dugong strategies, 89–90; endangered species process, *246*; flagship species, 248–49; Florida manatees, 35; genetics and demography implications, 173–74, 177–78; indicator species, 250; integrated framework, *247*; IUCN, 1–2; keystone species, 249; K-strategists, 14; manatees, 2; needs, 53; protected areas in, 251; scientists in developing countries, 243–45; sirenian, xiii–xiv; strategies, 3; summary, 251–53; umbrella species, 249–50; West Indian manatees, 36. *See also* Community conservation
Convention on Biological Diversity (CBD), 237–38
Convention on the Conservation of Migratory Species of Wild Animals (CMS, Bonn Convention), 237
Convention on International Trade of Endangered Species (CITES), 41, 60, 86, 101, 236–37
Convention of Migratory Species (CMS), 61
Convention for the Protection of the World Cultural and National Heritage, 101
Costa Rica, 44–45
Countercurrent heat exchangers, 12, *13*
"Counting Manatees for Their Own Protection," 180
Cox, N., 58, 63–64
CPPMA. *See* Centro de Pesquisa e Preservaçao de Mamíferos Aquáticos
Craig, B. A., 25, 190, 192
CSS. *See* Cold stress syndrome
Cultivation grazing, 10
Cultural significance: Australia and Pacific dugongs, 100–101; Cambodia dugongs, 63; China dugongs, 72; India dugongs, 76; Indonesia dugongs, 68; Japan dugongs, 81–82; Myanmar dugongs, 66; Sri Lanka dugongs, 74; Vietnam dugongs, 64
Cytology, 146–47

Dampier, William, 47
Das, H. S., 74, 91
Da Silva, Vera M. F., 204
Dayton, P. K., 14
DDT, 196, 198, 201
Dehnhardt, G., 18
De Iongh, Hans H., 58, 67
De Lima, Regis Pinto, 204
Demography. *See* Genetics and demography
Deutsch, Charles J., 23
Developing countries: conservation framework, 246–53; genetics and demography in, 177–78; law, 235–42; scientists in conservation, 243–45; tagging and movement in, 124–25
Dey, S. C., 74
Diet: Amazonian manatee, 5, *7*; dugongs, 4–7; Florida manatees, 8; manatees, 6–7, *7*; in marine environments, 5–8; seagrasses as, 5–11; sirenians, 7, *7*; Steller's sea cow, *7*, 7–8; West African manatee, 5, *7*; West Indian manatee, 5–6, *7*. *See also* Grazing
Digital Acoustic Recording Tag (D-tag), 123
Disease, 151, *152*
Distribution: Amazonian manatees, 7, *47*, 48; Arabia dugongs, 92–94; Asian dugongs, 58, *59*; Australia and Pacific dugongs, 102; Cambodia dugongs, 62; China dugongs, 71; dugongs, 4–5, *5*, *7*; Eastern African dugongs, 84–86, *85*; Florida manatees, 23–25, *24*; India dugongs, 74–75; Indonesia dugongs, 67; Japan dugongs, 78–80; manatees, 4–5, *5*, *7*; Myanmar dugongs, 65; Philippine dugongs, 69; sirenians, 4, *5*, *7*; Sri Lanka dugongs, 72–73, *73*; Steller's sea cow, *7*; Thailand dugongs, 60; Vietnam dugongs, 64; West African manatees, *7*, 36–37, *37*, 54, *55*; West Indian manatees, *7*, 38–39, *40T*
Dobbs, Kirstin, 99
Domínguez, H. M., 39
Dominican Republic manatee rehabilitation and captive programs, 212
Dominique, Lela, 56
Domning, Daryl, 4, 243
Do no harm principle, 28
Drowning, 150–51
D'souza, Elrika, 58
D-tag. *See* Digital Acoustic Recording Tag
Dugong Network Okinawa, 78
Dugongs: abundance, 4–5; allelic diversity, *177T*; bones, 15, 86, 87; China

research, 72; dentition, 5; diet, 4–7; distribution, 4–5, *5*, *7*; feeding trail, *8*, 77, *78*; future of, xiv; genetics and demography, 175–77; grazing, 9; grazing optimization hypothesis and, 10–11; habitat, 7; haplotypes, *176*, 177; hunting, 59, 64, 70, 79; IUNC status, *7*; life history attributes, 14; meat, 73, 82; medicines, 60–64, 66, 71, 82; migration and interbreeding, 176–77; molecular aging, 175; molecular sexing, 175; mtDNA phylogeographic analysis, 176–77; oil, 15, 71, 75, 86, 87, 100; pollutants found in, 15; population structure, 175; re-grazing, 10; reproduction, 13; rostral deflection, 5–6; in Southeast Asia, 1; study, xiii; tusks, 6, 18; Vietnam research, 64–65; weight, 4. *See also* Arabia dugongs; Asian dugongs; Australia and Pacific dugongs; Eastern African dugongs

"Dugongs along the Andaman Coast of Thailand," 111

"Dugong Uses and Myths," 87

Dunshea, G. J., 175

Durand, J., 47

Eastern African dugongs: accidental captures in gillnets, 86, *88*; aerial surveys, 90; conservation strategies, 89–90; distribution, 84–86, *85*; endangered, 90; exploitation for meat, 86; habitat assessment, 89; habitat destruction, 86–87; lack of environmental concern for, 88; legal status, 86; local culture and beliefs about, 88; meat, 88; mother-calf pairs, 90; overview, 84; political apathy toward, 87; population pressure, 86; population status, 85–86; regional issues, 87–88; research funding, 88; research priorities, 89; summary, 90; threats to, 86–88, *87T*

ECG. *See* Electrocardiography

EC-OCEAN database, 45

Ecotourism, 28, 70

Ecuador, 52, 53

Edwards, Holly, 186, 192

Electrocardiography (ECG), 141

Endangered species, 3; conservation process, *246*; history, 2; legislation, 29, 31

Endangered Species Act (ESA), 29, 31

Environmental Protection Agency (EPA), 196–97

Epibionts, 142, *154*

ESA. *See* Endangered Species Act

Facial morphology, 5

Falours, Samuel, 66

Feeding trails, 8, 77, *78*

Fernandes, L., 232

FIBA. *See* Fondation Internationale du Banc d'Arguin

Flamm, R. O., 189

Florida Fish and Wildlife Conservation Commission (FWC), 30, 32

Florida manatees (*Trichechus manatus latirostris*), *134*; anthropogenic mortality, 26–27; carrying capacity, 33–35; conservation, 35; crushing accidents, 27; diet, 8; entrapment, 27; habitat loss and degradation, 27; law enforcement and, 30; legal status, 29–31; management efforts, 31, *34T*; metabolic rates, 25; MIPS database, 45; photo-ID, 32, *136*, 151; population, 23, 25–26, 29, *34T*; range and distribution, 23–25, *24*; reproduction, 13; research efforts and needs, 31–35, *34T*; size, 18; status and conservation issues, 23–35; subpopulations, 25–26; successes and challenges, 35; threats to, 27, 29; tourism into ecotourism, 28; vital rates, *34T*; in warm-water network, *34T*; watercraft collisions, 27, 33; yearly count, 23

Florida Manatee Sanctuary Act (FMSA), 29, 31

FMSA. *See* Florida Manatee Sanctuary Act

Fondation Internationale du Banc d'Arguin (FIBA), 57

Fontana, A., 114

Food habits determination: by direct examination, *126*, 126–28; field methods and sample preparation, 130–31; NIRS, 126, 131–32; overview, 126; stable isotopes analysis, 128–30, *129T*, *130*, *131T*; summary, 132. *See also* Diet

Freeze bands, 133, *134*, *135T*

Frey, J. H., 114

FWC. *See* Florida Fish and Wildlife Conservation Commission

GAM. *See* Generalized Additive Models

Garcia-Rodriguez, A. I., 171, 172

Gastrointestinal tract (GI), 126–28

Generalized Additive Models (GAMs), 162, 164

Generalized Linear Models (GLMs), 162, 165

General summary of the distribution, habitats, and diet of sirenians, *7T*

Genetics and demography: in developing countries, 177–78; dugongs, 175–77; handling animal tissue, *168–70*; implications for conservation and management, 173–74, 177–78; manatees, 171–74; molecular aging, 170–71; molecular sexing, 170; molecular techniques, 168; mtDNA, 168–70, 172, *172*, *173*; SSRs, 170; terms and definitions, *170–71*

Geographic information system (GIS), 120, 159, 163, 167, 189; for aerial surveys, *194*, 195

Gerber, L. R., 229

GI. *See* Gastrointestinal tract

Giant otters, 2

Gillnets. *See* Accidental captures in gillnets

GIS. *See* Geographic information system

GLM. *See* Generalized Linear Models

Global Positioning System (GPS), 119

Gohar, H.A.F., 92

Gonzalez-Socoloske, Daniel, 179, 180–81

GPS. *See* Global Positioning System

GPS tags, 121–22, *122*

Grazing, 8–11

Grazing optimization hypothesis, 10–11

Grech, A., 104, 229

Guyana manatee rehabilitation and captive programs, 214

Habitat: Amazonian manatees, *7*, 48, 49–50; Arabia dugongs, *91*, 95–96; assessment, 2; assessment for Eastern African dugongs, 89; Australia and Pacific dugongs, *99*; degradation in Japan, 81; dugongs, *7*; Eastern African dugongs, 86–87; Florida manatees, 27; loss, 3, 27; manatees, *7*, 26; sirenians, *7*; Steller's sea cow, *7*; West African manatees, *7*; West Indian manatees, *7*, 36

Habitat delineation and assessment: GIS, 159, 163, 167; habitat requirements, 157–58; HSI, 159; limitations and advantages, 167; overview, 157; possible biases, 166–67; procedures, 158; quantitative modeling, 162–66; remote sensing, 159–62; satellite sensors, *160T*, 160–62, *161T*; variables and instruments, *158T*

Habitat Sustainability Index (HSI), 159

Halodule, 5, 6, 9–11, 128

Halophila, 6, 9, 9–11, 79

Handling animal tissue, *168–70*

Haplotypes, *176*, 177

Hard law, 236–37

Harvey, C. A., 146

Haynes, D., 200

Health assessment, West Indian Manatees: abdomen, 143; bacteriology, 146; blood samples, 144T, 145, 145–46; conclusion, 147; cytology, 146–47; data sheet, 140; digestive system, 143; ECG monitoring, 141; external examination, 140–41; feces, 143; hematology and blood chemistries, 143–44, 144T; interpretations, 146; microbiology, 146–47; mouth, 143; mycology, 146; overview, 139; physical examination form, 140; skin and epibionts, 142; urinary and reproductive systems, 142–43; virology, 146; vital signs, 141–42
Heinsohn, George, 102
Hematology and blood chemistries, 143–44, 144T
Herbivory, 8–9, 24. See also Grazing
Hertwig's solution, 126, 127, 127–28
Hindgut digesters, 18
Hines, Ellen, xiii, 58, 63, 65, 111, 246
Hispaniola, 38–39
Hodgson, Amanda, 4, 91
Homing, 120
Hooker, S. K., 229
HSI. See Habitat Sustainability Index
Human behavior, 35
Human coastal settlements, 2
Human development, 27
Human disturbance, 42–43
Hunting: Amazonian manatees, 48–49, 50; Arabia dugongs, 97; Australia and Pacific dugongs, 100; dugongs, 59, 64, 70, 79; sirenians, 15–16; West Indian manatees, 41–42; workshops, 52. See also Poaching
Husar, S. L., 39
Hybridization, 173–74, 174
Hydrodamalis gigas. See Steller's sea cow

IARC. See International Agency for Research on Cancer
IBAMA. See Brazilian Institute for the Environment and Renewable Natural Resources
ICAM. See Integrated Coastal and Marine Biodiversity
Ikeda, Kazuko, 77
Ilangakoon, Anouk, 58, 65–66, 75
Incidental catch, 15, 42
India, 74–76
Indigenous peoples, xiii, 223; Australia and Pacific dugongs and, 100–101; hunters, 3, 44; manatee fat and, 43; manatee meat and, 37, 42; manatee names, 47; manatee trading, 49
Individual identification: applied marks and tags, 133–35; genetic analysis, 137; interbreeding, fitness and disease issues, 137–38; overview, 133; photo-ID, 135–37
Indonesia, 66–68
Integrated Coastal and Marine Biodiversity (ICAM), 57
Interbreeding, 176–77
International Agency for Research on Cancer (IARC), 198
International Convention for the Prevention of Pollution from Ships 1973, as Modified by the Protocol of 1978 and Its Annexes (MARPOL), 238
International Union for Conservation of Nature (IUCN), 1–2, 29, 113, 229, 240; sirenian status, 7
Interviews: limitations and biases, 112–14; planning, 112; in research, 109–15; study examples, 110T; summary on, 114; techniques, 112; as tool, 109–12
in vitro dry matter digestibility (IVDMD), 10
IRMS. See Isotope ratio mass spectrometers
Isotope ratio mass spectrometers (IRMS), 130
IUCN. See International Union for Conservation of Nature
IUCN Red List of Threatened Species, xiii, 30, 40, 43, 57
IVDMD. See *in vitro* dry matter digestibility

Jamaica manatee rehabilitation and captive programs, 212
Japan, 2; accidental captures in gillnets, 81; aerial surveys, 77, 79; dugong cultural significance, 81–82; dugong distribution, 78–80; dugong legal status, 80; dugong research, 77–78, 82; dugong threats, 81; feeding trails, 78; habitat degradation, 81; NGOs, 83; protected areas, 80–81; seagrass, 79, 79T; summary, 83
Jethva, Bharat, 58
Jiang, Xia, 58
Jing, Xin, 58

Kataoka, T., 69
Keith, L., 54
Kendall, Sarita, 179, 180, 221, 225
Khmer Rouge, 62–63
Kiszka, Jeremy J., 84, 87
Kouadio, Akoi, 54–57
Kreb, D., 67
Kruska Wallis analysis, 185

K-strategists, 13, 14
Kwan, D. H., 13, 99

LaCommare, Katherine S., 179
Land-based surveys: applications and limitations, 185T; conclusion, 185; overview, 179; use and design, 184–85
Law: conclusion, 242; in developing countries, 235–42; in existing regimes, 235–36; hard law, 236–37; role in sirenian protection, 240–42; soft law, 238–39
Lawler, Ivan, 4, 99, 132, 186
Leatherwood, S., 74
Lefebvre, L. W., 39, 47
Legal status: Amazonian manatees, 48; Arabia dugongs, 97–97; Australia and Pacific dugongs, 101–2; Cambodia dugongs, 62–63; China dugongs, 71; Eastern African dugongs, 86; Florida manatees, 29–31; India dugongs, 75; Indonesia dugongs, 67–68; Japan dugongs, 80; Myanmar dugongs, 65; Philippine dugongs, 69; Sri Lanka dugongs, 73–74; Thailand dugongs, 60–61; Vietnam dugongs, 64; West Indian manatees, 40–41
León, M. A., 39
Letícia Zoo, 51
Limo, Regis Pinto De, 42–43
Live stranding or mortality, Australia and Pacific dugongs, 105T
Local Government Comprehensive Planning and Land Regulation Act, 29
Lopes, Maria José De Souza, 168
Lu, Shaoyong, 58

Magnification devices, 183T
Mamirauá Institute for Sustainable Development, 51, 52
Manatee Forum, 31
Manatee Individual Photo-Identification System (MIPS), 32
Manatee rehabilitation and captive programs: Amazonian manatees, 215–17; Belize, 210–212, 213; Brazil, 211, 214–17, 215, 216; Colombia, 213–314, 217; Dominican Republic, 212; Guyana, 214; Jamaica, 212; Mexico, 211, 213; Peru, 211, 217; United States, 206–8; Venezuela, 214; West Indian manatees, 206–14
Manatee rescue, 209; conclusions, 217; goals, 204; management and science, 206; partnerships, 205–6; program culture, 204–5; program success, 206; rehabilitation and captive programs, 206–17

Manatees, 1; abundance, 4–5; allelic diversity, *177T*; biodiversity value, xiii; bones, 15, 42, 45, 57; captive, 17, 52; conservation, 2; counting, 180; dentition, 5; diet, 6–7, *7*; distribution, 4–5, *5*, *7*; fat, 43, 50; future of, xiv; genetics and demography, 171–74; grazing, 4; habitat, *7*, 26; herbivores, 24; indigenous people's names for, 47; indigenous people trading, 49; IUCN status, 7; meat, 37, 42, 49, 50, 51, 55; medicines, 43, 50, 56, 113; metabolic rate, 18; oil, 15, 42, 45, 57; PCBs found in, 15; poaching, 166–67, 213–15, 218; rostral deflection, 5; teeth, 18; threats to, 26; vision and hearing, 16–17; weight, 4. *See also* Amazonian manatees; West African manatees; West Indian manatees
"Manatees in Hispaniola," 38–39
"Manatees in Nicaragua and Costa Rica, Central America," 44–45
Mani, S. B., 74
Marine angiosperms, 4
Marine Biology Research Center of the Autonomous University of Santo Domingo (CIBIMA-UASD), 39
Marine Mammal Commission (MMC), 31, 46
Marine Mammal Protection Act (MMPA), 29, 31
Marine Mammal Sanctuary of Estero Hondo, 39
Marine Protected Areas (MPAs), 239–40
Marmontel, Miriam, 2, 164, 221, 226, 227, 243
MARPOL. *See* International Convention for the Prevention of Pollution from Ships 1973, as Modified by the Protocol of 1978 and Its Annexes
Marsh, Helene, 4, 13, 59, 67, 228, 233
Marshall, Christopher D., 12
McDonald, Brenda, 104, 168, 175–77
Meat: Arabia dugongs, 97; dugongs, 73, 82; Eastern African dugongs, 86, 88; indigenous peoples and, 37, 42; manatees, 49, 50, 51, 55
Medicines: dugongs, 60–64, 66, 71, 82; manatees, 43, 50, 56, 113
MEPA. *See* Saudi Arabia Meteorology and Environmental Protection Administration
Mermaids, 66, 72, 77, 87
Metabolic rates, 18, 25
Mexico, 38, 166, 228; manatee rehabilitation and captive programs, *211*, 213
Mignucci-Giannoni, Antonio, 1, 36, 204, 243

Migration, 164, 176–77
MIPS. *See* Manatee Individual Photo-Identification System
MIPS database, 45
Mitochondrial DNA (mtDNA), 168–70, 172, *172*, *173*
MMC. *See* Marine Mammal Commission
MMPA. *See* Marine Mammal Protection Act
Molecular aging, 170–71, 175
Molecular sexing, 170, 175
Molecular techniques, 168
Morales, Benjamín, *202*
Morales-Arraut, Eduardo, 157, 164
Morales-Vela, Benjamín, 186, 204, 228, 247
Mortality. *See* Pathology and mortality assessment
Mote Marine Laboratory, 46
MPAs. *See* Marine Protected Areas
mtDNA. *See* Mitochondrial DNA
mtDNA phylogeographic analysis, 176–77
Muir, C. E., 84, 87
Mukai, Hiroshi, 77
Myanmar, 65–66

NAILSMA. *See* North Australian Indigenous Land and Sea Management Alliance
Nair, R., 75
National Environmental Significance (NES), 101
National Geographic Crittercam records, 123
National Institute for Amazonian Research, 51
National Rubbertapper Council, 51
Natural resources, 31
Natutama Foundation, 51
Near-infrared reflectance spectroscopy (NIRS), 126, 131–32, 163
Necropsy examination, *155*
NES. *See* National Environmental Significance
NGOs. *See* Nongovernmental organizations
Nicaragua, 44–45
NIRS. *See* Near-infrared reflectance spectroscopy
Nishiwaki, M., 67
Nongovernmental organizations (NGOs), 61, 63, 64, 70, 75, 77; Japan, 83; lack of in Middle East, 98
Non-paired chromosomes, *174*
North Atlantic right whales, 14
North Australian Indigenous Land and Sea Management Alliance (NAILSMA), 100–101, 105

Octachlorodibenzo-p-dioxins, 15
Ofori-Dansen, Patrick, 57
Oil: dugongs, 15, 71, 75, 86, 87, 100; manatees, 15, 42, 45, 57
Oil spills, 53, 70, 92
Olivera-Gómez, Leon D., 157, 165
Omacha Foundation, 51, 214, 217
Order Carnivora, 12
Order Cetacea, 12
Orellana, Francisco de, 47
Organic contaminants: biomarker assessment, 200; overview, 196; PBDEs, 199–200; PFOS, 199–200; POPs/PBTs contaminant group, 197–99, 203; priority, 196–97; sampling protocols and procedures, 201–3, *202*; studies, 200–201; value of study, 200
Ortega-Argueta, Alejandro, 109, 157, 166, 230
O'Shea, T. J., 15, 35, 200, 201
Ottenwalder, J. A., 39
Overfishing, 14

Packard, J. M., 192
Paintsticks, 133, *134*
Palmer, D. R., 175, 176
Paper parks, 45
Parasites, 142, 153
Parente, C. L., 43
Parr, Leslee, 168, 172
"Partnering for Success: Florida Manatee Photo-Identification," 32
Passive integrated transponder (PIT), 134–35, 137, 140
Patankar, Vardhan, 58
Pathology and mortality assessment, *148T*; anthropogenic causes, 148–51, *149T*; conclusions, 156; documentation, 155–56; natural causes, 151–54; necropsy examination, *155*, 155–56; overview, 148; recovery and history, 155; stochastic events, 154–55
PBDEs. *See* Polybrominated diphenyl ethers
PBTs. *See* Priority Persistent, Bioaccumulative and Toxic Pollutants
PCBs, 15
PCR products, *175*
Peduncle tagging equipment, *117*, 118, *118*
Pérez, Ignacio Jiménez, 44–45
Perfluorooctane sufonate (PFOS), 199–200
Persistent organic pollutants (POPs), 196
Peru, 53, *211*, 217

PFOS. *See* Perfluorooctane sufonate
Philippines, 68–70
Photographic documentation (photo-ID), *32*, 135–37, *136*, 151, 184; studies, 39
Phuket Marine Biological Center, 60, 62
Pink dolphins, 2
PIT. *See* Passive integrated transponder
Platform Transmitter Terminals (PTTs), 121
Poaching: manatees, 166–67, 213–15, 218; records, 76; sirenians, 113; West Indian manatees, 41–46
Pollution, 96
Pol Pot, 62
Polybrominated diphenyl ethers (PBDEs), 199–200
Pomeroy, R. S., 233
Poochaviranon, Sombat, 58
POPs. *See* Persistent organic pollutants
POPs/PBTs contaminant group, 197–99, 203
Population, 2; Amazonian manatee dynamic, 48; Dugongs' structure, 175; Eastern African dugong status, 85–86; Florida manatees, 23, 25–26, 29, *34T*; pressure on Eastern African dugongs, 86; West African manatees, 54–56, 173
Powell, J. A., 54
Pratt, P., 142
Preen, A. H., 9, 91
Prehistoric sirenians, 4
Priority Persistent, Bioaccumulative and Toxic Pollutants (PBTs), 196
Protected areas, 80–81; Arabia dugongs, 97; background information, 229–30; boundaries, 231–32; building community capacity, 232; community involvement, 231; conclusions, 234; in conservation, 251; design principles, 232; education plan, 233; effectiveness, 233–34; key features, *234*; management, 234; reasons for, 228–29; stakeholders in, 230–31, *231T*; steps for developing, 229–33; types, 229
PTT. *See* Platform Transmitter Terminals
PTT/GPS tags, 122–23
PTT tags, 121, *122*
Puerto Rico Manatee Conservation Center, 46
Puerto Rico manatee rehabilitation and captive programs, 208–12, *210*, *212*
Pugibet, E., 39
Pulster, Erin, 196

Quantitative modeling, 162–66

Race track pattern, 190
Ramsar Convention on Wetlands, 41
Red Data Book of Vietnam, 64
Red Sea, 92–93, 95–96
Red tide, 29
Reep, R. L., 16
Reeves, R. R., 54, 74
Regional Seas Plans (RSPs), 239–40
"Relationships between Amazonian Manatees and Amanã Reserve Inhabitants," 115
Relative growth rates, from published literature of some Australian tropical seagrasses, *9T*
Remote sensing, 159–62
Reproduction: Amazonian manatees, 48; dugongs, 13; Florida manatees, 13; in health assessment, West Indian Manatees, 142–43; sirenians, 13
Research: Amazonian manatees, 51–53; Arabia dugongs, 92, 98; Australia and Pacific dugongs, 102–5; Cambodia dugongs, 62, 63; China dugongs, 70–71, 72; Florida manatees, 31–35, *34T*; funding for Eastern African dugongs, 88; impediments for Arabia dugongs, 94–95; India dugongs, 74, 76; Indonesia dugongs, 66–67, 68; interviews in, 109–15; Japan dugongs, 77–78, 82; Myanmar dugongs, 65, 66; needs, 53; Philippine dugongs, 68–70; priorities for Eastern African dugongs, 89; regional database, 45; Sri Lanka dugongs, 72, 74; strategies, 2–3; Thailand dugong, 59–60, 61–62; Vietnam dugongs, 63–64; West Indian manatees, 37–38, 45, 57
Reynolds, John, 12, 23, 25, 190, 192, 196
Ricklefs, R. E., 13
Roff, J. C., 249
"Role of Law Enforcement in Conservation of the Florida Manatee," 30
Rommel, S. A., 18
Rood, Karl A., 32
Rosas, Fernando C. Weber, 204
Rostral deflection, 5–6
Roth, H. H., 54
RSPs. *See* Regional Seas Plans
R-strategists, 13
Rubber cradle, *119*
Runge, M. C., 25

Salm, R., 67
Sampling protocols and procedures, 201–3, *202*
Satellite-based tags: GPS tags, 121–22, *122*; PTT/GPS tags, 122–23; PTT tags, 121, *122*
Satellite sensors, *160T*, 160–62, *161T*
Saudi Arabia Meteorology and Environmental Protection Administration (MEPA), 92, 94
Save the Manatee Club, 46
"Save the Manatee" license tags, 33
Scientists, in developing country conservation, 243–45
Sea cows, 72
Seagrasses, 9, 43, 95; destruction, 63, 81; die-offs, 27; as diet, 5–11; digestibility, 77; Japan, 79, *79T*; mapping, 76; nutrition, 18; protecting, 15, 65; Thailand protection, 60–61. *See also specific seagrasses*
SeagrassNet, 66
Sea Sense, 88, 90
Sea to Shore Alliance, 46
Sea turtles, 69, 244
Self-Sullivan, Caryn, 36
Sheppard, James K., 157, 163, 177
Short nucleotide sequence repeats (SSRs), 170
Side-scan sonar, 180–81, *181*
Siegal-Willott, J. A., 141
Sighting map, *183*
Silas, E. G., 74
Sinclair, David, 102
Singh, T. P., 222
Sirenian International, 46
Sirenians: abundance, 4; adaptations, 19; in aquatic ecosystems, 4–11; biology, 124; conservation, xiii–xiv; dentition, 5; diet, 7, *7*; distribution, 4, *5*, *7*; exploitation, 13; facial morphology, 5; grazing, 8–9, 11; habitat, *7*; hindgut digesters, 18; hunting, 15–16; incidental taking, 15; IUCN status, *7*; K-strategists, 13; law and, 240–42; locomotion and speed, 14; poaching, 113; pollution and, 15–16; prehistoric, 4; reproduction, 13; role of, 11; rostral deflection, 6; span, xiii; surface-area-to-volume ratio, 22; tactile animals, 16. *See also* Dugongs; Manatees
Sirenian vulnerability: anatomy and function, 17–19; large size and life history attributes, 12–13; non life history attributes, 14; overview, 12; proximity to people, 15–16
Soft law, 238–39
Solanki, Parimal, 58
Somany, Phay, 58
Sorice, Michael G., 28

South-Western Indian Ocean Fisheries Project (SWIOFP), 88, 90
Spaghetti tags, 133
SPAW. See Specially Protected Areas and Wildlife
Specially Protected Areas and Wildlife (SPAW), 41
Sri Lanka, 72–74, *73*
SSRs. See Short nucleotide sequence repeats
Stable isotopes analysis, 128–30, *129T, 130, 131T*
Steller's sea cow (*Hydrodamalis gigas*), xiii; diet, *7*, 7–8; distribution, *7*; extermination, 7; habitat, *7*; IUCN status, *7*; size, 12; teeth, 5
Stochastic events, 154–55
Stockholm Convention, 196–99, 238–39
Sun, J., 71
Sutaria, Dipani, 58
SWIOFP. See South-Western Indian Ocean Fisheries Project
Symington, Keith, 58

Tagging and movement: attachment mechanisms, 117–19; in developing countries, 124–25; integrating equipment, 123; manufacturers contact information, *124T*; overview, 116; rubber cradle, *119*; satellite-based tags, 121–23; sirenian biology and, 124; techniques, 116–17, *117, 118*; telemetry, 119; VHF-only tags, 119–21. See also Individual identification
TDR. See Time-depth recorder
Tejo, Haydée Domínguez, 38–39
Telemetry, 119
Thailand, 59–62, 111, 224
The Nature Conservancy (TNC), 40
Thompson, K., 175
Threats: to Amazonian manatees, 48–51; to Arabia dugongs, 96–97; to Asian dugongs, 58–59; to China dugongs, 71–72; to Eastern African dugongs, 86–88, *87T*; to Florida manatees, 27, 29; to India dugongs, 75–76; to Indonesia dugongs, 68; to Japan dugongs, 81; to manatees, 26; to Myanmar dugongs, 65–66; to Philippine dugongs, 69–70; to Thailand dugongs, 61; to Vietnam dugongs, 64; to West African manatees, 54–56; to West Indian manatees, 41–43. See also Accidental captures in gillnets; Hunting; IUCN Red List of Threatened Species; Poaching; Watercraft collisions

Time-depth recorder (TDR), 123
TNC. See The Nature Conservancy
Tourism, 28. See also Ecotourism
Toxins, 151
"Transforming Manatee Tourism into Ecotourism," 28
Trauma, 150, *150*
Trichechus inunguis. See Amazonian manatees
Trichechus manatus. See West Indian manatees
Trichechus manatus latirostris. See Florida manatees
Trichechus senegalensis. See West African manatees
Tun, T., 58, 65–66

U.S. Geological Survey (USGS), 32
Ultra high frequency (UHF), 121
UNCED. See United Nations Conference on Environment and Development
UNCLOS III. See United Nations Law of the Sea Convention
United Arab Emirates' Heritage Club, 92
United Nations Conference on Environment and Development (UNCED), 239
United Nations Environment Programme, 15
United Nations Law of the Sea Convention (UNCLOS III), 236
United States Agency for International Development (USAID), 244
United States manatee rehabilitation and captive programs, 206–8
USAID. See United States Agency for International Development
USGS. See U.S. Geological Survey
"Using Side-Scan Sonar to Find Manatees," 180–81

Value: Amazonian manatees, 50; manatee biodiversity, xiii; West Indian manatees, 56–57
Van Vleet, E. S., 15
Vega, M., 39
Venezuela manatee rehabilitation and captive programs, 214
Very high frequency (VHF), 119
Vetter, W., 200
VHF. See Very high frequency
VHF-only tags, 119–21
Vianna, J. A., 43, 173, 174
Vianna, Juliana A., 168
Vietnam, 63–65
Virology, 146
Vital signs, 141–42

"Volunteer Wardens Return Manatee Calves to the Natural Environment," 227
Von Zharen, Wyndylyn M., 235

Waitkuwait, E., 54
Wallace, R. L., 31
Walls, G. I., 16
Walsh, M. T., 146
Wang, P., 71
Watercraft collisions, 27, 33, 42
Waycott, Michelle, 168
WCR. See Wider Caribbean
WCR manatees. See West Indian manatees
West African Manatee Conservation and Education Project, 57
West African manatees (*Trichechus senegalensis*): conclusion, 57; diet, 5, *7*; distribution, *7*, 36–37, *37*, 54, *55*; in freshwater environment, 8; grazing, 9; habitat, *7*; IUCN Red List of Threatened Species, 57; IUCN status, *7*; as K-strategist, 14; overview, 54; population, 54–56, 173; rostral deflection, 6; sightings, 54; size, 54; threats to, 54–56. See also Health assessment, West Indian Manatees
Western Indian Ocean (WIO), 84–85
Western Indian Ocean Marine Science Association (WIOMSA), 90
West Indian manatees (*Trichechus manatus*), *205*; aerial surveys, 38, 44; Amazonian manatees hybridization, 173, *174*; background, 36; conservation, 36; cultural and socioeconomic significance, 43–45; diet, 5–6, *7*; disease-resistance, 151; distribution, *7*, 38–39, *40T*; with epibiont, *154*; facilities holding, *207–8T*; grazing, 9; habitat, *7*, 36; historical research, 37–37; human disturbance, 42–43; hunting, 41–42; incidental catch, 42; IUCN Red List of Threatened Species, 40, 43; legal status, 40–41; magical significance, 44; manatee rehabilitation and captive programs, 206–14; photo-ID studies, 39; poaching, 41–46; research, 57; research needs, 45; rostral deflection, 6; size, 12; spatial distribution and gene flow, 172–73; subspecies designation, 171–72; summary, 46; tactile resolution, 18; threats to, 41–43; trapping, 55, *56*; value, 56–57; watercraft collisions, 42. See also Antillean manatee
Wetlands International, 57
Wetzel, Dana L., 15, 196, 201

Whale sharks, 45
"When Communities Are Not Consulted," 226
Whitehead, H., 47
WIDECAST. *See* Wider Caribbean Sea Turtle Network
Wider Caribbean (WCR), 36–37; countries, 38; management plan, 46
Wider Caribbean Sea Turtle Network (WIDECAST), 244
Wildlife Fund of Thailand, 61
Wildlife Protection Law, 48
Winter thermal refugia, 33
WIO. *See* Western Indian Ocean
WIOMSA. *See* Western Indian Ocean Marine Science Association

World Wildlife Fund, 57

Yadfon Association, 61
Yangon Zoological Garden, 65
Yaptinchay, A. A., 69
Yasuni National Park, 50

Zacharias, M. A., 249
Zayed, Sheik, 97